BIENVILLE'S DILEMMA

BIENVILLE'S DILEMMA

A
HISTORICAL GEOGRAPHY
OF NEW ORLEANS

RICHARD CAMPANELLA

CENTER FOR LOUISIANA STUDIES
UNIVERSITY OF LOUISIANA AT LAFAYETTE
2008

Center for Louisiana Studies
University of Louisiana at Lafayette
P.O. Box 40831
Lafayette, LA 70504-0831

http://cls.louisiana.edu

Printed in China

Library of Congress Cataloging-in-Publication Data

Campanella, Richard.
Bienville's dilemma : a historical geography of New Orleans / Richard
Campanella.
p. cm.
Includes bibliographical references and index.
ISBN 1-887366-85-7 (alk. paper)
1. New Orleans (La.)--Historical geography. 2. Landscape--Louisiana--
New Orleans--History. 3. New Orleans (La.)--Environmental conditions.
4. Human geography--Louisiana--New Orleans. 5. New Orleans (La.)--
Ethnic relations. I. Title.
F379.N557C238 2008
911'.76335--dc22
2008025952

Front cover: (top) *Veue et Perspective de la Nouvelle Orléans* by Jean-Pierre Lassus,
1726, courtesy French National Archives; (middle) *The City of New Orleans* by
Currier & Ives, 1885, courtesy Library of Congress; (bottom) aerial photograph
by Vincent Laforet, August 30, 2005, courtesy the Associated Press. Rear cover
and spine graphic by Richard Campanella using Landsat satellite imagery.

To My Wife, Marina

To My Parents,
Mr. and Mrs. Mario and Rose Ann Campanella
Brooklyn, New York

and

To Marina's Parents,
Sr. and Sra. Ernesto López and Porfiria Morán de López
San Juan Trujano, Oaxaca, México

I begin to understand the town a little…
and a curious town it is.

—Benjamin H. B. Latrobe, 1819

CONTENTS

URBANIZING THE LANDSCAPE

POPULATING THE LANDSCAPE

MANIPULATING THE LANDSCAPE

HUMANIZING THE LANDSCAPE

DEVASTATING THE LANDSCAPE

RESTORING THE LANDSCAPE

⚜

Introduction

dilemma (də-'le-mə), *n.* a problem involving a difficult
or unpleasant choice [which] will bring undesirable
consequences
    –*Merriam-Webster* and *Oxford English* dictionaries

Human experiences often play out as a sequence of greater and lesser dilemmas, in which every difficult choice engenders unknowable consequences. Could making a painful investment now relieve our children of far greater expenditures in the future? Or might treating today's minor inconveniences spawn major crises tomorrow? Should a settlement be built on the safest site, despite its inconvenience? Or should it exploit the most strategic situation, despite its risk? Should we remain in eroding marshes and continue centuries of tradition, or end our way of life and move inland so that aggressive coastal restoration may begin?

Dilemmas are as fascinating as they are distressing. Dilemmatic places—cities, for example, that are important yet costly, strategic but dangerous, triumphant and tragic—are among the most intriguing locales on Earth.

What better place to contemplate the notion of historical and geographical dilemma than New Orleans and coastal Louisiana? Described by geographer Peirce Lewis as the "inevitable city" in the "impossible" site,[1] New Orleans comprises a litany of polemical decisions and dramatic transformations. Here, the full spectrum of the human experience seems to manifest itself vividly in daily life and everyday cityscapes. A city once routinely predicted to rank among the world's greatest is now foreseen by some, in the wake of Hurricane Katrina and in light of eroding coasts, sinking soils, and rising seas, to have no future whatsoever. "If two words characterize all of southeastern Louisiana now," reflected environmental law scholar Oliver Houck, "they would be 'total uncertainty.'" So why would so many people fight to remain? "[B]ecause it's such a damned joy to live here."[2]

Bienville's Dilemma presents sixty-eight articles and essays on the historical geography of New Orleans. Not intended to be a traditional history of political figures and legislative acts, the book seeks to answer key questions guiding the discipline of geography: What is the shape, form, and origin of the physical landscape? How have humans transformed the landscape, and vice versa? How are phenomena distributed spatially, why, and how have the patterns changed through time? What distinguishes places from each other? How do people perceive place? What clues do we see in the present-day cityscape reflecting these questions? And how can geographical knowledge be used to restore and improve disturbed places? Most writings are new to this volume; others are updated derivations of my earlier research over the past thirteen years.

As often happens when writing about historical geography, the researcher must make certain structural decisions. Should time (history) serve as the volume's organizational vertebrae? Or should space (geography)? One must also choose between

15

breadth (comprehensiveness) and depth (analytical detail and approach).

I decided to organize the topics by the transformations and implications they wrought upon the landscape: formation, settlement, urbanization, population, manipulation, humanization, devastation, and restoration. I chose also to take an in-depth episodic approach, rather than a comprehensive one that touches lightly on everything. Scores of "mile-wide-inch-deep" books about New Orleans currently buckle bookshelves; what is lacking are focused, critical, in-depth studies. Relinquishing comprehensiveness means many important topics must be left out. To atone for these sins of omission, *Bienville's Dilemma* begins with an extensive timeline of historical events of geographical significance, intended to "fill in the blanks" left among the volume's articles. But this too falls short of a comprehensive chronology of local history: the timeline records selected historical events and trends that helped create the urban landscape we see today.

Emerging repeatedly throughout this volume is the theme of dilemma. It first appears in Bienville's momentous decision regarding where to establish New Orleans. It continues with the stories of levee construction, canal excavation, urban expansion, coastal erosion, and the myriad blessings and curses accompanying the transformation of a dynamic, fluid deltaic landscape into a rigid, controlled cityscape. It appears again in the dramatic story of Manuel Marquez, who found himself on the horns of a classic "lifeboat dilemma" as he and his family rode out the Great Storm of 1915. "Bienville's dilemma," metaphorically speaking, persists throughout New Orleans and coastal Louisiana society today, as citizens contemplate saving the place they love in the face of undeniable geological truths. Anyone who, since Hurricane Katrina, has grappled with rebuilding, considered moving out, contemplated moving in, debated either divesting or investing in New Orleans, or otherwise pondered the city's future, shares in Bienville's dilemma.

Problems end with solutions; dilemmas end with choices. Southeastern Louisiana must make excruciating choices regarding people, culture, and place if it is to survive. Entangled in those decisions are problems involving coastal restoration, economic diversification, environmental sustainability, social equity, and learning to live with risk. As a geographer, I believe these problems are solvable, so long as citizens muster the will to tackle them and the courage to confront the dilemmas underlying them.

It is my hope that the requisite willpower and valor will be summoned through the realization that these problems are not only solvable, but worth solving, and that the world would be a lesser place without New Orleans.

Acknowledgments

I wish to thank the following institutions for access to the research materials, datasets, and analytical tools used in this volume: Louisiana Collection and Special Collections of the Earl K. Long Library at the University of New Orleans; Louisiana Collection and Southeastern Architectural Archive in the Special Collections division of Howard-Tilton Library at Tulane University; New Orleans Public Library; The Historic New Orleans Collection-Williams Research Center; Catholic Archdiocese of New Orleans; *New Orleans Times-Picayune*; Tulane School of Architecture; Tulane School of Science and Engineering; Center for Bioenvironmental Research at Tulane and Xavier Universities; New Orleans City Planning Commission; Louisiana State Museum; Louisiana State University Department of Geography and Anthropology; Louisiana State University Computer-Aided Design and Geographic Information Systems (CADGIS) Lab; Louisiana GIS Digital Map; Louisiana Oil Spill Coordinator's Office; University of Louisiana at Lafayette; U.S. Census Bureau; U.S. Army Corps of Engineers-New Orleans District; U.S. Geological Survey; National Oceanographic and Atmospheric Administration; National Science Foundation; Library of Congress; Perry-Castañeda Library at the University of Texas at Austin; Port of New Orleans; GCR & Associates; Tulane University Department of Earth and Environmental Sciences; Vieux Carré Commission; and the New Orleans Notarial Archives.

Gratitude also goes to John Magill, Lawrence N. Powell, James D. Wilson Jr., Shelly Meaux, Laura Harris, Ronnie Cardwell, Mark Tullis, Amy Koritz, Mark S. Davis, Janet C. Gilmore, Thomas M. Ryan, Nina Lam, and many others for various insights and perspectives which influenced my research.

I am indebted to James D. Wilson Jr., Carl A. Brasseaux, and the staff of the Center for Louisiana Studies at the University of Louisiana-Lafayette, for their steadfast support of my work. I am particularly indebted to James for his hard work and wise counsel in terms of the content, design, and publication of this book.

My deepest gratitude goes to my wife, Marina Campanella; my parents, Mario and Rose Ann Campanella; brother Thomas J. Campanella; and uncle John Tambasco for their many years of love, support, and guidance.

Finally, I am grateful to New Orleans, for the way it enriches and inspires the world.

Timeline

Historical events of geographical significance in the New Orleans area

Prehistoric Indigenous peoples occupy Mississippi deltaic plain and explore and exploit networks of ridges, bayous, and bays. Knowledge of labyrinthine deltaic geography includes discovery of key shortcuts and portages between Gulf of Mexico and Mississippi River.

1519-1543 Spaniards Alonso Álvarez de Pineda, Pánfilo de Narváez, and Hernando de Soto explore lower Mississippi region; efforts lead to no lasting claims or settlements, but augment European knowledge of Gulf Coast/Mississippi River region. European diseases decimate indigenous populations following De Soto's expedition.

1682 Nine years after Marquette and Joliet's exploration of upper Mississippi, French Canadian René-Robert Cavelier, sieur de La Salle sails down Mississippi to Gulf of Mexico, confirming relationship among Great Lakes, river, and sea. His claim of Mississippi watershed asserts French dominion over one million square miles of North America, setting stage for foundation of French colonies near river's mouth. La Salle's attempt to return in 1684 ends in confusion and disaster, leaving France's Louisiana claim idle for fifteen years.

1699 Le Moyne brothers Iberville and Bienville explore Gulf Coast and lower river region and establish Fort Maurepas in present-day Ocean Springs, Mississippi. Expedition to found and colonize Louisiana signifies France's renewed interest in La Salle's 1682 claim, in large part to keep it out of hands of English (via migration from northeast and invasion from gulf) and Spanish (via Mexico and Florida).

1699 Bienville rebuffs English frigate *Carolina Galley* from entering French Louisiana. Incident (which gives "English Turn" its name) demonstrates English interest in lower Mississippi Valley and convinces Iberville of need to establish fort on Mississippi River, in addition to coastal settlements. Natives show Frenchmen various shortcuts among gulf, lakes, and river, one of which Bienville later selects for New Orleans site.

1700 Bienville founds Fort de Mississippi (Fort de la Boulaye) near present-day Phoenix in Plaquemines Parish. First European settlement within present-day Louisiana gives French experience in settling Mississippi deltaic plain.

1702 Seat of colonial government is moved from Fort Maurepas to new Mobile settlement, located north of present-day Alabama city of the same name. European population of lower Louisiana totals about 140 subjects, strewn out between Mobile Bay and Mississippi River.

1708   Some Mobile colonists are granted land concessions at Bayou St. John. Wheat crop near bayou's headwaters fails, but effort puts area "on the map" as first European settlement in future New Orleans proper.

1711   Mobile relocated to present-day site on bay. Move marks troubled era in early Louisiana history, with failed settlements, disease, and death matched by fading interest on part of French government.

1712   Disillusioned with Louisiana and preoccupied with other matters, French crown cedes colony as commercial monopoly to financier Antoine Crozat. Effort strives to discover gold and silver mines, raise tobacco on plantations, and trade with Spain. All three aims fail; Crozat retrocedes Louisiana to crown in 1717.

1715   King Louis XIV dies; five-year-old great-grandson Louis XV ascends to throne. Philippe, duc d'Orléans acts as regent of France.

1716   King issues edict regulating land grants and establishing *arpent* system in Louisiana (one *arpent* equals approximately 192 English feet), whereby riverine land is surveyed into long, narrow lots perpendicular to waterway. French "long lots" later influence formation of New Orleans' radiating street network, and demarcate much of southeastern Louisiana landscape to this day.

1717   Crozat's failure to develop Louisiana commercially opens opportunity for Scottish maverick financier John Law to propose elaborate land-development scheme. Befriending Philippe, duc d'Orléans, Law acquires monopoly charter for commercial enterprise in Louisiana, establishes Company of the West, and launches brazen marketing campaign across Europe to lure settlers and investors. Law's involvement reverses European perceptions of Louisiana as a burdensome New World backwater; colony is now the talk of Europe.

September 1717 Directive to found New Orleans issued in Company of the West ledger: "Resolved to establish, thirty leagues up the river, a burg which should be called Nouvelle Orléans, where landing would be possible from either the river or Lake Pontchartrain." Name of settlement honors Law's royal patron, Philippe, duc d'Orléans.

1718   In late March and early April, Bienville's men clear canebrake for foundation of New Orleans. Bienville's site exploits Bayou St. John/Bayou Road portage between Lake Pontchartrain and Mississippi River, shown to him by Indians nearly two decades earlier. Located on elevated natural levee and angled to confront approaching ships, site—present-day French Quarter—is highly problematic but superior to most in deltaic plain.

1718-1722 Bienville's siting of New Orleans is called into question by rival colonists, who debate relocating settlement to Bayou Manchac site (south of present-day Baton Rouge). Other suggested sites for company headquarters include Natchez, English Turn, Lake Pontchartrain shore, Natchitoches, Biloxi, Mobile, and Pensacola.

1719 Spring floods slow work on New Orleans. Headquarters of Louisiana colony relocated from Mobile back to Biloxi area; Bienville, an advocate of New Orleans remaining at its present site, reluctantly returns to Biloxi to build new fort.

1719 First large group of Africans arrives in chains, commencing fourteen decades of slavery in Louisiana. Over 5000 people, mostly from West African Senegambia region, are imported during 1719-31, first of two major waves directly from Africa. Racial subjugation through slavery, codified in 1724 *Code Noir*, profoundly influences New Orleans' social and urban geography. Compared to Anglo-America, racial identities and relationships become more complex and fluid in Caribbean-influenced French Louisiana.

1719-1721 Law's Company recruits thousands of French citizens (many from society's bottom rung), as well as German and Swiss farmers, to settle Louisiana, representing first major wave of Europeans to region. New Orleans by 1720 boasts houses for governor and director, company store, hospital, over 100 employees, and 250 concession-holders ready to work their land. But settlement is haphazardly laid out; disease takes its toll; and commercial effort struggles financially.

1720 "Mississippi Bubble" bursts; John Law's highly speculative development scheme for Louisiana fails.

1720s Germans settle *Côte des Allemands* upriver from New Orleans and help feed struggling New Orleans with their agricultural productivity. Teutonic population is later absorbed into French-speaking white Creole society, but retains some German ethnic identity for over a century.

1721 Adrien de Pauger, assistant to Chief Engineer Le Blond de La Tour, arrives to New Orleans and promptly adapts La Tour's designs for new Biloxi capital to New Orleans site, creating today's French Quarter. Pauger's impressive plans cast New Orleans in a positive light; primitive outpost grows into *bona fide* town.

1721 New Orleans population 519 (326 whites, 171 black slaves, twenty-one Indian slaves, one free black).

1721 On December 23, Company of the Indies officially transfers headquarters of Louisiana colony from Biloxi to New Orleans, boosting New Orleans' chances of surviving and prospering at its present location.

1722   September hurricane wipes away New Orleans' primitive structures and shoddy cityscape, serendipitously allowing Pauger to survey his planned street grid unimpeded. Present-day French Quarter bears most of original blocks, dimensions, and street names. Forty years after La Salle first sailed past site, foundation of New Orleans is complete.

1722   First substantial artificial levees erected. Started by La Tour and Pauger, levees by 1727 measure eighteen feet wide, three feet high, and one mile long, representing initial attempts to control Mississippi. Anthropogenic river control ultimately succeeds in preventing annual floods but inadvertently starves deltaic plain of critical sediments and freshwater, helping cause catastrophic land loss by late twentieth century.

1723-1727 Capuchin, Jesuit, and Ursuline religious orders arrive to city, playing major role in instilling Catholicism, French culture, education, care for orphans and infirm, and other civilizing aspects to frontier outpost. Ursuline Nuns are particularly influential in the education of girls and other activities, remaining active in city's spiritual culture to this day.

1726   New Orleans population 901 (793 whites, seventy-eight black slaves, thirty Indian slaves)

1727   New Orleans population 938 (729 whites plus 65 enlisted men, 127 black slaves, 17 Indian slaves)

1729   Natchez Indian uprising at Fort Rosalie kills 250 colonists, sending shockwaves through region. New Orleans responds by constructing primitive rampart and moat around street grid. Fortification remains in altered forms until early American years, affecting urban development of adjacent areas. Angles of old fort line remain visible today in certain parcels and building shapes between Barracks Street and Esplanade Avenue.

1731   Company of the Indies relinquishes Louisiana to king; era of private development ends after nearly twenty years of consistent under-performance. France thence views Louisiana, population around 7,000, as a disappointment at best and burdensome failure at worst, unworthy of renewed commitment.

1732   New Orleans population 1,294 (1,023 whites, 254 black slaves, nine Indian slaves, eight free blacks).

1736   Hospital founded. "Charity Hospital" later relocates four times to sites along backswamp edge, reflecting tendency to locate objectionable and threatening phenomena to "back-of-town." Final site (1833) marks location of present-day Charity structure and explains origin of today's Tulane Avenue medical district. Hurricane Katrina's floodwaters end "Big Charity's" history and leave structure's future in question.

1737   New Orleans population 1,748 (759 whites, 963 blacks, and sixteen Indians). City becomes majority-black in 1730s and remains so until 1830s.

1745   Ursuline Convent designed and built (1749-53) on present-day 1100 block of Chartres Street. Edifice, no longer a convent but still operated by Catholic Archdiocese, stands today as sole surviving complete structure from French colonial era, oldest documented extant building in Mississippi Valley and deltaic plain, and outstanding example of French colonial institutional architecture.

Circa 1750 Claude Joseph Villars Dubreuil excavates canal to power sawmill immediately below city. Waterway eventually establishes trajectory of Elysian Fields Avenue (1805) and Pontchartrain Railroad (1831), which influences layout of numerous street grids and neighborhoods between river and lake over next 200 years.

1754-1763 French and Indian War (Seven Years' War in Europe) pits France against England over claims in Ohio Valley; conflict draws in various European states and spreads around world. Defeat of France radically realigns colonial world: French North America, including Louisiana east of Mississippi, is ceded to England. Areas west of river, including New Orleans (thought to be an island, on account of Bayou Manchac distributary and lakes), avoid English possession, having been secretly ceded by King Louis XV in the Treaty of Fontainebleau to his Spanish cousin King Carlos III in 1762. City gains unwelcome new neighbor to north—British West Florida—to which many Anglo settlers migrate over next twenty years.

1755-1785 British exile French settlers from Acadie (present-day Nova Scotia). Thousands of displaced Acadians eventually find their way to Louisiana during 1764-85, drawn by French culture and geographical accessibility. Most Acadians settle west of New Orleans, forming agricultural and natural-resource-based rural society separate from, but important to, urban New Orleans. Corrupted local pronunciation of *Acadian* produces term *Cajun*.

1762-1769 Dominion of New Orleans passes from France to Spain in stages: secretly in 1762, publicly in 1764, politically in 1766, and militarily in 1769. Population remains largely Francophone in culture.

1763   New Orleans population 2,524 (1,646 whites, 826 black slaves, thirty-three Indian slaves, nineteen free blacks)

1775-1783 American Revolution fought mostly along Eastern Seaboard; Spanish in Louisiana seize British outposts in lower Mississippi and Gulf Coast region, with no immediate consequence to New Orleans. But war's outcome adds major new player to political geography and destiny of North America—and New Orleans.

1776-1781 Six hurricanes strike New Orleans area and cause extensive damage. One, in 1779, was experienced by William Dunbar, who later reported his meteorological observations in *Transactions of the American Philosophical Society*— among first to document cyclonic nature of tropical storms.

1777-1778 Spanish census enumerates 2,809 residents in New Orleans proper in 1777, and 3,059 in 1778, a six-fold increase since first French census in 1721. The 1,552 whites, 248 free people of mixed race, 105 free blacks, 213 mixed-race slaves, and 941 black slaves live throughout sixty-eight "isles," or blocks, comprising nearly the entire city proper.

1777-1783 Spanish government recruits residents of Granada, Malaga, and particularly the Canary Islands to settle in Louisiana, aiming to populate the colony's militia for possible war with English, augment agricultural production, and render Louisiana more culturally Spanish. Over 2,500 Canary Islanders ("Isleños") settle in present-day eastern St. Bernard Parish; others settle west of New Orleans, from Maurepas area to New Iberia. Isleño community remains in St. Bernard Parish today, where surnames such as Rodriguez, Nunez, Torres, and Hernandez abound.

1780   City's first food market, a small pavilion for butchers, opens; later evolves into French Market (1791) and becomes one of New Orleans' most famous features.

1780s   Second major wave of slave importations arrives directly from Africa, the first occurring in 1720s.

1780s-1790s With settlers trickling into Ohio and Mississippi valleys, river traffic begins to flow southward toward Spanish Louisiana. Primitive frontier vessels of late 1700s develop, by early 1800s, into steady stream of flatboats (for downriver travel) and keelboats (for returning upriver), delivering commodities and merchandise in and out of interior. New Orleans begins to benefit from nascent agricultural production in its distant hinterland.

1788   Population of New Orleans 5,388 (about 50 percent white, 35 percent enslaved black, and the remainder free people of color). Population of colony is over 25,000.

1788   Good Friday fire destroys 856 buildings in New Orleans, levelling 80 percent of city's structures and leaving about 70 percent of population homeless. Most original French colonial structures are lost. One of last examples of old French Creole house type, "Madame John's Legacy," is built on Dumaine Street immediately after conflagration.

1788   New Orleans' first suburb, Faubourg Ste. Marie (later called Faubourg St. Mary, now Central Business District) is surveyed upon former Gravier plantation above city proper, in response to population pressure and ruins of recent fire. Old plantation boundaries influence layout of emerging street network, as would transpire in many other areas.

1789   St. Louis Cemetery is laid out behind city, reflecting tendency to locate objectionable land uses to back-of-town. New cemetery embodies Spanish tradition of above-ground entombment; replaces old French subterranean burial ground on Burgundy and St. Peter. Still in operation today, "St. Louis No. 1" is resting place of many great local historical figures.

1791   French Market is founded along lower-city riverfront. Municipal market, originating from 1784 decision by Spanish Cabildo to centralize retail food vendors, displays city's multicultural face to amazed visitors throughout 1800s. Vending opportunities help launch generations of poor immigrants to financial independence, including Sicilians in early 1900s, who settle nearby. Market is also birthplace of American tropical-fruit industry; serves today as major node in tourist landscape and economy.

1793-1795 Eli Whitney invents cotton gin (1793); Jean Etienne de Boré successfully granulates Louisiana sugar (1795, near present-day Audubon Zoo). These technological breakthroughs help launch Southern cotton and sugar plantation economy, replacing old colonial-era crops such as tobacco and indigo. Both commodities enrich New Orleans into mid-twentieth century; also entrench slavery in region and play major roles in economic and cultural geography of city and South.

1794   Second major fire in six years—and second disaster in four months, following late-summer hurricane—destroys additional 212 structures in New Orleans. New Spanish building codes enacted after blaze phase out traditional "first-generation" Creole building styles. Structures built afterwards reflect Spanish colonial traits, often with local embellishments ("second-generation" Creole architecture). Village-like appearance of French New Orleans gives way to solid, walled, brick-and-stucco Spanish cityscape.

1794   Governor Carondelet directs excavation of canal from rear of city to Bayou St. John. "Carondelet Canal" supplants Bayou Road as route to Bayou St. John and Lake Pontchartrain; now shipments can be delivered efficiently by water from coast and lake directly to rear of city. Canal, which also serves as early drainage system, provides convenient right-of-way into downtown, used by railroads into twentieth century.

1795   Spain and U.S. sign Treaty of San Lorenzo, granting Americans open navigation of Mississippi River and right of deposit at New Orleans for three years.

1791-1804 Slave revolt in Saint-Domingue (present-day Haiti) threatens and eventually overthrows French regime.

1796   First significant yellow fever outbreak strikes New Orleans. Spread by *Aedes aegypti* mosquito (probably introduced from Africa through slave trade), yellow fever kills over 100,000 Louisianians and nearly 40,000 New Orleanians over next century. Plagues deeply influence economics, human geography, seasonal migration patterns, public image, and everyday life of city throughout nineteenth century.

1800   Apprehensive about United States' increasing interest in Louisiana, Spain, an empire in decline, secretly retrocedes Louisiana to militarily powerful France. Word of transfer soon reaches U.S.; alarms President Jefferson, who views New Orleans as critical to western expansion.

1802   Napoleon sends 20,000 troops to control situation in Saint-Domingue. Yellow fever decimates troops; slave revolt intensifies and eventually expels French regime, creating Latin America's first independent country (Haiti). Loss of extremely valuable sugar colony diminishes Napoleon's interest in France's cumbersome and problematic Louisiana colony.

1802   Spain rescinds American right of deposit at New Orleans (permitted since 1795), exacerbating tension between U.S. and colonial powers. President Jefferson launches effort to purchase New Orleans; threat of war emerges, with England casting eyes on Louisiana prize as well. Once perceived as a beleaguered backwater destined for failure, New Orleans is now coveted by three nations.

1803   Wary of over-extending its colonial empire, in need of money, and in light of impending war, Napoleon decides to sell not only Isle of Orleans but entire Louisiana colony to U.S.; treaty signed April 30. Formal hand-over of Louisiana, from Spain to France and thence from France to United States, occurs in Cabildo on December 20, closing colonial era. New Orleans, now in progressive American hands, is foreseen to become one of richest and most important cities in nation, hemisphere, and world.

1803   New Orleans population 8,056 (3,948 whites, 2,773 slaves, and 1,335 free people of color) residing in roughly 1,000 dwellings. Another 2,000 people live nearby.

1803-1840 New American city of New Orleans grows dramatically in population while also rising steadily in rank relative to other American cities' populations (see graph, "Tracking New Orleans' Ascent and Decline, 1790-2007").

Early 1800s Shifting river channel deposits sediment immediately above New Orleans, forming "batture" along Faubourg Ste. Marie riverfront. Geological formation instigates legal controversy regarding public versus private ownership of valuable new riverside land, reflecting differing Creole and American legal philosophies. Complex court case involves President Jefferson and lasts for decades; area is eventually incorporated into urban grid; includes today's Warehouse District. Laws regarding batture ownership remain complex and convoluted to this day.

1804-1825 Three attempts to improve public health through sanitation and nuisance-abatement regulatory boards arise and fail, due to minimal government support and commercial opposition to quarantines. New Orleans becomes nation's filthiest, least healthy, and most death-prone major city for much of nineteenth century, a fact oftentimes denied or covered up by city's commercial interests.

1805 New Orleans is incorporated as a municipal entity, legally establishing city government, mission, duties, privileges, and boundaries. Charter ends colonial-era notions of city management and makes New Orleans "official" American city. Process of Americanization is underway.

1805 Lower plantation of Bernard Marigny is subdivided for urban development. Faubourg Marigny becomes city's first expansion on natural levee in downriver direction. Neighborhood, known as the "poor Third" [municipality or district], becomes home to mostly working-class Creole and immigrant population during nineteenth century.

1806-1810 Upper plantations of Delord-Sarpy (Duplantier), Saulet (Solet), Robin, and Livaudais are subdivided for urban development. Faubourgs Duplantier, Solet, La Course, and L'Annunciation expand New Orleans onto wide natural levee in upriver direction; area is developed with working-class housing near river and grander homes inland. Neighborhood (today's Lower Garden District) becomes home to mostly American and immigrant population during nineteenth century.

1807 Act of Congress clarifies ownership of disputed lands in new American city; influences development of commons between the old city and Faubourg Ste. Marie. Act also reserves canal right-of-way planned to connect Carondelet Canal with river, paralleled by sixty-foot-wide public highways. Canal is never built; corridor instead becomes 171-foot-wide "Canal Street." Additionally, act confirms most land titles of settlers from colonial times, preserving old French *arpent* land-division system.

1809 Over 9,000 Saint-Domingue (Haitian) refugees arrive to New Orleans via Cuba. Refugees, roughly evenly divided among white, free people of color, and enslaved black, double city's population and revive city's Francophone culture. They integrate into Creole neighborhoods and society, adding new layers of ethnic complexity.

1809 Faubourg Pontchartrain planned at headwaters of Bayou St. John. Area promises to develop into attractive faubourg, but developers stay away until late

1800s, after settlement of complex Myrna Clark Gaines lawsuit, one of longest in U.S. history.

1810   New Orleans population reaches 17,224 (6,316 whites; 5,961 black slaves; and 4,950 free people of color), seventh largest among American cities.

1810   Plantation of Claude Tremé is subdivided for urban development. "Faubourg Tremé" spreads New Orleans toward backswamp, exploiting Esplanade Ridge/Bayou Road upland. Neighborhood, known for its black Creole and immigrant population, is described today as America's oldest black neighborhood, but was actually quite mixed.

1812   Louisiana admitted to Union as eighteenth state.

1800s-1860s Despite institutionalized social and economic oppression, enslaved black population is residentially integrated with whites in "classic Southern" urban settlement pattern of enslaved living in abodes adjacent to those of their masters. Free people of color reside mostly in lower city; emancipated blacks live mostly in poor back-of-town.

1812   First Mississippi River steamboat docks at New Orleans, having departed Pittsburgh in late 1811, evading the Great Falls of the Ohio, witnessing the Great Comet of 1811, and encountering recent devastation of the New Madrid earthquake in Missouri. Successful demonstration of emerging steam technology promises efficient upriver-bound transportation, replacing slow-moving keelboats for travel against current. "Steamboat era" begins in earnest by early 1820s, after technological, logistical, and legal barriers (namely monopoly granted to owners Robert Fulton and Robert Livingston) are surmounted. With city in American hands and hinterland under intensive cotton, sugar, and grain cultivation, new steamboat transportation puts New Orleans in strategic position to become principal Southern city.

1815   On January 8, local militia under command of Maj. Gen. Andrew Jackson defeats advancing British troops at Chalmette. Battle of New Orleans terminates English threat to young nation, brings city's society to national attention, and helps integrate isolated, once-foreign outpost into national fold. Anglo-American emigration increases, as does foreign immigration.

1816   Crevasse at Macarty's Plantation in present-day Carrollton floods backswamp to rear streets of city. Water damages city infrastructure and crops, but coats land with layer of sediment, building up elevation and helping enable early development of Carrollton. Flood actually saves lives by cleaning city and reducing death rate by over half.

1810s-1870s City expands steadily, mostly in upriver direction, on relatively broad natural levee in present-day uptown. Expansion occurs through piecemeal subdivision of old long-lot sugar plantations, and through political annexation of Lafayette (1852), Jefferson (1870), and Carrollton (1874). Plantations subdivided into uptown faubourgs during nineteenth century include Faubourg Nuns (des Religieuses), Panis Plantation (Faubourg Lafayette), Faubourgs Livaudais, Delassize, Plaisance, Delachaise, St. Joseph, Bouligny, Avart, Rickerville, Hurstville, Bloomingdale, Burtheville, Foucher Tract (Audubon Park and university campuses), Greenville, Friburg, and Macarty Plantation (Carrollton).

Late 1810s In response to War of 1812, U.S. War Department begins building "Third System" forts along Atlantic and Gulf coasts, including key waterways in and near New Orleans. Military later acquires riverfront land for barracks and naval bases, recognizing strategic location and vulnerability of city, which becomes one of nation's most fortified. Military presence increases with twentieth-century world wars; remains big local employer today.

1820 New Orleans population reaches 27,176 by some accounts; 41,351 by others (19,244 whites; 14,946 black slaves; and 7,188 free people of color). Inclusion of adjacent areas may account for difference.

Early 1800s Travelers from Europe and eastern seaboard visit New Orleans and marvel at booming port's social and physical distinctiveness, particularly its ethnic diversity. National perceptions about New Orleans as a unique and exotic city, or alternately as a wicked "Sodom and Gomorrah," begin to form.

1822 According to *The New Orleans Directory and Register*, city and suburbs count "1,436 brick, and 4,401 wooden dwellings; 1,258 brick and 1,567 wooden warehouses, workshops, &c.; 28 brick and 15 wooden public buildings, making in the whole 8,705 buildings of every description. New buildings are daily rising particularly in the upper part of New Orleans."

1824-1828 First Jewish congregations founded in New Orleans, notably Congregation Shangari Chassed (Gates of Mercy) in 1828, predecessor of Touro Synagogue. Later-arriving German Jews form small enclave at foot of Jackson Avenue, which would migrate to uptown/University area by turn of twentieth century. This older, established Reform Jewish population lived separately from Eastern European Orthodox Jews who settled near Dryades Street in late nineteenth century.

1823-1836 First true municipal water system, designed by Benjamin H. B. Latrobe, replaces various makeshift efforts. Located at foot of Ursulines Street, system uses steam pump to draw river water into three-story pumphouse, where it is stored in raised reservoirs and distributed to residential households through network of cypress pipes.

1825 Erie Canal in upstate New York connects Great Lakes with Hudson River. Waterway gives New York City access to western frontier, suddenly challenging New Orleans' monopoly on Mississippi Valley trade. Conservative New Orleans business community fails to diversify economy during ensuing decades, focusing instead on booming river trade. Seed for New Orleans' decline is planted, but is buried amid antebellum prosperity. Erie Canal spawns rampant waterway excavation elsewhere: more bad news for New Orleans.

1825-1830 Louisville and Portland Canal completed to circumvent waterfalls in Louisville, Kentucky, an obstacle to Ohio River navigation. Canal benefits New Orleans by providing fast, uninterrupted shipping to Pittsburgh, even as Erie Canal draws traffic away from New Orleans.

1828 and 1831 Abraham Lincoln guides flatboat down Mississippi to New Orleans, probably landing at Faubourg St. Mary wharves in today's Warehouse District. Tradition holds that sight of local slave markets makes lasting impression on young Lincoln.

1830   New Orleans population reaches 49,826 (21,281 whites; 16,639 black slaves; and 11,906 free people of color), fifth largest among American cities.

1830s   Esplanade Avenue is extended from river to Bayou St. John. Avenue is designed in French manner and developed as garden suburb for wealthy Francophones departing old city. Corridor exploits upraised Esplanade Ridge and forms axis of orthogonal street network of Sixth and Seventh wards, but does not replace its prehistoric predecessor, Bayou Road, which wanders across Esplanade at an angle all its own.

1830s   Black population in New Orleans, majority since 1730s, falls into numerical minority as Irish and German immigration augments city's white population. Urban slaves are often replaced by immigrant servants and laborers, contributing to steady decline in absolute number of black New Orleanians from 1840 to emancipation. City remains majority-white until late 1970s.

1831   Pontchartrain Railroad built to connect river and lake. Early railroad establishes Elysian Fields Avenue trajectory through backswamp a century prior to area's urban development. Railroad serves as ingress/egress for passenger traffic between New Orleans and Gulf Coast cities.

1832-1838 At cost of thousands of mostly Irish lives, New Basin Canal is excavated between rear of Faubourg St. Mary and Lake Pontchartrain, giving city (particularly uptown Anglo business community) improved access to lake trade. Waterway competes with circa-1790s Carondelet Canal and new Pontchartrain Railroad, both of which draw lake trade to Creole lower city. Canal and turning basin influence development of back-of-town and lakefront into mid-twentieth century.

1832   Cholera epidemic kills thousands, particularly newly arrived Irish immigrants.

1830s-1850s Main era of Irish immigration to New Orleans sees Irish settle in dispersed pattern throughout periphery of city, particularly along riverfront and back-of-town, while generally avoiding costly inner city. English-speaking Catholic churches are founded to serve this population.

1830s-1930s Sugar handling and trading creates "sugar landing" on upper French Quarter batture, riverside of present-day North Peters, from Toulouse to Iberville. Area develops into "Sugar District" in 1870s, with high-rise processing plants, storage sheds, shipping facilities, and exchange. Sugar processing moves to St. Bernard Parish in 1910s, but industry continues to use French Quarter riverfront until 1930s. Most facilities have since been demolished; area, now occupied by parking lots, is often eyed for new development.

1830s   Capt. Henry Shreve and State of Louisiana alter hydrology of Mississippi/Red/Atchafalaya region in central Louisiana, not foreseeing consequences. Shreve cuts off meander loop near Red-Mississippi juncture (1831) to aid navigation; severed section silts up ("Old River") in one part and sends Red River into Mississippi in another portion. Immense logjam prevents water from escaping down Atchafalaya distributary, but also retards navigation and development in south-central Louisiana. Shreve and state clear logjam during 1830s, unknowingly providing Mississippi with shorter path and steeper gradient to sea. Cleared logjam sends steadily increasing flow down Atchafalaya rather than Mississippi. Fearing catastrophic channel jump, engineers build Old River Control Structure in 1950s-60s to preserve lower Mississippi River channel—and New Orleans.

1833   City of Lafayette founded immediately above New Orleans. Jefferson Parish community draws German and Irish immigrants to its densely populated riverside blocks (present-day Irish Channel), and wealthy, mostly Anglo families to elegant garden suburb in its interior blocks (today's Garden District).

1834   First successful gas company brings new fuel to city for lighting and other purposes. Gas works are soon constructed near present-day Superdome, illustrating how back-of-town was used for operations too sprawling and objectionable to be located in front-of-town. Gas works remain in this area for over a century.

1835   New Orleans and Carrollton Rail Road installed on Nayades Street, present-day St. Charles Avenue. Streetcar plays important role in developing uptown New Orleans and guiding surveying of new streets, as old long-lot plantations are subdivided for residential blocks. Now oldest continually serving rail line in the world (excepting two-year post-Katrina interruption), St. Charles streetcar represents first component of an urban rail system that would grow steadily until the 1920s, then decline back down to its original line after 1964.

1835   Joseph Holt Ingraham publishes *The South-West by a Yankee*, writing "I have termed New-Orleans the crescent city…from its being built around the segment of a circle formed by a graceful curve of the river…. " "Crescent City" catches on and becomes city's premier nickname for well over a century.

1835   New Orleans Barracks constructed as U.S. military post in lowermost corner of Orleans Parish. Complex of outstanding Greek Revival structures within turreted walls forms landmark for visitors sailing upriver; serves as jumping-off point for troops in Mexican War and other operations. Renamed Jackson Barracks in 1866, installation is now home to Louisiana National Guard.

1836   Anglo displeasure with Creole political control and other ethnic tensions lead to creation of essentially three separate cities within New Orleans: lower First and Third municipalities are mostly Creole and immigrant; upper Second Municipality is mostly Anglo and immigrant. "Municipality system" is inefficient and divisive, but influential in ethnic geography of city, producing perception of Canal Street as dividing line between Creole and American cultures. City reunifies in 1852.

1836-1838 Municipal market system begins steady expansion. Public markets open above (Poydras Market, St. Mary's Market) and below (Washington Market) old city, while original French Market, established by Spanish administration, enjoys its own expansion. New Orleans' municipal market city grows steadily to thirty-four units in 1911, becoming largest such system in nation.

1837   Panic of 1837 and ensuing depression interrupts city's economic bustle; many wealthy citizens lose fortunes.

1837   Strong hurricane hits New Orleans, damaging structures and flooding marshes adjacent to Lake Pontchartrain.

1837-1842 Opulent "exchange hotels," built in First and Second municipalities, combine lodging, dining, banking, and conference space under one roof. St. Louis Exchange Hotel opens in predominantly Creole First Municipality; domed St. Charles Exchange Hotel opens in predominantly Anglo Second Municipality. Each becomes nuclei for competing Creole-Anglo interests, and are described as among most splendid hotels in America. Both cater to extended-stay guests during wintertime business season.

1830s-1840s New American aesthetics affect built environment: Creole architecture peaks and begins to decline in French Quarter; replaced by Greek Revival, which first arrived here in 1808 from Northeast. Stylistic shift reflects larger cultural changes in politics and society, from Creole to American.

1840   New Orleans population reaches 102,193 (59,519 whites; 23,448 black slaves;

and 19,226 free people of color). City is third-largest in nation, the highest ranking it would ever achieve.

1840 New Orleans is "rated ... as the fourth port in point of commerce in the world, exceeded only by London, Liverpool, and New York."[3]

1840 Antoine's opens in French Quarter. French restaurant represents new national phenomenon (first seen in New York City in 1830s) of "eating out" as delectable, high-end entertainment rather than mere necessity for hungry transients. Relocated to present-day St. Louis Street site in 1866 and now city's oldest continually operating enterprise, Antoine's represents culinary artifact of mid-nineteenth-century French cooking.

1840s Destrehan Canal dug to connect Mississippi River with Bayou Barataria and Barataria Bay. Canal helps develop West Bank; is expanded as "Harvey Canal" with modern locks in 1907 and widened as part of Gulf Intracoastal Waterway in 1924.

1840s-1910s New Orleans continues to grow in population, but declines in rank relative to other American cities. Increasing railroad and canal competition for Mississippi Valley trade partially explains why New Orleans begins to fall behind other cities (see graphs, "New Orleans' Meteoric Rise ... and Relative Decline, 1810-1860" and "Tracking New Orleans' Ascent and Decline, 1790-2007").

1846 War with Mexico breaks out following U.S. annexation of Texas. New Orleans plays prominent role as jumping-off point for troops and munitions; local *Picayune* newspaper becomes major source of war reporting for nation. Involvement symbolizes era (particularly 1830s-50s) when New Orleans served as favored site for launching campaigns of adventurism and intrigue into Latin America.

1840s-1850s Main era of German immigration to New Orleans. Like Irish, Germans settle in dispersed pattern throughout city periphery, particularly in Lafayette and Third Municipality. Somewhat better educated than Irish but burdened by language barrier, Germans instill rich cultural and institutional traditions into New Orleans society.

1840s-1850s Retailers migrate from narrow Royal and Chartres streets to commodious Canal Street, until now a mostly residential thoroughfare. Canal Street becomes South's premier downtown shopping destination until 1960s.

Mid-1840s After seven failed attempts since Louisiana Purchase, New Orleans launches a professionally staffed Board of Health to understand and improve city's terrible public-health crisis. Hard data and honest assessments of deplorable conditions are finally documented, yet death rate increases in ensuing decade, in part because of official complacency.

1848   Illinois and Michigan (I & M) Canal is completed across hundred-mile-long
"Chicago Portage," providing waterborne passage between Great Lakes and
Gulf of Mexico watersheds. New western commerce opportunity fuels development of Chicago, while diminishing New Orleans' once-monopolistic control of Mississippi River shipping traffic. I & M Canal is supplanted in 1900 by
larger Chicago Sanitary and Ship Canal.

1849   Crevasse in levee at Sauvé Plantation in Jefferson Parish diverts river water
into lowlands between natural levee of Mississippi and Metairie/Gentilly
ridges. Water fills backswamp and inundates city from rear, to within blocks
of riverfront; submerges 220 blocks, damages 2,000 structures, and displaces
12,000 residents. City infrastructure is rebuilt with funds from special tax.
"Sauvé's Crevasse" ranks as New Orleans' worst flood until Hurricane Katrina
levee failures of 2005.

1846-1856 Decaying *Place d'Armes* and surrounding buildings are renovated magnifi-
cently: St. Louis Cathedral and twin Pontalba Buildings constructed; Cabildo
and Presbytère renovated with Mansard roofs and cupolas; Andrew Jackson
statue installed; newly fenced and landscaped plaza renamed Jackson Square.
Outstanding work transforms dusty commons into place of splendor, completely intact today. Cast-iron galleries on Pontalba Buildings instigate local
fashion craze and forever change streetscape of French Quarter, as iron-lace
galleries are added to numerous townhouses and storehouses.

1847-1858 Yellow fever outbreak in 1847 claims lives of over 2,300 New Orleanians;
commences era of terribly costly epidemics killing at least 22,500 in upcoming
twelve years, disrupting nearly every aspect of life in New Orleans. High death
tolls are a product of poor municipal sanitation, perfect habitat for invasive
Aedes aegypti mosquito, and large numbers of vulnerable residents, primarily
Irish and German immigrants.

1850   New Orleans population reaches 119,460 (91,431 whites; 18,068 black slaves;
and 9,961 free people of color). Despite growing population and booming
economy, city drops in rank from third-largest in nation in 1840 to fifth-largest
in 1850.

1850   New telegraph lines speed city's communication links with adjacent cities and
points downriver.

1850   3,700 miles of canal are completed in U.S. since Erie Canal opened in 1825.
Waterway excavation in North further threatens city's grip on Mississippi and
Ohio Valley trade. But busy traffic on river obscures growing threat on horizon; New Orleans merchants focus on short-term opportunities and prosper
during antebellum "golden age."

1850s New railroads in Northeast give East Coast cities additional access to trans-Appalachian region, even when canals freeze in winter. Railroads further weaken New Orleans' command of Mississippi Valley trade; there are now numerous ways to get resources and cargo in and out of North American interior. Transportation costs decline for Western commodities in Eastern urban markets; city dwellers thus spend less on food and more on manufactured goods, fueling industrialization in North. Complacent business leaders in New Orleans are late in bringing railroads and industry to city, viewing traditional river transportation as salvation.

1850s As slavery becomes most divisive issue in nation, racial tensions increase locally and rights of free people of color are curtailed. City's traditional Caribbean-influenced three-tier racial caste system begins to give way to two-tier (white/black) notion favored in rest of nation. Some free Creoles of color respond by departing for Mexico, further diminishing city's nonwhite population in late antebellum years.

1851 52,011 immigrants arrive to New Orleans, almost equal to number arrived to Boston, Philadelphia, and Baltimore combined. City is primary immigration port in South and second in nation (behind New York) for most years between 1837 and 1860.

1852 Municipality system (1836) is abandoned; Lafayette incorporated into New Orleans. City emerges from municipality era with new Anglo-American ethnic domination and momentum toward upriver expansion. City's political and economic epicenter, including City Hall, is relocated from old city to Faubourg St. Mary. Old house-numbering system and ward boundaries are updated.

1850s Local publishing industry shifts its base from Chartres Street in old city to Camp Street in Faubourg St. Mary, reflecting increasing influence of American side of town. "Newspaper Row" remains in and around 300 block of Camp Street until 1920s.

1850s "Cotton District" forms around Gravier/Carondelet intersection. Cotton factors and merchants form busy financial district in heart of Faubourg St. Mary, nerve center of Southern cotton economy. District survives into 1950s.

1853 City's worst yellow fever epidemic claims at least 8,000 lives, probably closer to 12,000 (one-tenth the city); Irish and German immigrants suffer disproportionately. City streets are nearly deserted during summertime months. While local press notoriously underreports stories of plague to avoid affecting commercial interests, newspapers in rival Northern ports, particularly New York, document New Orleans' yellow fever miseries enthusiastically. Subsequent epidemics in 1854-55 continue suffering for city's underclass.

1855-1858 Three prominent national churches arise in former city of Lafayette, now Fourth District of New Orleans. Predominantly Irish St. Alphonsus Church (1855-58), German-language St. Mary's Assumption (1858-60), and Francophone Notre Dame de Bon Secours (1858) are erected in close proximity, symbolizing multiethnic nature of uptown New Orleans in late antebellum era. Similar situation prevails in Third District. Many of these geographically proximate church parishes are merged around turn of twenty-first century, due to limited resources.

1856 Hurricane strikes coastal Louisiana, soaking New Orleans and destroying utterly hotel resort on Isle Dernière ("Last Island"). Death toll of over 200 includes many prominent New Orleanians.

1857 Krewe of Comus formed by men from Mobile; helps transform celebration of Mardi Gras from private balls and disorganized street mayhem to public parades, fanciful royalty, and elaborate civic rituals. Mardi Gras, celebrated in Louisiana since 1699, soon develops into premier outward cultural trait distinguishing New Orleans from other American cities.

1858 Another 4,800 New Orleanians perish to yellow fever, city's second-worst plague. "Yellow jack" death toll declines nearly to zero during Civil War years, due in large part to sanitation efforts under federal occupation.

1860 New Orleans population reaches 174,491 (149,063 whites; 14,484 black slaves; 10,939 free people of color). Despite growing population, New Orleans' rank among American cities declines, from third-largest in 1840 to fifth-largest in 1850, to sixth-largest in 1860. Last antebellum year also marks city's highest ratio of whites to blacks: nearly six-to-one. By 2000, blacks outnumber whites by more than two-to-one.

1860 Thirty-one-thousand miles of railroad track crisscross U.S.; railroad and canal competition continues to cut into New Orleans' command of river trade.

1860 Three hurricanes buffet coastal Louisiana within two months, causing widespread damage and crop loss.

1860s Barges replace flatboats on the riverfront. Old flatboat landing is replaced by new docking facilities for powered barges; picturesque Mississippi flatboats from frontier era disappear from waterfront, except for coal transport. "Probably we will never again see the old days of flatboats revived."[4]

1861 Louisiana secedes from Union. Local Gen. P. G. T. Beauregard fires opening shots at Fort Sumter; Civil War begins.

1862 New Orleans, weakly defended by Confederacy, succumbs peacefully to federal troops executing "Anaconda Plan" to encircle South by seizing Mississippi River. War ends early for New Orleans as federal troops occupy city; South loses premier metropolis and critical grip on lower river. Region's slave-based plantation economy, which enriched white New Orleanians since colonial times, collapses forever; era of human slavery in New Orleans draws to a close after 143 years.

1862-1865 South and Southern agriculture devastated; shipping commerce to New Orleans interrupted; federal presence and post-war racial tensions alter social landscape.

1860s-1890s New social and urban factors affect built environment. Cottages, often with slave quarters and courtyards, diminish in popularity in French Quarter; replaced by shotgun houses, which peak in popularity during turn-of-century era. Individually crafted vernacular structures give way to quasi-mass-produced "catalog" houses.

1864-1866 Small but prominent Greek community founds first Eastern Orthodox Church in Western Hemisphere. Holy Trinity Church becomes religious center for Greek New Orleanians for century to come; Sixth Ward neighborhood around church's 1222 North Dorgenois site becomes geographical nucleus of Greek community.

1865-1871 Nine tropical storms and hurricanes batter Louisiana coastal region, causing varying amounts of damage.

1866 Violent riot breaks out at Mechanics Institute, in which mostly ex-Confederate white Democrats and their allies engage black Radical Republicans and their supporters, assembled for Louisiana Constitutional Convention. Tragedy claims dozens of lives (mostly black), injures over 100, and presages heightened racial tension and violence in Reconstruction-era Louisiana.

1866-1867 With city back under civilian control and no longer subject to military-enforced sanitation, public health troubles return. Cholera strikes twice in 1866; yellow fever outbreak in following year claims over 3,000 lives.

1867-1871 Sugar planters, seeking replacements for emancipated slaves, import Chinese workers from Cuban plantations. Effort fails, but brings small number of Chinese to city, some of who eventually settle in Third Ward and form "Chinatown" around 1100 block of Tulane Avenue. Others start family-owned laundries dispersed widely throughout city.

1868 Enterprise on Delachaise Street successfully manufactures and sells ice, one of first in nation. Year-round availability of ice allows corner grocers to carry perishables, previously limited by law (for health reasons) to city-controlled markets. Corner grocers, often run by Sicilian immigrants, appear throughout expanding residential areas. Parallel development of refrigerated shipping in this era enlarges meatpacking and other food industries from local to national scale, and expands list of commodities transhipped at New Orleans.

1868   New state constitution is among most progressive in nation, extending suffrage to blacks while calling for integrated public schools and accommodations. But entrenched racial order from antebellum times eventually trumps
constitution's aims, as racial tensions increase and federal troops depart in subsequent decade.

1869   State legislature takes action against public health nuisance created by city's
livestock and meat-processing industry. New law treats butchering as public utility, creating monopoly and centralizing and isolating slaughterhouse
activities away from city population. Outraged independent butchers sue;
"Slaughterhouse Case" arrives to U.S. Supreme Court, which decides in favor
of state monopoly in 1873. Locally, court's decision consolidates stockyards
and slaughtering to Orleans/St. Bernard parish line; nationally, it sets controversial precedent limiting interpretation of Fourteenth Amendment.

1860s-1870s Railroads are built across eastern marshes, connecting city with Rigolets,
St. Tammany Parish, Mississippi Gulf Coast, Mobile, and points east. Speedy
new transportation option unites New Orleans with coastal areas and diminishes passenger steamboat traffic to Port Pontchartrain on Elysian Fields Avenue lakefront. Recreation spots, summer escapes, fishing camps, and bedroom
communities for early commuters develop along railroad, particularly in Bay
St. Louis area.

1870s   International architectural styles begin to modernize cityscape. Creole architecture disappears almost entirely, as do antebellum American styles (particularly Greek Revival). Italianate facades, here since 1850s via English "Picturesque" movement, rise in popularity.

1870   New Orleans population reaches 191,418, ninth largest in nation. Emancipated slaves migrate to city in droves, doubling 1860 black population to 50,456
(26 percent of total 1870 population). Most settle in back-of-town; demographic pattern remains today, though backswamp is drained.

Late 1800s Settlement patterns change since antebellum years. Expanded streetcar networks allow affluent families, who traditionally lived in inner city, to move to
new garden ("trolley") suburbs, once occupied by poor Irish and German immigrants in antebellum times. Move opens up housing opportunities for poor
in inner city, where jobs also exist. Throughout late 1800s and early 1900s,
immigrants settle mostly in ring of inexpensive, conveniently located working-
class neighborhoods immediately surrounding CBD: the "immigrant belt."

1870s   New Orleans annexes Jefferson City, on uptown east bank, and Algiers, across
from French Quarter on West Bank, in 1870; Carrollton joins city in 1874.
Wards and municipal districts are adjusted to incorporate new city land. By
1880s, modern shape of Orleans Parish emerges.

1870s Sugar planters start recruiting peasants out of Sicily to work on Louisiana plantations in place of emancipated slaves. Sicilians, long part of New Orleans' tropical fruit trade, come by thousands between 1870s and 1900s. Most settle in lower French Quarter ("Little Palermo") and predominate in and near French Market until around World War II.

1870s Private company excavates drainage canals in lakeside marshes. Although project eventually fails, canals are later incorporated into successful municipal-drainage effort of 1896-1915, and remain in service today as the 17th Street, Orleans, and London Avenue outfall canals. All three waterways contributed to catastrophic flooding following Hurricane Katrina in 2005.

1871 Crevasse at Bonnet Carré sends river water into Lake Pontchartrain; June winds prevent lake's normal outflow to gulf, allowing water levels to rise in adjoining New Basin drainage canal. On June 3, levee breaches at Hagan Avenue and inundates area between Old Basin and New Basin canals up to Rampart Street. Worst flood since Sauvé's Crevasse, the Bonnet Carré Crevasse deluge illustrates how man-made navigation canals threaten population by bringing lake and gulf water into heart of city.

1872 Metairie Cemetery is laid out on former racetrack; becomes most famous of numerous cemeteries on Metairie and Gentilly ridges. Topographic features also host parks, fairgrounds, and other large-scale public land uses which require well-drained land and proximity to city population, but need too much acreage to be located in city proper.

1874 Violent riot between Democratic White League and Republican Metropolitan Police at foot of Canal Street represents flashpoint of post-war racial tensions. Conflict involves thousands and produces over 100 casualties. Monument to "Battle of Liberty Place" later dedicated at site becomes controversial reminder of racial discord in modern times; obelisk is eventually relocated and covered over with message of racial reconciliation.

1870s-1890s Orthodox Jewish people mostly from Poland and Russia settle between Dryades Street and St. Charles Avenue. The immigrants and their descendants form "Dryades Street neighborhood," New Orleans' only popularly recognized Jewish neighborhood, distinct from established Reform Jewish community of uptown. Jewish-owned shops on Dryades, and residences and religious institutions riverside of Dryades, remain into 1960s-70s.

Late 1800s Emancipation and post-war racial tensions polarize Louisiana's historically fluid sense of racial identification into exclusive white/black categories. Creole identity is redefined by white narrative historians as exclusive domain of white descendents of French and Spanish colonials, despite ample historical use of term for Franco-African-American community. Writers of the "local color" tradition romanticize city's history and Creole society; New Orleans mythology is born and survives to this day.

1875-1879 With sedimentation of river channel delaying shipping traffic at mouth of Mississippi, Capt. James Eads constructs parallel jetties at South Pass. Structures constrain water flow, increase velocity, mobilize sediment, and deepen channel, allowing ocean-going vessels to enter river promptly. Coupled with development of barges, growth of local railroad network, and improving economic conditions, Eads' jetties help city rebound from post-war slump. But engineering effort also diverts sediment away from Louisiana coast and onto edge of continental shelf, rather than building up marshes of birdfoot delta.

1877 Federal troops withdraw; New Orleans' turbulent occupation and Reconstruction era ends.

Late 1870s Garbage, waste, and excrement, traditionally dumped into Mississippi at various "nuisance wharves" along riverfront, are now loaded onto barges and dumped in the middle of river below city limits. Service is provided not by city but by private voluntary Citizens' Auxiliary Sanitary Association (1879), which also installs river pumps and pipes to flush out city streets.

1878 Worst yellow fever outbreak since 1850s claims over 4,000 lives.

1878 T. S. Hardee and Auxiliary Sanitation Association publish *Topographical and Drainage Map of New Orleans and Surroundings*, most accurate city map of era. 1879 version includes first comprehensive elevation measurements of city, at one-foot contour interval.

1879 Federal government creates Mississippi River Commission, ending era of local and state levee projects and commencing modern era of federal authority over flood and navigation control of Mississippi River.

1880 New Orleans population reaches 216,090; black population 57,617 (27 percent). By one account, city's ethnic mix comprised "some 70,000 French and Creoles, 30,000 Germans, 60,000 Negroes and mulattoes… 10,000 Mexicans, Spanish and Italians [and] 80,000 or 90,000… Anglo-Americans," including Irish.[5] City is now tenth-largest in nation, dropping steadily from rank of third in 1840.

1880 Growing city boasts 566 miles of streets, of which only ninety-four miles are paved. Of those, cobblestones cover 35 percent, pulverized oyster shells overlay 25 percent, stone paving blocks cover 24 percent, and the remainder are treated with stone fragments or planks.

1880 Railroads now link New Orleans to Cairo, Illinois and points upriver, to Mobile and points north and east, to Morgan City and points west, and to Donaldsonville across river (via ferries). Network of tracks complements city's shipping industry but pales in comparison to those connecting emerging Midwestern cities with northeastern metropolises.

Late 1800s-early 1900s Remarkable era of innovation, particularly in electrification, transportation, and communications, transforms cities and alters political and economic geographies. Progressive voices nationwide actively promote cleaning up cities, installing improved water, sewerage, and drainage systems, and creating city parks and playgrounds. Transformations foster development of Central Business District as non-residential inner core of high-rise office buildings, equipped with telephones and elevators. Office workers relocate to garden ("trolley") suburbs and commute on electrified streetcars and, later, automobiles. Globally, era witnesses shift in geo-political and economic power from one based on sea to one based on land. New Orleans, founded for its river/sea position and overly dependent on waterborne transportation, is ill-prepared for modern era.

Late 1800s-early 1900s "Local color" literary tradition flourishes in city. Writers such as George Washington Cable, Kate Chopin, Charles Gayarré, Grace King, and Lafcadio Hearn help mythologize New Orleans in public mind, forming foundation of modern-day tourism economy.

1882 Chinese Mission, founded on South Liberty Street, draws Chinese immigrants to Third Ward back-of-town; Chinatown forms around 1100 block of Tulane Avenue and survives until 1937.

1884-1885 World's Industrial and Cotton Centennial Exposition held at Audubon Park. Exposition fails commercially, but succeeds in helping develop semi-rural uptown into prosperous trolley suburbs with outstanding urban park and university campuses. Event also offers national and international venue for Louisiana artists and writers, who gain prominence afterwards.

1885-early 1900s First local cookbooks published, documenting city's foodways and helping form national cognizance of distinctive New Orleans cuisine. Publications coincide with rise in tourism, fueled by World's Industrial and Cotton Centennial Exhibition in Audubon Park, rising leisure class, railroad travel, and "local color" literary genre. Now a major source of local identity, city's food heritage is pillar of modern tourism industry.

1888 Strong hurricane, worst since 1837, strikes New Orleans; causes extensive structural damage, floods some areas with rainfall, and downs recently installed telephone and electrical lines.

1890 New Orleans population reaches 242,039, twelfth-largest in nation. Black population is 64,491 (27 percent).

1890-1891 Murder of Police Chief David Hennessy blamed on Sicilian mobsters; eleven Sicilians held at Parish Prison are lynched in retaliation. Incident leads to international crisis between Italy and U.S.; leaves deep scars in Sicilian community, contributing to its social isolation in "Little Palermo" (lower French Quarter) at turn-of-century.

1890s-1900s Arabi subdivision develops upon old Le Beau plantation immediately below New Orleans, bringing upper St. Bernard Parish area into urbanized area.

1890s-1920s Former Foucher tract and Allard Plantation landscaped into Audubon Park and City Park, respectively.

1891-1909 "Residential parks" created uptown along St. Charles Avenue. Rosa Park, Audubon Place, and other exclusive residential streets represent early form of zoning and "gating" of communities.

1893   Extremely powerful hurricane devastates coastal Louisiana and Gulf Coast, killing over 2,000.

1893-1895 City council empowers new Drainage Advisory Board to study and solve city's age-old drainage problem. Board collects vast amount of scientific and engineering data, develops large-scale topographic map, and proposes plan to drain water off natural levee to low point in central city, then pump it through canals into adjacent lakes. Construction begins in 1896 and progresses substantially following 1899 bond issue.

1894   Tulane University relocates uptown, after sixty years downtown as antecedent institutions. "University area" forms as Loyola University moves next door in early 1900s. Twin campuses impart vital character to uptown, helping form affluent neighborhoods with highly educated residential population, many from out-of-town.

1894   Erratic 1852 house-numbering system is replaced with logical system in use today, in which addresses increment by 100 per block, with odd numbers indicating lakeside or downriver sides. Effort reflects Progressive Era sensibilities of improved municipal services.

1890s-1900s Research conducted at Audubon Park refines methods for purifying river water for residential use. Shortly thereafter, purification and distribution plant is constructed in Carrollton, bringing city into modern age of municipal water systems. Carrollton site provides appropriate riverside location and elevation to draw water from Mississippi, remove sediment, add lime and sulfate of iron for softening, purify it with chloride gas, and store it. High-lift pumps then distribute water to city residents everywhere except Algiers, which is served through similar West Bank system.

1890s-1900s Steel-frame construction and concrete pilings are introduced to New Orleans; first generation of high-rises erected in CBD and upper French Quarter transforms city's skyline.

1893-1898 Streetcar lines are electrified throughout city.

1895 Conflagration destroys much of Algiers, last of great city fires. Algiers rebuilds in era of late Victorian architecture, giving modern-day Algiers Point neighborhood a quaint, turn-of-century ambience.

1896-1915 Following two years of research and design (and financing in 1899), a world-class drainage system is installed to remove runoff and standing water in low-lying backswamp. System radically alters geography of New Orleans: swamp and marshes disappear; urban development begins to spread toward lake; middle-class whites move off natural levee and into new lakefront suburbs (which explicitly exclude blacks through deed covenants). Crescent-shaped historic New Orleans gives way to modern twentieth-century metropolis.

1896 St. Augustine Catholic Church parishioner Homer Plessy tests post-Reconstruction Jim Crow laws by sitting in whites-only train car (1892). Legal case regarding his arrest backfires in historic 1896 Supreme Court decision: *Plessy v. Ferguson* establishes "separate but equal" legal precedent, entrenching segregation in South for next half-century. Public facilities in New Orleans, from streetcars to schools to department stores, are legally segregated by race. Case is viewed as the concluding chapter of the Americanization of New Orleans' Caribbean-influenced system of racial identity.

1897 Alderman Sidney Story sponsors ordinance to ban prostitution throughout city, except in fifteen-block neighborhood behind French Quarter. Subsequent ordinance creates second zone along nearby Gravier Street. Laws succeed in controlling prostitution, but inadvertently create vibrant and conspicuous red-light districts, dubbed "Storyville" and "Black Storyville" respectively. Storyville becomes nationally notorious and helps affirm New Orleans' ancient reputation for debauchery, while also incubating some of city's musical genius. Storyville closes in 1917 by order of U.S. Navy; forming "sporting houses" are demolished around 1940 for Iberville Housing Project.

1899-1902 Sicilian-born Vaccaro brothers and Russian-born Samuel Zemurray independently start importing bananas from Central America through New Orleans. Vaccaros' firm grows into Standard Fruit; Zemurray's Cuyamel Fruit later merges with United Fruit. Banana companies tighten city's grip on nation's tropical fruit industry, attained in antebellum times via shipping routes with Sicily. Companies establish close ties between city and Central American republics, particularly Honduras, deeply influencing political and economic landscape of Central America for years to come. Hondurans immigrate to city in modest numbers throughout twentieth century, giving New Orleans one of largest transplanted *Catracho* populations. Most currently reside in Kenner, Metairie, and Mid-City.

Turn-of-century Jazz musical style emerges from myriad local and regional influences; soon diffuses nationwide and worldwide with help from Tin Pan Alley music industry and nascent recording technologies. Jazz becomes "sound track" of Western world from 1920s to World War II, and is commonly recognized as New Orleans' most significant cultural contribution.

1900   New Orleans population reaches 287,104; black population 77,714 (27 percent). City remains twelfth-largest in nation

1900   Race riot erupts following violent exchange between police officers and back-to-Africa advocate Robert Charles. Incident, which occurs in poor, isolated back-of-town area settled by emancipated slaves, is often described as city's last major race riot, attesting to relatively peaceful race relations here. But neighborhood, present-day Central City, remains troubled today.

Early 1900s Steam-powered riverboats are gradually replaced by tug barges and other petroleum-powered vessels for freight shipping. Sights and sounds of steamboats crowding riverfront disappear from Mississippi River, except for excursion vessels, many of which carry local jazz bands to interior cities.

1901-1920s Dock Board modernizes port facilities, constructing riverside warehouses, grain elevators, canals, and new docking space.

1901   Louis Armstrong born in back-of-town, as jazz era emerges. New Orleans' most famous son greatly enhances city's image in eyes of world, but city fails to embrace Armstrong until years after his death, even demolishing his neighborhood in 1950s for new City Hall complex.

1904-1920 and 1926 Algiers resident Mayor Martin Behrman oversees important civic improvements, including modernization of drainage, sewerage, and water systems; expansion of city services and public education; and creation of Public Belt Railroad.

1905   Over 400 people die in city's (and nation's) last yellow fever epidemic. Poor Sicilian immigrants living in crowded conditions in lower French Quarter are blamed for outbreak. After *Aedes aegypti* is identified as vector, new drainage and potable-water systems (eliminating mosquito-breeding puddles and cisterns) finally end century-old public health problem.

1905-1910 New home construction commences in recently platted Lakeview subdivision, drained from marsh only a few years earlier. Lakeview develops mostly during 1910s-40s, becoming comfortable and stable middle-class inner suburb. Deed covenants restrict home ownership to whites only, affecting city's racial geography, as middle-class white families "leapfrog" over black back-of-town to settle in drained marshes.

1906   Continuing spirit of municipal improvements ongoing since 1890s, Olive Stallings establishes city's first playground for neighborhood children. Stallings leads new Playgrounds Commission in 1911 and eventually wills a portion of her estate to city's public playgrounds and pools, leading to birth of New Orleans Recreation Department.

1910   New Orleans population reaches 339,075; black population 89,262 (26 percent). City drops to fifteenth-largest in nation.

1910s   Architectural styles change: Creole cottages and shotgun houses decline in popularity, replaced by Craftsman, City Beautiful, and California-style bungalows. Three-bay townhouses give way to "catalog" framehouses, villas, and other structural typologies and styles.

1910s-1940s Gentilly is developed on and near Gentilly Ridge topographic feature in Seventh and Eighth wards. New suburb, with non-native architectural styles and spacious green surroundings, expands city toward newly drained lakefront. Deed covenants restrict sales to whites only.

1910s-1960 New Orleans continues to grow in population, while stabilizing in rank relative to other American cities at around the fifteenth-largest city in U.S. (see graph, "Tracking New Orleans' Ascent and Decline, 1790-2007"). Shipping and industrial activity relating to two world wars helps explain suspension of city's steady decline in national ranking.

1911   City's thirty-fourth municipal market opens, but proves to be last, as competition from ubiquitous corner grocery stores takes toll on old centralized stall markets. Automobiles, supermarkets, franchises, suburbanization, and globalized food production and distribution render system obsolete by mid-twentieth century.

1912   St. Charles Hotel launches national marketing campaign billing New Orleans as "The City Care Forgot." Effort helps instill slogan into national lexicon.

1914-1918 World War I rages in Europe; city benefits from war-related increase in river traffic. Local German community is devastated by stigma of enemy association; most German cultural institutions and public traditions in city are permanently silenced.

1915   Hurricane strikes New Orleans region, damaging 25,000 structures, causing flooding, inflicting $13 million in expenses, and killing 275 Louisianians, including twenty-four in tragic Rigolets incident. Eleven major churches lose their steeples or towers. Antebellum landmarks Old French Opera House and former St. Louis Hotel are heavily damaged; latter is subsequently demolished.

1917   Xavier University founded. Nation's only black Catholic institution of higher learning reflects New Orleans' distinct Creole heritage.

1918-1923 Dock Board excavates Inner Harbor Navigation Canal ("Industrial Canal") on old Ursuline Nuns holding in Ninth Ward; canal and locks connect river and lake, providing shortcut to gulf and opening up new deep-water wharf space. Much port activity shifts to Industrial Canal by mid-1900s, but returns to river by turn of twenty-first century. Canal benefits port but isolates Lower Ninth Ward from rest of city, while dangerously introducing surge-prone waterways into urban interior.

1919 Immense base for Army Quartermaster Corps is constructed at foot of new Industrial Canal, changing face of Ninth Ward riverfront and augmenting military presence in New Orleans. Base serves as Port of Embarkation during World War II. Army transfers base to Navy in 1966; Navy prepares to depart in 2009. Future of Naval Support Activity is currently under discussion.

1919 Old French Opera House burns. Demise of Bourbon Street landmark, built in 1859, symbolizes end of centuries-old cultural exchange between France and New Orleans; helps launch appreciation for decaying French Quarter.

1920 New Orleans population reaches 387,219, seventeenth-largest in nation; black population is 100,930 (26 percent).

1920s-1930s Writers, artists, and intellectuals are drawn to Quarter's bohemian ambience and cheap rents; many live within a few blocks of each other, fostering intellectual interaction. Together with "local color" era of late nineteenth century, "French Quarter Renaissance" puts New Orleans on map as great literary city.

1922 New Orleans Public Service Inc. gains control of all streetcar lines, electrical service, and natural gas distribution in city. Decade of 1920s marks apex for streetcar system, with over 220 track miles spanning from West End to Lower Ninth Ward and on nearly every uptown river-parallel street between Dryades and Tchoupitoulas. Ensuing forty years see gradual transition to rubber-tire buses and termination of 90 percent of mileage.

1922 Association of Commerce Convention and Tourism Bureau begins promoting New Orleans as "America's Most Interesting City," to counteract languid, anti-business connotations of "City that Care Forgot."

1926-1934 Ambitious Lakefront Project protects city from storm-driven lake and gulf surges while creating high, scenic acreage for residences, parks, facilities, and airport. Project radically alters shape and topography of city; accelerates movement of population toward Lake Pontchartrain.

1926-1935 With modern technology enabling road construction through swamps, new Airline Highway antiquates historic River Road as main terrestrial connection between New Orleans and Baton Rouge. Highway soon draws old riverfront communities away from Mississippi, but itself is superceded by I-10 forty years later.

1927   Great Mississippi River Flood inundates 26,000 square miles from Cairo to gulf; kills hundreds, displaces half-million, and threatens New Orleans. City is spared from river flooding, but controversial dynamiting of levee in St. Bernard and Plaquemines parishes to ensure metropolis' safety creates lasting ill-will between city dwellers and rural neighbors. Nation's worst natural disaster transforms federal river-control policy (through Flood Control Act of 1928) from "levees-only" to one of massively augmented levees, floodwalls, spillways, control structures, reservoirs, canals, revetments, and other devices throughout Mississippi Valley. Profoundly influential act puts federal government in flood control business, mandating federal financial and engineering responsibility for controlling Mississippi and other rivers, but immunizing government from liability should these systems fail.

1920s-1940s Old Basin (Carondelet) and New Basin canals, rendered obsolete by railroads, highways, and barges, are incrementally filled in, opening up valuable ingress/egress corridors to downtown. Former bed of New Basin Canal later becomes Pontchartrain Expressway right-of-way.

Late 1920s Highway 11 Bridge erected over eastern Lake Pontchartrain increases automobile access to Slidell and points east. New bridges over Chef Menteur and Rigolets passes speed up trip to coastal Mississippi.

1929   St. Charles Avenue between Lee Circle and Jackson Avenue is zoned for light industrial use, leading to demolition of old homes. Twenty-four years later, area is rezoned to eight-story commercial district, encouraging construction of large-scale edifices. Zoning changes alter character of once-elegant lower St. Charles to motley mix of retailers and open lots amid occasional old homes.

1930   New Orleans population reaches 458,762; black population 129,632 (28 percent). City is sixteenth-largest in nation.

1930s-1941 New Deal agencies Works Progress Administration and Public Works Administration execute numerous projects citywide, renovating historic structures, rebuilding aging infrastructure, and documenting city's past.

1934-1938 Public Works Administration renovates French Market, restoring circa-1813 Butchers Market, reconstructing Bazaar Market, remodeling Vegetable Market, demolishing Red Store, adding Fish Market, and razing Gallatin Street for new Farmers' Market and Flea Market pavilions.

1935   Huey P. Long Bridge, first across lower Mississippi River, links east and west banks of Jefferson Parish. Built for both railroad and automotive traffic, bridge ends era of train ferries and sparks development in semi-rural Jefferson Parish.

Hair-raising "Huey P" later proves inadequate for modern vehicular traffic; is currently undergoing widening.

1936   State constitution authorizes city to preserve French Quarter. Vieux Carré Commission guards nation's second legally protected major historic district (after Charleston); buildings deemed architecturally and historically significant are preserved and held to certain standards. By saving city's iconic neighborhood, effort creates bedrock of future tourism industry and helps inspire protection of other historic areas.

1937   Chinatown at 1100 Tulane Avenue is razed; small Chinese merchant community relocates to 500 block of Bourbon Street, where it survives in remnant form into 1980s.

1937-1943 Housing Authority of New Orleans (HANO) clears selected historic neighborhoods to construct subsidized housing projects. Six expansive areas, including former Storyville and portions of Tremé and the Irish Channel, are levelled, isolated from street grid, and rebuilt (1940-43) with garden apartments to be rented at subsidized rates to the poor. Those on higher elevation in the front-of-town are reserved for whites only; those in lower spots in the back-of-town are black-only. Later populated almost exclusively by the city's poorest African-Americans, the Iberville, River Garden (St. Thomas), Lafitte, Guste (Melpomene), C. J. Peete (Magnolia), B. W. Cooper (Calliope), St. Bernard, Florida, Fischer, and Abundance Square (Desire) public housing projects radically influence geographies of race and class in the late twentieth century. Viewed by many as "warehouses" for poverty and vice, some projects are demolished and rebuilt with mixed-income New Urbanist designs in early 2000s.

1940   New Orleans population reaches 494,537; black population 149,034 (30 percent). City is fifteenth-largest in nation, gaining slightly in rank due to Depression-era migration from rural regions, WPA-related job opportunities, and employment in industries relating to impending war.

1940   Moisant Airfield is established in isolated truck-farming community of Kenner, to supplant Lakefront Airport. Owned by City of New Orleans, Moisant begins commercial service in 1946 and is renamed New Orleans International Airport in 1960. Connected with city by Airline Highway, airport fuels growth of Kenner before East Jefferson Parish develops. Gap fills in entirely with completion of I-10 and Veterans Boulevard by 1970s. Airport is renamed Louis Armstrong-New Orleans International in 2001, but code MSY (allegedly "Moisant Stock Yards") remains. Airport's runway orientation and small size are now seen as obstacles to air traffic; new airport sites west and east of city are proposed in 1990s-2000s.

1941-1945 As nation fights World War II, New Orleans plays disproportionately significant role in war, as major ingress and egress for matériel and troops, base for ships and aircraft, and manufacturing center for Higgins landing craft (used during D-Day and other amphibious assaults). Navy commissions Naval Air Reserve Air Base on recently constructed lakefront, making area beehive of activity during war years. Troops on leave in city help transform Bourbon Street from bohemian nightspot to world-famous red-light district.

1940s Federal government encourages development of petrochemical refining capability in region. Bucolic River Road between New Orleans and Baton Rouge transforms from agrarian landscape of decaying antebellum homes to one of petrochemical refineries and industrial facilities. Region today is "Industrial Corridor" to some, "Cancer Alley" to others.

1940s Black Creoles begin migrating to war-related jobs in Jim Crow-free California. Railroad connections between New Orleans and Los Angeles give latter city a significant population of New Orleans Creoles (as well as Louisiana Cajuns), which remains to this day.

1942 German U-boat sinks *Robert E. Lee* near mouth of Mississippi, killing twenty-five, before it too is destroyed. Other enemy subs disrupt shipping in Gulf of Mexico and bring war to Louisiana coast. As in colonial days, New Orleans' position on river makes it valuable, but also vulnerable.

1944 G.I. Bill, passed in anticipation of millions of returning veterans, provides low-interest loans toward purchase of new homes. Housing shortages in most American cities lead young families to settle in new peripheral subdivisions, driving initial wave of post-World War II suburbanization. Infrastructure and commerce follow new suburbanites, encouraging further urban sprawl. In New Orleans, most post-war subdivisions occupy low-lying terrain drained only recently of swamp water.

1945 Geographer Gilbert F. White publishes *Human Adjustment to Floods*. Influential study finds that man-made flood-control structures paradoxically tend to *increase* flood damage, by inspiring overconfidence in the control of nature and encouraging humans to move into high-risk areas ("Floods are 'acts of God,' but flood losses are largely acts of man.") So-called "levee effect" occurs throughout coastal Louisiana during twentieth century, as swamp drainage and levee construction create valuable new real estate and lure more people into increasingly risky areas.

1946-1961 Mayor de Lesseps "Chep" Morrison oversees post-war modernization of city's infrastructure, reform of old-style political machines, and establishment of new commercial ties with Latin America. Brasilia-inspired City Hall complex, train station, airport, improved rail/street crossings, more buses, fewer streetcars, and bridges over both river and lake are among the changes of Morrison era.

1946   New York City building czar Robert Moses submits "Arterial Plan for New Orleans" to guide modernization of city's transportation system. Most controversial component entails connecting points east with West Bank by running elevated expressway in front of French Quarter. Funding arrives for "Riverfront Expressway" in 1964, launching bitter fight among New Orleanians for remainder of 1960s over fundamental notions of preservation and progress.

1946   Schwegmann Brothers Giant Supermarket opens on St. Claude and Elysian Fields; 40,000-square-foot grocery store is city's first modern supermarket. More follow, encouraged by increasing automobile dependence and flight to suburbs. Trends eventually spell doom for most corner grocery stores, street vendors, and municipal markets. Food retail, once micro-scale and spatially dispersed, becomes concentrated and less reflective of local food culture.

1947   Tennessee Williams' *A Streetcar Named Desire* debuts on stage. Play instills New Orleans mystique and sense of place into millions of theatergoers and later moviegoers; becomes most famous work of French Quarter literary community, active in 1920s-40s.

1947   Fourteen years after region's first offshore oil well is drilled, President Truman offers Louisiana all royalties and lease bids for near-shore wells and 37.5 percent of those farther out. State rejects offer in hope of more lucrative deal, which never comes. Decision costs state billions of dollars over next six decades; is only partially remedied when 2006 law directs 37.5 percent of future offshore royalties to four gulf states.

1947-1965 Upturn in tropical activity produces eight hurricanes affecting Louisiana coast, including two serious strikes to New Orleans proper.

1947   Late summer hurricane strikes New Orleans region while on northwestern track toward Baton Rouge. Winds of over 100 m.p.h. buffet city; small storm surge floods lightly developed eastern ramparts of metropolis as well as Jefferson Parish. Damages amount to $100 million; fifty-one people perish. Unnamed "Hurricane of 1947," as well as subsequent September 1948 storm, inspires additional levee construction along lake shore and adjacent marshes.

1949-1950s Federal Housing Act of 1949 leads to expansion of city's subsidized public housing developments. Second-generation structures lack the local designs, solid construction, and intimate settings of original circa-1940 buildings.

1950   New Orleans population reaches 570,445, sixteenth-largest in nation; black population 181,775 (32 percent).

1950   Louisiana Landmarks Society founded to preserve historically and architecturally significant structures; mission is later expanded to preserve historic neighborhoods and fight inappropriate development. Society saves many of city's famous buildings and fosters appreciation for historical architecture.

1950s Cut off by Industrial Canal, low-lying "New Orleans East" remains mostly rural except for ingress/egress services along Chef Menteur Highway and citrus orchards and recreational camps along Hayne Boulevard. First modern subdivisions appear along Dowman Road and Chef Menteur in the early 1950s, followed by aggressive development in the 1960s-70s when Interstate 10 is built. Installation of drainage system precedes urbanization; unlike the circa-1900 system west of the Industrial Canal, this one is designed to store sudden, heavy rainfall runoff in lagoons and open canals, thereby requiring less pumping capacity to remove it to Lake Pontchartrain.

1954 *Brown v. Board of Education* Supreme Court decision reverses locally originated 1896 *Plessy v. Ferguson* ruling on "separate but equal" public schools. Ruling sets legal stage for end of *de jure* segregation of schools and public accommodations in South. During next decade and particularly after Civil Rights Act in 1964, Jim Crow gradually disappears from streetcars, buses, department stores, schools, housing, restaurants, and facilities. Change is often accompanied by protests and tensions, but rarely violence.

1953 All but two streetcar lines—Canal and St. Charles—are discontinued in favor of rubber-tire buses.

1954 Union Passenger Terminal opens near present-day Loyola Avenue. New station unifies (hence the name) numerous passenger lines and leads to closing of turn-of-century stations located throughout city, including two picturesque structures near French Quarter. Consolidation of railroads tracks within recently filled-in New Basin Canal right-of way leaves many old rail corridors abandoned throughout city, many still owned by railroad companies.

1954-1962 Old River Control Structure is built to regulate flow among Mississippi, Red, and Atchafalaya rivers, addressing circa-1830s intervention which aided navigation interests but inadvertently altered system's hydrology. One of world's great engineering projects, "Old River" ensures that Mississippi will not abandon channel and jump into Atchafalaya (leaving New Orleans on elongated brackish bay) by allocating flow at government-approved seventy-thirty ratio between the two rivers.

1955-1956 New technology of packing cargo into standardized containers and handling them in mass-production mode from ship to truck or train rapidly transforms world's ports. Containerization ends centuries-old longshoremen culture in port cities, alters geography of urban waterfronts, and allows new small ports to compete with old major ports. With containerization, great ports no longer need great port cities. Port and city of New Orleans are deeply affected by new technology.

1955 Pontchartrain Park subdivision, with its distinctive curvilinear street network and golf course, is built in lakeside Seabrook section of Ninth Ward. First modern suburban-style development for black New Orleanians (funded by whites) draws middle-class families, many of them black Creoles, out of historical neighborhoods to settle in eastern lakeside section of parish.

1955   Lincoln Beach, a lakefront recreational destination for black New Orleanians prohibited through Jim Crow laws from using nearby Pontchartrain Beach, opens along Haynes Boulevard. An integral childhood memory of a generation of African-Americans, Lincoln Beach remains open until Civil Rights Act in 1964 prohibits discrimination at public facilities. A few vestiges of facility remain in ruins today.

1956   Federal Aid Highway Act is signed by President Eisenhower, commencing historic effort to build interstate highway system. New Orleans is eventually connected to nation via I-10 and I-610 plus nearby I-12, I-55, and I-59. One of world's longest causeways connects rural St. Tammany Parish with metropolitan Jefferson Parish, opening Florida Parishes to suburban expansion. "Across the lake" becomes "the north shore" in local parlance, particularly after second span is opened in 1965 and exodus increases. Region's first modern tunnels open on West Bank of Jefferson Parish, while now-infamous "Carrollton Interchange" is completed near Orleans/East Bank-Jefferson Parish line. Most major modern transportation corridors are built in the fifteen years following 1956, radically altering cityscape and urban geography of region.

1958   First downtown Mississippi River Bridge opens. Bridging of river furthers West Bank development; comes at expense of scores of historic structures in Lee Circle area. Second span is erected in late 1980s, creating "Crescent City Connection" and forming new iconic vista of downtown New Orleans.

1958   Navy relocates air station from East Bank lakefront across river to Belle Chasse. Move encourages new development in bridge-accessed West Bank portions of Orleans and Jefferson parishes, and brings upper Plaquemines Parish into metropolitan fold. Belle Chasse Naval Air Station-Joint Reserve Base is now major hub of military's presence in metropolitan area.

1958-1968 Mississippi River-Gulf Outlet Canal is excavated in St. Bernard and Plaquemines parishes. "MR-GO" gives ocean-going traffic shorter alternate route to Port of New Orleans and helps develop Industrial Canal as new center of port activity. But seventy-five-mile long waterway also causes coastal erosion and salt-water intrusion, requires constant dredging, and provides pathway for hurricane-induced storm surges to reach populated areas. MR-GO plays role in flooding following Hurricane Betsy in 1965, and infamously after Hurricane Katrina forty years later. "MR-GO Must Go" becomes battle cry of angry flood victims and environmentalists nationwide after 2005 catastrophe.

1959   After 107 years at historic Lafayette Square, City Hall and government offices are relocated to new Duncan Plaza complex. International-style office buildings, built upon recently demolished back-of-town neighborhood that included Louis Armstrong's birthplace, give city government more space and air of modernity. New complex fosters growth of city, state, and federal government office district on expanded Loyola Avenue.

1959   Cuban revolution and ensuing political tensions isolate Caribbean nation from Western world. New Orleans, chief shipping port to Bautista-era Cuba, loses major trade partner and centuries-old ties to former Spanish colony. Many Cuban exiles settle in city and state, drawn in part by sugar industry. When U.S. loosens trade embargo in early 2000s, local ports resume handling significant share of exports to Cuba, continuing historic relationship between city and island nation.

1960   New Orleans population peaks at 627,525, fifteenth-largest among American cities; black population is 233,514 (37 percent). Suburban Jefferson Parish population grows from 103,873 in 1950 to 208,769 in 1960. Roughly half of New Orleanians in 1960 reside above sea level, down from over 90 percent a half-century earlier. After 1960, New Orleans declines in both absolute population and in relative rank among American cities.

1960s   Decade witnesses profound transformations in society and infrastructure, affecting cityscape at every level. Declining population (first time since early 1700s), diminished tax base, increasing crime, suburbanization, globalization, gentrification, and other forces leave inner city with more derelict space, less public space, fewer neighborhood stores, less interaction among neighbors, and greater spatial disaggregation by race and class, even as *de jure* segregation ends. Traditional aspects of urban living—sidewalks teeming with shoppers, stoop-sitting, children playing in streets, bustling stall markets—diminish or disappear entirely from city experience.

1960-1964 Civil rights movement, court orders, and Civil Rights Act of 1964 hasten end of *de jure* segregation in New Orleans. Long in process but now empowered by national movement, struggle for racial equality in New Orleans comes to head with initial integration of public schools. Ugly street protests garner national attention, but city generally avoids violence seen in other Southern communities. "White flight" begins in earnest, setting Orleans Parish on ongoing trajectory of population decline.

1960s-1970s Hispanic immigrants, disproportionately from Cuba and Honduras, settle in working-class and middle-class areas of Irish Channel, Mid-City, and Ninth Ward. Most Hispanics live in Kenner, Metairie, and Mid-City according to 2000 Census.

1960s   Petroleum industry rises; port economy mechanizes. Coastal and offshore oil brings outside investment and professionals to New Orleans; triggers construction of downtown skyscrapers and "Houstonization" of city. Containerized shipping technology replaces many longshoremen and sailors; requires less waterfront space and frees up riverfront for recreational use. As oil industry rises, port-related employment declines.

1963-1972 Coast-to-coast I-10 is constructed through New Orleans. Major new infrastructure gives birth to modern metropolitan area; fosters middle-class exodus and suburban growth in eastward and westward directions. I-10 also destroys famous forested neutral ground of North Claiborne Avenue ("main street of black Creole New Orleans") and leads to decline of old ingresses/egresses, such as Airline Highway, Tulane Avenue, and Chef Menteur Highway.

1964 Civil Rights Act outlaws segregation in schools and public places. Blatant Jim Crow segregation disappears from public facilities, ironically putting many integrated retailers out of business, particularly on South Rampart and Dryades streets. Housing projects, segregated *de jure* since their opening around 1940, soon integrate but then re-segregate *de facto* as whites leave for suburbs.

1964 Reflecting nationwide switch from rails to buses and autos for urban transportation, all remaining streetcars except historic St. Charles line are terminated. Next twenty-five years mark low point in city's history of urban railways; 1964 decision is later regretted and reversed at turn of twenty-first century.

1964-1969 Federal funding arrives to build Riverfront Expressway, connecting bridge and CBD traffic with points east via French Quarter riverfront and Elysian Fields Avenue. Bitterly controversial plan, originally recommended by Robert Moses in 1946, divides citizenry and motivates unprecedented and ultimately successful campaign of resistance over next five years.

1965 Hurricane Betsy strikes New Orleans region in early September, causing extensive wind damage and flooding Ninth Ward and parts of Gentilly and New Orleans East. Disaster kills eighty-one Louisianians, injures 17,600, and causes $372 million in damage, about one-third in New Orleans. Betsy prompts Congress to authorize Flood Control Act of 1965, which includes Lake Pontchartrain and Vicinity Hurricane Protection Project. Influential act puts federal government in the business of storm protection; entails improvement and construction of hurricane-protection levees, flood walls, and gates (to what is now categorized as a Category-3 level storm) to protect developed areas as well as adjacent marshes. Envisioned new flood protection (never fully executed) increases real estate values and inspires new home construction in the very areas that flooded. During subsequent oil-boom years, over 75,000 homes are built in places such as New Orleans East, most of them on concrete slabs at grade level. Episode demonstrates so-called "levee effect" first identified by geographer Gilbert White in 1945: flood-control structures paradoxically increase flood damages, by luring homebuyers into flood plains. Forty years later, Katrina's floodwaters validate White's observation.

1966   Effort to compete with Houston and other ascendant Southern cities inspires widening of Poydras Street as "showcase" corporate corridor. Numerous historic structures are razed on lower side of street. Plan foresees need for major traffic-generating anchors at each end of Poydras: Rivergate Exhibition Hall (1968) is built at river end, Superdome (1975) at lake end.

1966   Simultaneous erection of International Trade Mart and Plaza Tower, city's first modern skyscrapers, symbolizes increasing oil-related wealth and new piling technology. Project sites are selected to spark competing skyscraper development on Poydras and Loyola, respectively. Poydras ultimately prevails.

1967   Saints NFL franchise brings professional football to New Orleans, making it a "big league city" mentioned in sports media in same breath as Dallas, Houston, Atlanta, and other competing cities. But a small market, declining population, and low per-capita income make city struggle to maintain "big league" perception. In early 2000s, Saints threaten to relocate to San Antonio or Mississippi Gulf Coast—unthinkable in earlier years. Team nevertheless remains wildly popular with regional residents, particularly after Hurricane Katrina.

1968   Rivergate Exhibition Hall is constructed at foot of Canal and Poydras streets. Bold freeform design adds stunning new vista to city's premier intersection; nurtures convention trade and fosters development of skyscraper hotels on lower Canal Street in early 1970s.

1968   Congress creates Nation Flood Insurance Program, pricing coverage at below-market rates to encourage participation. Program creates bonanza for real estate interests by encouraging development of flood zones, including coastal areas popular with wealthy second-home buyers.

1960s-1970s Ten blocks of historic Tremé, including many early-nineteenth-century vernacular houses, are levelled for Theater for Performing Arts and Louis Armstrong Park. Controversial urban renewal project, which displaced over a thousand residents, transforms Faubourg Tremé and is now regarded by many as a mistake.

1968-1969 After holding steady at 40,000 annually since *Brown v. Board of Education* (1954), white student enrollment at New Orleans public schools begins steady decline, while black enrollment doubles to 70,000. White exodus to suburbs and entrenchment of black underclass in Orleans Parish eventually lead to *de facto* re-segregation of New Orleans public schools. System that was one-to-one black-to-white in 1957 becomes five-to-one by early 1980s and nineteen-to-one in early 2000s.

1969   New hotels are prohibited in French Quarter, in attempt to balance tourist and residential use. Ban eventually encourages new hotel development on Canal Street, CBD, and Warehouse District. Attempt in 2004 to rezone parking lots riverside of North Peters for new hotels may foretell new construction in this area.

1969   Federal cancellation of bitterly divisive Riverfront Expressway project saves French Quarter's frontage with Mississippi; makes New Orleans one of first American cities to resist nationwide trend toward elevated expressways along downtown waterfronts.

1969   Category-5 Hurricane Camille strikes coastal Mississippi, obliterating significant portion of historic Gulf Coast. New Orleans suffers some wind and flooding, but is mostly spared what might have been a catastrophe.

1970   New Orleans population declines to 593,471; black population 257,478 (43 percent). City falls in rank from fifteenth- to nineteenth-largest in nation, at the time the largest ten-year drop in its history.

1970   Jazz and Heritage Festival is held at present-day Congo Square. Created by Massachusetts-born George Wein, inventor of the modern music festival, event grows into annual New Orleans Jazz and Heritage Festival (Jazz Fest), now second only to Mardi Gras in the cultural-tourism economy. Festival provides important venue for local musicians and helps instill "New Orleans sound" as essential part of American "roots" music; performs similar service for Louisiana food. Event's location at Fairgrounds on Gentilly Boulevard helps expose traditionally French-Quarter-bound visitors to non-tourist neighborhoods.

1971   Friends of the Cabildo publishes *New Orleans Architecture, Volume I: The Lower Garden District*. Study inspires new appreciation for historic architecture outside French Quarter and Garden District; sets scholarly tone for local historical research and stirs modern preservation movement. Nomenclature and boundaries used in series (currently eight volumes strong and growing) help revive historical place names and affect public's perceptions of place.

1971-1972 Galvanized by construction of out-of-scale Christopher Inn Apartments and empowered by subsequent historic district zoning (first since Vieux Carré protection in 1936), residents establish Faubourg Marigny Improvement Association. Group participates in political process, with eye toward historic preservation and neighborhood improvement; inspires residents of other historic neighborhoods, leading to both revitalization and gentrification. Old French term "faubourg" is revived in neighborhood nomenclature and adopted by real estate industry and press. Faubourg Marigny begins transforming from mostly working-class neighborhood of natives to professional-class neighborhood of transplants; becomes city's premier gay neighborhood.

1972   One Shell Square—697 feet high and resting on 200-foot pilings—rises as tallest structure in city and lower Mississippi Valley. Symbolizes apex of 1970s oil boom.

1972   Last full-scale Mardi Gras parades roll through French Quarter. Increasingly elaborate Carnival celebrations, including new "super krewes" (starting 1969), create safety hazard in Quarter's narrow streets. St. Charles Avenue becomes new route for most parades; French Quarter is left to inebriated revelry and lewdness. Neighborhood krewes gradually abandon their local parade routes and centralize along standard St. Charles route, even as parading tradition diffuses to suburbs and beyond. Beads and other "throws" grow in popularity, and now practically form a city industry (though trinkets are mostly manufactured in China). City's Mardi Gras celebration enters modern age during 1970s, as a major tourism-driven civic ritual attracting a nationwide audience.

1973   Second-worst Mississippi River flood on record threatens region. Old River Control Structure is damaged and later enlarged; Bonnet Carré Spillway opened to relieve pressure on levees.

1973-1974 Curtis and Davis architectural firm issues *New Orleans Housing and Neighborhood Preservation Study*. Landmark document identifies and delineates sixty-two official city neighborhoods, based on historical perceptions, natural geographical barriers and major transportation arteries, social and economic patterns, and census tract boundaries. Effort alters perceptions of place, space, and nomenclature in city; marks modern era of city planning. Designation of national and local historic districts starting in 1970s furthers trend toward perceiving neighborhoods as discrete, bounded, officially named entities with mutually agreed upon characteristics.

1970s   Renovation restores historic French Market structures, transforming complex from city marketplace vending foodstuffs to locals, to festival marketplace primarily oriented to visitors.

1970s   Post-Betsy flood control, Interstate 10, Industrial Canal, NASA Michoud plant, and new subdivisions make eastern New Orleans hot new real estate market, led by "New Orleans East" land development scheme.

1974   Preservation Resource Center is founded. Local non-profit group injects preservationist and "liveable city" philosophies into city discourse; becomes most influential group advocating adaptive reuse of historic structures and improvement of old neighborhoods.

1974   First "magnet schools" formed in New Orleans public school system. With fifty-fifty black/non-black racial quotas, magnet schools are designed to prevent further white flight. Relatively small number of white students tends to cluster in a few high-achieving schools, which soon become most racially integrated in city. Controversial quotas are banned in 1998 after protests; magnets later called "Citywide Access Schools."

1975   Moratorium is imposed on demolitions in CBD, after scores of nineteenth-century storehouses are razed for skyscrapers or parking lots.

1975   Louisiana Superdome is completed, marking peak of city's competition with oil-rich Houston. Spectacular domed stadium transforms skyline and breathes new life into CBD. Superdome serves as venue for high-profile events, publicizing city and its attributes to nationwide audiences on a regular basis.

Late 1970s Vietnamese refugees from post-war communist Vietnam arrive to New Orleans on invitation of Catholic Church. Archdiocese settles hundreds of mostly Catholic refugees in Versailles apartments in eastern New Orleans and in spots on West Bank. Versailles settlement forms unique neighborhood, one of city's most isolated and purest ethnic enclaves, known for elaborate multi-tier market gardens and open-air Saturday market. Neighborhood functions as nerve center for Vietnamese community dispersed throughout central Gulf Coast region.

1976   Riverfront promenade "Moonwalk" (honoring progressive Mayor Moon Landrieu) opens in front of French Quarter. Signifies change of riverfront use from port activity to recreation, as containerization and Industrial Canal docks concentrate and relocate shipping facilities off Mississippi.

Late 1970s New suburban subdivisions encounter unwelcome problem in former Jefferson Parish backswamp: soil sinkage. Subsidence of recently drained hydric soils causes structural damage to thousands of new ranch houses built on concrete slabs; issue makes headlines throughout late 1970s, particularly after some houses explode when gas lines break. New piling-based construction standards are subsequently adopted, but soils continue to sink.

1977   Lawsuit filed by environmental group successfully prevents Army Corps from building gates at mouth of Lake Pontchartrain, a flood-control measure envisioned in 1964 to prevent storm surge from entering lake. Corps later agrees to raise levee heights instead. Such an apparatus theoretically would have prevented Katrina-driven breaches on lakeshore outfall canals, though not those on eastern navigation canals.

1977   City, now majority-black for first time since 1830s, elects first black mayor, Ernest N. "Dutch" Morial, a descendent of Creoles of color (like many city leaders today). Mayor Morial serves from 1978 to 1986.

Late 1970s Audubon Zoo, constructed mostly during 1920s-30s and considered an out-of-date "animal prison" by modern standards, is redesigned and expanded into national-class zoological attraction and research facility.

1980   New Orleans population declines to 557,515; black population 308,149 (55 percent). City is now twenty-first largest in nation.

1980s   Cajun ethnic revival changes New Orleans tourism. Newfound appreciation of Cajun culture is exploited by French Quarter tourism venues; Cajun dishes, music, shops, and swamp tours become standard part of visitor experience. Chef Paul Prudhomme gains celebrity status through introducing nation and world to spiced-up Louisiana cuisine.

1983-1984 Worldwide oil crash hits city; devastates Gulf Coast and other petroleum-based economies. Bust costs New Orleans thousands of white-collar jobs in subsequent years and initiates dark era of job loss, middle-class exodus, and increasing crime rates which endures until mid-1990s. Louisiana's oil- and gas-related employment plummets from nearly 95,000 jobs in 1981 to about 41,000 in 2005.

1984 Louisiana World Exposition is held along present-day Convention Center Boulevard, on hundredth anniversary of World's Industrial and Cotton Centennial Exposition at Audubon Park. Like its predecessor, "World's Fair" fails financially but helps launch economic development in downtown and re-introduces citizens to riverfront. Historic "Warehouse District" is revitalized into convention, hotel, condominium, and arts district in subsequent years, as former fair structures are converted into Ernest N. Morial Convention Center and expanded to over one million square feet. Residential population of CBD/Warehouse District climbs from under one hundred in 1980 to over 1,300 in 2000.

Mid to Late 1980s Corps raises heights of city's levee system but neglects to account for new research on increased storm strength, surge height, coastal erosion, and soil subsidence. Concrete floodwalls are erected along riverfront and out-fall canal levees, but some are built with insufficiently long sheet piling. Corps' plans for "butterfly gates" to prevent surge from entering outfall canals are opposed by Sewerage and Water Board and Levee Board, because they would reduce ability to pump rainwater out of city. Shortfalls of flood-protection system are revealed twenty years later during Hurricane Katrina.

Mid-1980s "Festival marketplaces," like those pioneered by James Rouse, open along Mississippi River. Jax Brewery and Riverwalk further recreational/retail utilization of downtown riverfront, once reserved for maritime use. New Riverfront Streetcar (1988), first new line in decades, connects French Quarter with new attractions and Ernest N. Morial Convention Center.

1985 Unusual late-October Hurricane Juan floods coastal region, including portions of West Bank. Incident leads to raising of levees along metropolis' southern fringe.

1985-1986 New Orleans East land-development company, poised to urbanize over 20,000 acres of wetlands in eastern Orleans Parish, fails amid oil bust. Land is transferred to federal government and becomes Bayou Sauvage National Wildlife Refuge, reflecting new appreciation of once-scorned marshes and wetlands. Had area developed as envisioned, Hurricane Katrina's toll in lives and property would have been even higher.

1980s-1990s Numerous generations-old downtown department stores and restaurants—Holmes, Krauss, Maison Blanche, Godchaux's, Maylie's, Kolb's, and others—fold, due to middle-class exodus, growth of suburbs, crime concerns, parking crunch, and rise of tourism. Buildings are often converted to hotels for growing hospitality industry.

1987 Pope John Paul II's visit reaffirms New Orleans' place among nation's great Catholic population centers; draws worldwide attention to city's large Catholic African-American population.

1987 *The Big Easy* movie popularizes new nickname for city, introduced around 1970 from circa-1900 origins and now more prevalent than circa-1835 "Crescent City" moniker. Loaded with clichés and stereotypes, *The Big Easy* portrays New Orleans as eccentric, corrupt Cajun outpost obsessed with food and festivity; helps stoke tourism boom of 1990s.

1989 CNG Tower is constructed next to Superdome. Twenty-three years after erection of first modern high-rises, New Orleans' last office skyscraper to date (later named Dominion Tower) symbolizes declining petroleum-related wealth. Sixteen years later, following shift toward tourism, Donald Trump proposes 700-foot-high tower for Poydras Street—but for condominiums and hotel rooms, not offices. As of 2008, Trump investment is still promised but not yet commenced.

1990 New Orleans population drops below half-million mark to 496,938, ranking as twenty-fourth largest city in nation; black population is 307,728 (62 percent). Jefferson Parish population declines for first time, from 454,592 residents in 1980 to 448,306 in 1990, due in large part to oil crash.

1990-1991 Coastal Wetlands Planning and Protection Act ("Breaux Act") brings federal funds to Louisiana for coastal restoration; Caernarvon Freshwater Diversion opens below city, first major effort to reverse salt-water intrusion and rebuild wetlands around New Orleans.

Early 1990s Race relations deteriorate amid troubled economic times. Tensions are also a product of gubernatorial candidacy of former Klansman David Duke, Mardi Gras krewe integration controversy (which motivated three old-line krewes to cease parading), protests at Liberty Place monument on Canal Street, and record-high crime rates. Problems are exacerbated by lag between decline of oil industry and rise in tourism/service economy.

1990s Formosan termite infestations explode across city and region. Accidentally imported on shipping palettes from East Asia during World War II, invasive termites threaten housing stock (particularly historical structures) and urban trees; cost city hundreds of millions of dollars annually in control and damage costs. Threat leads to increased use of steel and aluminum in new construction and renovation.

1990s Hurricane evacuation planning transforms radically. Coastal erosion, subsiding soils, rising seas, and an upswing in hurricane frequency ends traditional notion of evacuating internally to sturdy schools and shelters within city limits. Now, citizens are urged to evacuate entire region in their own automobiles; rural coastal residents who once evacuated *to* New Orleans are now directed farther inland. Plans to evacuate the poor and others without cars are never fully articulated—a tragic oversight that would cost hundreds of lives during Katrina in 2005.

1990s-2000s Declining population forces archdiocese to close or reduce services at numerous historic churches, some of which are partially converted to homes for aged. Many religious elements of historical cityscape fall silent as local families relocate to suburbs and young, secular transplants move into old neighborhoods.

1992 Category-5 Hurricane Andrew, first of 1990s-2000s wave of mega-storms, pulverizes southern Florida and southcentral Louisiana. New Orleans is spared, but begins to recognize augmenting threat of storm surges amid eroding coast. Andrew ends notion of "riding out" storms in sturdy old schools; ushers in era of metropolitan evacuation. Light winds in city cause surprisingly heavy damage to live oaks, leading to discovery of extensive Formosan termite damage to urban trees.

1994 U.S. Environmental Protection Agency lists Upper Ninth Ward neighborhoods of Gordon Plaza, Press Park, and Liberty Terrace as Superfund sites. Once city's garbage dump from 1900s to 1960s, "Agriculture Street Landfill" was later covered with topsoil, developed, and populated with working-class, mostly black, families. High levels of lead and other contaminants in soil forced school closures and extensive clean-up during 1990s-2000s; many residents resisted remediation in favor of more costly solution of buyouts. Controversy garners attention of nationwide environmental justice movement.

Circa 1995 "Renaissance" begins. Worst of local recession passes; national economy heats up; convention and tourist traffic increases; crime rates begin to drop after 1994 peak. But damage is done: white-collar petroleum jobs retreat to Houston; blue-collar port jobs are largely replaced by automation. New Orleans becomes a tourist-oriented service economy.

1995 May 8 storm dumps up to eighteen inches of rainfall on metropolitan area; some areas get twelve inches in single hour. City's worst rainfall floods 56,000 homes and businesses and causes $761 million in damage throughout twelve-parish area; leads to half-billion dollars of mostly federal funds for new drainage projects. New Orleans increases pumping capacity with new pumps, canals, culverts, and backup generator, from three inches of rain every five hours to five inches in five hours.

1995   Amid protests, architecturally significant Rivergate Exhibition Hall is demolished for Harrah's at foot of Canal Street. Casino, opened in 1999 after turbulent construction period, is predicted to transform downtown, but eventually settles into modest niche between traditional French Quarter tourism and emerging Warehouse District convention trade. Gambling in New Orleans falls well short of exuberant expectations of early 1990s, indicating that visitors are more interested in enjoying city's unique attributes than in increasingly ubiquitous "gaming" opportunities.

1995-Present Upturn in tropical activity makes hurricanes a matter of nearly constant public apprehension during summer months. Storm threats with partial or total evacuations occur at pace of nearly every other year during this era. Persistent sense of uncertainty—vis-à-vis eroding coast, subsiding soils, rising seas, and warming climate—leads many to ponder city's long-term viability.

1996   *Brightfield* vessel collides with Riverwalk Mall, causing no fatalities but demonstrating risk of converting shipping wharves to public recreational and commercial uses.

Late 1990s-early 2000s Hotel capacity, mostly in CBD and Warehouse District, skyrockets to 37,000 rooms, to accommodate nearly ten million annual visitors. Numerous historic structures in CBD and Warehouse District are remodeled into "boutique hotels."

Late 1990s-early 2000s Scientific community and press bring coastal erosion issue to public attention. Increasing numbers of New Orleanians begin to understand connection between river, coastal wetlands, and city's sustainability; society grapples with possibility of city's mortality.

1998   City narrowly averts Hurricane Georges. Reminder of inevitability of "Big One," Georges teaches lessons on evacuation planning and street flooding in Mid-City area.

1999   New Orleans Arena opens, aiming to accommodate events too big for other venues but too small for nearby Superdome. With seating for 16,000-19,000 people, indoor arena succeeds in attracting Charlotte NBA franchise Hornets to city in 2002, plus numerous other entertainment and sports events.

1999-2005 In span of six years, dominant player in city's grocery market shifts from Schwegmann's to Winn-Dixie to Wal-Mart, reflecting transition in city's business sector from locally owned companies to regional and global firms. Televised media market saw similar transition over recent decades, from local to out-of-town ownership. Though local enterprises remain more common here than other cities, they comprise diminishing percentage of citywide economy, showing increasing influence of national culture in local urban life. Trend is partially reversed after Katrina, as Thibodaux-based Rouses expands into local grocery market (2007) and New Orleans-born Saints owner Tom Benson buys Fox affiliate WVUE (2008).

2000   New Orleans population declines to 484,674, thirty-first largest city in nation. Black population is 325,947 (67 percent). 2000 Census finds that metropolitan area's most ethnically diverse census tract is Fat City in suburban Metairie, while least diverse tract is in inner-city Lower Ninth Ward—exact opposite of earlier times. Thirty-eight percent of New Orleanians now reside above sea level, down from about half in 1960 and over 90 percent in 1910.

2000   D-Day Museum opens June 6, creating critical mass of cultural venues near Lee Circle. "Museum District" now comprises Ogden and Civil War museums, Contemporary Arts Center, and Julia Street art galleries. Highly successful attraction, renamed National World War II Museum, undergoes massive expansion starting in 2007.

2000   One of largest mapping efforts in state history entails measurement of topographic elevation through "light detection and ranging" (LIDAR) technology. High-resolution elevation maps of city and region, released to the public incrementally throughout the 2000s, dramatically illustrate effects of subsidence and coastal erosion. Datasets prove crucial in measuring depth of Hurricane Katrina flooding in 2005.

Early 2000s Federal government intervenes in city's public-housing crisis. "HOPE VI" philosophy (sixth version of a circa-1990 U.S. Housing and Urban Development program called "Homeownership and Opportunity for People Everywhere") entails ending concentration of poverty in isolated public-housing projects by replacing them with New Urbanism-inspired settings, while integrating poor families paying subsidized rents with modest-income families paying market rates toward home ownership. Desire, St. Thomas, Fischer, and other housing projects are demolished, to tears of some displaced residents and cheers of those who view them as incubators of poverty and crime. Relocated families carry elements of "projects culture" into residential neighborhoods, sometimes resulting in tension and gang violence. New construction, exhibiting revived historical architectural styles, begins on former St. Thomas site. Nearby Wal-Mart is subject of bitter controversy involving issues of preservation, gentrification, race, jobs, corporate subsidies, and new "tax-increment financing" (TIF) concept.

Early 2000s Popularity of downtown condominiums grows, triggering conversion of numerous historical structures and proposals for new Sunbelt-style condominium towers. Out-of-town buyers help drive up local real estate prices and intensify gentrification pressure on adjacent neighborhoods. Post-Katrina woes and cooling of national housing market temper condo trend in 2006-08.

2001-2005 Lower Garden District riverfront sees radical landscape alteration. Saulet apartment complex, re-engineering of Tchoupitoulas and Religious streets, new Wal-Mart and River Garden development, and renovation and demolition of old warehouses make area one of nation's most transformed inner-city riverfronts. Projects reflect city's ongoing "re-discovery" of river.

2001   Terrorists attack American targets. Ensuing homeland-security efforts view New Orleans as "top ten" potential target, for its port, petroleum facilities, and major public events. New security measures are enacted, affecting riverfront development plans.

2003   New Orleans population drops to Depression-era level of 469,032, representing loss of over 15,000 since 2000 (greater drop than during entire decade of 1990s). Fastest-growing parish in region is St. Tammany on north shore, which surpasses 200,000 for first time.

2003   Tourists spend over four billion dollars a year in Orleans Parish, generating over 61,000 jobs. Visitors to New Orleans account for 44 percent of state's tourism economy. Oil and gas sector fares much worse: city's Exxon-Mobil office relocates to Houston, continuing twenty-year trend of petroleum industry forsaking New Orleans and Louisiana for Houston area.

2003   Two-hundredth anniversary of Louisiana Purchase celebrated December 20 in front of Cabildo, site of original formal transfer of Louisiana from Spain to France to United States. Visions of city's greatness from early 1800s fall with declining relative importance of waterborne transportation in America. Once strategically located at sole ingress/egress to North American interior, city now competes with innumerable transportation options. Lack of industrial development, relative isolation, Civil War, over-reliance on river (and later oil), social problems, and other factors exacerbate city's woes. Poor, undereducated, physically vulnerable, and losing population, city relies increasingly on selling its past to visitors.

2004   New Orleans population declines to 462,269, barely ahead of Jefferson Parish's 453,590. City proper is now home to only 35 percent of seven-parish metro-area population, down from 80 percent a century earlier.

2004   Success of 1988 Riverfront line inspires reintroduction of streetcars to city's transportation system. Major new routes are installed on Canal Street (starting 1997) and Carrollton Avenue, designed to circulate tourists throughout city and foster rail commuting. Much-anticipated Canal line opens in April 2004 and succeeds in invigorating Mid-City businesses. Additional lines are foreseen for other areas to jump-start neighborhood restoration. Hurricane

Katrina derails most efforts, as floodwaters damage new streetcars and rearrange priorities.

2004   Major new containerized shipping facility at Napoleon Avenue wharf, coupled with environmental problems on MR-GO and bottleneck lock on Industrial Canal, returns river to position of prominence in local port industry. Opposite was foreseen in 1970s, when "Centroport" was planned to shift most business to MR-GO/Industrial Canal wharves. New uptown facility also concentrates port activity and frees up antiquated downtown wharves for other uses.

2004   Category-4 Hurricane Ivan spares city but devastates coastal Alabama. New "contraflow" plan, devised after Hurricane Georges in 1998, opens up incoming interstate lanes to outgoing evacuees. Horrendous traffic jams lead to refinement of evacuation planning. Ivan's sideswipe brings additional attention to urgency of coastal restoration; in retrospect, serves as "dry run" for next year's Hurricane Katrina.

2004-2005 City holds "riverfront charrette" to gather ideas for new land uses from Poland to Jackson avenues. With port activity now concentrated in uptown containerization facilities, city and developers eye abandoned wharves for replacement with recreational/tourist use. Plan emerges in which Port of New Orleans relinquishes its maritime servitude of riverfront to city in exchange for percentage of land sales and leases. If enacted, agreement would open up over four miles of riverfront, from Bywater to Lower Garden District, for massive redevelopment, mostly for recreational use. Rejuvenated in 2007-08 as "Reinventing the Crescent," effort now proposes $300 million from state, local, federal, and private coffers to fund new public green space.

2005   Pentagon recommends closure of Naval Support Activity in Algiers and Bywater. Twin locations straddling Mississippi made military sense when installation was created, but proved to be costly obstacle in modern times. City's loss of up to 2,700 jobs may be mitigated by growth of Naval Air Station in Belle Chasse and creation of "federal city," cruise terminal, and other facilities and amenities in vacated riverfront properties.

2005   Following Hurricane Ivan traffic-jam debacle, new "contraflow" evacuation plan is unveiled. With coast eroding, levees subsiding, sea level rising, and fresh memories of hurricanes Georges and Ivan, local officials and populace treat hurricane evacuation planning with paramount importance. New "contraflow plan" involves evacuating most vulnerable areas first, then diverting out-bound traffic onto in-bound lanes at four complex intersections, giving evacuees six different escape routes to safety.

July 2005 New Orleans population estimated at 452,170, down by 10,000 in a year and 32,000 since the 2000 Census.

August 23, 2005 Low-pressure system develops over southeastern Bahamas; loop current brings warm subsurface waters from Caribbean into Gulf of Mexico, where sea surface temperatures hit ninety degrees. Topical Depression 12 becomes Category 1 Hurricane Katrina; makes landfall near Miami on August 25 and enters gulf, where warm waters fuel increasing wind speeds.

August 27-28, 2005 Hurricane Katrina strengthens to Category 3, 4, then 5; forecast tracks edge westward, then stabilize on a New Orleans-area strike. City and region prepare for worst: residents board up homes and businesses; officials close floodgates and activate "contraflow" system; hundreds of thousands of residents evacuate. Those who will not or can not—around 100,000—remain home or take refuge in Superdome. Initial feeder bands arrive as last day of pre-Katrina New Orleans draws to close.

August 29, 2005 Hurricane Katrina, with diminishing Category 2-3 winds but an enormous residual-Category-5 storm surge, makes landfall at dawn in Barataria Basin, passes immediately east of New Orleans, and makes second landfall around 10 a.m. along Louisiana/Mississippi border. City endures fiercest winds between 8 and 10 a.m., causing extensive structural damage. Surge raises gulf levels by ten to thirty feet and lake levels by nine feet, ravaging coastal areas to east. Lakefront levees endure pressure, but lower-quality navigation and outfall canal levees and floodwalls are overtopped or overwhelmed. When winds die down in late afternoon, most people surmise that city "dodged bullet." In fact, multiple levee breaches let salt water drown vast expanses of metropolis.

August 29-September 4, 2005 Rising deluge from levee breaches turns windy disaster of Katrina into watery catastrophe of unprecedented proportions. Filthy floodwaters engulf entire neighborhoods. Thousands of residents, mostly poor and black, are trapped on rooftops or in Superdome and Convention Center, with no food or water. Looting, shooting, and fires break out citywide. Confused, delayed federal response exacerbates effects of inadequate planning at state and local levels. Shocking physical and social disintegration of New Orleans leads news stories worldwide for weeks. Supplies, buses, and troops finally arrive by weekend, bringing chaos under control and evacuating last residents. One week after Katrina, city's population drops to French colonial-era levels; in some neighborhoods, dead outnumber living.

September 2005 With a million citizens of southeastern Louisiana and coastal Mississippi scattered nationwide, "ghost city" of New Orleans begins long, slow process of recovery. Waters are pumped out faster than expected, electricity returns to selected areas, and some residents return at end of month, even as rescue squads discover more dead. Damage to historic district on high natural levee is mostly wind-driven and repairable; water-caused damage to twentieth-century neighborhoods near lake and eastward into St. Bernard Parish is utterly devastating.

September 23-24, 2005 Second "storm of century" in one month, Hurricane Rita, strikes Louisiana/Texas border region, destroying communities on southwestern Louisiana coast and raising gulf and lake levels in New Orleans area. Some hastily repaired levees breach again, re-flooding Lower Ninth Ward and adjacent areas. Communities in western Louisiana suffer similar degree of destruction seen in east during Katrina. Nearly half of Louisiana's population is directly affected by storms; economy and infrastructure is in shambles.

October 5, 2005 Residents are permitted back into city everywhere except Lower Ninth Ward, though only those in higher areas near river have basic utilities and services.

Mid-October 2005 Army Corps pumps out last traces of Katrina's and Rita's surges.

Late October 2005 Hurricane Wilma, third Category-5 storm in gulf in under two months and most intense hurricane ever recorded in region, strikes Florida and Mexico. Together with Katrina and Rita, Wilma lends dramatic credence to emerging worldwide discourse on global warming.

Late Autumn 2005 City struggles to regain footing as citizens grapple with decision to return, remain in FEMA-funded evacuation sites, or leave forever. Commissions form at local and state levels to devise plans for city's future; scores of public meetings convene to discuss and debate ideas. Orleans Parish population during mid-autumn doubles to roughly 144,000 after Christmas, as families return during school break. City exudes atmosphere of frontier town, with small population, high male-to-female ratio, extremely few children, large out-of-town workforce, ubiquitous military presence, curfews, and cash-based economy. Whites outnumber blacks substantially; lower economic classes are nearly absent, while Hispanic immigrant workers arrive in large numbers and convene daily at Lee Circle to await laborer jobs. Locally owned businesses return at much faster pace than national chains; Magazine Street becomes city's "main street." Locals outnumber tourists in French Quarter, which suffers financially because of cancellation of all conventions. With criminal element evacuated, once-violent city becomes one of safest in nation, while crime rates in some host cities increase. Overarching rebuilding question draws passionate debate: should city abandon heavily damaged eastern and lakeside subdivisions and rebuild primarily on higher ground, in expectation of smaller population? Or should city maintain prediluvian urban footprint under philosophy that planning for population shrinkage will only guarantee it? Despite heroic progress in clean-up and repair, New Orleans remains two cities divided topographically: higher areas near river bustle with activity; lower areas near lake remain dark, empty, and devastated.

Autumn 2005 to Present Steady stream of religious groups, college classes, students on break, and civic and professional organizations from across nation arrange "voluntourism" visits to the city, helping gut houses, clean parks, and build homes in collaboration with local citizens. According to Corporation for National and Community Service, approximately 1.1 million visitors performed fourteen million hours of work valued at $263 million during two years following storm, with pace increasing in second year. Remarkable phenomenon is viewed as triumph of civic spirit over bureaucratic lethargy.

Autumn 2005 to Present Speedy repair of storm-damaged I-10 "Twin Spans" reconnects New Orleans with points east; is followed by construction of new, higher lanes designed to rise above massive surges on rising seas. Mostly federally funded effort is largest transportation project in Louisiana history.

2005-Present State intervenes in city's long-troubled public education system, left in disarray after storm. Most public schools are now run under state-controlled Recovery School District or as semi-autonomous charter schools; only a few remain under purview of Orleans Parish School Board. By 2008, numerous charter schools strive to attract students citywide, forming one of the most competitive public-school markets in the nation. Nevertheless, abysmal public education continues to underlie city's most fundamental problems.

January 2006 "Bring New Orleans Back Commission" unveils initial recommendations for consideration by Mayor Ray Nagin, state's Louisiana Recovery Authority, federal officials, and public. "Action Plan for New Orleans: The New American City" recommends moratorium on rebuilding in heavily damaged low-lying areas; delineates thirteen planning districts and suggests forming neighborhood associations within each. Associations must demonstrate that at least half of households will return by May, else neighborhood would be bought out with federal help and converted to park or commercial zone. Plan also recommends "Crescent City Recovery Corporation" to oversee rebuilding, at expense of city government's authority. Proposals for light rail lines, bike trails, and parks are practically lost amid public response to potential neighborhood closures, which ranges from outrage to reluctant support. Charges of racism, red-lining, land-grabbing, and ethnic cleansing fly from plan opponents, while supporters speak of safety, reality, and pragmatism.

January 2006 Mayor Nagin rejects key recommendations of Bring New Orleans Back Commission. Unwilling (and probably legally unable) to close down far-flung, low-lying suburbs in favour of safer, higher areas, mayor opts for *laissez-faire* approach to rebuilding: "let people decide for themselves and government will follow." Decision rejects notion of shrinking the urban footprint, recommended by experts but wildly unpopular among vocal citizens and politicians. Incident demonstrates once again that disaster victims, shaken by tumult and craving normalcy, usually resist radical change, even if it promises to lower future risk.

February 2006 First post-Katrina Mardi Gras unfurls with small but enthusiastic and predominantly local crowds; festivities demonstrate city's ability to handle major functions. National and international reaction, initially skeptical, warms to one of endearment and admiration.

2006 Civic spirit and fear of "footprint shrinkage" inspires thousands of citizens to form numerous grassroots neighborhood associations citywide. Countless meetings produce series of neighborhood plans, many highly inspired and largely without financial or professional support. Impressive level of passionate civic engagement proves to be Katrina's silver lining.

Spring 2006 Campaign for mayor and city council, postponed during chaotic autumn of 2005, garners national attention as bellwether of city's postdiluvian racial and political makeup. Over twenty candidates, mostly whites, vie to replace Mayor Ray Nagin. "Footprint debate" becomes politically volatile; most candidates advocate rebuilding entire city. Mayor Nagin and Lt. Gov. Mitch Landrieu, respectively black and white, prevail in April election, in which thousands of displaced residents vote in statewide balloting locations. Despite dire warnings, election proceeds smoothly. Mayor Nagin's victory in May run-off election, as well as council and congressional outcomes, continue era of African-American leadership in local politics, contrary to experts' predictions immediately after Katrina. In late 2007, however, City Council becomes majority white.

2006 Women, disproportionately from wealthy uptown backgrounds, organize groups such as Citizens for 1 Greater New Orleans, levees.org, and Women of the Storm, urging reform in levee engineering, unification of levee boards, elimination of multiple tax assessors, and congressional attention to post-Katrina New Orleans. Their success recalls women of Progressive Era who led fight for drainage, potable water, and municipal improvements a century earlier.

Summer 2006 Two surveys estimate mid-2006 population of New Orleans at 200,725 and 223,388, down from 452,170 immediately prior to Hurricane Katrina. One survey estimates new racial composition as 47 percent black (down from almost 70 percent in 2000), 42.7 percent white (up from 28 percent), and 3.5 percent Asian; those of Hispanic ethnicity (regardless of race) comprised 9.6 percent, nearly triple their relative size from before Katrina. U.S. Census Bureau's American Community Survey, using different methodology, determined city's racial makeup as 59 percent black, 37 percent white, 3 percent Asian, and 4 percent Hispanic of any race. Differing figures reflect "soft" nature of city's postdiluvian population, and difficulty of measuring it.

August 29, 2006 First anniversary of storm is marked with wide range of civic remembrances. Worldwide news outlets return for update on city's progress—likely to become annual media ritual.

September 2006 Fulton Street pedestrian mall opens off lower Poydras Street, designed to give visitors a reason to patronize Warehouse District venues and Harrah's Casino, rather than explore traditional French Quarter/Bourbon Street circuit.

Fall 2006 FEMA trailers temporarily transform cityscape of flooded region, reaching their peak numbers a year after storm. Nearly 19,000 white tin boxes dot Orleans Parish, plus over 20,000 in adjacent areas, offering flood victims a convenient but cramped place to dwell as they repair their homes. Progress in rebuilding and concerns over formaldehyde cut trailer usage in half by early 2008.

2006-2007 Army Corps erects massive closable gates at mouths of outfall canals, to prevent repeat of surge-induced levee breaches during Katrina. Long recommended by Army Corps but resisted locally for fear of inhibiting canals' ability to remove runoff, gates represent significant improvement in flood protection for lakeside areas. Special by-pass pumps are installed to allow for rainwater runoff removal if gates are closed for impending storm. Industrial and MR-GO canals in east remain ungated.

Late 2006-Early 2007 Overlapping and sometimes competing urban-planning efforts, led by the City Council-hired Lambert/Danzey firms and the privately funded Unified New Orleans Plan (UNOP), keep citizens busy with numerous neighborhood meetings and planning charrettes.

Late 2006-Early 2007 With returning citizens comes a small but extremely violent number of criminals, reworking flood-affected drug-distribution economies and gangster turf. While the city's returned population doubles between last quarters of 2005 and 2006, murders and overall violent crimes increase nearly six-fold. Murders of two particularly civically engaged citizens—a black male music teacher and a white female filmmaker—incite a massive March Against Crime on January 11, 2007.

2006-2007 Canal Street is refurbished with granite sidewalks, palm trees, and other improvements, with aim of restoring artery's commerce and grandeur.

2006-2007 Storm-related bankruptcies, lack of affordable housing, and migrant-worker influx contribute to burgeoning homeless population. Closure of downtown shelters shifts geography of homelessness to beleaguered Ozanam Inn on Camp Street, "the Wall" at Elysian Fields levee, and to makeshift encampment under Duncan Plaza gazebo. Squatter colony of over 150 homeless people, camped immediately outside City Hall, forms striking statement on social problems of postdiluvian city.

2006-2008 Housing and Urban Development (HUD) and Housing Authority of New Orleans (HANO) move forward on pre-Katrina plans to demolish circa-1940s C. J. Peete, St. Bernard, B. W. Cooper, and Lafitte projects for new mixed-income New Urbanist developments, similar to River Garden/St. Thomas neighborhood. Small number of extremely vociferous activists, distrustful of promises to rebuild public housing, challenge any demolition-reconstruction effort as aimed at ridding the city of its poor African-American population. Their argument is weakened by the fact that many refurbished HANO apartments remain empty, but strengthened by city's general housing shortage and large homeless population. Agencies agree to demolish in stages, allowing some residents to return as work progresses, but insist that old-style projects represent failed policies that concentrated poverty, incubated social pathologies, and produced intergenerational dependency. Controversy climaxes on December 20, 2007, when City Council, amid violent scuffles inside and outside City Hall, unanimously votes to approve demolitions.

2007 Louisiana "Road Home" Program distributes billions of federal dollars to Katrina flood victims: $150,000 per eligible homeowner, minus insurance settlements and FEMA grants. Homeowners suffering greater than 50 percent damage opt to (1) repair or rebuild in place; (2) sell to state and purchase another home in Louisiana; or (3) sell to state and choose not to remain a homeowner in Louisiana. Lengthy and slow-moving paperwork process enrages citizenry, delays rebuilding decisions, and dooms Gov. Kathleen Blanco's reelection efforts. As of storm's second anniversary, less than one-third of the 140,000 eligible applicants closed on their payments.

2007 Plans for a gigantic medical complex comprising new LSU and Veterans Affairs hospitals promises economic development and health services for city, but also threatens demolition of nearly thirty blocks of historic Third Ward near Canal/South Galvez intersection. Plan distresses preservationists, but opposition is muted because of universally acknowledged importance of health care to city's recovery.

Summer 2007 Population of New Orleans estimated around 273,000, with thousands more living "between places" as Road Home monies trickle into flood victims' pockets and rebuilding decisions are finalized. Other estimates put city's July 2007 population at under 240,000 to over 300,000, depending on methodology. Return rate rises from about 50 percent of population on storm's first anniversary, to 60 percent by second anniversary. Portion of New Orleanians living above sea level rises to 50 percent.

August 2007 East Bank population centroid (theoretical center of balance among the distribution of households), located in the central Seventh Ward in 2000, shifts by August 2007 a mile to the southwest into the central Sixth Ward. Westward movement reflects slower return rates east of the Industrial Canal, while the southward movement signifies much higher return rates of the unflooded "sliver by the river" compared to heavily flooded lakeside neighborhoods.

Summer 2007 Three key entities—Army Corps, New Orleans Sewerage and Water Board, and Jefferson Parish—agree to relocate pumping stations for the 17th Street, Orleans, and London Avenue outfall canals from their historical inland locations (which marked the city's edge when they were installed a century ago), to new, higher lakefront locations. This would keep them out of flood-prone lowlands, allow for modernization, and most importantly, enable them to continue pumping runoff into Lake Pontchartrain even when new storm gates on outfall canals are closed for oncoming hurricanes. Rare multi-agency consensus constitutes first step toward seeking funding and eventually executing new plan.

Late 2007 Localism enjoys rare victory over national and global forces as Thibodaux-based Rouses grocery chain, known for its Louisiana foods and regional suppliers, takes over Sav-a-Center supermarkets. Change shifts city's food retail industry back into local hands, a position once enjoyed by locally owned Schwegmann's until Winn-Dixie and Wal-Mart moved into market in late 1990s-early 2000s.

2007-Onward Army Corps promises nearly $15 billion worth of improvements to region's flood control system over next four to five years, to ensure protection from storms with 1-percent chance of occurring in any given year. "Hundred-year protection plan" entails gating of outfall and navigation canals, raising of existing levee heights to account for rising seas and subsidence, construction of new levees, installation of pumping stations to allow for removal of interior runoff while gates are closed, and reinforcement of weak spots in existing floodwalls and levees. Project sends Army Corps on region-wide search for hundred-million cubic yards of clay needed for levee construction. If funded appropriately, effort will prove critical to future of region—but will fall short of "saving" it if not paralleled by equally aggressive coastal restoration.

2007-Onward New housing technologies in flood-affected zone alters city's inventory of building methods. Advances in "stick-built" (wooden frame) houses make wood more resistant to termites, mold, and wind; new poured-on-site concrete walls provide additional strength and insulation; "green building" becomes trendy buzzword. Modular homes, built off-site in factories and assembled rapidly on location, reduce costs but also design options while circumventing local craftsmen. Stylistically, debate rages between modernists and traditionalists on whether postdiluvian city should exhibit latest international trends in architecture, or respect traditional local aesthetics.

November 8, 2007 Louisiana enjoys productive day in Washington. Passage of Water Resources Development Act (over presidential veto) deauthorizes MR-GO

Canal while authorizing (but not yet appropriating) about $7 billion for Louisiana coastal restoration, levee construction, and related projects. Same-day passage of defense-spending bill allocates $3 billion toward shortfall in Road Home monies, ensuring homeowners will be reimbursed for federally caused flood damages.

Late 2007 Voting records from 2003 and 2007 gubernatorial elections reveal that black voters in Orleans Parish declined by over 54 percent (84,584 to 38,738), while white voters declined by 27 percent (46,669 to 33,937). Studies show that New Orleans will remain majority African-American, but by slimmer margin than before storm.

2007-2008 Army Corps releases flood-risk maps showing how "hundred-year protection plan," promised by 2011, will affect greater New Orleans. Basin-by-basin maps depict likely flood depths produced by medium to extreme storms under various scenarios, including before Katrina, in the present day, and after 2011, and with 0-, 50-, and 100-percent pumping capacity. Best-case scenario indicates light flooding in some low-lying suburban subdivisions; worst-case shows severe deluges in most below-sea-level areas. Most likely scenario shows marked improvements since 2005. Maps are aimed at helping residents understand that risk is not evenly distributed spatially, nor can it be eliminated entirely. Revealingly, Army Corps renames hurricane-protection levee system "Greater New Orleans Hurricane and Storm Damage Risk Reduction System."

2008 Thousands of flooded properties bought out from homeowners through Road Home program face uncertain future. Properties may eventually be turned over from state to New Orleans Redevelopment Authority (NORA), which will opt to repair or rebuild for market-rate or affordable housing, to convert to green space, or to enroll land in "Lot Next Door" program, in which homeowners may purchase adjacent parcels. NORA must decide similar fate for 10,000 blighted houses and possibly 15,000 additional substandard houses, putting city agency in charge of momentous decisions influencing future urban geography of New Orleans.

Winter-Spring 2008 B. W. Cooper, C. J. Peete, St. Bernard, and Lafitte housing projects are demolished and prepared for mixed-income redevelopment.

April 2008 Catholic archdiocese reorganizes its pastoral, social, and educational services to accommodate post-Katrina residential settlement patterns, incoming Latino immigrants, heavy uninsured storm damages, and declining number of priests. Reorganization leads to closure and consolidation of thirty-three parishes, some dating to antebellum times. Some congregations are merged with nearby churches, whose proximity is traceable to nineteenth-century ethnic settlement patterns.

April 2008 As Mississippi River nears flood stage (seventeen feet above sea level) at Carrollton Gauge, Army Corps opens Bonnet Carré Spillway for ninth time since its installation in 1930s, and first time since 1997.

Ongoing Hurricane Katrina story places New Orleans at center of nationwide and worldwide intellectual discourse on hotly contested topics, including global warming, urban resilience and sustainability, disaster preparation and response, appropriate role of government, race relations and poverty, and the future of old coastal cities. Countless post-Katrina symposia, conferences, journals, books, documentaries, and political dialogues render city part warning, part testbed, part metaphor, part prophet, and part inspiration.

Forming the Landscape

Mud, mud, mud…
this is a floating city,
floating below the surface of the water
on a bed of mud….

—Benjamin Henry Boneval Latrobe, 1819

Of Ice, Water, and Sediment
Geological origins of southeastern Louisiana and the New Orleans region

For millennia, the footprint of the earth's surface currently occupied by New Orleans and southern Louisiana altered between terrestrial and aquatic states. In times of cooling global temperatures, increasing quantities of the planet's water froze as glaciers, thus lowering sea level and dewatering coastal fringes. When temperatures warmed, terrestrial ice sheets transferred H_2O back to the world's oceans, raising their levels, expanding their volume, and subsuming coastal regions back into the hydrosphere.[6]

At the peak of the Ice Age, 18,000 years ago, vast quantities of water lay frozen upon earthen surfaces at the expense of the world's oceans. Ice sheets stretching as far south as present-day Cairo, Illinois radically changed the topography and hydrology of the North American continent, re-sculpting the Missouri River drainage system to the west and the Ohio River system to the east such that the two rivers joined at Cairo. Rising global temperatures then melted the glaciers and sent increasing amounts of water and sediment to that confluence. There, at the apex of an immense downwarping of the Earth's crust known as the Mississippi Embayment (forerunner of the Lower Mississippi Valley), a dramatically augmented Mississippi River delivered increasing quantities of sediment-laden water toward the Gulf of Mexico. Minor bluffs and terraces constrained the river to meander within a wide, flat alluvial valley until it passed below a line roughly between present-day Lafayette and Baton Rouge, where gulf waters lay. When moving water laden with sediment suddenly hits a slack water body, it loses its kinetic energy and dumps its sediment load. Alluvium began accumulating as a deltaic lobe at the mouth of the Mississippi, turning salt water into saline marshes and protruding the coastline into the Gulf of Mexico. Future southeastern Louisiana was beginning to form, approximately seven millennia ago.

As that alluvial deposit rose in elevation, the Mississippi sought paths of less resistance around it, and in doing so formed a new channel and extended the coastline outwardly in a new direction. The first deltaic lobe, if no longer replenished with soil and fresh water, would subside and erode back into the sea, as the new active delta grew nearby. Seasonal floods would spill muddy water beyond the banks of the river, depositing more sediment along its inundated flanks and raising still higher the height of the active delta.

Occasionally a *crevasse* (breach) opened in the bank, allowing a trickle, or a torrent, or even the entire water column to divert from the main channel and into adjacent wetlands, instigating the same land-building process in yet another area. The mouth of the Mississippi River in this manner extended farther and wider into the Gulf of Mexico, creating a network of active and abandoned complexes—a deltaic plain—

that would eventually become southeastern Louisiana and home to New Orleans.

One visitor arriving to New Orleans in 1828 observed delta-building processes forming the marshy eastern flanks of the city. "[W]e coasted along, past numerous small, sandy islands," he wrote, "over shallow banks of mud, and through several immense basins, such as Lake Borgne and Lake Pontchartrain, half fresh, half salt, and filled with bars, spits, keys, and...shoals [typical of areas] whose Deltas *are silently pushing themselves into the sea, and raising the bottom to the surface....*"[7] To the French geographer Elisée Réclus, who sailed up the river in 1853, those processes created a deltaic plain which resembled "a gigantic arm projecting into the sea and spreading its fingers on the surface of the water."[8] American geographer John McPhee described the lowermost river as jumping "here and there within an arc about two hundred miles wide, like a pianist playing with one hand—frequently and radically changing course, surging over the left or the right bank to go off in utterly new directions."[9]

Geologists have, since the 1930s, generally agreed on where this "hand" landed over the millennia, though its exact extent, movements, eras, and "fingers" (lobes) have been debated and refined (see map, "Deltaic Complexes of Southeastern Louisiana"). In the 1940s, geologists R. J. Russel and H. N. Fisk identified six delta complexes and subdivided them into a number of sub-deltas. In 1958, C. R. Kolb and J. R Van Lopik updated these findings with seven deltas of the Mississippi River, assigned some new names, and mapped them as distinctive lollipop-shaped lobes. The general consensus at that time was that the complexes, and thus the age of southeastern Louisiana, spanned roughly the last 5,000 years. According to the 1958 study, New Orleans proper was first directly coated by Mississippi alluvium by the Cocodrie Delta, starting about 4,500 years ago, then by the St. Bernard Delta. Sediments also layered the future New Orleans area during the years of the Plaquemines and Balize Delta, not because the Mississippi discharged there but because, during high water, it overflowed its banks and deposited sediments upon it.

The influential research of Kolb and Van Lopik is still widely cited today. In 1967, David E. Frazier advanced the science with radiocarbon dating and other new technologies. Frazier identified five deltaic complexes of the Mississippi River, subdivided them into sixteen lobes, determined that many functioned contemporaneously, and estimated that the entire land-building event transpired over 7,200 years. Other scientists have since added to the body of knowledge on the origins of southeastern Louisiana, but, according to geologist Roger Saucier, "Frazier's work remains the most definitive to date."[10] According to that research, the New Orleans region is mostly a product of the St. Bernard and Plaquemines deltaic complexes, starting at least 4,300 years ago—a time frame which aligns with earlier investigations.

New Orleans, then, stands not on the ancient, solid North American lithosphere, but on a thin, soft alluvial "doormat" cast recently out upon the continent's margin. Founded in 1718, the city has occupied this earthen surface for roughly 6 percent of the lifespan of its underlying geology, something few other major cities can claim. Certain live oak trees growing in City Park today have been around for about one-tenth the age of the landscape; some aged citizens have personally witnessed fully one-fiftieth of the city's geological existence. Not only is New Orleans' terrain the youngest of any major American city, but southeastern Louisiana is—as Mark Twain put—"the youth-fulest batch of country that lies around there anywhere" in the nation, and the entire lower Mississippi Valley, from Cairo to the sea, possesses the continent's youngest sur-face soils.[11]

By the time of French exploration, around 1700, most of the region's landscape formations had reached a stage recognizable today. The passes, bays, bayous, lakes, natural levees and backswamps which currently grace maps with Francophone names were in place and known well by the Native Americans and French colonists. But these features, at the dawn of the colonial era, were still geologically alive and shifting, driven by gravity, controlled only by the forces of nature. The Mississippi River periodically swelled over its banks and replenished the backswamp with new sediments; enough river water flowed toward the old Lafourche Delta to inspire early French explorers to name it "the fork;" and the Bayou Manchac distributary still injected fresh muddy river water into the region once similarly nourished by the old St. Bernard Delta.

All this geological dynamism is anathema to human settlement. Over the next 300 years, humans would seize this malleable and watery land and rework it to improve the safety and circumstances for the time frame in which they live: the moment and the immediate future. New Orleans as an urban system has since become one of the world's great engineering challenges, and southeastern Louisiana and the lowermost Mississip-pi River rank as one of the most anthropogenically altered regions in the hemisphere. Every blessing seems to be accompanied by a curse; every solution seems to spawn a future problem. The historical geography of New Orleans is, in large part, the story of the benefits, costs, and constant dilemmas associated with this geological tinkering.

The Topography of Ooze

The high stakes of low elevation

You will observe that the land [around New Orleans] is of peculiar forma-tion. Throughout nearly the whole country, the bank of a river is the lowest spot; here, on the contrary, it is the highest.[12]

—Father Vivier, 1750

Modern New Orleans is the lowest-lying and flattest metropolis in the nation. But both notions need further qualification.

Firstly, this deltaic city is not entirely "below sea level," as was proclaimed in-cessantly by pithy journalists and newly minted pundits following the Hurricane Ka-trina levee catastrophe of 2005. In fact, the prehistoric deltaic plain lay entirely *at* or *above* the level of the sea before man's recent interventions strangled off incoming sediment-laden fresh water and starved it into subsidence and erosion. Today, after decades of soil sinkage and rising seas, the metropolis straddles mean sea level: 51 percent lies at or slightly above sea level, and 49 percent falls below it (see map, "Topographic Elevation of Metro New Orleans"). Higher natural areas generally slope up to about +10 to +12 feet in elevation, with man-made areas peaking at +25 to +40 feet; lower zones dip to -5 or -10 in some neighborhoods, with some canal bottoms dropping to –15 feet or lower.[13] This partial sunkenness is unquestionably a problematic situation, but nowhere near as troubling as the unconditional phrase "below-sea-level city" implies.

Secondly, while the landscape may appear absolutely flat, its slight relative differences in elevation have deeply influenced the city's urban development. The reason: in a flood-prone coastal region, topographic elevation is a scarce resource that is in high demand for the protection it affords. A few inches here are as valuable as ten or a hundred feet might be in a hilly city. Barely perceptible elevations in New Orleans have influenced whether a neighborhood developed during the Napoleonic Age, the Jazz Age, or the Space Age. They also determined (along with levee-breach locations) which neighborhoods were flooded by Hurricane Katrina's surge and which were spared, oftentimes to the amazement of residents. "This is a little island," marveled one Esplanade Ridge man whose house evaded inundation because of its topographic perch. "Five blocks away, there was eight feet of water."[14]

The highest areas of the deltaic plain lie closest to the rivers and bayous— exactly the opposite, as Jesuit priest Father Vivier marveled in 1750, of erosion-formed areas. The Mississippi historically overflowed in the springtime, depositing largest quantities of the coarsest sediments immediately upon the banks of the river, with lesser amounts of finer-grained sediment settling away from the river. In time, areas closer to the river (natural levees) rose higher than riparian areas behind them (backswamp). This occurs in all alluvial and deltaic environments. Le Page du Pratz described the process in his 1758 *History of Louisiana*: the soils of this area, he wrote,

> are brought down and accumulated by means of the ooze which the Mississippi carries [during] its annual inundations; which begin in [early spring] and last for about three months. Those oozy or muddy lands easily produce herbs and reeds; and when the Mississippi happens to overflow the following year, these herbs and reeds intercept a part of this ooze, so that those at the distance from the river cannot retain so large a quantity of it, since those that grow next [to] the river have stopt the greatest part.... *In this manner[,] the banks of the Missisipi became higher than the lands about it.*[15]

Occasionally, a crevasse would develop along the high river bank, diverting a stream of water away from the river and through the backswamp. These "distributaries" formed natural levees of their own by dispensing "ooze" along their banks, thus forming ridges and eventually dividing hydrological basins into sub-basins. The major distributary in the New Orleans area once flowed out of the river near present-day River Ridge, and wended its way eastward to the sea. Its flooding cycle created a slight ridge—"a certain bulge, called in 'hill' in these parts...imperceptible to the naked eye, [perhaps] one meter high," according to visiting geographer Elisée Réclus.[16] The main channel of the Mississippi River once followed this path (now traversed by Metairie Road, City Park Avenue, Gentilly Boulevard, and Chef Menteur Highway), creating the present-day Metairie and Gentilly Ridge systems. Its offshoot, the Esplanade Ridge, comprises a slight upland beneath today's Esplanade Avenue from City Park to the French Quarter.

During the 1700s-1800s, the natural levees of the Mississippi and its distributaries formed the only well-drained habitable land in the region. Urban civilization in historic New Orleans was existentially correlated with topographic elevation; higher land meant relative safety, security, salubrity, beauty, comfort, even morality. Listen to Pierre Clément de Laussat, Louisiana's last French administrator at the time of the Louisiana Purchase, describe an excursion in 1803 on the well-drained Metairie Ridge system of present-day Jefferson Parish:

> I organized a trip on horseback along the Metairie road, toward the plantation of the three Hazeur brothers, real French knights... [T]he day was delightful, the sky serene, and the breeze from the northeast cooled off the heat of the sun. Trees were still thick with foliage.... Evergreens[,] [m]agnolias, vines, oaks, wild grapes, a great number of shrubs heavily laden with fruit... all form a lovely sight deep in the heart of these uninhabited wastelands and forests. Sprinkled here and there are log cabins and some cultivation. And most everywhere it is alive with herds and multitude of curious birds.
>
> Sundays were generally observed as holidays.... Whoever had a horse or a carriage was on [Metairie] road. Strollers dressed in their Sunday finery were many. Young folks everywhere tried their skills [while] Negroes and mulattoes...challenged each other to *raquette des sauvages*.... The road was full with an unbroken line of traveling coaches, *cabriolets*, horses, carts, spectators, and players.[17]

Contrast Laussat's festive foray on the Metairie Road topographic ridge with the following anonymous description, circa late 1840s, of the barbaric lowlands:

> This swamp is several miles wide, skirting the rear of the city...and into this mud hole, water and filth (what little passes off) are taken. This boiling fountain of death is one of the most dismal, low and horrid places, on which the light of the sun ever shone. And yet there it lies under the influence of a tropical heat, belching up its poison and malaria, [which sweeps] through the city, feeding the living mass of human beings who stand there [with] the dregs of the seven vials of wrath.... Another evil is, the city, by the bend of the river, is thrown so near the swamp [that] it is almost entirely under water...after a heavy shower, [and] becomes covered with a yellow greenish scum.... [18]

"The backswamp," "the woods," *prairies tremblantes*,[19] "the quarter of the damned:" low elevation formed a landscape of threat and fear for residents of eighteenth- and nineteenth-century New Orleans, depriving the community of arable land and living space while imparting miasmas and maladies. "[M]alignant disease," explained Thomas Ashe in 1809, "is generated by the lakes, swamps, and marshes, contiguous to the sea, and gradually diffuses itself up the river till checked by high lands and a higher latitude…."[20] "From land left saturated by receding floods, and from pools stagnating in sunken lots on the outskirts of cities," read an 1877 medicine advertisement, "rises a vapor pregnant with disease. Its name is miasma, and it is laden with the seeds of fever…."[21] This was the perception of the day. Perception drives reality, and reality meant striving to modify this hated topography as much as technology allowed.

Humans have altered the topographic elevation of New Orleans primarily for four reasons: to keep water out, to improve navigation, to remove water from within, and to create or shore up land (see later readings on all four of these topics).

Keeping river and lake water out of the city motivated the region's most influential landscape manipulation: the erection of artificial levees on the crest of the natural levees to prevent springtime overbank flooding of the Mississippi. Similar earthen embankments were later built along the Lake Pontchartrain shore to prevent lake water from inundating the city from the rear, and across the marshes (hurricane-protection levees) to protect the flanks. These man-made levees now rank among the highest earthen features in the region, though soil subsidence renders them slightly lower every year. Some failed during Hurricane Katrina, leading to catastrophic flooding of about half of the metropolitan area and over three-quarters of New Orleans proper.

The economic drive to accommodate shipping—the second motivation for topographic change—resulted in the excavation of navigation canals such as the Carondelet Canal (1794), New Basin Canal (1838), Industrial Canal (1923), and the Mississippi River-Gulf Outlet Canal (1960s), the first two now filled in, the latter two all too much part of the cityscape. While these waterways and their paralleling docks and wharves abetted the city's role as a port, they also served to divide the natural hydrological sub-basins into smaller ones, and to penetrate and score the metropolis with potentially deadly aqueous connections to surge-prone gulf waters. So too did a number of drainage (outfall) canals dug near the lakefront, part of the late-nineteenth-century effort to drain water from within the city.

As a result of anthropogenic topographic alteration, New Orleans' landscape, naturally sectioned into four sub-basins by the Metairie, Gentilly, Esplanade ridges and the natural levee of the Mississippi, today comprises roughly a dozen different hydrological sub-basins. Some are impounded by natural features, others by man-made features; all straddle the level of the sea to some degree, and all require mechanized pumps and outfall canals to relieve them of rainfall. That's because nature has no way of pushing water uphill—and uphill it must go, because the aforementioned topographic alteration has inadvertently deprived New Orleans' soils of replenishing water and sediment, causing half of it to sink below sea level.

As valuable as topographic elevation is to this nearly flat and flood-prone city, it is by no means the sole factor determining flooding potential. The safety of the entire metropolis depends, first and foremost, on the protection entailed by levees, floodwalls, drainage systems, and coastal wetlands. An above-sea-level home located in a hydrological sub-basin that suffers a levee breach, a pump failure, or a clogged drain is perfectly capable of flooding, even as below-sea-level areas in adjacent basins remain dry. This happened during Katrina: higher-elevation parcels in the Lower Ninth Ward neighborhood of Holy Cross flooded because of the severity of the levee failures east of the Industrial Canal, while lower-elevation areas west of the canal were spared because those levees fared better.

Nevertheless, because we cannot forecast where levees or pumps might fail and which basins might inundate, we are left with the one variable that we can predict: water seeks its level and inundates lowest areas first. Higher elevation (either topographic or structural) means that a particular household will either evade floodwaters altogether, or at least suffer lesser water depths, than its lower-elevation neighbors situated within that same flooded basin.

Meager topographic elevation thus forms a precious and scarce resource in this water-logged environment, and, as such, has influenced New Orleans' historical geography much like water scarcity has sculpted the history of the topographically rugged American West.

"Mud, Mud, Mud"

Soils as a stealth factor to New Orleans' historical geography

Pedologists—soil scientists—find below New Orleans thin layers of extremely finely textured alluvial soils, high in water and organic content, recent in their formation, and highly vulnerable to transformation though human activity. The particles derive from various parent materials scattered throughout the 1,243,700-square-mile Mississippi Basin, delivered here via the transporting, sorting, and depositing functions of the Mississippi River. The river carries about one billion pounds of sediment past New Orleans daily, a journey that starts in the uppermost reaches of the Mississippi and its tributaries.

Some particles erode into the system as stones (>75 mm in diameter), which settle quickly due to their weight. Others, from 75 mm to 2.0 mm (gravel) make it much farther down the system. Finer particles, measuring from 2.0 mm to 0.05 mm (sand), travel haltingly all the way to the Gulf of Mexico, settling in the bedload during times of low flow and remobilizing during high springtime flow. Silt (0.05 mm to 0.002 mm) and clay (the finest particles, less than 0.002 mm in diameter) dominate the sediments borne by the lowest stretches of the Mississippi, and spill out into the Gulf of Mexico in vast quantities. Only the finest, lightest sediment particles survive the pull of gravity and make it to the New Orleans region.

"At New Orleans there is nothing scarcer than stones," wrote one visitor in 1750. The alluvial soils forced Europeans to adapt traditional construction methods to new environmental conditions. "[B]ricks made on the spot are substituted for [stones].

Lime is made from shells, which are obtained [from] the shores of lake Pontchartrain. Hills of shells are found there [as well as] two or three feet below the surface" farther inland.[22] "An alluvial soil cannot be supposed to abound in rock," explained Maj. Amos Stoddard in his 1812 *Sketches, Historical and Descriptive, of Louisiana*. "Neither on the island of Orleans, nor along the immense flat country on the west side of the Mississippi...is even a single pebble to be found."[23]

As the Mississippi River historically flooded the New Orleans area and deposited water and sediment upon its swampy surface, coarser (heavier) sediments tended to settle first, at the crest of the natural levee, with finer and lighter particles settling progressively farther back from the river. Basil Hall, a geographically savvy visitor from Edinburgh, described this process beautifully as he sailed down the Mississippi from New Orleans in 1828:

> The effect of [the river's] overflowing is most interesting in a geological point of view. The larger materials, that is to say, the coarser grains of mud—for there is hardly any thing like sand—are first deposited; then the less coarse, and so on. In proportion as the velocity of this surplus water is diminished, by finding room to spread itself to the right and left, so will the materials which it carries along become finer, and in smaller quantities. Thus, a sort of natural embankment [forms] from the edge of [the Mississippi] towards the swampy country on either hand.[24]

The high, relatively well-drained natural levees are thus made of some sand (Hall overstated its rarity), much silt, and some clay. The sloping lands behind them comprise little sand, mostly silt, and more clay. The lowest areas in the backswamp are made of no sand, some silt, and mostly clay. As one moves away from the river, the amount of water and organic matter in the soil body increases, and the water table rises closer to the surface. Strewn throughout the soil body are layers of organic matter, such as decaying leaves and cypress stumps. Also found are relic barrier islands, such as the Pine Island Trend, a sandy deposit of the Pearl River which drifted westward with gulf currents before riverine sediments turned the water around it into land. Architect Benjamin Latrobe, while investigating the city in 1819, described the earthen gumbo of New Orleans soils and understood clearly its relationship with the river:

> Mud, mud, mud... [T]his is a floating city, floating below the surface of the water on a bed of mud.... The upper surface...is a marsh mud, extremely slippery [when] wet, with a small mixture of sand, & below this surface are decayed vegetables, water at 3 feet... abounding in large logs, or in large vacancies [from] logs which have rotted. Such a soil [is] the result of the gradual accumulation of the deposition of the river, & of the logs & trees which in astonishing quantities & of immense size are constantly descending the stream at every fresh.[25]

The soils of New Orleans have informed the city's historical geography through two general precepts. The *closer* to the river (or its distributaries), then the coarser the soil texture, the higher the land surface, the lower the organic matter and water table, the less the salinity, and the better drained and more fertile the soil. *Therefore*, the great-er the likelihood the area was once a plantation, the earlier the area was subdivided and urbanized, and the more likely it is now home to historical neighborhoods with eigh-teenth- or nineteenth-century architecture. Most of what people perceive as "classic New Orleans" stands on these soils, which go by the names of Commerce and Sharkey loams, among others.

The *farther* from the river (or its distributaries), then the finer the soil tex-ture, the lower the elevation, the higher the organic matter and water content, and the higher the salinity (particularly near the lake). *Therefore*, the less likely the area once hosted plantations, the more likely it urbanized later, the more likely it has subsided significantly once drained, the more vulnerable it is to flooding, and the more likely it exhibits twentieth-century architecture. Most modern suburban-style neighborhoods stand on these soils, among which are Harahan clay and the appropriately named Al-lemands Muck.

Soils have also helped make New Orleans an expensive place to urbanize. Transforming a natural landscape into a cityscape is a costly endeavor anywhere, but particularly in a semi-tropical deltaic environment with soft alluvial soils and a complex human history. A City Planning and Zoning Commission report from 1927 contended that New Orleans encountered "much higher [urbanization costs] than in other cit-ies built on different terrain." Initial surveying, for example, is complicated by contin-ued use of "the French system of measurements" and "the antiquity, inadequacy and inaccuracy of records," not to mention the difficult terrain. Clearing dense forest and underbrush is more demanding here than elsewhere, while excavating hydric soils of-ten means encountering enormous old cypress stumps lying layers-deep in the mucky earth. Then comes the costly engineering challenges of keeping unwanted water out (flood control), removing unwanted water from within (drainage), guiding potable wa-ter in one direction, and directing sewerage out the other. Finely textured soils loaded with organic matter and prone to sinkage make the grading and paving of streets and sidewalks that much more expensive. Underground infrastructure, namely sewer, gas, and water lines, also contends with the above soil-related problems. Large structures need to rest upon pilings hammered into the earth to keep from leaning, while high-rises require specialized pilings penetrating into hard suballuvial Pleistocene clays to remain upright. Add to this the effects of humidity, high rainfall, luxuriant vegetation growth, termites, mosquitoes, and occasional high winds and hard freezes to increase further the costs of urbanization. In the 1920s, New Orleans spent more per-capita on sanitation and streets than any major American city, not because it aspired to high standards but because it had to overcome a far more challenging starting point. (Inci-dentally, it ranked at or near the bottom in per-capita expenditures on public health, hospitals, schools, and libraries.)[26]

Soils played a stealth role in the flooding following Hurricane Katrina in 2005. As water levels rose in the city's network of navigation and outfall canals, pods of peaty organic matter allowed water to penetrate beneath the levees lining those waterways. Burdened additionally with intense lateral pressure on the concrete-encased sheet-piling floodwalls, levees breached in multiple locations and catastrophically inundated every hydrological sub-basin on New Orleans' East Bank. After the waters drained and New Orleanians returned to their wrecked homes, among the debris they encountered were the stumps and root systems of ancient cypress trees, uprooted from swamp soils for the first time in centuries by the surging torrent.

Gray, Turbid, and Broad

Magnitude and significance of the Mississippi River

To state that New Orleans is inextricably linked to the Mississippi River—physically, geologically, historically, culturally, economically—is axiomatic. Human agency, of course, created the city *per se*, but the river created its underlying terrain, drew indigenous and colonial attention to the site, connected it to trade systems, nurtured its crops and industries, sustained it, threatened it, unified external influences, and diffused internal traits. Tracing the Mississippi from headwaters to mouth (see map, "Mississippi River Drainage Basin") helps place New Orleans in its true context—as a river and sea port, so dependent on the artery that every resident literally imbibes its waters every day, from cradle to grave.

Starting with the traditionally recognized headwaters of 1,475-foot-high Lake Itasca, the incipient Mississippi—"its name in the Indian language [signifying] Parent of Rivers, or the eldest Son of the Ocean," according to a 1787 report[27]—forms a placid current of clear, cold water at times only a few dozen feet wide coursing through north central Minnesota. Seventy-five miles downriver, its flow runs at 443 cubic feet per second (c.f.s.), the equivalent of a twenty-one-by-twenty-one-foot wall of water passing a line in one second.[28] The St. Croix, Wisconsin, Rock, Des Moines, and Illinois rivers, plus many smaller tributaries, augment that rate to over 105,000 c.f.s. by the time the Mississippi undergoes its first major transformation, at the confluence with the 2,565-mile-long Missouri River.

"Big Muddy," born as Red Rock Creek in the Montana Rockies, drains nearly half the entire Mississippi Basin and outdistances the Mississippi by 200 miles. Though it contributes only 13 percent of the Mississippi's eventual maximum flow, the Missouri supplies the lion's share of the system's sediment load, eroded from western mountains and plains. Its confluence near St. Louis transforms the Mississippi to a muddy and turbulent river of 191,000 c.f.s. English traveler Charles Joseph La Trobe described the roiling convergence in 1833:

> [Our] boat glided suddenly from the clear water into a turbid yellow stream in which the mud could be seen boiling from below, [which subsequently] disappear[ed] for nearly ten miles. The surface of the river showed little or

no token of the adulteration of the current; and it was not till we got ... with-in a few miles of St. Louis, that we observed the two rivers, distinguishable from their difference of colour, flowing for a while distinctly side by side, till in fine mingling their waters they form one immense torrent.[29]

An even greater transformation occurs at Cairo, Illinois, where the Ohio River doubles the Mississippi's volume to over 484,000 c.f.s. Above Cairo, the Mississippi flows in a relatively well-defined channel through a bluff-lined valley one to six miles wide; below Cairo, the river meanders broadly across a pancake-flat alluvial plain twelve to twenty miles wide. The upper river runs *beneath* adjacent hills and collects their runoff; the lower river usually flows *above* its immediate surroundings, both shedding water into distributaries as well as collecting it via tributaries. Father Vivier of the Society of Jesus described the terrain, biota, and native ecological intervention along this section of the river in 1750:

> Both banks of the Mississipi are bordered ... by two strips of dense forests [beyond which] the country is more elevated, and is intersected by plains and groves [with] thinly scattered [trees]. This is partly due to the fact that the Savages set fire to the prairies toward the end of the autumn, when the grass is dry; the fire spreads everywhere and destroys most of the young trees. This does not happen in the places nearer the river, because, the land being lower, [is] more watery....
>
> The plains and forests contain wild cattle [American bison], which are found in herds; deer, elk, and bears; a few tigers; numbers of wolves ... wild-cats; wild turkeys and pheasants; and other animals, less known and of smaller size. This river [is] the abode of beavers; of a prodigious number of ducks, [plus] teal, bustards, geese, swans, snipe; and of some other aquatic birds, whose names are unknown in Europe, to say nothing of the fish of many kinds....[30]

By the time it flows past the loess bluffs (hills of wind-blown silt) of Vicksburg and Natchez, the Mississippi River reaches its peak single-channel volume, averaging 602,000 c.f.s. and surpassing 1,000,000 c.f.s. in high-water years—a theoretical foot-thick wall of water one-thousand feet wide and one-thousand feet high passing every second. "The Mississippi flows gray, turbid, and broad," wrote the Swedish traveler Fredrika Bremer of this area on a wintry day in 1850;

> its waters become more and more swollen every day, and the shores become still more flat and swampy, bordered with cotton-wood and cane-brake. Great blocks of timber, trees, and all kind of things float along the Mississippi, all telling of wreck and desolation. This great river seems to me like the waters of the [biblical] Deluge, and they bear along with them a vast register of sin.[31]

About fifty river miles south of Natchez, the Mississippi changes character for a third time. Historically, the Red River joined the Mississippi here while the Atchafalaya flowed out of the system as a distributary to the Gulf of Mexico. In the 1830s, Louisianians, in the interest of navigation, manipulated this hydrology by excavating shortcuts, clearing logjams, and dredging shoals. In doing so, they inadvertently allowed a steadily increasing flow of Mississippi water to escape down the Atchafalaya. Within a few decades, suspicions arose that this may someday pose a problem. Nathaniel H. Bishop, an adventurer who canoed alone down the Mississippi in the 1870s, learned from a local planter that the Atchafalaya River "was slowly widening its current, and would in time, perhaps, become the main river of the basin, and finally deprive the Mississippi of a large portion of its waters." The planter, since his boyhood,

> had watched the falling in of the banks with the widening and increasing strength of the [Atchafalaya's] current.... Once it was impassible for steamers; but a little dredging opened the way, while the Mississippi and Red rivers had both contributed to its volume of water until it had deepened sufficiently for the United States gunboats to ascend it during the late [Civil] war. It follows the shortest course from the mouth of the Red River to the Gulf of Mexico.[32]

"Shortest course" to the gulf means *steepest* course, a hydrological characteristic that flowing water invariably seeks. By the mid-1900s, scientists recognized that the Mississippi would eventually jump channels—substantially, possibly entirely, around 1975—abandoning New Orleans and converting Louisiana's invaluable river corridor to an elongated brackish bay. The future of New Orleans was in question: a severed Mississippi would stifle river traffic and allow ocean salinity to creep up to the city's municipal water intakes. To prevent this catastrophe, Army Corps engineers built the Old River Control Structure in 1954-62 to regulate the flow of the Mississippi into the Atchafalaya at a government-approved seventy-thirty ratio. The viability of New Orleans as a port and a city rests on this Herculean engineering project.

From Old River to Baton Rouge, flat alluvial bottomlands stretch out to the west while soft, rugged loess bluffs line the eastern bank. Louisiana's capital stands upon the last of these uplands. "We have passed Baton Rouge," continued Fredrika Bremer while sailing downriver in late 1850, "situated upon a high bluff....

> The Mississippi is at this point very broad. There are in the river sand-banks and verdant islands. Its waters are now clearer [because] the sun shines; the scenery of the shores is pleasing and quiet: plantations, orange groves, white slave villages amid the green fields, extensive views beneath the mild heavens.... The river is full of vessels, steamers, boats, and barges. We are approaching the gay city of New Orleans.[33]

Below Baton Rouge, flowing around 465,000 c.f.s., the Mississippi River finally exits its alluvial valley—"walled" at this point by meager terraces to the east (marked today by Baton Rouge's aptly named Highland Road), and by minor uplands to the west near Lafayette. From here on, the river flows between natural levees rising ten to fifteen feet above its surrounding deltaic plain. It is an incredibly productive environment, and historical visitors invariably noted the change in both the physical and human landscapes. "The soil [of the delta] is a deep black sandy alluvial, of great fertility, and seems not to deteriorate by cultivation," wrote one observer in the late 1840s. "This whole coast along the river is now occupied by the sugar planter, and for nearly eight months in the year the eye of the traveler sees nothing before him but the wavering sugar cane, presenting one unbroken living landscape of the most beautiful green ever beheld...."[34]

In these final 200 miles, the Mississippi River averages 2,000-3,000 feet wide, runs fifty to 200 feet deep, and flows at slightly below the rate gauged at Baton Rouge.[35] No more tributaries join the river in this deltaic region (the last one enters in North Baton Rouge); this figurative *cordillera* is a shedder of water, not a collector. Sugar cane still grows today on the adjacent landscape, but at a fraction of the acreage of antebellum times, and less so with every passing year.

To sail down this section of the Mississippi today is to experience a massively tamed river; levees not only constrain and guide the channel but disassociate it from adjacent banks. Entirely different was the experience in colonial times. Jesuit Father du Poisson described grueling days and nights on the wild lower Mississippi around present-day St. John the Baptist Parish during in the late spring of 1727:

> We set out at the time of highest water; the river had risen more than forty feet higher than usual; nearly all the country is lowland, and consequently... inundated. Thus we were exposed to the danger of finding no... land where we could cook and sleep. When we do find it...we begin by making a bed of boughs so that the mattress may not sink into the mud; then we spread upon it a skin.... We bend three or four canes in semicircles [to form a tent]; then we spread over this frail structure...a large canvass [*baire*].... In these tombs, stifling with heat, we are compelled to sleep....
> We are much more to be pitied when we find no camping-ground; then we fasten the pirogue to a tree, and if we find an embarras of trees we prepare our meal on it; [else] we go to bed without supper[,] exposed through the whole night to the fury of the mosquitoes. By the way, what we call an *embarras* is a mass of floating trees which the river has uprooted, and which the current drags onward continually. If these be stopped by a tree...or by a tongue of land, the trees become heaped upon one another, and form enormous piles; some are found that would furnish [a French city] with wood for three winters. These spots are difficult and dangerous to pass. It is necessary to sail very close to the embarras; the current is rapid there and should the pirogue be driven against these floating trees it would immediately disappear and would be swallowed up in the water....
>
> This was also the season of the greatest heat, which was increasing every day[;] there was always a burning sun above our heads.... [T]he height of the trees and the denseness of the woods—which extend along the entire route, on both sides of the river—did not permit us to enjoy the least breath of air....
>
> But the greatest torture [is] the cruel persecution of the mosquitoes. I believe the Egyptian plague was not more cruel.... This little creature has caused more swearing since the French came to *Mississipi* [sic], than...in all the rest of the world.... [W]e are eaten, devoured; they enter our mouths,

our nostrils, our ears; our faces, hands, and bodies are covered with them; their sting penetrates the clothing, and leaves a red mark on the flesh, which swells....

Such are the inconveniences of a Mississipi voyage.[36]

Only along certain banks and islands can one today experience a semblance of the untamed Mississippi. Even then, the water's channel, stage, flow rate, quality, sediment load, and biota would all reflect centuries of anthropogenic intervention. Even the mosquito population would differ: many species now in Louisiana were introduced since colonial times.

At River Mile 115, the Mississippi River enters metropolitan New Orleans and twists through it for the next twenty-seven miles. It is an especially wending section: two prominent "point bars" on the east bank, and three on the West Bank, have challenged navigators for 300 years. Point bars form on the concave side of a river meander, where the current slows and deposits sandy alluvium (*batture*) at the water's edge, extending the land outwardly. The term *batture* comes from the past participle of the French verb *batter*, "to beat," as in "beaten down by the river;" *leveé*, on the other hand, comes from *lever*, "to raise up." Battures figure prominently in Louisiana culture, both along the river and in the courthouse: what happened legally when a batture formed adjacent to private property oftentimes ended up in a lawsuit.

"The inhabitants consider themselves fortunate when a batture begins to form or continues to build up in front of their land," recalled Pierre Clément de Laussat in 1803. "But one bank builds up firmly only at the expense of the opposite bank, and a batture always means a bank cave-in [*éboulemens*]; one is always in proportion to the other."[37] The Frenchman was right: across the river from the point bar is the *cutbank*, where the river runs faster and deeper (*thalweg*) and erodes the bank more aggressively. Past the French Quarter, the thalweg swings across the channel, eroding the east bank in places such as Bywater and accreting on the west in Algiers. Army Corps levees, revetments, armoring, riprap, and other devices restrain the river from its normal functions, but the battle is ongoing—as are the legal cases involving batture ownership.

Ninety-five miles above the mouth sits the original city of New Orleans, where, coincidentally, lies the deepest point of the entire river, about 200 feet. Flow rates here typically range from 450,000 to 535,000 c.f.s. but can nearly triple during high water. Since consistent measurements have been kept, river stage in New Orleans has run as low as 0.71 feet above mean gulf level and as high as 19.98 feet, averaging about ten feet above the sea.[38] This means that the river surface is almost always higher than 56 percent of greater New Orleans, usually higher than 95 percent, and occasionally higher than 99.5 percent of the land surface (everything except the artificial levees).[39] At those times—specifically when the river surpasses seventeen feet in stage or 1,250,000 c.f.s. in volume—the Bonnet Carré Spillway is opened to divert up to 250,000 c.f.s. into Lake Pontchartrain. During extreme floods, the Morganza and Old River structures may also be activated to divert flow into the Atchafalaya River.

The sight from the levee of a swollen river gliding above the level of adjacent rooftops has long startled newcomers: "What struck me most," wrote a visitor from Edinburgh in 1828, "was the [Mississippi's] surface being six or seven feet higher that the level of the streets of New Orleans, and indeed of all the adjacent country.... [I]t seemed as if the smallest shake, or the least addition, would send it over the edge, and thus submerge the city."[40] But, as often happens in New Orleans, majesty and awe accompanied that sense of threat. Another visitor, also in 1828, waxed eloquently on New Orleans' future as he contemplated the great natural phenomenon before him:

> Standing on the extreme point of the longest river in the world, New Orleans commands all the commerce of the immense territory... exceeding a million of square miles. You may [sail for] 1000 miles from New Orleans up the Red river...up the Arkansas river; ... up the Missouri and its branches...to the falls of St. Anthony; [and] the same distance from New Orleans up the Illinois...the big Wabash...the Tennessee...the Cumberland, and... the Ohio up to Pittsburgh. Thus New Orleans has in its rear this immense territory, [plus] the coast of Mexico, the West India islands, and the half of America to the south, the rest of America on its left, and the continent of Europe beyond the Atlantic. *New Orleans is beyond a doubt the most important commercial point on the face of the earth.*[41]

Once past greater New Orleans, the river makes one last great meander at English Turn before straightening out and speeding up through Plaquemines Parish to the Gulf of Mexico. A wild, frontier-like ambience in both the physical and human environment prevails in this isolated region; one senses the culmination of a great natural process, and a proximity to the ragged edge of a continent.

At Head of Passes (River Mile 0), the channel trifurcates into a birdfoot-shaped embouchure known as the Balize Delta, or Plaquemines Complex. This feature comprises six sub-deltas, numerous splays and lobes, and three major passes: Southwest Pass (50 percent of flow and the route of most navigation activity), South Pass (20 percent), and Pass a Loutre (30 percent), which branches into North and Northeast Pass. The Balize is the seventh delta complex to have roamed across southern Louisiana in as many millennia, flooding, depositing, jumping channels, and building new land as earlier sediments sink and erode to the sea. The sediment load, discharged to the continental shelf, extends the lower deltaic plain into a subaqueous delta amid a sediment plume visible from space. In this great estuary, the telltale waters of the Mississippi, which reflect with unrelenting accuracy myriad environmental alterations in the North American interior, intermix with the sea. "The line of demarcation between the yellowish-brown water of the river, and the clear green water of the sea," wrote Joseph Holt Ingraham in 1835, "is so distinctly defined, that a cane could be laid along it."[42]

The Continental and the Maritime

Climate and weather in New Orleans

> Although the temperature was generally quite pleasant, its variations carried
> it rapidly from one extreme to the other…. One day may have been a real
> spring day; the following night would bring a violent wind…. The next day
> might be cold enough to call for heat; and the day after tropical…. A storm
> would break out, bringing [some] relief, [while] the mornings…were for
> the most part delightful. Such was May in Louisiana. We were to see what
> the summer months, about which people frightened us, were like.[43]
>
>   —Pierre Clément de Laussat,
>   recalling springtime in New Orleans in 1803

That the heat and humidity of a New Orleans summer constitute a "frighten-
ingly" oppressive climate—indeed, that it is even hot and humid—reflects, of course,
an anthropocentric perspective. Vegetation grows luxuriously under those very conditions that humans find oppressive; wildlife flourishes in the same subtropical coastal
wetlands that people describe as inhospitable. Simply put, New Orleans' climate "is
what it is:" inanimate atmospheric conditions produced by local, continental, or global
processes. Its influence on local society, however, is profound.

Latitude constitutes the most fundamental climate factor. New Orleans' position at 30 degrees north places it 6½ degrees beyond that portion of the Earth—the
tropics—that are exposed, because of the planet's 23½ degree tilt, to the most direct
and concentrated solar radiation. On the summer solstice, the sun's rays strike the
northern limit of the tropical region (the Tropic of Cancer) at a ninety-degree angle;
in New Orleans, the rays arrive at 83½ degrees. Latitude dictates sun angle, sun angle
drives solar radiation, and solar radiation increases temperature. If only latitude determined climate, New Orleans would experience warmer temperatures than all of North
America except south Florida, south Texas, and Mexico. But three other factors are at
play.

Position with respect to water bodies is a key one. Water serves as a "sink" for
solar radiation as well as a source of water molecules to evaporate into the atmosphere.
The tropically heated Gulf of Mexico warms the air mass above it and thence coastal
lands near it, including New Orleans. Warmer air bears more water molecules, giving
New Orleans a temperature and relative humidity higher than comparable inland areas
of the same latitude. Temperatures would go no lower than the 60s in the winter were it
not for the third factor driving climate: relative position on the continent.

Continental position exposes a place to certain prevailing winds and the conditions they bear. Winds in the mid-latitudinal northern hemisphere generally blow
west to east, which means that the western parts of continents are subjected to warmer,

more stable maritime climes, while eastern areas experience the more volatile continental conditions blowing in from the interior. Cold fronts, which arrive in lesser and
greater intensities roughly once or twice per fortnight from late October through early
April, drive autumn-to-spring weather conditions in New Orleans. Winter in particular is punctuated by the ebb-and-flow between warm, humid tropical air masses rising
from the Gulf of Mexico and frigid, dry air masses arriving from the Rockies, plains,
or polar region. This accounts for the city's notoriously varied wintertime weather,
suffered by the likes of newly arrived English visitor Charles Joseph La Trobe during
Christmas and New Year 1833-34:

> With a thermometer between 70° and 80°, and a constant drizzle...the
> streets were full of mud oozing up from the pavement, and it was a penance
> to be [in this] thick and unwholesome atmosphere.... [A]n impenetrable
> mist rested on the city, through which frequent flashes of lightning glim-
> mered portentiously;—then came a terrific storm...but with no abatement
> of the heat till the ensuing night, when the thermometer fell below the freez-
> ing point.

> Three days after the country was covered with snow, and many miserable
> wretches were found dead in the streets.... It continued freezing for four
> days, when the atmosphere again regained the former degree of heat. Such a
> chaos of mud can hardly be conceived.[44]

(Although such weather extremes are typical from December through February, the snow and extended freezes reported by La Trobe are rare. Most cold fronts lose
their frigid edge as they pass over the relatively warm waters of Lake Pontchartrain.)

Finally, topographic elevation—or in this case its absence—affects climate.
Sea-level New Orleans bears zero altitudinal influence on climate (roughly 3.3 degrees
F cooler for every thousand feet in elevation), but the lack of mountain ranges to the
northwest is consequential, because cold fronts are able to arrive unobstructed. These
interior influences make New Orleans' climate continental (read: wide range of temperatures and drier conditions), while proximity to the Gulf of Mexico renders it also
maritime (read: usually relatively warm and humid conditions). The following conditions characterize New Orleans' humid subtropical climate:[45]

- Daytime highs in the 90s and nighttime lows in the 70s-80s during the hottest
  months (July-August);
- Low-60s daytime highs to the mid-40s nighttime lows during the coldest
  months (December through February), with extremes ranging from the low
  80s to upper 10s;
- A season cycle defined mostly by cold fronts, with the first weak front marking
  the arrival of autumn (usually a few weeks after the equinox), the first strong
  front commencing winter (usually in late November), and the last strong and
  weak fronts passing in March and early May, respectively, ending winter and
  spring;
- A roughly 280-day growing season, with hard freezes occurring every few

years but some winters passing sans even a weak freeze;

- Relative humidity ranging from 65 percent on summer afternoons to 91 percent on summer mornings, and 66 to 85 percent on winter afternoons and mornings;

- An average of 63 inches of precipitation annually, with the most falling in summer (over 7" in July), the least in autumn (3.1" in October), and moderate amounts from December through May (around 5" per month);

- A norm of partly cloudy conditions, with sunlight reaching city streets during 60 percent of the drier months and around 45 percent of the wetter months. Clear days prevail 28 percent of the time; partly cloudy conditions comprise 32 percent, and cloudy days make up 40 percent of a typical year;

- Extremely rare snows, falling every decade or so and rarely amounting to more than a cold sleet or a dusting.

The impact of climate on New Orleans society is profound, but—excepting tropical storms—no more or less than it is wherever humans live. Climate allowed the large-scale cultivation of lucrative commodities, particularly sugar cane, for which New Orleans served enthusiastically as a trade and transshipment point. Architectural traits such as balconies, galleries, high ceilings, and steep roofs bear at least some provenance to climatic conditions. Summertime heat and humidity meant not only round-the-clock discomfit but the threat of death: a favorable climate enabled the African mosquito *Aedes aegypti* to establish itself here, spreading the yellow fever virus which killed tens of thousands of New Orleanians in the 1800s. Those of means, including Northern businessmen, responded by annually departing for more salubrious climes, leaving the summertime city disproportionately to Creoles (natives), immigrants, the poor, and the enslaved. One observer in the late 1840s estimated that, while the city's official population exceeded 100,000, "a transient population of thirty or forty thousand [departs] in swarms… as soon as the warm season commences, [and returns] as wild geese do from the North, on the first appearance of a flake of snow."[46] Thus, New Orleanians' response to climate seasonally altered the social, economic, ethnic, and racial dynamics of the city.

New Orleanians, in return, have influenced their climate. The urban heat island effect, in which the expansive concrete surfaces increase temperatures over metropolises, occurs in nearly all cities. Other environmental manipulations possibly affected local weather in more unusual ways. Englishman Thomas Henrys recorded in 1760 that "winters [in Louisiana] have been more severe, for some years past, than they were commonly known to be at the time when the *French* first settled here, occasioned, as is thought, by clearing the lands of the woods…."[47] Weather Bureau forecaster Isaac Cline, of Galveston hurricane fame, noted an eight-degree increase in summertime temperatures and a four-degree drop during winters between 1900 and 1918. His explanation:

> water absorbs heat more slowly than the earth during the day and loses it less rapidly at night. New Orleans, entirely surrounded by water and with

its soil saturated, formerly boasted of a more uniform climate. In late years, however, levees have prevented overflows, reclamation projects have effected the draining of swamps and, finally, sub-surface drainage … has eliminated surface water from the street drains [and] ground moisture [by] eight or ten feet.[48]

If Cline's analysis is correct, then New Orleans, by draining its backswamp, rendered itself more of a continental and less of a maritime climate.

Modern technology has tempered the effects of climate on New Orleans society. Domestic air-cooling technology transformed local streetscapes and culture, as New Orleanians traded the social space of stoops and front porches for the private space of climate-controlled living rooms. Yet the cycle of life in the city today is still fundamentally attuned to climate. The first cold front in October brings an up-tick in the tourism and convention trade, which peaks during the wintertime Carnival season (weather on Mardi Gras is notoriously varied). "Festival season" kicks into high gear during the delightful late winter and early spring, and when the last tunes die down at Jazz Fest, everyone knows "the Big Heat" is approaching. As in times past—but for very different reasons—those who can leave in the summer, do. The other 99 percent count the days to the next cold front—while living in dread of a climatic phenomenon that occurs locally for all of a few hours per century, yet threatens the very survival of the city: severe tropical storms.

Of the scores of such tempestuous low-pressure systems to strike New Orleans (see *The Fortuitous Storm of 1722, The Great Storm of 1915, Hurricane Betsy,* and *Hurricane Katrina*), the hurricane of 1779 was the first to be characterized meteorologically for the scientific record. Writing about New Orleans' climate for the *Transactions of the American Philosophical Society*, William Dunbar reported,

> August and September are called the hurricane months … I was at New Orleans during the [August 18, 1779 hurricane, in which] more than half of the town was stript of its covering, many houses thrown down in town and country, no ship or vessel of any kind was to be seen on the river next morning.

> The river … was forced over its banks, and the crops which were not yet collected, disappeared from the face of the earth. The forests [near] New Orleans assumed the dreary appearance of winter, the woods over large tracts were laid flat with the ground ….

Dunbar estimated that the storm spanned twelve miles and passed directly over New Orleans. He had the presence of mind to track the curiously changing directions of the wind:

> [I]t continued blowing from the East or S.E. for two or three hours with undescribable impetuosity, after which succeeded all at once a most profound and awful calm, so inconceivably terrific that the stoutest heart … could not look upon it without feeling a secret horror, as if nature were preparing to resolve herself again into chaos …. [After] 5 or 6 minutes, perhaps less, the

hurricane began to blow from the opposite point of the compass and very speedily regained a degree of fury and impetuosity equal if not superior to what it had before possessed.

Dramatically, Dunbar recounted how dead bodies, which had earlier blown upstream on the Mississippi's surging waters, now sped downstream with such velocity that they were more airborne than waterborne. He concluded his paper,

> It is probable that if similar observations are made upon all hurricanes, tornadoes and whirlwinds they will be found universally to consist of a vortex with a central spot in a state of profound calm....[49]

That observation, originating from New Orleans in 1779 and published in 1809 in one of early America's most influential scholarly journals, brought new scientific understanding to the phenomenon of tropical storms, and to the disciplines of meteorology and climatology.

New Orleans will figure prominently in the future of those and other scientific disciplines, given its front-line position vis-à-vis climate change, rising sea levels, eroding coasts, and other unfurling environmental dilemmas. In the meanwhile, weather patterns will continue to affect the daily life of New Orleans society as an ongoing battle between the continental and the maritime.

Settling the Landscape

Resolved to establish,
thirty leagues up the river,
a burg which should be called New Orleans,
where landing would be possible
from either the river
or Lake Pontchartrain.

—Company of the West ledger, September 1717

"Forest Primeval" Reconsidered

Indigenous occupation of the Gulf Coast region

That the pre-colonial Gulf Coast represented a pristine wilderness, populated by only a few scattered Indian tribes living in "harmony" with nature and implicitly "awaiting" the dawn of history, is a popular misconception. Native peoples in fact numbered many, altered their environment, and traveled and traded extensively. Modern-day New Orleans would be a very different place, and probably *in* a different place, had they not.

A Spanish expedition in 1519 recorded fully forty Indian settlements within the first few miles of what was probably the Mobile River. At the river's mouth, wrote one member, was "an extensive town," where "natives treated our men in a friendly manner."[50] Journals from Hernando De Soto's expedition (1539-1543) are replete with both peaceful and violent encounters with natives. Evidence that indigenous peoples cleared forest, burned fields, transported species, and raised crops prevails throughout historical accounts. A member of the La Salle expedition in 1682 described "fine corn fields and...beautiful prairies" in the otherwise densely forested region near present-day Natchez, Mississippi.[51] Pierre Le Moyne, sieur d'Iberville, upon first laying eyes on the future New Orleans site in 1699, described the area as "thickly covered with canes [which] burn readily," and spotted an Indian tending to a prairie fire nearby.[52] The grasses that grew following burning were ideal food for American bison, an important resource for the natives; Iberville's crew "saw three buffaloes lying down on the bank"[53] near what is now Jackson Square, plus a herd of over 200 farther upriver. Near present-day White Castle Iberville found the extensive Bayogoula Indian encampment, which he described as comprising "107 huts and 2 temples, [with] possibly about 200 to 250 men and few women and children,"[54] who tended "some cocks and hens"—domesticated chickens, a species not native to the New World. Another Frenchmen observed "fields where they cultivate their millet, [which] they break up ...with buffalo bones."[55] Above Baton Rouge, Iberville visited an Indian village of 140 huts "on the slope of a hill [covered with] corn fields...."[56]

The first-person accounts of abundant Indian life in pre-colonial Louisiana align with recent scholarship that increases traditional estimates of indigenous populations in pre-Columbian America. "There is substantial evidence," wrote geographer William M. Denevan in his 1992 article *The Pristine Myth: The Landscape of the Americas in 1492*, that "the Native American landscape of the early sixteenth century was a humanized landscape almost everywhere. Populations were large[;] forest composition had been modified, grasslands had been created, wildlife disrupted, and erosion was severe in places."[57] Indians, like anyone else, exploited their environment to the capacity of their technology. Those in Louisiana, as elsewhere, altered their landscape by setting fire to forests and prairies, tilting ecological cycles to their advantage for the cultivation of staples and the manipulation of fauna and flora habitat. They interacted and traded far and wide, intentionally or accidentally diffusing species and sometimes affecting the biological diversity and ecology of entire landscapes. Among those species were chickens, native to Asia, brought by the Spanish, and diffused up the Mississippi River via Indian trade routes. Wild pigs, smallpox, sugar cane, *Aedes aegypti* and the yellow fever virus, plus hundreds of other species deemed by humans to be either benign (azaleas, crepe myrtles, cotton) or malignant (nutria, kudzu, water hyacinth), would follow the trajectory of the Bayogoulas' chickens and help alter both the history and geography of Louisiana.

The presence of American bison (often recorded as "buffalo" or "wild cattle" in journals) in Louisiana also casts doubt on the "pristine myth." De Soto's expedition trekked thousands of miles throughout the Southeast in the 1540s and never mentioned bison.[58] Yet 160 years later, Iberville and his men repeatedly sighted them, and observed how natives utilized their hides for shelter, hair for clothing, meat for food, and bones for plowing. Bison abounded in Louisiana well into the colonial era: Jesuit Father du Poisson reported in 1727 that hunters "begin to find wild cattle [around Baton Rouge]; these animals roam in herds over the prairies, or along the rivers; last year a Canadian brought down to [N]ew Orleans four hundred and eighty tongues of cattle…killed during the winter."[59] Between De Soto's era and that of the French, bison seem to have massively expanded their range. Why?

Geographer Erhard Rostlund argued that the once-high Indian populations of early sixteenth-century North America kept bison herds in check on western plains (through hunting pressure), while precluding potential bison habitat in the southeast (through extensive land cultivation).[60] But after the European arrival, Old World diseases, primarily smallpox, decimated native populations by the thousands, even millions—"possibly the greatest demographic disaster ever."[61] Denevan puts the North American Indian's population decline at 74 percent (from 3.8 million down to one million) between 1492 and 1800. "When disease swept Indians from the land," wrote Charles Mann in his book *1491*, the "entire ecological *ancien régime* collapsed."[62] Bison were among the affected biota—as beneficiaries. The human die-off both diminished hunting pressure on bison in the west and liberated fine grazing habitat for their use in the southeast. Bison range, the theory goes, subsequently expanded southeastwardly toward the Gulf and Atlantic coasts. Iberville in 1699 viewed the animals at the fringe of their range, where they affected the local ecology and landscape.

Iberville also bore witness in 1699 to the terrible die-off suffered by indigenous peoples in the post-contact New World, reporting that "the smallpox…had killed one-fourth of the people" in a settlement near present-day Baton Rouge.[63] Former French officer Chevalier Guy de Soniat du Fossat, writing in 1791 of his memories of Louisiana in the 1750s, stated that the Indian "villages and…population have decreased about two-thirds in number since the advent of the Europeans, who introduced and brought among them diseases, desires, dissensions and all other abuses of civilization, heretofore unknown to them."[64] Soniat's eyewitness estimate from 1791 roughly concurs with Deneven's scholarly assessment from 1992.

The natives' demise, too, affected the landscape: fewer Indians meant fewer encampments, fewer forest clearings, fewer fires, fewer croplands, less hunting pressure, less use of natural resources, and more resources for other species. "[T]he Indian landscape of 1492," wrote Denevan, "had largely vanished by the mid-eighteenth century, not through a European superimposition, but because of the demise of the native population." Ironically, "the landscape of 1750 was more 'pristine' (less humanized) than that of 1492."[65]

Thus, the pre-colonial Gulf Coast and Louisiana deltaic plain comprised not the "forest primeval" romanticized in literature and popular history, but rather a landscape already transformed by sequential indigenous occupations more expansive and influential than commonly thought. The first Europeans did not "commence" history and document a benchmark landscape from which all subsequent transformations derived; they merely encountered a landscape continually under transformation—vastly by physical forces over millennia, and considerably by indigenous human forces over centuries.

The most significant contribution of pre-colonial indigenous peoples to the New Orleans we know today came not from these historical environmental manipulations, but from the sharing of critical geographical knowledge with early French explorers. Through extensive travel and trading, natives mastered the region's complex labyrinth of swamps, marshes, rivers, bayous, ridge systems, and bays. They revealed to the newcomers myriad portages, shortcuts, "back doors," safe routes, resources, and foods which would inform the Frenchmen's siting and settlement decisions.

"*The Indians made maps of the whole country for me*," reflected Iberville in 1699.[66] Without native geographical informants, Iberville and his brother Bienville, who founded New Orleans nineteen years later based principally on indigenous knowledge, would have "discovered" much less geography, and perceived it in a far less insightful manner.

Contact, 1519-1699

Initial Spanish and French forays into the lower Mississippi region

Earliest documented evidence of European exploration of the central Gulf Coast comes from Spanish explorer Alonso Álvarez de Pineda's 1519 expedition in search of a western passage. Pineda ascended "a river which was found to be very large and very deep, at the mouth of which [was] an extensive town."[67] He named the waterway *Río del Espíritu Santo*, presumed for centuries to be the Mississippi but now interpreted as probably the Mobile River.

Nine years later, Pánfilo de Narváez led an ill-fated imperialistic expedition from Cuba to Florida and westward along the coast. The expedition "came upon… a very large river [and] entered a bay…in which there were many islands. And there we came together, and from the sea we drank fresh water,"[68] probably the Mississippi estuary. Longshore currents then swept the expedition westward and wrecked it near present-day Galveston. There, Álvar Núñez Cabéza de Vaca led survivors on an epic 2,000-mile overland odyssey to the Pacific coastal town of San Miguel de Culiacán, Mexico, in 1536. His riveting account of sixteenth-century North America remains in publication to this day.

Cabéza de Vaca's report renewed Spanish interest in the North American interior, hitherto perceived as a mysterious and unpromising land. In May 1539, Hernando De Soto and 600 soldiers landed near present-day Tampa and proceeded to explore 4,000 miles throughout the future American South. They encountered the Mississippi River near present-day Memphis in 1541, becoming the first Europeans to sight the inland channel and gain "an adequate conception of the magnitude and importance of the Mississippi."[69] The arduous journey killed hundreds of soldiers (including De Soto himself, who was interred in the river) and probably thousands of natives, infected by newly introduced European viruses. Luis de Moscoso led the survivors down the Mississippi and possibly past the future site of New Orleans in July 1543, but again there is question: a 1544 map depicts a *Río del Espíritu Santo* that resembles the Mississippi in size and importance but not in shape and form, suggesting Moscoso took the Atchafalaya to the sea. If so, then no European left documented evidence of passing future New Orleans in the sixteenth century.

Moscoso's escape ended imperial Spain's initial probings of the lower Mississippi River. The Spaniards sought not settlement and colonization but riches; finding none, they left no permanent mark. The French in seventeenth-century North America also sought riches, but, invested as they were in New France, pursued a means—trade routes and empire—toward that end. Explorations of the Great Lakes region and upper Mississippi by Marquette and Joliet (1673) helped demystify the western frontier and refute the notion of a nearby Pacific Ocean, but no French explorer had yet confirmed the connection between the upper Mississippi and the Gulf of Mexico.

An ambitious young Norman named René-Robert Cavelier, sieur de La Salle set out to do just that. A resident of New France since 1666, La Salle petitioned "to endeavor to discover the western part of New France," to which King Louis XIV in 1678 "willingly [consented], because there is nothing we have more at heart than the discovery of this country…."[70] Thus authorized, La Salle formed an expedition, and, with surprising ease, sailed down the Mississippi in the winter of 1682 and neared the deltaic plain in late March. There, the expedition traversed country "so bordered with canes and so low…that we could not hunt," subsisting instead on "potatoes and crocodiles."[71]

In early April, La Salle, in his own words, "went ashore on the borders of a marsh formed by the inundation of the river" to confirm reports of a village that "the whole of this marsh, covered with canes, must be crossed to reach…."[72] The men soon came upon a recently destroyed Tangiboa [Tangibaho] village, which historian Marc de Villiers du Terrage surmised "must have lain very near the present site of New Orleans."[73] If so, these may be the first recorded descriptions of the future city's landscape.

After the expedition continued downriver, Father Membré described the historic moment that transpired as the party approached the Mississippi's birdfoot delta and smelled the salty waters of the Gulf of Mexico:

> [W]e arrived, on the sixth of April, at a point where the river divides into three channels [which] are beautiful and deep. The water is brackish; after advancing two leagues it became perfectly salt, and, advancing on, we discovered the open sea, so that on the ninth of April, with all possible solemnity, we performed the ceremony of planting the cross and raising the arms of France, [taking] possession of that river, of all rivers that enter it and of all the country watered by them.[74]

The Mississippi Basin, in La Salle's mind, now belonged to France; he named it after King Louis XIV, and *Louisiana* entered the vocabulary.

La Salle promptly returned to France and recommended to the Sun King the establishment of a fortification sixty leagues above the mouth of the Mississippi, for its "excellent position," "favourable disposition of the savages," fertile land, mild climate, military advantages, and opportunity to "harass the Spaniards in those regions from whence they derive all their wealth." The fortification would also serve as a base for preaching the Gospel, conquering the silver-rich provinces of Mexico, storing supplies, harboring and building ships, and exploiting the vast resources of newly claimed Louisiana. A league at that time measuring between 2.4 and three miles, La Salle's envisioned city probably entailed a site around Bayou Manchac. A "port or two" there, proclaimed La Salle, "would make us masters of the whole of this continent."[75]

La Salle set out in 1684 to found his city on the great river. What happened over the next three years is the subject of controversy among historians, though La Salle's tragic fate is not. The expedition missed the mouth of the Mississippi and landed at Matagorda Bay in present-day Texas; La Salle was murdered in March 1687 by mutinous crew, who subsequently died of disease or in Indian battles.[76]

La Salle's lieutenant, Henri de Tonti, mystified by La Salle's disappearance, returned to Louisiana in 1685 to search for his friend and comrade. At one point he left a letter for La Salle in a tree hole near the 1682 claim site, and another letter, dated April 20, with the Quinipissa (Quynypyssa) Indians at their upriver encampment. Hope faded, and he returned to France. There, Tonti kept alive the vision of settling Louisiana throughout the 1690s, warning the French about the English threat to the Mississippi River from the north and the Spanish interests from Mexico and Florida. His message arrived at a bad time, as France's attention was consumed by the War of the League of Augsburg. La Salle's claim languished even as it vexed the Spanish, who caught wind of it in Mexico City and subsequently deployed eleven Gulf Coast expeditions during 1686-93 to "re-discover" the Mississippi. All failed, though some came close.

Not until 1697 did French government officials return to Louisiana matters. What motivated them was not large-scale colonization akin to their successes in

French Canada and the West Indies; France at this time "had neither the material nor the moral resources" to make such a commitment. Rather, they decided to act on the Louisiana claim "primarily...to prevent a foreign foothold at the mouth of the Mississippi."[77] Minister of Marine Louis Phélypeaux, Comte de Pontchartrain thus directed thirty-six-year-old French Canadian warrior Pierre Le Moyne, sieur d'Iberville to seek "the mouth [of the Mississippi River,] select a good site that can be defended with a few men, and block entry to the river by other nations."[78]

The official charge for the founding of Louisiana had been issued.

Foundation of Louisiana, 1699

End of the exploratory phase, beginning of the settlement phase

Iberville, his younger brother Jean Baptiste Le Moyne, sieur de Bienville,[79] and their men arrived to the present-day Mississippi Gulf Coast in February 1699 and proceeded westward into the labyrinthine marshes of what is now St. Bernard and Plaquemines parishes. "When drawing near to the rocks to take shelter," Iberville wrote, "I became aware that there was a river. I passed between two of the rocks, in 12 feet of water, the seas quite heavy. When I got close to the rocks, I found fresh water with a very strong current." The rocks were an illusion—they were probably mud lumps—but the freshwater current was real. "We regarded this beautiful river with admiration," wrote Pénicaut the carpenter:

> The water is of a light color, very good to drink, and very light. The country, on its banks, appeared to be everywhere covered with splendid trees of every description, such as oak, ash, elm, and many others...upon which a vast number of wild turkeys roosted...fat and large [with a] nett weight [of] about thirty pounds![80]

Iberville wondered if this great river was the same that La Salle sailed seventeen years earlier. He proceeded up the delta (see map, "Iberville's Exploration of the Gulf Coast and Lower Mississippi River"). "All this land is a country of reeds and brambles and very tall grass," he wrote on March 3, 1699—which happened to be Mardi Gras. Six leagues farther was "a bend" the river "makes to the west...to which we have given the name Mardy Gras." With those words, Iberville introduced the ancient pagan and Catholic pre-Lenten feast into the colonial society he was about to found. Mardi Gras remains today the single most famous and distinctive cultural trait of Louisiana, and *Bayou Mardi Gras* ranks as the region's oldest French toponym (second only to *Louisiana* itself).

It was here also that Iberville spelled out what was probably by now quite apparent to him and his men: this entire landscape was a floodplain. "I climbed to the top of a nut tree as big as my body, but saw nothing other than canes and bushes. The land becomes inundated to a depth of 4 feet during high water. I made the decision to go upstream..."[81]

Iberville proceeded upriver in search of the legendary Bayogoula Indian encampment and later passed the bluffs of Baton Rouge. The expedition then returned downriver to Bayou Manchac, eastward through that distributary into two connected tidal lagoons they named lakes Maurepas and Pontchartrain, and back to the Gulf of Mexico. Meanwhile, younger brother Bienville made a remarkable discovery while visiting with the Mougoulacha Indians. It was the sad letter left by Henri de Tonti for his lost friend La Salle, dated April 20, 1685 and deposited at the village of the Quinipissa (Quynypyssa) Indians (see *Contact, 1519-1699*). By the time Bienville and Iberville read Tonti's words, La Salle had been dead for a dozen years. "This letter," wrote Iberville confidently, "removes all doubt that [the river I explored] is the Myssysypy."[82]

With that resounding confirmation, the early European exploratory phase of the Louisiana deltaic landscape (1519-1699) drew to a close and the settlement phase began. Concerned about the navigability of the mouth of the Mississippi River, Iberville favored the Gulf Coast for a settlement site and directed his men to build the first outpost, named Fort Maurepas, on the brink of Biloxi Bay in present-day Ocean Springs, Mississippi. Eighty-one men under the command of M. de Sauvolle, enumerated in the initial census in December, became the region's first French residents.[83] Iberville himself returned to France in May to report his success to the king: Louisiana was founded.

"Mud to One's Knees; Water to One's Waist"

The delta landscape in 1699

[N]othing more than two narrow strips of land, about a musket shot in width, having the sea on both sides of the river, which...frequently overflows....

So described one crewmember the turbulent, watery world of the Mississippi Delta as Iberville's expedition sailed upriver in 1699. On the banks were

cane-brake...so tall and thick [and] impossible to pass through...beyond [which] are impenetrable marsh.... [A]s you ascend, the banks appear more and more submerged, the land being scarcely visible. We saw a great quantity of wild game, such as ducks, geese, snipe, teal, bustards, and other birds.

We also saw a Mexican wolf, and a species of rat which carried its young in a sack under its belly.[84]

Along the verdant banks of present-day St. Bernard Parish, Iberville noted that "the trees and the ground are getting higher and are subject to 8-10 inch overflow. I have not yet noticed any walnut tree or fruit tree whatsoever." Blooming vines entangled mature live oaks and blackberry patches, forming a jungle-like scene. The crew spotted three alligators, "one of which was a monster;" and killed a buffalo.[85]

It is almost certain that Iberville first viewed the future site of downtown New Orleans on the calm Saturday of March 7, 1699, when he reported a sequence of wide river meanders "over a distance of 2 leagues" which corresponds to the bends the Mississippi makes through the modern-day metropolis. There, Iberville and his crew met a group of Annocchy Indians, with whom they traded tools and trinkets for buffalo meat, bear meat, and information on how to find the Bayogoula Indian encampment. American bison grazed on the natural levees of future New Orleans; that morning, the crew "saw three buffaloes lying down on the bank," which promptly disappeared into the "thick forest and cane-brakes."[86] The men spent that night somewhere along the present-day uptown riverfront. There, Iberville described elements of the cultural, physical, and biological landscape relevant to him at the moment—at the dusk of the region's prehistory and the dawn of its recorded history:

> [T]here are ten huts thatched with palmettos; near[by] is a small redoubt as high as a man, made of canes in the form of an oval, 25 yards wide and 55 long, having a few huts inside…. All the ground here becomes inundated a foot deep as far back as half a league in the woods, where I went. Both banks of the river, almost the entire distance above the sea, are so thickly covered with canes of every size…that one cannot walk through them. It is impenetrable country, which would be easy to clear. Most of the canes are dry; when set on fire they burn readily and, when burning, make as loud a report as a pistol shot. [They] have roots three and four feet in the ground, which look like a puppet.[87]

(The canes or reeds that Iberville and other earlier explorers repeatedly describe are a grass species, *Arundinaria gigantea*, which is the only bamboo native to North America. Once found throughout Southern riverine and riparian environments, "canebrakes" now constitute an endangered ecosystem, covering less than 2 percent of their former range.[88])

Iberville's geographical descriptions at this point become confusing. He recorded only 4.5 leagues of upriver travel against contrary winds and currents the next day, March 8, placing him anywhere from present-day Carrollton to Harahan to Norco. (The utter lack of prominent landmarks in this deltaic plain handicaps both the explorer and the reader of his journals.)

On March 9, Iberville recorded a significant realization:

> Two leagues from the place where we stopped for the night, the Indian… pointed out to me the place through which the Indians make their portage

to this river from the back of the bay where the ships are anchored. They drag their canoes over a rather good road, at which we found several pieces of baggage owned by men that were going there or were returning. He indicated to me that the distance from the one place to the other was slight…. From here to the sea it may be 50 leagues.[89]

Iberville learned from his Indian guides the existence of an alternative route to the Gulf of Mexico, by means of a tidal lagoon (Lake Pontchartrain) and a "rather good road" (an unnamed topographical ridge) rather than the sinuous Mississippi. Where exactly was that portage? It is difficult to say for certain. Based on the description, one possibility is the Bayou St. John/Bayou Road portage in New Orleans proper. But Iberville's recorded distances seem to indicate a location farther upriver. Perhaps it was the juncture made by Bayou Metairie/Metairie Road with Bayou St. John, but these features do not match the description. More likely it was a minor bayou and topographic ridge in St. Charles Parish, such as the Tigonillou/Bayou Trepagnier portage near the present-day Bonnet Carré Spillway.

Similar confusion arises from Iberville's records of his second voyage to Louisiana, early the next year. "I set out [from coastal Mississippi] with my brother De Bienville," he wrote on January 15, 1700, "to go to the portage from Lake Pontchartrain to the Mississippi, to see whether the barques could get in there." The landscape he subsequently described could be in the same St. Charles Parish vicinity Iberville visited the year before; it could also be in present-day Orleans Parish, along at the southern shore of Lake Pontchartrain, where Iberville encountered an inlet:

> I got to the mouth of the stream that leads to the portage. This stream is at the far end of the lake, toward the south; it is 20 yards wide, 10 feet deep, and 1 league long….

If this is in fact in present-day Orleans Parish, Iberville is positioned along present-day Robert E. Lee Boulevard between Wisner and St. Bernard Avenue, describing the mouth of Bayou St. John.

> I went to the portage, which I found to be 1 league long, and half the distance being full of water and mud up to the knee, the other half fairly good, part of it being a country of canes and fine woods, suitable to live in. I had three canoes carried over the portage.

After sailing up the crooked, log-strewn bayou, Iberville disembarked on a slightly elevated ridge, which could be the Bayou Road/Esplanade Ridge connecting Bayou St. John with the Mississippi River. Despite the elevation, the land hardly offered any better passage. Wrote Iberville's chaplain Paul du Ru of the trip, "From the head of [Bayou St. John?], we must cross through woods but on a path where there is water up to one's waist and mud to one's knees…. there was one occasion when I sank into it up to my waist."[90] Iberville and his men trudged across the ridge to the banks of the Mississippi—possibly to the site of the modern-day French Quarter, previously an Indian village:

I went and looked at the spot where the Quinipissas once had a village, 1½ leagues above this portage; here I found that the land did not become inundated, or did so very little. Trees have grown back in the fields as big as 2 feet around…. Today I had a small field cleared in which I had some sugar cane planted that I brought from St. Domingue…. The south side of the lake is bordered by a prairie half a league to one league wide, after which one comes to the tall trees. *This looks like a fine country to live in.*[91]

That was not the consensus.

"Bad Country, Bad People," 1699-1717

Troubled times in early Louisiana

Iberville's Louisiana explorations of 1699 spawned a nascent colonial French society scattered thinly along the Gulf Coast. Following the establishment of Fort Maurepas, outposts arose on the lower Mississippi River near present-day Phoenix, Louisiana in 1700 and at two sites near Mobile Bay in 1702 and 1711 (the latter of which is now modern Mobile). A small band of Mobile settlers cleared land at Bayou St. John in 1708, marking the first European development in present-day New Orleans. Scarcity, hunger, disease, natural disaster, official inattention, and a desperate lack of settlers (only around 300 lived throughout the entire colony in 1708) made life in early Louisiana a dreaded hardship.

Frustrated and pessimistic, the Crown in 1712 ceded a monopoly for the commercial development of Louisiana to a prominent financier named Antoine Crozat. Privatizing Louisiana released the government from the hassle of management, while opening up the possibility that commercialization might actually prove lucrative. But lack of mineral riches, scarcity of settlers for agriculture, and limited commercial interaction with Spain, coupled with mismanagement, feuding, and Indian tensions, doomed the speculative venture. "Bad country, bad people," is how Gov. Antoine de La Mothe Cadillac assessed the Louisiana colony in 1713.[92] When Crozat retroceded his monopoly in 1717, Louisiana's prospects seemed dim. Yet a number of important events occurred during the Crozat years.

First, in 1714, Louis Juchereau de Saint-Denis founded Natchitoches in present-day central Louisiana, establishing a French presence in the Red River region and trade connections with the Spanish to the south and west. Second, Antoine Cadillac established Fort Toulouse and Fort Tombecbé on key rivers in Alabama, to guard against English incursions from the north and east. Third, in 1716, Bienville founded a garrison—Fort Rosalie, now Natchez, Mississippi—creating a commanding riverside pres-

ence with fine soils nearby and an opportunity to monitor the potentially hostile Natchez Indians. These new French outposts formed clutches helping control and develop
the unwieldy and problematic Louisiana claim. It was also during the Crozat years that
King Louis XIV died (1715) and left the throne to his five-year old great-grandson,
Louis XV, for whom Philippe, Duc d'Orléans would act as Regent of France. Among
the Duc d'Orléans' many business associates was a flamboyant maverick peddling a
bold proposition. His name was John Law.

Born in Edinburgh in 1671, the gifted Law grew rich through high-risk financial affiliations with European aristocracy. He settled with his millions in Paris in the
early 1710s, allying himself with French royalty. Impressed with his financial wizardry,
the Duc d'Orléans authorized Law to establish the *Banque Générale* in 1716. When
Crozat surrendered his Louisiana monopoly the next year, Law pounced. He proposed
to the Duc d'Orléans a Louisiana land-development plan than would enrich all investors and the country. The scheming risk-taker found the right patron.

Less than a month after Crozat formally relinquished Louisiana, John Law's
new Company of the West received a twenty-five-year monopoly charter to develop
commercially the Louisiana colony, with a commitment to populate it with 6,000 settlers and 3,000 slaves during the next ten years. The Company then launched an unprecedented marketing campaign across the continent to drum up investment in Louisiana stock and land, and to entice the lower classes to immigrate there. Though based
on grossly exaggerated claims of commercial potential and doomed to fail, Law and
his Company of the West thrust Louisiana into the forefront of European attention
and, more importantly and more permanently, decided resolutely to found a city to be
called *La Nouvelle Orléans*.

Foundation of New Orleans, 1717-1718

The when, where, and why of Bienville's colossal decision

Resolved to establish, thirty leagues up the river, a burg which *should be
called* New Orleans, where landing would be possible from either the river
or Lake Pontchartrain.[93]

Those words, scribed in the register of John Law's Company of the West probably on September 9, 1717,[94] set in motion the foundation of the riverside city first
envisioned by La Salle thirty-five years earlier. The name honored the Duc d'Orléans,
Law's royal sponsor; the indicated site came from intelligence gathered from Indians
over the previous eighteen years regarding a strategic "backdoor" route to the Mississippi River. Rather than sailing up 100 treacherous miles of the lower Mississippi

(the "river route"), amid fog and debris and against the current and sometimes the wind, voyagers might instead traverse the usually calm waters of the Mississippi Sound, through a waterway known as the Rigolets, into the protected waters of Lake Pontchartrain, and up a small rivulet called Bayou St. John. Travelers would then disembark and follow a two-mile Indian trail—today's Bayou Road—along a slight upland now called the Esplanade Ridge, through the swamps to reach the banks of the Mississippi (see map, "Bayou St. John Portage, 1700s-2002"). To Bienville, this "lake route" circumvented the dangers of the river route and mitigated concerns (held primarily by his late brother Iberville, who had long favored coastal sites) about the feasibility of a riverside settlement.

Bienville fulfilled his charge during late March and early April 1718, when his men began clearing canebrake at a locale—today's French Quarter—he first viewed in 1699.[95] "We are working at present on the establishment of New Orleans thirty leagues above the entrance to the Mississippi,"[96] is about all Bienville wrote about New Orleans' earliest moments, scribed ten weeks after the effort commenced. An Englishman named Jonathan Darby, who landed the following year, recorded more detail. Bienville had

> arrived with six vessels, loaded with provisions and men. These were thirty workmen, all convicts; six carpenters and four Canadians… [t]he whole locality was a dense canebrake, with only a small pathway [Bayou Road] leading from the Mississippi to the Bayou [St. John] communicating with Lake Pontchartrain. [Residences were] made of standing boards and posts, with walls and chimneys of dirt and covered with cypress bark….[97]

Siting an outpost on that particular riverside perch offered the French a strategic position along a least-cost, minimum-distance route connecting, on one hand, the Gulf of Mexico/Caribbean/Atlantic World from whence they came, and on the other, the vast North American interior which they sought to develop. In addition to the portage, the advantages of slightly upraised land, fine soils, a well-positioned perch for river defense, and deep water for the docking of ships added to the site's appeal. The proximate cause motivating the foundation of New Orleans was the need for a convenient port and company office for the commercial development of Louisiana; the ultimate cause was the French imperial need to defend their Louisiana claim by fortifying its Mississippi River Basin gateway against the English and Spanish.

Establishing a settlement is one thing; ensuring its survival and prosperity is quite another. New Orleans faced numerous challenges and dilemmas, from both men and nature, in the years following its initial foundation.

Bienville's Dilemma

Questionable geography, questionable future: 1718-1722

Skepticism prevailed among partisans and observers regarding the wisdom of Bienville's site selection for New Orleans. Among the doubters was Father Pierre François Xavier de Charlevoix, the Jesuit traveler and author of *Histoire de la Nouvelle France,* who arrived to what he sardonically described as "this famous city of Nouvelle Orleans" in January 1722. Only a few weeks earlier, the Company of the Indies (successor to Law's Company of the West) officially designated New Orleans as capital of Louisiana, though word had not yet reached the struggling outpost.

New Orleans, according to Father Charlevoix, bore little semblance to a capital city. Not yet platted, the city comprised "a hundred barracks, placed in no very good order[;] a large ware-house built of timber[,] two or three houses which would be no ornament to a village in France; [and] one half of a sorry ware-house, formerly set apart for divine services."[98] A recent census enumerated 283 white men and women (mostly French but some German and Swiss), 171 African slaves, and twenty-one Indian slaves living in New Orleans proper, with another 791 people of all castes nearby.[99] "Imagine to yourself," Charlevoix wrote two weeks later,

> two hundred persons … sent out to a build a city … who have settled on the banks of a great river, thinking upon nothing but upon putting themselves under cover from the injuries of the weather, and in the mean time waiting till a plan is laid out for them, and till they have built houses according to it.

That plan, under development by Adrien de Pauger and his superior, Chief Engineer Le Blond de la Tour, circulated locally and reached Charlevoix's hands. "Pauger … has just shown me a plan of this own invention; but it will not be so easy to put into execution, as it has been to draw [on] paper." Pauger's magnificent design for the capital—preserved in today's French Quarter—reflected the high expectations that flowed from John Law's grandiose vision for Louisiana, even in the wake of the scheme's collapse in 1720.

Charlevoix harbored an ambivalence shared by many regarding New Orleans. At one point, he expounded on the outpost's potential, which he based

> on the banks of a navigable river, at the distance of thirty three leagues from the sea, from which a vessel may come up in twenty-four hours; on the fertility of its soil; on the mildness and wholesomeness of the climate …; on the industry of the inhabitants; on its neighbourhood to Mexico, the Havana, the finest islands of America, and lastly, to the English colonies. Can there be any thing more requisite to render a city flourishing?[100]

Sixteen days in New Orleans changed Charlevoix's mind. "The country [around] New Orleans, has nothing very remarkable;" he wrote, "nor have I found the situation of this so very advantageous...." He then laid out the dubious advantages alleged by New Orleans' defenders:

> The first is...a small river called *le Bayouc de Saint Jean*...which, at the end of two leagues, discharges itself into the lake Pontchartrain which has a communication with the sea, [for] trade between the capital Mobile and Biloxi, and with all the other posts we possess near the sea. The second is, that below the city the river makes a very great turning called *le detour aux Anglois* [English Turn], which is imagined would be of great advantage to prevent a surprize.[101]

Charlevoix dismissed both arguments, and was equally unimpressed with the marshy soils downriver from the city, whose "depth continues to diminish all the way to the sea." "I have nothing to add," he wrote dismissively, "about the present state of New Orleans."[102]

Charlevoix's conflicting feelings reflected a high-stakes debate that had raged across colonial Louisiana for years. Where should the capital of the colony—the Company's primary counter and port—be located? Suggestions ranged from as far east as Mobile and even Pensacola, to as far inland as Natchez and Natchitoches. The worthiest rival to Bienville's site was Bayou Manchac, the Mississippi River distributary south of Baton Rouge explored by Iberville two decades earlier. Manchac also boasted a shortcut to the Gulf Coast, and suffered few of the environmental problems of Bienville's site. Bienville himself, the eventual victor in the debate, expressed doubts years earlier in a February 1708 letter written to Minister Pontchartrain. "This last summer, I examined...all the lands in the vicinity of [the Mississippi] river. I did not find any at all that are not flooded in the spring." After calling for more agriculturists to settle the land, Bienville promised, "As soon as these settlers arrived at Lake Pontchartrain and at the Mississippi River they would be transported to the neighborhood of the Bayagoulas," a site located far upriver from the site he would eventually select for New Orleans. "*Those are the best lands in the world.*"[103]

Bienville's stance evolved over the years to favor strongly the French Quarter site. That he received substantial land concessions in that area probably influenced this advocacy. Bienville succeeded finally when the Company, apparently convinced of the strategic superiority of a river site over a coastal position and impressed with Pauger's new city plan, designated New Orleans as capital of Louisiana on December 23, 1721. "His Royal Highness having thought it advisable to make the principal establishment of the colony at New Orleans on the Mississippi River," beamed a satisfied Bienville to the Council, "we have accordingly transported here all the goods that were at Biloxi," the previous capital. He then lavished praise on his superiors: "It appears to me that a better decision could not have been made in view of the good quality of the soil along the river [and the] considerable advantage for...the unloading of the vessels."[104]

That historic—and fateful—decision derived largely from rational and carefully weighted geographical reasons of accessibility, defendability, riverine position, arability, and natural resources, plus a lack of better alternatives. Here is Bienville in his own words on the siting of New Orleans:

> [T]he capital city…is advantageously situated in the center of the French plantations, near enough to receive [their] assistance…and reciprocally to furnish the settlers with the things they need…from its warehouses. Bayou St. John which is behind the city is of such great convenience because of the communication which it affords with Lake Pontchartrain and consequently with the sea that it cannot be esteemed too highly.[105]

What Bienville failed to mention was that personal gain (he owned vast land holdings here and thus stood to benefit if the settlement progressed), bureaucratic inertia, momentum, and pure luck also played roles in the decision.

Ever since, second-guessing Bienville's geographical wisdom in his handling of the siting dilemma has become a favorite topic of local punditry. Bienville himself never recorded open regret about his New Orleans decision, but occasionally betrayed second thoughts in words that would resonate with later generations of New Orleanians:

> The river has been very high for three months and has overflowed in several places above New Orleans. It has destroyed several levees so that more than half of the lands of the inhabitants are submerged….

> This country is subject to such great vicissitude…. *Now there is too much drought, now too much rain. Besides the winds are so violent*…[106]

When the surges of hurricanes Katrina and Rita submerged those lands in August-September 2005, observers worldwide pondered how a major city could have been founded on so precarious a site. Some saw no future for the metropolis, save for its relocation to higher ground. In essence, the circa-1700s debate of the French colonials about where to locate Louisiana's primary city raged again—under very different circumstances, but with similar factors at play.

Indeed, this is a challenging site for a major city. Yet Bienville acted wisely in selecting it in 1718, because he knew what makes a city great is not its site, but its situation. "Site" refers to the city's actual physical footing; "situation" means its regional context and how it connects with the world.

A strategic situation near the mouth of North America's greatest river allowed French colonials to exploit and protect their vast Louisiana claim effectively from a single point.

Had Bienville located New Orleans farther upriver (such as at Bayou Manchac or Natchez), the city would have been too inconvenient for coastal traffic and unable to answer enemy incursions. In other words: good sites, but bad situations.

Had he located it farther east, such as at Mobile or Biloxi, he would have relinquished the critical Mississippi River advantage and still suffered flooding problems. Ditto for locations to the west: bad sites, bad situations.

Had he located the city farther downriver, the site would have been that much more vulnerable and precarious. The site he finally selected, today's French Quarter, represented the best available site within a fantastic geographical situation. French observer Francois Marie Perrin Du Lac captured succinctly in 1807 the horns of Bienville's dilemma:

> [T]here is not for a great distance a finer, more elevated, or healthier position [for New Orleans]. If higher, it would be too distant from the sea; if lower, subject to inundations."[107]

Bienville's wisdom became apparent around the time of Du Lac's visit, as New Orleans emerged as one of the most important cities in America. It was shown again after Hurricane Katrina, when the French Quarter and other historical areas all evaded flooding.

Why, then, is a major American city located in this problematic site? Because it made perfect, rational sense at the time of its founding—a time when man depended heavily on waterborne transportation, and when this particular site offered the best waterborne access to what proved to be the richest valley on Earth.

German geographer Friedrich Ratzel contemplated New Orleans' site-versus-situation dilemma in his 1870s assessment of urban America. "New Orleans," he judged, "is just as poorly located as a city, or more precisely as a dwelling place, as it is excellently located as a commercial site." He then added: "*This last-mentioned advantage has made up for all disadvantages.*"[108]

Eyewitness: New Orleans, circa 1730

A French woman and a Dutch man describe the early New Orleans cityscape

Primary historical documents about early New Orleans often record the activities of prominent men or the minutia of ship manifests, bills of sale, inventories, and the like. Eyewitness descriptions of the emerging cityscape and society, written by everyday residents, are valued exceptions. One came from a young woman in 1727; another from a young man during the late 1710s to 1730s

The arrival of the Ursuline Nuns to New Orleans in 1727 marked a significant milestone in the installation of French culture into New Orleans, vis-à-vis the Catholic faith, formal education, and the presence of women. Among the sisters was an articulate young postulant named Marie Madeleine Hachard de St. Stanislaus, who endeavored to dedicate her mission to her country's notoriously problematic Louisiana colony.

After a harrowing journey, Hachard and the nuns landed at New Orleans on August 6-7, 1727, finding "few persons on the wharf on account of the early hour"

(5 a.m.). They were escorted to their provisional quarters, a two-story house owned by Bienville on the present-day 300 block of Chartres Street.[109] There, the cloistered postulant wrote a series of lucid communiqués to her father in Rouen, who, duly impressed with what a later historian would describe as his daughter's "epistolary talent" and "wondrous experiences,"[110] subsequently had them published. "[O]ur city called New Orleans, capital of all Louisiana," she wrote,

> is situated on the bank of the Mississippi River, which is at this place wider than the Seine at Rouen. On our side of the river, there is a levée in good condition to prevent the overflow of the river[;] along [it] is a large ditch to receive the water that runs down the slope, with timbered palisades to confine it. On the other side of this river, there are wild woods with a few huts in which lodge the slaves of the Company of the Indies.

Her perspectives perhaps tinted by her relatively privileged circumstances, Hachard found a city that defied her low expectations.

> Our city is very beautiful, well constructed and regularly built[,] as I saw of it on the day of our arrival; for since that day we have always remained in our cloister. Before our arrival, we were given a very bad idea of [New Orleans]; but… people have labored [since then] for its improvement. The streets are very wide and straight; the principal one [now Decatur Street] is almost a league long. The houses are built with wooded-front and mortar, whitewashed, wainscoted and latticed. The houses are covered with shingles which are thin boards in the shape of slate, [with] all the appearance and beauty of slate. It suffices to tell you that here is sung publicly a song, in which it is said that this city has as fine an appearance as the City of Paris; thus, this tells you all.[111]

Hachard set New Orleans in the context of its regional geography: "I have been curious to inform myself about the state of the soil of this country…. You call this place sometimes Louisiana and at others Mississippi, but it ought to be Louisiana."[112] She then explained to her father the story of La Salle and the claiming of Louisiana, reflecting the historical perspectives at that time. "[T]he name of Mississippi is that of the river," she explained. Regarding toponyms, she had more to clarify:

> It is a river to which M. de la Salle gave the name of Colbert, because M. Colbert was then minister of state. But this name of Colbert has not been left to it and they have continued to name it the Mississippi River. [Others] name it at present River St. Louis. It is the largest river in all America except the St. Lawrence. A great many rivers flow into the Mississippi. It is from seven to eight hundred leagues from its source to the Gulf of Mexico into which it empties.

A league being 2.5 to three miles, Hachard's estimate is accurate: the Mississippi is about 2,340 miles from headwaters to mouth. "But it is not navigable," she continued.

> No vessels can ascend or descend on it except boats able to transport twelve or thirteen persons. Moreover, this river being bounded by forests of high

trees, the rapidity of its current caves and hollows the ground of its banks so that the trees fall in it [such that] the passage of the river is obstructed.

Hachard had by this time experienced a southern Louisiana summer. "We are here nearer to the sun than in Rouen," she wrote, "without, however, having very great heat. Winter is rather mild. It lasts about three months, but it has only slight white frosts." She then described the region's biogeography:

> We have been assured that Louisiana is four times larger than France. The lands are very fertile and yield several crops each year, not along the river, where there are mostly forests of oaks and other trees of prodigious size and height, and reed-canes which grow from fifteen to twenty feet high. But at a few leagues, there are prairies, fields, and plains [with] cotton-trees[,] syca-mores, mulberry trees, chestnut trees, almond trees, walnut trees, fig trees, lemon trees, orange trees, pomegranate trees, and others which make the beauty of the fields. If the soil were cultivated, there would not be any bet-ter in the world. But, for that, it would be necessary to have the place peo-pled…. [Generally] the people here live in idleness and apply themselves to scarcely anything except hunting and fishing.[113]

The insinuation that agriculture around New Orleans in 1727 occurred mostly in prairies distant from the river is curious. Hachard might have been referring to cul-tivations around the Bayou St. John area, or along the Metairie and Gentilly ridges, which had been cultivated as early as 1708. Or she may simply have been misinformed. The precocious young woman concluded her treatise on Louisiana geography with this note:

> You tell me, dear father, of your having bought two large maps of the state of Mississippi, and that you do not there find the city of New Orleans. Appar-ently, those maps must be very old, for this city, the capital of the country, would not have been omitted. I am sorry that it cost you a hundred and ten cents to buy maps on which you cannot find the place of our residence. I think they are going to make new maps, on which will be marked our settle-ment.[114]

Apparently the father's subsequent map purchase still fell short of Hachard's high cartographic standards. Writing in April 1728, she said,

> the map of Louisiana of which you inform me having made the purchase, in which the city of New Orleans is shown on the shore of a lake named Pontchartrain, at a distance of six leagues from the Mississippi River, is not correct; for our city is certainly not situated on a lake, but on the very banks of the Mississippi.[115]

On March 15, 1729, Marie Madeleine Hachard de St. Stanislaus, in the first such cer-emony within the present-day United States, became Sister St. Stanislaus Hachard.[116] The twenty-one-year-old nun served New Orleans for over thirty years, dying in the waning years of France's Louisiana dominion. The Louisiana Historical Society, writing in 1902, described Sister Madeleine Hachard as "the pious and charming woman whose letters form one of the most important historical documents for the study of [New Orleans'] early history...."[117]

Beneath Sister Hachard's Chartres Street cloister passed one Le Page du Pratz, who witnessed New Orleans evolve from a mere clearing in the late 1710s to an established community of the 1730s. "At my first arrival in Louisiana," he recollected in the 1750s, New Orleans

> existed only in name; for on my landing I understood M. de Biainville [Bienville], commandant general, was only gone to mark out the spot... He pitched upon this spot in preference to many others, more agreeable and commodious; but for that time this was a place proper enough; besides, it is not every man that can see so far as some others. As the principal settlement was then at Mobile, it was proper to have the capital fixed at a place from which there could be an easy communication with this post: and thus a better choice could not have been made....

He noted some advantages of New Orleans' situation:

> [T]he town being on the banks of the Missisippi, vessels, tho' of a thousand ton[s], may lay their sides close to the shore even at low water [and] need only lay a small bridge, with two of their yards, in order to load or unload, to roll barrels and bales, &c. without fatiguing the ship's crew. This town is only a league from St. John's creek [Bayou St. John], where passengers take water for Mobile....[118]

> The ground on which New Orleans is situated, being an earth accumulated by the ooze... is of a good quality for agriculture.... This land being flat, and drowned by inundations for several ages, cannot fail to be kept in moisture, there being... only a mole or bank to prevent the river from overflowing it; and would be even too moist, and incapable of cultivation, had not this mole been made, and ditches [dug] to facilitate the draining [of] the waters: by this means, [the region promises] to be cultivated with success.[119]

Yet Le Page (as he signed his name) did record some misgivings:

> I should imagine, that if a town was at this day to be built in this province, a rising ground would be pitched upon, to avoid inundations; [and] the bottom should be sufficiently firm, for bearing great stone edifices. [But] without seeing stone, or the least pebble, in upwards of a hundred leagues extent... such a proposition is impossible....[120]

Le Page then described the city proper, probably reflecting the years 1728-34, when he spent the most time there:

> The place of arms [now Jackson Square] is in the middle of that part of the

town which faces the river; [there] stands the parish church, called St. Louis, where the Capuchins officiate, whose house is to the left of the church. To the right stand the prison, or jail, and the guard-house; both sides of the place of arms are taken up by two bodies or rows of barracks. This place stands all open to the river.

All the streets are laid out both in length and breadth by the line, and intersect and cross each other at right angles. The streets divide the town in to fifty-five isles; eleven along the river lengthwise.... [E]ach of those isles is fifty square toises, and each again divided into twelve emplacements, or compartments, for lodging as many families. The Intendant's house stands behind the barracks on the left; and the magazine, or warehouse-general behind the barracks on the right, on viewing the town from the river side. The Governor's house stands in the middle of that part of the town, from which we go from the place of arms to the habitation of the Jesuits, which is near the town. The house of the Ursulin [*sic*] Nuns is quite at the end of the town, to the right; as is also the hospital of the sick, of which the nuns have the inspection. What I have just described faces the river.[121]

The greatest part of the houses is of brick; the rest are of timber and brick.... [T]here are many habitations standing close together; each making a causey [upraised path] to secure his ground from inundations, which fail not to come every year with the spring....[122]

Springtime river floods threatened human endeavors on water as well as land:

[A]t that time [of high water], if any ships happen to be in the harbour of New Orleans, they speedily set sail; because the prodigious quantity of dead wood, or trees torn up by the roots, which the river brings down, would lodge before the ship, and break the stoutest cables.[123]

Settlements not only spanned the forty or so river miles above and below New Orleans, but behind it toward the lake. In the following passages, we can discern Bayou St. John, the garrison later known as Spanish Fort, present-day Gentilly Boulevard, and the Rigolets and Chef Menteur passes:

A league behind the town, directly back from the river, we meet with a Bayouc or creek, which can bear large boats with oars.

From this creek to the town, a part of its banks is inhabited by planters; in like manner as are the long banks of another creek: the habitations of this last go under the name of Gentilly.

At the end of St. John's Creek, on the banks of the Lake [Pontchartrain], there is a redoubt [Spanish Fort], and a guard to defend it.

[T]raveling obliquely [from the lake], we meet the [Rigolets and Chef Menteur] Channels, which lead to Mobile.... [124]

Beyond the physical and urban geography of early New Orleans, Le Page meticulously cataloged the flora, fauna, and most significantly, the indigenous peoples and cultures of the region. His *History of Louisiana* remains a classic of early American geographical literature. Much of what we know of the early New Orleans cityscape comes from his observations, and those of a cloistered young postulant he probably never met.

Urbanizing the Landscape

A century from this date,
Orleans, like London, will [envelop]
every town and hamlet for miles around…
the largest city on the continent of America,
and perhaps in the world.

—Albert James Pickett, 1847

Imposing Order

Getting the wild deltaic landscape under control

Urban order came to New Orleans after three years of haphazard development. In 1721-22, Adrien de Pauger surveyed a symmetrical sixty-six-block grid around a central plaza fronted by institutions of church and state, surrounded by fortifications. Contrary to New Orleans' *laissez-faire* reputation, this first urban environment was "actually military in the insistence of its right angles, like the gridded camps Roman soldiers laid out at the wild edges of their empire…. The French Quarter looks like what it is—the elaboration of a colonial outpost designed by military engineers."[125]

French colonists, well aware of the site's challenges, set out altering the natural environment toward their sense of order. Seasonal overbank floods of the Mississippi ranked as a priority problem. The first significant effort to constrain the river through levees began in 1722-23, when Le Blond de la Tour and Pauger sketched plans for an earthen embankment about twelve feet wide atop the crest of the natural levee. By 1724, the first levee measured six feet wide, about 3000 feet long, and three feet high, but was readily breached by the river that spring.[126] A meager workforce constantly hampered reinforcement work; nevertheless, by 1727, a solid eighteen-foot-wide, three-foot-high levee (plus a parallel ditch to collect seepage water) lined one mile of the town's riverfront. Although river floods would plague the city into the late 1800s, these initial engineering efforts launched one of mankind's most massive manipulations of nature: the control of the Mississippi River.

Regionally, sedimentation at the mouth of the Mississippi challenged the viability of the colony, particularly the important coastal post known as the Balize. Built in 1722 off the easternmost "toe" (formerly East Pass, now North Pass) of the Mississippi Delta's "birdfoot," the Balize (probably from *valiza*, Spanish for "beacon") operated as a transshipment point for incoming vessels before they ascended the Mississippi. It served, among other things, to intercept Spanish maritime traffic that could not or did not want to venture upriver. "[T]he pass of The Balize is subject to continual changes which threaten to render it impractical for our vessels," warned Bienville in 1726.

> [T]he only [remedy] is to obstruct the east pass through which the current has been rushing [so that] all the water…would flow through the pass of The Balize carrying with it the mud that has collected there…. The enclosure of piles that is already well advanced will prevent…the [Balize] island from being eaten away by the sea, but it is necessary to transport a great deal of earth…to elevate the land of the island, make it inhabitable and to protect it against overflows. I agree it cannot be done without cost but this expenditure…is absolutely necessary.[127]

Bienville's proposal—Louisiana's very first coastal restoration plan—foretells the many vast hydrological engineering projects that would render the lower Mississippi River/Gulf of Mexico estuary one of the most anthropogenically altered major ecosystems on Earth. Themes familiar to the news headlines of southern Louisiana today—coastal erosion, river diversion, sediment transport, land-building, governmental financial commitment—began in the early 1700s.

Infrastructure was also needed: a call came "to establish bridges on three small streams that are between New Orleans and Bayou St. John for the convenience of carts," a reference to the tributaries which coursed through present-day Mid-City and impeded access to the bayou. The bayou itself, wrote Bienville in 1726, was "blocked in many places" and lined with "trees that hang over the banks and threaten to fall into it." Land grants were often used to motivate development: "A good settler on this bayou named Rivart offers to undertake this work," wrote Bienville, if the Company might be so kind as to "grant him as a concession … along this bayou."[128]

Bridges made of brick were needed in the city proper, to replace the flimsy wooden *banquettes* built by residents to cross the "little ditches in front of their houses, one or two feet in width by a foot or a foot and a half in depth, [dug] to drain off the water that seeps through the levee [and] from the rain…." Drainage and navigation improvements were in mind with a proposal for "a canal communicating between the river and Lake Pontchartrain,"[129] an engineering project appreciated as a challenge at the time and not executed until nearly two centuries later, when the Industrial Canal was excavated. To pay for various public-works projects, citizens would be taxed "five livres per head of negroes."[130]

Amidst this landscape manipulation came an appeal for forest conservation. "We [urge that] individuals preserve woods on their lands," wrote Governor Périer in 1729. "We are suggesting to them that they must leave one-third of" the trees standing. He predicted that the backswamp might be deforested within "fifty or sixty years," forcing New Orleanians to go north toward Manchac and Natchez for timber. Others shared his concerns. Le Page du Pratz, a resident of New Orleans between the late 1710s and the 1730s, wrote in 1758,

> The cypresses were formerly very common in Louisiana; but they have wasted them so imprudently, that they are now somewhat rare. They felled them for the sake of their bark, with which they covered their houses, and they sawed the wood into planks which they exported… The price of the wood now is three times as much as it was formerly.[131]

Such reports counter modern notions that natural resources in the colonial era were as abundant as conservationist sentiments were scarce (though Le Page probably overstated the rarity of cypress). Périer further wrote of "inducing the inhabitants to plant mulberry trees on their land," along drainage canals, and on plantation boundaries. Thought to be native to Louisiana but probably originally from Mexico, mulberry trees were particular valued because they supported silkworms and could thus foster the development of a local silk industry.[132] Toward this end, the Company of the Indies later adopted a resolution "forbidding the destruction of any mulberry-trees in the clearing of lands" and obliging "all the inhabitants to whom negroes are delivered" to "plant on their land the number of mulberry-trees per head of negroes that shall be fixed by the Council."[133]

Efforts to impose urban and agricultural order on the alluvial landscape depended heavily on a source of labor. Little, if any, reflection went into resolving the dilemma of labor shortage; with centuries of precedence in the West Indies, the solution seemed obvious: capture Africans, ship them to Louisiana, and institutionalize their enslavement. "All the colony is impatient to see some negroes, whom it greatly needs," wrote the colonists to Company directors in 1724. Forcibly extracted from the coastal Senegal region by a well-established slave trade, Africans arrived first in 1719, concurrently with the first major immigration wave.

African hands, according to white colonists, were needed not only for plantation agriculture but for public-works projects such as flood control, drainage, and defense. "When some negroes have come for us and the river permits us to take land on the bank we shall think of perfecting the length and breadth of the levee ....We shall see that willows are planted ...on top of the levee ...in order that the roots may be able to retain the land."[134] Recipients of newly imported slaves had to "pay" for their bondsmen by deploying them on grueling public-works projects for thirty days. "Several inhabitants have begun to furnish" their slaves, reported Governor Périer in 1728. "They are being employed to cut down the trees at the two ends of the town as far as Bayou St. John in order to clear this ground and to give air to the city and to the mill."[135] Colonists demanded slave labor to build land up for flood protection and to excavate moats as defense against potentially hostile Indians, particularly in the wake of the Natchez uprising of 1729. The King himself acknowledged in 1732 that "work on the moat ...to enclose the city of New Orleans ceased more than two years ago because the settlers do not have a large enough number of negroes to supply the statute labor...."[136]

Labor needs for public works and plantation agriculture motivated slavers to deliver increasing numbers of captured Africans to Louisiana's shores. In the two years prior to the census of November 24, 1721, the number of African slaves in the New Orleans area rose from zero to 533, then tripled to 1,561 over the next six years. Indians were also enslaved, though in lesser numbers: fifty-one in 1721; seventy-five in 1727. In circa-1721 New Orleans, 54 percent of the population owned the other 46 percent, a ratio that would remain roughly constant for the next 110 years.[137] Tree-cutting, canal excavation, mill work, levee construction, and other initial urbanization labor awaited the kidnapped Africans, followed by agricultural toil for the remainder of their lives and for generations of their descendents.

Much, indeed most, of the muscle that imposed urban order upon the wild New Orleans landscape came from newly enslaved African-born men.

Eyewitness: New Orleans, circa 1770

An Englishman and a Spaniard describe Spanish colonial New Orleans

England's defeat of France in the North American theater (French and Indian War) of the worldwide conflict known as the Seven Years' War radically realigned the geography of European empire. France retained only a few Canadian and Caribbean islands, while England won French Canada, French Louisiana east of the Mississippi, and Spanish West Florida. It would have gained Louisiana west of the Mississippi as well, had King Louis XV not secretly ceded those vast lands to his Spanish cousin, King Carlos III, a year earlier in the Treaty of Fontainebleau. Included in the clandestine offer was New Orleans, whose terrain was deemed an "isle" on account of the Bayou Manchac distributary, and was thus cartographically "detachable" from the east-of-the-Mississippi mainland. The clever and timely deal compensated a friend (Spain) for the loss of its territory (Florida) to the British, while keeping a strategic city (New Orleans) out of the hands of a triumphant enemy (England). One can only ponder what New Orleans might look like today had it become English. Instead, Spain accepted Louisiana in late 1762; after the secret transfer became public in 1764, the dominion of New Orleans passed from France to Spain politically in 1766 and militarily in 1769.

That year, Spain sent Francisco Bouligny, a Spaniard of French and Italian descent, to observe and advise the Crown on Louisiana affairs. England, meanwhile, moved quickly to establish a presence in its new possessions across Lake Pontchartrain. It sent Capt. Philip Pittman to survey the lands of British West Florida and to clear out the Bayou Manchac/Iberville River shortcut to the Gulf of Mexico—a critical route for British interests because it united West Florida with its new Gulf Coast possessions while avoiding Spanish New Orleans. Pittman and Bouligny, representing two very different cultures and perspectives on New Orleans, both left behind valuable eyewitness reports on the state of the city and region around the year 1770.

Pittman had the opportunity to visit the foreign colony during the interregnum period of 1765-69; his descriptions were published in London in 1770. "New Orleans['] situation is extremely well chosen," he wrote,

> as it has a very easy communication with the northern parts of Louisiana (now West Florida) by means of the Bayouk of St. John, a little creek, which is navigable for small vessels drawing less than six feet of water, six miles up from the lake Pontchartrain, where there is a landing place [present-day Bell Street vicinity] about two miles from the city [connected by Bayou Road]. The entrance of the Bayouk of St. John [present-day Wisner at Robert E. Lee boulevards] is defended by a battery of six guns and a sergeant's guard.[138]

Ocean-going vessels could not negotiate the lake/bayou route and thus had to use the river route to reach the city:

> The vessels which come up the Mississippi haul close along-side the bank
> next to New Orleans, [where they] discharge their cargoes…. The town is
> secured from the inundations of the river by a raised bank, generally called
> the Leveé; and this extends from the *Detour des Anglois* [English Turn], to
> the upper settlement of the Germans [Luling area], which is a distance of
> more than fifty miles, and a good coach-road all the way. The Leveé before
> the town is repaired at the public expense, [but] each inhabitant keeps that
> part in repair which is opposite to his own plantation.[139]

The Englishman found the French-turned-Spanish city in a rather decadent condition. Positioned behind St. Louis Cathedral, looking toward the river, he explained:

> The parade [ground] is a large square, in the middle of that part of the town
> which fronts the river; [behind it] is the church dedicated to St. Louis, a very
> poor building, framed with wood; it is in so ruinous a condition that divine
> service has not been performed in it since the year 1766, one of the king's
> storehouses being at present used for that purpose. The capuchins are the
> curates of New Orleans; on the left hand side of the church they had a very
> handsome and commodious brick house, which is totally deserted and gone
> to ruin; they now live on their plantation, and in a hired house in town. On
> the right side of the church is the prison and guard-house, which are very
> strong and good buildings. The two sides of the square were formerly oc-
> cupied by barracks for the troops, which are entirely destroyed. The square
> is open to the river, and on that side are twenty-one pieces of ordnance…
> which are fired on public rejoicings.

The Good Friday Fire of 1788 claimed the primitive French-era St. Louis Church described by Pittman. The Spanish cleared away the ruins in 1789 and by 1794 completed a more substantial Spanish-style edifice with distinctive bell-shaped towers. Except for the front wall, the 1794 church was entirely reconstructed in 1849-51 in the Greek Revival style popular at the time, forming the St. Louis Cathedral that overlooks Jackson Square today. A generation after Pittman's visit, the structures on either side the church would be replaced by the Spanish Colonial-style Presbytère and Cabildo, both later adorned with mansard roofs and cupolas also still standing today.

"All the streets are perfectly straight," he continued,

> and cross each other at right angles, and these divide the town into sixty-six
> squares, eleven in length by the river's side, and six in depth; the sides of
> these squares are one hundred yards each, and are divided into twelve lots,
> for the establishment of the inhabitants. The intendant's house and gardens
> take up the right side of the parade [ground], the left side is occupied by
> the king's store-houses and an artillery-yard…. The convent of the Ursu-
> lines and general hospital, which is attended by the nuns, occupy the two
> left hand squares facing the river: these buildings are strong and plain, well
> answering the purposes for which they were designed.[140]

The intendant's house occupied the present-day corner of Toulouse and De-catur streets; the king's storehouse was located three blocks downriver, at Dumaine. The Ursulines' convent and hospital occupied a double-block bounded by present-day Decatur, Ursulines, Chartres, and Barracks streets. Only the Old Ursulines Convent, designed in 1745 and built in 1749-53 by Claude Joseph Villars Dubreuil according to designs by Ignace Broutin, remains today—the oldest documented structure in the Mississippi Valley and deltaic plain, and the most aged in the city by a margin of about thirty years.

Pittman commented on the French Creole- and West Indian-inspired housing style and typology in New Orleans:

> The general plan of building in the town, is with timber frames filled up with brick; and most of the houses are but of one floor, raised about eight feet from the ground, with large galleries round them, and the cellars under the floors level with the ground; it is impossible to have any subterraneous buildings, as they would be constantly full of water. I imagine that there are betwixt seven and eight hundred houses in the town, most of which have gardens. The squares at the back and sides of the town are mostly laid out in gardens; the orange-tress…in the spring afford an agreeable smell.[141]

Only one surviving French Quarter house—Madame John's Legacy, built two decades after Pittman's visit—conforms to his characterizations. It stands on Dumaine Street as the last, best example of what New Orleans looked like prior to the 1788 and 1794 fires (see *Transformation by Conflagration*).

Pittman's description of city defenses alludes to tensions within local society:

> There are, exclusive of the slaves, about seven thousand inhabitants in town…. The fortifications are only an *enceinte* of stockades, with a *banquette* within and a very trifling ditch without; these can answer no end but against Indians, or negroes, in case of an insurrection, and [to] keep the slaves of the town and country from having any communication in the night. There are about four hundred soldiers kept for the police of the town and coun-try; these belong to the detached companies of the marines: there are also ten companies of militia, four chosen from the inhabitants of the town, the planters and their servants form the remainder.[142]

A few years after Pittman cast his eyes upon early Spanish colonial New Or-leans, Francisco Bouligny, the Spanish officer advising the Crown on Louisiana affairs, scribed a *Memoria* on the colony's status and potential. The influential report, written in 1776 based on Bouligny's experiences of 1769-75, focused on policy recommen-dations regarding trade, economic development, and Indian relations. It began with a comprehensive geographical overview of the New Orleans region.

Like Pittman, Bouligny situated New Orleans among a network of key wa-ter bodies—the Mississippi, Pontchartrain, Manchac, Bayou St. John, and "an infinity of inlets"—reflecting the degree to which geographical perceptions at that time were driven by navigable waterways. The British threat also underscored Bouligny's report: "The English can and do go easily from Mobile to Manchac via the lakes," he wrote, in reference to the efforts of Pittman and others to clear out the Bayou Manchac/Iberville River route. That task was a challenging one: "Although this route is shorter than via the Mississippi when the latter is high, it cannot be used when the Mississippi is low. And, at all times, the English can only go through the lakes with very small or very flat boats." Bouligny went on to describe, with great accuracy, the topography of New Orleans:

> All the lands on both banks of the Mississippi are higher when nearer to it, and [decline by] of four feet per twenty *arpents* of distance from the banks of the river. Thus, however, much it rains, not a drop of water that falls on the fields enters the river. This slope generally follows the same ratio with so much evenness that it is impossible for men to level it with the same exactness.[143]

With the French surveying unit *arpent* measuring about 192 feet, a declivity of four feet over a distance of twenty *arpents* equates to about one vertical foot per thousand horizontal feet, or roughly 2.5 inches per city block. Today, land in downtown New Orleans measured backward from the crest of the natural levee typically slopes downward by over triple that ratio, due to levee- and drainage-induced soil subsidence. The degree of sinkage over the past two centuries is revealed further when Bouligny pointed out how colonial New Orleans experienced storm surges from lakes Pontchartrain and Borgne:

> When the southerly winds swell the lakes, the waters usually come near the houses which are situated on the banks of the river. For this reason and because of the lack of fresh water, the banks of those lakes are not inhabitable.[144]

That wind-blown lake water regularly approached the rear of the French Quarter indicates the extent to which present-day lakeside New Orleans comprised a saline marsh that communicated liberally with gulf waters. Had the lake formed an earthen rim at its edge, as was erected over a century later, those dikes would have prevented surges from reaching the city. But those very man-made barriers (plus drainage apparatus) caused the marsh to subside in places by over ten feet. The fact that roughly half of modern New Orleans falls below sea level is an anthropogenic condition created over a century after Bouligny wrote his report. The landscape he witnessed—low and flat as it was—lay entirely *above* sea level.

A good geographer, Bouligny advised on the "many advantages gained from the slope which the land has toward the interior." "[T]here are some places," he pointed out, "where the land is somewhat higher and capable of cultivation," presumably a reference to the Metairie and Gentilly ridges. "[I]t would be advantageous to establish some families there in order to be closer to and in sight of the English who cross the lake."[145] Additionally, the topographic slope allowed "constructing mills on both banks," to exploit "the immensity of the woods in all that country." Such a sawmill operated on present-day Elysian Fields Avenue throughout the Spanish colonial era, powered by diverted river water. "[O]pening canals to communicate with the lakes which are behind the city" would, he continued, "facilitate the transportation of lumber and products from the interior lands." That advice was taken two decades later, when Spanish Governor Hector Carondelet ordered a canal excavated to connect the city with Bayou St. John and the lake. Bouligny also noticed that "when the river is high, it gives a certain dampness to the fields" and enhances their arability, particularly for rice cultivation.[146]

Like Pittman, Bouligny observed the area's housing stock, focusing on farm and plantation houses near New Orleans rather than city structures. He characterized them as

> comfortable, relative to the climate which prevails there. All have a very broadly covered gallery or balcony which surrounds them to guard against the strong heat of summer, and all the rooms have chimneys for shelter from winter which on days can also be rough.

> The houses are made with wood, brick, and lime, in the style of this Court. The kitchens are separated from the houses about twenty paces. Behind all of the houses, particularly in the countryside, there is a garden or *huerta*, which almost all cultivate themselves, helped by their children and the domestics.... This garden provides them with all the vegetables and fruit they can consume, and many of them send the surplus to sell in [New Orleans], especially those closest to it.

> All the houses are about thirty of forty paces distant from the edge of the river because the people are thus happier, and because of the ease with which they embark and disembark since everything is transported by water.[147]

It is interesting that Bouligny described certain local architecture traits, which were predominantly French Creole and West Indian at this time, as "in the style of this [Spanish] Court." In fact, Spanish urban architecture would not be introduced *en masse* into the Francophone city until after the 1794 fire, and never really took hold in rural Louisiana.

Capt. Philip Pittman and Francisco Bouligny, representing two colonial regimes new to Louisiana and at odds with each other, might have crossed paths during their respective deployments. Apparently the men took well to their Louisiana assignments: the surname Pittman endures among the population of the Florida Parishes; Bouligny, for his part, "married a French girl and stayed" in New Orleans, fathering the illustrious Bouligny lineage, prominent in local society to this day.[148]

Despite differences in language, culture, and agendas, their journal descriptions together form a comprehensive eyewitness geography of circa-1770 New Orleans.

Antecedent Cadasters, Antecedent Axes

The influence of old plantations, railroads, and canals on the modern streetscape

Glancing at a map of New Orleans, streets seem to emerge from a nebulous mid-crescent origin and radiate outwardly toward the arching river, like blades in a handheld fan. Viewed from the perspective of the river, the effect resembles the skeleton of a sinuous snake (see map, "The Antecedent Cadaster"). Deeply influential in the experience of the city, the radiating pattern happened neither by chance nor by plan. Its antecedent is a cadastral (land parceling) system developed in north-central Europe around the end of the first millennium.

The logic behind the system is compelling. Given (1) a valued linear resource at one end (usually a waterway or a road), (2) unproductive land at the other end (marshes or mountains), and (3) fertile land in between (natural levees or valley bottoms), one can maximize the number of farms enjoying access to the valued resource by delineating the fertile land into narrow strips. Excess width diminishes the number of farms created, while insufficient depth deprives some farms of access to the waterway or road. The surveying of narrow, long parcels of land thus allocated two scarce resources—accessibility and arability—optimally.[149]

It was primarily the French who transferred the tradition to the New World. The "long lot" system arrived officially to Louisiana when the Crown, exasperated with overly generous land concessions granted to certain colonists, stipulated in the Edict of October 12, 1716 that land delineation occur "in the proportion of two to four arpents front by forty to sixty in depth."[150] Surveyors used the unit *arpent* to measure the cadasters (parcels), which equates to 180 French feet (191.835 American feet) lineally and 0.845 American acres superficially. Settlers were allotted riverside or bayou-side land usually spanning two to eight *arpents de face* (frontage arpents), and extending back to the swamp by forty or eighty *arpents*, depending on the width of the natural levee.[151]

By the 1720s, most riverine land near New Orleans had been delineated into *arpent*-based long lots. Straight portions of the river yielded neat rectangular long lots; where the river meandered, lots diverged on the convex side and converged on the concave side, forming a radiating pattern of elongated triangles or trapezoids.

Jesuit Father du Poisson described the state of land distribution and development in and around New Orleans in 1727:

> [L]and *granted* by the Company of the Indies to a private individual [or] partnership, for the purpose of clearing that land and making it valuable, is called a "concession." [T]he concessionaries are…the gentlemen of this country, [who, when they departed for Louisiana], equipped vessels and filled them with superintendents, stewards, storekeepers, clerks, and work-

men of various trades, with provisions and all kinds of goods. They had to plunge into the woods, to set up cabins, to choose their ground, and to burn the cane-brakes and trees....

A smaller portion of land granted by the Company is called a "habitation." A man with his wife or his partner clears a little ground, builds himself a house on four piles, covers it with sheets of bark, and plants corn and rice for his provisions; the next year he raises a little more for food, and has also a field of tobacco; if at last he succeed [sic] in having three or four Negroes, then he is out of his difficulties.... [B]ut how many of them are as nearly beggars as when they began!

A district where there are several habitations not far from one another, which make a sort of Village, is called a *settlement*. Besides the concessionaries and the habitants, there are also in this country people who have no other occupation than that of roving about....[152]

In time, concessions and habitations became plantations and farms of varying sizes, and the agrarian civilization of the Louisiana delta, long lots and all, inscribed itself into the delta alluvium.

After the 1788 fire leveled most of New Orleans, demand for new land put pressure on adjacent plantations. Starting with the Gravier family, which subdivided its plantation into Faubourg Ste. Marie soon after the blaze, planters independently considered whether they could make more money continuing in agriculture, or by developing their plantations for residential living.

One by one, over many years, owners eventually made the decision to develop, and hired surveyors to design and lay out street grids. Of course, those grids had to conform to the limits of their client's property. The upper and lower limits of the plantation usually became the bordering streets of the new subdivision, the middle was often reserved for a broader avenue, and all other areas became side streets and house lots.

Where the river ran straight and the abutting plantations formed elongated rectangles (such as below Elysian Fields Avenue), orthogonal street networks fit neatly into the antecedent cadaster.[153] But uptown, where the river yawned broadly, surveyors were forced to "squeeze" street grids into wedge-shaped plantations. Odd angles, jogs, and multi-sized blocks often resulted when surveyors forced orthogonal street grids into angular cadasters.

Because of this piecemeal development and the lack of a central planning authority, the geometry of the colonial-era *arpent* system became "burned into" the expanding street network of the growing American city. Although full housing density would not occur until around 1900, most long lots within the New Orleans crescent had transitioned from plantation to faubourg between 1788 and the Civil War, in this manner:

Plantation Owners	Name of New Subdivision	Initial Subdivision	Location
Jesuits/Gravier	Faubourg Ste. Marie	1788	Common roughly to Howard
Jesuits/Delord-Sarpy/ Duplantier	Faubourg Duplantier	1806-10	Roughly Howard to Felicity
Jesuits/Solet	Faubourg Solet		
Jesuits/Robin	Faubourg de La Course		
Jesuits/Livaudais	Faubourg de L'Annunciation		
Ursuline Nuns	Faubourg des Religieuses	1810	Felicity to St. Andrew
Panis/Poultney	Faubourg (later City of) Lafayette	1813-24	Josephine to Philip
Livaudais	Faubourg Livaudais	1832	Philip and Harmony
Livaudais/Delassize	Faubourg Delassize	1834	Harmony to Toledano
Wiltz	Faubourg Plaisance	1807	Toledano to Delachaise
Wiltz/Delachaise	Faubourg Delachaise	1855	Delachaise to Amelia
Avart	Faubourg St. Joseph	1849	Amelia to General Taylor
Avart/ Hampton/Bouligny/ Millaudon/Kohn	Faubourg Bouligny	1834	General Taylor to Upperline
Avart	Faubourg Avart	1841	Upperline to Valmont
Ducros/Beale/ Walden/ Ricker	Rickerville	1849	Valmont to Joseph
LeBreton/Hurst	Hurstville	1834-37	Joseph to "Lower Bloomingdate Line"
LeBreton/Avart/ Green	Bloomingdale	1836	"Lower Bloomingdate Line" to "Upper Bloomingdale Line"
Boré/Burthe	Burthesville	1854	"Upper Bloomingdale Line" to Exposition Boulevard
Fontenot/Foucher	Never subdivided; now Audubon Park, Tulane, and Loyola Universities	Acquired by city in 1871; becomes park in 1879; campuses in 1894-1910	Exposition to Walnut
LeBreton/Foucher/ Ogilvie/ Green	Greenville	1836	Walnut to Lowerline to Freret
Derbigny/LeBreton	Friburg	1837	Freret to swamp, from Walnut to Lowerline
LeBreton/Macarty	Carrollton	1833	Lowerline to river

The ancient agrarian logic of the *arpent* system to this day defines the urban texture of uptown New Orleans. Clues to its influence abound; they are obscure at first, but ubiquitous once discovered. The system explains why certain uptown streets suddenly terminate in a "T," forcing motorists to seek alternative routes to proceed. It explains why narrow, grassy slivers split occasional streets, and why structures built thereupon are shaped like New York's Flatiron Building. It also explains why driving in a straight line on a river-parallel street (St. Charles Avenue, Prytania, etc.) above Lee Circle means you are driving *within* an old plantation, while turning your steering wheel ever so slightly means you're *crossing* an old plantation line: most bends in river-parallel uptown streets correspond to old long-lot plantation lines.

Angled Intersections with St. Charles Avenue	Magnitude of Angle[154]	Historical Significance of Intersection (year indicates time of subdivision)
Felicity Street	14 degrees	Boundary between L'Annunciation plantation (1807) and Ursuline Nuns property (1809); once approximate upper edge of Jesuits plantation.
St. Andrew Street	8 degrees	Boundary between Ursuline Nuns property (1809) and Panis plantation (1813).
Philip Street	5 degrees	Boundary between Panis property (1813) and Livaudais plantation (1832).
Pleasant/Toledano Street	10 degrees	Toledano separates Delassize property (circa 1833) and Wiltz plantation (1807).
Foucher/Amelia/Peniston Street	14 degrees	Amelia separates Delachaise plantation (1855) and Faubourg St. Joseph portion of Avart plantation (1849).
Bordeaux/Upperline/Robert Street	31 degrees	Upperline separates Bouligny plantation (1834) and Faubourg Avart portion of Avart plantation (1841).
Nashville/Eleonore/State Street	10 degrees	"Bloomingdale Line" (between Eleonore and State) separates Hurst plantation (circa 1833) and the Bloomingdale portion of the Avart plantation (1836).
Lowerline Street	5 degrees	Boundary between Greenville portion of the Foucher plantation (1836) and Macarty plantation (1833).

It may seem paradoxical that arbitrary and cryptic cadastral patterns often have a greater and longer-lasting impact on cityscapes than massive structures of brick and mortar. But buildings are subject to the elements and the whims of their owners, whereas cadastral systems are inscribed in legal and political realms and are rooted deeply in fundamental national philosophies. Excepting revolutionary changes of government, cadastral patterns usually endure under new administrations and continue their imprint upon the landscape. The French *arpent* system persisted even when Spanish dominion replaced the French, and American replaced the Spanish. Its geometry survived after plantation agriculture gave way to faubourgs, and faubourgs became urban neighborhoods.

The term *arpent* abounds in historical documents of former French colonial regions of North America, and occasionally appears today in real estate signs and transactions. French long-lot fields and farms persist in eastern Canada, the Great Lakes region, the central Mississippi Valley, and most famously throughout the Francophone region of Louisiana. Those long-lots are all gone from New Orleans proper, but their ancient geometrical rationale affects the daily life of citizens today, testifying to the significance of the antecedent cadaster.

❧

While antecedent cadastres influenced the street pattern in the nineteenth-century river side of New Orleans, antecedent transportation axes affected the urban design of the twentieth-century areas near the lake.

The relatively unfertile silty-clay swamps and marshes north of the Metairie and Gentilly ridges remained largely uncultivated and undeveloped during historical times. Yet they had to be crossed to access Lake Pontchartrain, which communicated with the coastal cities of Biloxi, Mobile, and Pensacola and the abundant natural resources across the lake. Muddy Bayou Road and twisting, log-strewn Bayou St. John provided this access from 1718 until 1794, when the Carondelet Canal (later Old Basin Canal) was excavated to connect the city more efficiently with the bayou. It too proved inadequate for the growing city; a better, faster, river-lake connection was needed.

Two competing responses were launched. In 1831, downtown investors installed an early railroad between the Faubourg Marigny and the lake along what is now Elysian Fields Avenue. With no reason whatsoever to design a curve in the trackbed, the Pontchartrain Railroad penetrated the wide-open backswamp with a perfectly straight south-to-north line, a trajectory traceable to a sawmill canal first dug by plantation owner Claude Joseph Villars Dubreuil around 1750 (see A Trip Across the Back-swamp).

Two years later, uptown bankers also seeking lucrative trade opportunities funded the excavation of what came to be called the New Basin Canal. Starting with a turning basin at the present-day Loyola/Julia intersection and an angle at the Metairie Ridge, this waterway thence also ran straight northwardly to the lake (see Scoring and Scouring the Land). These two transportation corridors inscribed initial axes into the city's otherwise vacant lakeside marsh.

As various drainage systems were attempted during the 1850s-70s and finally (successfully) in the 1890s, outfall canals such as the 17th Street, the Orleans, and the London Avenue were excavated—again with perfectly straight, south-to-north geometries—to remove water pumped from low spots in the middle of the crescent. Municipal drainage allowed New Orleans to expand off the riverside natural levee and into the lakeside lowlands, but not before engineers and surveyors laid out street networks and parcels for new homes. Planners were naturally inclined to survey new neighborhoods within this existing framework of railroads, navigation canals, adjacent shell roads, and drainage canals. In this manner, antecedent axes influenced the orthogonal street grid of the lakefront, just as antecedent cadasters affected the radiating streets of the riverfront.

The tendency continued into the twentieth century, when the Inner Harbor Navigation (Industrial) Canal was excavated (1918-23) in eastern Orleans Parish. Planners laying out the modern suburbs of New Orleans East in the 1950s-70s aligned many of their street grids to the axis established by the Industrial Canal.

Like the arpent-based sugar plantations in uptown, the Pontchartrain Railroad and the New Basin Canal are both disappeared, rendered obsolete by progress and removed in 1932 and 1950, respectively. Yet their imprint remains, influencing how New Orleanians live in, drive about, and experience their city every day. They show how seemingly arcane landscape decisions made ages ago proceed to shape cityscapes and human lives for centuries to come.

Architectural Chronology, 1700s to 2000s

A brief history of stylistic phases

Architectural styles arrived by ship to this port city, rather like fashions in clothing, to be successively draped on the same persisting and evolving [structural] bodies.[155]

So wrote the late Malcolm Heard in his 1997 architectural guide *French Quarter Manual*. Indeed, styles phase in and out gradually, through the adoption of earlier aesthetic traits, the modification of others, and the introduction of new ones. Demarcating this continuum into discrete eras is therefore about as subjective as classifying the styles themselves.

In his 1966 publication *The Vieux Carré—A General Statement*, Bernard Lemann identified the historic architectural phases of the French Quarter as Colonial Period (1720-1803), Early Federal Period (1803-1825), Antebellum (1825-1860), Paleotechnic (early industrial age architecture, 1850-1900), and Modern.[156] The architectural historians behind the influential *Plan and Program for the Preservation of Vieux Carre* (1968) delineated the major stylistic eras as French and Spanish Colonial; Transitional Styles (1803-1835); Greek Revival (1835-1850); Ante-Bellum Period (1850-1862); Later Victorian Period (1862-1900); and Twentieth Century.[157] The late Lloyd Vogt, architect and author of the classic *New Orleans Houses: A House-Watcher's Guide* (1985), categorized styles popular throughout New Orleans (not just the French Quarter) into the following periods:

- Colonial Period (1718-1803): French Colonial style
- Postcolonial Period (1803-1830): Creole style
- Antebellum Period (1830-1862): Greek Revival
- Victorian Period (1862-1900): Gothic Revival, Italianate, Second Empire, Eastlake, Bracket, Queen Anne, and Richardson Romanesque styles
- Early Twentieth (1900-1940): Georgian Colonial Revival, Neoclassical Revival, Tudor Revival, Bungalow style, and Spanish Colonial Revival
- Modern Period (1940-Present): International and Suburban Ranch styles[158]

Two additional architectural trends may warrant inclusion in the above chronology. Post-Modernism—the incorporation of eclectic historical ornamentations into the facades of Internationalist designs—arrived famously with Charles Moore's influential Piazza d'Italia monument (1978) in the CBD, followed by a number of skyscrapers and other structures built in the 1980s. Recent years have also witnessed a local embrace of revived historical house styles and typologies. Designing new structures to resemble outwardly their old neighbors has been practiced in the French Quarter at least since the 1960s, but contextualizing them in village-like New Urbanist settings, with porches, minimum setback distances, close proximity to neighbors, sidewalks, and green space, did not arrive to New Orleans until the early 2000s.

To date, the city's premier example of New Urbanism is the River Garden mixed-income housing complex built on the former St. Thomas projects site, which embodies pastel-colored New Orleans-style designs and ornamentations. Public response to the "faux faubourg" ranges from adoration among many residents, to ambivalence within the historical preservationist community, to outright loathing by many academic architects and planners.

After Hurricane Katrina, many neighborhood associations and housing developers in the flooded region embraced the philosophy of New Urbanism—to the chagrin of Modernists, who resist the notion of "prescription" and intellectually "going back" in history rather than engaging new concepts and challenges. Tension between the two schools underscored much of the neighborhood planning activity and demolition/reconstruction controversies of the postdiluvian years. It remains to be seen whether a "New Urbanist Period"—or for that matter, a "Post-Postmodern Modernist Period"—will warrant inclusion in New Orleans' chronologies of architectural style. It does seem likely that future architectural historians will recognize a "Post-Katrina Period" for the thousands of manufactured homes, "green buildings," revived historical forms, and functional structures that have arisen since the storm. Regardless of stylistic variations, most postdiluvian houses share a certain architectural trait that dates back to the Colonial Period, only to have been foolishly abandoned during the Modern Period: raised construction on piers.

In a coarse sense, the geography associated with historical architectural eras is quite simple: Earlier styles predominated in the original city (and still do), and as the city spread, it did so with styles popular during that developmental period. A faubourg created in the early 1800s probably boasts Creole and Greek Revival styles; a 1920s neighborhood usually hosts a fair share of bungalows and Spanish Revival villas; and a post-World War II subdivision likely abounds in slab-at-grade ranch houses. Having a good architectural eye in New Orleans means also having a fair sense of the developmental history of the city, its topographic elevation, its soils and hydrology, and its cultural and ethnic fabric: the layers are correlated. Complicating these relationships, of course, is the fact that old buildings in old neighborhoods oftentimes get replaced with new ones with new styles. Such complexification, one can argue, is healthy; it enriches the cityscape.

Also complicating these historical trends and patterns is the damage and destruction wrought by Katrina's floodwaters (see map, "Threatened Historical Architecture"). Where will new neighborhoods arise? Will they look like the past, or something wholly new? Will *they* enrich the cityscape?

The two essays that follow focus on the 1710s through 1860s, when the city made its most significant contributions to the architecture heritage of this nation.

Architectural Geography, 1710s to 1810s

Spatial diffusions and dispersions of early New Orleans architecture

Architecture speaks to cultural geography in three ways. The appearance of certain styles or typologies in a new place sheds light on that locale's cultural source regions and external diffusion patterns. Secondly, a style's spatial distribution within that place informs on internal historical, geographical, demographic, economic, and social forces. Finally, building materials and architectural traits oftentimes reflect adaptations to a region's natural resources and environmental conditions.[159]

Nearly all mid-eighteenth-century New Orleans structures exhibited a Franco-West Indian style described variously as "French Colonial" or "French Creole." Traits included a single principal story raised upon piers, large double-pitched pavilion-like roof, broad wooden galleries supported with delicate colonnades and balustrades, exterior staircases, and walls made of brick or mud mixed with moss (*bousillage*) set within a load-bearing skeleton of timbers. Center chimneys, French doors and shutters, and a lack of hallways and closets characterized interiors. An Englishman who visited New Orleans in 1765-69 explained that "the general plan of building in the town, is with timber frames filled up with brick...." This distinctive brick-between-post construction, often covered with clapboards, prevails throughout eighteenth- and early-nineteenth-century structures still standing today. He continued,

> most of the houses are but of one floor, raised about eight feet from the ground, with large galleries round them, and the cellars under the floors level with the ground; it is impossible to have any subterraneous buildings, as they would be constantly full of water.[160]

These galleried residences reflected a housing arrangement more suited to rural or semi-rural conditions; that it also prevailed in early New Orleans attests to the nascent city's village-like state.

Four interrelated hypotheses have been offered on the genesis of Louisiana's Creole architectural heritage. One popular proposition holds that it was "invented" locally as a rational adaptation to the environment. Many people embrace this deterministic hypothesis for its clear and causative explanations: Heavy rains explain steep roofs. Waterlogged soils cause raised construction. Hot weather leads to breezy galleries.[161]

Undoubtedly there is some truth to these relationships, but evidence indicates that, in general, cultural antecedents have weighed more heavily than independent invention in the appearance of architectural traits. Only later are they modified locally according to environmental and practical limitations. Note, for instance, the counterintuitive presence of galleried houses in frigid French Canada, or the Spanish use of flat roofs in rainy New Orleans. "That full-blown Creole galleried houses ... were being built only a dozen or so years after colonization began,"[162] pointed out Jonathan Fricker, also casts serious doubt on the invention hypothesis. Unless they glean intriguing new construction techniques from natives, pioneering settlers in risky, unforgiving frontier environments generally embrace "knowns" and eschew experimentation, particularly in a high-stakes endeavor like home construction. They are more likely to carry on what their forebears taught them, modifying those traditions to new conditions and tastes only as time progresses, as new knowledge is gained, and as risk declines.

A second hypothesis views Louisiana Creole architecture as a descendent of Canadian houses derived from the Normandy region of France, modified in the West Indies and Louisiana to reflect local needs. This proposition suggests that Creole architecture diffused *down* the Mississippi Valley. A related hypothesis emphasizes the derivation of Louisiana Creole houses directly from France, particularly Normandy, ascribing less importance to the modifications made by Canadians and West Indians, and even less to local environmental conditions.

A fourth and favored hypothesis sees Creole architecture (particularly its signature gallery) as an extraction from a West Indian cultural milieu, influenced by a wide range of European, African, and indigenous traditions (particularly the Arawak Indian *Bohio* hut). The appearance of galleried houses throughout the Caribbean—not solely in French colonies but in Spanish and British ones as well, as early as 1685—leads advocates of this hypothesis to de-emphasize the French role in the origin of Creole architecture. While underlying French and French Canadian house types were brought to the New Orleans region by former Canadians, the founders and early settlers also brought with them significant West Indian contributions and modifications, which were locally altered to taste and need by later generations. This hypothesis suggests that Creole architecture diffused *up* the Mississippi Valley from the Caribbean, rather than down from Canada or directly from France. Anthropologist Jay Dearborn Edwards viewed this West Indian/Creole influence consequential enough to warrant the inclusion of the Caribbean region as "another major cultural hearth for the domestic architecture of eastern North America," along with England, France, Spain, Germany, Holland, and Scandinavia.[163]

Frenchman Pierre Clément de Laussat, the prefect who reluctantly handed over Louisiana to the Americans in 1803, might have agreed with Edwards' statement. Wrote Laussat in his memoirs,

> I imagine that Saint-Domingue was, of all our colonies in the Antilles, the one whose mentality and customs influenced Louisiana the most. Frequent intercourse existed between the two, [and many] exiles from the island prefer Louisiana as refuge.[164]

Irish traveler Thomas Ashe, writing in 1809, also viewed New Orleans as a component of the West Indian/Caribbean region. "The merchandize for the Mississippi is exactly similar to that of the West India trade—the race of people being nearly the same, and the climate not essentially differing."[165] It follows reasonably that architectural traits and traditions diffused throughout that cultural region.

Whatever its origin, this "first-generation" Creole tradition prevailed in New Orleans even after Spain assumed dominion in the late 1760s, because the inhabitants remained Franco-Caribbean in their culture and the new Spanish rulers did not aggressively seek to change this. But population growth and urban development increasingly rendered these structures inadequate, wasteful of space—and dangerous. Over a thousand were destroyed by the great conflagrations of 1788 and 1794, and almost all others succumbed over the years to decay, demolition, storm, and fire. Only one institutional example survives today from the French colonial era (the Old Ursuline Convent, designed 1745, completed 1753), while perhaps the best example of an early Creole residential structure (Madame John's Legacy, 1788), remains at 632 Dumaine Street. The remarkable circa-1780s Ossorno House (913 Gov. Nicholls) would have been an equally fine example were it not for the later modification of its hip roof to a gable.

After the 1794 fire, the Spanish colonial administration decreed new building codes, looking to their own traditions to foster a sturdier urban environment (see *Transformation by Conflagration*). Wood was discouraged in favor of brick; steep roofs went out in favor of flat or gently sloping ones; brick-between-post walls were covered with stucco; wooden shingles were replaced with clay tiles. Other Spanish features unrelated to fire safety accompanied the new traits, such as arched openings on the ground floor, pilasters, balconies, and courtyards. The fenced gardens and wooden galleries of a French village gave way to the massive stark walls and wrought-iron balconies of a Spanish city. "As such structures proliferated," wrote architect Malcolm Heard, "the physical character of the Quarter evolved accordingly—the influence of northern French building traditions, transmitted to some degree through the cold Canadian provinces, waned in favor of the more Mediterranean forms of the Spanish."[166] Derivations of those forms abound throughout the Quarter today, but surviving examples of pure Spanish Colonial Style are uncommon. Twenty-five edifices—about one of every hundred buildings in the Quarter—exhibit this style, of which twenty-two were built in the Spanish colonial era (all after 1789). Most are loosely clustered within two blocks of the Toulouse/Royal intersection, plus on Chartres from St. Louis to St. Ann. Of the three that postdate the Spanish years, two are quite famous: the Old Absinthe House at 240 Bourbon, built in 1806, and the Girod (Napoleon) House at 500 Chartres, built in 1814, with a wing dating to 1797.

Spain would control New Orleans for only a few years after its architectural style finally gained a foothold. After the Spanish dons departed in 1803, but before Anglo-American culture came to predominate, New Orleanians found themselves with an amalgam of architectural traditions and building skills, some by way of France, some by way of Spain, others by Canada, the West Indies, Africa, Latin America, and elsewhere. From this admixture emerged what may be called "second-generation" Creole style. Traits include Spanish-style arched openings, stucco-covered walls and stucco entablatures with moldings, a steep hip roof, narrow wrought-iron balcony, unadorned windows, multiple stories, and narrow passageways between buildings. While only two or three specimens of the previously discussed eighteenth-century "first-generation Creole" structures survive in the French Quarter, about 740—roughly one of every three extant structures in the district—exhibit this subsequent architectural style that is also called Creole. (The 600 block of Royal Street is replete with fine examples.) Dating mainly from the 1820s and 1830s, this tradition exhibits an indigenous New Orleans look and design that harks back to colonial antecedents, but with local modifications and variations. A visitor from Edinburgh in 1828 recorded his impressions of this cityscape in terms that would resonate with a first-time visitor today:

> [W]hat struck us most [about New Orleans] were the old and narrow streets, the high houses, ornamented with tasteful cornices, iron balconies, and many other circumstances peculiar to towns in France and Spain; and pointing out the past history of this city fated to change its masters so often.[167]

Graceful, smooth simplicity, uninterrupted by cluttering detail, typified these second-generation, Spanish-influenced Creole styles.

Beautiful as they were, their days were numbered as new political, demographic, and cultural waves swept into New Orleans at the dawn of the nineteenth century.

Architectural Geography, 1810s to 1860s

Spatial patterns of New Orleans' antebellum architecture

The Anglo-Americans trickling into New Orleans after the Louisiana Purchase at first conformed to the local architectural traditions, having little choice but to move into existing structures or hire local builders to build what they knew. Some adjusted and modified their structures, but existing styles and typologies generally persisted.[168]

When the emigrant trickle grew to a torrent in the 1810s and 1820s, the newcomers increasingly brushed aside local architectural traits in favor of their own imported concepts—and their own architects. Had they arrived a generation or so earlier, they might have brought with them the classical styles that were all the rage in the North and upper South at that time, such as Georgian, Federal, and what is now called Jeffersonian Classicism.[169] But arriving as they did in the early 1800s, the Americans preferred the latest architectural fad sweeping the Northeast: the aesthetics of ancient Greece.

The earliest known surviving structure in Louisiana with a prominent Greek trait (Doric columns) is the circa-1814 Thierry House at 721 Gov. Nicholls Street, designed by twenty-one-year-old Henry Latrobe and Arsène Lacarrière Latour. Latrobe's father, the famed English-born architect Benjamin Latrobe, first introduced Greek styles (not to mention Philadelphia bricks and other Northeastern stonework and mill-work) to New Orleans in 1807-09, when he designed and built the Custom House for the recently arrived U.S. government.[170]

Within a few years, Greek Revival spread throughout the city and region—on plantation houses, townhouses, storehouses, cottages, and (later) even shotgun houses. Creole-influenced arched doorways were replaced with squared-off openings and Greek "keyhole" entrances; side and center hallways appeared to provide more domestic privacy; brick "jack arches" went out in favor of heavy granite lintels; stucco entablatures with moldings gave way to attic windows and dentils. On plantation hous-es, delicate colonnades disappeared for massive classical columns. Creole architecture gave way to Greek Revival as Creole culture relinquished to American.

Greek Revival formed the first major American architectural contribution to New Orleans, visible today on hundreds of French Quarter structures and thousands throughout the city. Georgian, Federal, and Jeffersonian Classicism, on the other hand, are rare in the Quarter and citywide, as are Gothic and other Northeastern styles that "missed" the major wave of Anglo settlement in Louisiana. Only eighteen extant struc-tures in the Quarter exhibit Federal, Georgian, or Gothic styles; Greek Revival, on the other hand, adorns 614 structures, more than one in every four extant Quarter build-ings. American history, and Louisiana's place in it, is written into these patterns.

History is also inscribed in the historical trends of Creole versus American styles. Creole styles (second-generation, that is) peaked in the 1830s then fell off pre-cipitously, while Greek Revival hit its zenith a decade later and fell off more gradu-ally. This architectural transition from Creole to Greek Revival corresponds to the 1830s-40s shift of cultural and political power in the city, from Creole to American elements.[171] It transpired gradually and sometimes piecemeal, with some townhouses exhibiting both second-generation Creole as well as Greek Revival traits. Revealingly, these "transitional" structures mostly arose precisely when the Creole/American cul-tural rivalry peaked, in the late 1830s. Afterwards, momentum swung permanently to-ward the Americans, and as it did, the old colonial-inspired Creole styles declined and Greek Revival and other new American styles caught on. As architect Malcolm Heard observed, "[t]he conflicted process by which Creoles assimilated American influence became architecturally manifest in the large number of Creole townhouses built in the French Quarter during the 1830s."[172]

The *geography* of Creoles and Americans is also written in brick. Creole cul-ture in antebellum times was by no means strictly limited to the confines of the French Quarter, nor did Anglo-Americans reside exclusively above Canal Street, as legend has it. In fact, both ethnic groups (plus many others) could be found throughout the Quar-ter, with Creoles predominating in the lower area and Anglos in the upper blocks by Canal Street. This ethnic-geographical pattern, observed by a number of nineteenth-century travelers to the city (see *Streetscapes of Amalgamation*), drove a correlated geog-raphy of architecture which can be witnessed to this day: Greek Revival specimens out-number Creole examples in the upper "American" blocks, particularly above St. Louis Street, while the reverse is true in the Creole-dominant blocks below that street. St.

Louis Street is significant because, in 1822, the famous Creole aristocrat Bernard Marigny identified it as a *de facto* dividing line between American and Creole interests.[173]

At the block level, the trend is even more dramatic. In the heavily Americanized blocks between Iberville and Bienville streets, which visually resemble Manhattan or Boston more so than the lower Quarter, Greek Revival buildings outnumber Creoles by an eleven-to-one ratio. But from St. Ann to Gov. Nicholls Street, an area that can pass for a southern European or Caribbean village, Creole structures outnumber Greek Revivals by more than a 2.5-to-1 ratio. This architectural geography is a direct descendent of the ethnic geographies of nineteenth-century New Orleans, when the city underwent its historic and sometimes painful transition from a Creole past to an American future.

By the 1850s and certainly by the Civil War, new architectural fashions hatched in Europe and arrived lately to America, such as Victorian Italianate, finally overwhelmed the local Creole architectural tradition. "[T]he truly significant period of New Orleans architecture was brought into jeopardy by the [Louisiana] Purchase and brought to an end by the Civil War," wrote James Marston Fitch. "The Americanization of the Crescent City has long been completed, at least architecturally; and the whole nation is the poorer for it."[174] Other new styles arrived, and subsequent generations of New Orleans architects continued the city's fine reputation for the building arts.

The Creole tradition, however, never truly revived. We are fortunate indeed, and deeply indebted to pioneer preservationists, to keep within our stewardship (mostly in the French Quarter, Faubourg Marigny, Faubourg Tremé, and Bayou St. John) the nation's largest concentration of this unique and beautiful tradition.

Shotgun Geography

The where and wherefore of the South's most famous house type

While architectural styles represent ever-changing tastes and fashions "draped" upon structures rather interchangeably, typology, or type, refers to the underlying form, shape, orientation, and layout of a building. Typology represents "a philosophy of space, a culturally-determined sense of dimension,"[175] reflecting the needs, wants, and means of a structure's builders and owners. Cultures that value privacy often sacrifice living space to make room for hallways, while gregarious societies are comfortable with rooms adjoining directly. Individuals with abundant means, and a desire to display it, may opt for a spacious house type with multiple floors and amenities, while those of humble means have to settle for less.

Four structural types account for 81 percent of the 2,244 street-fronting buildings in the French Quarter. The *townhouse* (comprising 35 percent) is a multistory, three-bay brick structure, often with shared walls, designed for the residential occupancy of its affluent owners. The *storehouse* (22 percent) is outwardly similar but serves a commercial purpose on the ground floor, and may afford either residential or commercial (including storage) use on the upper floors. The *cottage* (15 percent) is a rectangular or square residential structure (lest it be on a corner, where it often serves a retail functions as well), usually one to one-and-a-half stories plus an attic, whose roofline is parallel with the abutting street. The *shotgun* house (9 percent) is a simple, narrow, linear residential structure oriented perpendicularly to the street, usually built with working-class or poor occupants in mind. Variations of these four structural types abound: townhouses and storehouses might have steep or flat roofs, balconies or galleries, or arched or square openings; cottages and shotguns might have hip or gable roofs, brick or wooden walls, or single or double bays. But the underlying form usually remains unmistakable.[176]

Of these typologies, the famous shotgun house stands alone as the most ubiquitous traditional vernacular house type in New Orleans and throughout the South. From whence and how did this curious structure trace this expansive geography?

Folklore holds that the term "shotgun house" derives from the ability to fire bird shot through the front door and out the rear without touching a wall. Another story claims that the house's shape recalls a single-barrel shotgun, a duplex thus resembling a double barrel. The term itself postdates the house type by many years, rarely appearing in print prior to the 1900s (though it probably circulated in vernacular speech earlier).[177] Folklorist John Michael Vlach defined the typology of the shotgun as "a one-room wide, one-story high building with two or more rooms, oriented perpendicularly to the road with its front door in the gable end," but added that "other aspects such as size, proportion, roofing, porches, appendages, foundations, trim, and decoration have been so variable that the shotgun is sometimes difficult to identify."[178] The outstanding exterior characteristic is its elongated shape, sometimes in length-to-width ratios approaching ten-to-one. Inside, what is salient is the lack of hallways, which implies a lack of privacy: occupants and visitors need to pass through rooms—including private bedrooms—to get to other rooms.

Scholarly interest in the shotgun house dates from geographer Fred B. Kniffen's research in the 1930s on Louisiana folk housing, which explored structural typology as a means to delineate cultural regions. Debate has ensued among cultural geographers, architectural historians, and anthropologists as to the shotgun's origins, form, function, and diffusion. New Orleans shotguns present a special problem, for nowhere else are they so common and so varied. A number of hypotheses have been offered.

Geographer William B. Knipmeyer saw parallels between the shotgun house and the Native Louisianian "palmetto house," pointing out its rectangular shape and "high pitched gable roof...oriented with its greatest length perpendicular to the bayou, path, or road."[179] Knipmeyer traced a lineage from the structural form of pre-European Choctaw huts to indigenous palmetto houses to wooden frame camps and eventually to the shotgun, which he viewed as a fairly late development enabled by the late-1800s lumbering trade.[180] But another scholar argued that indigenous building types and techniques in North America, unlike those of other continents, proved "totally inadequate for even the lowest levels of European requirements," and were largely ignored by colonizers beyond the most rudimentary settlements.[181]

John Michael Vlach also disagreed with the Native American hypothesis in his 1975 dissertation, noting the abundance of shotgun-like houses throughout present-day Haiti. Vlach traced the essential shotgun typology to the eighteenth-century enslaved populations of Haiti, formerly Saint-Domingue, who had been removed by slavers from the forested peri-coastal areas of the western and central African regions known at the time as Guinea and Angola. Vlach described a gable-roofed housing stock indigenous to the western coastal regions of modern sub-Saharan Africa, specifically those of the Yoruba peoples, and linked them to similar structures in modern Haiti with comparable rectangular shapes, room juxtapositions, and ceiling heights. Vlach suggests that the exodus of Haitians to New Orleans after the insurrection of 1791-1803 brought this vernacular house type to the banks of the Mississippi. "Haitian émigrés had only to continue in Louisiana the same life they had known in St. Domingue. The shotgun house of Port-au-Prince became, quite directly, the shotgun house of New Orleans."[182]

The Haitian/African origin hypothesis for New Orleans shotguns is favored by many scholars. One strand of indirect support comes from the distribution of shotgun houses throughout Louisiana. Geographer Fred Kniffen showed in the 1930s that this house type generally occurred along the waterways and bayous of southeastern Louisiana as well as the Red, Ouachita, and Mississippi riverine areas in the northern part of the state.[183] These areas tended to be, and remain, more Francophone in their culture, higher in their proportions of people of African and Creole ancestry, and older in their historical development. Beyond state boundaries, shotguns occur throughout the riverine areas of the lower Mississippi Valley, spatially correlated with antebellum plantation regions and with areas that, historically and currently, host large black populations.[184] If in fact the shotgun diffused from Africa, to Haiti, through New Orleans and up the Mississippi Valley, this is the North American distribution we would expect to see. But there are economic variables at play here as well—these areas tend to be poor, and poor people are more likely to live in simpler houses—and they may trump cultural factors in explaining the spatial distribution of the shotgun.

Others speculate that while the shotgun resembles house types of other cultures, its manifestation in New Orleans and the South is related to them only because its ease of construction and conservation of resources (building materials, labor, space) made it equally attractive in many areas. One may reason that, given a mild climate, a builder need not rely on the wisdom of ancestors to design a rudimentary edifice that accommodates a narrow street-side or bayou-side lot while minimizing materials and labor. The lack of hallways simply reflects a desire to maximize living space in a cramped environment, even if it sacrifices privacy. A shotgun, according to this theory, is simply a least-cost solution that any rational individual would invent independently, given certain constraints. Advocates of this theory point to the traditionally narrow parcels of New Orleans blocks, and the slender *arpent* lots along waterways in Louisiana, as causative agents for the occurrence of narrow, elongated structures. "[T]he reason there are shotguns," stated a *Times-Picayune* article, is because "they were an efficient way to house a lot of people on limited land in skinny 30-by-120-foot lots," like New York City's "railroad flats" or Philadelphia's "trinity" houses.[185] Lending some apparent support for the "invention hypothesis" is the activity of Roberts & Company, a New Orleans sash and door fabricator formed in 1856 which developed prefabricated shotgun-like houses in the 1860s and '70s and even won awards for them at international expositions. Whether Robert & Company truly invented the design or simply "capitalize[d] on a local traditional form"[186] is the key question. Others have suggested that shotguns were invented in response to a city real estate tax code which pegged taxation to street frontage rather than total area—even though no one seems to be able to identify that exact law.

The "invention hypothesis," despite it popular appeal, suffers weaknesses. It fails to explain why the shotgun is not always found wherever narrow lots or frontage-based taxes exist, yet *is* found when these conditions do not exist, such as throughout rural plantation regions. Nor does it explain why the shotgun failed to catch on until many years *after* the delineation of narrow lots. Could cultural factors outweigh local invention in the development of the shotgun? Jay Dearborn Edwards points out, "anthropologists have long realized that independent invention is rare in human cultural development. People are far better at borrowing the ideas of their neighbors than they are at inventing their own out of whole cloth."[187]

Shotgun singles and doubles came to dominate the turn-of-the-century housing stock of New Orleans' working-class and poor neighborhoods. Yet they were also erected as owned-occupied homes in middle- and upper-middle-class areas, including the Garden District. New Orleans shotguns exhibited numerous locally inspired variations: with hip, gable, or "apron" roofs; with "camelbacks" to increase living space; with hallways for privacy; with grand Greek Revival and Neo-Classical porticos; and with elaborate Victorian gingerbread. "Bungalows," which arose between the world wars, arguably represent the final modification of the shotgun house typology. Local society by this time desired more privacy and living space than earlier generations; increasing affluence and new technologies such as mechanized kitchens, indoor plumbing, air conditioning, automobiles, and municipal drainage helped form new philosophies about residential space. Professional home builders responded accordingly: the slab-at-grade ranch house became the "default" house type for new construction in the city after World War II. Shotguns, by mid-century, went extinct.

For years, architectural historians rolled their eyes at the run-of-the-mill 1890s Victorian Italianate shotgun house, and did not protest their demolition, even in the French Quarter, as late as the 1960s. In recent decades, however, many New Orleanians have come to appreciate the sturdy construction and exuberant embellishments of the classic shotgun. Today they are a cherished part of New Orleans culture and a favorite target for historical restoration—although, revealingly, incoming occupants often "de-shotgun" their new abodes by incorporating hallways, adding wings, or converting two narrow doubles into one ample single.[188]

Beyond selected gentrified neighborhoods and towns of the South, shotguns remain a symbol of poverty and are hardly cherished by those who call them home. When lined up along barely paved streets on the "wrong sides" of towns like Donaldsonville, St. Francisville, Natchez, and Vicksburg, they form both picturesque vistas of Southern life, and poignant reminders of a troubled past.

How the Poor Third Became the Lower Ninth

Three centuries of urban transformation in the Lower Ninth Ward

Note: Two years after Hurricane Katrina, actor and sustainable-architecture advocate Brad Pitt launched the Make It Right Foundation, aiming to develop affordable and environmentally sound housing for residents to return to the Lower Ninth Ward. The organization asked me to write a brief history of that neighborhood's urban development. The following essay is scheduled to appear in a book the foundation is planning to release.

The Lower Ninth Ward the world came to know after Hurricane Katrina in 2005 bore neither that name nor that form for the first two centuries of its historical development. A sequence of human interventions—some gradual, some swift—since the early 1700s transformed that natural deltaic landscape into the cityscape we know today.

During the era of indigenous occupation, that landscape comprised part of a gradually sloping hydrological basin bordered on the south by the ten-foot-high natural levee of the Mississippi River, and on the west and north by the slight Esplanade and Gentilly topographic ridges, rising two to four feet above sea level. Any rainfall or high river water spilling into that basin flowed eastward out Bayou Bienvenue toward Lake Borgne and the Gulf of Mexico.

Springtime high water on the Mississippi overtopped the river's natural levees every few years. Those periodic floods did not constitute disasters; in fact, they created the entire Louisiana deltaic plain, over a period of 5,000 to 7,000 years, by depositing layers of sand, silt, and clay at a pace faster than natural subsidence or wave action could reduce them. In this manner, the present-day Lower Ninth Ward and its deltaic environs arose from the Gulf of Mexico through periodic nourishment by sediment-laden river water. The highest lands, which lay closest to the Mississippi, declined by roughly one vertical inch for every hundred feet of distance away from the river. The lowest lands stood at or near the level of the sea, *not below it*. A semi-tropical climate, abundant rainfall, and rich alluvial soils allowed verdant vegetation to grow, but not all plant communities grew everywhere. Along the river arose dense bamboo-like reeds; immediately behind them grew jungle-like hardwood forests laced with vines. Farther back, at lower elevations, were palmetto-strewn cypress swamps, which petered out to grassy saline marshes where Bayou Bienvenue flowed into the sea.

"All this land is a country of reeds and brambles and very tall grass," wrote Pierre Le Moyne, sieur d'Iberville in March 1699 as the French explorer sailed up the

Mississippi for the first time.[189] About eighty miles upriver, a sharp meander (present-day English Turn) challenged Iberville's expedition by positioning its ships against prevailing winds. Once past this obstacle, the Mississippi straightened out for about eight miles, then curved sharply again. Between those two meanders, on the eastern bank, lay the present-day Lower Ninth Ward, undistinguished and unnoticed by its early European visitors.

Over the next two decades, Iberville, and later his younger brother Bienville, would establish a French colonial society throughout the region, culminating with the foundation of New Orleans in 1718 (see *Settling the Landscape*). Bienville located his settlement—the present-day French Quarter—on the natural levee at the cusp of that second meander, exploiting a portage route which allowed for faster and safer access to the Gulf Coast.

As New Orleans grew in the 1720s to a population of 500 to 1,000 people, fertile lands above and below the city were surveyed into French "long lot" plantations. Their elongated shape ensured that every plantation would garner a share of the most arable land, while gaining access to the Mississippi for transportation purposes. On a typical Louisiana plantation, the manor house occupied the crest of the natural levee near the river; behind it were dependencies, workshops, sheds, and slave cabins, followed by croplands and backswamp. Planters raised tobacco, indigo, rice, plus grains and vegetables, using the labor of enslaved Africans first brought to Louisiana in 1719. Maps from around 1730 indicate that such plantations had already been established around the present-day Lower Ninth Ward, their forests probably cleared by recently arrived slaves. Reported Gov. Etienne de Périer in 1728, "[slaves] are being employed to cut down the trees at the two ends of the town as far as Bayou St. John in order to clear this ground and to give air to the city and to the mill." [190]

Colonial-era New Orleans struggled throughout the eighteenth century with sparse population, disease, disaster, and low prioritization under French and Spanish dominion. Then, a sequence of events around the turn of the nineteenth century reversed the city's fortunes. First, a slave insurgency in Saint-Domingue (present-day Haiti), which began in 1791 and eventually expelled the French regime, diminished Napoleon's interest in the seemingly unpromising Louisiana colony, and eventually motivated him to sell it to the United States in 1803. Concurrently, the cotton gin (1793) and the successful granulation of Louisiana sugar cane (1795) facilitated the rapid expansion of lucrative cotton and sugar production in the hinterland, both of which would profit New Orleans enormously. Finally, the introduction of the steamboat to Mississippi River commerce starting in 1812 allowed the new American city to exploit fully its strategic position in world shipping. Within two decades (1790s-1800s), New Orleans blossomed from an orphaned outpost of two descendent Old World powers, into a strategically sited port city of an ascendant, business-oriented, expanding New World nation. Prominent observers regularly predicted New Orleans would become the most affluent and important city in the hemisphere.

In 1805, the new American administrators incorporated New Orleans as a municipal entity, legally establishing its government, duties, privileges, and boundaries. Shortly thereafter, the city's lower limit became fixed roughly three miles downriver from the present-day French Quarter, an area within which lies the present-day Lower Ninth Ward. Designating those rural outskirts as being within New Orleans (Orleans Parish) limits would, in time, affect their use, population, and destiny. Features and phenomena that (1) people did not want to be located in the heart of the city, (2) *could* not be located above the city because it would pollute the water source, but (3) nevertheless *had* to be located within the city's limits, often ended up in the city's lowermost corner. This would become a familiar theme for the future Lower Ninth Ward: first on the list for urban nuisances, last in line for amenities.

Being the farthest-downriver corner of New Orleans also meant being the first that ships would encounter while heading upriver. For this and other reasons, the U.S. Government established New Orleans Barracks near the parish line in 1835. Now known as Jackson Barracks, home of the Louisiana National Guard, the installation served as the premier embarkation point for military operations throughout the region. It was also the first designed development within the future Lower Ninth Ward.

As New Orleans Barracks was under construction, its upriver neighbors included fifteen plantations or other land holdings principally dedicated to the cultivation and processing of sugar cane. Modern-day street names recall this now-extinct agrarian landscape: "Sister Street" once lined the convent and land holding of the Ursuline Nuns (where the Industrial Canal now lies), while nearby Deslonde, Reynes, Forstall, Caffin, and Delery streets all commemorate plantation owners from the 1830s.[191] "Flood Street" was named not for the natural disaster but for another plantation owner, Dr. William Flood, who played an important role in the Battle of New Orleans in 1815.

With the rapid agricultural development of the Mississippi Valley and only one way to deliver those commodities to market effectively—by shipping down the Mississippi—New Orleans' economy boomed. So too did its population, which more than doubled between the Louisiana Purchase (1803) and 1810, and nearly doubled decennially until 1840, when New Orleans counted 102,193 residents and ranked as the third-largest city in the nation. It was also the South's largest city and its premier immigration destination, home to arguably the most ethnically, racially, linguistically, and culturally diverse population in the nation. Thousands of English-speaking, mostly Protestant Anglo-Americans had emigrated to the opportunity-rich port city after the Louisiana Purchase, where they encountered thousands of French-speaking Catholic Creoles who seemed to view nearly everything—government, law, religion, race, architecture—differently. People of African descent, both free and enslaved, as well as tens of thousands of immigrants from Ireland, Germany, France, Haiti, Cuba, Mexico, Italy, Greece, and nearly every other nation, made antebellum New Orleans like no other American city.

New Orleans' urban footprint expanded accordingly, as former "long lot" sugar plantations were subdivided as faubourgs (suburbs) and built up with new homes. Because the wealthier Anglo population tended to settle above the original city (present-day uptown), where the natural levee was wider and the river flowed free of inner-city refuse, New Orleans spread predominantly in an upriver direction, by a two-to-one ratio over downriver development. It expanded only slightly away from the river, where low-lying swamplands prevented most urban development.

The downriver expansion that did occur began in 1805 with the surveying of Faubourg Marigny, and continued into the 1810s-40s with the subdivision of plantations comprising the present-day neighborhood of Bywater. The population that settled here tended to be markedly poorer than that of the upper city, mostly comprising Creoles, Irish and German immigrants, and representatives of smaller groups from southern Europe and Latin America. Officially, the area was designated as the Third Municipality, which spanned from Esplanade Avenue downriver to the parish line, including the present-day Lower Ninth Ward. To some, the Third Municipality comprised "the Creole faubourgs;" to others, it was the "old Third," the "dirty Third," the "poor Third," and only occasionally, and ironically, the "glorious Third."[192] After 1852, the lower regions of New Orleans gained a new nomenclature: wards.

Wards as a political-geographical unit date to the 1805 chartering of the city. Serving a number of municipal purposes, wards were redrawn four times over the next forty-seven years. After the city's unsuccessful sixteen-year experiment with semi-autonomous municipalities, the reunified city government (1852) redrew ward lines for a fifth time. Because Felicity Street had long marked New Orleans' upper boundary, the new ward enumeration began at Felicity (First Ward) and continued consecutively downriver. To equalize populations within wards, the high-density French Quarter was sliced into the narrowest wards (Fourth, Fifth, and Sixth), while the lower-density "Creole faubourgs" allowed for broader units. The lowermost outskirts remained so rural that a single mega-ward—the Ninth—enveloped the entire area. Hence the birth of the Ninth Ward. City planners then returned above Felicity Street and demarcated upriver lands, and later Algiers on the West Bank, as wards ten through seventeen. The modern-day map of New Orleans wards, unchanged since the 1880s, thus reflects the city's piecemeal growth since 1852.

Urbanization first arrived to the present-day Lower Ninth Ward around 1840. While the Charles Zimpel map of 1834 indicates a solid line of plantations from the Ursulines' parcel to the U.S. Barracks, the Maurice Harrison map of 1845 shows roughly one-third of that area subdivided into vacant streets and blocks. As each planter decided he could make more money subdividing his plantation than cultivating it, more and more croplands became platted with urban grids. Names for old streets running parallel to the river (Chartres, Royal, Dauphine, etc.) were extended from the original city downriver to the U.S. Barracks, while new river-perpendicular streets often adopted the names of their anteceding plantations. Thus, the geometry of the old French long-lot surveying system drove the urban form of the emerging neighborhood.

Historical population figures for what is now the Lower Ninth Ward are difficult to ascertain because nineteenth-century censuses aggregated populations by wards, not at sub-ward levels. The vast majority of Ninth Ward residents clustered not in the present-day Lower Ninth but at the upriver end of the ward, in what is now called Bywater by the river. We do know that enough residents lived in the present-day Lower Ninth to warrant the establishment of St. Maurice Catholic Church in 1857. Fourteen years later, the Brothers of the Holy Cross established an orphanage which would later become the Holy Cross Catholic High School campus. Horse-drawn streetcar service arrived to the area in 1872, which brought more residents to the once-rural district.[193]

By the time the 1883 Robinson map was published, the area had been subdivided at least as far north as Urquhart Street, just one block beyond the aptly named Marais ("marsh") Street. Roughly two-thirds of those blocks (present-day Holy Cross section of the Lower Ninth Ward) were further subdivided into parcels, and of those, approximately half had homes.[194] The neighborhood in the late nineteenth century formed a low-density dispersion of cottages and frame houses, usually with fenced gardens, arranged in a village-like setting amid open fields and an occasional West Indian-style plantation home left over from the antebellum era. Also there were railroads, a cotton press, a military hospital, warehouses, and a livestock landing and slaughterhouse— an enormous malodorous operation enabled by a controversial 1873 U.S. Supreme Court decision approving the consolidation of the city's stockyards and slaughtering facilities. It comes as no surprise that this urban nuisance got located downriver from the city proper but within city limits—that is, in the lowermost corner of the Ninth Ward. With it came railroads, soap makers, rendering plants, and related operations. They provided working-class jobs, but also drove down property values. So too did the American Sugar Refining Company, which built a fourteen-story industrial sugar-refining plant (complete with its own docking and railroad facilities) across the parish line in 1909-12. The year 1912 also saw the realignment and augmentation of the Mississippi River levee in the area, improving flood protection for the increasing number of working-class families moving into the neighborhood.

The single most influential transformation of the Ninth Ward's environment occurred in the late 1910s. Competition among ports motivated city leaders in that era to advocate streamlining navigation routes and creating new dock space off the crowded riverfront. The vision soon evolved into the "Inner Harbor Navigation Canal." Officials in 1918 identified the corridor for the so-called "Industrial Canal:" a five-mile-long, 600-foot-wide, mostly undeveloped right-of-way splitting the Ninth Ward in two. From the city's perspective, the proposed route made the most sense: it lay within city limits, crossed a relatively narrow land strip between river and lake, exploited a convenient position for shipping and docking activity, and was either city-owned or readily acquirable. From the Ninth Ward's perspective, the canal represented job opportunities—but also a major disruption, a barrier, and a potential threat that would have been resisted fiercely by citizens had it been proposed for the heart of the city.

Excavation took a little over a year; construction of the intricate lock system, to handle the differing water levels of the river and lake, took another three years. When the Industrial Canal opened in 1923, it succeeded in enhancing port activity in the area. It also severed the lowermost portion of the city from the urban core, inspiring the term *Lower* Ninth Ward. From now on, residents of this isolated neighborhood (who mostly relied on a single streetcar line for transportation into the city center) would have to dodge drawbridges and railroad crossings to interact with the rest of their city. More ominously, the Industrial Canal introduced gulf water into city limits, held back only by flimsy floodwalls and inadequate levees. Worse yet, the installation of the municipal drainage system around the turn of the twentieth century—and a few decades later to the Lower Ninth Ward—drained the backswamp and allowed its finely textured sediment particles to settle and subside. Soon, former swamp and marshlands throughout the city began to subside below sea level, even as their populations increased. Artificial levees were built along the periphery to keep water out. The topography of New Orleans began to assume the shape of a bowl—or rather, a series of bowls, one of which comprised the Lower Ninth Ward.

The human geography of the Lower Ninth Ward in the early twentieth century iterated the area's topography. The 5,500 New Orleanians who resided there in 1910 (1.6 percent of the city's total population) shared certain traits: most ranked no higher economically than the working- or lower-middle class, and nearly all were born and raised locally. Those settling on higher ground closer to the river, in the so-called front-of-town, were predominantly white, usually of Irish, German, Sicilian, French, Creole, or Latino stock, who in previous generations lived in the "Poor Third" or in the French Quarter. Those who settled in the back-of-town (north of St. Claude Avenue and later Claiborne Avenue, an area that remained largely undeveloped into the 1920s-30s) were mostly African-American and either poor or working-class. Some were black Creoles (Franco-African-Americans) with generations of heritage in the city; others had emigrated from rural areas after emancipation, or later, following the mechanization of Southern agriculture. Immediately behind the back-of-town blocks lay the city's sewage treatment plant—yet another municipal disamenity which had to be located downriver from the city proper (and its water source), but had to remain within city limits. Behind the treatment plant, another navigation canal—the Intracoastal Waterway—was excavated in the 1940s to facilitate east-to-west barge traffic. By World War II, the 11,556 residents of the Lower Ninth Ward, long severed from the other 97.7 percent of the city's population by the Industrial Canal, were now surrounded on three sides by water bodies, even as their underlying soils subsided.[195]

The 1960s brought more tumultuous transformations. Resistance to school integration—which was fierce within the working-class white Ninth Ward population—and other factors led to the wholesale departure of whites downriver into the neighboring suburban parish of St. Bernard. Once racially mixed with a predominantly white front-of-town and black back-of-town, the Lower Ninth Ward became increasingly African-American. At the same time, excavation commenced on a third major navigation canal: the Mississippi River-Gulf Outlet (MR-GO) Canal, designed to connect the earlier man-made waterways directly with open gulf water. Its excavation entailed the widening of the Intracoastal Waterway and the turning basin at the Industrial Canal junction. Like the earlier waterways, the MR-GO promised jobs and economic dividends; in actuality, it delivered little more than environmental degradation and urban hazard. This was demonstrated when Hurricane Betsy struck in September 1965, its surge inundating the four major hydrological sub-basins straddling each side of the man-made navigation canals. Hardest hit of all was the Lower Ninth Ward. Numerous Industrial Canal levee breaches along the Southern Railroad tracks, plus overtopping, deluged the poor, mostly black rear section of the neighborhood by three to five feet along St. Claude Avenue, and to nine feet along the back levee. Only the streets closest to the Mississippi River—present-day Holy Cross—evaded Betsy's deluge. Severe flooding damaged or destroyed thousands of homes and hundreds of businesses throughout the Lower Ninth Ward.[196]

The next thirty-five years saw the Lower Ninth Ward's population decline from its 1960 peak of over 33,000 (5 percent of the city's population) to under 19,500 (4 percent) by century's end. Once racially mixed, the neighborhood in 2000 was over 95 percent black. By no means was the Lower Ninth Ward the poorest or lowest-lying neighborhood of the city. It actually boasted a higher home-ownership rate than the city as a whole, and its lowest-lying areas (four feet below sea level) lay three to four feet *above* the lowest zones of Lakeview and Gentilly, and eight feet higher than the lowest spots in New Orleans East. Its riverside section (Holy Cross National Historic Register District) stood six to eight feet above sea level, and boasted sturdy, raised, historically significant homes mostly dating to the 1870s-1920s. Its rear section, particularly the blocks lakeside of Claiborne Avenue, possessed a humbler housing stock dating mostly from the 1920s-70s, many of which were built on concrete slabs at grade level. Isolated from public view, dismissed by the historical and architectural community, and plagued by the same social ills found throughout inner-city America, the rear sections of the Lower Ninth Ward seemed like a world unto itself—cherished by its residents, avoided by everyone else.[197]

At 5:00 a.m. August 29, 2005, Hurricane Katrina's low pressure and residual Category-Five storm surge penetrated the MR-GO/Intracoastal Waterway "funnel," overtopped meager levees, and introduced gulf water immediately behind the Lower Ninth Ward and St. Bernard Parish. Water stage rose dangerously in the Industrial Canal to fourteen feet above normal levels. Around 7:45 a.m., a massive section of floodwall collapsed and sent a violent torrent of brackish water eastward into Lower Ninth Ward homes. Shortly thereafter, the surge overtopped the rear levee and inundated the neighborhood from the north. More water surged westward from St. Bernard Parish. Flood levels rose by ten feet in twenty minutes. Scores of people, who either could not or would not evacuate, perished in their own homes under harrowing circumstances. Others climbed to attics or rooftops, even as their houses bobbed and drifted. Bloated gulf waters would continue to pour into the Lower Ninth Ward and every other hydrological sub-basin on the East Bank of Orleans Parish for days after the passage of Hurricane Katrina. By week's end, water levels stabilized at three to four feet deep in the highest areas of the Lower Ninth Ward, and ten to twelve feet or deeper in the lowest sections. For all the social tensions that existed between the Lower Ninth Ward and St. Bernard Parish, the two areas suffered sadly similar fates.

The federal levee failures induced by Hurricane Katrina and the preceding century of environmental deterioration altered utterly the destiny of the Lower Ninth Ward. The neighborhood ranked unquestionably as the hardest-hit of the entire metropolis, and, not surprisingly, was the last to see utilities, municipal services, and residents return. Two years after the storm, roughly one-quarter of the Holy Cross-area population and under 10 percent of the north-of-Claiborne section had returned, the two lowest return rates in the city.

The Katrina flood also brought great notoriety to the Lower Ninth Ward, rocketing it from local obscurity to worldwide infamy as the most beleaguered urban neighborhood in world's wealthiest nation. With the infamy came sympathy and concern, which in turn brought legions of advocates, researchers, church groups, student volunteers, documentary filmmakers, politicians, and the just-plain-curious to the once-ignored neighborhood. With its odd and ominous name, the Lower Ninth Ward seemed to bear witness and impart wisdom on a wide range of complicated and po-lemical topics. Poverty. Race. Social justice. Environmental deterioration. Geographi-cal risk. Global warming. Urban and cultural sustainability. Green architecture. Decent citizens nationwide fell into two schools of thought regarding the Lower Ninth Ward's future. Some viewed the entire region as equally at-risk and dependent on levees for flood protection, and interpreted the closing-down of heavily damaged, low-lying neighborhoods as an outrageous cultural affront that should be resisted on humanistic and economic grounds. They pointed to the Netherlands as a model for how to solve this problem. Others, who could not deny the scientific realities of soil subsidence, coastal erosion, and sea level rise, encouraged the densification of higher-elevation his-torical districts and the relinquishing of hazardous areas to nature. This school viewed massive Netherlands-style floodwalls as dangerously deleterious to coastal wetlands, which would further increase urban risk. To the outside world taking sides in the de-bate, the Lower Ninth Ward became a flashpoint, a symbol, a metaphor.

To the inside world of its residents, however, the Lower Ninth Ward repre-sented very different things. Family. Friends. Schools and churches. Heritage and leg-acy. Home.

The Make It Right Foundation's effort to develop affordable and environmen-tally sustainable housing in the Lower Ninth Ward—indeed, at the very site of the levee breach—stands at the nexus of these conflicting visions. No one vision is categorically false or improper; each one represents parallel truths and values, projected upon an unknowable future.

This much is certain: whatever progress the Foundation makes will influence the future transformation of the Lower Ninth Ward.

Geography of Urban Growth, 1788-2008

Explaining the patterns of New Orleans' expansion

Cities emerge either as planned endeavors or unplanned occurrences. The former are executed top-down by a centralized authority with the aid of engineers and surveyors, who lay out networks of streets and blocks. The latter derive from the bot-tom up, forming spontaneously as people aggregate at river confluences, heads of navi-gation, break-of-bulk points, road intersections, portages, valued resources, forts, and other convenient locales. Unplanned cities expand in irregular star-like patterns; only when permanency seems assured do they come under governmental authority—and planning.

New Orleans is the epitome of a planned town, conceived in 1717 by the Company of the West, initiated in 1718 by Bienville, and designed and surveyed in 1721-22 by Le Blond de la Tour and Adrien de Pauger. The community remained within that platted grid until 1788, when a catastrophic fire forced inhabitants to look beyond city limits for their growing numbers (see *Transformation by Conflagration*). From 1788 to the early 1900s, New Orleans expanded in a manner planned at the intra-subdivision scale, but unplanned at the citywide scale, guided invisibly by a series of conditions and unwritten "rules."

The first condition was *immediate adjacency to an already urbanized area*. The nature and scale of pedestrian traffic (read: minimized walking distances) encouraged new developments to occur quite literally across the street from existing ones. Faubourg Ste. Marie, New Orleans' first suburb, was laid out in 1788 immediately upriver from the original city, while the Faubourg Marigny was founded in 1805-06 directly below it. Faubourgs Duplantier, Solet, La Course, and Annunciation (1806-10) abutted Faubourg Ste. Marie once its blocks urbanized with parcels and structures. Faubourg Tremé (1810) also closely adjoined an established urbanized area, across the old fort line from the original city. Existing development, then, was a strong predictor of the location of future development—until new transportation systems altered spatial relationships.

Roads, canals, and railroads diminished the need for immediate adjacency, broadening the expansion "rule" to *accessibility*. Bayou Road allowed a tiny agricultural community to thrive at Bayou St. John about two miles away from the city since early colonial times, but it was not subdivided into Faubourg Pontchartrain (St. John, 1810) until the Carondelet Canal made it accessible to the old city. Navigation canals also made distant Spanish Fort and West End into lakefront mini-ports and resorts in the early- to mid-1800s. Ridge-following roads enabled development along present-day Metairie Road and Gentilly Boulevard years before the metropolis enveloped these areas. The Pontchartrain Railroad (1831) turned Milneburg into a busy lakefront port, while the New Orleans & Carrollton Railroad (1835) fueled the establishment of Lafayette, Jefferson, Carrollton, and other communities now comprising Uptown, which were at the time otherwise unattached to the city proper. With these new conveyances, New Orleanians could now live farther from the city center yet still partake of its attributes; real estate developers were more than eager to accommodate them.

In addition to adjacency and accessibility, land in New Orleans needed to be "high and dry" before urban development could occur. This important topographic rule restricted the city to the crescent-shaped natural levee of the Mississippi River, and to a lesser extent the smaller Esplanade and Metairie/Gentilly ridges, for most of its first two centuries. The natural levee crested at ten to fifteen feet above sea level near the riverfront (the "front-of-town") and sloped downward to uninhabited swamp and marshland which lay inches above sea level. The backswamp edge roughly aligned with present-day Claiborne Avenue during the era in question—a few blocks closer to the river in the earlier decades; a few blocks closer to the lake by 1900, as early drainage efforts took effect. Neighborhoods near the backswamp edge were generally known as the "back-of-town," a term still heard today.

Land also had to be legally acquirable for subdivision. Sugar plantations surrounded New Orleans; as the city spread, planters had to decide whether they could make more money by continuing to cultivate their holdings or by surveying them into blocks and selling the real estate. Nearly all eventually chose the latter—though at different times and with the service of various surveyors, who independently designed street grids into the long-lot plantations (see *Antecedent Cadasters, Antecedent Axes*).

A few government-owned commons also succumbed to private-sector development. The Canal Street corridor is one such example: for twenty-two years, it comprised a dusty commons between the old city (at present-day Iberville) and Faubourg Ste. Marie (at present-day Common Street—hence the name). It was finally subdivided in 1810, at an angle that unified the extant street grids of its neighbors.

A terrain's expansiveness and adjacency to the more prosperous, amenity-rich, desirable section of town also drove development patterns. Because of the broad point-bank meander of the Mississippi in uptown, natural levees there sprawled wider than those abutting the straight section of river flowing below the French Quarter. Developers thus had more fine land to subdivide uptown than in the lower city. Fortuitously, those same uptown areas were also physically adjacent to the economically vibrant and socially fashionable part of New Orleans. This was the American section, where English predominated, business and industry reigned, and American culture prevailed. Horsedrawn streetcars and hackney cabs transported uptown residents to their downtown offices and stores in St. Mary (anglicized from Faubourg Ste. Marie), now the city's economic and professional heart.

Uptown also benefited from a basic hydrological advantage over lower areas: refuse flows downriver. Areas upriver from the urban core thus evaded most of the local sewage, debris, carcasses, and other pollutants that ended up in the Mississippi. For this and aforementioned reasons, New Orleans grew faster, bigger, and grander in an upriver direction, compared to downriver or away from the river.

Downtown communities, by contrast, looked more toward a European past than an American future. This predominantly Creole and immigrant section mostly spoke French, practiced a religion that differed from the American norm, and culturally referenced the fading colonial worlds of France and Spain and their Caribbean sphere of influence. Granted, the lower city boasted its share of professional districts, fancy hotels, theaters, and other amenities, but they could not match those of St. Mary. The faubourgs carved from lower-city plantations were thus usually poorer and humbler—"the Poor Third," meaning the Third Municipality below Esplanade Avenue—than those uptown. Money and urban amenities tended to gravitate upriver; indigence and urban nuisances often ended up downriver (or away from the river). Planters who subdivided their lower-city parcels for urbanization saw little of the quick economic success enjoyed by their uptown counterparts; neighborhoods a mile below the French Quarter took sixty to eighty additional years to reach the urban-density levels realized by areas a mile above the Quarter as early as the 1810s. It is no coincidence that present-day Bywater is home to the last riverfront plantation home on the city's east bank—the Lombard House, which presided over one of the area's last agrarian riverfront parcels. It is also no coincidence that the Lower Ninth Ward ended up as one of the city's poorest and most isolated neighborhoods, and among to slowest to urbanize.

Thus nineteenth-century New Orleans steadily expanded upriver more so than downriver, as sugar plantations were subdivided into grids, transformed into low-density villages, merged municipally with New Orleans, and finally developed into modern urban garden-suburb environments. Albert James Pickett described this transformation in 1847, and, with varying degrees of precognition, projected the trend into the future. "The city proper," he wrote, measures

> five miles long [and] three-fourths of a mile wide. Then commences Lafayette [present-day Garden District and Irish Channel, which together with New Orleans proper] may be considered as one vast place.... After a succession of splendid mansions, farms, and other houses, the whole resembling a continued village, Bouligny [Napoleon Avenue area] and Carrollton unite with the chain of commerce. A century from this date, Orleans, like London, will [envelop] every town and hamlet for miles around, [becoming] the largest city on the continent of America, and perhaps in the world.[198]

Uptown's developmental success is reflected in the various adjustments of Orleans Parish's official borders. The upper limits of New Orleans expanded upriver six times between 1797 and 1874, from its original location along present-day Iberville Street to its final position on Monticello Street, over eight river miles upriver. The lower parish line, on the other hand, has *contracted* over the past 200 years, from the eastern marshes of what is now St. Bernard Parish to within a few hundred feet of present-day Jackson Barracks, three miles below the French Quarter.[199]

The city's geography of growth is also inscribed in its present-day municipal districts (not to mention its wards—see *Wards, Faubourgs, and the Perception of Place*). In 1836, ethnic tension between Anglo-Americans and Creoles resulted in the division of the city into three semi-autonomous municipalities. When that cumbersome system was abandoned in 1852, the three municipalities were renumbered and renamed "Municipal Districts," but they kept their geographical limits—and, to an extent, their political sub-cultures. That year also saw the annexation of Lafayette (formerly of Jefferson Parish) which became the Fourth Municipal District. Algiers (1870), Jefferson (1870) and Carrollton (1874) followed in annexation, becoming respectively the Fifth, Sixth, and Seventh districts of New Orleans but still maintaining some political self-identity. From this intra-urban parochialism emerged, among other things, the ability of each district to assess its own real estate taxes through seven separately elected tax assessors. This grossly inefficient multiple-assessor system, entrenched through generations of political patronage and unique among American cities—lasted into the twenty-first century. It took a citizens' revolt against government incompetence, mobilized in the wake of Hurricane Katrina by the grassroots organization "Citizens for 1 Greater New Orleans," to reform the system through a statewide constitutional amendment vote in 2006. The seven-assessor system, scheduled to end in 2010, is traceable to the seven separate political entities of the mid-nineteenth century, whose limits and enumerations cartographically summarize New Orleans' geography of urban growth.

One final criterion sorted the destiny of Orleans Parish lands for urban development. Areas closer to risky, noisy, smelly, unsightly or otherwise offensive nuisances and hazards—flood zones, railroads, canals, dumps, wharves, industry—tended to develop for lower-class residences and commercial or industrial land uses, while areas further from such sites attracted higher-end development for a more moneyed crowd. Housing for the city's poorest residents, usually African-American, was such a low priority for developers that other urbanization "rules," particularly for drainage and accessibility, carried little weight. This left the poor and the disenfranchised to settle in social and geographical isolation in the low-amenity, high-nuisance, high-risk back-of-town (see *"Two Centuries of Paradox"* and *The White Teapot*).

In the early twentieth century, progressive municipal activism and new technology radically rewrote the "rules" that drove the geography of New Orleans' urban growth. Engineers installed a world-class municipal drainage system to remove standing water from the lakeside lowlands, while concurrently augmenting artificial levee systems to prevent river and lake water from entering the city (see *Constraining and Controlling the River* and *"Drained Dry and Covered With Gardened Homes"*). The advances seemingly neutralized topography and hydrology as constraints on urban growth, allowing the city to spread northward to the lake then laterally to adjacent saline marshes. It was a pattern witnessed many times before and since: real estate interests and their government allies install flood-control devices in an uninhabited area; once the water is drained, street networks, transportation arteries, utilities, and residential and commercial development follow. People move in, buy into the value, nurture it, and seek to repeat the process into adjoining flood-prone areas. Before long, more and more people move closer and closer to danger. So secure were New Orleanians in their technological salvation from floods that the centuries-old tradition of building houses raised on piers was abandoned, after Word War II, for faster, cheaper slab-at-grade foundations.

By no means were drainage and flood control the only new "rules" guiding twentieth-century New Orleans; complex social phenomena involving race, class, crime, transportation, education, economics, lifestyle, cost of living, and gentrification also weighed heavily in driving metropolitan morphology from World War II to the early 2000s.

Hurricane Katrina and the ensuing deluge of 2005 reminded New Orleanians that the historical rules still warrant our attention—indeed demand it. Satellite images of Katrina's floodwaters bore a haunting resemblance to historical city maps. Neighborhoods spared the deluge occupied the same higher ground developed in the eighteenth and nineteenth centuries (dubbed "the sliver by the river"); areas inundated mostly comprised former backswamp developed in the twentieth century. Topography and hydrology had *not* been neutralized; building at grade level was a *terrible* idea. Levees and drainage had lured people off safer grounds and into dangerous ones—the so-called "levee effect," in which flood-control structures paradoxically increase flood damage by encouraging floodplain development. "Floods are 'acts of God,'" wrote geographer Gilbert F. White famously in 1942, "but flood losses are largely acts of man."[200]

If New Orleans is to attain environmental sustainability, its future urban geography must pay more attention to that of its past.

Populating the Landscape

Truly does New-Orleans represent
every other city and nation upon earth.
I know of none where is congregated
so great a variety of the human species,
of every language and colour.

Not only natives of the well known
European and Asiatic countries are here…
but occasionally Persians, Turks, Lascars, Maltese,
Indian sailors from South America
and the Islands of the sea, Hottentots, Laplanders,
and, for aught I know to the contrary,
Symmezonians.

—Joseph Holt Ingraham, 1835

Creolism and Place

The convoluted and controversial history of New Orleans' home-grown ethnicity

New Orleans is the only American city that can reasonably claim to have rendered its own ethnicity. Creole is a place-based ethnicity, as fundamental to the understanding of New Orleans as Hispanicism is to Latin America. Creole is also a complex, fluid, and controversial identity, whose definition varies on the axes of time, place, context, and perspective.

Most scholars agree that Creole is the anglicization, and *Créole* the gallicization, of *Criollo*, a noun derived from the Spanish verb *criar*, meaning *to create, to raise*, or *to breed*. Others cite a compatible Portuguese etymology. The *Academia Real Española* holds that the word was coined by early Spanish colonials in the West Indies "to refer to persons born of European parents in the islands as well as to locally born blacks."[201] Creole would come to describe those of Old World parents born upon New World soils, with no first-hand knowledge of the mother country. The notion diffused from the West Indian core as colonialism and slavery spread to the periphery of the Caribbean region. Louisiana represented the northern apogee of that cultural region, and to its shores Creole arrived soon after the establishment of French society in the early eighteenth century.

Creole remained a subtle and generally irrelevant identity in eighteenth-century New Orleans, because no outside threat compelled residents to unify around a common heritage. That changed in the early nineteenth century, when Saint-Domingue refugees, European immigrants, and most significantly English-speaking Protestant Anglo-Americans, arrived by the tens of thousands. Those of old colonial stock—described as "ancient Louisianians" by the territory's first American governor, William C. C. Claiborne—soon found themselves fighting against "modern Louisianians" (incoming Anglo-Americans, including Claiborne) for economic, political, and cultural sway in a city that was once entirely theirs.[202] From this native-versus-newcomer struggle (see *Nativity as Ethnicity in New Orleans*) arose a modified variation of Creole, now meaning *native-born*. Creoles in this era generally traced their ancestors to colonial times and exhibited the cultures of those Latin societies; they anteceded the era of American domination, forming the local population that newcomers "found" here upon arrival. Creoles of the early nineteenth century might be white, black or racially mixed; they were almost always Catholic and Latin in culture, and usually had significant amounts of French or Spanish blood. But they could also be of German, African, Anglo, Irish, or other origin, so long as they extracted from local society. "All who are born here, come under this designation [of Creole], without reference to the birth place of their parents," wrote Benjamin Moore Norman in 1845.[203] " 'Creole' is simply a synonym for 'native,' explained Joseph Holt Ingraham in 1835; "To say 'He is a *Creole* of Louisiana' is to say 'He is a *native* of Louisiana.' "[204]

Racial identification within the Creole ethnicity usually derived from context. Advertisements offering "Creole Slaves," including fourteen-year-old "Eugenie, creole…good child's nurse and house servant" and sixteen-year-old "Sally, creole…tolerable cook"[205] implied that these were black Creoles, while an article on Creole voting trends would indicate that these were white Creoles, because blacks were denied suffrage. The *gens de couleur libre* (free people of color—mixed in racial ancestry, Catholic in faith, and proudly French in culture) occupied a special caste between white and black, and were often described as Creoles of color, or simply Creoles, again depending on context.

Ethnic tensions between Creoles and incoming American emigrants and immigrants, on the rise since the Louisiana Purchase, underscored social, political, and economic life in antebellum New Orleans. As early as 1806, one visitor noted the newcomers' domination of lucrative positions: "Virginians and Kentuckeyans [*sic*]," he wrote, "reign over the brokerage and commission businesses, [while] the Scotch and Irish [conduct] exportation and importation…." Creoles seemed to be relegated to lesser functions: "the French keep magazines and stores; and the Spaniards do all the small retail of grocers' shops, cabants, and lowest orders of drinking houses. People of colour and free negroes, also keep inferior shops, and sell goods and fruits.[206]

The division peaked in the 1820s-30s. On one side was an uneasy alliance between Francophone Creoles, foreign French (that is, immigrants from France and refugees from Saint-Domingue), and Latin immigrants; as the numerical majority, this Catholic group maintained political and cultural control. On the other side were Anglophone Americans of Protestant religions, plus their allies, who enjoyed commercial dominance. Each group criticized the other's wielding of power and influence, not to mention their habits and idiosyncrasies. "There is, as everyone knows," wrote the English sociologist-philosopher Harriet Martineau in the 1830s,

> a mutual jealousy between the French and American creoles in Louisiana…. The division between the American and French factions is visible even in the drawing room. The French complain that the Americans will not speak French; will not meet their neighbors even half way in accommodation of speech. The Americans ridicule the toilet practices of the French ladies; their liberal use of rouge and pearl powder…. Till lately, the French creoles have carried everything their own way, from their superior numbers.[207]

After years of discord, the Americans in 1836 won legislative consent to divide New Orleans into three semiautonomous municipalities. Most Creoles and foreign French would be concentrated in the First Municipality (the French Quarter) and Third Municipality (below the Quarter, which also had a high immigrant population), while most Americans would govern themselves in the Second Municipality (above Canal Street, also home to many Irish and German immigrants).

From the perspective of the wealthier Second Municipality, the system fostered economic development and alleviated ethnic tensions. From the viewpoint of the mostly Creole-and-immigrant First and "Poor Third" municipalities, the arrangement engendered isolation and discord. "Had the Legislature sought, by the most careful efforts," wrote the Third Municipality's *Daily Orleanian* in 1849, "to create a war of races, to make distinction between Creole and American, they could not have chosen a better means for these objects, than the present division operates."[208] It was during this era that Canal Street assumed its legendary role as an ethnic Rubicon, strictly separating the allegedly warring factions with its symbolic "neutral ground." Yet city directories and census data indicate that while Anglos and Creoles did indeed outnumber the other in their respective districts, the ratio was roughly three-to-one in each case. In other words, exceptions abounded.

The municipality system proved inefficient and ended in 1852—but only after the Americans had allied with uptown German and Irish immigrants to guarantee numerical superiority over the Creoles. The reunified city was now under Anglo control; Anglos subsequently began winning city elections. "[T]he 'American' candidate for Mayor was elected by over 2,000 majority," reported the *New York Times* on citywide elections a few years later; "with the exception of two Assistant Alderman, the entire American Ticket was elected."[209] City Hall moved out of the Creole quarter and into the American sector; the fulcrum of commerce and publishing did the same; speakers of English increased their numbers; and Creole cultural influence gradually waned. "New Orleans has long been known as a 'very gay city,' " wrote the observant Swedish traveler Fredrika Bremer in the last year of the municipality system,

> but has not so good a reputation for its morality, into which French levity is strongly infused. This, however, it is said, decreases in proportion as the Anglo-American people obtain sway in the city. And their influence grows even here rapidly. The French population, on the contrary, does not increase, and their influence is on the decline.[210]

New Orleans society in the mid-nineteenth century moved steadily away from all that was Franco and Creole and toward that which was Anglo and American. In doing so, it gradually abandoned its traditional Caribbean-influenced notion of a racial "gradient" between black and white, an intermediary caste occupied by the free people of color and at least nine different combinations of white and black blood, not to mention Indian. In its place came a strict sense of racial separation, prevalent in the rest of Anglo-America. Ethnic tensions that once revolved around nativity now, in the 1850s, dwelled more and more on race. Some Creoles of color, bearing the brunt of the emerging new racial order, fled to the Mexican ports of Veracruz and Tampico.[211] Wrote Barbara Leigh Smith Bodichon in 1857,

> Every year the regulations concerning free negroes are more annoying. No sailors or cooks, etc. (if free coloured people) can land from the vessels unless by a pass from the Mayor and security from the Captain. No freed negroes can stay in the state unless born here and no free coloured people can enter, so that the free coloured population can only increase by birth…. It is a most unnatural state of things! I never was in a country where law interfered so wickedly with right."[212]

A few years later, the nation split into belligerent regional factions. Four years of violence ensued.

In the bitter aftermath of the Civil War, with emancipation and black Reconstruction government restructuring life in New Orleans, new tensions rose between whites and those of African ancestry. While the unquestioned hegemony of whites in antebellum times might have allowed for a certain level of "pan-racial creolism,"[213] in which peoples of different racial ancestries openly shared a common nativity-based ethnicity, such feelings dissipated after the South's crushing defeat. Embittered whites increasingly rejected "the racial openness of Louisiana's past"[214] and assumed a newfound antipathy toward blacks of all shades, regardless of ethnicity. White Creoles in particular, dreading suspicion of possessing traces of African blood, vociferously proclaimed the impossibility of a black Creole. Racial identification, once fluid and complex, increasingly polarized into black or white. The old nativity-based use of the word Creole inconvenienced the emerging postbellum racial order, necessitating a revisionist definition—one that revolved not around birthplace or local heritage, but around a very specific five-word criterion: *pure French or Spanish blood.*

Thus, many New Orleanians who had long identified themselves as Creole, particularly the descendents of the *gens de couleur libre*, were denied their heritage by the most influential voices of the day. Charles Gayarré, the famed white Creole narrative historian, lectured a Tulane University audience in 1885, "It is impossible to comprehend how so many intelligent people should have so completely reversed the meaning of the word *creole*, when any one of the numerous dictionaries within their easy reach could have given them correct information of the subject…. It has become high time to demonstrate that the Creoles of Louisiana … have not, because of the name they bear, a particle of African blood in their veins…."[215] In *The Creoles of Louisiana* (1884), George Washington Cable answered his question, "What is a Creole?" with "any [Louisiana] native, of French or Spanish descent by either parent, whose non-alliance with the slave race entitled him to social rank. Later, the term was adopted by—not conceded to—the natives of mixed blood, and is still so used among themselves."[216] Notwithstanding that definition, Cable would later cast doubt on the white racial purity of Creoles in his writings, earning him enemies in New Orleans high society and a famous feud with writer Grace King. Other "local color" writers carried the no-black-blood insistence into the twentieth century, while helping construe what historian Joseph Tregle would later describe as a quasi-religious belief in the mythological Creole—the genteel aristocrat, the charming romantic, the disdainer of physical labor, the *bon vivant.*

Word of the revised definition never quite made it to the masses, and mixed-race Francophone Catholics who had long thought of themselves as Creoles continued to do so. It was in this era that Rodolphe Lucien Desdunes (1849-1928), born a free person of color, penned *Nos Hommes et Notre Histoire*, the first history of New Orleans Creoles of color. It was written in French, published first in Montreal in 1911, and not fully translated to English and published in Louisiana until 1973.

Geographically, wealthier Creole families began departing the French Quarter around the 1860s. Some moved to the tony new garden suburbs of Esplanade Avenue in the 1850s; others lost their businesses and fortunes to the Civil War and left their mansions for humbler abodes in the lower faubourgs. The spacious townhouses they left behind in the French Quarter were often "cribbed" into tenement apartments, which attracted poor Sicilian immigrants to the neighborhood (dubbed "Little Palermo") in the late 1800s. Some Creoles of color, alarmed by the increasing racial tensions of the day, left Louisiana for Mexico, Haiti, Cuba, and France. By century's end, concentrations of Creoles in New Orleans shifted from the French Quarter, Tremé, and Marigny farther into the Fifth, Sixth, Seventh, Eighth, and Ninth wards, between the Mississippi River and the backswamp.

Louisiana's century-long transformation from the Caribbean-style fluidity of racial identification to the American sensibility of strict distinction culminated with the 1896 *Plessy v. Ferguson* Supreme Court decision, which legalized segregation of whites from those with any amount of black blood. Not coincidentally, the case involved a light-skinned Catholic Creole of color from Faubourg Tremé, Homer Plessy.

Creole would continue to evolve into modern times. Despite the safety of the revisionist definition, many white Creoles in race-conscious Louisiana gradually released themselves from explicit identification as Creole, removing all potential doubt of their whiteness by severing ties with the equally genuine Creoles of black and mixed-race backgrounds. Fewer whites unconditionally self-identifying as "Creole" meant that those who continued to embrace personally the term were more likely to have some African blood. In time, the popular understanding of Creole in the streets of New Orleans came to mean a Franco-African-American—a local person of mixed racial ancestry, usually Catholic, often with a French surname, often well-established in business and society, and always with deep roots in the city's Francophone history, particularly in the downtown wards.

Drainage technology installed around 1900 allowed urbanization to spread out of the historical riverside city and into the lakeside marshes. White Creoles, who by now rarely identified themselves unconditionally as Creoles and melded with whites of Anglo, German, Irish, Italian, and other ancestries, departed for new lakeside developments such as Lakeview and Gentilly in the 1910s-40s, and for Jefferson Parish later in the century. Some black Creoles departed for Los Angeles around World War II, seeking war-related jobs and escaping Jim Crow segregation. Those who remained tended to move from the old riverfront faubourgs lakeward into the Seventh, Eighth, and upper Ninth wards. Prompting this shift was the nationwide post-war preference for suburban living, the outlawing of racist deed covenants which excluded blacks from new subdivisions, and the structural and social decline of the inner city. Many Creoles, including much of the city's black middle and upper class, moved again in the 1970s-90s to the even newer suburbs of eastern New Orleans. The central Seventh Ward remains the neighborhood most associated with the modern-day Creole population.

The ranks of Creole thinned yet again during the Civil Rights Movement, which viewed Creolism as a divisive and elitist faction incompatible with the movement's goals.[217] That many Creoles of color descended from the *gens de couleur libre*, who often owned slaves and enjoyed a relatively privileged status, surely added to the tension. Forced to "choose sides" in the modern-day racial dichotomy, some Creoles departed for the West Coast; others "passed" for white (*passe blancs*); and most chose to declare their primary public racial identity as black or African-American. By the 1970s, many black New Orleanians of Creole ancestry, like their white counterparts earlier, abandoned public self-identification as Creole in favor of clear-cut black racial solidarity. They did so for fear of dividing the black community; whites had done so earlier for fear of being considered *part of* the black community.

The election of Ernest "Dutch" Morial—a Creole of color who could easily pass for white—as the city's first black mayor in 1977 solidified the newfound political unity of the Creole and non-Creole black communities. Recalled his son Marc Morial in 1994, who himself would serve as mayor for the next eight years, "At that time, the black community had historically been divided…between light-skinned blacks and dark-skinned blacks…Catholic blacks and Protestant blacks…uptown blacks and downtown blacks. My father's political genius was that he was able to convince the overwhelming majority of the black community that they had singular common causes…." (Morial's references to light-skinned downtown Catholic blacks are allusions to black Creoles—Franco-African-Americans, as opposed to the Anglo-African-Americans who tend to be darker-skinned Protestants who live uptown.) "The Creole experience," continued Sybil Morial, Marc's mother and the matriarch of the Morial family, "is a part of history and we should never deny our history. But in this time, *I think attempted designations today of who is Creole and who is not are totally irrelevant. I am an African-American, not a Creole…. Much that is good came from the Creole experience. But it also produced much that was bad, including artificial differences that were used to prevent black unity.*"[218] Most black New Orleanians shared that sentiment, and Creole faded from publicly expressed ethnic identity, even as the term (as an adjective, usually for food) was bandied about relentlessly by the steadily growing tourism industry. So depleted had grown the ranks of Creole by the late twentieth century that a 1998 anthropological paper on Creolism found it apt to proclaim in its opening sentence, "There is good reason to believe that there are creoles in Louisiana."[219]

Yet, as researcher Mary Gehman wrote, "to anyone who observes New Orleans social, political, and racial patterns, it is very clear that "Creole" is a term used frequently by blacks among themselves for those who carry on the names, traditions, family businesses and social positions of the free people of color…. Though rarely discussed in the media or other open forums, this intra-racial situation affects the politics, social order, jobs and businesses of the city in many ways."[220] Code words heard in the African-American community to refer to its Creole subset include "yellow," "high yellow," and the old French term *passé-blanc*.

Only recently has a Creole revival movement gained steam, inspired by the success of the Acadian (Cajun) resurgence of the 1970s-80s and by recent popular and scholarly interest in multiculturalism. Creole activists emphatically lay claim to their *own* identity—not European-American, not African-American, not some hyphenated race-based amalgam, but a unique ethnicity with its own names, dates, and legacies. They face ample challenges ahead, from both political activists intent on racial solidarity and cultural activists so sympathetic to the cause that they expand the definition of Creole to meaninglessly inclusive extremes.

Defining Creole, meanwhile, remains as contentious as ever. The discourse is as fascinating to observe as it is to participate in. People with absolutist inclinations tend to view social information—in this case the meaning of a word—as flowing from the top down (witness the aforementioned definitions offered by the *Academia Real Española* and Charles Gayarré), and dismiss any later modifications in word usage as mere misunderstandings made by ignorant masses (witness George Washington Cable's explanation). This school usually favors the "New-World-offspring-of-Old-World-parents" or the "pure-French-or-Spanish-blood" definitions, and sees the others as recent revisionism driven by politically correct academics. Other people, who have more relativist tendencies, tend to view word meanings as flowing from the bottom up—that is, driven by popular usage—and insist that those who write history simply *cannot* deny the ethnic heritage and identity claimed explicitly by hundreds of thousands of people and their ancestors. This school usually embraces the "native-to-New-Orleans" or the "Franco-African-American-Catholic-from-Louisiana" versions, and particularly disdains the "pure-French-or-Spanish-blood" criterion as racially motivated revisionism left over from the postbellum age. The Creole controversy is alive and well, intrinsic to Louisiana culture; it reveals as much about present-day society as it does about the past.

For those who *live* Creolism rather than debate it, the latest challenge may be the greatest: Hurricane Katrina's floods devastated the Creole-dominant neighborhoods of the Seventh, Eighth, and Ninth wards, scattering their residents nationwide. Two years after the catastrophe, only about half had returned. Time will tell if Creole ethnicity, borne of a sense of importance attached to being *from here*, can survive being elsewhere.

Extraordinary Multiculturalism, Extraordinarily Early

New Orleans as America's first genuinely multicultural metropolis

No city perhaps on the globe, in an equal number of human beings, presents a greater contrast of national manners, language, and complexion, than does New Orleans.

—William Darby, 1816

Q. They say that in New Orleans is to be found a mixture of all the nations?
A. That's true; you see here a mingling of all races. Not a country in America or Europe but has sent us some representatives. New Orleans is a patchwork of peoples.

—M. Mazureau, interviewed by Alexis de Tocqueville, 1832

Americans, English, French, Scotch, Spaniards, Swedes, Germans, Irish, Italians, Russians, Creoles, Indians, Negroes, Mexicans, and Brazilians. This mixture of languages, costumes, and manners, rendered the scene one of the most singular that I ever witnessed.... [They] formed altogether such a striking contrast, that it was not a little extraordinary to find them united in one single point. If there is a place [representing] the confusion of tongues at the Tower of Babel, it certainly is New Orleans.

—C. D. Arfwedson, 1834

Jews and Gentiles, the Frenchman, Italian, Spaniard, German, and American, of all conditions and occupations.... What a hubbub! what an assemblage of strange faces, of the representatives of distinct people! What a contact of beauty and deformity, of vulgarity and good-breeding! What a collection of costumes...!

—H. Didimus (Edward Henry Durell), 1835-36

When we state that in no city in the New or in the Old World is there a greater variety of nations represented than in [New Orleans], we are but asserting an established truism. New Orleans is a world in miniature, subdivided into smaller commonwealths, [in which] distinctive traits of national character are to be seen, and the peculiar language of its people is to be heard spoken.[221]

—*Daily Picayune*, 1843

The New Orleans market furnishes, perhaps, the best opportunity for the ethnological student, for there strange motley groups are always to be found. Even the cries are in the quaint voices of a foreign city, and it seems almost impossible to imagine that one is in America.[222]

—Nathaniel H. Bishop, 1879

That nineteenth-century visitors regularly marveled about New Orleans' ethnic diversity offers more than mere anecdotal evidence for the Crescent City's distinction in this regard. Such observers tended to be worldly, erudite, and, by the very nature of their waterborne arrival, usually familiar with other cosmopolitan ports. Their comments may thus reflect fair comparisons to many other great cities worldwide. They align with the assessments of prominent historians.

"Almost from the beginning," wrote the late Joseph Logsdon, "South Louisiana had a diverse population of Frenchmen, Germans, Italians, Indians, Africans, and Spaniards. It contained a mixed population well before Chicago, Boston, New York or Cleveland.... [New Orleans' diversity] amazed early travelers, [who] could find comparisons only in such crossroads of the world as Venice and Vienna."[223] Far more immigrants arrived to the United States through New Orleans—over 550,000 from 1820 to 1860, with 300,000 in the 1850s alone—than any other Southern city in the nineteenth century. For most of the late antebellum era, New Orleans ranked as the nation's number-two immigrant port, ahead of Boston and behind only New York.[224] Moreover, New Orleans "was an almost perfect microcosm...of the entire pattern of human movement into the United States prior to 1860."[225]

The diversity could be heard as well as seen: visitors often invoked the biblical

Babel in describing the mix of foreign tongues audible in the markets and streets. By one estimate, fully two-thirds of the city's population spoke no English fifteen years after Americanization.[226] "Louisiana was the most compactly multilingual place in the country," wrote English language scholar Richard W. Bailey; "Amerindian and African languages, Caribbean creoles, German, Spanish, French, and English were all routinely spoken by persons permanently resident in New Orleans—and the brisk trading along the levee brought still more languages."[227]

Numbers corroborate these assessments of New Orleans' superlative ethnic diversity. The 1850 Census, the first to record birthplace, shows that the city was home to more significantly sized ethnic groups (measured by ancestry, nativity, race, and enslavement status) than any other American city. That is, when we break major American cities' populations into the sub-groups tabulated by the 1850 census, seven groups in New Orleans each comprised at least 5 percent of the city's total population. No other city had more than five such groups.[228]

Adding also to the mix were thousands of American emigrants, who, extracted from nearly every state in the union, found themselves within their own country yet in a seemingly foreign culture. The Americans "have all nicknames," reported one 1838 account:

> There's the hoosiers of Indiana, the suckers of Illinoy, the pukes of Missuri [sic], the buckeyes of Ohio, the red horses of Kentucky, the mudheads of Tennessee, the wolverines of Michigan, the eels of New England, and the corn crackers of Virginia. All these, with many others, make up the population, which is mottled with black and all its shades, 'most of all supplied by emigration. It is a great caravansary filled with strangers, disperate [sic] enough to make your hair stand on end, drinkin' all day, gamblin' all night, and fightin' all the time.[229]

It may well be that New Orleans represented America's first genuinely multicultural metropolis—no small thing for a nation founded on the notion of pluralism and destined for an even more demographically diverse future. At the very least, New Orleans exhibited an extraordinarily high degree of diversity extraordinarily early in the nation's development. A writer around 1880 offered fairly accurate numbers on the city's various racial and ethnic groups, regardless of birthplace. He began with the obligatory visitor's rhapsody:

> What life in these streets! What a mingling of peoples! Americans and Brazilians; West Indians, Spanish and French; Germans, Creoles, quadroons, mulattoes, Chinese, and Negroes surge past us.... This manifold population includes some 70,000 French and Creoles, 30,000 Germans, 60,000 Negroes and mulattoes, and 10,000 Mexicans, Spanish and Italians. Therefore, the Anglo-Americans cannot number more than 80,000 or 90,000.... Each nationality moves in its own circles and mingles little with the others. Each has its [own] daily press....[230]

What impact did this diversity have on the city's character? Conventional wisdom today holds that multiculturalism in general invigorates and enriches societies, and, in the case of New Orleans, underlies nearly all of its distinguishing charms: food, music, architecture, etc. Popular consensus in the nineteenth century was, to say the least, decidedly more exclusionary, if not downright caustic. This correspondence from the *Boston Post* described New Orleans society in 1863:

> Instead of a healthy American population, speaking the language of Webster, we have gouging Jews, dark Spaniards, treacherous Sicilians, rat-catching Chinamen, lurking Creoles, lazy negroes, and a sprinkling of Yankees … bent on making a fortune.[231]

Frederick Law Olmsted, who distinguished himself with his inquisitive 1853-54 traveling study of the slave states before gaining fame as a landscape architect, reflected on New Orleans' multiculturalism with thoughtful ambivalence:

> I doubt if there is a city in the world, where the resident population has been so divided in its origin, or where there is such a variety in the tastes, habits, manners, and moral codes of the citizens. Although this injures civic enterprise … it [nurtures] individual enterprise, taste, genius, and conscience; so that nowhere are the higher qualities of man—as displayed in generosity, hospitality, benevolence, and courage—better developed, or the lower qualities, likening him to a beast, less interfered with, by law or the action of public opinion.[232]

Antebellum Ethnic Geographies
Residential settlement patterns from Americanization to the Civil War

People do not distribute themselves randomly across the cityscape. They gravitate toward areas that, first and foremost, offer available housing, and thence that are perceived to maximize their chances of success (in terms of housing, employment, services, amenities, convenience, safety, and existing social networks) while minimizing costs and obstacles (such as price, distance, crime, discrimination, noise, danger, and environmental nuisances). The resultant spatial patterns, which range from intensely clustered to thoroughly dispersed, vary dynamically by group, place, and time. This essay describes New Orleans' ethnic geography during antebellum times, when American emigration and foreign immigration rendered New Orleans arguably the most diverse city in America. The next essay investigates turn-of-the-twentieth-century patterns.

In pre-industrial cities, prosperous members of charter groups usually resided in the inner city, with domestic servants and slaves living in adjacent quarters, and middle- and working-class families residing in a ring of adjacent neighborhoods. Indigents, among them immigrants, tended to settle at the city's ragged outskirts or waterfronts. The pattern is an ancient one—"in many medieval cities in Europe, the city centres were inhabited by the well-to-do, while the outer districts were the areas for the poorer segments of the population"[233]—and it carried over to New World cities. Lack of mechanized conveyances drove the pattern: pedestrian-scale movement made inner-city living a convenient and expensive luxury, which spatially sorted the classes and castes into certain residential-settlement patterns.

In antebellum New Orleans, the charter groups mostly comprised the upper classes of French Creole (as well as *Français de France*) and Anglo-American society, who tended to live in townhouses in the French Quarter and the Faubourg St. Mary, respectively. Observed Elisée Réclus in 1853, "The oldest district of New Orleans, the one usually called the French Quarter, *is still the most elegant of the city,*" where houses had been "mostly purchased by American capitalists."[234] We see evidence of this pattern today: the central French Quarter is replete with opulent antebellum townhouses, often ornamented with expensive iron-lace galleries.

Encircling the highly desirable commercial/residential inner core was an annulus of middle- and working-class blocks in the lower and rear fringes of the French Quarter (where, to this day, we see a humbler cityscape of cottages and shotgun houses) plus adjacent faubourgs. Further out, along the wharves, canals, backswamp, and upper and lower fringes of the city, lay a periphery of muddy, low-density village-like developments—shantytowns in some places. Here resided thousands of immigrants and other working-class and poor, including manumitted blacks. During the first great wave of immigration to New Orleans (1820s to 1850s, corresponding to national trends), laborer families mostly from Ireland and Germany arrived by the thousands and settled throughout this semi-rural periphery. They predominated in the riverside upper fringe (upper Faubourg St. Mary and into the adjacent city of Lafayette), the backswamp around the turning basins of the New Basin and Old Basin canals, and the lower faubourgs (the "Poor Third" Municipality).

First-person witnesses to antebellum ethnic geographies abound. Wrote the influential *Commercial Review* editor J. D. B. De Bow in 1847, "immediately [beyond] the corporate limits of New Orleans,...Lafayette has been chiefly settled by a laboring population, mostly German and Irish emigrants, who literally fulfil the scriptural command of eating their bread in the sweat of their brow." Farther away from the riverfront's nuisances and closer to the convenient new passenger streetcar line on what is now St. Charles Avenue, a more languid urban environment emerged, and with it a different ethnic composition:

> But [the laboring population] is not the only class which is pouring into this
> rapidly advancing city. The rear of Lafayette is most beautifully situated for
> dwelling-houses. The ground is high and dry, and vegetation flourishes...
> with amazing luxuriance. Here are collected many of our wealthy citizens,
> who have built handsome villas, with gardens and large yards....[235]

In those "handsome villas" lived, more often than not, Anglo-Americans who grew wealthy pursuing port-city opportunities and erected palatial homes on spacious lots in the American manner. This portion of old Lafayette is today's well-preserved

Garden District; the section by the river now comprises the modern-day Irish Channel, whose functional housing stock enjoyed far less appreciation—and preservation— over the years.

The enigmatic moniker "Irish Channel" first appeared in print in 1893. In that year, seventy-three-year-old Capt. William H. James recollected that in the 1830s, poor Irish immigrants settled primarily along or near the banks of the New Basin Canal at the rear edge of the Faubourg St. Mary; around present-day Gallier Hall in the heart of St. Mary, and

> at and above Tchoupitoulas and Canal streets. To this quarter was the given the name, probably as a souvenir of the land of their nativity, of the 'Irish Channel.' Here dwelt many engaged in the work of hauling cotton and Western produce.[236]

Geographically, James is describing Irish settlement in the rear, upper, and riverside fringes of antebellum New Orleans. Thomas K. Wharton witnessed the second of these demographic patterns at an 1854 New Year's Eve mass at St. Teresa of Avila Church on Camp Street:

> Passing by the church of St. Teresa on our way from St. Mary's market, all Ireland seemed to be streaming from its portals. It is astonishing how large an element [the Irish] form in our resident population.... A stranger from Dublin or Londonderry might fancy himself quite at home again in our streets....[237]

Irish and Germans shared remarkably similar residential settlement patterns. So German was the area between present-day Howard Avenue and Felicity Street— which includes the aforementioned highly Irish area near St. Teresa's—in 1843 that the *Daily Picayune* (using "Dutch," a corruption of *Deutsch*, to mean "the natives of Holland, Prussia, and all the German States") wrote,

> [Y]ou will see nothing but Dutch faces and hear nothing but the Dutch language, every word as rough as a rock of granite... This part of the city is so thoroughly Dutch that the very pigs grunt in that language; you may well imagine yourself to be on the precincts of Amsterdam."[238]

Even the heart of the Irish Channel, around Adele Street in Lafayette, teemed with as many Germans as Irish. Wrote H. Didimus (Edward Henry Durell) in 1835-36:

> The city of Lafayette is busy behind me—a mere suburb of rusty, wooden houses; on my left I hear a confused Babylonish dialect, sounds harsher than harshness, the patois, provincialisms, and lingual corruptions of all the Germanic tribes—it is the German quarter....[239]

Abraham Oakey Hall made passing reference in the late 1840s to immigrant settlement patterns and their relationship to underlying Creole/Anglo geographies:

One section of New Orleans, the First Municipality, is the old city, left to the tender mercies of the French and Creole population; narrow, dark, and dirty (meaning either their city or the people). One, in the Second Municipality, the new city; with here a little of Boston, there a trifle of New York, and some of Philadelphia.... The third section a species of half village, half city, (unmistakable in its French Faubourg look,) is given over to the tender mercies of the Dutch and Irish, and the usual accompaniments of flaxen-polled babies and flaxen-tailed pigs.[240]

As Hall sailed upriver from New Orleans, he noticed the changing land use, housing density, and ethnic composition of the city's upper periphery:

We swept by the city. A mile or so of shipping to eye, with here and there some caravanserai [inns for transients]...cotton-yards...and...houses [with] longer separation between them. Here was Lafayette [present-day Jackson at Tchoupitoulas], the asylum of anglicised Dutchmen....[241]

While the immigrants of the semi-rural periphery congregated more in certain areas and less in others, rarely did they cluster intensely and exclusively. While they generally avoided the inner city, rarely were they wholly absent from any particular area. Intermixing predominated: the so-called Irish Channel was home to many Germans and other groups, just as Little Saxony near the lower-city riverfront housed as many Irish and Creoles as Saxons. Like the Milky Way galaxy, the patterns formed greater and lesser concentrations overlaid on top of each other, with no intense clusters and no complete absences. Why?

Low-skill employment in this era—dock work, flatboat wharf jobs, warehousing, stockyard and tannery work, rope walks, public-works projects, canal excavation, railroad construction—lay scattered throughout the outer fringe, rather than among the offices and shops of the exclusive inner core. Slaves once were assigned these grueling and dangerous hard-labor tasks, but because they yielded higher profit on sugar plantations, a niche opened for poor unskilled immigrants. Between the 1830s and 1840s, white immigrants mostly from Ireland and Germany took most of the unskilled labor, dock worker, drayman, cabman, domestic, and hotel servant jobs from blacks (both free and enslaved).[242] While some of the better working-class jobs existed downtown, the lion's share of hard-labor jobs were on the outskirts. Also there was cheap, low-density, cottage-scale housing, which fortuitously afforded open lots for "truck farming," a favorite extra-income activity particularly among Germans. Immigrants of the antebellum era thus avoided the inner city for its lack of unskilled-labor employment, its high real estate prices and crowding, and because mechanized transportation (early horse-drawn streetcars) for commuting was limited and costly. Better-off Irish and Germans, who likely arrived earlier (such as the "lace-curtain" Irish establishment of the Julia Street area), worked in downtown-based professions and lived in costly downtown dwellings; they generally blended in with charter groups and rarely rubbed shoulders with their poorer, recently arrived brethren.

People born in France comprised the third-largest immigrant group in antebellum New Orleans, followed by smaller numbers from a wide range of southern European and Latin lands, such as Spain, regions within modern-day Italy, Cuba, Mexico, Haiti, West Indian islands, and Central and South America. These Catholic peoples of the Latin world usually settled in the working-class neighborhoods on the lower, Creole side of New Orleans, below the central French Quarter. With the exception of some "foreign French," Latin-culture Catholic immigrants were uncommon in predominantly Anglo-culture uptown. Much of the rest of the world, from Scandinavia to China to India to the Philippines, contributed at least some immigrants or transients to antebellum New Orleans society.

The antebellum geography of New Orleanians of African ancestry consisted of enslaved blacks intricately intermixed with the white population, while free people of color predominated in the lower half of the city. Anecdotal evidence of these patterns comes from an 1843 article in the *Daily Picayune*:

> The Negroes are scattered through the city promiscuously; those of mixed blood, such as Griffes, Quarteroons, &c., [Creoles of color] showing a preference for the back streets of the First [French Quarter, Faubourg Tremé] and part of the Third Municipality [Faubourg Marigny and adjacent areas].[243]

Urban slavery drove this pattern: the enslaved were kept in close quarters by their enslavers, for reasons of convenience and security (see *"Two Centuries of Paradox"*).

The ethnic geography of antebellum New Orleans, then, comprised:

- a commercial nucleus around the upper Royal and Chartres intersections with Canal Street;
- a mostly Creole and Francophone-culture populace below that commercial nucleus, local in nativity, Latin in culture, Catholic in faith, French in tongue, and white or mixed in race;
- a mostly Anglo-culture populace living above the commercial nucleus, born in the North or the upper South, Protestant (and in lesser part Jewish) in faith, English in tongue, and white in race;
- elite residential living (townhouses) in the inner cores of both the Creole and Anglo sections;
- slaves and domestic servants residing in close proximity to wealthier residents of both the Creole and Anglo sections, often in quarters appended to townhouses;
- a widespread dispersion of Irish and German immigrants throughout the periphery and waterfronts of the city, particularly Lafayette and the Third District, with very few living in the inner city;
- smaller numbers of southern European and Caribbean immigrants, particularly French, Italians, and Haitians, settling in the Creole area for its language, culture, and Catholic environment;
- a poor free black (manumitted slave) population along the backswamp edge.

The antebellum dispersion pattern explains why, to this day, the precise location of the Irish Channel remains a hotly debated subject, and why no one particular neighborhood claims a German sense of historical place. (It is hard to pin down the exact location of a dispersed phenomenon.) The antebellum clustering of the wealthy in the inner city is also evident today: elegant townhouses outnumber humble cottages in the French Quarter, while the reverse is true in the adjacent faubourgs of Marigny and Tremé. Racially, one of the most fascinating spatial patterns of antebellum times was the numerical predominance of free people of color over slaves in the Creole lower city, and the exact reversal of this ratio in the Anglo upper city.[244] This trend reflects the Creole adherence to the Caribbean-influenced three-tier (white, free people of color, and enslaved black) racial caste system, versus the Anglos' recognition of a strict white/ black dichotomy.

Some of these demographic patterns persist today. The Franco-African-American descendents of the free people of color, for example, generally remain downtown, particularly in the Seventh Ward, while Anglo-African-Americans predominate uptown, mainly in Central City. Immigrant settlement patterns, however, changed markedly as American cities, including New Orleans, came of age in the late nineteenth century.

The Rise and Fall of the Immigrant Belt

Residential settlement patterns around the turn of the twentieth century

The millions of southern and eastern Europeans who arrived to the United States (and the thousands who came to New Orleans) during the second great wave of immigration, 1880s to 1920s, encountered a rapidly changing urban landscape. Industrialization, the installation of urban streetcar networks, and the rise of centralized, high-rise business districts triggered two important repercussions.

First, in New Orleans, the gentry moved out of the inner city and resettled in "garden suburbs," particularly along St. Charles Avenue, uptown, Esplanade Avenue, and the City Park area. In some cases, wealthy families departed their opulent townhouses because they lost their fortunes to the Civil War or struggled economically in its aftermath; in other cases, they simply moved away from new urban nuisances and risks, and toward new amenities. Unsightly and smelly breweries, warehouses, and sugar refineries arose in the French Quarter in this era, a block or two from once-elegant mansions. Faubourg St. Mary began to look less like a faubourg and more like a congested downtown. Inner-city living lost its appeal. With convenient new streetcar lines affording rapid access to professional jobs in downtown offices, one no longer had to prioritize for pedestrian access in choosing where to live. Why not move to a spacious new Victorian home in a leafy suburban park? This exodus, which can be traced to the 1830s-50s but was mostly a postbellum trend, opened up scores of spacious inner-city townhouses as potential apartment housing for working-class folk. As recently as 1939, fully 78 percent of the city's antebellum-era dwelling units were occupied by tenants rather than owners, and most of these units were located in or near the inner city.[245]

Second, employment opportunities for the unskilled poor moved from the semi-rural periphery, where they existed in the agrarian days before the War, to the urban core, where postbellum modernization created new opportunities. Labor-intensive jobs disappeared from the periphery because those very lands were being developed into the garden suburbs for the relocating upper class, and because much of the needed infrastructure (canals, railroads) was already in place. Whereas an 1830s Irish laborer might have been drawn to the backswamp to dig a canal, or an 1840s German worker to the Lafayette wharves to unload flatboats, a Sicilian, Russian, Polish, or Chinese immigrant in the 1890s gravitated downtown to market housewares, peddle fruit, prepare food, or sell notions. Newly arrived immigrants not only had a reason to settle close to downtown, but an affordable apartment to rent there as well (see map, "Racial and Ethnic Geographies of Early 1900s New Orleans").

Thus, unlike their antebellum predecessors, immigrants of the late nineteenth century eschewed the semi-rural periphery, favoring instead to live in a concentric zone of neighborhoods immediately beyond the inner commercial core. This "immigrant belt" offered enough advantages (proximity to work, convenience, housing) to make life easier for impoverished newcomers, but suffered enough nuisances (crowded conditions, decaying old building, noise, vice, crime) to keep the rent affordable. It offered to poor immigrants a place to work, a nearby and affordable abode in which to live, and (after an enclave developed) a social support haven including religious and cultural institutions. The immigrant belt ran loosely from the lower French Quarter and Faubourg Marigny/Bywater, through the Faubourg Tremé and into the Third Ward back-of-town, around the Dryades Street area, through the Lee Circle area and toward the riverfront in what is now called the Irish Channel. In this amorphous swath, immigrants and their descendents clustered well into the twentieth century, such that their enclaves earned popular monikers ("Little Palermo," "Chinatown") or strong people-place associations, such as "the Orthodox Jews of Dryades Street" or "the Greeks of North Dorgenois Street."

Although ethnic groups clustered more intensely in the postbellum immigrant belt than in the antebellum semi-rural periphery, ethnic intermixing still predominated. With the exception of certain black back-of-town areas, rare was the block or neighborhood in which only one group could be found. Page after page of census population schedules record Sicilians living next to African-Americans, Irish sharing a double with Greeks, Filipinos living across the street from Mexicans—even in enclaves in which a particular group numerically predominated. Ethnic intermixture is an integral childhood memory of most New Orleanians who came of age prior to the 1960s, and it is striking how often this observation arises in their reminiscences.

The postbellum era also saw the migration of thousands of emancipated slaves into the city from nearby plantations. Victims of disdain, discrimination, and destitution, their settlement patterns were driven in large part by the geography of environmental hazards and nuisances. Flooding, mosquitoes, swamp miasmas, noisy railroads, smelly wharves and canals, industries, pollution, odd-shaped lots, lack of city services, inconvenience: these and other objectionable circumstances drove down real estate prices and thus formed the lands of last resort for those at the bottom rung. The natural and built environment of New Orleans dictated that most nuisances monopolized the two lateral fringes of the metropolitan area: the immediate riverfront and the backswamp edge. Poor African-Americans, the majority of who were culturally Anglo rather than Creole, clustered in these troubled areas, particularly the back-of-town, while others settled within walking distance of their domestic employment jobs in uptown mansions. Creoles, particularly those of color, remained in their historical lower-city location, and migrated lakeward as drainage technology opened up the backswamps of the Seventh Ward and adjacent areas. Other sections of the new lakefront subdivisions laid out in the early twentieth century explicitly excluded black residency through racist deed covenants. By that time, wealthier whites resided in the convenient, low-nuisance swath sandwiched between the riverfront and the backswamp (particularly along the St. Charles/Magazine corridor), and in the new lakeside neighborhoods, while working-class whites intermixed throughout the front-of-town.

New Orleans prides itself on its uniqueness, sometimes to the point of extolling peculiarities where none exists. In fact, the Crescent City's ethnic distributions mimic those of other American cities, from antebellum times to today. The expression of immigrant enclaves, wrote one social geographer, commonly "takes the form of a concentric zone of ethnic neighbourhoods which has spread from an initial cluster to encircle the CBD"[246]—very much what occurred in New Orleans. In *Cities and Immigrants: A Geography of Change in Nineteenth Century America*, David Ward stated that researchers are "generally able to agree that most immigrants congregated on the edge of the central business district, which provided the largest and most diverse source of unskilled employment."[247] The concentric-ring phenomenon is standard material in urban-geography literature, where it appears diagrammatically as Ernest W. Burgess' classic "Concentric Zone Model," part of the so-called Chicago School of Urban Sociology, which first viewed cities as social ecosystems in the 1920s. According to Burgess' model, a theoretical city's central business district was surrounded first by a "zone in transition," then a "zone of workingmen's homes," a "residential zone," and finally a "commuters' zone." In that transitional zone could be found "deteriorating…rooming-house districts" and "slums," populated by "immigrant colonies" such as "Little Sicily, Greektown, Chinatown—fascinatingly combining old world heritages and American adaptations." "Near by is the Latin Quarter," Burgess added, "where creative and rebellious spirits resort." In the "zone of workingmen's homes," Burgess predicted Germans, German Jews, and other second-generation immigrants to settle, and in the residential and commuter zones, he foresaw restricted residential districts and bungalow suburbs.

Burgess had Chicago in mind when he devised his Concentric Zone Model, but to a remarkable degree, he could have been describing circa-1900 New Orleans. Little Palermo, Chinatown, the Greek area, and the Orthodox Jewish neighborhood all fell within Burgess' transitional zone (which I am calling the "immigrant belt"). Germans, German Jews, Irish, and other earlier immigrants and their descendents settled in the workingmen's zone (former Lafayette, the Third District, and other areas of the old semi-rural periphery). And Burgess' restricted residential zone and commuter zones describe the leafy garden suburbs (also known as "trolley" or "streetcar suburbs," for the developmental role played by that conveyance) of uptown, Esplanade Avenue, Lakeview, and Gentilly—right down to the bungalows. Even his Latin Quarter model found local representation: "creative and rebellious spirits" have long gravitated to the French Quarter.[248]

In the closing decades of the twentieth century, the factors that once drew immigrants to that amorphous belt around the CBD diminished or evaporated entirely. They reappeared in different and distant form: in the new subdivisions and strip malls of suburbia. Immigrants in New Orleans today—few in number but enough to form residential patterns—generally settle far away from the inner city, in the extreme western suburban periphery of Kenner (home of "Little Honduras"), or Versailles in extreme eastern Orleans Parish ("Little Saigon"), or to the fringes of the West Bank. Others live in Metairie and elsewhere in Jefferson Parish. It is in these modern ranch-house/strip-mall suburbs that new immigrants find affordable housing, maximized economic opportunities, and minimized obstacles, including a decent environment to raise and educate their children. Once again, New Orleans is not alone in this remarkable trend: it is playing out in most major American metropolises. "In 1900," stated a recent *Preservation Magazine* cover article entitled *The New Suburbanites*, "immigration meant taking a ferry from Ellis Island to a tenement on the Lower East Side. Today, it often means taking the airport limo to a three-bedroom house in the suburbs."[249] A drive along Williams Boulevard in Kenner finds a plethora of Latin and Asian businesses, an ethnic "suburbscape" that makes downtown New Orleans look homogeneous by comparison. "Suburbs are on their way to becoming the most common place of residence for Hispanic- and Asian-Americans;" as of the late 1990s, 43 percent of the nation's Hispanics, and 53 percent of Asian-Americans, called suburbia home, and the trend has only strengthened in the decade since.[250]

That most immigrants in greater New Orleans prior to Katrina lived in relatively comfortable suburban conditions attests to the fact that while this metropolis attracted few people from foreign lands, most who did come were fairly economically stable and arrived into established and nurturing social networks. Pre-Katrina New Orleans simply did not offer a sufficiently robust economy to attract large numbers of poor immigrants; thus its old inner-city immigrant belt vanished and most newcomers opted for suburban lifestyles. An inspection of a 2000 census map of greater New Orleans' ethnic groups (recorded as "ancestry") shows an even dispersion throughout the metropolitan area *beyond* old New Orleans. Immigrants today—Hispanics and Asian Indians in Kenner, the Chinese of West Esplanade Avenue in Metairie, the large Vietnamese community of the Versailles neighborhood, the Filipinos on Lapalco Boulevard on the West Bank[251]—generally reside at the very fringes of the metropolitan area. Ironically, they often live next door to descendents of circa-1900 immigrants; West Esplanade Avenue in particular abuts a number of census tract in which high concentrations of locals of Italian, Greek, Chinese, and Jewish ancestry may be found.

So utterly reversed is the present-day ethnic geography of New Orleans that formerly lily-white Metairie—Fat City, no less—ranked in 2000 as the most ethnically diverse census tract in the metropolitan area. Even more stunning was the least diverse tract: the Lower Ninth Ward, once practically the Brooklyn of the South.[252] The same trend is seen in public schools: most in New Orleans are racially homogeneous (overwhelmingly African-American), whereas those in the once all-white suburbs are now held up as "exemplars of successful integration."[253] Equivalents of this statistical irony can be found in most other modern American metropolises. "So vast is the change taking place in the suburbs of many of our cities that the definition of suburbia needs rewriting."[254]

Hurricane Katrina added a new twist to the history and geography of immigration to New Orleans. Extensive opportunities in the construction trades attracted thousands of poor migrant workers—overwhelmingly male, predominantly from Mexico, and many undocumented—to the city and region. An extreme shortage in housing in late 2005-06 forced many workers to live in tents in parks and parking lots, or in cars and abandoned houses. Others lived in distant towns and commuted in the beds of pick-up trucks. By 2007, as flooded houses returned to the rental market and rents declined somewhat, Katrina immigrants began to settle in a dispersed fashion, including in the flood-affected region. The cityscape reflected their presence: workers queued at rendezvous to await day jobs; signs in Spanish appeared outside home-improvement stores; taco trucks set up at busy intersections; Latin American foods made their way into local cuisine; schools started accommodating Spanish-speaking youngsters; and the *Times-Picayune* began running its want ads (*Empleos*) in Spanish.

It remains to be seen what percentage of these workers, who are doing the lion's share of the heavy lifting in the rebuilding of New Orleans, will settle permanently into local society—and write the next chapter of the ethnic geography of New Orleans.

"Two Centuries of Paradox"

The geography of the African-American population

Embedded in the complex geography of New Orleans' African-American community are multitudes of historical and recent influences. Among them, to name a few, are the city's Franco-Afro-Caribbean heritage, urban slavery, Civil War and emancipation, Southern race relations, urban amenities and nuisances and their corresponding land values, and the catastrophe of the Katrina flood. The modern city, as a result, exhibits a spatial distribution of African-Americans that is *de facto* segregated in many ways, yet still more racially integrated than many major American cities.

Premier among the antebellum black settlements was the so-called "back-alley" pattern. Urban slaves often labored as domestics and resided in the distinctive slant-roof quarters appended behind townhouses and cottages. Other enslaved blacks, many of them skilled craftsmen and artisans, lived in detached quarters on back streets and alleys, close to the abodes of their masters. This settlement pattern imparted an ironic spatial integration into New Orleans' antebellum racial geography, despite the severe and oppressive social segregation of chattel slavery. Not unique to New Orleans, the intermixed back-alley pattern has been documented in other urban slave centers, such as Charleston, Washington, and Baltimore.[255]

Slaves accounted for roughly two-thirds of the African-ancestry population of antebellum New Orleans; *gens de couleur libre* (free people of color) comprised most others. Many members of this somewhat privileged mixed-race caste, a product of the city's Franco-Afro-Caribbean heritage, excelled in professions, studied abroad, and gained middle- or upper-class status. Some even owned slaves. Throughout most of the antebellum era, more free people of color called New Orleans home than any other Southern city, and occasionally more than any American city, in both relative and ab-solute terms. Their presence helped distinguish New Orleans and Louisiana society from the national norm. "It is worthy of remark," read an 1856 article in the *New York Times*,

> that this class of population, free colored persons, should be so differently regarded in Louisiana from any other of the Southern States.... [They have] acquired a *status* and influence unknown in any other city, even in the Free States.... [O]ne in eleven [in New Orleans work as] clerks, doctors, drug-gists, lawyers, merchants, ministers, printers and teachers... It will thus be seen that the free colored population of New-Orleans are acquiring an as-similation to the whites in education and influence, (whether for good or evil, is the problem) superior to that of any other State or city.... It is a sub-ject of study for the philosopher, the philanthropist, and the statesman.[256]

Spatially, this notable population clustered in the lower French Quarter, Bayou Road, the faubourgs Tremé, Marigny, New Marigny, Franklin, and those making up the present-day neighborhood of Bywater. Why here? This was the Francophone, Catholic, locally descended (Creole) side of town, a social environment largely created by free people of color (as well as white Creoles) and more conducive to their interests. The mostly Anglophone Protestant world on the upper side of town was not only culturally foreign terrain, but its white inhabitants were oftentimes more hostile to the very no-tion of a free person of color.

The antebellum geography of black New Orleans, then, consisted of slaves in-tricately intermixed citywide—"scattered through the city promiscuously," as the *Daily Picayune* put it in 1843—and free people of color predominating in the lower neigh-borhoods.[257] With the minor exception of the back-of-town, where very poor manu-mitted blacks and others lived in squatter-like huts, there were no expansive, exclusively black neighborhoods in antebellum New Orleans.

New Orleans' black population surged by 110 percent between the censuses of 1860 and 1870, bracketing the trauma of Civil War and emancipation. It rose another 54 percent by the turn of the century.[258] Caught up in its own woes, the unwelcoming city nevertheless offered better opportunities to freedmen than the sugar fields. In 1870, black men, who made up one-quarter of the labor force, worked 52 percent of New Orleans' unskilled labor jobs, 57 percent of the servant positions, and 30 to 65 percent of certain skilled positions.[259]

Where were these emigrants to settle? Unaffordable rents and racially antagonistic neighbors prevented the freedmen from settling in most front-of-town areas. The townhouses in the inner city, recently vacated by wealthy families, had since been subdivided into low-rent apartments, but these hovels were more likely to be leased to poor immigrants than to poor black emigrants. Nor could the freedmen easily take refuge in the downtown neighborhoods of the former free people of color, who often scorned the freedmen as threats to their once relatively privileged (but now rapidly diminishing) social status.

Destitute and excluded, most freedmen had little choice but to settle in the ragged back-of-town, where urban development petered into amorphous low-density shantytowns and eventually dissipated into deforested swamps. The back-of-town offered low real estate costs because of its environmental hazards, urban nuisances, inconveniences, and lack of amenities and city services. Together with many local ex-slaves who also found themselves, for the first time, seeking their own shelter, the freedmen joined those blacks already settled at the backswamp margin in the formation of the city's first large-scale, exclusively black neighborhoods. Concurrently, emancipation diminished the "back-alley" intermingling pattern of black residency in quarters behind white abodes. (Irish and German servants had already replaced many domestic slaves in the 1850s, turning "slave quarters" into "servants' quarters.") The city's back-of-town grew increasingly black in both absolute and relative numbers, while the front-of-town became more white.

Yet complicating patterns persisted from earlier times. Creoles of color continued to choose their neighborhoods on their terms, for reasons of tradition, family, religion, culture, convenience, economics, or real estate, and usually remained on the downtown side of the city. Other black families, whose fathers worked on the docks and wharves, settled near the riverfront for its proximity to the port. Others settled in areas that, unlike the low-lying back-of-town, lay high on the natural levee and free from flood threat—but whose other environmental nuisances nevertheless rendered them less desirable and lower in rent. These areas included blocks near wharves, battures, mills, warehouses, factories, industrial sites, dumps, cemeteries, hospitals, and particularly along canals and railroad tracks. Still others settled in uptown clusters that have been described as "superblock" patterns (see *The White Teapot*).

Thus, even as the city's racial geography gradually disaggregated after the Civil War, it remained far more spatially heterogeneous than those of Northern cities. The German geographer Friedrich Ratzel noticed the pattern in 1874, a decade after emancipation, and offered three hypotheses:

> New Orleans has a larger colored population than Charleston or Richmond, but you would not believe it if the statistics did not say so—*so much less is the distance separating these people from the whites*. This is partly because

of the great preponderance of mulattoes (who call themselves "yellow"...
as opposed to "black"...), partly because of prosperity that prevails in these
circles, and partly, though not least of all, *because the French in Louisiana
never set themselves off so strictly from their slaves and freed men as the Anglo-
Americans did in the other slave states.*[260]

Two national trends around the turn of the twentieth century further spatially
disaggregated New Orleans' heterogeneous racial geography. One commenced—or
rather climaxed—with *Plessy v. Ferguson* in 1896. That landmark Supreme Court decision (on a New Orleans-based case) to legalize "separate but equal" statutes represented the culmination of decades of increasing racial tension in the wake of emancipation,
as well as a major final act in the century-long process of Americanizing New Orleans'
old Franco-Caribbean Creole culture. Legally sanctioned racial segregation would affect real estate sales, deed covenants, access to public schools, jobs, public housing, and
nearly every other aspect of life.

The second trend entailed the Progressive Era, which, in New Orleans and
elsewhere, brought significant improvements to municipal services: water distribution,
sewerage, public health, electrification, telephony, transportation, and most importantly for this deltaic city, drainage and flood control. These technologies "neutralized"
the lakefront's low elevation and waterlogged terrain as sources of environmental risk,
and allowed modern amenities to be extended into the former backswamp. Automobiles arrived serendipitously, followed by modern transportation arteries. Developers
eagerly built new subdivisions—Lakeview and Gentilly, for example—in the spacious,
modern California style, quite the antithesis of the antique housing stock that predominated in the rest of the city. They also installed racist deed covenants explicitly prohibit-
ing sale or rental to black families.

The new subdivisions were a hit. During the 1910s-40s, middle-class white
families, formerly residents of the historical front-of-town, "leapfrogged" over the black
back-of-town and settled in the low-lying, whites-only lakeside subdivisions. The intricately intermixed racial geography of old had further disassociated; in the two generations since emancipation, white and black New Orleanians had moved away from each
other *en masse*. The trend would only strengthen.

Tremendous social transformations forged new racial relationships in mid- to
late-twentieth-century New Orleans. Chief among these were *Brown v. Board of Education* (1954), the Civil Rights Act of 1964, and the ensuing desegregation of public facilities, integration of public schools, and overall increased opportunities in education,
employment, and housing for African-Americans. Jim Crow disappeared with less violence and resistance here than other Southern cities; black and white New Orleanians
subsequently found themselves working, shopping, and dining together in increasing
numbers. Yet *living* together did not necessarily follow the trend; in fact, residential
integration diminished. Suburban-style subdivisions in lakefront and eastern New Orleans, in Jefferson, St. Bernard, and St. Tammany parishes, even as far as coastal Mississippi, drew white New Orleanians by the tens of thousands between the censuses of
1960 and 2000. Middle-class African-Americans, for their part, mostly moved lakeward

to the neighborhoods east of City Park and thence into the subdivisions of eastern New Orleans. The greater New Orleans metropolitan area, by century's end, had racially dichotomized into a white west and a black east, with notable exceptions traceable to historical times (see maps, "1939-1960-2000 Metro New Orleans Population"). Greater New Orleans' racial geography by the early 2000s ironically formed more segregated spatial patterns than it did in the early 1800s. "Two centuries of paradox" is how one researcher described the phenomenon.[261]

Perhaps the most pernicious driver of *de facto* racial segregation began as a progressive federal and city government program designed to help the poor. Following the U.S. Housing Act of 1937, the Housing Authority of New Orleans (HANO) cleared a number of old neighborhoods, replete with nineteenth-century architectural gems but considered unsightly slums at the time, to make room for subsidized housing for poor families. Three-story, common-wall brick apartments, tastefully designed to reflect local architectural style and scale, were built in geometrical arrangements among grassy walkways and oak trees. In accordance with the Jim Crow laws of the day, each complex was racially segregated: two white-only developments were higher in elevation and closer to the front-of-town, while the four black-only projects occupied lower-elevation areas in the back-of-town. The complexes were expanded following the Housing Act of 1949. After desegregation of the projects in the 1960s, whites promptly left the units for affordable-living alternatives in working-class suburbs, and poor blacks took their places. Within a few years, tens of thousands of the city's poorest African-Americans became intensely consolidated into a dozen or so projects, all of which were isolated from adjacent neighborhoods and cut off from the street grid. With that concentrated poverty came the full suite of social pathologies, including fatherless households, teen pregnancy, government dependency, drug trading, gang activity, and incessant violent crime. (Whether the projects bred and exacerbated social ills, or merely concentrated them, is a matter of ongoing debate.) So bad did matters get by the 1990s that the federal government, which had come to view public housing as warehouses of indigence and cyclers of dependency, intervened. The new philosophy, encapsulated in a controversial scheme named Project HOPE ("Homeownership and Opportunity for People Everywhere"), called for the demolition of the most troubled projects and their replacement with mixed-income New Urbanist communities, in which subsidized rental units for the poor abutted market-rate rentals and purchasable homes aimed at modest-income families. The HOPE philosophy rested on two geographical notions: that a physically improved and aestheticized place creates a better society, and that class intermixing restrains delinquency and dependency among the poor. (While both concepts are subject to varying levels of debate, among geographers and the public in general, most agreed that the public-housing *status quo* could not continue.) In the early 2000s, amid vocal opposition but with the overwhelming support of the general population, the solidly built structures of the St. Thomas, Desire, Fischer, and other projects were demolished and redeveloped with pastel-colored New Urbanist designs. Opponents read bitter irony into the policy, noting that New Orleans' circa-1940 housing projects, with their modest scales, airy verandahs, and shady courtyards, seemed to embody New Urbanist principles a half-century before the term was coined. Paralleling Chicago's Cabrini Green and Atlanta's East Lake experiments with mixed-income public housing (which really did replace ugly, dehumanizing high-rises), New Orleans' grand social experiment got under way.

Hurricane Katrina interrupted that experiment in 2005, and rendered the HOPE effort even more polemical amid the postdiluvian housing shortage of 2006-07. When HUD and HANO proceeded with pre-storm plans to demolish and rebuild the circa-1940s C. J. Peete, St. Bernard, B. W. Cooper, and Lafitte projects, a small number of extremely vociferous activists challenged the effort as designed to deny poor, displaced African-Americans their right to return to the city. Given the housing shortage and high homeless population of the time, their case rested upon the bird-in-hand-is-worth-two-in-bush argument: why destroy existing high-quality housing stock when the promise to redevelop it may not be kept, and when basic financing had not yet been secured? Those favoring the demolition pointed to forty years of deteriorating structural and social conditions as sufficient reason to proceed with HOPE. They also noted that many refurbished HANO apartments had failed to attract tenants, indicating that displaced residents were *not* being denied their wish to return. While the public-housing residents in question were overwhelmingly black, both sides in the controversy claimed the full range of the city's racial and class diversity among their supporters; the dispute explicitly did not break down along race and class lines.

Contending that the projects represented failed policies which concentrated poverty, incubated social pathologies, and produced intergenerational dependency, the agencies insisted on proceeding with the HOPE concept (though they did agree to stagger the demolition and reconstruction so that some residents could return as work progressed). All that kept the bulldozers from rolling was the approval of the City Council and mayor. The controversy climaxed on December 20, 2007, when the City Council, amid violent scuffles inside and outside City Hall, unanimously voted to approve the demolitions. Mayor Nagin concurred, and in early 2008, signed off on the demolition permits. By spring of that year, the C. J. Peete, St. Bernard, and B. W. Cooper projects lay in rubble, while Lafitte awaited the same fate. Plans currently entail replacing the "Big Four" complexes' 4,500 units with 3,343 subsidized apartments, 900 market-rate apartments, and another 900 homes for sale.[262] Because New Orleans' public-housing population is about 99 percent black, the eventual success or failure of the HOPE vision will deeply influence the city's future racial geographies.

Katrina's flood shattered the centuries-old geographies of African-American New Orleanians. Nearly all of their population of 324,000 dispersed nationwide after the excruciating debacle that started with the hurricane's strike on August 29, 2005, deteriorated immeasurably with the federal levee failures, and ended when the last stranded residents were evacuated in early September. Approximately 221,000 black New Orleanians—more than two-thirds—lived in areas that were deeply and persistently flooded.[263] Those who lived in unflooded areas—particularly home-owners—generally returned by mid-2006 and continued those historical settlement patterns, while those who flooded—particularly renters—continue to face unraveled lives, uncertain futures, and likely displacement after generations of local lineage. By summer 2006, fewer than 90,000 black New Orleanians had returned, equaling the city's black population in the year 1910. That figure is contested because of the difficulty of measuring population in a society recovering from a major catastrophe. The American Community Survey of 2006 estimated the city's black population at 131,441, still about 60 percent below its pre-Katrina size.[264] Whatever the actual figure, New Orleans' African-American population and its total population both increased over the next two years, but at diminishing rates. A comparison of voting records from the 2003 and 2007 gubernatorial elections revealed that black voters in Orleans Parish declined by over 54 percent (84,584 to 38,738), while white voters decreased by 27 percent (46,669 to 33,937). Voter turnout is by no means a perfect indicator of population (for which we will have to wait until the 2010 Census), but it is a fair surrogate. Most studies show that New Orleans will remain majority African-American, but by a slimmer margin than before the storm. The demographic shift will affect New Orleans' culture, economics, and politics. "The city now has a more racially balanced electorate," said political scientist Ed Chervenak. "The days when local candidates could appeal to Orleans' overwhelmingly black electorate and receive a handful of white votes to win office may be a thing of the past."[265]

The shift will also affect the city's human geography. Earlier upheavals, such as the Civil War, occasioned the region-wide concentration of African-Americans into New Orleans. Katrina, as of 2008, has had the reverse effect, scattering them throughout the region and nation. Time will determine the permanency of the New Orleans black Diaspora, and what intricate historical settlement patterns—the historical intermingling, the downtown Creole cluster, the old back-of-town, the riverfront concentration, and the ongoing paradox of residential segregation amid social integration—will persist.

The White Teapot

Explaining a peculiar demographic pattern

Map out nearly any socio-economic data about New Orleans—election returns, income, family size, population density—and an odd, teapot-shaped cartographic feature emerges (see map, "The 'White Teapot'"). The plotted statistics correlate to an underlying racial geography: a contiguous swath of historical neighborhoods, stretching from Carrollton to Bywater, comprises only 10 percent of the city's human-occupied footprint, but houses 42 percent of its white population (58,000 out of 136,000 in 2000).[266] How did this demographic pattern form?

Explaining the origins of the "white teapot" draws heavily on three realities: (1) urban amenities, geographical hazards, and environmental nuisances are not evenly distributed across the New Orleans cityscape; (2) the white population on average has always been better educated, more privileged, and significantly wealthier than the black population; and (3) many whites have passively discouraged, actively excluded, or simply fled from black neighbors, particularly in the mid- to late-twentieth century.

When uptown developed in the nineteenth century, hazards and nuisances and other undesirables that people did not want in their backyards predominated at the extreme ends of the natural levee. Toward the rear lay the swampy, flood-prone, mosquito-infested backswamp, while along the immediate riverfront were malodorous wharves, noisy railroads, warehouses, and work yards. The middle ground in between—a few blocks either side of the Royal Street/St. Charles Avenue/Prytania Street corridor—lay far enough from the backswamp to buffer its environmental risks, and just as far from the riverfront wharves and railroads to abate their unpleasantness. When investors installed the New Orleans & Carrolton Rail Road—present-day St. Charles Streetcar Line—through this middle ground in 1833, they both reflected and reinforced the desirability of this middle corridor. Building a costly commuter rail along busy riverfront wharves would not create upscale residential real estate, and locating it along the backswamp edge would make even less sense. By running it down present-day St. Charles Avenue, the engineers created a new urban amenity in an area that already enjoyed environmental advantages. Wealthy families soon started building ample homes along and near St. Charles Avenue, particularly in the Garden District, which formed in the 1830s-50s between St. Charles and Magazine. The proverbial "other side" of St. Charles Avenue (quite literally "the other side of the tracks") would have been too close to the swamp, while the "other side" of Magazine came too close to the riverfront wharves. Simpler abodes arose in those areas, and humbler folk occupied them.

In this deltaic Southern metropolis, where urban landscapes were not all homogenous and people were not all treated equally, those with the financial wherewithal—usually whites— gravitated to better-drained, lower-nuisance, lower-risk zones, which had higher property values. Those without the means—usually blacks—had to make do with low-rent marginal lands. Poor people, particularly recently emancipated African-Americans, settled in large numbers along the backswamp (present-day Central City), where land and housing were cheap. Working-class families of all backgrounds settled along the riverfront, in places such as the Irish Channel. Builders erected housing stock accordingly—substantial homes in the desirable area, simple cottages elsewhere—which, of course, reinforced the pattern, since no affluent family would move into a hovel and no poor family could afford a mansion. Thus, by the latter decades of the nineteenth century, the teapot's "spout"—the predominantly wealthy, mostly white, amenity-rich corridor buffered on both sides from undesirables—started to form.

The 1884 World's Industrial and Cotton Centennial Exposition initiated a building boom of leafy "streetcar suburbs" around what would become beautiful Audubon Park. Next door to that urban oasis came the graceful campuses of Tulane and Loyola universities (1894-1910), adding further appeal to the neighborhood. It did not hurt, also, that nearby Carrollton occupied a slightly higher and wider swath of the natural levee, giving the area added protection from floods. These factors all drove up property values. By World War I, well-off whites predominated throughout the greater Carrollton/Universities/Audubon Park area, with some notable exceptions. The "kettle" of the teapot had formed.

Those few exceptions tell a geographical story of their own. Because many blacks worked as domestics for wealthy uptown whites, they (together with working-class whites) often settled in small cottages and shotgun houses developed in the "nucleus" of "superblocks"[267] outlined by the great mansion-lined avenues such as St. Charles, Louisiana, Napoleon, and Carrollton. Those avenues were developed for upper-class residential living because of their spaciousness, magnificence, "see-and-be-seen" perches, and proximity to streetcar service; smaller streets within the nucleus of the avenue grid were built up with much cheaper housing stock. The grand avenues thus formed a "lattice" of upper-class whites around cores of working-class blacks and whites, who oftentimes worked as domestics in those nearby mansions and conveniently walked to their jobs.

Later in the twentieth century, working- and middle-class whites departed for the suburban parishes in greater numbers than did blacks or wealthy whites. Formerly mixed neighborhoods of longshoremen along the river became almost entirely black, as did the uptown "superblock nuclei" and the once-integrated Sixth, Seventh, Eighth, and Ninth wards of downtown. Increasing percentages of African-Americans in areas surrounding the white teapot, and decreasing percentages therein, had the effect of sharpening the spatial delineation of this demographic feature.

Finally, the recent gentrification of historical neighborhoods around Coliseum Square, Faubourg Marigny, and Bywater brought whites into areas that had been mixed or majority-black in prior decades. This extended the teapot's "spout" nearly all the way to the Industrial Canal. The curious feature, traceable to the late 1800s, thus came into its present-day form by the latter decades of the 1900s.

What impact does the white teapot and the surrounding majority-black areas have on the New Orleans cityscape? Since white New Orleanians earn roughly double the average household income of African-Americans, the teapot spatially correlates with patterns of myriad socio-economic phenomena: politics, property values, single-parent homes, average monthly rent, blighted housing, crime, health and education disparities, and more. It even correlates with nativity, one of the few social characteristics that does *not* correlate well with racial geographies elsewhere in the metropolis (see *Nativity as Ethnicity in New Orleans*).

The teapot's impact, then, is dramatic. Crossing streets like St. Claude in Bywater (tip of the spout) or St. Charles/Carondelet in the Lower Garden District (trunk of the spout) takes a pedestrian across distinct race and class lines, and into strikingly different cityscapes. Guide books routinely warn tourists exploring the French Quarter not to exit the demographic pattern (though never so bluntly and not in those terms), while many African-Americans feel equally unwelcome and suspect upon entering it. So distinct are the urban characteristics within and beyond the white teapot that the two areas almost seem like sub-cities, separate communities that happen to abut each other, but otherwise do not interact.

Vertical Migration

Residential shifts from higher to lower ground

Nearly all New Orleanians lived above sea level for most of the city's first two centuries. Those higher natural levees abutting the Mississippi River offered sturdier, better-drained urbanization opportunities, not to mention proximity to the lucrative riverfront, compared to the low-lying backswamp. The cypress swamp and saline marshes close to Lake Pontchartrain, low as they were, had not yet been choked off from adjacent water bodies by levees and pumps, and thus remained at or near their original sea-level elevations. Those few people who did live along the lakeshore and marshes still resided at or close to the level of the sea, usually in raised wooden "camps." Into the early 1900s, well over 90 percent of the more than 300,000 people in New Orleans resided above sea level (see map, *Vertical Migration: Population Distribution with respect to Topographic Elevation*, 1700s-2000).

That era saw the augmentation of the artificial levees, the excavation of the outfall canals, and the installation of the Wood screw pumps and associated municipal-drainage apparatus. Soon, the flood-protected and runoff-drained lowlands transformed from seemingly useless backswamp into developable real estate, even as it subsided. "The entire institutional structure of the city was complicit" in the ensuing urbanization of the lowlands, wrote local historian John Magill; "developers promoted expansion, newspapers heralded it, the City Planning Commission encouraged it, the city built streetcars to service it, [and] the banks and insurance companies underwrote the financing."[268] New Orleanians, convinced that the topographical and hydrological factors that once constrained them to the natural levee had now been neutralized by technology, migrated enthusiastically off the natural levee and settled into trendy new suburbs with names like Broadmoor, Fontainebleau, Gentilly, and Lakeview. Popping up along the new orthogonal street grids and spacious suburban lots were thousands of California bungalows, Spanish Revival villas, English cottages, Midwestern ranch houses, and other homes of non-native architectural styles. Into those abodes moved thousands of families. Between 1920 and 1930, nearly every census tract lakeside of the Metairie/Gentilly Ridge *at least* doubled in population. Low-lying Lakeview saw its population increase by about 350 percent, while parts of equally low Gentilly grew by 636 percent. Older neighborhoods on higher ground, meanwhile, lost residents: historic faubourgs Tremé and Marigny dropped by 10 to 15 percent; the French Quarter declined by one-quarter. The high-elevation Lee Circle area lost 43 percent of its residents, while low-elevation Gerttown increased by a whopping 1,512 percent.[269] Similar figures could be cited for the 1910s and 1930s-50s.

The 1960 census recorded the city's peak population of 627,525, roughly double the number at the beginning of the century. But while over 90 percent lived above sea level in 1900, only 48 percent remained there in 1960. Fully 321,000 New Orleanians had "vertically migrated" off the high lands near the Mississippi to the low lands near the lake—which had, by this time, subsided by a number of feet below sea level.[270]

Subsequent years saw tens of thousands of New Orleanians migrate *horizontally* as well. They departed Orleans Parish neighborhoods for social and economic reasons, not for any sense of environmental hazard. In some areas, the demographic exodus occurred dramatically, stoked in large part by the school integration crisis of 1960-61. "I remember Midnight Mass, 1962," recalled one resident of the Irish Channel; "[t]hey had to close Constance Street to traffic because the crowd was spilling out of [St. Alphonsus] church onto the street. By 1964, it was all gone," so quickly had those parishioners decamped for the suburbs.[271] Fifteen years later, St. Alphonsus closed for lack of a congregation. Similar stories played out citywide. In all, the Crescent City's population dropped by 23 percent from 1960 to 2000, representing a net loss of 143,000 mostly middle-class whites to adjacent Jefferson, St. Bernard, and St. Tammany parishes or beyond. Testifying to the level of unimportance ascribed to topographic elevation—and implicitly the level of faith in drainage and flood-control technology—most white-flighters unknowingly moved vertically onto lower (or low*ering*) ground even as the sprawled out horizontally.

Suburban exodus coupled with urban sprawl *within* Orleans Parish meant that remaining residents were literally putting more distance among themselves. In 1960, 627,525 New Orleanians lived mostly on 36.8 square miles of occupied neighborhoods (excluding parks, cemeteries, campuses, undeveloped marshes, and other non-residential areas), equating to 17,053 people per square mile. By 2000, only 484,674 lived on 66.7 square miles, a density of 7,266 per square mile.[272]

Within the remaining Orleans Parish population, 121,000 New Orleanians—many of them middle-class blacks—internally migrated vertically, from higher historic neighborhoods to low-lying subdivisions mostly in New Orleans East. Within the span of a century, New Orleans' above-sea-level population, in relative numbers, declined from over 90 percent in the early 1900s, to 48 percent in 1960, to 38 percent in 2000. In absolute figures, the above-sea-level population remained steady at around 300,000 from the early 1900s to 1960, then dropped to 185,000 by 2000.

Hurricane Katrina's surge wreaked disproportionate havoc on the same below-sea-level regions to which hundreds of thousands of New Orleanians confidently flocked decades prior. Two years after the catastrophe, the portion of the New Orleans population residing above sea level increased to 50 percent—12 percentage points higher than in 2000 and 2 percentage points more than 1960.[273] By another measure, 55 percent of the city's 143,825 households receiving mail as of February 2008 (a fair but not perfect indicator of repopulation) lay above sea level.[274] Relative numbers thus seem to show that New Orleanians are shifting back to higher elevation.

Absolute numbers, however, tell a different story. Above-sea-level areas, despite their less-damaged status, still lost tens of thousands of residents since the storm. Although that population decline represents a much smaller drop than below-sea-level areas (which diminished by over 100,000), it indicates that New Orleanians after Katrina are *not* flocking to higher ground. The increased percentage now living above sea level mostly reflects the slower repopulation pace of harder-hit low-lying areas, more so than a renewed social value placed on higher ground. Even those wishing to move uphill oftentimes find themselves stymied by insurance stipulations, Road Home restraints, and a tight real estate market, and resign themselves to rebuild in place. If any elevation-related historical tradition regained popularity since the storm, it's raising structures above the grade, not clustering on higher ground.

These figures will change as the recovery progresses. Not until the 2010 and 2020 censuses will we learn with reasonable confidence to what extent New Orleanians stay put, rebuild, or vertically or horizontally migrate again.[275]

New Orleans' Ethnic Geography in a National Context

Similarities and distinctions compared to other American cities

Wrote geographer Peirce F. Lewis, "it is easy to conclude…that New Orleans' urban growth…obeyed special rules which applied only to it—and nowhere else. It is a tempting conclusion, but untrue."[276] Indeed, an important lesson to be drawn from New Orleans' shifting ethnic and racial geographies is that they generally parallel those observed elsewhere. The correlation of African-American and other minority and poor populations with areas of high environmental risk and nuisance areas has been documented far and wide, spawning the environmental justice movement. Likewise, the centrifugal pattern of immigrant settlement in antebellum times, the centripetal clustering in the turn-of-the-century era, and the centrifugal suburban settlement of recent decades have all been witnessed in other large American cities. Ernest W. Burgess' classic "Concentric Zone Model" (see *The Rise and Fall of the Immigrant Belt*) was among the first (1920) to describe the concentric patterns of class and ethnicity around American cities' central business districts. Burgess' investigation of Chicago's early-twentieth-century ethnic geography revealed striking parallels to those of New Orleans in the same era.

Nevertheless, some unusual aspects distinguish New Orleans' experience from the norm. The Crescent City is arguably the oldest genuinely multicultural city in the nation, and may well have witnessed certain ethnic spatial patterns before other cities replicated them on grander scales. Its Franco-Hispanic colonial heritage, deeply influenced by Afro-Caribbean cultures and further rendered by sheer isolation, spawned the enigmatic notion of Creole, a home-grown ethnicity that in time would manifest itself spatially in New Orleans. (How many cities render their own ethnicity?)

Sudden political Americanization, followed by gradual cultural Americanization, would create perhaps the greatest ethnic-geographical chasm in New Orleans history: the downtown Creoles and the uptown Anglos. This underlying dichotomy informed the residential geographies of numerous other groups: Saint-Domingue refugees, foreign French, and Italians, for example, gravitated to the Creole side, while Jews, Scandinavians, and emancipated African-Americans settled on the Anglo side.

New Orleans was also one of the few places in the United States to harbor a three-tier racial caste system (white, free people of color, and enslaved black), which further differentiated Creole/Anglo ethnic geographies. The Creole side of town, for example, exhibited a three-to-one ratio of free people of color to slaves in 1860; the Anglo side of town had the exact opposite.[277]

Physical geography also differentiated New Orleans' experience: the city's deltaic topography constricted urbanization to the narrow natural levee between riverfront wharves and the backswamp, creating a bifurcated environment in which empowered groups gravitated to the more desirable middle ground, and the disenfranchised poor clustered along the troubled margins. These aged patterns—akin in theory, if not in form, to the cinturónes de miséria (misery belts) surrounding Latin American capitals—remain vividly apparent in modern racial distributions. In some areas today, the interface between black and white neighborhoods (such as Central City and the Garden District) marks the edge of the backswamp at the time of emancipation. Most cities have natural barriers that restrict expansion, but New Orleans' backswamp formed an adjustable constraint: with drainage, it receded and eventually disappeared, leaving behind its imprint in the distributions of humanity. Soils of the former backswamp also subsided substantially, giving New Orleans a dynamic vertical dimension to its residential settlement patterns—a claim few other cities can, or would want to, make.

How does New Orleans' racial geography compare to other American cities? It depends on how one measures integration and segregation. One tool is the "dissimilarity index," which calculates the percent of one group that would have to move to another geographical unit (block, census tract, etc.) to match the distribution of the other group. Perfect integration produces a dissimilarity index of zero, while a completely segregated city would measure 100. Most large American cities have dissimilarity indices in the 60s, 70s, and 80s, meaning that roughly three out of four people of one group would have to relocate in order to integrate with the other group.[278] Compared to the nine largest American cities in which nonwhites outnumber whites, New Orleans' dissimilarity index of 70.6 ranked more integrated than those of Chicago (87.3), Atlanta (83.5), Washington, D.C. (81.5), Philadelphia (80.6), Cleveland (79.4), and Baltimore (75.2). Only Memphis (68.6) and Detroit (63.3) produced lower (more integrated) indices.[279] Looking to other American cities, New Orleans ranked more integrated than New York (85.3), Miami (80.3) Boston (75.8), Houston (75.5), and Los Angeles (74.0), not to mention nearby Baton Rouge (75.1) and other prominent cities. But three Southern ports most historically comparable to New Orleans—Mobile (63.3), Pensacola (65.3), and Charleston (63.8)—ranked more integrated than the Crescent City. Perhaps, in these data, we are seeing vestiges of the ancient "back-alley" pattern (see "Two Centuries of Paradox") persisting in these oldest Southern entrepots. According to these measures, the popular impression of a relatively high level of racial integration in New Orleans proper (albeit much less than it used to be, and perhaps not as much now after Hurricane Katrina) seems founded.

The ethnic geographies of New Orleans are notable, too, vis-à-vis the city's cultural source regions. This was a city that looked not to England and northern Europe to people its land and inform its society, as did most elder cities of this nation, but to France and Spain, the Caribbean, Latin America, and Africa. This was a Catholic city in a Protestant nation, a mixed legal jurisdiction in a land of English common law, and a historically racially intermixed society in a nation traditionally divided strictly between white and black. New Orleans represented the expanding American nation's first major encounter with sophisticated, urban foreignness. From the perspective of *America's* ethnic geography, then, New Orleans indeed plays a starring role.

It has been said that America Americanized New Orleans. But it may also be said that New Orleans Americanized America.

Roofscapes of downtown New Orleans, 2003-2007.
Bottom photo by Ronnie Cardwell; all others by Richard Campanella.

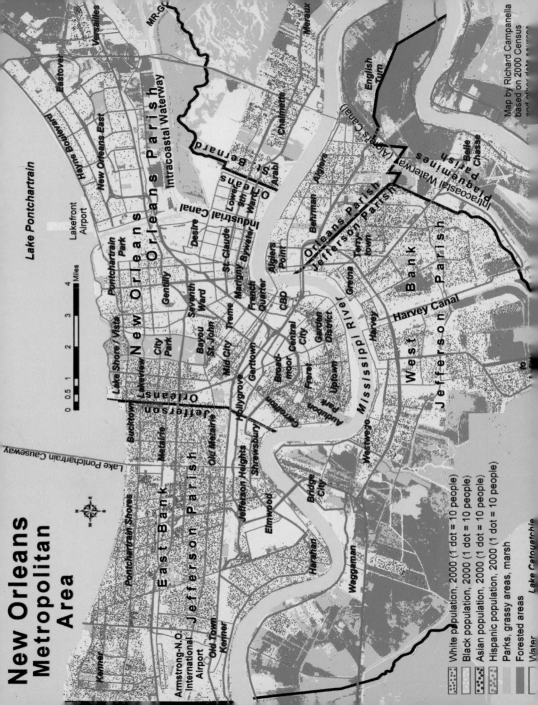

New Orleans Metropolitan Area

Lake Pontchartrain

Lake Pontchartrain Causeway

0 0.5 1 2 3 4 Miles

White population, 2000 (1 dot = 10 people)
Black population, 2000 (1 dot = 10 people)
Asian population, 2000 (1 dot = 10 people)
Hispanic population, 2000 (1 dot = 10 people)
Parks, grassy areas, marsh
Forested areas
Water

Map by Richard Campanella
based on 2000 Census
and other data sources

Lake Catouatchie

Mississippi River

West Bank
Jefferson Parish

Orleans Parish
Jefferson Parish

Plaquemines Parish

Intracoastal Waterway (Alger's Canal)

St. Bernard

Intracoastal Waterway

MR-GO

English Turn

Belle Chasse

Violet
Meraux
Chalmette
Arabi
Orleans
Lower 9th Ward
Bywater
Marigny
French Quarter
CBD
Garden District
Central City
Uptown
Audubon
Freret
Broadmoor
Gert Town
Hollygrove
Gentilly
Seventh Ward
Treme
Mid City
Bayou St. John
City Park
Desire
St. Claude
Industrial Canal
Pontchartrain Park
Lakeview
Lake Shore / Vista

New Orleans
Orleans
Jefferson

Algiers
Algiers Point
Behrman
Gretna
Terrytown
Harvey
Westwego
Waggaman
Bridge City
Elmwood
Shrewsbury
Jefferson Heights
Old Metairie
Metairie
Bucktown
Pontchartrain Shores
Harahan
Kenner
Old Town Kenner
Armstrong-N.O. International Airport

Harvey Canal

Lakefront Airport

New Orleans East

Hayne Boulevard

Versailles

Estelle

East Bank
Jefferson Parish

N
W   E
S

New Orleans Metropolitan Area

Lake Pontchartrain

Lake Pontchartrain Causeway

Lake Catouatchie

New Orleans / Orleans Parish

Jefferson Parish / East Bank

Jefferson Parish / West Bank

Orleans Parish

St. Bernard

Plaquemines Parish

Mississippi River

Intracoastal Waterway

Industrial Canal

Inner Harbor Navigation Canal

Harvey Canal

Jefferson

Orleans

Lakefront Airport

Hayne Boulevard

New Orleans East

Versailles

MR-GO

Meraux

Chalmette

Arabi

Lower 9th Ward

Desire

St. Claude

Marigny

Bywater

French Quarter

Treme

Seventh Ward

Bayou St. John

City Park

Gentilly

Gert Town

Mid City

Pontchartrain Park

Iris Shore Vista

Lakeview

Bucktown

Metairie

Pontchartrain Shores

Old Metairie

Jefferson Heights

Shrewsbury

Hollygrove

Carrollton

Broadmoor

Central City

CBD

Garden District

Uptown

Frerel

Audubon Park

Algiers Point

Algiers

Behrman

English Turn

Belle Chasse

Terrytown

Gretna

Harvey

Westwego

Bridge City

Elmwood

Harahan

Waggaman

Kenner

Armstrong-N/O International Airport

Old Metairie

to Lafitte

N
W   E
S

Miles
0 0.5 1   2   3   4

Map by Richard Campanella
using LSU-processed 2002
Landsat TM / SPOT satellite
image merge.

Detail of the circa-1732 *Carte de la côte de la Louisiane* (above) shows the heart of French coloni[al] Louisiana roughly a generation after its founding. Natchez in present-day Mississippi appears at u[p]per left; Baton Rouge, Manchac, and the Bayagoula region are visible at center left; New Orlea[ns] appears at center; Biloxi is at center right; and Mobile's original and eventual sites are visible at f[ar] right. The famous 1885 Currier & Ives *City of New Orleans* bird's-eye view (below) captures the city['s] development a century and a half later. Images courtesy Library of Congress.

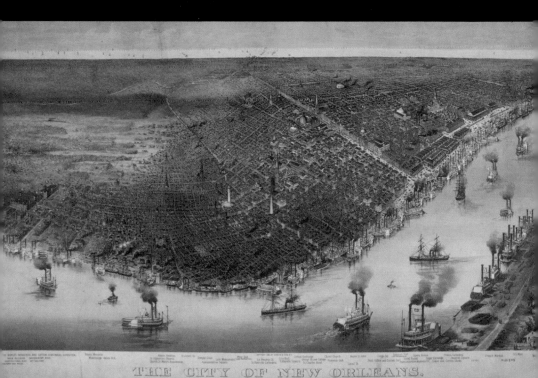

THE CITY OF NEW ORLEANS.
AND THE MISSISSIPPI RIVER. LAKE PONTCHARTRAIN IN DISTANCE.

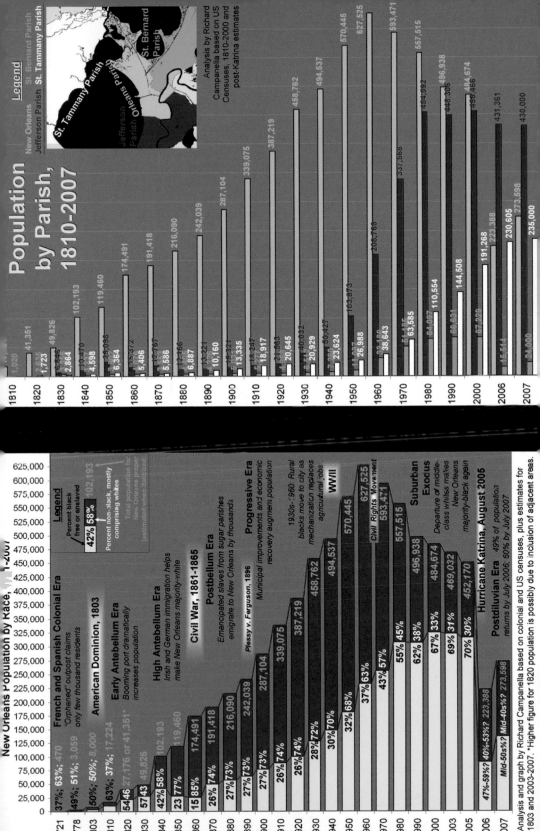

Population by Parish, 1810–2007

Legend
New Orleans (Orleans Parish)
Jefferson Parish
St. Bernard Parish
St. Tammany Parish

New Orleans Population by Race, 1721–2007

Legend
Percent black free or enslaved
Percent non-black, mostly comprising whites
Total population for New Orleans proper (estimated when italicized)

French and Spanish Colonial Era
"Orphaned" outpost claims only few thousand residents

American Dominion, 1803

Early Antebellum Era
Booming port dramatically increases population

High Antebellum Era
Irish and German immigration helps make New Orleans majority-white

Civil War, 1861–1865

Postbellum Era
Emancipated slaves from sugar parishes emigrate to New Orleans by thousands

Progressive Era
Municipal improvements and economic recovery augment population
Plessy v. Ferguson, 1896

1930s–'960: Rural blacks move to city as mechanization replaces agricultural jobs

WWII

Civil Rights Movement

Suburban Exocus
Departure of middle-class whites makes New Orleans majority-black again

Hurricane Katrina, August 2005

Postdiluvian Era 49% of population returns by July 2006; 60% by July 2007

Year		
1721	37%; 63%; 470	
1778	49%; 51%; 3,059	
1803	50%; 50%; 8,000	
1810	63%; 37%; 17,224	
1820	54%46% 27,176 or 41,351*	
1830	57 43 49,826	
1840	42% 58% 102,193	
1850	23 77% 119,460	
1860	15 85% 174,491	
1870	26% 74% 191,418	
1880	27% 73% 216,090	
1890	27% 73% 242,039	
1900	27% 73% 287,104	
1910	26% 74% 339,075	
1920	26% 74% 387,219	
1930	28% 72% 458,762	
1940	30% 70% 494,537	
1950	32% 68% 570,445	
1960	37% 63% 627,525	
1970	43% 57% 593,471	
1980	55% 45% 557,515	
1990	62% 38% 496,938	
2000	67% 33% 484,674	
2003	69% 31% 469,032	
2005	70% 30% 452,170	
2006	47%–59%? 40%–53%? 223,388	
2007	Mid-50s%? Mid-40s%? 273,598	

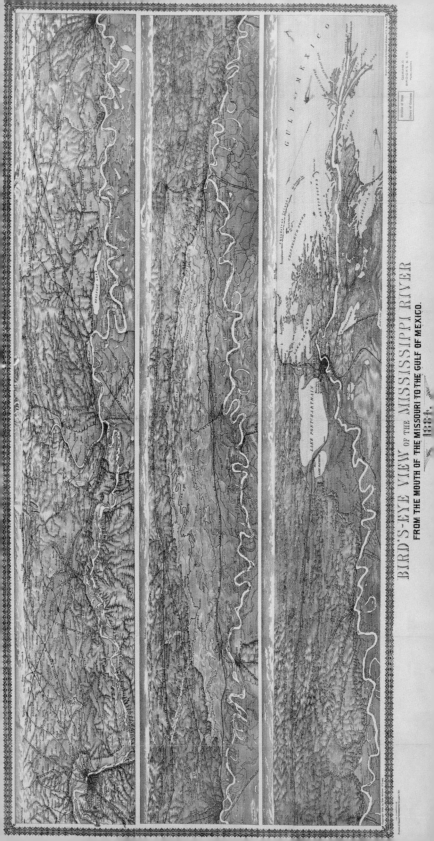

BIRD'S-EYE VIEW OF THE MISSISSIPPI RIVER

FROM THE MOUTH OF THE MISSOURI TO THE GULF OF MEXICO.

1884.

GULF OF MEXICO

LAKE PONTCHARTRAIN

Mississippi River at Natchez (top), where it reaches peak volume; at Baton Rouge, just before it exits its alluvial valley; and at Convent (middle), as it flows through its deltaic plain. Aerial view (bottom left) shows the forested batture and artificial levee separating river from natural levee of Jefferson Parish near the Huey P. Long Bridge. Computer-generated image at bottom right shows Mississippi wending through New Orleans and heading toward the Gulf of Mexico. *Bird's-Eye View of the Mississippi River, 1884 courtesy Library of Congress; photos by Richard Campanella, 2006-2007*

Mississippi River Drainage Basin

Headwaters, Missouri River

Lake Itasca Headwaters, Mississippi River

Headwaters, Ohio River

Missouri River Basin

Upper Mississippi Basin

Wisconsin R.

Ohio River Basin

Headwaters, Arkansas River

Missouri River

Upper Mississippi

Illinois R.

Headwaters Tennessee Ri.

Platte River

St. Louis

Cairo

Ohio River

Arkansas River

Lower Mississippi R.

Memphis

Tennessee River

Headwaters, Red River

Canadian River

Arkansas River

Arkansas River Basin

Red River

Lower Mississippi Basin

Vicksburg

Natchez

Baton Rouge

New Orleans

Mouth of Mississippi River

Gulf of Mexico

Basin spans 1,750 miles from Montana to Pennsylvania, and 1,450 miles from Alberta to Louisiana, covering total of 1,243,700 square miles. Map by Richard Campanella.

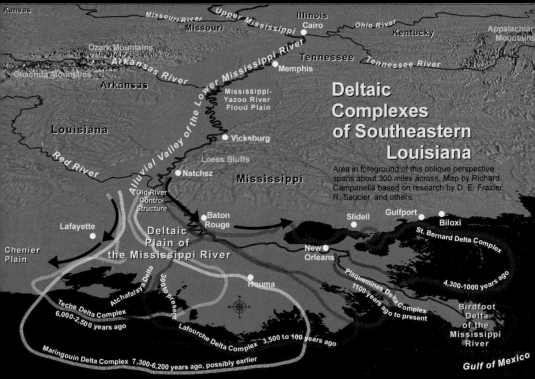

Deltaic Complexes of Southeastern Louisiana

Kansas

Missouri River

Upper Mississippi

Illinois

Cairo

Ohio River

Kentucky

Appalachian Mountains

Missouri

Ozark Mountains

Arkansas River

Lower Mississippi River

Tennessee

Tennessee River

Ouachita Mountains

Arkansas

Memphis

Mississippi-Yazoo River Flood Plain

Louisiana

Alluvial Valley of the Lower Mississippi River

Vicksburg

Loess Bluffs

Area in foreground of this oblique perspective spans about 300 miles across. Map by Richard Campanella based on research by D. E. Frazier, R. Saucier, and others.

Red River

Natchez

Mississippi

Old River Control Structure

Lafayette

Deltaic Plain of the Mississippi River

Baton Rouge

Slidell

Gulfport

Biloxi

St. Bernard Delta Complex

Chenier Plain

New Orleans

Atchafalaya Delta

3000 to present

Houma

Plaquemines Delta Complex 1100 years ago to present

4,300-1000 years ago

Teche Delta Complex 6,000-2,500 years ago

Lafourche Delta Complex 3,500 to 100 years ago

Birdfoot Delta of the Mississippi River

Maringouin Delta Complex 7,300-6,200 years ago, possibly earlier

Gulf of Mexico

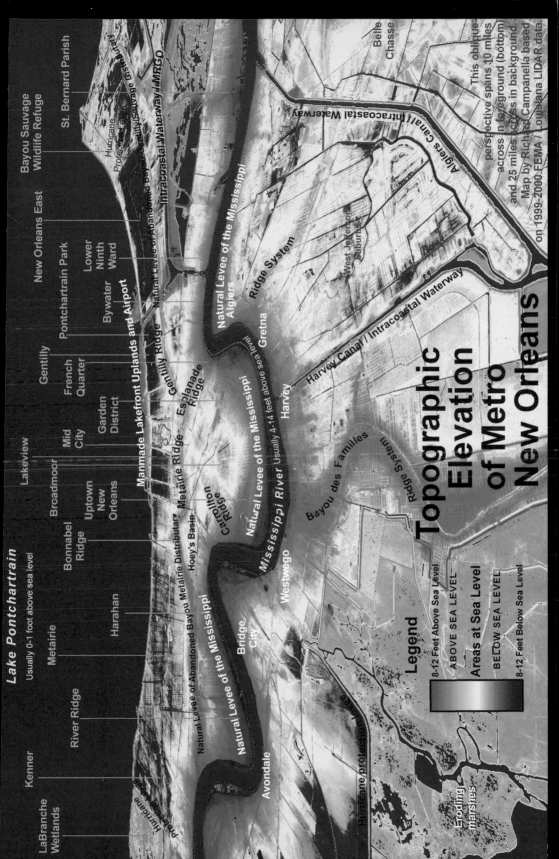

Topographic Elevation of Metro New Orleans

This oblique perspective spans 10 miles across in foreground (bottom) and 25 miles across in background. Map by Richard Campanella based on 1999-2000 FEMA / Louisiana LIDAR data.

Legend

8-12 Feet Above Sea Level

ABOVE SEA LEVEL

Areas at Sea Level

BELOW SEA LEVEL

8-12 Feet Below Sea Level

Lake Pontchartrain
Usually 0-1 foot above sea level

LaBranche Wetlands

Kenner

River Ridge

Metairie

Bonnabel Ridge

Broadmoor

Lakeview

Harahan

Uptown New Orleans

Mid City

Garden District

French Quarter

Gentilly

Pontchartrain Park

New Orleans East

St. Bernard Parish

Bayou Sauvage Wildlife Refuge

Belle Chasse

Manmade Lakefront Uplands and Airport

Gentilly Ridge

Esplanade Ridge

Metairie Ridge

Carrollton Ridge

Hoey's Basin

Natural Levee of Abandoned Bayou Metairie Distributary

Natural Levee of the Mississippi

Bywater

Lower Ninth Ward

Natural Levee of Abandoned Bayou Gentilly/Sauvage Distributary

Intracoastal Waterway / MRGO

Hurricane Protection Levee

Natural Levee of the Mississippi

Algiers Ridge System

West Jefferson Suburbs

Algiers Canal / Intracoastal Waterway

Natural Levee of the Mississippi Usually 4-14 feet above sea level

Gretna

Harvey

Harvey Canal / Intracoastal Waterway

Bayou des Familles Ridge System

Mississippi River

Westwego

Bridge City

Avondale

Natural Levee of the Mississippi

Hurricane protection levee

Eroding marshes

February-March ~ 1699

Iberville's Exploration of the Gulf Coast and Lower Mississippi River

Interpretation and map by Richard Campanella based on Iberville's journals, satellite image courtesy ESRI

Present-Day Louisiana

Present-Day Mississippi

Present-Day Alabama

11 Turn-around in Old River region

Red pole (Baton Rouge) sighted on bluffs *March 17* **10**

9 Bayogoula Indian Camp visited *March 14*

Return through Bayou Manchac **12** *March 24*

River-lake portages discovered *March 9* **8**

Pass Manchac **13** *March 28*

14 Future New Orleans Lakefront *March 29*

Future New Orleans riverfront sighted *March 7* **7**

Future **6** English Turn navigated *March 6*

Rigolets and Mississippi Sound **15** *March 30*

Reunion with ships at Biloxi Bay; founding of Fort Maurepas **16** *March 31-April 8*

5 Bayou Mardy Gras named *March 3*

2 Landing at Ship Island *February 10*

Mouth of Mississippi entered **4** *March 2*

Mud lumps sighted **3** *March 2*

Landing at Massacre (Dauphine) Island *February 2, 1699* **1**

Arrival from Leoganne, Ste. Domingue (Haiti) departed December 31, 1698

Gulf of Mexico

1749

Bayou St. Jean

Marsh

Chantilly

"Chantilly" (Gentilly)

"Metairie"

Chemin au Bayou St. Jean

Swamp

Higher Ground

N.lle ORLEANS

Swamp

Today

Bayou St. John

Below sea level

Gentilly Ridge

Gentilly Boulevard

City Park
Metairie Ridge
Avenue

Below sea level

Bayou Sauvage Road
Gentilly Road

Below sea level

Above sea level

Bayou St. John Portage, 1700s-2000s

Interpretation and graphic by Richard Campanella based on Saucier, F., Carr
particulière du cours du fleuve St. Louis depuis le village sauvage, 174

The Antecedent Cadaster

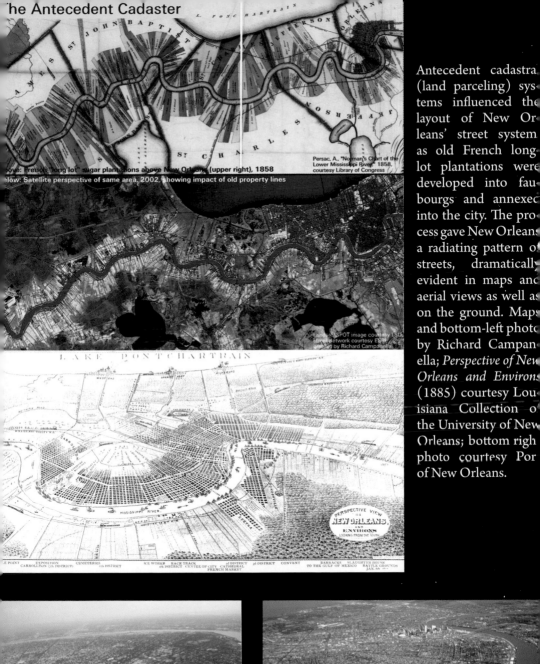

Above: French "long lot" sugar plantations above New Orleans (upper right), 1858
Below: Satellite perspective of same area, 2002, showing impact of old property lines

Persac, A., "Norman's Chart of the Lower Mississippi River," 1858, courtesy Library of Congress

Landsat/SPOT image courtesy LSU; street network courtesy ESRI; graphic by Richard Campanella.

LAKE PONTCHARTRAIN

PERSPECTIVE VIEW of NEW ORLEANS AND ENVIRONS LOOKING FROM THE SOUTH

Antecedent cadastral (land parceling) systems influenced the layout of New Orleans' street system as old French long-lot plantations were developed into faubourgs and annexed into the city. The process gave New Orleans a radiating pattern of streets, dramatically evident in maps and aerial views as well as on the ground. Maps and bottom-left photo by Richard Campanella; *Perspective of New Orleans and Environs* (1885) courtesy Louisiana Collection of the University of New Orleans; bottom right photo courtesy Port of New Orleans.

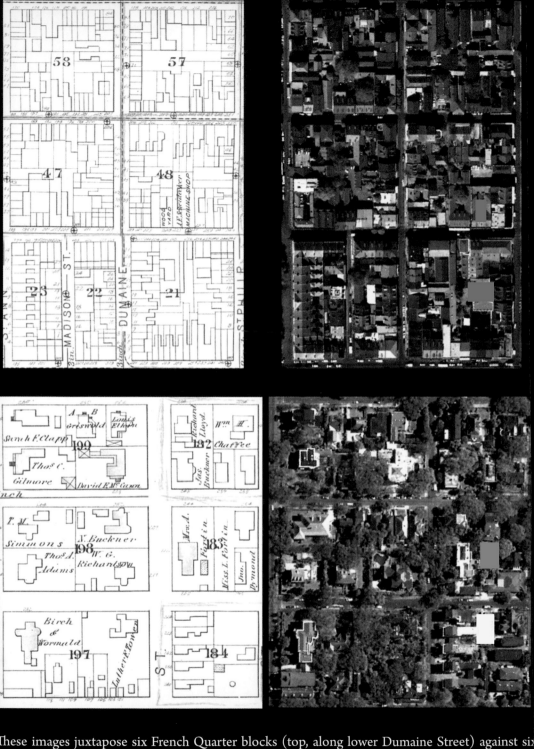

These images juxtapose six French Quarter blocks (top, along lower Dumaine Street) against six Garden District blocks (bottom, Prytania at Third and Fourth), to illustrate differences in housing density, setback distances, garden space, and foliage between European-influenced downtown and American-influenced up█████ New Orleans. 1883 *Robinson Atlas* detail courtesy N██ Orleans No█ █arial Archives; satellite imagery courtesy DigitalGlobe.

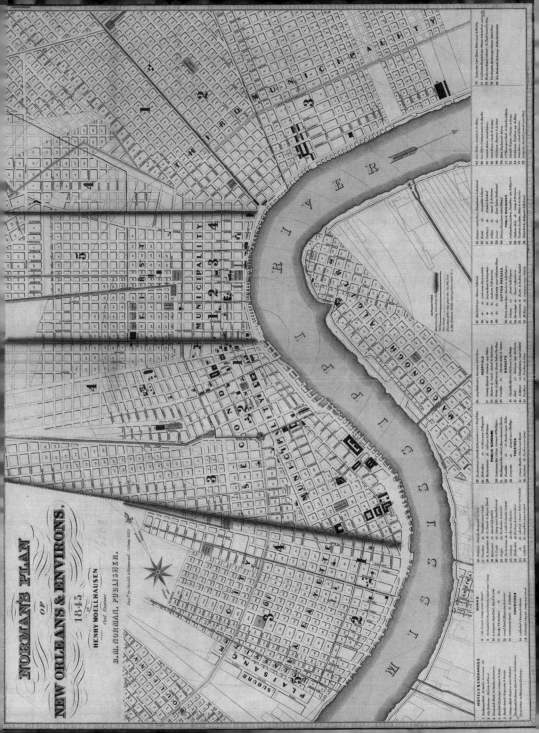

NORMAN'S PLAN OF NEW ORLEANS & ENVIRONS.

1845

HENRY MOELLHAUSEN, Civil Engineer.

B. M. NORMAN, PUBLISHER.

Top row: Rare "first-generation" Creole houses of West Indian design, mostly dating from the lat 1700s. Second row: "second-generation" Creole townhouses and storehouses, reflecting Spanish ir luence and dating from the early 1800s. Third row: Greek Revival townhouses, dating from 1830s 850s. Fourth row: Cottage typologies, mostly early- to mid-1800s. Bottom row: Shotgun typolo ries, mostly from late 1800s and early 1900s. Photos by Richard Campanella, 2004 2007

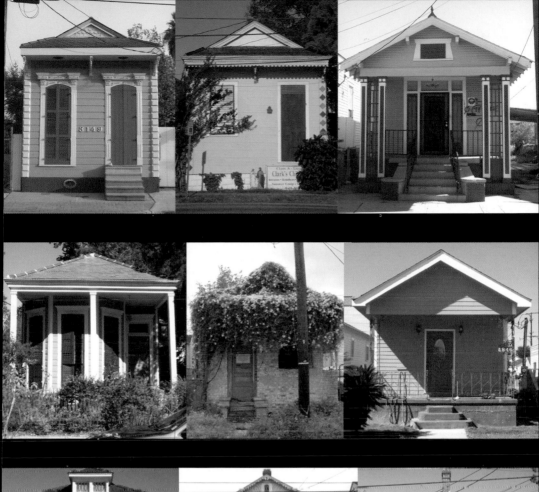

The shotgun house typology in New Orleans, shown in various sizes and architectural styles, dating mostly from the 1880s-1910s. Photos by Richard Campanella, 2007.

The shotgun house typology in the Deep South. These photos were taken in St. Helena Parish an Donaldsonville in Louisiana, and Natchez and Vicksburg in Mississippi. Photos by Richard Cam panella, 2003-2007.

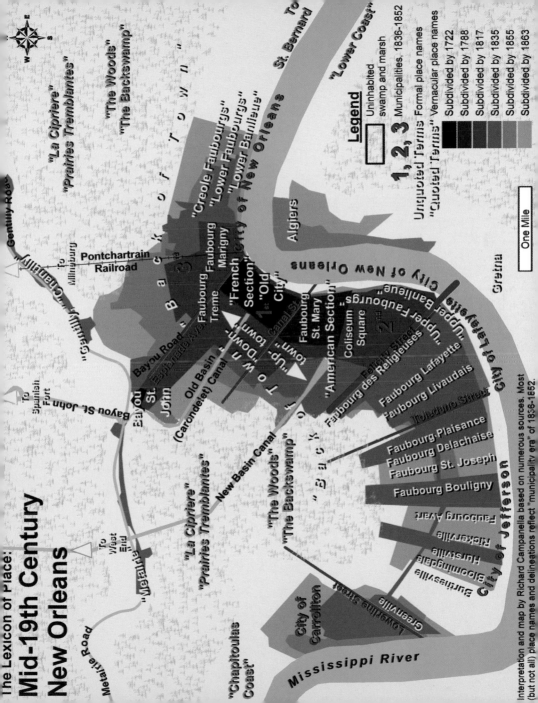

The Lexicon of Place: Mid-19th Century New Orleans

Legend

Uninhabited swamp and marsh

Municipalities, 1836-1852

1, 2, 3

Unquoted 'Terms' — Formal place names
"Quoted 'Terms'" — Vernacular place names

- Subdivided by 1722
- Subdivided by 1788
- Subdivided by 1817
- Subdivided by 1835
- Subdivided by 1855
- Subdivided by 1863

One Mile

Interpretation and map by Richard Campanella based on numerous sources. Most (but not all) place names and delineations reflect "municipality era" of 1836-1852.

"La Cipriere" "Prairies Tremblantes"

"The Woods" "The Backswamp"

"Lower Coast"

To St. Bernard

"Creole Faubourgs" "Lower Faubourgs" "Lower Banlieue"

"Back of Town"

To Milneburg "To Chantilly"

Pontchartrain Railroad

Gentilly Road

To Spanish Fort

Bayou Road

Bayou St. John

St. John Bayou

Faubourg Treme

Faubourg Marigny

Old Basin (Carondelet) Canal

Esplanade Avenue

"French Section" "Old City"

1st "City of New Orleans"

Algiers

City of New Orleans

Canal Street

"Up-town" "Down-town"

Faubourg St. Mary

"American Section"

Coliseum Square

Felicity Street

2nd "Upper Faubourgs" "Upper Banlieue"

Faubourg des Religieuses

Gretna

"To West End"

"Metairie"

Metairie Road

"La Cipriere" "Prairies Tremblantes"

"Chapitoulas Coast"

New Basin Canal

"The Woods" "The Backswamp"

"The Woods" "The Backswamp"

"Back o' Town"

Faubourg Lafayette

Faubourg Livaudais

Toledano Street

City of Lafayette

Faubourg Plaisance

Faubourg Delachaise

Faubourg St. Joseph

Faubourg Bouligny

Faubourg Avart

Rickerville

Hurstville

Bloomingdale

Burtheville

City of Jefferson

Lowerline Street

Greenville Street

City of Carrollton

Mississippi River

1732

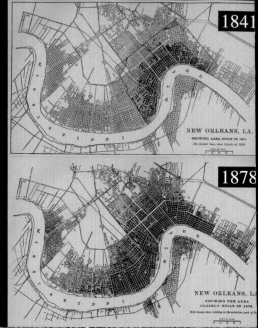

1841

1878

NEW ORLEANS, LA.
SHOWING AREA BUILT IN 1841.

NEW ORLEANS, LA.
SHOWING THE AREA
CLOSELY BUILT IN 1878.

1922

2001

Top left: Detail of *Carte du cours du fleuve St. Louis depuis dix lieues au-dessus de la Nouvelle Orleans* (circa 1732). Top right: Urbanized area (darkened shades) of New Orleans in 1841 and 1878, as depicted in *Report on the Social Statistics of Cities*, 1886. At center right is a rare 1922 aerial mosaic of the city; at bottom right is a satellite image of the same area in 2001. Maps courtesy Library of Congress and Perry-Castañeda Library Map, University of Texas at Austin. Photos courtesy Port of New Orleans and Ikonos.

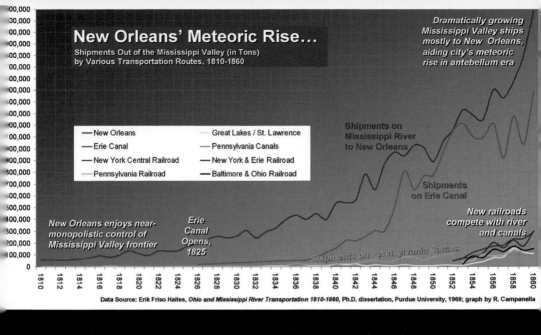

New Orleans' Meteoric Rise...

Shipments Out of the Mississippi Valley (in Tons) by Various Transportation Routes, 1810-1860

Dramatically growing Mississippi Valley ships mostly to New Orleans, aiding city's meteoric rise in antebellum era

Shipments on Mississippi River to New Orleans

Shipments on Erie Canal

New railroads compete with river and canals

New Orleans enjoys near-monopolistic control of Mississippi Valley frontier

Erie Canal Opens, 1825

Shipments on Pennsylvania Canals

Legend:
— New Orleans
— Erie Canal
— New York Central Railroad
— Pennsylvania Railroad
— Great Lakes / St. Lawrence
— Pennsylvania Canals
— New York & Erie Railroad
— Baltimore & Ohio Railroad

Data Source: Erik Friso Haites, *Ohio and Mississippi River Transportation 1810-1860*, Ph.D. dissertation, Purdue University, 1969; graph by R. Campanella

uch of New Orleans' meteoric rise in the early nineteenth century (above) can be traced to the dra-atically increasing population and agricultural productivity of the trans-Appalachian West, which d little choice but to ship downriver to New Orleans to deliver its commodities to market. Bu en as these shipments increased in absolute numbers, an emerging network of eastern and Mid estern canals, railroads, and roads gave New Orleans unwanted new competition for Mississipp lley trade. The city's relative share of the market (below), once at over 99 percent, declined t out 50 percent by the eve of the Civil War. New Orleans' population would continue to grow fo century to come, but its rank among American cities would steadily sink after peaking as the third rgest in the nation in 1840. [See "Lessons in Over-Reliance" for details.]

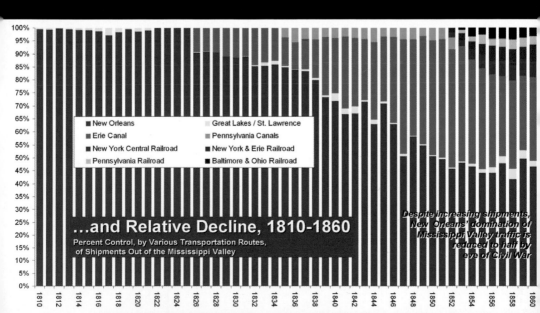

...and Relative Decline, 1810-1860

Percent Control, by Various Transportation Routes, of Shipments Out of the Mississippi Valley

Legend:
■ New Orleans
■ Erie Canal
■ New York Central Railroad
■ Pennsylvania Railroad
■ Great Lakes / St. Lawrence
■ Pennsylvania Canals
■ New York & Erie Railroad
■ Baltimore & Ohio Railroad

Despite increasing shipments, New Orleans' domination of Mississippi Valley traffic is reduced to half by eve of Civil War

Data Source: Erik Friso Haites, *Ohio and Mississippi River Transportation 1810-1860*, Ph.D. dissertation, Purdue University, 1969; graph by R. Campanella

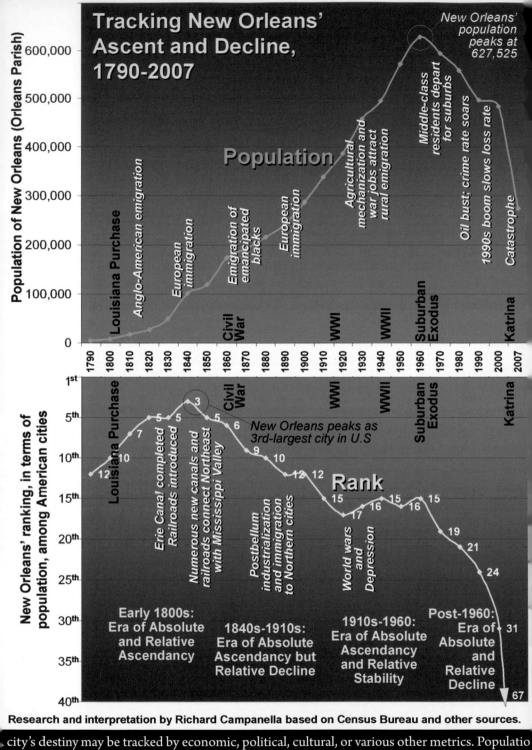

Tracking New Orleans' Ascent and Decline, 1790-2007

Population of New Orleans (Orleans Parish)

New Orleans' population peaks at 627,525

Population

- Louisiana Purchase
- Anglo-American emigration
- European immigration
- Emigration of emancipated blacks
- European immigration
- Agricultural mechanization and war jobs attract rural emigration
- Middle-class residents depart for suburbs
- Oil bust; crime rate soars
- 1990s boom slows loss rate
- Catastrophe

- Civil War
- WWI
- WWII
- Suburban Exodus
- Katrina

New Orleans' ranking, in terms of population, among American cities

- Louisiana Purchase
- Erie Canal completed
- Railroads introduced
- Numerous new canals and railroads connect Northeast with Mississippi Valley
- Postbellum industrialization and immigration to Northern cities
- World wars and Depression

New Orleans peaks as 3rd-largest city in U.S

Rank

- Civil War
- WWI
- WWII
- Suburban Exodus
- Katrina

Early 1800s: Era of Absolute and Relative Ascendancy

1840s-1910s: Era of Absolute Ascendancy but Relative Decline

1910s-1960: Era of Absolute Ascendancy and Relative Stability

Post-1960: Era of Absolute and Relative Decline

Research and interpretation by Richard Campanella based on Census Bureau and other sources.

city's destiny may be tracked by economic, political, cultural, or various other metrics. Populatio ffers perhaps the most straightforward. These graphs pair New Orleans' population (top) with i nking by population size among American cities (bottom) for 1790-2007. Certain relevant histor al events and trends are overlaid on the graphs. The data reveal four distinct eras of municipal as endancy and/or decline. New Orleans' population has been declining in both absolute and relativ rms since 1960, particularly since Hurricane Katrina in 2005. [See "Lessons in Over-Reliance"]

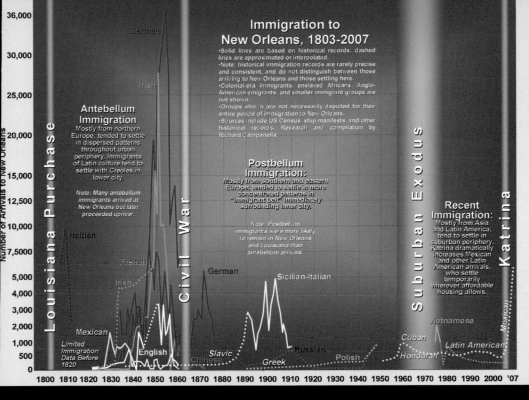

Immigration to New Orleans, 1803-2007

- Solid lines are based on historical records; dashed lines are approximated or interpolated.
- Note: historical immigration records are rarely precise and consistent, and do not distinguish between those arriving to New Orleans and those settling here.
- Colonial-era immigrants, enslaved Africans, Anglo-American emigrants, and smaller immigrant groups are not shown.
- Groups shown are not necessarily depicted for their entire period of immigration to New Orleans.
- Sources include US Census, ship manifests, and other historical records. Research and compilation by Richard Campanella.

Antebellum Immigration
Mostly from northern Europe; tended to settle in dispersed patterns throughout urban periphery. Immigrants of Latin culture tend to settle with Creoles in lower city.

Note: Many antebellum immigrants arrived at New Orleans but later proceeded upriver.

Postbellum Immigration:
Mostly from southern and eastern Europe; tended to settle in more concentrated patterns in "immigrant belt" immediately surrounding inner city.

Note: Postbellum immigrants were more likely to remain in New Orleans and Louisiana than antebellum arrivals.

Recent Immigration:
Mostly from Asia and Latin America; tend to settle in suburban periphery. Katrina dramatically increases Mexican and other Latin American arrivals, who settle temporarily wherever affordable housing allows.

Louisiana Purchase

Civil War

Suburban Exodus

Katrina

German, Irish, Haitian, French, Irish, Mexican, English, German, Sicilian-Italian, Chinese, Slavic, Greek, Russian, Polish, Cuban, Honduran, Vietnamese, Latin American, Mexican

Limited Immigration Data Before 1820

Y-axis: Number of Arrivals to New Orleans — 0, 500, 1,000, 2,000, 3,000, 4,000, 5,000, 7,500, 10,000, 12,500, 15,000, 20,000, 25,000, 30,000, 36,000

X-axis: 1800 1810 1820 1830 1840 1850 1860 1870 1880 1890 1900 1910 1920 1930 1940 1950 1960 1970 1980 1990 2000 '07

This 1919 aerial photograph of downtown New Orleans (French Quarter at upper center; Lee Circle at lower right; Lake Pontchartrain in distance) captures the "belt" of working-class neighborhoods around the CBD where immigrants, in the late 1800s and early 1900s, settled in large numbers. Southeastern Architectural Archive, Special Collections, Tulane University Howard-Tilton Library.

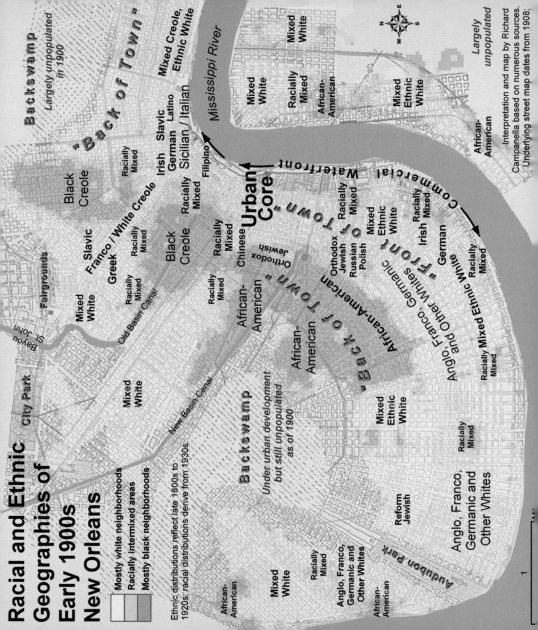

Racial and Ethnic Geographies of Early 1900s New Orleans

Mostly white neighborhoods
Racially intermixed areas
Mostly black neighborhoods

Ethnic distributions reflect late 1800s to 1920s; racial distributions derive from 1930s.

Interpretation and map by Richard Campanella based on numerous sources. Underlying street map dates from 1908;

Backswamp
Largely unpopulated in 1900

Mississippi River

Largely unpopulated

Mixed Creole, Ethnic White

Mixed White

Mixed White

Racially Mixed White

African-American

Mixed Ethnic White

African-American

"Back of Town"

Black Creole

Slavic

Franco / White Creole

Greek

Irish
German
Slavic
Latino
Sicilian / Italian

Racially Mixed

Filipino

Urban Core

Waterfront

Commercial

"Front of Town"

Mixed White

Racially Mixed

Black Creole

Racially Mixed

Chinese

Orthodox Jewish

Racially Mixed

Racially Mixed

Orthodox Jewish
Russian
Polish

Mixed Ethnic White

Irish Mixed

German

Racially Mixed Ethnic White

Racially Mixed

City Park

Fairgrounds

Bayou St. John

Mixed White

Old Basin Canal

New Basin Canal

African-American

Racially Mixed

African-American

African-American

"Back of Town"

Germanic, Franco, and Other Whites

Anglo, Franco, Germanic and Other Whites

Backswamp
Under urban development but still unpopulated as of 1900

Mixed Ethnic White

Racially Mixed

Racially Mixed

Mixed White

Anglo, Franco, Germanic and Other Whites

Reform Jewish

Anglo, Franco, Germanic and Other Whites

African-American

African-American

Audubon Park

1

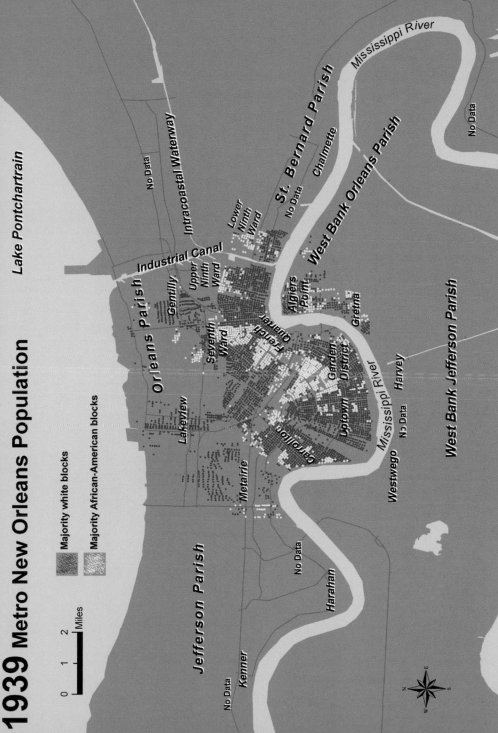

1939 Metro New Orleans Population

Majority white blocks

Majority African-American blocks

0 1 2
Miles

Lake Pontchartrain

Jefferson Parish

Orleans Parish

St. Bernard Parish

West Bank Orleans Parish

West Bank Jefferson Parish

Mississippi River

Mississippi River

Intracoastal Waterway

Industrial Canal

Gentilly

Lakeview

Metairie

Carrollton

Seventh Ward

Upper Ninth Ward

Lower Ninth Ward

French Quarter

Garden District

Uptown

Algiers Point

Gretna

Chalmette

Harvey

Westwego

Harahan

Kenner

No Data

No Data

No Data

No Data

No Data

No Data

No Data

Analysis and map by Richard Campanella based on "Report on Survey of Metropolitan
New Orleans Land Use" (1941) by Sam Carter. Street network reflects modern situation.

N E S W

1960 Metro New Orleans Population

Every dot represents ten (10) residents distributed evenly at the census-tract level.

White population

African-Americans and other nonwhites

Miles
0 1 2

Lake Pontchartrain

New Orleans East

MR-GO Under Construction

Intracoastal Waterway / MR-GO

Mississippi River

St. Bernard Parish

Chalmette

Industrial Canal

Pont-chartrain Park

Lower Ninth Ward

West Bank Orleans Parish

Gentilly

Upper Ninth Ward

Seventh Ward

Marigny/ Bywater

Algiers Point

Lakeview

Orleans Parish

Mid City

French Quarter

Gretna

No Data for Belle Chasse

Gert Town

Garden District

West Bank Jefferson Parish

Carrollton

Central City

Uptown

Harvey

Mississippi River

Metairie

Westwego

East Bank Jefferson Parish

Harahan

Kenner

Kenner

Analysis and map by Richard Campanella, using 1960 census tract data spatially adjusted to exclude uninhabited areas. Street...

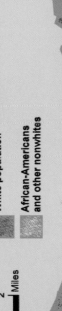

2000 Metro New Orleans Population

Every dot represents ten (10) residents distributed evenly at the census-block level.

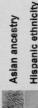

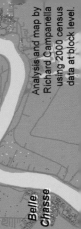

Legend:
- White population
- African-American
- Asian ancestry
- Hispanic ethnicity

Analysis and map by Richard Campanella using 2000 census data at block level.

Lake Pontchartrain

Kenner

East Bank Jefferson Parish

Metairie

Harahan

Kenner

Lakeview

GerTown

Carrollton

Mid City

Orleans Parish

Gentilly

Pont-chartrain Park

Seventh Ward

Upper Ninth Ward

Industrial Canal

Intracoastal Waterway / MR-GO

New Orleans East

Versailles

Lower Ninth Ward

St. Bernard Parish

Chalmette

Central City

Uptown

Garden District

Marigny/ Bywater

French Quarter

Algiers Point

Gretna

Harvey

Westwego

West Bank Jefferson Parish

West Bank Orleans Parish

Belle Chasse

Mississippi River

Mississippi River

0 1 2 Miles

The "White Teapot"

Teapot-shaped region of predominantly
white residential settlement in historical
New Orleans neighborhoods

Every dot represents five
residents distributed evenly
within census blocks.

· Whites
· Blacks
· Hispanics
· Asians

Analysis by Richard Campanella

Industrial Canal

Upper
Ninth
Ward

Seventh
Ward

Bywater

"Spout" Marigny
of teapot

Treme

French
Quarter

Algiers
Point

Gretna

CBD

Former backswamp edge

Lower
Garden
District

"Kettle"
of
teapot

Central
City

Garden
District

Irish
Channel

"Spout"
of teapot

St. Charles Avenue

Riverfront wharves and railroads

Tulane
Loyola

Audubon Park

Carrollton

"Handle"
of teapot
("superblock"
settlement patterns)

Mississippi River

Miles
0   0.5   1

Vertical Migration

Population Distribution with respect to Topographic Elevation, 1700s to 2000

1941 Land Use Survey, 1960 Census, 2000 Census, and others. Analysis and mapping by Richard Campanella; see chapter for details.

1700s

One dot signifies one residential block

Lake Pontchartrain

Lowest Ground

Higher Ground

Lower Ground

Highest Ground

Higher Ground

Lower Ground

Highest Ground

Mississippi River

Mid-1800s

One dot equals 50 people at the census tract level.

Early 1910s

One dot equals 25 people at the enumeration district level.

Late 1930s

1960

2000

One dot equals 25 people at the block level.

Population by Race and Elevation in New Orleans, 1939

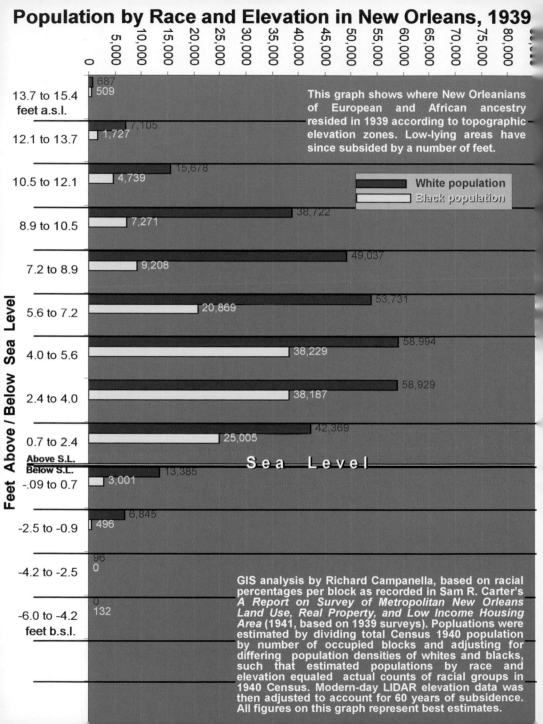

This graph shows where New Orleanians of European and African ancestry resided in 1939 according to topographic elevation zones. Low-lying areas have since subsided by a number of feet.

White population
Black population

X-axis: 0, 5,000, 10,000, 15,000, 20,000, 25,000, 30,000, 35,000, 40,000, 45,000, 50,000, 55,000, 60,000, 65,000, 70,000, 75,000, 80,000

Y-axis label: Feet Above / Below Sea Level

Elevation	White	Black
13.7 to 15.4 feet a.s.l.	687	509
12.1 to 13.7	7,105	1,727
10.5 to 12.1	15,678	4,739
8.9 to 10.5	38,722	7,271
7.2 to 8.9	49,037	9,208
5.6 to 7.2	53,731	20,869
4.0 to 5.6	58,994	38,229
2.4 to 4.0	58,929	38,187
0.7 to 2.4	42,369	25,005
-.09 to 0.7	13,385	3,001
-2.5 to -0.9	6,845	496
-4.2 to -2.5	96	0
-6.0 to -4.2 feet b.s.l.	0	132

Above S.L.
Below S.L.

S e a   L e v e l

GIS analysis by Richard Campanella, based on racial percentages per block as recorded in Sam R. Carter's *A Report on Survey of Metropolitan New Orleans Land Use, Real Property, and Low Income Housing Area* (1941, based on 1939 surveys). Popluations were estimated by dividing total Census 1940 population by number of occupied blocks and adjusting for differing population densities of whites and blacks, such that estimated populations by race and elevation equaled actual counts of racial groups in 1940 Census. Modern-day LIDAR elevation data was then adjusted to account for 60 years of subsidence. All figures on this graph represent best estimates.

Population by Race and Elevation in New Orleans, 2000

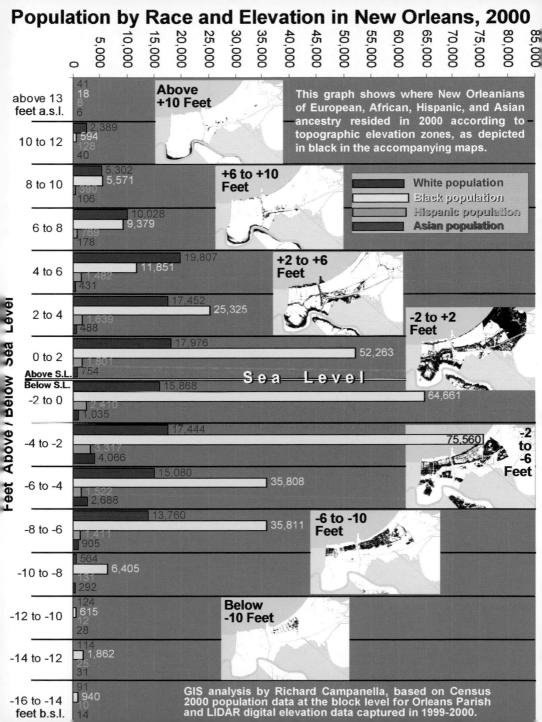

Feet Above / Below Sea Level

Elevation	Above +10 Feet
above 13 feet a.s.l.	41 / 18 / 8 / 6

This graph shows where New Orleanians of European, African, Hispanic, and Asian ancestry resided in 2000 according to topographic elevation zones, as depicted in black in the accompanying maps.

10 to 12 — 2,389 / 594 / 128 / 40

+6 to +10 Feet

8 to 10 — 5,302 / 5,571 / 390 / 106

- White population
- Black population
- Hispanic population
- Asian population

6 to 8 — 10,028 / 9,379 / 769 / 178

4 to 6 — 19,807 / 11,851 / 1,482 / 431

+2 to +6 Feet

2 to 4 — 17,452 / 25,325 / 1,639 / 488

-2 to +2 Feet

0 to 2 — 17,976 / 52,263 / 1,801 / 754

Above S.L.

Sea Level

Below S.L.

-2 to 0 — 15,868 / 64,661 / 2,410 / 1,035

-4 to -2 — 17,444 / 75,560 / 3,317 / 4,066

-2 to -6 Feet

-6 to -4 — 15,080 / 35,808 / 1,522 / 2,688

-8 to -6 — 13,760 / 35,811 / 1,411 / 905

-6 to -10 Feet

-10 to -8 — 564 / 6,405 / 131 / 292

-12 to -10 — 124 / 615 / 12 / 28

Below -10 Feet

-14 to -12 — 114 / 1,862 / 25 / 31

-16 to -14 feet b.s.l. — 91 / 940 / 10 / 14

GIS analysis by Richard Campanella, based on Census 2000 population data at the block level for Orleans Parish and LIDAR digital elevation data captured in 1999-2000.

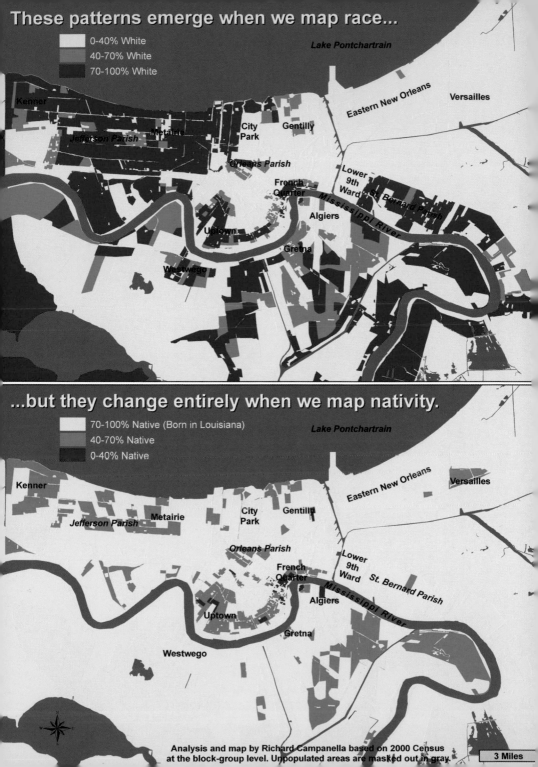

These patterns emerge when we map race...

- 0-40% White
- 40-70% White
- 70-100% White

Lake Pontchartrain

Kenner

Jefferson Parish Metairie

City Park

Gentilly

Eastern New Orleans

Versailles

Orleans Parish

Lower 9th Ward

St. Bernard Parish

French Quarter

Mississippi River

Algiers

Uptown

Gretna

Westwego

...but they change entirely when we map nativity.

- 70-100% Native (Born in Louisiana)
- 40-70% Native
- 0-40% Native

Lake Pontchartrain

Kenner

Jefferson Parish Metairie

City Park

Gentilly

Eastern New Orleans

Versailles

Orleans Parish

French Quarter

Lower 9th Ward

St. Bernard Parish

Mississippi River

Algiers

Uptown

Gretna

Westwego

Analysis and map by Richard Campanella based on 2000 Census at the block-group level. Unpopulated areas are masked out in gray.

3 Miles

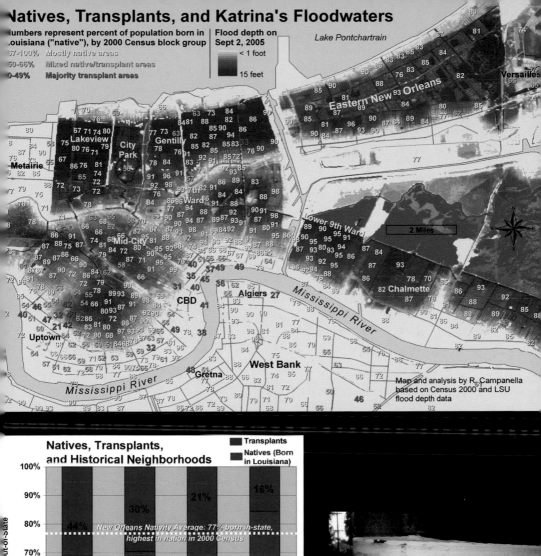

Natives, Transplants, and Katrina's Floodwaters

Numbers represent percent of population born in Louisiana ("native"), by 2000 Census block group | Flood depth on Sept 2, 2005

57-100% Mostly native areas
50-66%   Mixed native/transplant areas
0-49%   Majority transplant areas

< 1 foot

15 feet

Lake Pontchartrain

Eastern New Orleans

Versailles

Lakeview

City Park

Gentilly

Metairie

9th Ward

Lower 9th Ward

2 Miles

Mid-City

Mississippi River

Chalmette

CBD

Algiers

Uptown

Gretna

West Bank

Mississippi River

Map and analysis by R. Campanella based on Census 2000 and LSU flood depth data

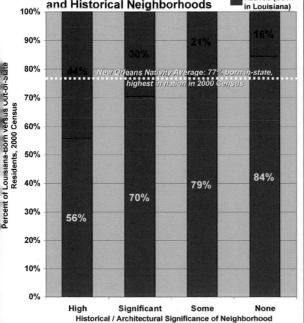

Natives, Transplants, and Historical Neighborhoods

Legend:
- Transplants
- Natives (Born in Louisiana)

Y-axis: Percent of Louisiana-born versus Out-of-state Residents, 2000 Census

New Orleans Nativity Average: 77% born in-state, highest in nation in 2000 Census

Historical / Architectural Significance of Neighborhood	Transplants	Natives
High	44%	56%
Significant	30%	70%
Some	21%	79%
None	16%	84%

Analysis and graph by Richard Campanella using Census 2000 nativity data and official city neighborhoods. "High" historical value included French Quarter, Treme, Garden District, CBD, Marigny, Lower Garden District, and Bywater; "Significant" included most of Uptown and Mid City / Bayou St. John, Warehouse District, Algiers Point, Central City, St. Roch, Holy Cross, St. Claude, Six and Seventh Wards; "Some" included all neighborhoods in greater Gentilly, Lakeview, and along lakefront, plus Broadmoor, Leonidas / West Carrollton, Gerttown / Zion City, Tulane / Gravier, Hollygrove, McDonogh, Pontchartrain Park, and Lower Ninth Ward. "None" category comprised all other areas, particularly in New Orleans East, West Bank, and housing projects.

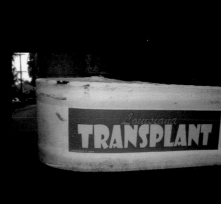

"Louisiana Transplant" bumper sticker in the Faubourg Marigny, one of New Orleans' most historic but least native-born neighborhoods. Photo by Laura Harris, 2006.

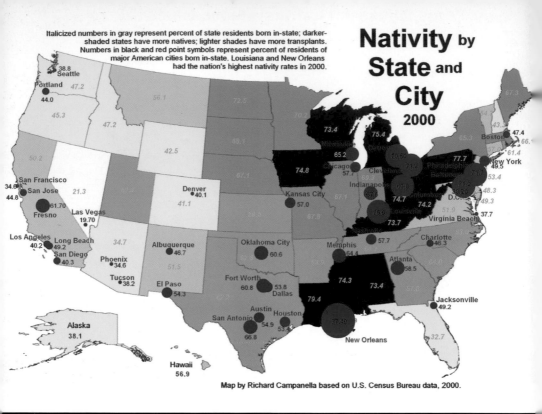

Italicized numbers in gray represent percent of state residents born in-state; darker-shaded states have more natives; lighter shades have more transplants. Numbers in black and red point symbols represent percent of residents of major American cities born in-state. Louisiana and New Orleans had the nation's highest nativity rates in 2000.

Nativity by State and City 2000

Map by Richard Campanella based on U.S. Census Bureau data, 2000.

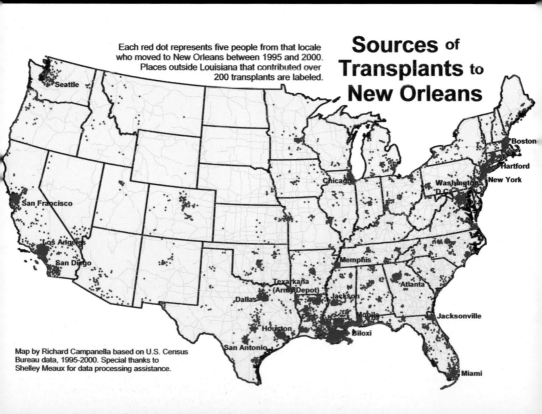

Each red dot represents five people from that locale who moved to New Orleans between 1995 and 2000. Places outside Louisiana that contributed over 200 transplants are labeled.

Sources of Transplants to New Orleans

Map by Richard Campanella based on U.S. Census Bureau data, 1995-2000. Special thanks to Shelley Meaux for data processing assistance.

...ty nicknames and slogans are significant ...cause they both reflect and drive mass ...rception about a place, and how it devi- ...es from other places. At right is a chronol- ...y of New Orleans' various monikers. Be- ...w: Joseph Holt Ingraham claimed to have ...med New Orleans "the Crescent City" ...his 1835 publication, *The Southwest by* ...Yankee. He seems to be correct: the nick- ...ame is exceedingly rare prior to 1835 and ...ry common afterwards. Bottom left: The ...ueen & Crescent Hotel on Camp Street ...aces its name to a railroad line connecting ...incinnati ("the Queen of the West") with ...ew Orleans ("the Crescent City"). Bottom ...ght: "The City [that] Care Forgot" slogan ...ppeared in a 1910s nationwide marketing ...mpaign for the St. Charles Hotel. [See ...he Lexicon of Place" for details.] Ad from ...iladelphia Inquirer; graphic and photo by ...ichard Campanella.

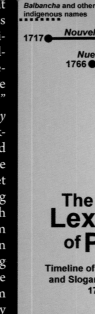

Research by Richard Campanella, see chapter for sources

The Lexicon of Place

Timeline of Names, Nicknames, and Slogans for New Orleans, 1700s-2000s

Balbancha and other indigenous names

Nouvelle Orléans — 1717

Nueva Orleans — 1766–1803

New Orleans — 1803

"Sodom and Gomorrah," "Great Southern Babylon," "Wet Grave," "Necropolis of the South," etc.

"Crescent City" — 1835

"Queen of the South"

"City That Care Forgot" — 1912

"America's Most Interesting City" — 1922

"Birthplace of Jazz"

"The Big Easy" — 1970

1700 · 1750 · 1800 · 1850 · 1900 · 1950 · 2000

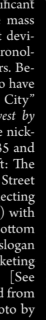

2
THE

SOUTH-WEST.

BY A YANKEE.

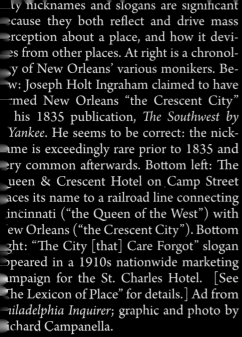

forming a magnificent thoroughfare along the whole extensive river-line. From this highway streets shoot off at right angles, till they terminate in the swamp somewhat less than a league back from the river. I have termed New-Orleans the crescent city in one of my letters, from its being built around the segment of a circle formed by a graceful curve of the river at this place. Though the water, or shore-line, is very nearly semi-circular, the Levée-street, above mentioned, does not closely follow the shore, but is broken into two angles, from which the streets diverge as before mentioned. These

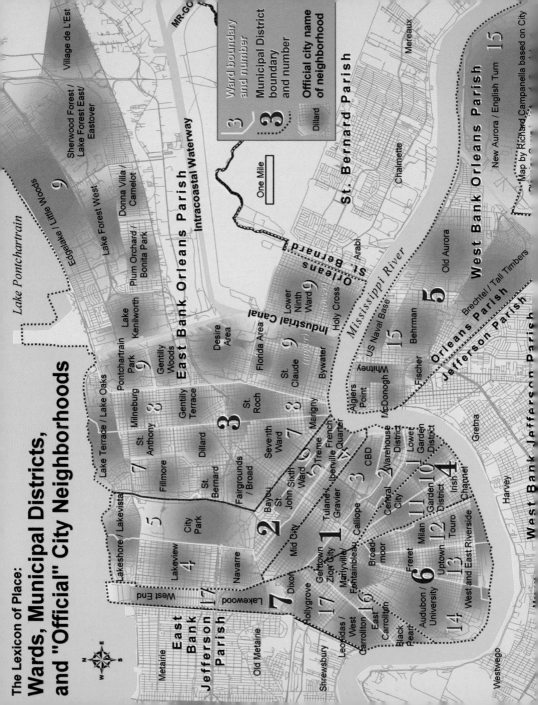

The Lexicon of Place:
Wards, Municipal Districts, and "Official" City Neighborhoods

Map by Richard Campanella based on City

Legend:
- 3 — Ward boundary and number
- 3 — Municipal District boundary and number
- Dillard — Official city name of neighborhood

One Mile

N
W E
S

Lake Pontchartrain

East Bank Jefferson Parish
- Metairie
- Old Metairie

East Bank Orleans Parish

Intracoastal Waterway

St. Bernard Parish

- Village de L'Est
- Sherwood Forest / Lake Forest East / Eastover
- Eggelake / Little Woods
- Lake Forest West
- Donna Villa / Camelot
- Plum Orchard / Bonita Park
- 9

- Lake Terrace / Lake Oaks
- Lake Kenilworth
- Pontchartrain Park
- Gentilly Woods
- 9
- Mereaux
- Dillard

- Lakeshore / Lakevista
- West End
- St. Milneburg
- St. Anthony
- Gentilly Terrace
- Desire Area
- Florida Area
- Dillard
- 8
- Chalmette
- Arabi
- Orleans / St. Bernard

- Lakeview
- City Park
- Navarre
- 5
- Fillmore
- St. Bernard
- Dillard
- St. Roch
- 3
- St. Claude
- 9
- Lower Ninth Ward
- Holy Cross
- Bywater
- Industrial Canal
- 9

- Lakewood
- 4
- Fairgrounds / Broad
- Seventh Ward
- 7
- Marigny
- 8
- Mississippi River

- Dixon
- Mid City
- Bayou St. John
- John Sixth Ward
- 6
- Treme
- Iberville
- French Quarter
- 2
- Whitney
- Algiers Point
- McDonogh
- Fischer
- Behrman
- Old Aurora
- 5

- Hollygrove
- 17
- Gert Town
- Zion City
- Tulane / Gravier
- Calliope
- CBD
- 3
- Warehouse District
- Central City
- 2
- US Naval Base
- 15
- **West Bank Orleans Parish**

- Shrewsbury
- Leonidas / West Carrollton
- East Carrollton
- Black Pearl
- Audubon University
- 14
- Freret
- 6
- Uptown
- 13
- Milan
- 11
- Touro
- 12
- Garden District
- 10
- Lower Garden District
- Irish Channel
- 4
- West and East Riverside
- Gretna
- Harvey
- Westwego
- Brechtel / Tall Timbers
- New Aurora / English Turn
- 15

- Broadmoor
- Marlyville / Fontainebleau
- 16
- 1

Orleans Parish
Jefferson Parish

West Bank Jefferson Parish

MR-GO

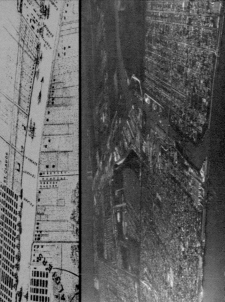

Flooding caused by Sauvé's Crevasse in 1849 (upper left) compared to modern-day topographical metropolitan area (inundated), in which dark-green shades are above sea level, yellow areas are at sea level, and red... below sea level... city's worst flood... Katrina in 2005, Sauvé's Crevasse occurred... weak spot on the... a Jefferson Parish sugar plantation, close to the former distributary which formed the Metairie/Gentilly ridge system. Photo at bottom left shows vicinity of Sauvé's Crevasse, along levee-top bike trail in River Ridge. Map from *Report on the Social Statistics of Cities* (1886), courtesy ...y-Castañeda Library, University of Texas at Austin; photo and topographic map by Richard Campanella based on Louisiana/ FEMA LIDAR data.

Detail of *Perspective of New Orleans and Environs* (1885, upper right) shows the mostly rural Ninth Ward of lower New Orleans. The Inner Harbor Navigation Canal (Industrial Canal, 1918-1923) severed the Ninth Ward into "upper" and "lower" portions, and was later joined by the Intracoastal Waterway (visible in upper right corner of the 1950s photo, lower right) and Mississippi River-Gulf Outlet Canal. These and other man-made canals have allowed salt water to kill marshes and swamps and intruded into the very heart of the levee-protected metropolis. Images courtesy Louisiana Collection of the University of New Orleans and Army Corps of Engineers-New Orleans District.

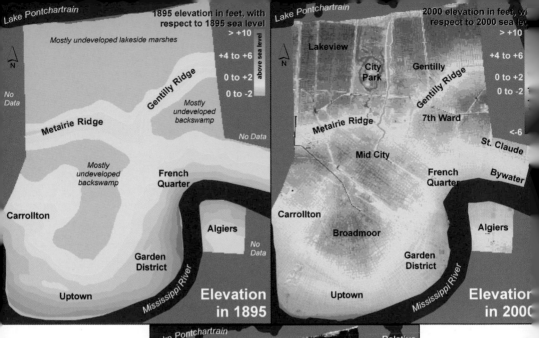

1895 elevation in feet, with respect to 1895 sea level

Mostly undeveloped lakeside marshes

> +10
+4 to +6
0 to +2
0 to -2

above sea level

Lake Pontchartrain

N

No Data

Gentilly Ridge

Metairie Ridge

Mostly undeveloped backswamp

Mostly undeveloped backswamp

French Quarter

No Data

Carrollton

Algiers

Garden District

No Data

Uptown

Mississippi River

Elevation in 1895

2000 elevation in feet, with respect to 2000 sea level

> +10
+4 to +6
0 to +2
0 to -2
<-6

Lake Pontchartrain

N

Lakeview

City Park

Gentilly

Gentilly Ridge

Metairie Ridge

7th Ward

St. Claude

Mid City

French Quarter

Bywater

Carrollton

Algiers

Broadmoor

Garden District

Uptown

Mississippi River

Elevation in 2000

A Century of Soil Subsidence in New Orleans

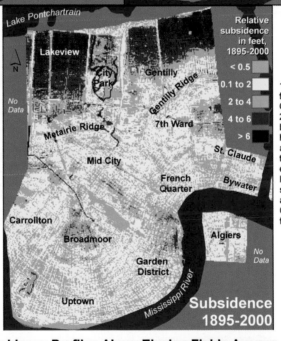

Relative subsidence in feet, 1895-2000

< 0.5
0.1 to 2
2 to 4
4 to 6
> 6

Lake Pontchartrain

N

Lakeview

City Park

Gentilly

No Data

Gentilly Ridge

Metairie Ridge

7th Ward

St. Claude

Mid City

French Quarter

Bywater

Carrollton

Algiers

Broadmoor

Garden District

No Data

Uptown

Mississippi River

Subsidence 1895-2000

1895 elevations processed from "Contour Map of New Orleans," by L. W. Brown; 2000 elevations from Louisiana LIDAR dataset. Historic elevations were adjusted from Cairo Datum to modern standards. All elevations are relative to level of sea at time of survey. GIS analysis, maps and graphs by Richard Campanella; see chapter for further details.

Elevation / Soil Subsidence Profiles Along Elysian Fields Avenue, 1895 and 2000

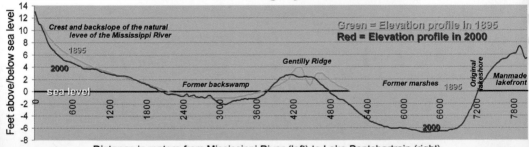

Feet above/below sea level

Crest and backslope of the natural levee of the Mississippi River

1895

2000

Green = Elevation profile in 1895
Red = Elevation profile in 2000

Gentilly Ridge

Former backswamp

Former marshes

1895

Original lakeshore

Manmade lakefront

sea level

2000

Distance in meters from Mississippi River (left) to Lake Pontchartrain (right)

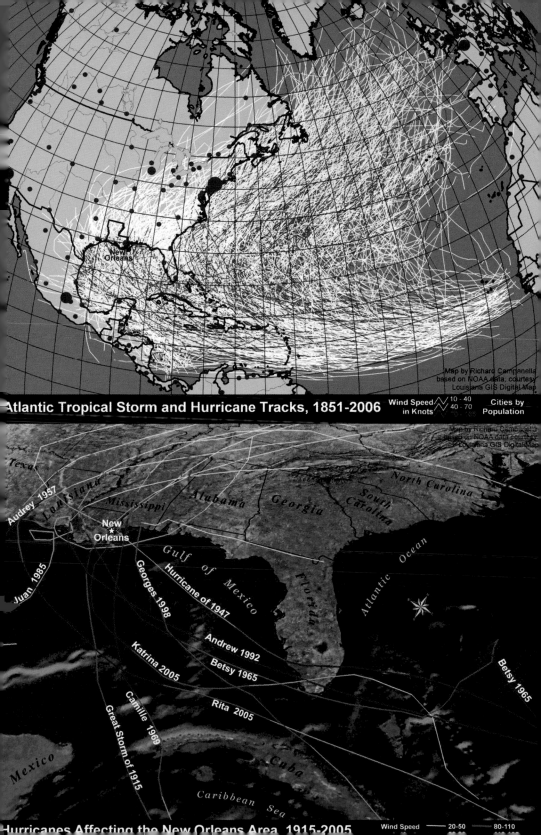

Atlantic Tropical Storm and Hurricane Tracks, 1851-2006

New Orleans

Map by Richard Campanella
based on NOAA data, courtesy
Louisiana GIS Digital Map

Wind Speed
in Knots   10 - 40
            40 - 70
            70 - 85

Cities by
Population

Map by Richard Campanella
based on NOAA data courtesy
Louisiana GIS Digital Map

Texas

Louisiana

Audrey 1957

Mississippi

Alabama

Georgia

South
Carolina

North Carolina

New
Orleans

Juan 1985

Gulf   of   Mexico

Georges 1998

Hurricane of 1947

Florida

Atlantic   Ocean

Andrew 1992

Betsy 1965

Katrina 2005

Betsy 1965

Camille 1969

Rita 2005

Great Storm of 1915

Mexico

Cuba

Caribbean   Sea

Hurricanes Affecting the New Orleans Area, 1915-2005

Wind Speed   20-50   80-110

Detail of 1884 drawing by Edward Molitor shows the Louisville & Nashville railroad tracks traversing the Rigolets landbridge (upper center) eastward toward the Mississippi Gulf Coast. It was in this remote corner of New Orleans that Manuel Marquez and his companions found themselves in a dramatic life-and-death moral dilemma during the Great Storm of 1915 [see "Manuel's Dilemma"]. Middle and bottom: freight train and tracks in the Rigolets today. *Bird's-Eye View of the Mississippi River, 1884* courtesy Library of Congress; photos by Richard Campanella, 2007.

Hurricane Betsy flooding of the Lower Ninth Ward in 1965; Hurricane Katrina flooding of same area (and far beyond) in 2005. Betsy image courtesy Army Corps of Engineers-New Orleans District; Katrina image courtesy of the Associated Press.

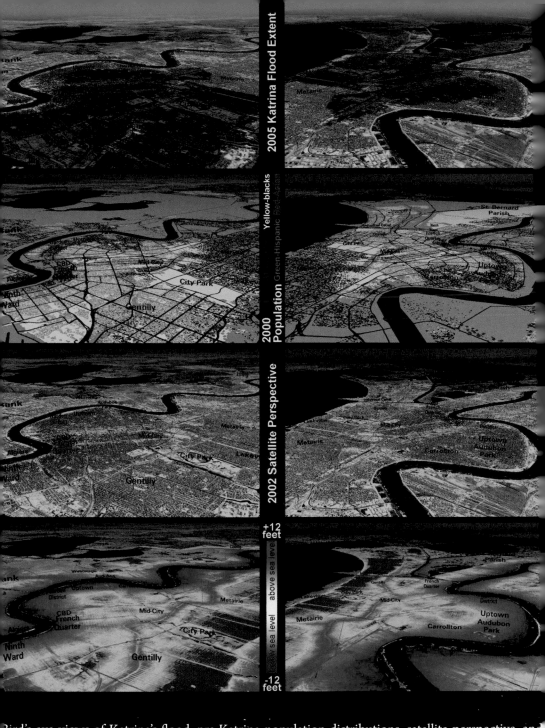

2005 Katrina Flood Extent

2000 Population Yellow-blacks Green-Hispanic Red-Asian

2002 Satellite Perspective

+12 feet
above sea level
below sea level
-12 feet

Bird's eye views of Katrina's flood, pre-Katrina population distributions, satellite perspective, and topographic elevation. Views on left are from the northeast looking southwest; views on right are from the west-southwest looking east-northeast. Computer images by Richard Campanella

Cityscapes of devastation: New Orleans, autumn and winter 2005-2006.
Photos by Richard Campanella.

Landscapes of devastation: Lower Ninth Ward (top left), Plaquemines Parish (top right and middl[e] [l]eft) and Waveland, Mississippi (middle right), October 2005. Pair of photos below shows the au[t] [t]hor's former house in Waveland, before and after Hurricane Katrina (note blue steps and crook i[n] [p]ine branch at right). Photos by Richard Campanella.

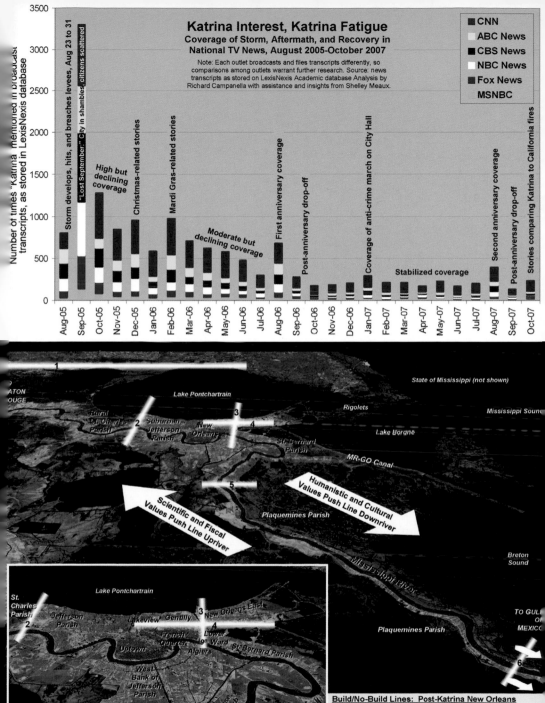

Top: A measure of Katrina press coverage, 2005-2007. Bottom: generalized suggestions of various stakeholders of where to draw the "build/no-build line." Research and graphics by Richard Campanella; special thanks to Shelley Meaux for assistance with Lexis-Nexis searches.

Threatened Historical Architecture

Relationship between Historical
(pre-WWII) Architecture and
Katrina's Floodwaters

Milneburg
Lakeview
Dillard
Gentilly
Terrace
Fairgrounds
Old Metairie
Navarre
Bayou
St. John
Seventh
Ward
Upper
Ninth
Ward
Six
Ward
St. Roch
St. Claude
Mid
City
Lower
Ninth
Ward
Hollygrove
Third
Ward
Treme
Gravier
Holy Cross
Gerttown
Shrewsbury
Fontainbleau
Broad-
moor
Central
City
Mississippi River

Building data cover only
residential areas predating
1939. Map by Richard
Campanella based on 1941
Survey of Metropolitan New
Orleans Land Use, by Sam
R. Carter, and flood extent
data from LAGIC-LSU, FEMA,
NOAA, Times-Picayune, and
other sources.

0 0.5 1
Miles

Median Era of Construction of Buildings per Block as of 1939

- 1859 or before
- 1860-1884
- 1885-1904
- 1905-1919
- 1920-1924
- 1925-1929
- 1930-1939
- *Post-1939 blocks are not shown*

Flood extent as of August 31, 2005
Flood extent as of September 8, 2005

Katrina's flood made New Orleans' architectural legacy and future a controversial topic. Citizens discussed and debated demolition, deconstruction, house raising, footprint shrinkage, green space, environmental sustainability, New Urbanism, and the merits of historicity versus modernism. Photos at center show two early twentieth-century houses raised above base flood elevations; photo at bottom shows actor Brad Pitt's "Make It Right" vision for Lower Ninth Ward, in which pink tents stand in for environmentally sustainable houses to be built inexpensively for former neighbors. Map and photos by Richard Campanella, 2007.

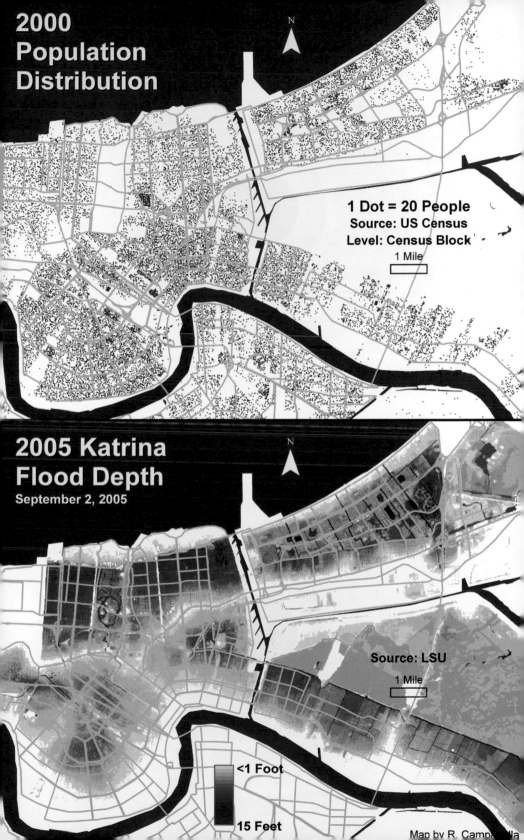

2000 Population Distribution

1 Dot = 20 People
Source: US Census
Level: Census Block

1 Mile

2005 Katrina Flood Depth

September 2, 2005

Source: LSU

1 Mile

<1 Foot

15 Feet

Map by R. Campanella

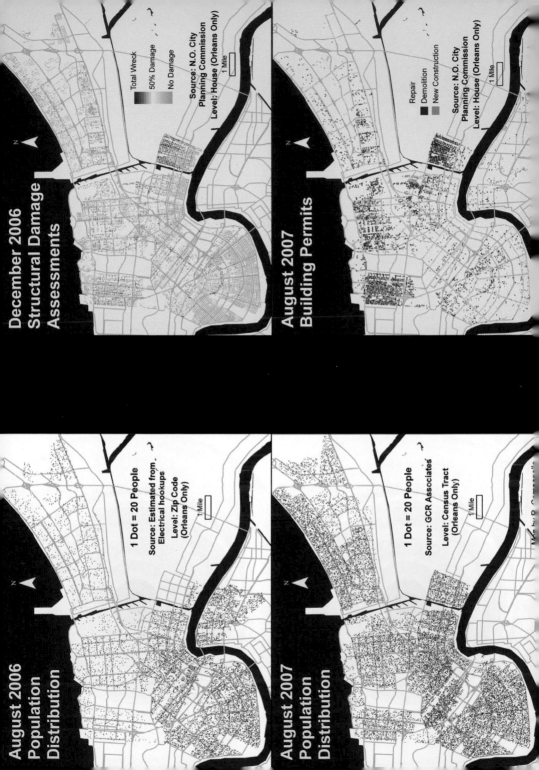

August 2006 Population Distribution

1 Dot = 20 People

Source: Estimated from Electrical hookups

Level: Zip Code (Orleans Only)

1 Mile

N

December 2006 Structural Damage Assessments

Total Wreck
50% Damage
No Damage

Source: N.O. City Planning Commission

Level; House (Orleans Only)

1 Mile

N

August 2007 Population Distribution

1 Dot = 20 People

Source: GCR Associates

Level: Census Tract (Orleans Only)

1 Mile

N

August 2007 Building Permits

Repair
Demolition
New Construction

Source: N.O. City Planning Commission

Level: House (Orleans Only)

1 Mile

N

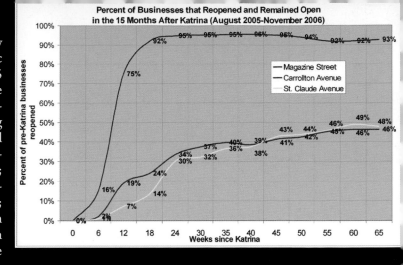

Percent of Businesses that Reopened and Remained Open in the 15 Months After Katrina (August 2005-November 2006)

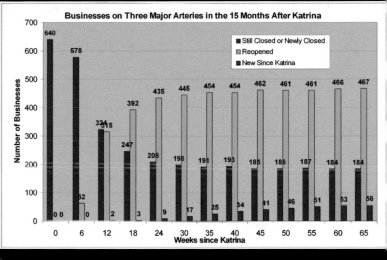

Businesses on Three Major Arteries in the 15 Months After Katrina

ew Orleans in many ys demonstrated heroic silience after the 2005 lug... op and middle an... show the re-open... businesses along major commercial teries (unflooded, pros-rous Magazine Street; ght flood..., working-as... Claude Avenue; ... North and South arrollton Avenue, which perienced... nywhere or zero to deep flood-g) during the fifteen onths following Hur-can... Katrina. Bottom rap... ...ts a crude mea-re of the remarkable vic engagement among ew Orleanians following e s... by counting the ne... civic association ... neighborhood asso-ati... appeared in the cal newspap... espite ...ager spirit to rebuild, ... of thousands of pre-atrina residents opted to ...tt... sewhere, leaving fected... ighborhoods ...arked ... populated. ew can argue that this re-ity represents "urban re-lience" in its purest form. ew Orleans rebounded fter disasters ... a stronger ash... historical times, ...hen... occupied higher roun... amid a healthier eltai... plain and a more ital... onomy. Business-eturn survey... author; ...pecia... thanks to Shel-...y Meaux for assistance ... civic engagement re-...earch.

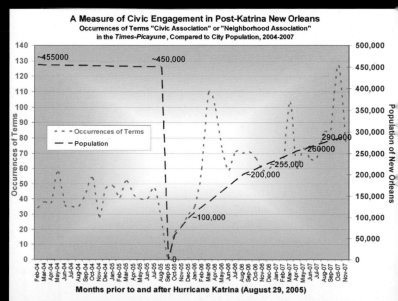

A Measure of Civic Engagement in Post-Katrina New Orleans
Occurrences of Terms "Civic Association" or "Neighborhood Association" in the *Times-Picayune*, Compared to City Population, 2004-2007

Cityscapes of recovery.
Photo of 17th Street Canal (bottom left) shows new gate and by-pass pumps installed in 2007.
Photos by Richard Campanella, 2005-2007.

Manipulating the Landscape

No place in America
fights Mother Nature
the way New Orleans does.

Chris Erskine, 2008

Agriculture in the Colonial Era

*Two Frenchmen, an Englishman, and a Spaniard
describe the lackluster colonial agricultural economy*

"The men who [settled] Biloxi Bay in 1699," wrote Nancy Surrey in her 1916 treatise on commerce in French colonial Louisiana, "were interested chiefly in mining and trading, with scarcely even a secondary interest in agriculture."[280] Precious minerals proved to be non-existent in Louisiana, and colonists' ensuing efforts to export pearls, buffalo hides, dried fish, and other sundries also fell short of expectations. With the hope of quick riches fading, Louisiana's destiny as an agricultural colony became apparent, albeit greatly hindered by a paucity of labor. France had to import sustenance to keep the colony alive in its first few years—not quite the relationship the mother country had envisioned.

A sequence of events in the late 1710s advanced Louisiana agriculture to a second level. In 1716, the Crown, exasperated with the granting of too much land to too few colonists, issued an edict delineating fertile lands into narrow "long lot" plantations and distributing them to a greater number of planters (see *Antecedent Cadasters, Antecedent Axes*). In 1718, Bienville founded a riverside port and counter-office—New Orleans—that would, in time, serve as the premier transshipment point for crops raised on those plantations. In 1719, in response to the labor shortage, French colonials imported the first African slaves to Louisiana. Agricultural productivity would rely on the toil of enslaved men and women of African descent for the next 143 years. At roughly the same time, the first major wave of Europeans arrived to Louisiana, among them hard-working German and Swiss farmers who settled the nearby *Côte des Allemands* and proceeded to cultivate crucial food crops for the colony.

With the basic components of an agricultural economy in place, the 1720s witnessed Louisiana exports expand from raw materials such as peltry, lumber, pitch, and tar, to include tobacco, indigo, and rice.[281] Those three crops, plus grains and garden vegetables, predominated along the lower Mississippi throughout the colonial era.

A generation later, four colonial officials—two Frenchmen, an Englishman, and a Spaniard—documented Louisiana's growing agricultural landscape and trade economy, complete with the spins and biases of the day.

An anonymous French officer, displeased with the state of New Orleans (see *Passing Judgment on New Orleans Society*), described in 1744 an agriculture- and forestry-based frontier exchange economy involving commodities and supplies moving among France, Caribbean colonies, and Indians in the interior:

> We trade at present with the Americans, to whom for their stuffs and rum we [give] chiefly peas and beans, which are very rare [in the French West Indies]; we also supply them with timber for building ships. To the merchants who bring stuffs, cloth, wine, brandy, liquors, arms, and meal from France, we give in exchange tobacco, rice, *mahis* [maize], cotton, indigo, skins, pine wood, cypress, cedar, log wood, pitch, tar, or piastres, [which are] paper bills having no currency but in the colony.

> Lastly we supply the savages [Indians] with fusils [flintlock muskets], powder, shot, knives, needles, razors, vermillion, woollen [*sic*], ribbons, blankets, skirts, blue and red cloth, and brandy…for which we get skins of wild oxen, kids, otters, beavers, venison, or wild fowl….[282]

Frenchman Michel de la Rouvillière, the commissary at New Orleans, scribed in September 1752 the "present situation of the colony in regard to its settlements, its products, and its commerce" to his superior in France, Minister Antoine Louis Rouillé. Michel's report provides a view of French Louisiana's modestly expanding agricultural production as well as New Orleans' emerging role in France's New World trade economy:

> The [Crown's] vessels came very late this year. This caused all kinds of merchandise to be scarce and expensive here…. [The price] declined upon the arrival of these vessels, which came, fifteen in number, almost together.

Ships loaded and unloaded Campeachy wood (dark heartwood from the logwood tree of Campeche, Mexico, used to extract a purple dye), "timber of all sorts and in abundance; tobacco in the form of snuff and twists, …indigo[,] and many more peltries than in the preceding [years], since more of them have come down than usual from the Illinois [country] and the Choctaws."

"The harvests of rice and corn will be rather bountiful in the interior of the colony," he predicted.

> Indigo will not yield so much because of the abundant rains…. The Illinois [country] has furnished much flour[;] enough has already come down to supply all the posts on the way and even the Natchitoches…. The plantations of wax trees that several individuals have made in the interior of the colony were astonishingly productive last winter. Sieur Dubreuil…alone has made at least six thousand pounds of this wax…and several have gone into the woods by the sea to gather it from the wild trees of this species. The public here uses no other material at all to furnish it light, and commerce has profited by a part of it for France and for America.

Michel is describing bayberry trees, also known as wax myrtles, whose berries yield a yellow-green wax when exposed over hot water. Early New Orleans was a major regional producer and exporter of candle wax made from this native coastal Louisiana tree. Planters also experimented successfully with cotton: wrote Michel, "I have seen some…cotton I found to be splendid," though, "together with the seeds, [t]hey are rather difficult to detach." The same Dubreuil who produced wax also attempted to solve the cotton ginning problem: "Sieur Dubreuil has just constructed a wheel that by means of two cylinders of copper, iron, or hard wood, joined together and turning one over the other like those of sugar mills, detaches these seeds quickly enough to make it possible to profit from it in commerce." (Claude Joseph Villars Dubreuil, a noted builder responsible for the extant Old Ursuline Convent, operated a sawmill powered by diverted river water at the present-day foot of Elysian Fields Avenue. Perhaps this was the site where Dubreuil designed his cotton gin. Successful or not, it would take another forty years for a mechanical cotton engine to transform plantation agriculture in the South—and New Orleans' destiny.) On the overall climate for plantation agriculture in Louisiana, Michel gushed:

> All the other products grow perfectly. All the seasons are perfectly distinct. Each one makes itself felt as it ought to. The climate is splendid. The summer is, to tell the truth, a little too warm and stormy, but that is exactly the time when the river is high.

High water struck Michel not as a liability, but an asset: "One can dispose of its water as one wishes without trouble or expense and at the same time…waters and…enriches one's land with the mud that the water leaves on it." Michel was equally upbeat about urban New Orleans:

> The settlers…have come out of their lethargy. They are all asking for negroes and really cannot succeed without that. Things are moving along very well. The colony is growing every day by itself. It is necessary, so to speak, only to spur it on. In the three years that I have been here about forty fine houses of brick have been built in New Orleans; several fine plantations have been organized and perfectly established; several sawmills and a number of settlers have been placed on new lands where they are living rather wretchedly while waiting for some negro workers who can help them to develop and clear them. Some…have sent me money…to have some negroes brought from the Cape [Français].

Michel issued a three-part recommendation for the colony's success: "send here good peasants, farmers, and decent people, and a supply of negroes"—and no bad soldiers, like those who recently proved to be "almost a total loss. The majority have already run away or died of drunkenness, of debauchery of all sorts, and of venereal diseases [and] scurvy…." Michel suggested recruiting settlers to Louisiana from the French islands of the Caribbean, "especially of Martinique…where they find themselves too cramped and limited for their plantations…."

Fitting a man dedicated to commercial development, Michel summarized that Louisiana "is, to tell the truth, my lord, the best land that there is in the world and the finest colony that the King could possess."[283]

Two years later, war broke out between French and English colonial interests in the territorially contested Ohio River Valley. The conflict spread worldwide in the late 1750s, increasing in both bloodshed and stakes. French forces in North America mostly succumbed by 1760, but fighting continued elsewhere for three more years. Foreseeing defeat, King Louis XV in 1762 secretly ceded France's claims west of the Mississippi, plus the "isle" of New Orleans, to his Spanish cousin King Carlos III, in compensation for Spain's loss of its Florida possession to the British. When France signed the Treaty of Paris in 1763, nearly all of the rest of French North America, including Louisiana east of the Mississippi as well as French Canada, became British territory. Francophone New Orleans not only lost its mother country for the unwanted Spanish dons, but gained an unwelcome new neighbor to north: British West Florida. English Capt. Philip Pittman was among those new neighbors.

Pittman, deployed to survey his country's new lands, described New Orleans' geography and plantation agriculture in the late 1760s:

> There are some plantations on the Bayouk [sic] of St. John, and on [Bayou Road] from thence to New Orleans. The settlements of the Gentilly are one mile from the Bayouk of St. John, on the side of a small creek [now-filled Bayou Gentilly], which also communicates with the lake Pontchartrain.
>
> Cannes Brulé, Chapitoula, and the German settlements [Kenner, Harahan, and Hahnville areas, respectively] join each other, and are a continuation of well cultivated plantations of near forty miles from New Orleans, on each side of the river....
>
> The different articles [grown on these plantations] are indigo, cotton, rice, maiz, beans, myrtle wax-candles, and lumber. The indigo of this country is much esteemed for its beautiful colour and good quality; the colour is brighter than that which is fabricated at St. Domingo. The cotton, though of a most perfect white, is of a very short staple, and is therefore not in great request. The maiz, different sorts of beans, rice, and myrtle candles, are articles in constant demand in St. Domingo.
>
> Some of the richest planters, since the year 1762, have begun the cultivation of sugar, and have erected mills for squeezing the canes; the sugar produced in this country is of a very fine quality, and some of the crops have been very large; but no dependence can be had on this, as some years the winters are too cold, and kill the canes in the ground.[284]

Agricultural production in Louisiana, most of which passed through New Orleans, increased markedly at the close of the French era. The colony exported 672,000 *livres'* worth of produce in 1755 and ten times that number in 1762 (6,662,000 livres), with tobacco accounting for the lion's share.[285]

By the 1770s, plantation agriculture dominated the lower Mississippi River landscape. Francisco Bouligny, a Spanish officer advising the Crown on Louisiana affairs, witnessed the growth of the colony during 1769 to 1775. While "the first ten leagues [thirty miles] upon entering the river are uninhabitable," he wrote, "after them both banks of the river are cleared and cultivated up to Manchac," near Baton Rouge.

This means about 175 riverine miles on both sides of the Mississippi, to 2,000 feet depth on either side, were in agricultural production, with livestock grazing on pasture behind the plantations and timber harvested from the woods behind the pastures. Bouligny then described how the plantations were delineated:

> Land is measured by river frontage, and all these lands, or most of them, belong to various individuals according to their abilities. But as a rule...they have 500 to 600 *varas* of river frontage, with 2,400 in depth. This is the usual concession; but beyond this distance, as the interior of the lands is not inhabitable, the concession is usually augmented in depth.[286]

Bouligny is describing the French custom (encoded in the 1716 edict) of delineating long lots perpendicular to river, measured by the unit *arpent*. Bouligny, a Spaniard, translated *arpent* to Spanish unit *vara*, which equates to about 2.8 English feet. Early Louisiana long lots typically ran four to ten *arpents* in frontage by forty in depth, which generally align with Bouligny's estimates. Where the river meanders and the natural levee stretches farther back, long lots spanned in depth to eighty arpents or more. Names for canals, levees, and streets reflecting the so-called "forty arpent line" or "Eighty Arpent Line" are still found throughout southern Louisiana today, a relic of colonial-era plantation agriculture.

Bouligny's description of the emerging elite planter class, and its dependence on institutionalized African slavery, foretells the agriculturally based aristocracy that would dominate Louisiana and New Orleans for much of the upcoming century:

> In all the countries of the world, the men who dedicate themselves to the cultivation of the soil are generally mere day-laborers.... On the contrary, in Louisiana there reigns a noble and proud vanity because the greatest praise that can be made of a boy is to call him a good planter, that is, a man intelligent in the toils of the field.[287]

> The majority of the planters who live [around] New Orleans are the most decent people.... Many of them are former officers from the time of the French[;] others are merchants who, having gained a certain well-being, have employed it in buying Negroes and a piece of land. [This] provides them with the ease to increase their capital.... They gather frequently to eat with their neighbors; and their conversations are always directed to the state of the harvest.... Each one has a gang of Negroes according to his ability, and the wealth of each one is measured by naming the Negroes he has.[288]

Events forthcoming in the new American century would augment the "reign" of the "noble and proud" planter class, and help make the lower Mississippi River plantation region home to one of the nation's highest concentration of millionaires. They would also subject thousands of Africans—to whom Bouligny referenced in the off-handed manner usually reserved for mere objects—to decades of enslavement on those lucrative lands.

Agriculture in the American Era

Sugar and cotton transform the South—and New Orleans

A sequence of events around the turn of the nineteenth century utterly transformed Louisiana agriculture, and launched New Orleans into the world economy.
First, in 1791, a slave rebellion destabilized the extremely profitable French sugar island
of Saint-Domingue. Troops sent by Napoleon failed to overcome insurgents and yellow
fever, and by 1804 the colony declared independence as Haiti. The loss diminished
Napoleon's interest in the costly and cumbersome Louisiana colony, which he viewed
as little more than a granary for Saint-Domingue. Wary of over-extending his colonial
empire, in need of money, and in light of impending war, Napoleon decided to sell the
entire Louisiana territory to the United States. Suddenly, New Orleans, for decades
the orphan of two declining, distracted Old World colonial empires, now found itself
strategically positioned to prosper under the dominion of an ascendant, unabashedly
capitalistic New World democracy. River commerce, once controlled by "individuals
purchasing the rights of monopoly from the king of Spain," in which "wealth circulated
in a very partial manner," now fell under "the American commercial system … of tolera-
tion and competition," which "diffuses [wealth] to all around." Anglo-American settlers
arrived in droves to Louisiana—some to New Orleans to work as merchants, others
to the lower Mississippi Valley as planters. "The influx of American speculators was so
great" after the Louisiana Purchase, wrote a disapproving but nevertheless impressed
Thomas Ashe in 1809, "that the character of commerce instantaneously changed, and
violence and competition, which in America means contention, reigned triumphant-
ly…." The number of merchants in New Orleans, he wrote, increased fifty-fold in six
years.[289]

As these geopolitical events unfurled, three agriculturally related technological
breakthroughs transpired over twenty years. In 1793, Eli Whitney invented the cotton
engine, or "gin," which dramatically improved the separation of cotton lint from seed.
In time, cotton cultivation spread into newly cleared Mississippi Valley lands mostly
north of Baton Rouge. Two years later, Jean Etienne de Boré of New Orleans succeeded in granulating sugar cane locally—a process practiced for centuries in the tropical
West Indies, but elusive in semi-tropical Louisiana—and replicated the success commercially. Serendipitously for Louisiana, the turmoil in Saint-Domingue decreased the
supply of West Indian sugar and increased demand for new Louisiana cane just as many
sugar-savvy Haitians arrived to New Orleans and helped launch a local sugar industry.
Sugar cane cultivation swiftly replaced fading colonial-era crops throughout the lower
Mississippi River region. "It is worthy of remark," wrote one visitor in 1810, "that the
plantations … from Natchez to New Orleans and still lower down, were formerly appropriated to the culture of indigo and rice, but the demand for these articles … being on

the decline, the attention of the planters is now turned to that of sugar and cotton, both of which [make] excellent shipments ...."[290] New Orleans served as the transshipment and marketing node, and later as processing center, for the region's exploding sugar and cotton exports. The two commodities spectacularly increased port traffic. "The exportation commerce of Louisiana, fifteen years ago, was carried on with thirty ships of moderate size," wrote Frenchman Francois Marie Perrin Du Lac in 1807 after visiting the region in 1801-03. "Since the cultivation of sugar and cotton, it has so increased, that above two hundred are employed."[291]

Finally, in 1812, the first Mississippi River steamboat docked at the city's riverfront. After a few years of working out technological, logistical, and legal barriers (namely the ill-advised monopoly granted to inventors Robert Fulton and Robert Livingston, overruled by the Supreme Court in 1824), steam shipping rapidly antiquated slow-moving keelboat traffic to upriver destinations, providing efficient transportation for hinterland exports and exterior imports to reach New Orleans' wharves.[292] Cotton ginning, sugar granulation, and steamboat transportation also helped entrench slavery in the region, and again, New Orleans was positioned to benefit—in the crassest commercial sense—becoming the busiest slave mart in the South.

"The products of Louisiana are already quite considerable," wrote former Napoleonic prefect Pierre Clément de Laussat later in life, as he scribed his memoirs of the Louisiana Purchase era. Laussat's description of American agricultural expansion into the Mississippi Valley at that time, though sardonically hyperbolic, divulges both grudging admiration for the new American nation and exasperation with Old World powers:

> Wherever the Anglo-Americans settle, land is fertilized and progress is rapid. There is always a group of them who act as trailblazers, going ... into the American wilderness ahead of the settlers .... They clear it, populate it, and then push on again and again.... They set up their temporary shanties, fell and burn trees, kill the Indians or are killed by them, and disappear ... either by death or by soon relinquishing to a more stable farmer....

> When a score or so of such new colonists have congregated into one location, two printers arrive—one a federalist, the other an antifederalist—then the doctors, then the lawyers, and then the fortune seekers. They drink toasts, nominate a speaker, set up a town, and raise many children. Finally, they advertise the sale of vast tracts of land [then] exaggerate the population [to] form an independent state ... and so another star appears on the flag of the United States!

> A district under the Spanish or French regime might begin, end, start again, get lost again, and so successively until its fate is sealed ... Under the Anglo-Americans, a newly born state...keeps on growing and strengthening.[293]

That growth meant more shipments to New Orleans, where additional legions of Anglo-American merchants, as well as Creole and foreign businessmen, oversaw handling and transshipment to ocean-going vessels bound for world ports.

The turn of the nineteenth century thus saw New Orleans transform from an isolated colony engaged in a regional-scale frontier exchange economy, to a key cog of a vast, export-driven Atlantic World economy. Out went colonial Louisiana's low-value, hither-and-thither exports, catalogued in 1791 as "indigo...skins of wild beasts, timber, lumber, planks, shingles, rice, tobacco, and corn...;"[294] in their place came vast, monocultural, slave-labor plantations of cotton and sugar, the former above Baton Rouge, the latter throughout the Louisiana deltaic plain southward to the sea. New Orleans' ensuing prosperity revolved around the financing, marketing, handling, storage, processing, and shipping of those two premier commodities.

Voyagers on the antebellum Mississippi witnessed the fruits of this agricultural productivity lining the river as well as floating down it. "In the whole distance to New Orleans, plantation touches plantation," marveled Timothy Flint in 1823; "I have seen in no part of the United States such a rich and highly cultivated tract.... Noble houses, massive sugar-houses, neat summer-houses, and numerous negro villages succeed each other [like] one continued village.... [It is the] richest agricultural district in the Union."[295] Wrote English geologist Charles Lyell as he sailed near Baton Rouge in the late winter of 1846, "A great many handsome country houses, belonging to the proprietors of sugar plantations, give a cultivated aspect to this region...."

> [T]he scenery is enlivened by a prodigious number of schooners and large steamers sailing down from the Ohio and Red rivers, heavily laden with cotton. This cotton has already been much compressed...but it undergoes, at New Orleans, still greater pressure, by steam power, to diminish its bulk before embarkation for Liverpool.

> The captain calculated that within the first seven hours after we left [downtown New Orleans], we had passed no less than ten thousand bales going down the river...amounting to 350,000 dollars. All this merchandize would reach *the great emporium* within twenty hours.... [296]

Much of the "great emporium's" professional class served as middlemen—agents, factors, lawyers, advisors, bankers, representatives—for wealthy planters. Each commodity spawned its own economic district within the city: the "Cotton District" formed around the intersection of Carondelet and Gravier streets, home to the Cotton Exchange and numerous factor offices; the "Sugar District" formed on the French Quarter levee around the foot of Bienville Street, where the Sugar Exchange and industrial sugar refining facilities operated.

The Civil War radically disrupted New Orleans' agricultural dependency, but only temporarily. Within a year, operators began recruiting Chinese field hands out of Cuba and, later, Italians out of Sicily to replace emancipated slaves as labor sources in the sugar fields. (Their effort would inadvertently create a "Chinatown" and a "Little Palermo" at opposite ends of downtown New Orleans.) With mostly low-paid black labor, cotton and sugar agriculture remained fundamental to the city's economy well into the twentieth century.

A series of factors dethroned King Cotton and its Crescent City retainers in the 1910s-30s, among them federal regulations, foreign imports, railroad and trucking competition with river transportation, and the westward shift of cotton cultivation to drier areas. Cotton acreage in Louisiana declined from almost two million acres in 1930 to a few hundred thousand in later decades. In New Orleans, the total number of cotton-related businesses listed in city directories declined from 152 in 1921 to 47 in 1945-46. Cotton factors, the quintessential power profession of antebellum times, declined from ninety-three in 1880, fifteen in 1921, and only one in 1949.[297]

The city's sugar industry suffered a similar fate. The new Chalmette Sugar Refinery moved the sugar processing industry from the French Quarter levee to semi-rural St. Bernard Parish in 1912. Disease, low yields, price drops, and foreign competition followed. Sugar factories (mills) in rural parishes diminished from 300 in 1900 to 54 in 1926. Louisiana's share of the national market fell from 11 percent around 1900 to 4.5 percent in 1937.[298] In New Orleans' Sugar District, brokers, factors, and firms almost completely disappeared by the early 1930s. The state's sugar cane industry regained its footing by the 1950s, counting over 2,300 farms and forty-eight mills, but subsequent free trade, increased competition, dropping prices, rising costs, low yields, and uncooperative weather steadily eroded its status. By 2005, only 730 sugar cane farms and thirteen mills remained in operation statewide.[299] Sugar cane cultivation remains a major part of southern Louisiana culture, but less and less so every year. A recent publication entitled *Delta Sugar*, by John B. Rehder, encapsulated the trend in its subtitle: "Louisiana's Vanishing Plantation Landscape."

Petroleum, shipping, and, now, the tourism and convention trade have long since supplanted the handling of early American-era agricultural commodities as the city's premier calling. Yet the modern cityscape is replete with their influences, from cotton factors' offices in the CBD, to sugar merchants' mansions in the Garden District, to the immense U.S. Custom House on Canal Street—once among the largest government buildings in the nation, built to process receipts on the vast agricultural riches of the Mississippi Valley as they passed through the Queen City of the South.

Constraining and Controlling the River

The blessings and curses of levee construction on the Mississippi

Springtime river floods quickly convinced French colonials in New Orleans that the natural *levée* (from *lever*, "to raise") provided insufficient protection from the Mississippi. The first organized effort to heighten and reinforce it began in 1722-23, when city engineers Le Blond de La Tour and Adrien de Pauger planned an earthen embankment about twelve feet wide reinforced with a double palisade of timbers. Original plans had to be scaled back because of an insufficient labor force and the death of La Tour in late 1723. By 1724, the first levee measured six feet wide, 3000 feet long, and probably three feet high, but was readily breached by the high waters of the Mississippi that spring. Three years later, a solid eighteen-foot-wide and three-foot-high levee (plus a parallel ditch to collect seepage) lined one mile of the town's riverfront. For manpower, the city at first obligated slave owners to assign their bondsmen thirty days' labor on public works, then adopted a tax instead.

Throughout the French colonial era, "extension of the levee line [beyond the city] was almost entirely the work of private land developers supervised at the local level, first by commandants, then by parish and county governments."[300] By 1732, riverfront levees extended twelve miles below New Orleans to thirty miles above it; by 1752, the berms spanned twenty miles below the city to thirty miles upriver, and advanced in that direction by about one mile per year.[301]

The traditional of localism continued under the Spanish, as each concession recipient bore the responsibility of levee construction, drainage ditch excavation, and road clearing. Le Page du Pratz, who resided in New Orleans from its founding to the 1730s and published his *History of Louisiana* in 1758, wrote

> On [both] banks of the river runs a causey, or mole [road following crest of levee] from the English Reach quite to the town, and about ten leagues beyond it; which makes about fifteen or sixteen leagues on each side the river; and which may be travelled in a coach or horseback, on the bottom as smooth as a table.[302]

A league measuring 2.5 to three miles, Le Page's estimates generally concur with those of an English captain who visited New Orleans in the late 1760s:

> The Leveé...extends from the *Detour des Anglois* [English Turn], to the upper settlement of the Germans, which is a distance of more than fifty miles, [with] a good coach-road all the way. The Leveé before the town is repaired at the public expense, [but] each inhabitant keeps that part in repair which is opposite to his own plantation.[303]

No integral flood-control infrastructure can be decentralized and "outsourced" to individuals in this manner. Failure of any one landowner to install and maintain properly his portion of the levee would compromise the entire system. An early attempt at centralized oversight came with Spanish Governor Carondelet's levee ordinance of 1792, which required syndicated residents to raise levees to the recent high-water mark of the river, while reinforcing their sides by filling in ditches and planting grass to conserve the soil. Livestock grazing was strictly forbidden, and in the most vulnerable places, "the owner will have to have at all times a deposit of pickets, planks, Spanish moss and other articles necessary to stop the crevasses under penalty of a fine of one hundred piastres."[304]

A weak federal government and rural isolation allowed localism to continue under American dominion. In New Orleans, the City Council gradually gained control over the waterfront and set standards (1810) for levee construction: at least three feet above the river at normal stage, one foot above high-water line, and five to six feet wide at the base for each foot in height. The effort at this time fell under the direction of City Engineer Jacques Tanesee, who designed embankments that, unlike today's trapezoidal berms, faced the river with a wall of wooden pilings reinforced by an earthen backslope which doubled as a wharf. Levees in adjacent areas rarely conformed to those standards, thereby reducing the system's overall effectiveness to that of the weakest link.

Yet, as American expansion ensued, levees of varying standrds expanded upstream at a rapid pace. Circa-1770 levees paralleled the river from English Turn up to the German Coast; by 1812 they extended up to Old River; and by 1844 the dikes reached beyond Greenville, Mississippi.[305] A visitor during 1819-21 described the region's "artificial embankment" as

> thirty or forty yards from the natural bank of the river, four to six feet high, and six to nine feet broad at the base, [extending] 130 miles on the eastern, and about 170 on the western side of the river.... [I]ts preservation is secured by the obligation which the law imposes on every individual to maintain in good repair that part which is before his own land...enforced by commissioners who are appointed to inspect and direct repairs.[306]

Fifteen years later, Joseph Holt Ingraham described New Orleans' system in his travelogue, *The South-West by a Yankee*:

> [The levee] extends, on both sides of the river, to more than one hundred and fifty miles above New-Orleans. This *levée* is properly a dike, thrown up on the verge of the river, from twenty-five to thirty feet in breadth, and two feet higher than high-water mark; leaving a ditch, or fossé, on the inner side, of equal breadth, from which the earth to form the levée is taken. Consequently...when the river is full...the surface of the river will be *four feet higher* than the surface of the country....[307]

Disaster inspired reform in flood-control policy. A crevasse in the levee of Pierre Sauvé's Jefferson Parish plantation on May 3, 1849 flooded over 200 blocks in New Orleans, by filling up the backswamp and inundating the city from the rear. "Sauvé's Crevasse" ranked as the city's worst flood until Katrina in 2005 (see *"May Heaven Avert Another Such Catastrophe!"*), and forced the federal government to consider its role in overseeing lower Mississippi River flood control. Washington responded by offering federally owned swamplands to states in the Mississippi Valley in exchange for their commitment to build levees, drain the swamps, sell the land, and recoup their investment. The Swamp and Overflow Land Act of 1850 spurred more levee construction, but fell short of expectations. Also at this time, the federal government engaged in matters of the navigability and control of the Mississippi by funding two landmark (and competing) surveys. One was led by Andrew Atkinson Humphreys, which would recommend a "levees-only" policy to control the Mississippi; the other, by Charles Ellet, suggested a comprehensive approach that included levees to constrain the river, and outlets and reservoirs to accommodate it. Humphreys' research would lead to increased federal involvement in levee development later in the century (and to great reconsideration in the wake of the 1927 flood, when the wisdom of Ellet's research proved true).[308]

The state also entered the picture. In 1854, the Louisiana state legislature formed four flood districts and a Board of Swamp Land Commissioners to oversee levee development. In time, this entity would evolve into the "levee district," a consortium of governmental bodies that manages levee work and possesses the power to levy taxes.[309] The age of localism was ending. But then war clouds gathered, derailing progress for over a decade. Miles of existing levees in Louisiana deteriorated during the Civil War.

Flood control came of age in the civil-engineering era of the late nineteenth century. Locally, city engineers in New Orleans proposed in 1871 an integrated system of protection levees and urban drainage networks, though full execution would take another generation. Statewide, in 1886, Louisiana created levee districts to begin coordinating levee maintenance efforts. Most significantly, at the national level, Congress created the Mississippi River Commission in 1879 and directed it to work with the Army Corps of Engineers in controlling the lower Mississippi. With the Commission "offering advice, serving as a clearing house for technical data, and providing two thirds of the funding required for construction, levees in Louisiana reached a new level of sophistication."[310] In 1890, the state created the Orleans Levee District and the Board of Levee Commissioners, charging them with the "construction, repair, control and maintenance of all levees in the District, whether on river, lake, canal or elsewhere...."[311] By 1892, a half-million cubic yards of soil went into the construction of five miles of new levees and the reinforcement of twenty-four existing miles. Over a million more cubic yards were added to the city's levees in 1892-96. In 1907, earth-moving machines were introduced, reducing construction costs by half while speeding work and improving quality. By the late 1920s, the Orleans Levee Board's workers had moved an additional fifteen million cubic yards of soil to the New Orleans riverfront levees in accordance with the exacting standards of the Mississippi River Commission.[312]

While the massive earthen wall arising around New Orleans gave its citizens a sense of security, the emphasis on levees alone as the defense against floods—the "levees only" policy advocated by Humphreys and others, including the public, since the mid-1800s—backfired during the Great Flood of 1927. Levees are critical to the control of a river but, without backup mechanisms, they raise the river's level and power and thus worsen the chances and consequences of a crevasse. In other words, they alleviate the annual nuisance of minor flooding but increase the risk of an occasional catastrophic deluge. Levees also sever the annual replenishment of sediment and freshwater that the river historically imparted to the deltaic plain.

The 1927 deluge flood inspired quick passage of the Flood Control Act, which cemented the federal government's financial responsibility for, and engineering commitment to, a massively augmented Mississippi River flood control system. Immense alteration of the Mississippi Valley's physical and human geography was forthcoming: levees would be raised, broadened, strengthened, and extended; floodways, spillways, and runoff channels were to be excavated; reservoirs, locks, dams, weirs, and other structures would be installed. The changes, mostly executed in the 1930s-60s, radically affected millions of people, where and how they lived, and how they perceived their environmental security or risk. The tradeoff: the Flood Control Act also specified that the government would not be liable for losses should those flood-control systems fail.

Locally, as a result of the Flood Control Act of 1928, levees were realigned, reinforced, and raised, creating the earthen berms Louisianians know today. Backing up the traditional levee control of the river were the Bonnet Carré and Morganza spillways, built to accommodate the will of the Mississippi by providing "safety values" to divert dangerously high water into adjacent water bodies. No major Mississippi River levee breaches have occurred in the New Orleans metropolitan area since 1927.

Until recently, the Orleans Parish Levee Board maintained, according to the design grades of the U.S. Army Corps of Engineers, twenty-eight miles of levees and floodwalls and seventy-three floodgates along the Mississippi River, plus another 101 miles of levees and 107 floodgates along Lake Pontchartrain and the navigation and outfall canals.[313] While the latter failed infamously during Hurricane Katrina in 2005, exposing engineering flaws at Army Corps and leading to the unification of parish levee boards, the riverfront levees succeeded in keeping a twelve-foot-above-normal gulf surge flowing *up* the Mississippi from pouring into New Orleans. That provided little comfort to the tens of thousands of homeowners who flooded because of canal levee breaches—failures for which, according to the 1928 Flood Control Act, the government was not liable.[314]

The control of the Mississippi River, an effort spanning three regimes and nearly three centuries, represents one of humanity's grandest manipulations of a natural system. It has rendered nearly as many blessings—productive croplands, a livable New Orleans, a society flourishing on a bountiful deltaic plain— as it has curses: coastal erosion, subsidence, saltwater intrusion, ecological decline, and levee-dependent land-development schemes that lure settlers into hazardous flood plains. Spatially, the effort resolved the threat of Mississippi River flooding to New Orleans proper—only to transfer that threat to the rising, encroaching Gulf of Mexico. Temporally, it succeeded in preventing frequent minor floods—but increased the chances of an occasional mega-catastrophe.

Levees, in short, both enable and endanger human life—a classic Louisiana dilemma.

Scoring and Scouring the Land

The benefits and costs of canal excavation in a delicate environment

Why score and scour thin, delicate soils and invite dangerous water bodies into the heart of a bowl-shaped metropolis? That question perplexed many outside observers as the Katrina saga played out in the late summer of 2005. Motivations for canal excavation that seemed rational in the past now bear greater scrutiny.

Pressure to improve access between the Mississippi River and Lake Pontchartrain inspired canal plans as early as 1718. One proposal appeared on what may be the earliest city plat, *Plan de la Ville de la Nouvelle Orléans projettée en Mars 1721*. Technologically too ambitious for the era, the envisioned canal never passed the conceptual stage. Nor did Gov. Périer's suggestion in 1727 to dig a channel from city limits to Bayou St. John. Most waterway excavation in early colonial times took the form of minor ditches for draining runoff from muddy streets, which residents crossed on raised sidewalks (*banquettes*) and wooden bridges.

Around 1750, Claude Joseph Villars Dubreuil directed his slaves to excavate a river-diversion canal to power a *moulin à planches* (sawmill) on a plantation immediately below New Orleans. That project, later called the Marigny Canal, eventually influenced the rectilinearity of Elysian Fields Avenue when the Faubourg Marigny was laid out in 1805. Despite the potential danger of provoking a crevasse, diverting the river for hydrological energy was not uncommon in colonial times. English Capt. James Pittman reported in 1770 that "many of the planters" near New Orleans "have saw-mills, which are worked by the waters of the Mississippi in the time of the floods, and [go] day and night till the waters fall."[315] The practice continued into the American years. Wrote Fortescue Cuming in 1810, "a number of mill races [have been] cut through the levee. On these races saw mills are erected for sawing plank, boards for building houses, and others for making sugar boxes...exported to the Havannah."[316]

Canal excavation for transportation promised far more profit than those dug for energy. New Orleanians in the late 1700s still relied on ancient Bayou Road to reach Bayou St. John and Lake Pontchartrain, limiting cargo and passenger movement between city and lake. Spanish Gov. Hector Carondelet addressed this problem in 1794 by directing the excavation of a canal to the bayou, an idea first broached by Governor Périer almost seventy years earlier. The initial narrow ditch, used for drainage, would be widened for schooners and lined with tree-lined banquettes, providing a promenade for citizens as well as freight access to the lake.[317] Completed by 1796 at a width of fifteen French feet, and later privatized and widened in the early American years, the Carondelet Canal developed into a key commercial waterway for "cotton, tobacco, lumber, wood, lime, brick, tar, pitch, bark, sand, oysters, marketing...furs and peltries,"[318] while also serving to drain runoff from city streets. Appreciative citizens "erected a monument...in the English, French, and Spanish languages, purporting, that, ' This canal was designed, planned, and executed by the Baron de Carondelet, for the convenience of the city.' "[319] Maj. Amos Stoddard described the waterway in 1812:

> This canal rises in a basin...sufficiently capacious to accommodate several small vessels. It extends in a direct line about two miles to St. John's creek, and is about twenty feet wide. This is of great advantage to the city, particularly as the products of the lake and back country, such as fish, lime, tar, [and] pitch...find an easy water access to the inhabitants; whereby a difficult and expensive cartage of three miles [on Bayou Road] is avoided.[320]

The waterway gave the city access to lakeshore and coastal trade as well as to the piney-woods regions behind them. When a flatboat navigated successfully in 1824 from the wild headwaters of the Pearl River in central Mississippi all the way to the Carondelet Canal's turning basin, it was hailed as "a new and interesting experiment in the inland commerce of this country [which] will lead to events of incalcuable benefit to the trade of New Orleans."[321] A contributor to the *New York Times* later remarked on the bustling spectacle of that turning basin, located immediately behind the city at present-day Basin and Orleans streets:

> The commerce of Carondelet Canal ... is annually increasing[;] a large trade is carried on with the river and seaboard towns of Alabama, Mississippi, Florida, &c.... The large fleet of brigs, schooners, sloops, and steamers, which come up to the city in the rear, at once strikes the attention of the stranger, and he wonders how the vessels ever got up ... into the heart of the city.[322]

Anglo-American businessmen in the upper city responded to the lower (predominantly Creole) city's successful canal project, as well as its recent Pontchartrain Railroad, by planning their own city-to-lake waterway. The New Orleans Canal and Banking Company invested four million dollars in 1831 to excavate a channel to the lake, measuring sixty feet wide, accommodating six-foot-draft vessels, lined with a levee and a paved toll road, and terminating in a turning basin near Julia Street's present-day intersection with Loyola Avenue. For labor, the company recruited poor Irish "ditchers," who died by the thousands from disease and brutal work conditions.

The New Orleans Canal, completed in 1838 and nicknamed the New Basin Canal to distinguish it from the Carondelet ("Old Basin") Canal, soon proved a success. The waterway brought to the inner city a steady stream of sand, gravel, and shell for fill; lumber, firewood, and charcoal; fruits, vegetables, cotton, and seafood, and myriad other cargo from the lake and coast. Both navigation canals, their adjacent shells roads, and the Pontchartrain Railroad all helped connect New Orleans with its neighbors while circumventing slow and costly trips across the land or down the river. "The citizens seem *determined* to avoid the one hundred and ten miles of river navigation," wrote one visitor in 1832, when two of these projects were under development.[323] That observation encapsulates much of the motivation for the scoring and scouring of the New Orleans landscape.

Drainage explains most of the rest. The Old and New Basin canals were joined by a series of drainage ("outfall") canals excavated in the 1870s as part of the emerging municipal drainage system, which came to fruition at the turn of the twentieth century. Unlike earlier gravity-fed drainage ditches, massive pumps propelled rainwater through these wider waterways and into adjacent water bodies. Because they had to be lined with levees, the drainage canals formed new hydrological sub-basins in the lakeside marshes, because they bisected the ever-so-slight topography of the natural basins with severe and sudden barriers. The 17th Street, Orleans, London Avenue, and other later drainage canals (some open, others covered) escorted unwanted rainwater out of the topographic bowl, but also allowed a channel of lake water to sit within and above the bowl, a few feet from newly developing residential neighborhoods. This is usually not a problem, so long as the levees hold.

Competition among ports motivated city leaders in the 1910s to advocate streamlining navigation routes and creating new dock space off the river. The vision soon evolved into the "Inner Harbor Navigation Canal." A committee organized in 1918 identified various benefits that the so-called "Industrial Canal" would bring to New Orleans: the creation of ship-building sites within a protected, fixed-level harbor; the development of new water frontage that could be privately held (river frontage in New Orleans was traditionally held in the public trust); the creation of space for new facilities to handle, store, and transport cargo; and the extension of the Intracoastal Canal.[324]

In May 1918, the corridor for the canal was selected—a 5.3-mile-long swath with a 1600-foot-wide right-of-way located roughly two miles downriver and parallel to Elysian Fields Avenue (where, incidentally, a similar canal was foreseen ninety years earlier). The selected corridor boasted definite advantages, being (1) within Orleans Parish limits; (2) across a relatively narrow land strip between river and lake; (3) mostly undeveloped; (4) convenient to existing shipping lanes and port activity; and (5) either city-owned or readily acquirable. Its riverside half followed a tract owned by the Ursuline Nuns since 1821 (plus adjacent Convent Street and some nearby blocks), which the nuns, "[w]ith exceptional generosity,"[325] donated to the city in 1911. The orientation of the nuns' property and the surrounding street network in the Ninth Ward (present-day Bywater and Holy Cross neighborhoods) determined the northeasterly orientation of the lower portion of the Industrial Canal; once the corridor got past the developed area along the natural levee, designers dog-legged the path in a northwesterly direction to achieve a shorter route to the lake. Thus physical, historical, economic, and political geography all played roles in siting the Industrial Canal.

With the Dock Board in charge and the renowned George W. Goethals Company as consulting engineers, ground was broken on June 6, 1918. Digging a major canal through a swamp connecting a powerful river and a bay of the Gulf of Mexico presented numerous engineering challenges. For one, levees had to be built along the excavation, to prevent flooding of the lowlands. A lock was necessary, because the tidally influenced lake lay only inches above the sea while the river flowed anywhere from one to twenty feet above that level. Turning basins were needed to accommodate larger vessels.

Dredges had to enter the dig site via the lake and Bayou Bienvenue because boring in directly from the Mississippi was too risky. Preventing waterlogged soils from sliding into the excavation proved challenging, while occasional cypress trunks embedded in the muck jammed the suction dredges and slowed progress.[326] The recently installed drainage system at Florida Walk had to be siphoned beneath the canal, and existing railroads had to be rerouted. At one point, the Dock Board decided to double the bed size from the lock to the lake, requiring further excavation. With labor gangs, mechanized excavators, pile drivers, dredges, dynamite, and other implements, the city's largest single-site construction project to date redefined the geography of metropolitan region.

As the main channel reached completion in September 1919, attention turned to the great lock.[327] Located about 2,000 feet in from the Mississippi, the lock measured 640 feet long, only 74 feet wide, and 50 feet deep. The five-gate motorized device raised and lowered vessels between the average-ten-foot-high river and the sea-level lake. An engineering landmark, the lock ranked among the largest in the nation at the time and lay upon soils far less stable than any previous project of this type.

Envisioned for over two centuries, New Orleans finally accomplished its dream of connecting lake and river on January 29, 1923. Eight days later, the fire tug *Samson* carried Gov. John M. Parker and distinguished guests through the lock, opening the canal for navigation.[328] At the May 5, 1923 dedication ceremony of the Industrial Canal, Governor Parker declared that the waterway would "equip New Orleans to be, in the broadest sense, the gateway of the Mississippi Valley for its interchange of products with the markets of the world."[329]

Soon after its completion, the Dock Board adapted the canal into an inner harbor, accommodating not just the passage of vessels but their docking and loading needs. Among the new features was the six-block-long shedded Galvez Street Wharf, added in 1924. The modification reflected the sentiment that the dispersed, end-to-end nature of the old river wharves would someday necessitate the development of compact, economical dock space somewhere other than the Mississippi. Excavation of the Intracoastal Waterway ("ICWW," 1940s), a barge route running through protected waters from Texas to Florida, furthered that vision. The ICWW, jutting through cypress swamp eastwardly from the Industrial Canal, gave metropolitan New Orleans another watery access route to gulf waters.

The Industrial Canal played an important role in the city's World War II effort. The Florida Avenue Wharf opened to handle increased business; legendary shipbuilder Andrew Jackson Higgins built LCM tank-carriers, FS ships, and PT boats at a sprawling facility near Gentilly Boulevard; and the Army Quartermaster Corps (1919), at the river end of the canal, served as the Port of Embarkation for troops departing for the front lines.

For the port and navigation interests, the Industrial Canal proved a success. For St. Bernard Parish and many Ninth Ward residents, the waterway severed them from the urban core (see *How the Poor Third Became the Lower Ninth*), inconvenienced their daily commutes, and lowered their property values. For the metropolis in general, the canal dangerously introduced adjacent water bodies into the urban heart, and necessitated the erection of new levees and floodwalls along areas that had subsided below sea level. The adjacent ICWW formed another gulf-connected waterway, its guide levee potentially funneling surges into the Industrial Canal and yards away from people's homes.

Still more pressure for efficient navigation access came from the shipping industry. As the vision for the Industrial Canal arose with World War I on the horizon, the idea to connect the Industrial Canal (and thence the river) directly with the Gulf of Mexico via a "Mississippi River-Gulf Outlet Canal," later dubbed MR-GO, originated when war clouds gathered again in the early 1940s. Local government authorities and business leaders met with the U.S. Army Corps of Engineers in 1943 and agreed that a tidewater canal would put New Orleans and the Mississippi Valley's vast inland-waterway network back in competition with routes that utilized the Panama Canal for east-west shipping. Participants disagreed, however, on the route of the seaway: some advocated an east-bank path from the Industrial Canal to the Gulf of Mexico; others favored a west-bank route from Intracoastal Canal to Grand Isle.

The war delayed the plan until the late 1940s, when local leaders and politicians in Washington made headway promoting the project. Funding was lost, however, when Sen. Russell Long withdrew an amendment that would have authorized $67 million for the project when he sensed that opposition from advocates of the competing St. Lawrence Seaway would ruin the effort. Similar legislation met the same fate twice again by 1953. "Apparently, upper Mississippi Valley supporters of the Louisiana seaway were more interested in the St. Lawrence seaway, which New Orleans opposed, and withdrew their votes until the St. Lawrence project passed Congress," wrote historian Gary Bolding. "After Congressional approval of the St. Lawrence seaway in 1954, opposition to the New Orleans project faded."[330] A bill for New Orleans' seaway finally passed and was signed into law by President Eisenhower on March 29, 1956.

The first phase of the project (1958-59) altered twenty million cubic yards of local topography and bathymetry by enlarging the ICWW between the Industrial Canal and Paris Road. Phase two (1959-61) dredged a narrow access channel from the ICWW to the Breton Sound, affecting twenty-seven million cubic yards in St. Bernard Parish. The third and fourth phases (1960-65 and finalized in 1968) enlarged this access channel, from Paris Road to the –38-foot bathymetric contour in the Gulf of Mexico, an excavation of 225,000,000 cubic yards of saline marsh. Spoil was accumulated on a 4000-foot-foot-long guide levee paralleling the lower MR-GO in St. Bernard Parish, while spoil from the excavation of the spacious turning basin in New Orleans (at the point where the Industrial Canal, MR-GO, and ICWW all intersect) went to shore up the area now occupied by the Jordan Road Terminal.[331]

The completed MR-GO channel measured 36 feet deep and 500 feet wide in its inland stretch, and slightly larger in its offshore portion. It eliminated 37 shipping miles between New Orleans and the open gulf, and provided ample opportunities for dockside development within the Port of New Orleans. "Sailing time, ship turnaround time, navigation hazards, and congestion all tend to be reduced by the [MR-GO]," reported the Army Corps of Engineers.[332]

Nevertheless, the MR-GO fell short of economic expectations. While annual traffic on the seaway averaged 7,193,000 tons of freight in 1984-93, tonnage declined steadily in the 1990s, accounting for 11 percent of port activity in 1990 and only 5 percent in 1998.[333] The project failed to draw the wharves and dockside facilities away from the Mississippi to become the CENTROPORT that was envisioned in the 1970s. At that time, observers predicted that the Mississippi would be free of port facilities by 2000. Instead, by the millennium, the vision and the trend had decidedly reversed back to the historical circumstance of riverside wharves. Recognizing the difficulty of large container ships in navigating the MR-GO to dock in the Industrial Canal, the Dock Board decided to create a "mega-wharf" by combining and expanding the uptown river terminals at Napoleon and Nashville Avenues. The sophisticated new uptown container wharf, coupled with worsening delays on the narrow and shallow eastern navigation canals, effectively shifted the fulcrum of port activity back to the Mississippi by the early 2000s. The MR-GO remained open for a few shipping interests.

Environmentally, the MR-GO ranks among the region's—or rather, the federal government's—worst mistakes. The project destroyed 8,000 acres of wetlands during its inception, subsequently caused severe coastal erosion and salt-water intrusion, and permanently forged a minimum-friction pathway for gulf storm surges to enter the metropolis. During hurricanes Katrina and Rita in 2005 (not to mention Betsy in 1965), guide levees along the Y-shaped junction of the Intracoastal Waterway and MR-GO "funneled" an eighteen-foot-high surge into the Industrial Canal, raising the level and speed of the current. Levees along all three navigation canals either were overtopped, disintegrated, or in the case of the Industrial Canal, breached catastrophically at the expense of many lives. It was not the first time that a man-made navigation exacerbated a disaster: in 1871, a breach on the New Basin Canal levee allowed high Lake Pontchartrain water, fed by a Mississippi River crevasse at Bonnet Carré, to inundate the rear portions of the Second, Third, and Fourth wards. The Bonnet Carré Flood ranked as the city's second-worst deluge until 2005.[334]

It took hundreds of lives in St. Bernard Parish, the Lower Ninth Ward, and New Orleans East to convince the Army Corps and other key authorities that the MR-GO must be closed. As of late 2007, congressional authorization for the waterway's partial closure is in place, but funding appropriation is not. "Closure" can mean any number of things; the Corps currently envisions deauthorizing the waterway from the Intracoastal Waterway junction to the gulf, and constructing a twelve-foot-wide, seven-foot-above-sea-level rock dike across the channel at Bayou La Loutre, a project that would cost $24.7 million and take about six months. Literally filling the channel would have cost nearly three billion dollars, taken decades to complete, and required over one-third of a trillion cubic yards of sediment to fill only half of the MR-GO — a disquieting commentary on just how much environmental havoc the project wreaked.[335] Meanwhile, terminal operations formerly dependent on the MR-GO connection to the Industrial Canal (which itself was silted-up by Katrina's surge and remains bottlenecked by a narrow lock) are relocating back to the natural banks of the Mississippi, where their predecessors did business since 1718. Environmental historians today consider the MR-GO a poster child for NEPA legislation (passed a few years after the canal was completed), which subjects federal projects to far more rigorous environmental-impact analysis.

Retrospection obligates us to recall the historical context in which these ill-fated decisions were made. City authorities in times past rightfully worried about the diminishing importance of the Mississippi River due to Northern canal excavation, railroad construction, industrial development, and other challenges to New Orleans' transportation advantage (see *Lessons in Over-Reliance*). Given limited levels of ecological and geological understanding, they responded in a rational way—by answering the competition with canals and seaways of their own. The public and private sectors thus scored, scoured, and scarred the delicate soils of the New Orleans region because the near-term need for drainage, navigation, and resource extraction seemed more pressing than theoretical storm surges and coastal erosion seemed threatening. The effort, until recently, hardly even rose to the level of an acknowledged dilemma: authorities generally viewed such projects as purely advantageous until they proved to be partially lethal. Little deliberation or reflection appears in the historical records of these decisions.

Now we know better. It is hoped that no major canal or seaway will ever be dug in or around New Orleans again, while existing waterways whose costs outweigh their benefits will be gated and, if possible, closed. Reversing two centuries of canal excavation is the order for the next century.

A Trip Across the Backswamp

Eyewitness descriptions of New Orleans' now-disappeared marshes and swamps

> [B]eyond the city... all is level as the ocean, with the dark woods growing gray in the distance, then blue, and fainter blue, as they vanish over the rim of the world.[336]
>
> —John Mitchell, describing the backswamp
> from the roof of the Custom House in 1858

While riverside New Orleans in the 1820s bustled with population and commerce, those dark, gray, and rather ominous expanses by Lake Pontchartrain lay mostly vacant and wild. Impenetrable bamboo-like reeds covered the lakeshore's thin spongy soils, while myriad inlets and minor bayous intersected the salt grasses and terminated in lakeside shell banks and detritus. Farther inland, cut-over cypress forests offered an equally foreboding environment. Few reasons compelled New Orleanians even to visit, let alone live amid, the marsh and backswamp near the Lake Pontchartrain shore.

Across the lake and eastward to the Gulf Coast, however, lucrative commercial opportunities beckoned. The growing metropolis needed lumber, tar, bricks, firewood, game, and other raw materials from the piney woods of the Florida Parishes; its citizens wanted quick and comfortable access to Biloxi, Mobile, Pensacola, and beyond. Bayou St. John, Carondelet Canal, and their adjacent shell roads—the only passages across the marsh at the time—left much to be desired for both cargo and passenger travel. A visitor from Mobile in 1828 typified the experience of confused travelers arriving to New Orleans from the Gulf Coast in that era:

> We landed at a place called, I think, the Piquets [probably Spanish Fort, along the Lake Pontchartrain shore], about six or seven miles from New Orleans.... This short distance we passed over on a road skirting a sluggish Creek [Bayou St. John] running in the midst of a swamp overgrown with cypress and others thirsty trees, rising out of a thick, rank underwood.[337]

A slow, bumpy carriage through a threatening swamp made for a sorry ingress and egress to a city destined for greatness. There had to be a better way.

A group of lower-faubourg businessmen that same year endeavored to solve this problem with an exciting new transportation technology: railroad. The men formed a company in 1829, won a state charter in 1830, gained rights to a direct, unobstructed, five-mile route connecting river and lake, and commenced work clearing the track bed. On April 23, 1831, the horse-drawn Pontchartrain Railroad made its inaugural run. Six stagecoach-like cars bearing state and local dignitaries, a band, and the company stockholders

> moved in the most imposing manner to the sound of music amidst a large concourse of admiring spectators, who lined each side of the road, and reached the lake by happy coincidence at the moment the Mobile steamboat arrived for the first time at Port Pontchartrain with the mail. The mail and passengers were immediately forwarded to the city... and reached the head of the road in half an hour.[338]

The Pontchartrain Railroad became the first railroad west of the Appalachians, and first in the nation to complete its track system. Seventeen months later, it introduced steam rail locomotion to the city, "to the great admiration and wonder of a vast concourse of our citizens, who were assembled...to witness this novel and interesting sight."[339]

Rickety and primitive as the line was (Abraham Oakey Hall called it in 1847 a "relic from the infantile days of the art of steam propulsion" and its locomotive "one thousand mosquito power"[340]), the Pontchartrain Railroad had a significant impact on the economics and geography of the lower city. It gave New Orleanians, for the first time, thirty-minute access to the lakefront. It bolstered numerous enterprises needing cargo moved northward or eastward. It also transformed Elysian Fields Avenue into a wide, straight, and ever-lengthening thoroughfare. Thousands of passengers arriving to New Orleans after 1831 sailed not up the Mississippi to the world-renown riverfront levee of New Orleans—its "front door"—but through the Rigolets channel to tiny Milneburg (present-day Elysian Fields intersection with Leon C. Simon), where, sometimes confused and disoriented, they boarded "Smokey Mary" and rode down Elysian Fields through the city's "back door." Among these visitors were presidents, dignitaries, celebrities, illustrious names of the day—and travel memoirists, usually from the Northeast or Europe, who toured the nation's major cities with pen in hand. Some left behind rich descriptions of the trip across the backswamp.

One of the first visitors to describe the Pontchartrain Railroad and the Elysian Fields landscape was Joseph Holt Ingraham, around 1833-34. "Its advantages to New-Orleans are incalculable," he wrote; the line represented "an avenue of wealth" on which "a great trade is carried on with Mobile and other places along the Florida coast...with safety and rapidity."[341] He paid six "bits" for the round-trip passage to Milneburg and boarded the eight-to-ten-car train (which, incidentally, was segregated by race) at an elongated station at the foot of Elysian Fields. With the clanging of a bell, "our fiery leader moved forward, smoking like a race-horse, slowly and steadily at first—then, faster and faster, till we flew along the track with breathless rapidity." Ingraham then observed the physical landscape, embracing the widespread nineteenth-century view of the natural world as a threatening and foreboding place:

> The rail-road, commencing at the Levée, runs for the first half mile through the centre of a broad street, with low detached houses on either side. A mile from the Levée we had left the city and all dwellings behind us [near the North Claiborne intersection], and were flying through the fenceless, uninhabited marshes, where nothing meets the eye but dwarf trees, rank, luxuriant undergrowth, tall, coarse grass, and vines, twisting and winding their long, serpentine folds around the trunks of the trees like huge, loathsome water-snakes. By the watch, we passed a mile-stone every three minutes and a half; and in less than nineteen minutes, arrived at the lake. Here, quite a village of handsome, white-painted hotels, cafés, dwellings, store-houses, and bathing rooms [Milneburg] burst at once upon our view; running past them, we gradually lessened our speed, and finally came to a full stop on the pier…. The pier, constructed of piles and firmly planked over, was lined with sloops and schooners, which were taking in and discharging cargo, giving quite a bustling, business-like air to this infant port. Boys, ragged negroes, and gentlemen amateurs, were fishing in great numbers farther out in the lake; others were engaged in the delicate amusement of cray-fishing, while on the right the water was alive with bathers….[342]

After brushing shoulders with French- and English-speaking locals raising a ruckus at Milneburg's smoked-filled cafés and billiard halls, Ingraham reboarded. Alas, the return trip did not go so smoothly: somewhere between the Gentilly Ridge and the city, the locomotive struck and completely severed a cow.

In 1839, the Englishman James Silk Buckingham arrived from Mobile to Port Pontchartrain and boarded the train through "a perfect swamp or morass…with impervious woods and thickets on either side" for the half-hour journey to New Orleans. He was more attuned to the cultural landscape than the physical one. Here he describes the Faubourg Marigny:

> The avenue by which we entered the city was called Les Champs Elysées; and every thing that caught our attention reminded us strongly of Paris. The lamps were hung from the centre of ropes passing across the streets, as in France; women were seen walking unbonneted, with gay aprons and caps; the names of all the streets and places we passed were French; the car-drivers, porters, and hackney-coachmen, spoke chiefly French; the shops, signs, gateways, pavements, and passengers moving in the streets, all seemed so perfectly Parisian, that if a person could be transported here suddenly, without knowing the locality, it would be difficult for him to persuade himself that he was not in some city of France.[343]

The English geologist Charles Lyell arrived by a Lake Pontchartrain steamer on Mardi Gras 1846, and traveled the Pontchartrain Railroad bound for the St. Charles Hotel. The train

> conveyed us in less than an hour to the great city, passing over swamps in which the tall cypress, hung with Spanish moss, was flourishing, and below

it numerous shrubs just bursting into leaf. In many gardens of the suburbs, the almond and peach trees were in full blossom[;] the blue-leaved palmetto, and the leaves of a species of iris ... were very abundant. We saw a tavern called the "Elysian Fields Coffee House," and some others with French inscriptions. There were also many houses with porte-cochères, high roofs, and volets, and many lamps suspended from ropes attached to tall posts on each side of the road, as in the French capital. We might indeed have fancied that we were approaching Paris, but for the negroes and mulattos, and the large verandahs reminding us that the windows required protection from the sun's heat. It was a pleasure to hear the French language spoken....[344]

During his tour of the South in 1853-54, a disoriented Frederick Law Olmsted encountered a substantially more developed and deforested environment along Elysian Fields Avenue.

There were many small buildings near the jetty, erected on piles over the water—bathing-houses, bowling-alleys, and billiard-rooms, with other indications of a place of holiday resort—and, on reaching the shore, I found a slumbering village. [Then] a locomotive backed, screaming hoarsely, down the jetty; and I returned to get my seat.

Off we puffed, past the restaurant ... through the little village of white houses ... and away into a dense, gray cypress forest. For three or four rods [about 60 feet], each side of the track, the trees had all been felled and removed, leaving a dreary strip of swamp, covered with stumps.... So it continued, for two or three miles; then the ground became dryer [Gentilly Ridge], there was an abrupt termination of the gray wood ; the fog was lifting ... disclosing a flat country, skirted still, and finally bounded, in the background, with the swamp-forest [near present-day Interstate 610 intersection]. A few low houses, one story high, all having verandahs before them, were scattered thinly over it.

At length, a broad road struck in by the side of the track [established portion of Elysian Fields Avenue]; the houses became more frequent; soon forming a village street, with smoke ascending from breakfast fires; windows and doors opening, maids sweeping steps, bakers' wagons passing, and broad streets, little built upon, breaking off at right angles....

I asked the name of the village [Faubourg Marigny], for my geography was at fault. I had expected to be landed at New Orleans by the boat, and had not been informed of the railroad arrangement, and had no idea in what part of Louisiana we might be....

There was a sign, "*Café du Faubourg*," and, putting my head out of the window, I saw that we must have arrived at New Orleans. We reached the terminus, which was surrounded with *fiacres* [hackney cabs waiting at the foot of Elysian Fields] in the style of Paris. "To the Hotel St. Charles," I said to a driver....[345]

William Howard Russell, a correspondent from London who covered the

South's secession from the Union, arrived to Confederate New Orleans a month after the bombardment of Fort Sumter in 1861. His trip on a steamer from Mobile attested to the times: rumors flew about armed cruisers from the United States threatening Southern coastal positions; armed men in uniform eyed the vessel as it steamed past Biloxi-area beaches; some military men on board nearly came to blows over an argument; and "a thin, fiery-eyed little woman...expressed a fervid desire for bits of "Old Abe"—his ear, his hair; [either] for the purpose of eating or as curious relics....'." Continued Russell:

> At night the steamer entered a dismal canal [Rigolets channel], through a swamp which is infamous as the most mosquito haunted place along the infested shore.... When I woke up at daylight, I found the vessel lying alongside a wharf with a railway train alongside, which is to take us to the city of New Orleans....

> A village of restaurants or "restaurats," as they are called here, and of bathing boxes has grown up around the terminus [Milneburg]; all the names of the owners, the notices and sign-boards being French. Outside the settlement the railroad passes through a swamp, like an Indian jungle, through which the overflowings of the Mississippi creep in black currents. The spires of New Orleans rise above the underwood and semi-tropical vegetation of this swamp. Nearer to the city lies a marshy plain, in which flocks of cattle, up to the belly in the soft earth are floundering among the clumps of vegetation. [We approached] a suburb of exceedingly broad lanes [lower Elysian Fields Avenue through Faubourg Marigny], lined on each side by rows of miserable mean one-storied houses, inhabited...by a miserable and sickly population.[346]

By the time of Russell's visit, the Pontchartrain Railroad's heyday was beginning to pass. In the late 1850s, new railroads such as the New Orleans, Mobile and Chattanooga line connected the city directly with the Gulf Coast, leaving only lake traffic to the Pontchartrain. No longer would dignitaries descend Elysian Fields Avenue from points worldwide; increasingly, the Pontchartrain Railroad primarily served day trippers to Milneburg, which became more of a resort and less of a port.

In 1880, a half-century after its formation, the Pontchartrain Railroad was acquired by the Louisville & Nashville Railroad Company. James S. Zacharie, using the unmistakable cadence of a modern-day tour guide, described the circa-1885 Elysian Fields landscape to tourists seeking the picturesque and the interesting—a far cry from the culturally exotic and physically threatening environment reported by his predecessors:

> Leaving the city, the road goes direct to the lake in a straight line, four miles, which is the narrowest point between the lake and river. Washington square, with the Third Presbyterian Church (on left) at Goodchildren street (on right) Shell Beach R.R. depot to Lake Borgne. At the Gentilly Ridge (on left), a Jewish cemetery; passing through old fortifications erected in 1862, and the swamp, Milneburg is reached, a small village, named after Alexander Milne, a benevolent old Scotchman. This village is composed of a se-

ries of restaurants and bathing houses. At the end of the long pier is a light house....[347]

Note that Zacharie makes only fleeting reference to the once-vast and threatening backswamp.

Urbanization continued to expand northward up Elysian Fields Avenue. New rail lines, streetcars, canals, roads, and later automobiles enabled easy access to the lake. An urban railroad that formed a valued asset in the early nineteenth century became a noisy urban nuisance in the early twentieth century. Protesting neighbors played their part in the demise of the Pontchartrain Railroad, but it was direct-line railways, automobiles, and buses that sealed its fate.

In 1930, the Louisville & Nashville Railroad Company, which kept the Pontchartrain running solely to maintain its franchise on the route, began divesting itself of the century-old line. "Abandonment of the railroad will remove the last barrier in the way of a proposed thoroughfare from the Mississippi river to Lake Pontchartrain via Elysian Fields avenue,"[348] predicted the *Times-Picayune* that year. Also in 1930, the Milneburg entertainment district, where generations of New Orleanians recreated and where great jazz musicians played, closed to make way for the seawall and lakefront project. On March 15, 1932, after 101 years of service, "Smoky Mary" made her last run down the Pontchartrain Railroad. Tracks on Elysian Fields Avenue were removed partially in 1935 and entirely in 1954. By that time, the adjacent backswamp had been cleared, drained, platted, developed, and populated.

Elysian Fields Avenue today lacks the mansions, oak canopies, clanging streetcars, and Mardi Gras parades that bring fame and iconic status to St. Charles Avenue. Its only claims to fame are its cameos in Tennessee Williams' *A Streetcar Named Desire* and Walker Percy's *The Moviegoer*, earned more for its convenient metaphorical implications than as a real place. But to thousands of people a century and a half ago, Elysian Fields Avenue formed the back door to the Queen of the South, and a rare first-hand experience across the storied New Orleans backswamp.

"Drained Dry and Covered with Gardened Homes"

The history and consequences of municipal drainage

Distributaries, tidal inlets, and runoff flowing off the Mississippi's natural levee rendered the flat lakeside flanks of Orleans Parish a vast wetland, wooded with cypress in some parts and grassy with tidally influenced brackish water in others. The uninhabitable backswamp seemed to most New Orleanians to produce little more than miasmas, mosquitoes, and mud, while inhibiting urban growth and travel. Residents and visitors dreaded the hydric landscape, anthropomorphizing it as ugly and evil (see *The Topography of Ooze*). Efforts to neutralize this perceived threat through hydrological engineering anteceded most of the growth spurts of the expanding metropolis.

Colonial-era attempts at drainage involved ditches dug around city blocks to feed a makeshift network of outflow canals, over which wooden bridges and raised sidewalks (*banquettes*, a term still heard today) were built for pedestrians. In 1794, Spanish Governor Carondelet had prisoners and slaves excavate a canal at the rear of the city for drainage and navigation to Bayou St. John. "Carondelet Canal" scored the cityscape for well over a century but hardly solved New Orleans' drainage problem. Likewise, the Melpomene and Poydras canals dug in the American Sector, and the Marigny Canal on Elysian Fields Avenue, did little to dry the streets and drain the swamps.

By the late 1850s, engineers guided by a drainage plan envisioned by city surveyor Louis H. Pilié had built four steam-powered paddle wheels to push water through brick channels toward Lake Pontchartrain. The system fell into disrepair when war broke out. A more serious attempt occurred in 1871, when the Mississippi and Mexican Gulf Ship Canal Company dug thirty-six miles of drainage canals (predecessors of the present-day 17th Street, Orleans, and London Avenue outfall canals, of Hurricane Katrina infamy) before it too went out of business. Failed private initiatives landed the formidable task back into municipal hands by the 1880s, at which time the city's inadequate system could only remove at most 1.5 inches of rain per day.

A public consensus, driven in part by uptown women of means, finally arose during the Progressive Era of the 1890s in support of a serious drainage effort. The New Orleans City Council responded in February 1893 by directing the Drainage Advisory Board to gather data and design a solution, funding it with $700,000. No lethargic bureaucratic committee, the Drainage Advisory Board assembled the best and the brightest in the city, "successful engineers, international experts on public health…men who believed New Orleans's history of inconclusive skirmishes with…nature could end in a rousing victory for the city."[349]

The engineers' findings, presented in January 1895, included a summary of past drainage attempts, a new large-scale topographic map, and fresh meteorological and hydrological data. Their proposed solution: use natural topography to drain runoff from within New Orleans' various hydrological sub-basins to low points therein, then install pumps to propel the water uphill through outfall canals and into adjacent lakes. A network of waterways of varying magnitudes would facilitate the intricate dendritic drainage system: Street gutters would collect surface flow and direct it into covered branch drains; branch drains would flow into main drains; main drains would flow into gravity-fed branch canals; branch canals would flow into a central main canal at the lowest spot in the city, where pumping stations would speed the draw of water into it. Another set of pumps would then propel the water uphill through the outflow canals (already in place since the 1870s) and finally into adjacent lakes Pontchartrain and Borgne.[350]

Construction, which began in 1896, received an additional boost in June 1899 when voters (including women, who had the suffrage in this special municipal-bond referendum and enthusiastically supported municipal improvement) overwhelmingly approved a two-mill property tax to fund waterworks, sewerage, and drainage. This important moment in local democracy launched the Sewerage and Water Board of New Orleans, then and now the organization responsible for these Herculean tasks.

By 1905, workers completed forty miles of canals, hundreds of miles of pipelines and drains, and six pumps draining 22,000 acres with up to 5000 cubic feet per second (c.f.s.). This effort represented only 44 percent of the original plan, but it already transformed the landscape. Wrote George Washington Cable,

> there is a salubrity that could not be when the mosquito swarmed everywhere, when the level of supersaturation in the soil was but two and half feet from the surface, where now it is ten feet or more.... The curtains of swamp forest are totally gone. Their sites are drained dry and covered with miles of gardened homes.[351]

A victim of its own success, the drainage system abetted urbanization and increased impermeable acreage and thus runoff, forcing in 1910 the Drainage Advisory Board to reconvene and expand the system—something that reoccurred throughout the early to mid-twentieth century. What originally comprised a "wet" drainage system, in which acres of open land absorbed a fair amount of runoff, gradually grew into a "dry system" incapable of storing the accumulation of sudden intense rainfalls, thus forcing up the pumping capacity and giving the system zero leeway in pumping that water out.

Among the board employees was a quiet young Tulane engineering graduate named Albert Baldwin Wood, a descendent of the prominent Bouligny family. In 1913, Wood presented his design for a "screw pump," an enormous impeller that would draw water out of the suction basin and into the discharge basin rapidly and efficiently. Eleven "Wood pumps" were installed by 1915; many are still in use today. The brilliant and modest Wood devoted his career to New Orleans' drainage challenge; his patented Wood screw pumps were adopted in China, Egypt, India, and the Netherlands. While Wood is often credited with draining New Orleans, he actually made an existing system faster and more efficient.

New Orleans' home-grown drainage technologies effectively neutralized the city's age-old topographical and hydrological constraints. A land rush from the old riverside city into trendy new lakeside suburbs ensued; assessed property value citywide grew during 1900-14 by 80 percent, to $250 million. Death rates that ranged around 7 percent in the late 1700s (seventy annual deaths per one thousand population) and 4.3 percent in the 1800s, declined to 1.8 percent in the two decades following the installation of the drainage system.[352] Malaria and typhoid deaths decreased tenfold, and yellow fever disappeared forever after one last epidemic in 1905.

By 1925, the New Orleans drainage system served 30,000 acres with a 560-mile network of canal, drains, and pipes and a total pumping capacity of 13,000 c.f.s. Neighborhoods with names like Lakeview and Gentilly Terrace arose in the spacious style of suburban California, a world away from the traditional local cityscapes a mile or so away. Pumps that were originally located behind the city's old neighborhoods were now in front of its new ones.

The Sewerage and Water Board in modern times drains over 61,000 acres in Orleans and neighboring Jefferson Parish of nearly thirteen billion cubic feet of water annually. Ninety miles of covered canals (many beneath neutral grounds), eighty-two miles of open canals, twenty east bank pumping stations, two West Bank stations, and ten underpass pumps combine to siphon rainwater into neighboring water bodies at 45,000 c.f.s., ten times the 1915 capacity and "enough to fill the Louisiana Superdome in 35 minutes."[353] Most of New Orleans, from uptown to the French Quarter to Gentilly and Lakeview plus "Hoey's Basin" in Old Metairie in Jefferson Parish, drains northward through the 17th Street, Orleans, and London Avenue canals into Lake Pontchartrain. Bywater and the Upper and Lower Ninth wards, once a single natural hydrological basin until it was bisected by the Industrial Canal, drain into that man-made waterway. New Orleans East drains mostly northward into the lake, except for the area south of Chef Menteur Highway, which flows into the Intracoastal Waterway and out to the gulf. Algiers, also it own basin, drains into the man-made Algiers Canal and southward into Bayou Barataria. Drainage of the "old city," west of the Industrial Canal, is dependent on the immediate action of engineers to power-up the pumps and get that runoff mobilized out to Lake Pontchartrain as soon as possible, before it accumulates "in the bowl." There are no retention ponds for temporary water storage. More recent systems, such as in New Orleans East, were wisely designed to be more forgiving: there, lagoons and open canals store a certain amount of runoff, giving the system some leeway before requiring it to pump the water out. Thus, less pump capacity is needed, and response time is extended.

The draining of the New Orleans backswamp radically altered nearly every imaginable geography of New Orleans, from patterns of urban infrastructure and architectural style to spatial distributions of ethnicity, race, and class (see *"Two Centuries of Paradox"*). It reworked hydrology and topography by slashing open the marshes with canals and lining them with earthen berms, thus creating new sub-basins and dangerously penetrating the city's heart with surge-prone waterways. It changed New Orleans vertically, allowing freshly drained hydric soils to subside by as many as ten feet. It might have also affected local climate: temperatures in New Orleans increased by eight degrees in summer and dropped by four in winter between 1900 and 1918. The Weather Bureau attributed the polarization to the recent swamp drainage, which reduced surface water and its stabilizing effect on air temperature.[354]

Municipal drainage represented the single most dramatic transformation of the New Orleans cityscape, delivering many blessings but also creating the circumstances that rendered Hurricane Katrina's floodwaters not merely disastrous, but catastrophic. The brilliant engineering solution that "drained dry" the dreaded backswamp and allowed it to be "covered with gardened homes," had indeed created scores of beautiful neighborhoods and thousands of happy homeowners. It also enticed people into harm's way with a fatally false sense of security.

"Ornament to the City"

The Lakefront Project, 1926-1934

Five miles from the bustling quay of the Mississippi lay historic New Orleans' "other" waterfront: the grassy shore of the semi-brackish inland bay known by the quasi-misnomer of Lake Pontchartrain. Low, marshy, and remote, the lakeshore remained a wilderness in the early decades and a shantytown of fishing camps and jerry-built shacks into the early twentieth century. The only exceptions were West End, Spanish Fort, and Milneburg, which served as lakefront resorts for city dwellers and mini-ports for the waterways and railroads connecting with downtown.

The municipal drainage project of the early 1900s transformed those marshes into valuable real estate. As white middle-class New Orleanians eagerly moved out of old riverside neighborhoods and into the new lakeside suburbs, engineers turned their attention toward reinforcing the lakeshore against hurricane-induced storm surges, such as the one caused by the Great Storm of 1915. At first, the Orleans Levee Board built a levee about 300 feet inland from the marshy shore (now Robert E. Lee Boulevard), but the high humus and water content of the soils resulted in shrinkage and subsidence. A more ambitious solution had been envisioned decades earlier, by city surveyor W. H. Bell, whose *Plan of Property Improvements for the Lake Shore Front of the City of New Orleans* (1873) first broached the idea of combining flood protection with residential and recreational land creation. Why settle for a flimsy levee when you can build a solid seawall and create high, dry scenic real estate at the same time?

In 1924, chief engineer Col. Marcel Garsaud was commissioned to develop the concept, and within the year emerged with a plan so ambitious that the Levee Board needed additional constitutional authority to approve it. A curving levee reinforced by a stepped concrete seawall, over five miles long and a half-mile offshore, would be built in the lake; bottom sediments would then be dredged and pumped into the bemired enclosure behind it, creating new land over five feet high. Colonel Garsaud's plan also called for the improvement and sale of the new land to offset the original $27 million price tag.

Work on the "Lakefront Improvement Project" began in 1926. A temporary wooden bulkhead was constructed 2,500-3,500 feet offshore to an elevation of two feet above lake level. Lake-bottom sediment was then hydraulically pumped behind it until flush with the levee top. The bulkhead was then strengthened and raised by four feet, then filled again to the brim. The entire process took over three years; the result was 2000 new acres of lakefront land, averaging four to six feet above lake level or roughly half the elevation of the natural levee. A stepped concrete seawall, designed after similar structures on the Florida coast, completed the project in 1930.

What to do with this scenic new land? One plan allocated most acreage to recreational parkland use; another proposed lagoons and canals among parklands and residences. A compromise allowed for the public recreational development of lands between Lakeshore Drive and the lake, and residential and public-facility develop- ment (sans lagoons) of remaining areas. Land sold to pay off the Levee Board's bonds spawned new residential neighborhoods such as Lake Vista, Lakeshore, Lake Terrace, and Lake Oaks, developed during 1939-60. The Lakefront was also home to Pontchar- train Beach (for whites only; blacks bathed at Lincoln Beach from 1955-64), an amuse- ment park, marinas, recreational facilities, and a branch of Louisiana State University that became the University of New Orleans in 1975.[355] "Lakefront was and is an orna- ment to the city," wrote geographer Peirce Lewis, "one of the very few places where twentieth century city planning has truly improved a large area of an American city."

"It is some measure of the project's scale," continued Lewis, "that a municipal airport was added to the Lakefront scheme almost as an afterthought,"[356] through the efforts of politically connected Levee Board president Abe Shushan. Built in 1931-33 on a triangular peninsula jutting into the lake, Shushan Airport required no real estate acquisition, did not interfere with existing infrastructure, provided obstruction-free approaches and departures, and allowed for inexpensive expansion farther into the lake.[357] At the time one of the finest airfields in the nation, Shusan Airport, along with the Naval Air Station, played an important role in preparation for the air war against Germany and Japan. Today, the 300-acre man-made peninsula, now Lakefront Airport, hosts a 6,879-foot-long airstrip, a terminal with great Arc-Deco styling, and extensive use by corporate and private aircraft.

Now more than one-quarter the age of the city, the Lakefront pads the north- ern edge of New Orleans from the Jefferson Parish line to the Industrial Canal. In utter contrast to the old riverfront city, Lakefront New Orleans today is spacious, sprawling, suburban, relatively prosperous, and privy to expansive horizon-wide vistas of water and sky. It presents a subtropical coastal ambience associated more with modern day coastal Florida hundreds of miles away, than with historic riverine New Orleans five miles away.

Despite its success in creating new residential land, the Lakefront Project was primarily designed to resist gulf-fed storm surges. It served this function well during Hurricane Katrina, remaining mostly dry while preventing ten-foot-high lake waters from spilling into eight-foot-low residential neighborhoods. The same cannot be said for the slender levees and floodwalls lining the city's outfall canals—the very canals that enabled urban expansion toward the lake, and necessitated the Lakefront Project.

Buckets, Gutters, Cisterns, and Taps

Potable water problems in a city surrounded by water

New Orleanians once obtained their domestic water by purchasing it from street vendors—one *picayune* for four buckets—or scooping it themselves from the Mississippi. Homemakers would then remove the sediment with stone, alum, or charcoal filters and store the "cool and transparent" water in earthen jars.[358] For all the impurities, it ranked as the best fresh water source around. "When filtrated, it is transparent, light, soft, pleasant, and wholesome," reported Maj. Amos Stoddard in 1812. "The salubrious quality of [Mississippi River] water is attributed in part to the nitre and sulphur [and the river's] deep and rapid current...."[359] Another observer in 1802 ascribed miraculous powers to the resource:

> The Creoles say the Mississippi water, which they drink, has a tendency to make them prolific. It is a fact, that women who in other parts of world could never breed, have become pregnant in a year after their arrival in Louisiana.[360]

Water for other domestic uses came from shallow, muddy wells dug in courtyards. The great river flowing but one block away went largely underutilized for lack of a mechanized system to pump it over the levee and distribute it throughout the city.

A system worthy of Biblical times was attempted in 1810 on the levee at Ursulines Street. Slaves pumped river water into a raised tank, which thence flowed by gravity through hollow cypress logs to subscribers. Famed architect Benjamin H. B. Latrobe designed a vastly improved system a few years later: a steam pump mounted in a three-story pumphouse would draw water from the Mississippi, store it in raised cast-iron reservoirs, and distribute it to nearby basins and through a network of cypress pipes to residences. Over a decade in the making and fraught with legal problems, Latrobe's waterworks were finally completed three years after the architect's death (to yellow fever), and served the city from 1823 to 1836. His son, John H. B. Latrobe, witnessed the operation in 1834:

> The water works erected by my father are in operation...I saw this morning the water bubbling up from the pipes into the large cast iron box around them, and running off in a rapid stream through the gutters. At every corner were crowds of negro women filling their buckets and water carts supplying themselves from a less defiled place than the margin of the river. After my father[']s death these works, in an unfinished state, fell into the hands of the corporation, and [their present state] is much less efficient than they were capable of under a proper management.[361]

Today, a beautiful little park at Decatur and Ursulines honors Latrobe's achievement.

The city's rapid growth in this era spawned new private water companies. Premier among them was the Commercial Bank of New Orleans (1836), whose waterworks system served parts of the Second Municipality now comprising the Lower Garden District, Garden District, and Irish Channel. Sixty-horsepower steam pumps located at Tchoupitoulas and Richard streets drafted water from twelve feet beneath the Mississippi's surface at a pace up to 2,280 gallons per minute, and propelled it through an eighteen-inch-wide, 200-yard-long iron pipe into a raised reservoir spanning an entire city block. From there, a network of smaller cast-iron pipes delivered the gravity-fed water to commercial and domestic clients, who paid a rate of three dollars per head. By one account, nearly 1,300,000 gallons per day were distributed in this manner in 1847.[362]

The Commercial Bank oversaw commercial operations from 1836-69, after which the city took over until 1878, when it deeded the system over to the New Orleans Water Works Company. Monopoly status, upheld in court, precluded the rise of competing systems. By the 1880s, about eight million gallons per day were pumped through seventy-one miles of cast-iron pipe, creating a small domestic water supply for those few who were connected to the system. Lack of modern purification processes, plus mismanagement and unreliability, rendered the system inadequate and forced residents to satisfy their potable-water needs through what one writer described in 1893 as "one of the strangest and most distinctive features of New Orleans[:] collecting-tanks for rain-water in almost every door-yard."

> Rising above the palms, the rose-trellises, and the stately magnolias are these huge, hooped, green cylinders of wood. They suggest enormous watermelons on end and with the tops cut off.... Nine-tenths of the water used for cooking and drinking is this cistern water....[363]

Into the 1890s, "practically the whole city depended on rain water caught on their roofs and stored in cisterns as the source of drinking water."[364] This meant that, during dry spells, many residents of this water-surrounded city actually suffered water shortages, particularly the poor living in the back-of-town. During droughts, water was sometimes "delivered" simply by pumping it through the open gutters. This tactic, in 1883, serendipitously provided another Mississippi River resource to New Orleans: "Many of these gutters are alive with small fish and river shrimp, and they furnish a harvest to the boys who catch them...."[365]

The progressive municipal-improvement era of the late 1800s finally inspired the development of a full-scale modern municipal water system (as well as drainage and sewerage systems) in New Orleans. Research conducted at Audubon Park in the 1890s helped determine optimal methods for purifying sediment-laden river water, debunking claims that only artesian wells or Lake Pontchartrain could provide potable water. The New Orleans Sewerage and Water Board, established in 1899, sited the new waterworks plant in the extreme upriver neighborhood of Carrollton. This location occupied, at the time, the semi-rural edge of the city, upstream from sources of urban pollution and above the salt-water intrusions occasioned by extremely low river stages or hurricane-induced gulf surges.[366] The site also provided the maximum amount of head for distribution to houses, because it tapped the river at a slightly higher stage that in other parts of the city. (The river gains about 1.5 inches in stage per river mile heading upriver in the metro area; thus the river at the Carrollton intake flows on average over one foot higher than at the French Quarter.) Locating the plant 3000-4000 feet from the river kept it safe from shipping activity, wharves, and railroads, while siting it just within the Orleans Parish line kept it within local government control, even if it did supplant some residential blocks.

The Carrollton Water Works Plant, started in 1905 and opened in 1908, drew water from the Mississippi by an intake pipe and pumped it into a "head house," the controlling node at the center of a series of reinforced concrete reservoirs. The water then passed slowly over the "grit reservoir," where the coarsest particles settled out, then returned to the head house to be pumped into the "lime mixing reservoir," where lime and sulfate of iron were added for softening. Next, the water returned to the head house to be sent to the "coagulating reservoir," where finer particles of suspended sediment were precipitated out. Finally, the water was again sent back to the head house, strained through sand filters, poured into "equalizing reservoirs," treated with a small dosage of chloride gas, and stored in the clean water well to await delivery. Eight pumps then propelled the purified water through distribution mains to city residents everywhere except Algiers. Water mains were laid starting in 1905; by 1910 they extended 512 miles; by 1926, they measured around 700 miles and spanned most of the urban footprint. The number of water meters soared from around 5,000 installed in 1900 (one per fifty-seven people) to 22,600 in 1910; 56,600 in 1920; and nearly 96,000 in 1927—one for every four people, or roughly every household. In this manner, modern engineering technology delivered a tiny fraction of the runoff of the North American interior   33,000,000 gallons per day in the 1910s, or 0.01 percent of normal river volume—into the kitchens and courtyards of New Orleanians.[367]

Today, a greatly enlarged Carrollton Plant operates on the same century-old site; while the treatment process is modernized, some key antique infrastructure remains. Water is drawn from the Mississippi through two screened intakes straddling the parish line: the three-pump, 210-million-gallon-a-day New River Station built on the Jefferson side in 1982, and the backup Old River (Oak Street) Station, with four circa-1928 pumps on the Orleans side. Drawn water flows downhill for about eight blocks toward the East Bank Water Treatment Plant, where lime, ferric sulfate, and polyelectrolytes are added. The water is then (1) slowly paddled through mixing and settling basins, where fine-grain river sediments are mechanically removed and returned to the river; (2) disinfected for bacteria with polyphosphate, chlorine, ammonia, and treated with lime to adjust pH, soften the water, and control corrosion; (3) pumped through a second complex of large reservoirs for further settling and disinfection; (4) treated with fluoride for tooth protection; then (5) passed through two sand-filtration facilities for final treatment. The tap-ready H_2O is either stored in ten large round tanks lining South Claiborne Avenue, or pumped through the South Claiborne or Panola Street stations to thousands of East Bank customers. The West Bank and adjacent parishes are handled through separate, similar systems.[368]

Into the twenty-first century, the Carrollton and Algiers plants distributed 125 million gallons of river water per day through 1,610 miles of water mains (ranging in diameter from three to 4.5 feet along trunk lines to eight to twelve inches under French Quarter streets) to 160,000 service connections and virtually the entire population. This abundant water supply remains one of the city's greatest and most reliable blessings—cheap, at about $0.03/gallon, and surprisingly high in quality.

The problem is the infrastructure, primarily the power stations and the pipe network, of which one-third is roughly a century old. Concerns remained tolerable, patchable, and largely hidden until Hurricane Katrina arrived in late August 2005. Winds uprooted trees, rocked houses, and broke underlying water lines, but the pumps kept water flowing through the system. After the levees broke, however, floodwaters swamped the century-old South Claiborne electrical power plant, stilling the movement of the life-sustaining resource to the thousands of people trapped in the city. Many New Orleanians who remained during Katrina remember well that unsettling moment on Wednesday, August 31, when a twist of the tap yielded a spit of rusty water, a sputter of air, and a dark new outlook on the city's future. There was now no water to drink, no indoor sanitation, no showers to escape the heat, and, most ominously, no hydrant water to extinguish fires. Blazes claimed scores of structures, even as water inundated them.

Heroic action and creative jury-rigging on the part of the Sewerage and Water Board allowed reasonably safe tap water (as well as sewerage and drainage) to return to unflooded areas by late September, and to most of the city months later. The system, however, remains gravely compromised, with 50,000 patched leaks, a billion dollars in storm-related damages, $3.2 billion needed to replace the aging distribution system, and $125 million to update the antique twenty-five-cycle South Claiborne electrical plant—one of the last of its type in the nation—with modern sixty-cycle motors.[369]

Serious as these problems are, they are solvable. New Orleanians remain blessed with an abundant and reliable supply of fresh water, especially in light of the municipal water shortages in urban areas across the nation and globe. A water surplus in the Crescent City and a shortage in Florida have led some to ponder the economics of exporting Mississippi River water as a commodity.[370] The water is here, the shipping lanes and port facilities are established, the technology is available; the only obstacle is cost, and if present trends continue, willing buyers may someday call. More ominously for New Orleans, future water shortages in the urbanizing Southeast may motivate the diversion of certain eastern tributaries of the Mississippi, much like northern California rivers have been rerouted to quench the thirst of the state's southern metropolises.

Indeed, New Orleans has in its hands what may prove to be the most coveted natural resource of the twenty-first century.

Lessons in Over-Reliance

The once-lofty and now-diminished economic importance of the Mississippi River

The Port of New Orleans recently ranked as the fourth busiest shipping port in the nation, with 6,000 ocean-going vessels calling per year and 2,000 depositing or loading nearly ninety million tons of cargo. When combined with the nearby Port of South Louisiana along the River Road, it easily ranks first nationwide. Before Katrina, the city's port supported over 107,000 jobs, pumped $13 billion into the local economy, earned an additional $2 billion, and contributed $231 million to state tax coffers annually. Important as the shipping industry is to the city, it is nowhere near as fundamental as it was in historical times, when New Orleans enjoyed a near-monopoly on Mississippi Valley trade.

As the trans-Appalachian region developed in the early nineteenth century, its emerging frontier society produced immense supplies of agricultural commodities in search of sources of demand. A Missouri hunter, an Illinois corn farmer, a Mississippi cotton grower, or a Louisiana sugar planter had little choice but to ship his harvest downriver to reach urban markets on the Eastern seaboard and Europe. Shipping out of the trans-Appalachian West, which nearly tripled from approximately 60,300 tons in 1810 to 176,400 tons in 1825, went down the Mississippi to New Orleans to a degree of over 99 percent; only a tiny portion found its way out the Great Lakes and St. Lawrence River or other routes to eastern markets.[371] As the premier transshipment point before reaching open seas, New Orleans prospered in financing, marketing, and handling these commodities. Planters also used the river to get to New Orleans to conduct business, meet with financiers, buy supplies for their estates, educate their children, or socialize and entertain. Few other transportation options existed, particularly when bulky commodities needed to be moved long distances. The lion's share of New Orleans' spectacular wealth and meteoric rise between the Louisiana Purchase and the Civil War can be traced to river-related activity, as a cotton and sugar port and later as a handler of coffee, tropical fruit, and myriad other freight. The antebellum riverfront bustled with carefully managed shipping activity; protruding docks and wharves spanned well over two miles, with certain sections reserved specifically for flatboats, steamboats, schooners, ferries, ocean-going sailing ships, and "planters' pirogues."[372] "So long as New Orleans enjoys her present advantages by location on the Mississippi river," wrote the *New Orleans Bee* in 1836, "so long will her commerce continue to be augmented, and her property ensured."[373] Nearly everyone agreed. "Mississippi Obsession" is how one historian would later characterize the city's supreme confidence in its geographical advantage.[374]

The advantage did not last so long, at least not in its purest form. Competition started in 1825, when the newly completed Erie Canal gave New York City and the

Eastern Seaboard waterborne access to the trans-Appalachian region. Excavation commenced a decade later on the Illinois and Michigan (I & M) Canal, which would give
the emerging city of Chicago a piece of Mississippi River trade. More canals followed;
emigrants flowed westward, and new river towns and cities sprouted on the western
frontier. Stated a later government report,

> [before] 1835 transportation had been north and south on the river, and
> New Orleans from advantage of position had developed commercially with
> little effort on her part. In 1835 the trade was to some extent diverted to an
> east and west direction by the opening of the Erie and other canals, [while]
> Pittsburg and Cincinnati were rapidly developing....[375]

In the 1830s, according to one historian, "an increasing percentage of western produce traveled on the canals directly to the East. New Orleans' share of the total western output was decreasing, but the tremendously rapid rate of growth taking
place in the agricultural West concealed New Orleans' declining position."[376] Whereas
Western shipments to New Orleans comprised at least 80 percent of the port's total
receipts in 1840, they fell to only 18 percent by 1858; that activity increasingly flowed
eastward on the Ohio, across the Great Lakes, and through man-made canals, or rolled
on an every-increasing network of railroad tracks. By another measure, New Orleans
controlled over 99 percent of trans-Appalachian shipping up to 1825, but only 80 to
90 percent in the 1830s, 60 to 70 percent in the 1840s, and around 50 percent in the
1850s. By the eve of the Civil War, New Orleans' former Mississippi Valley monopoly
had to be shared with the Erie Canal, the I & M Canal, the New York Central Railroad,
the New York & Erie Railroad, the Pennsylvania Railroad, the Baltimore & Ohio Railroad, and an emerging network of other transportation options throughout the Midwest.[377] "[T]he flow of western trade reversed itself," wrote two prominent historians;
"the economic unit known as the Mississippi Valley had been turned on its head, so
that the Mississippi River was flowing north."[378]

Getting a shrinking share of a dramatically growing antebellum economy (see
graphs, "New Orleans' Meteoric Rise...and Relative Decline, 1810-1860"), New Orleans concentrated on short-term enrichment. After all, Mississippi Valley shipments
to New Orleans increased *thirty-six-fold* from 1810 to 1860, when over 2,187,000 tons
of domestic commodities kept the city's wharves bustling.[379] The city grew spectacularly too, boasting in 1860 over twenty times the population from late colonial times.
Why waste time preparing for a rainy day when business is booming right here and
now? Even after the Civil War, New Orleans' population continued to grow by tens of
thousands per decade, and the river remained the city's most reliable source of income.
It was still faster and cheaper to ship agricultural commodities down the Mississippi
through New Orleans to Liverpool (forty cents per bushel and thirty-one days), than
to send them on rail to Chicago, to Buffalo by lake, to New York by canal, and then to
Liverpool (sixty-four cents per bushel and fifty-two days).[380]

But "[p]hysiologists make a distinction between the growth and the development of an organism," pointed out historian John G. Clark. "New Orleans [in the
nineteenth century] experienced growth, but...did not demonstrate a developmental

capacity comparable to that of other major urban centers, [doing] little to expand upon or improve her natural advantages."[381] Over-relying on the Mississippi River, New Orleans' conservative business class faltered in developing back-up competitive advantages in value-added industries and investing in the latest transportation technologies. In particular, competition from railroads—from nonexistent in 1830, to 9000 miles of railroad track in 1850, to 193,000 miles in 1900—eroded the city's once-exalted destiny. New Orleans' ranking among American cities in terms of population helps illustrate the ironic pairing of absolute growth with relative decline: when the city overwhelmingly controlled the Mississippi Valley, its population *and* rank increased, from seventh-largest in 1810 to fifth-largest in 1820 and 1830 to third-largest in 1840, its all-time peak. But as canals and railroads began directing wealth elsewhere, New Orleans dropped to fifth place in 1850, sixth in 1860, and ninth and tenth after the calamity of the Civil War.[382]

New Orleans' economic dilemma—exploiting today's boom versus preparing for tomorrow's bust—was not lost on the city's business class. On the contrary, leaders fretted constantly about encroaching competition. "We have been accustomed to look to the Mississippi as the protector of our greatness," wrote one shrewd editorialist in 1850;

> We have thought that as long as the mighty... Father of Waters continues to roll past our city, our superiority in a commercial point of view, never can be successfully attacked. Time, the corrector of all errors, has demonstrated the fallacy of our belief. It has shown us that we are by no means impregnable; that our position, unequalled though it may be, can be made useless to us, when railroads and canals, intersecting the valley of the Mississippi in every direction, offer to the producer a cheaper and readier transit...
>
> New York has her great Erie Canal, Boston her Western Railroad, Philadelphia her canals and railroads, Baltimore her communications with the Ohio Valley—by all of which a large portion of our legitimate trade is diverted from us. Charleston, Savannah, and even Mobile are now preparing to grasp at a share of the spoil....
>
> In the meantime New Orleans has contented herself with contemplating the Mississippi, boasting of her magnificent position and unbounded resources, and yet has done nothing at all to preserve the advantages which nature has conferred to her.... [S]he has begun to discover that the steam engine or even an artificial ditch is a powerful rival....[383]

Local businessmen did take action, but it proved negligible in the face of daunting economic-geographical realities. Railroads eventually came to New Orleans, but, isolated as the region lay from the great Northern metropolises, could never rival the intricate web of tracks that unified the Midwest and the East. Some value-added industries arose in the early twentieth century, but they mostly handled petroleum and chemicals, employed relatively few laborers, and arguably occasioned more costs than benefits to the local society. Major shipping canals would also come, dug in the 1910s-60s toward the worthwhile goal of making the port more competitive. But in a tragic irony, the artificial waterways allowed salt water and hurricane-induced storm surges to penetrate city limits and, in 2005, nearly caused the death of the very city they were supposed to enrich (see *Scoring and Scouring the Land*).

Ever-expanding Northern waterways, seaways, railways, highways, airways, and pipelines meant that, by the 1900s, the monopoly once enjoyed by New Orleans on Mississippi Valley traffic now looked more like monopolistic competition. Whereas waterborne transportation moved nearly all freight in early-nineteenth-century America, only about 15 percent of intercity commercial freight travels on inland waterways today; the rest is handled by railroads, trucks, pipelines, and aircraft. A modern-day cotton or sugar producer, unlike his ancestor, now has numerous transportation options to get his commodity to market, few of which involve either the Mississippi or the Crescent City. He might only need to come to New Orleans for a trade show—*by air*.

In the 1950s and 1960s, a technological breakthrough transformed the shipping industry. To speed the handling of freight in individualized odd-shaped units, engineers developed standardized "containers" gripped by cranes and gantries in mass-production mode, like a factory. The simple but revolutionary idea allowed for the efficient handling of cargo between vessel and train or truck, with a minimum of labor and dock space. Containerization swept through the shipping industry within a few years and radically altered the geographies, economies, and cultures of port cities worldwide. It meant that great ports no longer really needed great port cities; rival ports expanded in smaller population centers (witness Gulfport, Mississippi), or opened in remote areas (witness Port Fouchon, Louisiana). In New Orleans, thousands of longshoremen, stevedores, dock workers, and other riverfront laborers gradually lost their jobs to machines, or to competing ports and their machines. Worse yet, most vessels currently calling at the Port of New Orleans constitute tankers or cargo vessels, which generate even fewer local jobs than containerized ships. The hospitality industry now trumps port activity as the city's premier source of employment.

Containerization also meant that great ports no longer needed to occupy so much waterfront space. Mechanization meant concentration. In New Orleans, many riverfront wharves and warehouses deteriorated and were cleared away for recreational and tourism-related venues, such as the Moonwalk, Woldenberg Park, and the Riverwalk festival marketplace (1970s-80s). The process of "reclaiming" the riverfront for people continues today, as planners propose a contiguous stretch of public facilities and green space from Poland to Jackson avenues. This is a healthy trend—and, oddly, a reversion to historical times, when citizens "promenaded" nightly along the riverfront to enjoy waterfront breezes. But it also reflects a probably irreversible downturn in the industry over which New Orleans was founded to reign. The Port of New Orleans is still critically important to City of New Orleans, employing thousands of people and generating millions of dollars, but, in truth, the city today needs the port more than the port needs the city.[384]

By its commanding position in this vast country, New Orleans will...become one of the richest markets in the New World.
> —James Pitot, circa 1802

New Orleans will be forever, as it is now, the mighty mart of the merchandise brought from more than a thousand rivers[;] no such position for the accumulation and perpetuity of wealth and power [has] ever existed.
> —Thomas Jefferson, 1804

...a port or two [here] would make us masters of the whole of this continent.
> —René-Robert Cavelier, sieur de La Salle, circa 1684

Many factors explain New Orleans' failure to achieve those heady visions from centuries past. Chief among them is the ineluctable reality that the Mississippi River, despite its magnitude and importance, now represents but one of a number of transportation options in and out of the world's richest valley. "[F]aith in the invulnerability of geographic location dulled the mind and tempered the energies of the business community of New Orleans," wrote historian John G. Clark, "preventing its leaders from calculating accurately and quickly the significance of threats to their commercial hegemony."[385] Once the third-largest city in the U.S., New Orleans fell to the thirty-first largest in 2000, and as low as the sixty-seventh largest city in the country one year after Hurricane Katrina (see graph, "Tracking New Orleans' Ascent and Decline, 1790-2007").

The historical splendors of old New Orleans that remain with us today may be viewed as a grand and splendid vestige of an economic geography that no longer exists.

Biological Manipulation

Human agency in the translocation of species—
and transformation of the environment

Describing species as "native" or "alien" to a particular place presupposes a certain order in the world, a perception that selected life forms "belong" to delineated ranges. In reality, species move about as much or as little as circumstances or serendipities permit; some cross entire hemispheres seasonally while others unintentionally wander permanently to new regions and continents. Humans have participated in this biological diffusion by dispersing themselves as well as thousands of other species, intentionally or accidentally. Categorizing species as native or alien, and thence presuming the former to be benign and the latter malignant, is a human construct, one that ignores spatial and temporal continuums—not to mention our own place in nature.

Yet one cannot refute that the pace of species translocations has radically accelerated with the technological advances and economic globalization of the past century. Nor can one deny that for every introduced species that proves to be lucrative and beneficial (such as, in Louisiana, sugar, cotton, and soybeans) or otherwise desirable (such as cherished "Southern" ornamentals such as azaleas and crepe myrtles), others are indisputably destructive and costly. Anthropogenically translocated species in general are known as "introduced," "non-indigenous," or "alien" species; those that are viewed as pests are ascribed the adjectives of "invasive" or "nuisance." The tags are subjective, and sometimes contested.[386]

Louisiana's humid subtropical climate, myriad waterways, and productive coastal wetlands make it ideal habitat for the establishment of species that evolved elsewhere. Centuries of shipping traffic have occasioned the accidental relocation of hundreds of species to this new environment, while deliberate introductions of agricultural crops, animals, and ornamental plants account for even more biological reshuffling. Railroads, canals, roads, and interstates perform critical economic functions but also serve as conduits for further biological diffusion. The result: roughly a thousand species of flora and fauna once unknown to Louisiana now thrive in the state. Of the world's 100 "worst" invasive species according to the French environmental organization *Fondation d'Entreprise*, at least thirteen occur in southern Louisiana. One-third of The Nature Conservancy's "Dirty Dozen" list of the most destructive invasive species in the U.S. are found in Louisiana, a state that comprises only 1.4 percent of the nation's conterminous land area. The U.S. Geological Survey's database of non-indigenous aquatic species shows that Louisiana has more introduced aquatic plants (thirty-two) than any other state except Florida, which has forty-five. It is home to almost two-and-a-half times the average number of introduced aquatic plants per state.

Four particular invasive species have caused disproportionate damage to southern Louisiana ecology and society. Two were introduced accidentally, two deliberately. Historically, *Aedes aegypti* ranked as the most detrimental, even as it went all but unnoticed. This mosquito, native to Africa, arrived to the Caribbean and later French colonial Louisiana in the early 1700s, probably in water stored on slave ships. *Aedes aegypti* itself was merely a pest, but it carried the yellow fever virus which claimed the lives of over 100,000 Louisianians, and 40,000 New Orleanians, between 1796 and 1905. Discovery of the culprit in the early 1900s remains one of history's great medical breakthroughs. Mosquito control has since eradicated yellow fever in the region and nation, but *Aedes aegypti* still thrives in New Orleans, and continues to transmit dengue and yellow fever throughout the tropics.

Water hyacinth, a lush aquatic plant with a beautiful purple flower, was deliberately introduced as an ornamental at the 1884 World's Industrial and Cotton Centennial Exposition at Audubon Park. Other individuals around the same time imported it directly from South America. Finding ideal habitat in the highly productive freshwater wetlands of southern Louisiana, hyacinth established itself throughout the region, clogging waterways, out-competing native aquatics, starving water of light and oxygen, and creating mosquito habitat. National newspaper reports attested to the incredibly rapid spread of the aquatic plant; the following piece appeared in Illinois in 1895 under the title "Navigation Impeded by Flowers."

> An assisted immigrant is making a lot of trouble in Louisiana. It is a plant, a water hyacinth, which a man from New Orleans saw and admired about three years ago while on a visit to Colombia. He brought some bulbs [home] and grew them in tubs in his front yard. In about two years patches of the flower appeared in Bayou St. John.... In another year the bayou was full of it, so that navigation was impeded. Now all the canals near New Orleans are overrun and covered up with this invading flower; great masses of it are floating in the lake; rivers running into the lake are choked with it, and it has traveled a hundred miles to the westward of New Orleans.[387]

Two years later, Congress appropriated funds "to investigate the obstruction of the navigable waters of Florida, Louisiana and other south Atlantic and gulf states by the plant known as the water hyacinth"[388]—a costly and constant battle which continues to this day.

Even more damaging to coastal wetlands are nutria, a large furbearing rodent from Argentina originally imported to California for fur in 1899. Specimens made their way under controlled circumstances to breeders in St. Bernard Parish, who sold some to the McIlhenny family (of Tabasco Sauce fame) during the Depression. Intentionally released animals (1940-45) and escapees subsequently spread from Avery Island throughout the coastal marshes, oftentimes aided by state fish and game officials, who viewed nutria as a boon to the state's fur trapping industry. They were—until the 1980s, when fur fell out of fashion in favor of leather for women's coats. Prices dropped from over ten dollars a pelt to as low as a dollar; trappers looked for other lines of work, and the nutria population exploded. The rodents devoured marsh grasses in expansive, contiguous areas known as "eat-outs," exposing thin, silty coastal soils to wind and water erosion and exacerbating the degradation of hundreds of thousands of acres of coastal marsh. They also displaced native muskrat populations. A state bounty program offering four to five dollars per tail has motivated some trappers to pursue nutria again, resulting in 1.6 million kills since 2002 and reducing nutria-damaged marsh from around 80,000 acres per year to 34,000 in 2007.[389] But, with phenomenal reproductive rates and a geographical range now spanning all three continental-U.S. coasts, nutria are likely to remain a permanent part—and cause—of the shrinking Louisiana landscape.

During the World War II era, ships arriving from East Asia unknowingly brought in a tiny winged pest which today costs New Orleanians $300 million annually. Formosan termites, infested in wooden shipping pallets, found an agreeable climate and plenty of wooden housing stock in the port cities of Houston, Mobile, and New Orleans; they soon spread throughout the Gulf South via shipping lanes and relocated lumber and railroad ties. For years, the household pesticide Chlordane drove the Formosans out of treated structures and into urban trees, weakening them structurally and oftentimes causing their collapse. When Chlordane was banned in 1988, Formosan termites proceeded to infest houses, showing a particular taste for the old timbers of historical structures. Recent control attempts by the U.S. Department of Agriculture and local entities have, at best, only stabilized the problem, which has since spread to the entire southern tier of the United States. Formosan termite control efforts are now literally embedded in the cityscape: during the 1990s, custom-designed traps topped with unmarked aluminum disks were drilled into French Quarter sidewalks, their purpose baffling to newcomers.

Few would argue that any "good" came from these four biological introductions, among many others. Similarly, few would claim that other importations, such as wheat, soybeans, popular ornamentals such as azaleas, and game birds such as ring-necked pheasants represent costly ecological evils that must be eradicated. (Indeed, were it not for two non-native species, cotton and sugar, New Orleans never would have grown as dramatically as it did during its nineteenth-century heyday.) Only this is certain: species introductions demonstrate that humans are active agents in the biological manipulation of their environs; a freak accident or a naïve tinkering in the distant past may yield untold consequences in the future.

Humanizing the Landscape

The instant the [sun] sets,
animation begins to rise,
the public walks are crowded…
the inhabitants promenade on the Leveé…
the billiard rooms resound,
music strikes up,
and life and activity
resume their joyous career….

—Thomas Ashe, 1806

Sagamité: Geography of a Food– or Geography of a Word?

Explaining a curiously ubiquitous indigenous food of eighteenth-century North America

Wrote historical anthropologist Shannon Lee Dawdy, "archaeological [evidence] indicates that the charter generation in New Orleans attempted to replicate the diet they knew in France," but as time wore on and ties to the motherland loosened, local diets "turned more towards wild, native resources…becoming more *sauvage* through a process of creolization."[390]

Marie Madeleine Hachard, a young postulant from Rouen who arrived with the Ursuline Nuns in 1727, left behind evidence that sheds light on Dawdy's observation. In a series of remarkable letters to her father, Hachard recorded detailed accounts of (among other things) early New Orleans food culture, a topic of particular interest for a city that would gain worldwide fame for its culinary contributions.

"Bread costs ten cents a pound," wrote Hachard, "and is made of Indian corn meal; eggs from forty-five to fifty cents a dozen; milk fourteen cents a gallon." She continued:

> We eat meat, fish, peas, and wild beans and many kinds of fruit and vegetables, such as pineapple which is the most excellent of all the fruits; watermelon, sweet potatoes; pippins which are much the same as the russets…of France; figs, bananas, pecans, cashewnuts, which, as soon as eaten, seize the throat; pumpkins and a thousand other things….
>
> [W]e live on wild beef, deer, swans, geese and wild turkeys, hares, hens, ducks, teals, pheasants, partridges, quails and other fowl and game of different kinds. The rivers are teeming with enormous fish, especially turbot [brill, flounder] which is an excellent fish, ray, carp [probably catfish] and many other fishes unknown in France. They make much use of chocolate with milk and coffee [mocha, café au lait]. A lady of this country has given us a good provision of it. We drink it every day. During Lent, meat is allowed three times a week, and, during the year, meat is allowed on Saturday as in the Island of St. Domingo. We accustom ourselves wonderfully well to the wild food of this country. We eat bread which is half rice and half flour. There is here a wild grape larger than the French grape, but it is not in clusters. It is served in a dish like plums. What is eaten most and is most common is rice cooked with milk….[391]
>
> During Lent, we ate meat four days a week, with the Church's permission; and outside of that season we abstain only on Fridays. We drink beer. Our most ordinary food is rice cooked with milk, wild beans, meat and fish….

Butchers kill only twice a week, for it is hard to keep the meat fresh. Hunting lasts all winter, which commences in October. It is made at ten leagues from the city. Wild oxen [bison] are caught in large numbers.... We pay three cents a pound for that meat, and the same price for venison, which is better than the beef or mutton which you eat in Rouen. Wild ducks are very cheap. Teals, geese, waterhens, and other fowl and game are also very common.... There are oysters and carps of prodigious size which are delicious.... We also eat watermelons and muskmelons, [and] sweet potatoes[,] cooked in hot ashes as you cook chestnuts.... [P]eaches and figs, which are in abundance...are sent to us in so great a quantity from the habitations, that we make preserves and blackberry jelly....[392]

Some of these rustic edibles remain rudimentary to Louisiana food ways today, particularly oysters, catfish, and *café au lait*. One dish in particular dates from prehistoric times and, at least by one description, endures on local breakfast tables to this day. It is called *sagamité*.

Early French explorers reported this native food with remarkable frequency, though they described it with equally remarkable inconsistency. One of Iberville's crew explained *sagamité* as "nothing more than the groats of Indian corn mixed with water and lard to season it, then baked." Pénicaut, Iberville's carpenter, described it as "a soup" made from "a kind of oats" produced by native cane grass, also used to make bread, but later characterized it as "a boiled dish, made of corn and beans." Le Page du Pratz described "Sagamity" as a "maize-gruel"—adding, with no sarcasm—"which to my taste surpassed the best dish in France." He noted that Indians ate it "as we eat soup, with a spoon made of a buffalo's horn."[393]

In fact, missionaries and settlers in New France recorded *sagamité* as early as 1615.[394] Jesuit Father Paul Le Jeune, speaking of the Lower Algonquin peoples, left behind a detailed description of the food in his *Relations of 1633*:

> I shall say here that the Savages are very fond of sagamité. The word 'Sagamiteou' in their language really means water, or warm gruel. Now they have extended its meaning to signify all sorts of soups, broths, and similar things. [It] is made of cornmeal; if they are short of that, we sometimes give them some of our French flour, which, being boiled with water, makes simple paste. They do not fail to eat it with appetite, especially when we place in it a little 'pimi;' that is to say, oil, for that is their sugar. They use it with their strawberries and raspberries....

Reuben Gold Thwaites, who edited the Jesuit Relations in the 1950s, explained further that the word *sagamité* derived from *sôgmôipi* ("the repast of chiefs") and referred to hominy corn "usually pounded into meal...boiled in water, with the addition of meat, fish, or oil," if available. Sometimes, "beans, peas, pumpkins" and other seasonal vegetables "were boiled with the corn, especially when the latter was still green: a survival of this usage remains in our modern 'succotash'...."[395]

Sagamité appears repeatedly in frontier journals, particularly from French Canada, the Great Lakes, and the Mississippi Valley, and rarely do the descriptions concur. Henri Joutel's 1714 account of La Salle's disastrous 1684 expedition recorded that the food was made by "pounding the *Indian* Corn and Baking the Meal, or making the Pottage of the said Meal, by [the natives] call'd *Sagamite* ... their Sort of Hasty-Pudding."[396] Folklorist Margaret Sargent reported that the Huron Indians made *sagamité* to celebrate special events or welcome distinguished guests, and described it as "a stew of green corn, beans, and animal brains."[397] Jesuit Father du Poisson, traveling the lower Mississippi in 1727, described a French and an Indian variation of the ubiquitous dish:

> The most ordinary food of this country[,] especially for travelers—is *gru*. Corn is pounded ... to remove the outer skin, and then is boiled a long time in water, but the Frenchmen sometimes season it with oil; and this is *gru*. The Savages, pounding the corn very fine, sometime cook it with tallow [rendered animal fat], and more often only with water; this is sagamité. However, the *gru* answers for bread; a spoonful of *gru* and a mouthful of meat go together.[398]

Another Jesuit, Father Pierre Laure, writing from Quebec in 1730, clarified that the word *sagamité* "never had the signification given to it through a misconception of its [meaning]; for it means nothing but 'the water'—or 'the broth—is hot,' *tchi sagamiteou*.... He then described how Indians in that region saved seal fat to season their *sagamité*. This description, like others from northern climes, views *sagamité*'s form as a broth, rather than the corn ingredient, as its defining characteristic.[399]

The dish—and the word—remained part of eastern Canada's culture at least into the late nineteenth century. Wrote Johann Georg Kohl in his 1861 *Travels in Canada*,

> I found that the old Indian national dish called *Sagamité*, so often mentioned in the earliest reports of the Jesuits, is a favourite among the Canadian peasants. What the word means I have in vain inquired, but the dish consists of maize boiled in milk [or] water.... [S]ince it formed for a hundred years the daily bread of so many pious missionaries in the wilderness, there is a kind of historical interest attached to it. It is often met with at the tables of respectable citizens in Montreal and Quebec.[400]

Sagamité was far less known in the American South, but not entirely lost to history. As the region prepared for war in 1861, a Georgia newspaper recommended the food as nourishment for "our boys ... before going on the march:"

> Sagamite—Portable Food for Scouts—The old historians and travellers, and Indian fighters, tell us of an admirable and easily portable food, which the Red men carried with them in their pouches.... It was a combination of Indian meal and brown sugar, three parts of the former to one of the latter, browned, together over the fire. This food, in small quantities, not only sufficed to arrest hunger, but to allay thirst. This is the famous sagamite of the Red men....[401]

Sagamité made it to the pages of Louisiana literature in the late nineteenth century. George Washington Cable referred to it fleetingly his 1879 novel *The Grandissim-*

es, in which colonists "sat down to bear's meat, sagamite and beans" during a fictional 1699 encounter with Louisiana Indians.[402] His literary rival, narrative historian Grace King, interpreted "sagamity" as "hominy cooked with grease and pieces of meat or fish," and speculated that it represented "the original of the Creole Jambalaya, in which rice has since been most toothsomely substituted for corn."[403] Indeed, at least one historical source—from Louisiana in 1744—blurred the line between the two starchy ingredients: "The Slaves," it reported, "are fed with Rice, or with Mahis [maize] husked and boiled, which is called *Sagamité*."[404]

Sagamité resembles a wide range of modern New World corn dishes, including New England's succotash and hasty pudding, the South's cornbread and hush puppies, Acadiana's *macque-choux*, Mexico's *tamale* and corn soup *pozole*, and Meso-America's sweet drink *atole*.[405] By no means does this insinuate that all, or even any, originate from *sagamité*: there are, after all, only so many ways to render corn edible, and disparate cultures are likely to develop those ways independently.

But are disparate cultures likely to *name* them all the same way? How did this indigenous word gain such an expansive geography? Did natives throughout eastern North America use *sagamité* to describe a wide range of corn-based concoctions, implying extensive social and economic interaction among distant tribes?

Or, on the other hand, did Europeans learn the word from indigenous sources in one region and apply it liberally to similar foods in other regions as *they* diffused, describing them all as *sagamité* in their journals? After all, it was mostly the French, not the Indians, who left behind the documents we read today.

The latter hypothesis is more likely the case. The diverse meaning and range of *sagamité* suggests that Frenchmen and other Europeans learned it from Indians early on and recorded it in their journals, which in turn were read by other Frenchmen, who thence applied it loosely to similar foods and passed the term on to the next generation, then the next, and so on. The result: one word with many meanings in various places. Jesuit Paul Le Jeune and Pierre Laure seemed to allude to this transformation of definition in their previously cited explanations from 1633 and 1730.

Folklorist Janet C. Gilmore, whose research I came across after I developed the above hypothesis, studied *sagamité* in the Great Lakes region and arrived independently at a similar conclusion. Characterizing *sagamité* as "a boiled, one-pot meal, with flexible ingredients [which] can be made very simply as basic, everyday fare [or] dressed up to be a feast food," Gilmore concluded,

> French missionaries and explorers...applied a Native American-based designation, "sagamité," to a family of indigenous concoctions that had a much more varied range of terminology, processes, and conceptual relationships within and across [Native] peoples, legitimating the native cuisine while simultaneously homogenizing and reducing it to a single concept.[406]

If this explanation is accurate, the story of *sagamité* is not so much the geography of a food, but the geography of a word. Its spatial diffusion mimics the spread of France's other Old World cultural traits in the New World, including language, religion, law, economics, architecture, surveying systems, place names, and other food ways.[407]

Some of those traits have disappeared; others thrive to varying degrees, in places like Quebec and New Orleans. Take, for example, one description of *sagamité* that bears a striking resemblance to a modern Southern dish, with a minimum of interpretative liberty. It comes, not surprisingly, from our articulate young informant of circa-1727 New Orleans, Marie Madeleine Hachard. "The people of Louisiana," she wrote, "find very good a food called '*sagamité*,' which is made of Indian corn crushed in a mortar, then boiled in water, and eaten with butter or cream.[408]

Butter and cream on ground Indian corn: a blending of that which was transported from France with that which was derived locally, unified in a single dish that is consumed regularly throughout New Orleans today. *Sagamité*, according to this description, is grits.

The French Market and the Historical Geography of Food Retail

How New Orleanians made groceries since Spanish colonial times

The wholesaling and retailing of foodstuffs in colonial times occurred in an ad-hoc manner, mostly on the levees and in the streets. Spanish administrators in the 1770s grew concerned about the difficulties of inspecting and regulating foods in such a decentralized way, and in 1780, erected the city's first public market: a sixty-by-twenty-two-foot wooden pavilion used mostly for meat. It was replaced by a sturdier, covered structure in 1782, also dominated by butchers.[409]

Distribution of other foodstuffs occurred at two levels. Hunters and farmers brought in "salt meats of all grades, oil, suet and pork lard...rice, corn, peas, beans... chickens and turkeys"[410] and other fresh game and produce to the riverfront levee, where they were permitted to retail directly to the public for a period of three hours. Afterwards, under the watchful eye of Spanish authorities, they were restricted to wholesaling to a ragtag throng of independent vendors, who then roamed the streets to sell to housekeepers. "Making groceries" in 1780s-New Orleans meant either arriving at the right time on the levee, or tracking down the right peddler in the street. The system benefited neither the buyer, who had to seek out vendors of the desired foods; the vendor, who had to lug perishables exposed to the elements; nor the Spanish city government (*Cabildo*), which sacrificed a potential revenue stream and hindered its ability to inspect for quality and regulate for price. A second market was needed. On September 10, 1784,

> the Cabildo decided to construct a market large enough to accommodate
> all the daily food supplies...in order to have all the retailers in one place, as

their number has increased…. This public market will be large enough to receive the merchandise and accommodate the peddlers and will protect them from the bad weather and excessive heat which spoils the provisions, as well as from the heavy rains and extreme cold weather that damages and alters their quality, and this public market should be centrally located.[411]

Announcements posted to advise the peddlers of the new rules provide insight into New Orleans food culture of the 1780s. Peddlers of "fresh beef, fresh pork, salted meat and sausages…mutton, venison…, rice, fresh and dry vegetables, wild fowl of all kinds and fresh fish" were instructed to arrive to the market on a fixed day where they would be assigned a stall for "a small fee." Fishermen, who traditionally sold their catch "in the plaza [and] in the heat of the sun" on street corners, often caused a public nuisance when they dumped "blood, gills and other waste" in front of people's houses. They, too, were ordered "to a designated place" in the market, where they could only sell their fish by the pound (unless it was a rare fish, marketable by the cut).

Hunters, for their part, sometimes offered spoiled meat in the hope of squeezing the last *picayune* out their rapidly depreciating offering. "This abuse being bad for the public health," authorities threw the meat into the river "in [the hunter's] presence" and slapped a fine on the offender. Penalties for vendors selling outside the market were more severe: "8 days in jail and a discretionary fine" for free people, and a "lashing if they are slaves" selling for their own gain. Only those slaves affiliated with local market gardens (truck farms) had the freedom to vend either in the streets or in the market.[412]

As in any economy, various sectors competed aggressively and petitioned authorities to intervene on their behalf. Store merchants disdained street peddlers and asked the Cabildo to prohibit their activity. Both merchants and peddlers lost retail business to the wholesalers on the levee. City inspectors and tax collectors wrangled with all sectors: certain members of the Cabildo, for example, resisted the construction of a dedicated fish market on grounds of cost and cleanliness. Spanish officials in general meddled brashly in setting prices, taxing, and stipulating providers, particularly for beef and flour, the subjects of ongoing controversies in the Cabildo's deliberations.[413] Not willing to let the free market allocate resources and set prices on its own, the Cabildo, in one case, raised the price of bear fat—not because of the scarcity of bears, but the gunpowder and ammunition needed to kill them.[414]

Peddlers continued to play a role in the retail economy for years to come: Benjamin Latrobe reported in 1819 that "in every street during the whole day [enslaved] black women are met, carrying baskets upon their heads calling at the doors of houses."[415] Most working-class citizens, however, availed themselves to the convenient new centralized public market system for their retail needs, making it a resounding success. When the market structures were destroyed by the Good Friday Fire of 1788, the city government replaced them during 1790-92 with an open-air market and soon remodeled it into an enclosed stall market where St. Ann Street meets the levee. Tradition holds this milestone (specifically 1791) as the foundation of the French Market, although antecedent entities date back to 1780.

The market grew in 1799 to accommodate the controversial fish market, and shortly thereafter for the display of veal, pork, and lamb. Colloquially called the "French Market" or "Creole Market" (because uptown Anglo-Americans and visitors dubbed everything in the old city as "French" or "Creole" regardless of its true ethnic affiliation), New Orleans' first municipal market expanded periodically over the next 140 years. The original meat market at St. Ann was destroyed by a hurricane in 1812 and replaced by an extant pillared Roman-style arcade; a vegetable market arose at the St. Philip intersection in the 1820s, followed by a fish and wild game market (1840), a fruit market, and a bazaar market (1870) for dry goods. Finally, in the 1930s, Gallatin Street was cleared away for the open shed that now hosts the French Market flea market stalls. The entire municipal market system also expanded, starting in 1836-38 with the St. Mary, Poydras, and Washington markets in adjacent faubourgs, and continuing with the Tremé, the Dryades, and a dozens of others into the early twentieth century.[416]

The French Market gained widespread fame in the antebellum era, thanks to the steady stream of visitors who wrote about the spectacle upon setting foot on the levee. Most waxed—with varying degrees of eloquence—on the market's incredible ethnic diversity ("all nations under the sun have here vomited forth their specimens of human cattle"[417]), or on the dizzying linguistic soundscape ("….a confusion of languages various as at Babel…"). A visitor from Edinburgh in 1828 noted that "the fishermen were talking Spanish," possibly Isleños from St. Bernard Parish, "while amongst the rest of the crowd there was a pretty equal distribution of French and English." His inventory of foods for sale during his late April visit imparts some idea of the city's food culture at the time:

> …cabbages, peas, beet-roots, artichokes, French beans, radishes, and a great variety of spotted seeds, and caravansas [a type of bean]; —potatoes both of the sweet and Irish kind;—tomatoes, rice, Indian corn, ginger, blackberries, roses and violets, oranges, bananas, apples;—fowls tied in threes by the leg, quails, gingerbread, beer in bottles, and salt fish….

> [At] every second or third pillar sat one or more black women, chattering in French, selling coffee and chocolate [and] smoking dishes of rice, white as snow, which I observed the country people eating with great relish, along with a very nice mess of stuff, which I took to be curry…. But I found it was called gumbo, a sort of gelatinous vegetable soup, of which…I learnt afterwards to understand the value. [418]

Some noted not only the languages, ethnicities, and foodstuffs of the French Market, but also the pretty girls. This lyrical description dates from 1852:

> Sunday morning in the Creole Market….We dash into the crowd, like a bold swimmer, desperate to make our way; but ho! our step is arrested by a blue-eyed lassie, fresh and innocent from the vineyards of the Danube or the Rhyne, whose offered cup of smoking "Mocha" temps the appetite, and we pause to sip the fragrant beverage…

> Lo! On our right stands a burly butcher, red to the elbows…. In the middle of the market….we fight our way gallantly [through] the well-filled baskets,

overrunning with meats and vegetables that soil our vestments....

[F]ish that swam in waters long dried up are offered on the altars of Epicurus; and birds of strange feather, the date of whose demise is wrapt in the mystery of forgotten times. There are eels from Lake Borgne, croakers and crabs from Pontchartrain, red fish from the briny surf, and...shad preserved in ice, imported from the far East. There is picking for the larder of the very best, and if you choose not guardedly, of the worst, too.[419]

Swedish traveler Fredrika Bremer, who toured the market in January 1851, found it "in full bloom on Sunday morning each week," reflecting, she observed, the difference between French and Anglo observance of the Sabbath. "The French Market is one of the most lively and picturesque scenes of New Orleans," wrote Bremer.

One feels as if transported at once to a great Paris *marché* [except] that one here meets with various races of people, hears many different languages spoken, and sees the productions of various zones. Here are English, Irish, Germans, French, Spanish, Mexicans. Here are negroes and Indians. Most [who sell] are black Creoles, or natives, who have the French animation and gayety, who speak French fluently....

On the outskirts of the market you found Indians[,] wrapped in their blankets, with their serious, uniform, stiff countenances, and downcast eyes.... [O]utside the market-place, Indian boys were shooting with bows and arrows to induce young white gentlemen to purchase their toy weapons. These red boys were adorned with...brilliant ribbon round their brows, and with feathers....

I wandered among the stalls, which were piled up with game, and fruit, and flowers, bread and confectionery, grain and vegetables, and innumerable good things all nicely arranged.... The fruit-stalls were really a magnificent sight; they were gorgeous with the splendid fruits of every zone, among which were many tropical ones quite new to me. Between two and three thousand persons, partly purchasers and partly sellers, were here in movement, but through all there prevailed so much good order and so much sunny, amiable vivacity, that one could not help being heartily amused. People breakfasted, and talked, and laughed just as in the markets at Paris...[420]

Wrote a local journalist upon visiting the market in 1859,

About midnight the markets begin to show signs of life; the coffee tables are decorated with their array of cups of steaming Mocha, and visited by many for business or amusement....

[T]he dull sound of cart wheels is heard, and the butchers and vegetable vendors bring their quota of the daily food of New Orleans. The noise of the hammer and the cleaver is heard, as beefsteaks, chops and ribs are separated and hung up temptingly, while pyramids of vegetables, mountains of game, and cart loads of fish are spread out upon the stalls....

Daylight appears, and the crowd of visitors keeps increasing; servants with their baskets, gentlemen enjoying an early smoke… fine ladies out for an early walk; and good housewives who do their own marketing. The dense crowd [keeps] moving in a double human stream [through] peddlers and dealers of every imaginable kind. Here the Italian, with his basket of eggs, there the Yankee, with a table covered with cakes of soap, trinkets and nick nacks; squatted on this side, the Indian squaw looks calm and indifferent, with the bunches of sassafras roots, aromatic plants from the forest, and the small bag of *gombo* powder.… [A] little further, the plantation negro will offer you honey, palmetto brooms and young chickens[,] rabbits, Guinea pigs and choice Shanghai or Bantam fowl. The Frenchmen solicits your attention to his cheap, fine goods, while you are startled by the hoarse voice of the Spanish oystermen, crying "salt oysters!"[421]

Nathaniel H. Bishop, who canoed alone down the Mississippi to New Orleans around 1876, described the market's "strange motley groups" with the standard cadence of flowery exoticism and ethnic stereotyping:

We see the Sicilian fruit-seller with his native dialect; the brisk French madame with her dainty stall; the mild-eyed Louisiana Indian woman with her sack of gumbo spread out before her; the fish-dealer with [an] odd patois; the dark-haired creole lady with her servant gliding here and there; the old Spanish gentleman with the blood of Castile tingling in his veins; the graceful French dame in her becoming toilet; the Hebrew woman with her dark eyes and rich olive complexion; the pure Anglo-Saxon type, ever distinguishable from all others; and, swarming among them all, the irrepressible negro, –him you find in every size, shape, and shade, from the tiny yellow picaninny to his rotund and inky grandmother, from the lazy wharf-darky… to the dignified colored policeman….[422]

New Orleans' municipal market system enjoyed its heyday in the late nineteenth century. What thwarted its domination in the latter years were the increasingly ubiquitous corner grocery stores, many of which were established by Italians and other immigrants who got their start in the French Market. Their intentionally dispersed geography gave the corner grocers a major competitive advantage over centralized markets: convenience. The city fought back with a 1901 law that prohibited groceries to open within nine blocks of a municipal market, and in 1911, the system expanded to its thirty-fourth unit (double the number from 1880). New Orleans at the time boasted the highest per-capita number of public markets among major American cities, and quite possibly the highest absolute number as well.[423]

Municipal markets, nevertheless, became increasingly ill-suited for twentieth-century city life. Nearby corner grocery stores continued to draw consumers away from the drafty halls of the picturesque old stall markets. Then, automobiles, supermarkets, franchises, suburbanization, and finally nationalized and globalized food production and distribution redefined utterly the geography of food retail. Within a few decades, progress rendered the market system—and to some degree its old nemesis, the corner grocery—obsolete. Most markets closed by the late 1950s, their structures either demolished or retrofit for other uses. Yet their geography survives: a number of modern-day commercial clusters, along corridors such as Magazine, Prytania, Decatur, and Claiborne, reveal the old market locations.

After the demise of markets and corner stores, local retail chains (namely Schwegmann's), plus increasing numbers of regional and national chains (such as Winn-Dixie and later Sav-a-Center), came to dominate the New Orleans food market. By century's end, Schwegmann's closed and Winn-Dixie, Sav-a-Center, and finally Wal-Mart garnered the lion's share of the market. While some single-location independents and small local chains (Langenstein's, Ferrara's, Zuppardo's, among others) still dotted the cityscape, most New Orleanians spend most of their food dollars at national big-box chains. The rapid transformation reflected the shift in the city's business sector from locally owned companies to regional and global firms. That trend reversed somewhat two years after Hurricane Katrina, when the unstable postdiluvian business environment spooked the national Sav-a-Center chain out of the region. In its place came Thibodaux-based Rouses, which to the delight of many New Orleanians, brought back many traditional local food specialties to the city's supermarket shelves.

The same cannot be said of the French Market, which essentially operates today as a "festival marketplace," catering to visitors' want of souvenirs rather than residents' need for food. Many local historians, unable to see past the trinkets and the bead-draped tourists, generally disdain the place, loudly lamenting the passing of the "real" market of decades ago. They are missing something. At least in the Flea Market and Fruit and Vegetable portions of the complex, stall-based vendors still create an open marketplace ambience which loosely matches the descriptions recorded in historical journals. More significantly, the vendors, most of them immigrants, continue the French Market's ancient legacy as a place of extraordinary ethnic diversity, where working-class newcomers can launch their own businesses and determine their own destiny. The market itself survives as the sole vestige of the old Spanish public market system, tracing a direct lineage to the Cabildo deliberations of over two centuries ago.

Reflected one observer of the French Market in 1859,

> There is something there not to be found elsewhere, and to our mind, the study of the living panorama [at] the old market would give the observer a correct idea of the combined elements that make New Orleans the most incomprehensible city in the States.[424]

"Concerns Akin Assemble Together"

Business districts and commercial clusters in New Orleans

Firms often cluster with their competitors to tap the infrastructure, resources, labor pool, services, and customer base upon which all in the industry depend. New

Orleans, the South's premier city for over a century, boasted an intricate network of industry districts. Examples from the early nineteenth century include a "banking district" at the intersection of Royal and Conti streets and a cluster of publishers along upper Chartres Street. Many more districts formed in the bustling late antebellum years. Reported *The Daily Picayune* in 1859:

> Carondelet Street was devoted entirely to cotton and shipping; Canal [hosted] the dry goods trade; Chartres was expected to retain the variety trade; St. Charles, with its various places of amusement, could retain only certain classes of offices, besides coffee saloons and cigar stores; Magazine had a near monopoly on the wholesale boot and shoe and a goodly part of the wholesale dry goods trade; from Tchoupitoulas to the levee, Canal to Lafayette, Western produce reigned; Poydras claimed as a specialty bagging and rope.[425]

In the 1870s-1900s, "exchanges" formed in certain commodity-based industries, serving as central meeting places for information-sharing, negotiation, investing, trading, marketing, and socializing. Exchanges typically took the form of an elaborate building sited in the heart of the respective industry's district, becoming a sort of "capitol" for that business community. Cotton firms formed a centralized Cotton Exchange at Carondelet and Gravier in 1871; produce merchants followed with their Produce Exchange on Magazine Street in 1880 (which later evolved into the Board of Trade). Sugar merchants launched the Louisiana Sugar Exchange in 1883 on the French Quarter levee's "sugar district," and expanded it to include rice in 1889. A Stock Exchange formed among the brokers of Gravier Street in 1906, making that area New Orleans' answer to Wall Street.[426] Other exchanges—the Mechanics, Dealers and Lumbermen's Exchange; the Mexican and South American Exchange; the Auctioneers' Exchange; and the Fruit Exchange, to name a few—both reflected and reinforced the geographical concentration of competing firms. A 1904 streetcar map listed the districts that flourished during the city's turn-of-the-century economic boom:

> PRINCIPAL SHOPPING DISTRICT. Canal Street, at Bourbon and Dauphine Streets.
> GENERAL OFFICE DISTRICT. Carondelet and Common Streets.
> SHIPPING DISTRICT. Canal Street, at Canal Street Ferry Landing.
> WHOLESALE COTTON DISTRICT. Carondelet and Gravier Streets.
> WHOLESALE GROCERY DISTRICT. Poydras and Tchoupitoulas Streets.
> WHOLESALE SUGAR AND RICE DISTRICT. North Peters and Customhouse Streets.
> NEWSPAPER DISTRICT. Camp Street, between Gravier and Poydras Streets.
> HOTEL DISTRICT St. Charles and Common Streets.
> THEATRE DISTRICT. Canal and Baronne Streets and St. Charles Street.[427]

In these districts are represented three major Louisiana crops—cotton, sugar, and rice—and New Orleans' two long-standing major industries: shipping and tourism, represented by the hotel district. The remaining districts reflect New Orleans' role as a local and regional hub for business, retail, journalism, and the arts.

A publication by George W. Engelhardt in the same year described Canal Street as the "retail quarter," Tchoupitoulas as the "wholesale grocery district," and Camp Street as the "financial, jobbing, and newspaper street." His identification of the Cotton Exchange at Carondelet and Gravier as the hub of the "money quarter of the city" reflected the importance of cotton to the city's economy. Between this fiscal precinct and the Mississippi River was what Engelhardt called "the wholesale business of the city," meaning its warehousing, manufacturing, and shipping district. Wrote Engelhardt:

> The produce and fruit trade…has a street or two of its own ; lumber…takes to the basins terminating the [Old Basin and New Basin] Canals ; and in general it is to be said that here, as in the greater cities everywhere, *concerns akin assemble together.* Thus the grocery and provision lines, the import coffee trade, the iron works, the printing and publishing houses, the horse and mule markets have each their own special locality somewhere in or about this particular quarter of trade.[428]

Perhaps the most renowned "industry" cluster of historic New Orleans—Storyville, the red-light district bounded by Basin, St. Louis, Robertson, and Iberville/Canal—formed by default when Alderman Sidney Story had prostitution banned (1897) from the rest of the city. By the early 1900s, nearly every structure within those eighteen blocks served some aspect of the sex industry, from filthy cribs to lively saloons to gaudy "sporting houses." Storyville declined in the mid-1910s and closed by order of the Navy Department in 1917; most of its structures were demolished around 1940 for the Iberville Housing Project.

Prostitution was not the only trade clustered by law. Another less famous but far more significant case involved historic New Orleans' most disdained urban nuisance: the animal slaughtering industry. Livestock landing and slaughtering were once restricted to "Slaughterhouse Point" in Algiers, but convenience led the industry to relocate to the city's side of the river. Suitable wharves, cheap land for stockyards, plentiful immigrant labor, and adjacency to the rapidly growing upper half of the metropolis destined most livestock shipments in the mid-1800s to the banks of Lafayette and Jefferson cities immediately upriver from New Orleans—and its drinking water source. There the animals awaited purchase by the city's hundred-plus butchers, most of who hailed from the Gascony region of France and operated shops citywide. The "Gascon butchers" had the right to slaughter on their own premises, which minimized their costs and inconveniences while empowering them to time the killing according to market demand. Largely unregulated and lacking municipal garbage disposal, many butchers dumped blood, entrails, excrement, carcasses, and other offal in the nearby backswamp, on adjacent lots, or worse, into the river at points above the drinking-water intakes. Nearly every neighborhood suffered malodorous and unsanitary conditions on account of the butchers' dispersed geography. Citizens, following the lead of numerous other cities, petitioned the state to relocate, concentrate, and regulate New Orleans' *abattoirs.*

The biracial Reconstruction-era state legislature complied in 1869 with "An Act to Protect the Health of the City of New Orleans, to Locate the Stock-Landings and Slaughter-Houses, and to Incorporate the Crescent City Live-stock Landing and Slaughter-house Company."[429] The law called for centralizing slaughtering activity across the river and granting a monopoly to one group to carry out this trade. Many citizens applauded the new law, and some invested in the publicly traded stock. A makeshift livestock landing and slaughterhouse complex arose quickly once land was acquired in Algiers. [430]

Others, however, were outraged, principally the Gascon butchers. Abetting them were those who philosophically opposed monopolies, suspected corruption, or simply resisted all actions of the Reconstruction state legislature for political, racial, or anti-Northern reasons. The butchers filed nearly 300 lawsuits, some of which arrived to the docket of the U.S. Supreme Court. Their argument rested on the recently ratified Fourteenth Amendment, which (the butchers' ex-Confederate lawyer ironically contended) ensured broad federal protection against state infringements on basic rights such as practicing one's trade. In the meanwhile, they formed their own association to rival the monopoly, and built an east bank facility along the lower parish line, immediately below Jackson Barracks. The monopoly eventually acquired this new facility, and when workers "were given a choice between the company's fairly makeshift original abattoir [in Algiers] and larger, better-equipped one located on the same side of the river as the city, the vast majority quickly abandoned the west-bank facility." [431]

In 1873, the U.S. Supreme Court ruled in favor of the monopoly. Justices in the slim majority limited their interpretation of the Fourteenth Amendment to protecting the rights of newly freed slaves only, while expressly avoiding altering the postbellum balance of power between the federal government and the states. They also sanctioned certain levels of state police power in the interest of public health. The decision in the so-called *Slaughter-house Cases* has since been viewed by historians as among the most controversial and influential in the Court's history, contested by both liberal and conservative legal scholars.

Locally, the *Slaughter-house Cases* resulted in the concentration of *abattoirs* below the city proper, namely the lowermost corner of the Ninth Ward, now present-day Arabi. This locale kept the smelly, noisy, messy operation downriver from the city's water source, sufficiently far from the population to minimize offensive odors yet close enough to supply meat markets and consumers, and positioned on the more convenient east bank of the river. Countless animals were slaughtered in this *de jure* industry district into the early twentieth century, when growth pressure led to the area's urbanization. Relocated again, the city's last abattoir closed in 1963. Vestiges of the old slaughterhouse and its ancillary functions can still be found in the present-day Arabi and Lower Ninth Ward cityscapes, while ramifications of the famous Supreme Court case abound in the American legal landscape. [432]

During the Depression, at a time when industry district formation began to weaken, Works Progress Administration writers observed some old and some new concentrations:

Most of the fur dealers are still to be found along North Peters and Decatur Sts. Royal St. has become one of antique shops.... Coffee roasters and packers are ... along Magazine and Tchoupitoulas Streets from Canal to Howard Ave. Farther uptown, Poydras St. from Camp to the river is the wholesale fruit, produce, and poultry center, while the principal meat packers are found near Magazine and Julia Sts. The section between Camp St. and the river, and Canal St. and Jackson Ave., contains most of the wholesale jobbing houses and many of the manufacturing plants. Carondelet St. has always been the street of the cotton brokers and bankers.[433]

The circa-1960s middle-class exodus and ensuing decline of downtown bear some blame for the disappearance of New Orleans' historical industry districts. Weightier factors include national and global technological changes in the various industries and the flow of finances and data therein, which often eliminated the need for players to cluster spatially. In other cases, the industry leader relocated while its competitors folded. "Newspaper Row," which formed on Camp Street near Natchez Alley in the 1850s, declined once the *Times-Picayune* moved to Lafayette Square in the 1920s and its competitors went out of business. The French Quarter levee's Sugar District declined once the premier sugar processing facility moved to St. Bernard Parish in 1912. The Cotton District disappeared by the early 1960s after federal involvement in cotton pricing rendered the Cotton Exchange obsolete.

Yet some old clusters survive, and some new ones have formed. Bourbon Street gained worldwide fame as nightclub and bar district around World War II, a reputation that grows deeper with every subsequent generation. The recently "discovered" Warehouse District is, despite its name, today more of a hotel, restaurant, and convention-services zone than one of warehousing. An arts and museum district formed in the early 2000s in the vicinity of Julia, Camp, and Andrew Higgins Drive, anchored by the highly successful and ever-expanding National World War II (D-Day) Museum, the up-and-coming Ogden Museum of Southern Art, and the stalwart Civil War Museum at Confederate Memorial Hall. Royal and Chartres streets still comprise the antiques district in the French Quarter, as they have for over a century, while Magazine Street plays that role uptown. The city's medical district on lower Tulane Avenue, traceable to the siting of Charity Hospital there in 1833, bustled until recently with the clinical, educational, and research activities of Tulane University Medical School, Charity Hospital, University Hospital, Veteran's Administration, Louisiana State University Health Sciences Center, Delgado Community College and other entities. A few blocks away, the Orpheum, Saenger, Joy, and State Palace made the Canal/Basin intersection the city's theater and entertainment district.

Katrina-related flood damage darkened the theater district and led to the closing of the historical Charity Hospital nucleus of the medical district. With most other old districts now defunct, one is tempted to consider the business-clustering trait to be a thing of the past.

Not quite. In 2005, an effort to recognize and promote a "Greater New Orleans Biosciences Economic Development District" gained momentum, aiming to exploit the Tulane Avenue medical cluster to foster a new biomedical research industry.

Hurricane Katrina temporarily derailed that effort, but it spawned another: The state legislature's call for the geographical consolidation of civil and criminal courts in 2006 inspired a one-billion-dollar "Justice Facilities Master Plan" for the area bounded by Tulane, Broad, I-10, and Jefferson Davis Parkway. Viewed by supporters as a rational way to unify co-dependent functions and share resources, the clustering plan is bitterly opposed by CBD-based law firms and those who depend on them.

It remains to be seen if New Orleans intentionally develops a new biomedical or legal district. Yet at a smaller level, spontaneous business clustering thrives. Wrote a *Times-Picayune* journalist two years after Katrina,

> Call it the gas station phenomenon: that capitalist oddity in which business-
> es decide to cluster along the same block or intersection as their competi-
> tion, rather than spread out across the city to capture different streams of
> customers. Take the two gelato shops in the 3000 block of Magazine Street.
> And the grocery stores along Tchoupitoulas Street.
>
> Now two of the city's largest private hospitals have announced plans to open
> imaging centers directly across the street from each other at the intersection
> of Napoleon and Claiborne avenues.[434]

Indeed, "concerns akin" continue to "assemble together."

Passing Judgment on New Orleans Society

A city's striking ability to inspire passionate reaction

An anonymous "Officer at New Orleans," writing in 1744, found little in French colonial New Orleans society to admire. That his letter circulated in London on the eve of an English war with France may explain its caustic tone (and perhaps com-promise its objectivity). "The French live sociably enough," he allowed,

> but the officers are too free with the town's people; and the town's people
> that are rich are too proud and lofty. Their inferiors hardly dare to speak to
> them.... [A]n upstart fellow thinks that others are not worthy to look at
> him. Every one studies his own profit; the poor labor for a week and squan-
> der in one day all they have earned in six[;] the rich spend their time in
> seeing their slaves work to improve their lands, and get money which they
> spend in plays, balls, and feasts.[435]

New Orleanians' favorite "pastime," he continued, "is women," and of the 500 or so he estimated in the city, "I don't believe without exaggeration that there are ten of them of a blameless character...." Men fared little better in the officer's eyes: "the rich man knows how to procure himself justice of the poor...." Those lacking money nevertheless "are seldom without wine in their cellars; the tradesmen is seldom a week without drinking it beyond moderation; but that is nothing in comparison with the soldier."

No wonder New Orleans society failed to impress. "The country," explained the officer, "was at first settled by lewd, good-for-nothing people sent from France," including those with "no fathers, taken ... out of the hospitals at Paris and L'Orient." The ne'er-do-wells apparently passed on their vulgar genes to the present [1740s] generation: "A child of six years of age knows more here of raking and swearing than a young man of 25 in France; and an insolent boy of 12 or 13 years of age will boldly insult and strike an old man."[436]

The officer's critique of French soldiers' indulgences offers a glimpse into the street culture and economics of the circa-1740s city:

> Liquors are a pistole a bottle; brandy, three livres fifteen sols; rum and wine, fifty sols; bread, twelve sols a pound; butcher's meat, six sols; a suckling pig, 100 sols; a turkey, three or four livres; a goose, fifty sols; a duck, twenty-five; a teal, twelve; a small salad, thirty; and if one will pass a quarter of an hour with a female, white, red, or black, or tawny, you must reckon upon a bill of fifty sols.[437]

With a *pistole* worth around two dollars, a *livre* about twenty cents, and a *sol* one-twentieth of a *livre*, a dinner of brandy, bread, and goose followed by fifteen minutes with a prostitute cost $1.87 in French colonial New Orleans.

Though little is known of this anonymous officer and the accuracy of his descriptions, a reader is struck by the number of modern-day New Orleans stereotypes he invoked: a haughty elite, loose morals, balls and revelry, drinking and prostitution, all amid tensions of race and class. The letter was not published in France and did not come to the attention of historians until 1887.

Nearly a half-century after the anonymous officer's missive, Chevalier Guy de Soniat du Fossat, who first arrived to New Orleans as a French officer in 1751, penned a "Synopsis of the History of Louisiana, from the Founding of the Colony to End of the Year 1791," which his descendent, Charles T. Soniat, translated in 1903. Though mostly a light history and description, the pamphlet contains interesting perspectives informed by Soniat's personal experiences in the colonial city. "After having spoken of Louisiana and of its soil, we ought to say something of the Creoles who inhabit it," he begins.

> Creoles are defined to be "the children of Europeans born in the colony." They, in general, measure about five feet six inches in height; they are all

well shaped, and of agreeable figure; they are lively, alert and agile, and not-withstanding the great heat of the climate, are laborious. They are born with ambition, and an honest self esteem. They are endowed with a natural disposition for all sciences, arts and exercises that amuse society. They excel in dancing, fencing, hunting, and in horsemanship. Nature has favored them with a penetrating and active mind, and they are capable of being easily instructed. The lack of teachers renders their education somewhat incomplete, and it must be said, in all justice, that...they possess...politeness, bravery, and benevolence. They are good fathers, good friends, and good kinsmen.

The women, besides having the qualities above enumerated are agreeable in figure, and seldom deformed. They make good mothers, and are devoted to their husbands and their children; and in their marital relations seldom are they unfaithful....

[T]he stranger arriving in this wild and savage country will be surprised to see in this capital, as exist in all countries of Europe, brilliant assemblies where politeness, amiability, and gayety reign supreme.[438]

Soniat, while himself not Creole (on account of his French birth), fathered the quintessential old-line aristocratic white Creole family, so it is plausible that his rather flattering and romanticized "Portrait of the Creole" reflects this personal circumstance. The popular usage and understanding of the term Creole would transform throughout the next two centuries, at first abandoning the children-of-Europeans-born-in-the-colony definition in favor of a native-to-Louisiana meaning, and later either including or adamantly excluding those with African blood (depending on who was doing the defining). One aspect of Soniat's Creole portrait which thrives in the popular imagination today is that of the likely and chivalrous *bon vivant*—the Creole as a cultured, fascinating, slightly mysterious, and ultimately unknowable specimen of humanity. Quite unlike the anonymous officer of 1744, Soniat extended those generous characterizations to New Orleans itself— "where politeness, amiability, and gayety reign supreme."

Spanish officer Francisco Bouligny, who resided in Louisiana from 1769 to 1775 and subsequently wrote an influential *Memoria* for the Crown, shared Soniat's favorable views of local society. Indulging in hyperbole, he painted a rosy picture of the colony for his superiors:

Without a doubt this province, the most favorable to population in the world, the salubriousness of its climate, the amenity and fertility of its fields, the abundance and shadiness of its forests, and the ease of canal construction to penetrate its hinterlands, makes this country an earthy paradise.

He then projected the healthy physical environment upon the occupying society:

The women are all fertile and there is no marriage which does not have abundant children. The creoles are of a healthy temperament and capable of the hardest exercise.... Their industry and application are no less since it is rare for a head of family not to have the best books [on] agriculture and the exploitation of the woods. There are few houses whose furniture has not been made by the owner's own hands. Very well off men do not disdain to spend entire days at the foot of a plow, in the mill, in carpentry, or in a blacksmith shop. It can be truthfully said that the population base there today is the most favorable for indefinite development, as much for industry as for population and commerce.

Bouligny viewed Louisiana women not only as fruitful, but savvy Darwinians:

The women themselves, in their classes, distinguish and praise the most intelligent and diligent men, a policy strong enough for that country to be able to reach the greatest perfection.

Bouligny read chivalry into Creole gender relations, a theme shared by many future interpreters of Creole culture:

[Creole men] quickly leave the plow...to offer their hand to a lady and assist her across the furrows they have made. The elegance of their ways and the propriety with which they reason [inspires] admiration among strangers.[439]

Bouligny was no less upbeat on race relations and human bondage: "The Negro slaves have only the name slave since in reality they are as happy as the day workers of Europe...." Their contentment, he suggested, derived from benevolent masters providing them a barrel of corn, a parcel for gardening, another parcel for raising animals, and a cabin "like those they make here in Spain." "They all live healthy and robust to such a point that some [visitors] have been astonished on seeing them so agile, radiant, and strong."[440]

Poverty might have existed in Bouligny's New Orleans, but did not show itself. "Not a single poor person is seen asking for alms in all [Louisiana]." Visiting sailors who attempted begging from local housewives got a lecture on laziness instead of a handout. Concluded Bouligny,

[T]he present population of Louisiana is the most favorable to provide an infinite development and [a bulwark against] its neighbors, however strong and forceful they might be.[441]

Bouligny's New Orleans, much like Soniat's, was robust, fruitful, industrious, content, genial, and indomitable.

Pierre-Louis Berquin-Duvallon, a Saint-Domingue planter who fled the slave insurrection for Louisiana and settled in New Orleans for two and a half years, scribed in 1802 an acerbic little volume about his adopted home. It was translated to English

by an American, John Davis (who infused his own agenda into the text), and published four years later under the title *Travels in Louisiana and The Floridas in the Year 1802, Giving a Correct Picture of Those Countries.*

Embittered by his losses and eager to rebuild them in Louisiana, Berquin disdained the condition of Spanish-governed New Orleans and directed special contempt at its Creole population. He viewed a return of French dominion, coupled with new American investment (an angle advanced by translator Davis), as Louisiana's salvation. This hidden agenda deeply colored Berquin's "correct picture" of the colony—and of Creole society.

Berquin reported certain traits of Creole women—for frivolity, vanity, sexual prowess, and *joie de vivre*—that occur regularly in later literature:

> The female Creoles being in general without education, can possess no taste for reading, music or drawing; but they are passionately fond of dancing[,] passing whole nights in succession in this exercise.

> The ladies of New-Orleans dress themselves with taste, [while] the women in the country… are less pompous [but] love [their apparel] equally well. Their little hearts beat with tumult at the sight of a new dress…. Their waists are every day getting short, their arms more naked, and their bosoms more bare.[442]

> Vanity is a passion… found wherever there are human beings. But I know no part of the globe where it is so prominent a feature of the moral character as in Louisiana….[443]

> [Creole women] are very prolific, bear early and long. They are seldom married seven years without having half a dozen children…. It is a very common thing for the mother and daughter to be big at the same time; sometimes the grand-daughter… makes a trio of big bellies.[444]

Many themes in Berquin's progressively more vitriolic narrative persist today as deeply embedded citywide stigmas—of lavish living amidst poverty, of corruption, of moral decadence.

> Luxury… has made great progress through the colony. Every thing in the town is tinctured with ostentation. An air of expense distinguishes the apparel, vehicles, furniture of the inhabitants. Simplicity has taken flight, parade has usurped its place. This luxury is dangerous in a rich nation, but to regions ever doomed to mediocrity it is a mortal poison.[445]

"Luxury and corruption go hand in hand," he lectured his readers. "This is strongly exemplified at New-Orleans by the number of white infants, the fruit of illicit commerce, exposed nightly in the streets, a maternal sacrifice to false honour." He viewed New Orleanians not only as morally lax, but also loquacious, mendacious, narcissistic, and cruel:

> Falsehood has attained to such a height, that no one lies here for the plea-

sure of lying. No people in the world have such a tendency to hyperbolical amplification.[446]

A man represents himself here twice as rich as he is. The most ordinary habitation is a terrestrial paradise. The men are always frank and generous, the women never old, nor the girls ever ugly.[447]

Our Creoles likewise choak [*sic*] themselves in talking of the illustriousness of their families... They are the greatest egotists in the world; their conversation is eternally about themselves. They are vulgarly familiar with their equals, insolent towards their inferiors, cruel to their slaves, and inhospitable to strangers.[448]

Not one to discriminate in his discriminations, Berquin viewed free people of color with equal contempt:

The mulattoes are in general vain and insolent, perfidious and debauched, much giving to lying, and great cowards. They have an inveterate hatred against the whites, the authors of their existence....

The mulatto women have not all the faults of the men. But they are full of vanity, and very libertine; money will always buy their caresses.... They live in open concubinage with the whites.... [449]

On enslaved Africans, Berquin was no less or more vicious:

Negroes are a species of beings whom nature seems to have intended for slavery; their compliancy of temper, patience under injury, and innate passiveness, all concur to justify this position....

[T]he negro slave of Louisiana... is lazy, libertine, and given to lying, but not incorrigibly wicked.

I do not consider slavery either as contrary to the order of a well regulated society, or an infringement of the social laws. Under a different name it exists in every country. Soften then the word which so mightily offends the ear; call it dependence.[450]

New Orleanians, to Berquin's ear, "have a disgusting drawling method of pronouncing their words;" they "lame and disfigure certain [French] words," perhaps because of a "physical...defect in [their] organ of speech...."[451] He mocked their pretentiousness: "A *tutoiement* prevails in the familiar conversation of domestic life. It is never *you*, but always *thee* and *thou*. It has, however, no particular force. It is the babble [that] owes it origin to the base birth, the vulgar manners and low discourse of the first colonists." That base birth, Berquin patiently explained, accounted for the loathsomeness of the people of New Orleans:

Louisiana...has always been a colony more or less poor, and insulated, for a long time, from the rest of the globe. The country miserable in its soil was not less so with regard to its inhabitants.[452]

> [T]he Creoles of Louisiana being all of base extraction…were naturally il-literate, ignorant and rude…. [T]he present race seem to have degenerated from their ancestors, they are rude, envious, interested, avaricious, and pre-sumptuous…. [T]heir ignorance exceeds all human credibility.[453]

It is no wonder, then, that the New Orleans of Pierre-Louis Berquin-Duvallon was a city of illiteracy and brutishness:

> There is neither a college, nor a library here, whether public or private…. A librarian would starve [here] unless he could teach his readers the art of doubling his capital…. There is only one printing office in the city [and one] meagre weekly newspaper….[454]

> A Creole told me…that a never failing method to make him fall asleep, was to open a book before him.[455]

> Men of cultivated talents are very rare here.—There are few good musi-cians, and I know but one portrait painter…. I am persuaded there are not ten men of polite literary attainments [among the] ten thousand souls [of] New-Orleans.

> The standard of individual merit in this country is, first a man's riches, and secondly his rank. Virtue and talents obtain no respect.[456]

Berquin concluded his prejudicial diatribe by portraying himself as the heroic bearer of a moral burden:

> If I have been acrimonious in my strictures on certain classes of [Louisi-ana's] inhabitants, it was with a desire to mark vice with infamy, and expose meanness to contempt….Let the stricken deer go weep; the sorrow of the wicked provokes no sympathy.[457]

Although differing entirely in their assessments, the commentaries of the anonymous French officer, of Soniat, of Bouligny, and of Berquin trace a course that runs through numerous historical observations of New Orleans society. Commenta-tors, both visiting and resident, seemed hell-bent on *passing judgment* on the city and its people—draconian and absolutist judgment, with little nuance and qualification. Many admired and extolled the city; many others loathed and excoriated it; few fell in between.

New Orleans' ability to inspire passionate and polarized reaction continues to this day. First-time visitors are usually either appalled or enamored with the city's raff-ish air and tolerated vices, either disturbed or fascinated by its elegance and decadence. Fervent reaction to New Orleans ratcheted up even higher after Hurricane Katrina sub-jected the city's troubles and glories to international discourse.

Ask an informed American citizen today to ruminate on Dallas or Atlanta or Phoenix, and you will probably get small talk, lukewarm pleasantries, and a brief conversation. Ask them what they think about New Orleans, and you are in for not only an opinionated retort, but a sentimental smile, a scolding finger, a treasured memory, a shaking head, or an exasperated shrug over the course of a conversation spanning the spectrum of the human experience. This enigmatic capacity to rile and inspire, to scandalize and charm, to liberate and fascinate, helps explain why thousands of people have rejected the amenities and opportunities of the lukewarm Dallases and Atlantas and Phoenixes of the world, and chosen instead to cast their lot with this troubled old port—embracing all its splendors and dilemmas, all its booms and busts, all its joys and tragedies.

> *Because thou art lukewarm, and neither hot nor cold, I spew thee from my mouth.*
>
> —Revelation 3:16

Ethnic Tensions, circa 1802:
Incident at a New Orleans Ball

Geopolitics and ballroom dancing in a tumultuous era

His riches lost to the slave insurrection in Saint-Domingue, Pierre-Louis Berquin-Duvallon (see previous reading) sought refuge in circa-1800 New Orleans and schemed to rebuild his fortune. Thwarting his ambitions, in Berquin's view, were the appalling conditions of the Spanish colonial city and the despicable character of its Creole people. He set out on a literary mission to expose this scandalous state of affairs.

Berquin's book, *Travels in Louisiana and The Floridas in the Year 1802, Giving a Correct Picture of Those Countries,* viewed a return of French dominion plus new American investment as Louisiana's salvation. That hidden agenda underlies his account of an incident at a New Orleans ball, the scene of many near-violent ethnic tensions in the years around Americanization.[458]

According to Berquin, attendees mostly of French Creole ancestry had commenced forming *contre-danses Francais* when

> [t]he eldest son of the [Spanish] governor, not liking the French country dances, [substituted] English country dances; an innovation the company tolerated from deference for his distinguished rank. This act of complaisance in the assembly was misunderstood by the youthful Spaniard; he abused it grossly.

Interrupting the French country dances,

> our young illustrious Spaniard calls out, *"Contre-danses Anglaises!"* and the
> dancers[,] inflamed at his want of moderation…ordered the music to play
> on, exclaiming unanimously, *Contre-danses Francais!* The son of the gover-
> nor soon found partizans, who joined with him in the cry of *"Contre-danses
> Anglaises!"* while the dancers, firm to their purpose, reiterated *"Contre-danses
> Francaises!"* It was *confusion worse confounded*, a vociferation without end. At
> length the illustrious Spaniard finding the dancers obstinate, called out to
> the fiddlers, "Cease playing, you rascals!" The fiddlers instantly obeyed.
>
> The officer who was stationed with a guard of soldiers to maintain order in
> the place, thought only of enforcing the will of the illustrious Spaniard; he
> ordered his men to fix their bayonets, and disperse the dancers. The scene
> now beggared all description. Women shrieking and wringing their hands,
> girls fainting and falling on the floor, men cursing and unsheathing their
> swords. On one side grenadiers with fixed bayonets stood in a hostile atti-
> tude; on the other the gallant dancers were opposed with drawn swords.[459]

Berquin then added two additional ethnic dimensions to the impending brawl:

> During this squabble and uproar, how did a number of Americans act, who
> were present at the ball? Men of a pacific nature, and habituated to neu-
> trality, they neither advocated the French nor English country dances.…
> [Instead] they ran to the assistance of the fair ladies who had fainted away;
> and, loaded with their precious burdens, carried them through drawn swords
> and fixed bayonets to a place of safety.
>
> It was at the moment a conflict was about to take place…likely to termi-
> nate in a tragedy, that three young Frenchmen, lately arrived from Europe,
> mounted the orchestra and harangued the crowd. They spoke with an elo-
> quence prompted by the occasion. They declaimed on the superiority of
> concord over dissention; they entreated, conjured, and exhorted the par-
> ties, as they respected the safety, preservation, and lives of the ladies not to
> make a field of battle of a place that was consecrated to soft delight. Their
> exhortations restored peace and harmony to the society.… The ball was
> even resumed [and] remained in possession of the advocates for the French
> country dances….[460]

Perhaps events transpired precisely as Berquin recorded them, in that crowded
New Orleans ballroom two centuries ago. That is unlikely. His narrative, with its foolish
Spaniard, its frivolous and hot-headed Creoles, its heroic and gallant Americans, and
its eloquent, peace-loving Frenchmen "lately arrived from Europe," aligns suspiciously
well with Berquin's political objective, as infused by his American translator's agenda:
to excoriate Creole society, attract American investment, restore French colonial power, and rebuild in Louisiana the fortune he lost in Saint-Domingue.[461]

History overtook Berquin's agenda. Even as the ink dried on Berquin's man-
uscript, France negotiated away its last best hope for a major North American pres-

ence. The French prefect who relinquished the colony during the Louisiana Purchase ceremony described Berquin's book—which "caused a considerable stir" when copies began circulating locally—as "bilious" and "filled with sarcasm," the man himself "narrow and warped."[462] Creole society, it turned out, needed none of Berquin's rebuking: severed culturally and politically from its French Caribbean source region, it gradually melded with American culture.

Only one of Berquin's goals—increased American investment—came to fruition, perhaps more so than the cantankerous old misanthropist would have preferred.

Streetcapes of Amalgamation

*Creole/American cultural hybridization in the
nineteenth-century streets of New Orleans*

"During most of the nineteenth century," wrote historians Arnold R. Hirsch and Joseph Logsdon,

> New Orleans remained in counterpoint to the rest of urban America. Newcomers...recoiled when they encountered the prevailing French language of the city, its dominant Catholicism, its bawdy sensual delights, or its proud free black population—in short, its deeply rooted creole traditions. Its incorporation into the United States posed a profound challenge, the infant republic's first attempt to impose its institutions on a foreign city.[463]

Anglo influence arrived in tiny doses to colonial Louisiana, well before the birth of that American republic. It commenced in 1699, when Bienville famously rebuffed Capt. Louis Bond's *Carolina Galley* at English Turn; it continued in 1719, when an Englishman named Jonathan Darby set foot in New Orleans proper.[464] Anglo presence increased greatly, with tension, as France lost the Seven Years' War and with it its North American colonies, leaving New Orleans with unwelcome Spanish *dons* in the *Cabildo* and unwanted English neighbors across Lake Pontchartrain. It ratcheted up in the late 1790s, when American immigrants began to move to Spanish New Orleans, which granted to the infant republic the treasured right of deposit upon its wharves for shipments on the Mississippi.

Spain grew increasingly apprehensive about the westward-leaning United States' interest in the lower Mississippi frontier. With Latin American colonies demanding its attention and resources, Spain secretly retroceded Louisiana to militarily powerful France; Napoleon accepted, envisioning the cumbersome colonial orphan as a breadbasket for France's extremely lucrative Saint-Domingue sugar colony. But when a major slave insurrection on that Caribbean island succeeded in expelling French troops and creating the Western Hemisphere's second independent nation (Haiti), Napoleon's only remaining interest in Louisiana was to keep it out of English hands. When American diplomats broached purchasing New Orleans, Napoleon offered them the entire colony instead. On December 20, 1803, the vast Louisiana claim transferred to American dominion, and Creole New Orleans became, on paper, a U.S. city. Ambitious Northern businessmen eyed the new American port on the southwestern frontier as a potentially lucrative opportunity. Many lost no time in emigrating.

"The Americans [are] swarming in from the northern states," recollected Pierre Clément de Laussat, the last French official to oversee Louisiana, barely four months after the raising of the American flag.

> Each one turned over in his mind a little plan of speculation[;] they were invading Louisiana as the holy tribes invaded the land of Canaan. Their tendency, and…instinct, is to exclude from these privileged regions any generation but their own.[465]

Some Anglo-American emigrants derived from English stock and hailed from New England and the Mid-Atlantic states; others were of Celtic, Upland Scottish, or Irish Southerner heritage and arrived from the upper South. Nearly all were Anglophone Protestants of American culture and nationality. More still came after the Battle of New Orleans in 1815, in which Louisianians once again rebuffed an English intrusion, this time with violence and finality. "Americans are pouring in daily," remarked an amazed Benjamin Latrobe four years after the battle.[466] Creoles—that is, natives—held little in common with their new compatriots, but increasingly had to share space, sway, and say with them.

The slow and oftentimes painful absorption of post-colonial Creole New Orleans into the Anglo-American United States defined the city's experience for the remainder of the nineteenth century. The transformation infiltrated all manifestations of culture, in a way that often mystified newcomers. "What is the state of society in New Orleans?, asked Latrobe rhetorically in 1819. One "might as well ask, What is the shape of a cloud?"[467] The process of cultural amalgamation played out in politics, economics, religion, law, linguistics, and architecture, as well as in music, food, drink, dance, festivity, and recreation. Irishman Thomas Ashe's description of New Orleans nightlife in 1806 captured the city's oft-observed twilight personality shift, not to mention its penchant for pleasure:

> The instant the [sun] sets, animation begins to rise, the public walks are crowded…the inhabitants promenade on the Leveé…the billiard rooms resound, music strikes up, and life and activity resume their joyous career…. The [dining] table is excellent, being covered with fish, soup, fowls, roasted, broiled, and stewed meats, with vegetables… Coffee is served soon after dinner (…dinner-hour is three…), after which it is customary to enjoy a *siesto*.[468]

That decidedly European ambience soon began to Americanize. At times the amalgamation occurred subtly; other times it transpired loudly and visibly in the streetscapes, as witnessed and recorded by observant visitors. Among them was Charles Sealsfield, who, in his book *The Americans As They Are* (1828) noticed the emergence of the "refined" Greek Revival style—the Americans' first major architectural import—against the otherwise "crude" buildings of Creole New Orleans:

> [T]he houses are rapidly changing from the uncouth Spanish style, to more elegant forms. The new houses are mostly three stories high, with balconies, and a summer-room with blinds. In the lower suburbs, frame houses, with Spanish roofs, are still prevalent.[469]

One particular Creole cultural trait consistently offended Protestant sensibilities: disregard of the Sabbath. "The general manners and habits are very relaxed" in New Orleans, noted an English visitor in 1819. "The first day of my residence here was Sunday, and I was not a little surprised to find in the United States the markets, shops, theatre, circus, and public ball-rooms open. Gambling houses *throng* the city..."[470] Sealsfield concurred in 1828:

> It was on a Sunday that we arrived; the shops, the stores of the French and creoles, were open as usual...the coffee-houses, grog-shops, and the *estaminets* [drinking holes] of the French and German inhabitants, exhibited a more noisy scene. A kind of music, accompanied with [singing] resounded in almost every direction. This little respect paid to the Sabbath is a relic of the French revolution and of Buonaparte [*sic*], for whom the French and the creoles of Louisiana have an unlimited respect, imitating him as poor minds generally do....
>
> To a new comer, accustomed in the north to the dignified and quiet keeping of the Sabbath, this appears very shocking. The Anglo-Americans, with few exceptions, remain even here faithful to their ancient custom of keeping the Sabbath holy.[471]

Creole and Anglo ethnic predomination in the lower and upper city thus produced, at least on Sundays, two very different street scenes—one bustling and festive, the other reverent and quiet.

Joseph Holt Ingraham, in his travelogue *The South-West by a Yankee*, described in 1833-34 the emerging Anglo-American street scenes in a neighborhood once dominated by Francophone Creoles:

> After passing Rue Toulouse, the streets began to assume a new character; the buildings were loftier and more modern—the signs over the doors bore English names, and the characteristic arrangements of a northern dry goods store were perceived.... We had now attained the upper part of Chartres-street, which is occupied almost exclusively by retail and wholesale dry goods dealers, jewellers, booksellers, &c., from the northern states, and I could almost realize that I was taking an evening promenade in Cornhill [England], so great was the resemblance.[472]

Ingraham then proceeded down Canal and doubled back on Levée Street (now Decatur). He continued: "The stores on our left were all open, and nearly every one of them, for the first two squares, was…a clothing or hat store…kept by Americans; that is to say, Anglo Americans as distinguished from the Louisiana French…." It was not until he approached the market, about five blocks down, that "French stores began to predominate, till one could readily imagine himself, aided by the sound of the French language, French faces and French goods on all sides, to be traversing a street in Havre or Marseilles."[473]

An observer in 1842 detected the full range of cultural differentiation in downtown street scenes, ranging from the geopolitical to the architectural, linguistic, gastronomic, and musical. "Almost entirely unlike any other city in the world," he began, "is New Orleans." That uniqueness, he implied, rested on the Creole/American dichotomy:

> So unharmonious was the intercourse between the French and American population, that some years since [1836] a divisional line was drawn between them [on Canal Street]…. In crossing the line, it is as passing from an American into a French city. No change is so visible, as the customs of the two. The buildings in the French portion [exhibit] an antiquated appearance, and almost unique, though modelled from the Spanish with a semblance of the French style…. The shops…bear a greater resemblance to Paris, than of any city in the Union.
>
> The language used is a mongrel of the French and Spanish…. The mode of living is widely dissimilar to that of the American, though of late some few dishes have been introduced on the American tables [of the most] fashionable boarding house….
>
> The soft music of the guitar, or the thumbing of the tamborin, or the croaking of the hand organ, greet the ears of the stranger in every direction; *for unlike the cities of the north, street music is tolerated in New Orleans.*[474]

Frederick Law Olmsted, a keen student of landscapes if ever there was one, read the cultural amalgam in the streetscape as he rode a cab up present-day Decatur Street to the St. Charles Hotel in 1854. In the lower Quarter, Olmsted witnessed "narrow dirty streets, among grimy old stuccoed walls; high arched windows and doors, balconies and entresols, and French noises and French smells, French signs, ten to one of English." In the upper Quarter, he reported that "now the signs became English, and the new brick buildings American." Upon crossing Canal and heading up St. Charles Avenue, he saw "French, Spanish, and English signs, the latter predominating."[475]

London-based war correspondent William Howard Russell recorded rare street-level descriptions of Confederate New Orleans as he arrived under tense circumstances a month after the bombardment of Fort Sumter. "[S]uch a whirl of secession and politics[!]" he remarked as he took in the scenes:

> The Confederate flag was flying from the public buildings and from many private houses. Military companies paraded through the streets, and a large proportion of men were in uniform…

The streets are full of Turcos, Zouaves, Chasseurs [French infantry units and other foreign soldiers who wore distinctive uniforms]; walls are covered with placards of volunteer companies; there are Pickwick rifles, La Fayette, Beauregard, MacMahon guards, Irish, German, Italian and Spanish and native volunteers.... Tailors are busy night and day making uniforms....

There are some who maintain there will be no war after all.... No one imagines the South will ever go back to the Union voluntarily, or that the North has power to thrust it back at the point of the bayonet. [476]

Despite the excitement of the moment—a New York firm had just fled town; a frightened artist associated with an abolitionist paper ensconced himself from hostile locals—Russell still took time to critique the ethnic cityscape. "A great number of the men and women had evident traces of negro blood in their veins," he observed as he disembarked the Pontchartrain Railroad in the Faubourg Marigny,

and of the purer blooded whites many had the peculiar look of the fishy-fleshy population of the Levantine [eastern Mediterranean] towns...all were pale and lean.

There is an air thoroughly French about the people—*cafés*, restaurants, billiard-rooms abound, with oyster and lager-bier saloons interspersed. The shops are all *magazins*; the people in the streets are speaking French, particularly the negroes, who are going out shopping with their masters and mistresses, exceedingly well dressed, noisy, and not unhappy looking... [T]he richness of some of the shops, the vehicles in the streets, and the multitude of well-dressed people [gave] an impression of [the] wealth and comfort of the inhabitants.

The markets...swarm with specimens of *the composite races* which inhabit the city, from the [pure-blooded] negro, who is suspiciously like a native-born African, to the Creole who boasts that every drop of blood in his veins is purely French. [477]

Russell settled at the St. Charles Hotel—"an enormous establishment, of the American type, with a Southern character about it." Shortly thereafter, news arrived that federal troops had invaded Virginia. The first major battles ensued that summer, and within a year of Russell's visit, New Orleans succumbed to Union forces.

After the war and Reconstruction, the German travel memoirist Ernst von Hesse-Wartegg read as much cultural fusion into the New Orleans streetscape as his antebellum predecessors. Regarding Canal Street, he rhapsodized:

Here the South lies at one end of [this] international thoroughfare, the tropical West Indies at the other. The contrasts collide in one city, it seems, and in *this* street. Situation, prospect, traffic, the splendor of shops, all of life as lived in a street—in a word, *everything*—says we stand on the boundary between two great but distinct cultures. Anglo-Saxon and Latin meet *here*. Everything says we tread the contiguous edges of geographical zones. Tropical and temperate intersect *here*.

Canal Street divides New Orleans as the Straits of Dover do England from France. Indeed, English culture and French—better called Anglo-Germanic and Latin—could not be more precisely and more surely set at intervals than here, on either side of our broad Canal Street. From the Mississippi inland, everything to the left [of Canal Street] is Anglo-Saxon, and to the right it is Spanish, Italian, and French...the bastion of Creole culture. West of Canal, then, we hear *street, cents,* and *mister* without exception; east, *rue, centimes,* and *monsieur* also without exception. Ask directions in public and get the answer in English to the left, in French to the right. Each nation dwells as a separate society, isolated from one another, not mingling.[478]

Hesse-Wartegg, Olmsted, Ingraham, and other travel writers, for all their exertions at decoding streetscapes, nonetheless were first-time visitors who relied on initial impressions to form their assessments. Had they spent more time in the city and tracked its day-to-day idiosyncrasies, they probably would have confirmed what Benjamin Latrobe predicted in 1819: that Creole culture was slowly succumbing to Anglo-American society. True, it predominated in the early years of Americanization, especially after 9,000 Francophone Haitian refugees arrived in 1809 and reinforced the city's French Caribbean cultural ambience. But loosening ties to the motherland, increasing numbers of American emigrants and European immigrants, and growing entanglements with American political, legal, economic, religious, and social networks left Creole society threatened, reactionary, and receding.

Tensions, occasionally coming "perilously close to armed violence,"[479] mounted in the 1820s. Bills circulated—and nearly passed—to "convert the whole [of New Orleans] into two cities, to be called the Upper and Lower city...arising from the opposing influence of American (as they are called) and French interests."[480] Americans finally won legislative consent in 1836 for a similar plan, dividing New Orleans into three semiautonomous units essentially to free themselves of Creole predomination. The inefficient "municipality system" was abandoned in 1852, but only after the Americans established alliances with uptown German and Irish immigrants to ensure numerical superiority over the Creoles. The reunified city was now politically Anglo-dominant; city government relocated from the old Spanish-style Cabildo on Jackson Square to the new Greek Revival City Hall on Lafayette Square; the fulcrums of commerce, politics, and communications shifted from the Creole old city to Anglo Faubourg St. Mary. The keenly observant French social geographer Elisée Réclus, who visited the city as a young man the year after the city's reunification, noticed the emerging cultural Americanization:

In fact, the French are only a small minority here [in the French Quarter;] most of their houses have been purchased by American capitalists.... The American section, located west [across] Canal Street, [is] the center of political life.

The population of New Orleans...includes barely 6,000 to 10,000 French, or one-twentieth, [plus] the same number of Creoles who are not yet completely Americanized.

It is clear that the French language will increasingly disappear.... Soon the Anglo-Saxon idiom will dominate unchallenged, and all that will remain [of the old ways] will be the names of streets: Tchoupitoulas, Perdido, Bienville, etc. At the French Market, which foreigners once visited without fail in order to hear the medley of languages, one now hears only English conversations.

Even the [opera house] is proof of the gradual disappearance of foreign or Creole elements. Formerly, this theater showed only French plays, comedies, or vaudeville, but to continue to be profitable, it was forced to change its playbills and its name. Today it is patronized by the American public.[481]

Twenty-four years after Réclus' amalgamation interpretation, and around the same time that Ernst von Hesse-Wartegg assured his readers of the continued vitality of New Orleans' "two great but distinct cultures," an interesting "Letter from New Orleans" (1877) appeared in Northern newspapers. It concurred with Réclus' 1853 assessment about as much as it contradicted Hesse-Wartegg's contemporary take. The anonymous piece presents a valuable critical analysis of the still-visible yet waning French Creole culture in the streets of the Crescent City:

New Orleans is gradually, but very perceptibly, parting with its distinctive French character. It may be two generations before it will have become sufficiently Anglicised to present no marked features of contrast with the other large cities of the United States. But the inroads of the Anglo-Saxon, the Celtic and Teutonic races are such that it is only a question of time, and a comparatively short time at that, when the descendents of the Latins will be swallowed up and disappear in the embrace of their more hardy and vigorous neighbors.

The writer then breaks with nineteenth-century travelogue tradition by—quite accurately—dismissing the notion of a purely French Creole quarter separated resolutely from an equally purely Anglo-American sector:

The boundary which separates the French from the English portion of the city exists now only in name. In the long, narrow streets of Frenchtown there is scarcely a square where the Germans, the Irish and the Americans have not established themselves in active competition with the French. Side by side with the coffee and the absinthe shops are the lager beer saloons and the gin mills. Next to signs bearing the poetical and high-surrounding names with which the French language so abounds, you read "Smith," "Brown," "Thompsons," &c in great variety.

Nor did another staple of the antebellum travel writer—a trip to the French Market—impress this critic. "The French market was formerly the object of much interest and curiosity to visitors," he allowed, "and no one who came to New Orleans thought he had 'done' the city if he did not rise at daylight on Sunday morning and go to the French market." He continued:

The stranger who now jumbles out of his bed at dawn ... sees [at the Market] a great display of fruits and flowers and numberless little coffee stalls; he bears a great deal of jabbering in a villainous patois that sounds perhaps a little more like French than does Cherokee. He looks in vain for the pretty flower girls, the type of the French peasantry, for the tambourine and the castanets, for the side-shows which are so picturesque an accompaniment of French market places. He cannot play the gallant to the sallow, toothless old hags who chatter and grin at him like so many monkeys while they importune him to buy their wares. Everything looks dirty and smells bad, and it is a very short time before you have all you want of the French market.

Recovering from his disappointment, the visitor returns to the theme of Creole cultural decline:

Up to 1868 the courts kept duplicate copies of their records in French and English. Now [they] are transcribed in English exclusively. L'Abeille, (the Bee,) a French daily newspaper, which has been in existence fifty years, is still printed. It is quite large a sheet and looks moderately prosperous, although the signs of decay are very perceptible to the experienced eye, and the day is not far distant when L'Abeille will be no more. *The amalgamation process is seen in everything, and the end is a mere question of time.*[482]

In 1914, the state legislature rescinded the law that required certain legal documents to be published in French, a stipulation that had kept *L'Abeille* in business even after Creole French grew rare. Nine years later, the paper folded.

Cultures rarely truly disappear; rather, they hybridize—or, as the previously cited source put it, "amalgamate"—into a new form, which may reflect any combination or outgrowth of its antecedents. Some saw it coming: English-born architect Benjamin Latrobe, who reflected on the impending cultural Americanization in 1819, wrote

The state of society [in New Orleans] is puzzling. There are in fact three societies here: 1. the French, 2. the American, & 3. the mixed. The French society is not exactly what is was at the change of government, & the American is not strictly what it is in the Atlantic cities.

[One] cannot help wishing that a *mean*, an *average* character, of society may grow out of the intermixture of the French [Creole] & American manners.[483]

To a degree, Latrobe's wish came true. Creole culture is by no means dead in modern New Orleans: thousands of residents identify themselves (in certain contexts) as Creole, or black Creole, and certain neighborhoods—particularly the Seventh Ward—are widely recognized as cultural hearths of Creolism. As recently as 1970, fully 41,719 U.S.-born residents of Orleans Parish (one of every fourteen) claimed French as their "mother tongue," the language spoken in their childhood home.[484] Creole foods remain popular, as are civic traditions such as Mardi Gras and All Saints Day. Remnant French Creole words and phrases are occasionally heard in conversation. Downtown neighborhoods such as the French Quarter, faubourgs Tremé and Marigny, Bywater, and the back-of-town to Bayou St. John are replete with Creole architectural styles, typologies, and buildings crafts—in short, with Creole streetscapes.

But every surviving Creole trait is outnumbered enormously by those reflecting national and global culture. History seems to have proven Benjamin Latrobe right when he predicted in 1819,

> In a few years…this will be an American town. What is good & bad in the French manners, & opinions must give way, & the American notions of right & wrong, of convenience & inconvenience will take their place…. [E]verything French will in 50 years disappear. Even the miserable patois of the Creoles will be heard only in the cypress swamps.[485]

Nativity as Ethnicity in New Orleans

The significance of being—and not being—from New Orleans

Deep in the digital catacombs of the 2000 Census, in Summary File 3 of the estimates made from nineteen million "long-form" questionnaires, is an interesting statistic: 77.4 percent of New Orleans' 484,674 residents were born in Louisiana, the highest rate of in-state nativity among major American cities (see map, "Nativity by State and City").[486] In the wake of Hurricane Katrina, city advocates upheld that figure as evidence of a strong sense of place-rootedness and love-of-place ("topophilia") on behalf of New Orleanians. Perhaps. But it also reflects the city's inability to attract new blood, because of limited opportunities and myriad quality-of-life challenges. Indeed, nativity rates at the state and city level nationwide tend to correspond to depressed, declining areas such as the Rust Belt, seemingly corroborating that a rejection by outsiders trumps the dedication of insiders in determining the percentage of people born locally.[487] In New Orleans, socio-economic problems motivated tens of thousands of families to flee their supposedly beloved city, helping drop its peak population by one-quarter since 1960.

Yet thousands of people have bucked the trend by moving *into* New Orleans in that same era. Many, particularly in the professional and creative classes, were specifically drawn by New Orleans' intriguing charms, and unlike natives, were self-selected for "Orleanophilia" from a nationwide pool of millions. Some newcomers might be what Eric Weiner, author of the recent bestseller *The Geography of Bliss*, described as "hedonic refugees:" people who "have an epiphany, a moment of great clarity when they realize, beyond a doubt, they were born in the wrong [place]," and transplant themselves to another offering a better "cultural fit"—and greater happiness.[488] Other new New Orleanians seem to have more in common with expatriated Americans living in Europe or the tropics—"expats"—than with their compatriots who have simply moved to another American city. Despite their relatively small numbers and recent arrival, non-natives, or "transplants," often revel in their adopted community and become surprisingly influential cultural forces there.

This has long been the case in New Orleans. The city's history is replete with culturally influential transplants, including (to name but a few) Rhode Island-born Judah Touro and Baltimore-born John McDonogh, Irish architect James Gallier, the Mobile-based founders of the Krewe of Comus, Greek-born writer Lafcadio Hearn, and most notably, Mississippi-born playwright Tennessee Williams, who throughout his life eloquently and consistently embraced New Orleans as his "spiritual home." The phenomenon continues today, when, contrary to popular perceptions, New Orleans' artistic, musical, culinary, literary, historical, and preservationist communities disproportionately comprise non-natives. Transplants abound among the organizers of public festivals, the patrons of the Contemporary Arts Center, the authors at literary events, the renovators of historical homes, the revelers of the ribald Krewe de Vieux, the gallery-hoppers of Julia Street, and the night-clubbers of Frenchmen Street.[489] This is not to say that locally born people eschew such activities: prosperous uptown "blue bloods" and Jewish families, most of them with eighteenth- and nineteenth-century local lineages, generously patronize the city's cultural and social institutions, while the African-American community forms a veritable reservoir of deeply rooted local cultural traditions. Rather, it simply recognizes that transplants are statistically overrepresented in outwardly visible cultural endeavors.

Transplants form certain geographies. Those from out-of-state hail disproportionately from southern California; major Texas cities; Chicago; Atlanta; Memphis; Washington D.C.; Miami; San Francisco; Hartford; nearby Biloxi, Mobile, and Jackson; Jacksonville, Boston, and New York City (see map, "Sources of Transplants to New Orleans").[490] They usually settle in New Orleans' historical areas, comprising one-third the residency of eighteenth- and nineteenth-century neighborhoods compared to less than one-fifth of twentieth-century subdivisions. Calculated another way, 44 percent of the residents of neighborhoods of the "highest" historical significance are transplants, compared to 30 percent of "significantly" historical areas, 21 percent of "somewhat" historical neighborhoods, and only 16 percent of "non-historical" areas (see graph, "Natives, Transplants, and Historical Neighborhoods").[491]

Why? People who choose to move to New Orleans often expressly seek to escape the perceived homogeneity of the rest of America, and therefore gravitate to houses and neighborhoods that reflect the distinctive historical essence of the city. Why flee Midwestern blandness only to settle for an equally banal ranch house in a modern New Orleans subdivision? A galleried townhouse, a colorful shotgun, or a quaint Creole cottage is far more appealing. Accordingly, New Orleans' iconic neighborhoods—the French Quarter, the downtown faubourgs, the Garden District and uptown—are usually home to the highest number of transplants. Sixty-one percent of the French Quarter's 2000 population, and 55 percent of the Garden District's, were not even born in Louisiana, let alone New Orleans. One must visit the modern subdivisions of the lakefront, eastern New Orleans, or the West Bank—places routinely dismissed as "placeless" and "historically not significant"—to find native-born denizens predominating by over 80 and 90 percent. And only the poverty-stricken subsidized housing projects boast nativity rates approaching 100 percent.

Mapping out New Orleans' nativity patterns yields a whole new cultural geography compared to standard interpretations based on race, class, and other factors (see map, "These Patterns Emerge..."). The stark divide between the mostly black Lower Ninth Ward and mostly white St. Bernard Parish completely disappears when one plots nativity, as nearly everyone in both areas was born here. New Orleans East and Westwego seem very different when we segment society by race, but quite similar when we do so by nativity. Conversely, Uptown and Lakeview seem the same in terms of race and class, but quite different in terms of nativity (the "white teapot," it turns out, is also a "transplant teapot"). Remarkably, the Vietnamese enclave of Versailles, often viewed as an exotic exception to "classic New Orleans," turns out to be more native-to-Louisiana than the world-famous French Quarter and Garden District, which get all the attention. St. Bernard Parish boasts the metro area's highest parish-level nativity rate—86.4 percent, arguably making it a treasure trove of genuinely local culture—yet few books extol "da parish," hardly any dissertations are written about it, and few documentary filmmakers lug their cameras there.[492]

The residential geography of natives and transplants proved consequential during the Hurricane Katrina catastrophe (see map, "Natives, Transplants, and Katrina's Floodwaters"). Transplants' predilection for historical houses placed them, more often than not, on higher ground, because most old neighborhoods occupy the better-drained natural levee which generally did not flood. Natives, on the other hand, who lived for generations in cramped historical housing stock and were more inclined to flee to spacious modern lakeside suburbs in the early- to mid-1900s, unwittingly placed themselves upon lower-lying terrain. Those areas flooded deeply. Katrina's flood disrupted the lives of New Orleanians of all backgrounds, but disproportions did exist, and one of them regarded nativity.

The cultural influence of transplants often flies beneath the radar of discourse about the city. Perhaps this is because transplants do much of the chattering about the city (you're reading one now), and ascribing cultural significance to themselves seemingly undermines the very attributes of deep-rooted localism which attracted many transplants to New Orleans in the first place. Or perhaps it involves transplants' omnipresent angst over cultural "authenticity:" if *native* implies *authentic* and *real*, then *transplant* must mean the opposite—and who wants that?

Such worries should be set aside. Yesterday's transplants are today's natives; today's transplants are tomorrow's natives. As for locally distinctive cultural traits, cities and other human communities both *produce* and *attract* people with certain characteristics. The societies of New York City or Los Angeles do not necessarily produce disproportionate numbers of great artists and performers; they *attract* them from across the globe. The same is true for software engineers in Seattle, policy-wonks in Washington, and scholars in Boston. Both groups—those produced by, and those attracted to, certain cities—help form those places' distinctive local cultures. A New Orleans musician originally from Des Moines, a Nebraska-born French Quarter chef, or a Gentilly playwright originally from San Francisco all legitimately help form local New Orleans culture simply by nature of the city's ability to draw them here.

Still, transplant and native populations see things quite differently.[493] Transplants (setting aside immigrants for the purposes of this discussion) are more likely to be white, professional, better-off in terms of income and education, and childless, or at least less fruitful, compared to their locally born neighbors. They also tend to be more socially liberal, less culturally traditional, and more secular than natives. Many, probably the majority, of the city's openly gay population is non-native. Tulane University, whose faculty and student body are even more out-of-town than the rest of the city is native, is culturally and geographically central to the transplant universe. Transplants' accents tend to be of the neutral Midwestern variety, and conversations with strangers often begin with the question, "So, where are you from?" They tend to describe various parts of the city in terms of faubourgs or historic districts, or in reference to popular restaurants, nightclubs, specialty food stores, or other entities relevant to their interests. Transplants are more likely to listen to National Public Radio and listener-supported WWOZ than commercial stations, and tend to be "Jazz Fest people" more so than "Mardi Gras people." They predominate disproportionately at events involving the arts, culture, and social, urban, and environmental causes. In urban controversies, transplants often embrace aesthetic or idealistic values—"save the architecturally significant structure;" "preserve the historical character of the neighborhood," "protect the environment"—because those values fortify the very reasons why they moved here. Revealingly, many transplants exhibit a hypersensitive aversion to all things touristy (particularly Bourbon Street), a strategy designed to distance themselves as far as possible from dreaded notions of cultural inauthenticity and "fakeness."

The native-born population, on the other hand, tends to be less moneyed, less educated, more religious and traditional in culture, and more likely to be African-American (in large part because so many native-born middle-class whites departed). Natives also count among their ranks many influential "old money" families, who may share a common race and class with their prosperous transplant neighbors, but little else. Natives of the working class often speak with a port-city accent, use vernacular expressions such as "where y'at" or "making groceries," and are more likely to eat traditional foods on a weekly schedule, such as red beans and rice on Monday and fish on Friday. Natives of the upper class tend to pronounce their city's name with the tri-syllabic Or-le-ans. Natives in general tend to regionize the city into wards, school districts, or church parishes, and are oftentimes unfamiliar with trendy revived faubourg names or historical districts. Their conversations often begin with, "So, what school did you go to?" or "What church do you belong to?" In municipal controversies, natives often advocate for the pragmatic—"we need economic development;" "our young people need jobs"—over the abstractions favored by many transplants. Natives tend to prefer Mardi Gras over Jazz Fest, the public University of New Orleans over the pricey and exclusive Tulane, and commercial radio over public stations. Natives predominate overwhelmingly (sometimes exclusively) in the memberships of old-line krewes and uptown social clubs, among the attendees of the plebeian Gretna Heritage Festival and St. Bernard Parish Crawfish Festival, and in just about any event affiliated with a church.

Nativity informs many urban-policy controversies in New Orleans, oftentimes trumping the race- and class-related factors which tend to get more attention. During the raucous 2006-07 debate about the future of public housing (which explicitly did *not* break down along racial lines), those protesting the proposed demolitions angrily pointed out that three of the four redevelopment firms came from out-of-state, while those favoring demolition huffed at the large numbers of out-of-town activists among the protestors. In the testy post-Katrina planning meetings of 2005-06, irate New Orleanians oftentimes responded to out-of-town experts' recommendations to close down certain low-lying, heavily damaged neighborhoods by citing their nativity—"Well I'm *from* here, born and raised, six generations…"—as if it were a credential. In some ways, it is: nativity reflects commitment to place, and ratchets up one's status as a stakeholder.

The differences between natives and transplants almost seem to form, or at least *in*form, two separate sub-cultures, perhaps even two ethnicities. There is historical precedence for blurred lines between nativity and ethnicity in New Orleans: the common denominator unifying the city's ethnic Creole population in the early nineteenth century was not principally race or class, but deep-rooted Louisiana nativity. Rivalry between native Creole and newly arrived transplants—Anglo-Americans as well as immigrants—practically defined New Orleans society between the Louisiana Purchase and the Civil War.

The little-researched notion of nativity as ethnicity is explored more broadly in the next reading.

Nativity as Ethnicity in America

Dynamics between natives and transplants within the United States

Social science research commonly deconstructs American society along the fault lines of race, ancestry, gender, class, education, religion, political leaning, and orientation. Yet much cultural differentiation transcends those lines, or complicates the social terrain therein. This essay posits that nativity—where one is born, and the depth of one's roots in that place—ranks high among those segmentations, serving as a unifying bond inextricably linked with parallel cultural traits such as accents, customs, foods, spirituality, relationships with nature, politics, and overall worldview. Nativity, in some cases, almost functions as a sort of ethnicity.

Early nineteenth-century New Orleans offers one example. When English-speaking Protestant Anglo-Americans transplanted themselves to this seemingly exotic and foreign city on the southwestern frontier, they encountered here a more sedentary and conservative people of varied backgrounds—French, Spanish, Hispanic, African,

Caribbean—who looked, dressed, spoke, worshipped, governed, worked, recreated, socialized, and thought differently. What bonded these diverse New Orleanians together, and distinguished them from the incoming Anglo-Americans, was their own shared colonial-era Louisiana nativity: their Creole ethnicity. They were *from here*, and attached importance to it.

Hispanicism represents another example. The Hispanic (or Latino) ethnicity unites peoples of diverse backgrounds—the majority of indigenous and/or Spanish blood, plus others of African, German, Italian, English, Asian, and Jewish ancestry— who all share a nativity to Latin America.

That a common nativity binds people of otherwise varying backgrounds comes as no surprise. Nation-states bank on this notion (to varying degrees of success), be they the indigenously dominated nations of the Old World or immigrant-based societies of the New World. Nativism at the national scale fueled the Know-Nothing movement against Catholics and immigrants in the 1850s, while regional nativity stoked the South's violent resistance to Union advances during the Civil War. History is replete with nativity narratives; they operate at various spatial scales and intensity levels, and yield both the best and worst in human relations.

This hypothesis goes further than the axiomatic nativity-is-important theme. It suggests that nativity—particularly when those who possess it feel threatened by those who do not—forms a *strong* sense of unifying identity. Nativity is relevant even among Americans born in the United States, with all its supposedly geography-neutralizing telecommunications technology and move-every-five-years restlessness. Nativity is culturally significant: Americans who are native to a certain place often see things very differently than their newly arrived neighbors, and that divergence often plays out in the public arena. Many land-use controversies in rural areas are better understood as dynamics between natives and transplants, rather than as struggles of class, race, or gender. A public hearing on timber policy in Oregon or a predator-control initiative outside Yellowstone National Park, for example, is likely to break down along native/ transplant lines, the former usually supporting timbering, mining, or ranching activity, the latter siding with environmental health and ecological values. Likewise, urban controversies in places like San Francisco or New Orleans often pit natives, who tend to favor pragmatic economic development and job creation (reasons for them to stay here), against transplants who are likely to prioritize for abstractions such as historicity, sustainability, and urban livability (the very reasons why they moved here).

Exceptions and complicating variables abound with regard to these generalizations, but they do not negate the importance of place in group identity. Yet scholarly research on this dynamic between natives and transplants is hard to find. A literature review proves to be a frustration in semantics: key terms such as "native," "nativity," "local," and "place rootedness" can be pegged against "transplant," "transplantedness," "newcomer," and "mobility," but none roll off the tongue, none grab the essence, and all suffer from multiple meanings. Most scholarly articles on "nativity" use the term in reference to national birthplace vis-à-vis immigration, rather than the state-, region-, or city-level nativity I am focusing on here. The word "native," of course, also yields literature on indigenous peoples—yet another dimension to the dynamic. Other searches call forth investigations in the area of regional identity, which comes the closest to the angle discussed here. Sociologist John Shelton Reed, for example, has explored concepts of "regional sociology" throughout his body of work on the South and Southerners, whom he terms a "'quasi-ethnic' regional group."[494] A fair amount of literature exists on the nativity-based notion of Creolism, possibly the best historical documentation of the phenomenon.

Why researchers have not appreciated the significance of nativity in modern America may derive from its low profile: it is often overshadowed by the more conspicuous social segmentations of race, gender, class, and ancestry, which have become the prevailing coin of the academic realm in recent decades. Native/transplant tensions oftentimes play out against a backdrop of gentrification, and are thus categorized—and sometimes mischaracterized—as race and class issues, rather than place-related ones. Nativity-based interpretations of conflicts also do not lend themselves to the sort of progressive social activism practiced by researchers in the advocacy tradition of academia. The shrugging response to nativity may also stem from the fact that most scholars themselves lead the mobile lives of transplants, and overlook place-rootedness as a legitimate source of perspective-difference simply because it is not their personal life story.

While the native/transplant dynamic appears to be little-studied, the act of residential relocation preceding it—the mobility rate—is carefully measured by demographers and tracked by economists. Nearly fifty million Americans—one in six—move to new residences every year, and of those, over eight million cross state borders. Attracting the interstate movers are Nevada, Alaska, Wyoming, Idaho, Arizona, Oregon, and other states in the booming West and South; supplying them are California, Ohio, New York, and other places primarily in the northern and eastern United States. Mobility rates correlate to age: twenty-somethings made up 14 percent of the total population in 2006 but accounted for 57 percent of movers; those over age fifty comprised 27 percent of Americans but only 14 percent of movers.[495] Unlike nativity, American mobility is a favorite topic of social scientists and writers; James M. Jasper explored it in his 2000 publication, *Restless Nation: Starting Over in America*, as did David Popenoe in *Private Pleasure, Public Plight* (2001). Robert Putnam touched upon it in his influential bestseller *Bowling Alone* (2000). Contrary to popular belief, mobility rates have been fairly stable for decades and have even declined by some measures, leading some to debunk the old "America's-increasingly-mobile-society" cliché as a myth.[496] Despite the ups and downs of the mobility rate, however, the nation's *nativity* rate is unquestionably diminishing. Mobility is episodic; Americans move at greater or lesser rates depending on demographics, economics, and other factors. Nativity, on the other hand, is binary. You only have to move once to lose forever your status as a native by birth. Thus, even if mobility rates decline, the ranks of transplants grow, and the number of deeply rooted natives shrinks.

Nativity occurs along temporal and spatial continuums. Given enough time, transplants matriculate into the ranks of natives; exactly how much time depends on various factors. Someone who moved to Alaska in the 1970s might convincingly claim native status as he sneers at a transplant who arrived in the 2000s, so rapidly is that state attracting newcomers. A third-generation resident of Portland, Oregon may boast a stronger claim to nativity in that young West Coast boomtown than a third-generation Charlestonian, who may defer to one who goes back six or seven generations in that old Southern port. A resident of the suburbs of Westwego or Kenner might proudly claim nativity to New Orleans, only to be dismissed by another who hails from New Orleans proper. New Orleanians whose ancestors arrived in the 1800s often joke about their rejection from certain social circles by the descendents of those who arrived in the 1700s. American Indians proudly hold their superlative nativity status as an argumentative trump card, stuffing a sock in the mouths of nativity-claiming whites who, of course, arrived millennia later. Nativity is a complex, fluid phenomenon; like Creolism, people adjust their claim to it depending on the audience, context, time, and place. Even quantitative measurement is a challenge: U.S. Census nativity data aggregated at the block-group level (the highest spatial detail publicly available) reflect only the birth state (or birth nation for immigrants), which means that researchers cannot quantify nativity at the city or town level where much of this dynamic plays out.

Nativity in America serves as a reliable source of self-pride, as evidenced by the popularity of T-shirts and bumper stickers reading "CALIFORNIA NATIVE," "FLORIDA NATIVE," "WYOMING NATIVE: ENDANGERED SPECIES," etc. This is a bit paradoxical, since *non*-nativity, in a larger sense, is a legacy shared by most Americans. A willingness to risk everything and leap into the geographical unknown to find a better life might be the closest thing Americans have to a unifying ethos, or possibly even a gene. One might expect Americans to be proud of mobility. Yet we glance downwardly when we admit we "just moved to the area" (have you ever seen a "FLORIDA TRANSPLANT" bumper sticker?) and puff with pride when we announce we're "born and raised here, five generations." Perhaps pride in nativity varies directly with perceptions of transplant threat. For all the native pride in Louisiana, rarely does one see a "LOUISIANA NATIVE" bumper sticker—perhaps because, with the nation's highest nativity rate (79.4 percent), native-born Louisianians do not truly feel threatened by transplants.[497]

Pride may explain only part of the urge to declare nativity. Perceptions of cultural threat or feelings of inferiority vis-à-vis a wealthier, better-educated, more cosmopolitan transplant "invasion" may also be at play. (*Forbes Magazine*'s recent list of America's twenty-five "smartest cities" was entirely dominated by communities with high transplant and low nativity rates.[498]) This is where nativity gets complicated, as it often travels hand-in-hand with class and education differences. To whom are native-pride messages directed? Is the driver of a vehicle with a GEORGIA NATIVE bumper sticker scorning all those recently arrived Hispanic immigrants filling bottom-rung jobs in the construction and service economy? (Indeed, many academics, predisposed to standard conflict narratives, might view anti-Hispanic racism as the driver's motives.) Or is the bumper sticker really directed at all those brash, worldly, well-heeled young professionals who moved recently to "his" state—people who may look like him, but who don't speak his accent, don't eat his foods, don't worship, vote, or recreate his way, and don't seem to have anything to say to him the few times they interact?

Transplants' views of natives are equally complex, indeed paradoxical. At an abstract level, transplants often embrace the native population endearingly, if not pa-tronizingly, as "colorful" or "authentic" elements of their adopted towns and cities. But on an individual level, transplants often disdain locals as uneducated, coarse, lower-class neighbors with dubious values, and socialize with them only passingly.

The tension has its own lexicon. Natives use anti-transplant code words and phrases such as "city slickers," "Easterners," "Northerners," "Carpetbaggers," "Yankees," or variations of "these folks who move in from…." In disagreements, natives pointedly remind transplants "look, you're not from here," or suggest "if you don't like it, go back to…." Transplants respond with, "hey, you don't own this place" or "this is a free coun-try." They betray anti-native sentiments when they affect exaggerated local accents, poke fun at local customs, or say things like "good ol' boys," "local yokels," "rednecks," "hillbillies," "crackers," or "they've been here since the beginning of time."

The dynamic also limns a certain geography. It is strongest in cities and towns with (1) robust, expanding economies, particularly in the white-collar professions and information technologies, and/or (2) high scenic, recreational, historical, cultural, cli-matological, or quality-of-life attributes. These two factors—economic opportunity and an appealing environment—drive much non-immigrant transplantation.[499] Some places score high on both accounts and attract transplants in droves: Seattle, Portland, Austin, the Colorado Rocky Mountain Front, and Las Vegas (80 percent non-native, the highest in the nation) are the best examples, followed by cities like San Francisco and New York.[500] Other places offer a sound economy and a reasonably attractive cli-mate and atmosphere, and draw outsiders to lesser but still substantial degrees: Atlanta, Asheville, and Nashville, for example. Still others provide the sound economy but less so the atmosphere (Minneapolis comes to mind), or plenty of atmosphere amid a lousy economy (New Orleans), and thus draw transplants to varying levels of significance. Places like Washington D.C., Virginia Beach, and San Diego exhibit very high transplant rates because government jobs or military service compel outsiders to move there.

Certain "boutique communities" offer such highly desirable scenic, historic, or cultural attributes that transplantation transforms their societies utterly. Sante Fe, Key West, and Jackson, Wyoming are among the premier examples. Picturesque col-lege towns in New England, the Appalachians, the Rockies, or the West Coast are also native/transplant hot-spots, though here the dynamic (sometimes referred to as "town-gown" antagonisms) is complicated by differing class and educations levels: less-educated, working-class natives versus better-educated, upper-middle-class trans-plants affiliated with the university. Boulder's University of Colorado, Ithaca's Cornell University, and New Haven's Yale University are three of hundreds of examples.

If current trends continue, the native/transplant dynamic will likely augment in the twenty-first century, as more and more Americans pull up roots from the places of their ancestors. But eventually it seems destined to decline, as the notion of multi-generational place-rootedness gives way to periodic place-hopping, and local culture becomes interchangeable with national culture.

We would be a lesser nation for it.

The Lexicon of Place

Deconstructing New Orleans' names, nicknames, and slogans

Nicknames tend to get ascribed to that which deviates from the norm. This is usually true for people; it's certainly true for places. Archetypal American suburbs like Scottsdale, Arizona or Longmont, Colorado earn no widely recognized nicknames, neither as terms of endearment nor disdain. Some communities, sensitive about their own banality, nickname themselves in the hope of instilling an identity and convincing visitors that one exists. Rarely do such conscientiously promoted monikers stick. Even locals don't buy that Slidell, Louisiana is "The Camellia City," or Waveland, Mississippi "The Hospitality City."

Mention "The Big Apple," "Beantown," "City of Brotherly Love," or "City of Light," however, and their respective urban associations are universally understood. The sobriquets do wonders in imparting a sense of appealing distinction to those places, not to mention a desire to visit. That New Orleans bears arguably the most nicknames and slogans of any American city, ranging from the elegant ("Crescent City," "Queen City of the South," "Creole City") and the disapproving ("Great Southern Babylon," "Sodom and Gomorrah," "The Wet Grave"[501]) to the self-promoting ("America's Most Interesting City," "Gateway to the Americas," "Birthplace of Jazz") and the blithe ("City that Care Forgot," "Big Easy")—can thus be interpreted as an effect, perhaps also a cause, of the city's widely perceived deviation from the national norm.[502] New Orleans' veritable glossary of lasting monikers seems to imply that *something different happened here.*

Nicknames are significant. If geography may be understood as that which inscribes *character* to *place*, then city nicknames operate as accessible, widely circulating "buzzwords" that drive, for better or worse, the mental imagery and stereotypical characteristics held by millions of people about certain locales. For this reason, nicknames should not be dismissed as trivial; they warrant scholarly investigation because they help form mass perception.

History does not record the various names given to the future New Orleans site prior to colonialism. One amateur historian, writing in 1889, reported that the area was called *Balbancha*, Choctaw for "the place where there is unintelligible talk," referring to the various languages spoken among those who sought refuge here from belligerent tribes to the west.[503] That name has also been ascribed to the lower Mississippi River.

Naming of the colonial city came about in more conventional ways. A September 1717 entry in the register of John Law's Company of the West read, "Resolved to establish, thirty leagues up the river, a burg which *should be called* New Orleans, where landing would be possible from either the river or Lake Pontchartrain."[504] The name honored Philippe, duc d'Orléans, who, as Regent of France acting on behalf of seven-year-old King Louis XV, sponsored Law's monopoly to develop Louisiana.

French historian Baron Marc de Villiers du Terrage, working off primary documents in 1920, judged that the envisioned settlement first gained its name "not by the [French] Marine Board, nor by the directors of the Company of the West, but by Bienville and L'Epinay, in their report of May, 1717, on the new posts to be established." The savvy Bienville, understanding that toponyms drive perceptions and were therefore consequential, had previously suggested renaming other outposts already burdened with dubious names. The indecisive-sounding "Mobile," for example, should become "Fort Immobile," while the nearby barrier island originally branded awfully as "Massacre" (for the human bones found there in 1699), might do better as "Dauphine" Island. Bienville also appreciated how the "very exotic" names of "Biloxi" and "Natchitoches" struck Parisian ears. One record from July 1717 shows that the name "Orleans" nearly went to Massacre Island. In the end, the name "New Orleans" seems to have made it from the Bienville-L'Epinay letter of May 1717 to the company register of September 1717, after which it quickly became known both in Paris and Louisiana.[505]

New Orleans thus gained its name in the time-honored manner continued by countless institutions: as an attempt to flatter a patron. That the name somehow gained a feminine grammatical gender, contrary to the French custom of casting cities as masculine, has provided fodder for generations of metaphorically inclined literary types. Wrote Father Charlevoix in 1722, "Those who have given [the city] this name, must have imagined Orleans was of the feminine gender. But of what consequence is this? Custom, which is superior to all the laws of grammar, has fixed it so."[506] According to Marc de Villiers du Terrage, "the reason for the feminising of New Orleans was probably euphonic. *Nouveau-Orléans* would have been too offensive to the ear. It is true that *Nouvel-Orléans* might have passed. Perhaps *Nouvelle-Orléans* was adopted by analogy with *Nouvelle-France, Nouvelle-York*, etc."[507]

Had the city been relocated to the Bayou Manchac distributary, as was proposed a number of times, that locale probably would have been christened under the same name. But had it been transferred to pre-existing settlements at Mobile, Biloxi, or Natchez, the syllables "Nouvelle Orléans" might have disappeared from the French colonial Gulf Coast.

It succeeded, of course, despite myriad challenges and regime changes. "Nouvelle Orléans" was hispanicized to "Nueva Orleans" when the colony transferred from France to Spain in the 1760s, although the translated name predominated more in official documents and maps than in the spoken word of the still mostly Francophone population. (The new name's gender, unlike that of the French version, aligned with the Spanish linguistic tradition of characterizing cities as feminine.)

"Nueva Orleans" was officially anglicized to the gender-neutral "New Orleans" when the American flag arose on December 20, 1803; colloquially, however, both the French and English versions circulated in the early nineteenth century, reflecting the city's era of cultural transition. As the city Americanized and English became its *lingua franca*, the English version "New Orleans" became inextricably intertwined with this particular crescent of the Mississippi.

While there is only one "New Orleans," the toponym "Orleans" was later adopted by at least ten towns, townships, or counties across the United States. They occur mostly in states touched at least tangentially by the French in America, such as Vermont, New York, Michigan, Indiana, and Iowa. Another 220 minor cartographic features also bear the name. Worldwide, "Orleans" occurs as a civil toponym about twenty-five times, again in a spatial pattern reflecting France's influence: nine times in the mother country, five times in Algeria, twice in the West Indies, and most others in former French America.[508]

Nicknames for New Orleans began to be coined once this remote and exotic city began to be enveloped into the American fold. Most of the earlier ones called attention to its reputation for frivolity, filthiness, and—that salacious nineteenth-century word—*wickedness*. Disapproving slogans reflecting these sentiments, including "the Great Southern Babylon," "Necropolis of the South," and particularly "Sodom and Gomorrah," appear regularly in literature of the times. An 1812 *New-York Gazette* piece saw New Orleans' recent bouts with hurricanes and fires as products of its reputation as "a second Sodom...exhibiting, particularly on the Sabbath, scenes of the most licentious wickedness."[509] An 1815 Boston article reported on the characterization of the Louisiana Purchase as "a wicked waste of the people's money" and New Orleans "as a place that has disgraced America by its worthlessness and vice...very little better than old *Sodom* and *Gomorrah*."[510] An 1819 article in the *Boston Recorder*, which reported New Orleanians celebrating the Fourth of July even when it occurred on a Sunday, editorialized that "New Orleans has been long represented as the Sodom of our country, [where] the institutions of religion are not regarded either by the civil or military authorities...."[511] A missionary minister visiting in 1823 reminded his readers that "New Orleans is of course exposed to greater varieties of human misery, vice, disease, and want, than any other American town.... Much has been said about [its] profligacy of manners... morals...debauchery, and low vice... [T]his place has more than once been called the modern Sodom.[512]" An anonymous booklet authored "by a resident" in 1850 catalogued the city's crimes in extensive sub-chapters entitled "Illegitimate Families," "Concubinage," "Kept Mistresses," "Extent of Licentiousness," "Regular Prostitutes," "Prostitution of Wives," "Amalgamation," "A Man Selling His Own Children," "Slave Girls Hired As Bed Companions," "Disregard of the Sabbath," "Bull Fighting," "Drinking Houses," "Vagrants," "Women Whipping on the Plantations," "Chain-Gangs of Women," and "Depravity of Slaveholders," among others. He held back when he characterized New Orleans as "this Babel of all Babels, this Sodom of all Sodoms...this modern Golgotha"[513]

As the city's stature and prosperity rose, so did the implications of its nicknames. Joseph Holt Ingraham, a Northerner born in 1809 who visited the Old Southwest around 1833 and wrote a travelogue in 1835, claimed to have coined the nickname that would become the city's premier for over a century to come. "I have termed New-Orleans the crescent city in one of my letters," wrote Ingraham, "from its being built around the segment of a circle formed by a graceful curve of the river at this place."[514] He certainly was not the first to associate the region's graceful river meanders with the word "crescent." Bienville himself used the French equivalent of that word repeatedly during the foundation era—"one of the finest crescents of the river…," "the very fine crescent of the port of New Orleans…," etc.—prompting French historian Baron Marc de Villiers du Terrage to comment in 1920,

> This expression, found in a memoir drawn up in 1725 or thereabouts, shows that the crescent, which was later to give New Orleans her nickname, had been observed almost from the start.[515]

The word occurs in other early sources. In his 1758 account of Louisiana, Le Page du Pratz described the hairpin meander of English Turn as forming "the figure of a crescent, almost closed."[516] An 1818 Gettysburg newspaper quoted a Kentuckian saying that New Orleans "is built in the shape of a crescent, the curve of the river constituting a safe and commodious harbor,"[517] and ten years later, a Georgia newspaper described the bend as a "vast crescent" connecting "sloops, schooners, and brigs" docking at one end with ocean-going vessels and steamboats at the other.[518]

But such descriptions fall short of nicknames. We do know that by 1839, four years after Ingraham's book, a "Crescent City" shipping line was in operation, and by 1840, a local newspaper named *The Crescent City* circulated. The next year, *The Weekly Crescent City* hit the streets.[519] In 1842, Louis Fitzgerald Tasistro used "Crescent City" three times in his book *Random Shots and Southern Breezes*; two uses appeared in quotations, suggesting that the term was new and conscientiously borrowed, heard enough to be invoked without explanation but not enough to be invoked inconspicuously.[520] A review of Tasistro's book appearing in *The United States Democratic Review* that same year made passing reference to "the 'Crescent City,' as New-Orleans has been called," again implying recent coinage.[521]

Dignified and mellifluous, "Crescent City" stuck. In 1846-47, another Northerner visitor (and future mayor of New York City), Abraham Oakey Hall, wrote sketches about his destination and published them in 1851 under the title *The Manhattaner in New Orleans; or Phases of "Crescent City" Life*. Scottish geologist Charles Lyell, who visited on Mardi Gras 1846, also repeated the term in his 1849 travelogue.[522] So prevalent had the appellation become by the 1850s that some visitors conscientiously reflected upon it. French geographer Elisée Réclus, who visited what he termed "the metropolis of the South" in 1853, found its nickname "poetic" and suggested updating it to "the Double Crescent City," because the recent annexation of Lafayette gave New Orleans "two graceful curves."[523] An observer scanning the cityscape from the roof of the Custom House in 1858 wrote,

> Beyond rolls the river, sweeping round in the curve which has … given [New Orleans] its name, 'twin sister to the Crescent Moon.'[524]

Such publications, which hit the streets during New Orleans' heyday as one of the most important cities in the nation, helped instill "Crescent City" as the universally accepted nickname for the ascendant metropolis. A number of businesses, associations, vessels, and rail lines reinforced popular usage by incorporating the term into their names.

Digital database searches lend further support to Ingraham's coinage claim. A search on "Crescent City" in Cornell University's "Making of America" online database, which accesses over 110,000 volumes of books and periodicals published between 1815 and 1926, yielded not a single occurrence prior to 1840, but one in 1842, twenty-four during 1845-50, and fifty-one during 1850-55, by which time the moniker was entrenched.[525] Queries of the *Archive of Americana* database, which stores millions of newspaper articles dating from 1690 through 1922, show that "Crescent City" occurred not once before 1835, but 18,314 times afterwards (starting in 1839-40), in contexts almost always relating to New Orleans.[526] Likewise, the commercial database *newspaperarchive.com*, which digitized 73 million pages from 239 years' worth of newspapers from 753 cities, yielded zero hits for the key words "New Orleans" and "Crescent City" from 1759 to 1835, but 9,446 from 1836 to 2007. A number of other historical databases produced no pre-1835 uses of "Crescent City."

Also corroborating Ingraham's claim is his literary reputation for coining terms and embracing colloquialisms. Scholars of American English have identified his *The South-West by a Yankee* as the first documented source of a number of Americanisms, including "Bermuda grass," "Havana cigar," "flower-pot plant," and "sporting gentleman."[527] Their research, however, makes no mention of what may be his most significant linguistic contribution. Ingraham later settled in Natchez, Mississippi, becoming locally prominent as a lawyer, author, teacher, and clergyman. He died in 1860.

"Queen City of the South," or "Queen of the South" (note again the feminine gender) is a bit more fluid—and contested—than Ingraham's term. Lacking the alliterative brevity of "Crescent City," the phrase operates more along the lines of a slogan than a nickname, and might have been used more often to describe New Orleans retrospectively, after its prestigious era had begun to wane. An 1847 *Scientific American* article saluted Cincinnati as the "Queen City of the West" but bestowed no equivalent Southern title upon New Orleans, despite its mention on the same page. Two 1850 occurrences of "Queen City of the South" crowned Charleston with that honor, and Atlanta as "destined to become" that noble metropolis. *Harper's Magazine* in 1858 dubbed St. Louis as the "Queen City of the Mississippi Valley," but again failed to honor New Orleans when it was cited later on the same page.[528] An 1883 article in *Harper's Magazine* further validated Cincinnati's claim to the nickname:

> Cincinnati is rich in *sobriquets*. That of the "Queen City" is so widely known
> as to be a synonym [for] Cincinnati [that] would be understood from Maine
> to California.

The article goes on to say that "the sobriquet for Cincinnati now most in vogue is that of "the Paris of America"—a claim that might appall a New Orleanian.[529]

A *Harper's Weekly* article published as Union troops seized the city in May 1862 reminded its readers that "New Orleans, as every one knows, is the queen city of the South… The city is built around a bend in the river, from which circumstances it bears the sobriquet of "The Crescent City."[530] A later national article published in 1885, recounting the 1862 events, ascribed the *Queen City* title retrospectively—and with a dash of cynical irony—to the city:

> The Chalmette batteries [prepared] to meet our fleet…. Farragut made
> short work of them, however, and our fleet, meeting with no further resis-
> tance, passed on and anchored before New Orleans. The Queen City of the
> South lay at the conqueror's feet, unable to do anything in the way of de-
> fense….[531]

Of all the city's slogans (distinguished here from nicknames), the one that
circulates most frequently today is "The City That Care Forgot." At once world-weary
and liberating, the enigmatic phrase is curiously, perhaps intentionally, ambiguous, depending on whether one interprets "care" to mean kindness or worry. It seems to have
entered the literary lexicon at latest by the early twentieth century, though its exact origins remain foggy. Historian Robert C. Reinders, author of the 1964 publication *End
of an Era: New Orleans, 1850-1860*, stated in a chapter entitled "The Good Times" that
"one hundred years ago, as today, New Orleans was billed as "the city care forgot."[532] It
is not clear, however, if Reinders meant to cite the slogan figuratively or literally; his
accompanying quotations from the 1850s substantiate the spirit of the phrase but not
its precise phraseology. Digital database searches on over a hundred million pages of
historical newspapers dating back to the eighteenth century failed to return a single
usage until the early twentieth century—no surprise if the term circulated primarily in
local slang.

Confirmed early usages start to appear as part of a circa-1910s tourism marketing campaign by the famed St. Charles Hotel. The February 9, 1912 *Daily Picayune*
featured a four-column advertisement that read

NEW ORLEANS
"THE CITY CARE FORGOT"
The St. Charles
"The Center of the City's Hotel Life"[533]

Management of the St. Charles went national with the campaign: a March
1912 *Des Moines Capital*, a January 1913 *Philadelphia Inquirer*, and other papers repeatedly ran an advertisement that read,

NEW ORLEANS
"THE CITY CARE FORGOT"

QUAINT HISTORIC
NEW ORLEANS
America's Carnival and Convention City

The St. Charles
Finest all year Hotel in the South[534]

The marketers paralleled their campaign with a photo booklet entitled *Souvenir of NEW ORLEANS, "The City Care Forgot,"*[535] which, by 1917, reached its third

edition. The campaign's liberal use of the slogan seemed to imply that it resonated with familiarity among readers. It went unexplained in the text, lest one construes the pamphlet's generous coverage of Carnival revelry, luxurious accommodations, and leisurely sight-seeing as ample evidence for the city's capacity as a refuge from worldly cares.

Another ad posted by the Texas and Pacific Railroad in the *Fort Worth Star-Telegram* (1915) echoed similar tones of exoticism and escapism posed to lure travelers: "Occasion Extraordinary—New Orleans—"The City Care Forgot"—Spend Three Glorious Days in New Orleans."[536] Similar usages appeared in other American newspapers in the 1910s-20s; the *Fort Worth Star-Telegram*, for example, ran the circa-1913 St. Charles ads repeatedly in 1922. Also that year, a major *New York Herald*-copyrighted article on "atmosphere seeker" tourism in New Orleans appeared under the headline *"Life Throbs Anew in Vieux Carre of City Care Forgot."*[537]

A 1926 promotional publication by the New Orleans Federation of Clubs, entitled *New Orleans: Key to America's Most Interesting City*, offered an insightful perspective of the slogan and its implications. "New Orleans," it explained,

> is lovingly referred to throughout the length and breadth of the United States as "The city that care forgot" and it is this implanted idea in the minds of Americans that still gives it a flavor of present day romance and results in such a tremendous influx of visitors [each] winter.

If "The City That Care Forgot" garnered such widespread association with New Orleans in the mid-1920s, then the slogan's roots might indeed grow deeper than the previous decade. As for its implications, the Federation quickly assured potential investors that, in fact,

> New Orleans is not entirely a "City that care forgot" for it is one of the most up-to-date and modern American cities, home to an ever growing and expanding business spirit and center of finance....[538]

The title of the aforementioned document, and the pointed disassociation from the implications of a leisurely, care-free city, reflect a formal decision in 1922 by the Association of Commerce's Convention and Tourism Bureau to promote New Orleans as "America's Most Interesting City." Wrote historian Anthony J. Stanonis in his recent treatise on tourism,

> through the distribution of one hundred thousand stickers bearing the phrase ["New Orleans—America's Most Interesting City"], to be used on packages mailed [worldwide], local businesses hoped to relegate to the scrap heap the familiar descriptions of New Orleans as the "City That Care Forgot" and the "Paris of America." These old slogans needed correction if not erasure from the public mind...making life in New Orleans seem little more than "a series of parades and Bacchanalian debaucheries."[539]

In fact, both slogans were used to promote commerce in this era. Those in finance and industry preferred the new one; those in tourism liked both.

The above examples show that "The City That Care Forgot" first circulated broadly in the 1910s and 1920s to attract visitors by depicting New Orleans positively as a quaint and charming refuge from worries. It did not come about in a rueful attempt to impugn New Orleans as a rough and unforgiving port city, though it could be construed that way. (Activists imploring improvement of the city's social conditions oftentimes rework the phrase to read "The City that Forgot to Care.") Whether the original slogan was *coined* for those escapist purposes is difficult to ascertain; indeed, it may never have been specifically coined at all, but rather extracted loosely from variations circulating in late-nineteenth-century parlance, as suggested by the historian Reinders. One possible precursor appeared as a subtitle to a nostalgic 1890 article on "The Old Crescent City," which read, "Where Time Fleets Carelessly."[540]

The slogan reached larger audiences when it appeared in the influential Federal Writers' Project *New Orleans City Guide* (1938) and in Edward Larocque Tinker's *Creole City: Its Past and Its People.* Those widely read sources helped instill the phrase in the literary lexicon, although its length and awkwardness precluded it from emerging as a truly ubiquitous nickname.

Not so "Big Easy." Succinct, languid, and slightly provocative, that term seems to have emerged from the music and nightclub scene of the early 1900s. Jazzman Pops Foster, born on a plantation in 1892, recalled performing around 1908 "over in Gretna [at] the Big Easy Hall and the Drag Nasty Hall (it's still in Gretna)," in an interview recorded in 1967.[541] Other secondary sources claim the legendary joint was located in Storyville or somewhere uptown; neither of Foster's halls appear in the Gretna listings of *Young and Co. Business Directory for 1908-1909*, suggesting that their monikers were nicknames or that the venues operated off-the-books. When Pops Foster died in 1969, a newspaper story with a San Francisco dateline reported that

> About 300 came to church to see him off, New Orleans style, [as] Turk Murphy's band played the same tunes Pops slapped out years ago in places like Funkeybucket's Hall, Henry Metrango's and the Big Easy.[542]

"The Big Easy" apparently circulated sufficiently in the vernacular speech of certain socio-economic circles, historically and contemporarily, to inspire *Times-Picayune* reporter James Conaway to adopt it as the title of his 1970 novel about police corruption in New Orleans. That book brought the term to wider attention. Some of the first nationwide appearances of "Big Easy" as a nickname for New Orleans arose subsequent to Conaway's publication. One occurred in an insightful 1972 Associated Press article by Sid Moody entitled "Mardi Gras in New Orleans: Is It Worth It?," subtitled "Fat Tuesday in the Big Easy." The journalist described the

> constant nightroar of the kids of Bourbon St., pierced by rebel yells in the city they call "The Big Easy," swilling Boone's Farm, grabbing flesh, [and] rapping with cops....[543]

Note that Moody felt a need to introduce the nickname to his readers, implying limited usage or recent coinage.

Around the same time, "The Big Easy" appeared repeatedly in the gossip columns of local journalist Betty Guillaud, who, according to a colleague, "used it in her *States-Item* column [in the early 1970s] to contrast life in New Orleans with the rat race of the Big Apple."[544] Guillaud's later *Times-Picayune* gossip column, "Big Easy Does It," further reinforced the nickname. Said Guillaud years later, "[p]eople have credited me with inventing it and have asked me to use it for lots of things…. Sandy Cash wrote a song by that title and there was a TV series [in 1982] which didn't fly. Someone even wanted to use it for a restaurant."[545] According to columnist Chris Rose, Guillaud, "more than anyone else, gave the city's nickname cache and relevance and made it stick."[546]

Hollywood might have played a bigger role in entrenching the nickname. When a movie about police corruption was changed from a Chicago setting to New Orleans, its star, actor Dennis Quaid, suggested entitling it "The Big Easy."[547] The movie's 1987 release and subsequent popularity helped stoke the local tourism industry by delivering 108 minutes of nonstop clichés and stereotypes—exaggerated accents, voodoo ceremonies, loose morals, official corruption, and incessant obsessions with food and festivity—all set to Cajun music and packaged under the title *The Big Easy*. What a travelogue had accomplished for "Crescent City" in the 1830s, a Hollywood production did for "The Big Easy" in the 1980s. In the two years prior to the film's release, major American newspapers used the term "Big Easy" in their articles only once, while "Crescent City" appeared forty-one times. After the movie came out, "Crescent City" continued its same pace (forty-three occurrences during 1987-88), whereas "Big Easy" surged to 109 times. During the year following Hurricane Katrina, when journalists filed thousands of articles about New Orleans, "Crescent City" appeared 672 times in the headlines and lead paragraphs of major American newspaper articles, while "Big Easy" occurred 898 times.[548]

The success of "The Big Easy" is no mystery. Playing off New York City's "Big Apple," the tag resonated with familiarity and ease of recollection. Its economy of words and syllables rendered it friendly to headline editors, travel writers, and glib television personalities. Its odd yoking of two adjectives conveyed a swaggering, nonchalant roguishness that seemed to satisfy popular expectations about the city's carefree attitude—the same expectations, incidentally, that "The City that Care Forgot" helped instill. "Big Easy," in short, was not only convenient and cool, but also rang true to outside ears. That the nickname's popularity rose precisely as tourism replaced petroleum and shipping as the city's premier economic sector was no coincidence: a marketer could not have invented a better term to convince visitors to partake of the city's opportunities for escapism. The suggestive nickname worked almost too well: at one point, the city's tourism promoters—like their predecessors in 1922 vis-à-vis "The City that Care Forgot"—backed away from "The Big Easy," according to one historian, "out of fear that it detracted from their growing efforts to appeal to touring families."[549]

The shift from the elegant "Crescent City" to the raffish "Big Easy" may symbolize, to some, New Orleans' transformation from an affluent, ascending metropolis with a genuine *raison d'être*, to a poor and descending one married to a phony tourism construct. This interpretation is complicated, at the very least, by the fact that New Orleans was quite troubled even during its so-called "golden age," as reflected by certain decidedly unflattering historical nicknames.

"Crescent City," "Queen of the South," "Sodom and Gomorrah," "City that Care Forgot," "America's Most Interesting City," "The Big Easy:" What can we learn about New Orleans through its lexicon of names, nicknames, and slogans? Some early ones reflect outsiders' sense of disapproval of that which offended their presumed cultural norms: New Orleans as the alien, the condemned, the threatening "other." Others arose from an embracing appreciation of geographical and cultural beauty and distinction: New Orleans as colorful, curious, romantic, unique. Still others were conscientiously coined by vested interests (oftentimes by exploiting reputations and images imparted by earlier nicknames) and promulgated for economic aims, namely tourism and shipping: New Orleans as product, service, experience. The nicknames reveal a wide range of images, judgments, and agendas, imposed both externally and internally, oftentimes contested, and implying either compliment or critique.

On one point almost all can agree: this lexicon of place both reflects and drives popular perceptions that, compared to other American cities, *something different happened here.*

Wards, Faubourgs, and the Perception of Place

How New Orleanians delineate, label, and argue about their urban space

New Orleanians perceive, delineate, and label their urban spaces in myriad ways. Some use faubourgs, municipalities, districts, and wards; others refer to church parishes and school districts; still others spatialize the city by ethnic groups; by neighborhood age and atmosphere; by economic class and public safety ("good" and "bad" areas); by nodes, nuclei, and landmarks; and vis-à-vis Canal Street, the lake, or the river. The spatial perceptions vary complexly over time and within sub-segments of the population. While some pedantic aficionados insist that neighborhoods are named absolutely and delineated officially, like matters of law or physics, such perceptions of place are more appropriately viewed as the human constructs they are, wonderfully individualized and wholly subject to interpretation. Therein lies their significance.

The subjectivity begins with the city's first neighborhood. "French Quarter," "the Quarter," "old city," "original city," Vieux Carré (Old Square), and Vieux Carré de la Ville usually describe those blocks bounded by present-day Iberville Street, North Rampart Street, Esplanade Avenue, and the Mississippi River. In informal contxts, they also includes the "100 blocks" between Iberville and Canal, although this strip did not fall within the original city and remains today beyond the jurisdiction of the Vieux Carré Commission. Portions of blocks along North Rampart and Esplanade also spanned beyond the original plat but are now officially "in" the French Quarter. In historical records, the

French Quarter comprised part of the First Municipality when the city experimented with semi-autonomous municipalities in 1836. After reunification in 1852, the French Quarter became part of the new Second Municipal District, which was in turn sliced into the Fourth, Fifth, and Sixth wards, all of which remain in use today. Some locals shrug off these arcane bureaucratic limits and refer generically to all quaint, historic neighborhoods below Canal Street as "the French Quarters"—plural—or simply as "da quarters."

Faubourg or fauxbourg (literally "false town") is the French term for an inner suburb. Sometimes used synonymously with the term banlieue ("outskirts" or "suburbs"), it described the subdivisions laid out within old plantations beyond the limits of the original city, starting in 1788. Both terms faded as French disappeared from local speech in the late 1800s and early 1900s, but faubourg was revived in the 1970s through the efforts of preservationists, neighborhood organizations, and real estate agents. The first neighborhood to re-embrace the term was the Faubourg Marigny, which many view as the quintessential New Orleans faubourg. The term is now commonly used as a synonym for "historic neighborhood" throughout New Orleans, excepting (by definition) the French Quarter. Popular with culturally aware history buffs (many of them transplants), the term faubourg is ironically uncommon among deep-rooted locals (particularly native-born elders) who came of age when the term was defunct.

Faubourg Ste. Marie, "Faubourg St. Mary," "St. Mary," "Second Municipality," "American Sector," "American Quarter," "Central Business District," and "CBD" all refer to the area loosely bordered by present-day Canal Street (or Iberville Street), Claiborne or Loyola avenues, Howard Avenue or the Pontchartrain Expressway, and the Mississippi River. In certain historical contexts, the "Canal Street corridor" (between Iberville and Common) is considered separate, because this swath remained a dusty commons for twenty years after the faubourg's 1788 platting. Faubourg Ste. Marie is generally used for discussions recounting the late 1700s and early 1800s, while Faubourg St. Mary, St. Mary, and the American Sector usually connote nineteenth-century contexts. "Second Municipality" implies exclusively the municipality era of 1836-52, while "Central Business District" and "CBD" refer to the area in the twentieth and twenty-first centuries. Today, the CBD falls within the First Municipal District and mostly the Third Ward. One real estate investor is currently spearheading an effort to designate officially and market the CBD as "The American Sector," playing off the world-famous cachet of the French Quarter.

Everyone has a particular feel of where "downtown" becomes "uptown" in New Orleans (and, relatedly, whether the words should be capitalized as proper nouns or lower-cased as general urban regions). Many people today divide the two places-of-mind along the Pontchartrain Expressway, which roughly separates the harder, congested streets of the commercial sector from softer, leafier residential environs. Others refer exclusively to the Garden District or the University area as "uptown" and the French Quarter and Central Business District as "downtown." Years ago, Canal Street would have been seen as the demarcation—a notion still held by many New Orleanians, despite the fact the most local usage of "downtown" and "uptown" implies otherwise. Understanding the two distinctive yet nebulous regions is enabled by embracing their various and adamantly defended definitions, rather than by dogmatically attempting to reject all but one.[550]

The term "Garden District" (in use at least since the 1850s) connotes the wealthy historic neighborhood bounded generally by Magazine Street and Jackson, Louisiana, and St. Charles avenues, historically the inland portion of the former Jefferson Parish city of Lafayette. Here, wealthy families of predominantly Anglo-American stock built spacious mansions (1830s-50s) set back from the streets and surrounded by greenery, a very different urban environment compared to the French Quarter. Exact limits of the Garden District depend on whether one is referencing official city neighborhood delineations, local historic districts, or national historic districts. Even then, many locals and most visitors use "Garden District" to mean all prosperous, foliated uptown historic neighborhoods.

Wards as a political-geographical unit were introduced with the 1805 chartering of the city, replacing a Spanish equivalent from colonial times. Serving as voting districts, demographic units for censuses, and other municipal purposes, wards were delineated and redrawn four times over the next forty-seven years. After the city's unsuccessful sixteen-year experiment with semi-autonomous municipalities, the reunified city government (1852) redrew ward lines for a fifth time. Because Felicity Street had, for many years, marked the Jefferson/Orleans parish line, the new wards were enumerated starting from Felicity (First Ward) and continuing consecutively downriver to the Orleans/St. Bernard parish line near present-day Jackson Barracks (Ninth Ward). Each ward extended perpendicularly from the river, where most people lived, straight back into the uninhabited backswamp. To equalize population sizes within wards, the high-density French Quarter was sliced into the narrowest wards (Fourth, Fifth, and Sixth), while the lower-density upper and lower faubourgs spanned broader swaths. The lowermost outskirts of the city were so depopulated that a single mega-ward—the Ninth—enveloped the entire area. City fathers then "swung around" above Felicity Street and demarcated newly annexed Lafayette as wards Ten and Eleven. The enumeration continued upriver as more Jefferson Parish communities merged with New Orleans: Jefferson City became wards Twelve, Thirteen, and Fourteen in 1870, then Algiers on the West Bank was annexed as Ward Fifteen. Upriver expansion concluded when the city annexed Carrollton, which became wards Sixteen and Seventeen. As development spread toward the lake, old ward lines that once projected neatly off the sinuous Mississippi were extended and angled somewhat awkwardly to intersect the smooth west-to-east arc of the lakeshore. The modern-day map of New Orleans wards, unchanged since the 1880s, thus reflects the city's piecemeal growth since 1852.

An additional adjustment in ward geography came in the 1920s, when the newly excavated Industrial Canal severed the Ninth Ward into "upper" and "lower" sections (a reference to the flow direction of the river, not topographic elevation). By the late twentieth century, the riverside sections of the upper and lower Ninth wards became respectively known by the more appealing monikers of Bywater and Holy Cross, while areas behind St. Claude and Claiborne generally remained anonymous. Their higher degree of historical and architectural significance brought Bywater and Holy Cross to the table of urban planners and preservationists, thus subjecting them to specialized naming and greater attention—more evidence for the significance of place names and nicknames. Real estate agents, who know this well, are universally enamored with mellifluous historical monikers under the theory that more people would rather live in "the Faubourg Bouligny" than in "the Thirteenth Ward."

Place perceptions and labels inform on nativity, race, and other social dimensions. New Orleans natives with deep local roots often use the ward system in perceiving urban space, probably because it formed the premier space-delineation option prior to the official urban-planning and historic-districting era that began in the 1970s. Recent transplants, many of who specifically moved to the city for its historical and cultural charms, tend to recognize space vis-à-vis recently revived historical names, like Faubourg St. John, "the Marigny," and Faubourg Tremé (see *Nativity as Ethnicity in New Orleans*).

Because nativity rates are much higher among black residents than whites, wards are particularly common as a spatial reference in the African-American community. Elderly natives of any race are often unfamiliar with the trendy revived faubourg names, just as many recently arrived transplants and college students are at a loss when asked what ward they live in. Native-born New Orleanians, who tend to be culturally traditional and family-oriented, are more likely to identify landmarks and regionize the city by churches, church parishes, and school districts, a spatial lexicon that does not work for many young, secular, childless transplants. What is "the Seventh Ward" to a native-born black Creole may be "Faubourg New Marigny" or "the Jazz Fest neighborhood" to a white transplant; what is the "Upper Ninth Ward" to the working class may be "Bywater" to artists and bohemians. Older members of the black community still speak of the "back-of-town" and "front-of-town," even though the swamps and marshes that gave meaning to those ancient spatial perceptions (see *Geographies of Nuisance and Risk*) have long been drained away.

Spatial references often reveal subtle (or not-so-subtle) social, racial, and political narratives. Politicians in New Orleans cleverly deploy localized spatial references (to wards, uptown, downtown, or the back-of-town) to certify their authenticity, establish their "street cred," or allude to racial dynamics. When Mayor Ray Nagin famously assured black residents that post-Katrina New Orleans will remain a "chocolate" city, he pointedly shrugged off "what people are saying in Uptown," implying that residents of that urban region bore other racial designs.[551] The adjectives "inner-city" and "suburban," which originally carried geographical meaning, are now widely and openly used as race and class euphemisms—despite the fact that many inner cities are gentrifying while suburbs grow increasingly diverse. Sometimes prejudices are revealed when observers unconscientiously describe the same area differently, depending on context. "When something bad happens," lamented one New Yorker, "[this] neighborhood is called Harlem. When something good happens, it is the Upper West Side.[552]"

Like city dwellers anywhere, New Orleanians also break down space through landmarks such as favorite restaurants, stores, places of worship, or nightspots. Landmarks often work better than street addresses or intersections in communicating location. Say "4133 South Carrollton Avenue," or "the intersection of South Carrollton and Ulloa," and even long-time residents may ponder a while before picturing that particular locale; say "near the Rock-N-Bowl" and, for many, the picture clarifies significantly. Such landmarks form a perceptual map which can be shared within one's social network, but not necessarily beyond it. Someone from New Orleans East with no interest in either music or bowling might prefer a straightforward street address than some unfindable reference to an unfamiliar venue. So central was a health-food store to the identity of an Esplanade Avenue neighborhood that some residents jokingly called the area "Faubourg Whole Foods," a reference that might baffle those neighbors who could not afford to shop there.

Gangs a century ago often identified themselves by referencing neighborhood landmarks: the "St. Mary's Market Gang" and "Shot Tower Gang," for example, were named for two prominent features in the Irish Channel area. Gangs today usually spatialize their identity by ward (e.g., "10th Ward Posse"), something regularly seen in graffiti and on commemorative T-shirts sold at gangster funerals. Curiously, some gangs based in housing projects adopt ward-based names that do not reflect the actual ward locations of their home turf. Wards often pop up in rap lyrics; one rapper in 2005 dubbed himself "Fifth Ward Weebie."

Government agencies and advocacy groups eschew nuanced, fuzzy perceptions of place, preferring instead bureaucratic and legal clarity in the sub-regionalization of the city. To this end, they periodically impose rigid boundaries and official monikers upon the cityscape. In 1973-74, the architectural firm Curtis and Davis' *New Orleans Housing and Neighborhood Preservation Study* identified and delineated sixty-two "official" city neighborhoods (later increased to seventy-three), cartographically depicted as tidy little polygons based on census tracts, natural barriers, transportation arteries, and social and economic patterns. Planners have widely adopted the Curtis and Davis map in the past three decades, yet most New Orleans would be at a loss to identify three-quarters of its "official" neighborhoods.

Another imposed official delineation of space and place in New Orleans is by historic district. The city boasts some of the largest urban National Register Historic Districts in the nation. Inclusion in the U.S. Department of the Interior's National Register of Historic Places is largely an honorary designation; the only material benefits involve certain tax credits and special consideration vis-à-vis federally funded projects. Yet these delineations have proven highly influential, in large part because the Preservation Resource Center, New Orleans' largest historic-protection advocacy group, embraced them in a widely distributed and very influential map and website. Local historic districts, on the other hand, span far less acreage and are less known by the public, but have more "teeth" in protecting architecturally and historically significant structures. They are overseen by the Historic District Landmarks Commission, with involvement from the City Planning Commission and other groups.

New Orleans' most distinctive spatial perception involves not place but direction. Rather than the cardinal directions, which only serve to confuse in crescent-shaped New Orleans, *lakeside, riverside, upriver* (or *uptown*), and *downriver* (or *downtown*) are universally used as surrogates for northward, southward, westward, and eastward. Confusing at first, the system works well (except perhaps in the jumbled Bayou St. John/Mid-City area) and makes more sense locally than allusions to distant poles and stars. Logical as it is, the terminology does not travel well. Residents of urbanized St. Bernard Parish, for example, do not go "downriver" to get to the rural coastal region, but rather "down the road." Likewise, fishermen in places like Yscloskey and Shell Beach go "up the road" to shop or do business in Meraux or Chalmette.[553]

The Hurricane Katrina catastrophe turned worldwide observers into new speakers of New Orleans' lexicon of place. Hundreds of *arrivistes* from journalism and academia trooped into the city in the wake of the deluge and eagerly embraced the clearly defined official neighborhood maps for their reporting and research. Two of the hardest-hit areas—Lakeview and the Lower Ninth Ward—emerged in media reports as metaphors for the socio-economic and cultural-geographical chasms within the beleaguered metropolis. *Lakeview*, on the one hand, lent its name to symbolize all that was suburban, white, and middle-class: a typical American twentieth-century subdivision implicitly wealthy enough to enjoy a *view* of the *lake* but innocent enough to misunderstand the water's threat. It flooded terribly. The *Lower Ninth Ward*, on the other hand, spoke to all that was poor, black, underprivileged, and disenfranchised: *Lower*, implying class, isolation, and topography (even though Lakeview lies lower); *Ninth*, as in "bottom-rung;" and *Ward*, that gritty, antiquated political unit unknown to many Americans except as a place for society's lunatic fringe. It flooded worse than Lakeview. Scores of other neighborhoods also suffered the deluge, from working-class white Chalmette to wealthy black Eastover, to the Vietnamese enclave at Versailles and the small Hispanic cluster in Mid-City. But media outlets construed Lakeview and the Lower Ninth Ward to symbolize all angles of the tragedy that viewers needed to know.

Had they listened closely to New Orleanians, they would have heard much more complex, nuanced, and fascinating perceptions of place.

"The Cradle of Civilized Drinking"

Ruminations on New Orleans' ancient reputation for escapism

[T]o all men whose desire only is to be rich, and to live a short life but a merry one, I have no hesitation in recommending New Orleans.[554]
—Henry Bradshaw Fearon, 1819

On a per-capita basis, the Yellow Pages recently listed more bars for New Orleans—55.3 per 100,000 population—than any other major American city. The Crescent City and San Francisco claimed approximately double the per-capita number of drinking establishments of Denver, Boston, Portland, Phoenix, and Las Vegas, and over five times the rate from other large cities.[555]

This pre-Katrina statistic corroborates popular perceptions of New Orleans as a drinking town, a reputation nearly as old as the city. An anonymous critic writing in 1744 roundly rebuked the city's society, noting that even men of little means "are seldom without wine in their cellars; the tradesmen is seldom a week without drinking it beyond moderation; but that is nothing in comparison with the soldier."[556] Wine and liquor comprised fully one-third of Louisiana imports in 1788.[557] An indignant newcomer visiting later in the Spanish colonial era wrote of New Orleanians,

> In their parties there is no delicacy. All is grossness, and noise, and uproar. Wine, not conversation, is sought. The men will not only get tipsy, but stagger and reel in the presence of the ladies; this intemperance … incurs no disgrace; … the ladies laugh at the eccentricity of their walk.

> The city abounds with tippling houses. At every cross street of the town and suburbs, one sees those places of riot and intoxication crowded day and night. The low orders of every colour, white, yellow, and black, mix indiscriminately…. [558]

The stigma of intemperance increased markedly in the early American years, as shipping activity bustled, transients abounded, and reputations spread. "This place is one of the worst I ever witnessed," wrote a homesick new resident in 1817; "the chief amusements are gambling and drinking … quarrels and even murders are very frequent here."[559] Reported John H. B. Latrobe, who visited in 1834,

> In all the streets around, cafés and barrooms [on the Sabbath] were open and in the receipt of a full and noisy custom. Rum and gin, Monongahela [rye whiskey], and Tom and Jerry [sweetened hot rum] here live in palaces … of taste[,] elegance and refinement…. The drinking room is large[;] a whole army of bottles, with contents of all colours line the shelves in close array…. [560]

Another man, describing in 1847 the city's varied and low-priced eateries, reported that "the profit is on the liquor," as evidenced by "the immense patronage these establishments enjoy, and their multiplication within the last year…. Many of these lunch and drinking establishments are coining money; they monopolize the corners of every square; whole rows of them may be found in some localities, and new ones are springing up every day."[561] "The city's more than twenty-five hundred taverns are always filled with drinkers … especially during election time," wrote the French geographer Elisée Réclus during his 1853 visit;

> [They] fuel the most violent passions with brandy and rum … If [a political candidate] doesn't know how to drink a cocktail with style, he will lose popularity and be branded a traitor. When political adversaries meet in a bar, drunk or sober, insults followed by fistfights or gunshots are not unusual. More than once, the conqueror has been seen drinking over the corpse of the conquered.[562]

An 1850 anonymous expose on the city's licentious ways, *New Orleans As It Is (Truth is Stranger Than Fiction)*, excoriated the local embrace of spirits:

Of [all] the sources of evil and cause of contamination, there is none...
so glaring as the immense number of drinking houses in every part of the
city....

[G]rog shops... are found in whole blocks—on three of every four corners,
where one street crosses another, and ranges of building from street to street,
every door leading into a drinking house. The style and splendor of [some
bars and saloons surpasses] the mansion of any millionaire in this country.

[Drinking] is the great propelling power that drives on the maddening car of
human passion into every other scene of vice and pollution.... This practice
of almost constant drinking through the day, pervades all classes of society.
Not only the male portion, with scarcely an exception, but the *ladies*....

[W]ines and liquors of all kinds constitute the principal offerings in the
courtesies of every day life.... [T]hree-forths of the men... are confirmed
drunkards, [taking] up to twenty-five to thirty [drinks] a day, and yet these
are all high-minded, *sober*, and respectable *gentlemen*, full of *Southern chivalry*[!][563]

The cocktail, though not invented in New Orleans as is often claimed, certainly
gained fame here, and it was here more so than any other American city that absinthe,
the notorious greenish-hued European spirit, flowed. Modern New Orleans, described
recently as "The Cradle of Civilized Drinking," is home to some of the nations' oldest and most famous bars, among them Lafitte's Blacksmith Shop, the Old Absinthe
House, the Napoleon House, and Pat O'Brien's. Many today relish this ancient reputation: a coffee-table book celebrating New Orleans saloons, *Obituary Cocktail*, became a
local bestseller in the late 1990s. A festival dedicated to the cocktail recently drew over
12,000 people. A legislator in 2008 filed a bill to declare the Sazerac as Louisiana's "official state cocktail," indicating the mischievous and defiant sense of pride held by many
residents for their putative tolerance for drinking.[564]

New Orleans' historical affinity for alcohol thrives today, though under more
controlled circumstances than in the days of grog shops and dram houses. Beer by the
pint is sold at the most mundane public events, and first-time visitors are often stunned
by the casual legality of open containers. "Booze is part and parcel of just about every
event and occasion in town, from debutante balls to jazz funerals to peewee league T-
ball games," wrote columnist Chris Rose, with barely an ounce of hyperbole.[565] The impression is not lost on the nation: a 2004 Internet survey of 500,000 people ranked New
Orleans as America's number-one city for bar-hopping, night life, and dining out—and
dead last, incidentally, in cleanliness. A similar 2007 poll concurred: first in "cocktail
hour," "going out all night," and "wild weekends;" last in safety and cleanliness.[566]

A number of factors explain the city's modern-day embrace of drinking, spanning from the historical and geographical to the cultural and the economic. Port cities
as a general rule boast lively night scenes. Sailors, travelers, visiting businessmen, and
other transients, liberated by their anonymity and decoupled from the responsibilities
and restraints of home, gravitate to opportunities for immediate gratification, in which

alcohol usually plays a primary role. (Sex is a close second—and, not coincidentally, accounts for another historical reputation associated with this city.) Sailors at sea for extended periods of time demand such services immediately upon disembarking; port cities happily oblige, calling off traditional bans on late-night and Sunday sales to accommodate those arriving at odd times. (The words "Last call!" are rarely heard in New Orleans.) Port cities, with their diverse ethnic stock, are also typically more cosmopolitan and liberal than interior cities. So we should not be surprised that New Orleans, San Francisco, and Boston score among the highest bar rates in aforementioned Yellow Pages survey.

A second possible reason explaining New Orleans' lead in this area is its Latin cultural connection, informed by Southern European and Mediterranean Catholic societies which view alcohol as part of the daily bread. Germans, who arrived in large numbers in the 1830s-50s, did their part by introducing beer (rather successfully) to what was very much a "wine town." More conservative areas of the South, usually with greater Protestant Anglo influence and less immigration, tended to view alcohol as an escapist's vice, and still do today. In Louisiana, hard liquor is available in any supermarket, even K-Marts and Wal-Marts, and Daiquiris are sold legally in go-cups at drive-throughs. In neighboring states, only special liquor stores vend hard liquor, and many counties, particularly in Texas, prohibit alcohol entirely. Drinking is simply part of the culture in Louisiana, especially in New Orleans—and some may argue that is for the better. After acknowledging the widespread availability of spirits, the previously cited circa-1847 resident commented,

> We have TOLERATION [here in New Orleans]—freedom to think,—to do and live as you please…. This is the very happiest state of society…. There are few great crimes committed. Even drunkenness, considering the facilities, is exceedingly rare, and there is [here] an utter absence of that abandonment and degradation, which infests large classes of the population of other cities."[567]

For all the availability and acceptability of alcohol in Louisiana, the state regularly ranks average in terms of both alcohol use and abuse. While the New Orleans area had, as of 2004, a higher percentage of citizens (8.33-8.4 percent) reporting recent alcohol dependence or abuse than the state (8.15 percent) and the nation (7.66 percent), the differences were not huge. The figures generally fell in the middle range of American states, and well short of the nation's highest (13.5 percent, in Wyoming). Regions with the highest percentages of their citizens reporting regular alcohol usage consistently clustered in the north central United States—an area not know for its ports, immigrant populations, or Latin heritage.[568]

An above-average number of bars vis-à-vis an average level of alcohol consumption logically implies that visitors comprise many of the bar patrons. Many, perhaps most, of the Yellow Pages listings represent bars located in the French Quarter and CBD which cater to tourists and conventioneers and their "party town" expectations, rather than locals living out their daily lives. The perception of New Orleans as The City That Care Forgot might have developed over centuries via sailors and visitors letting loose in this remote and exotic port, but with the mechanization of shipping and the advent of other transportation options, those bar hoppers of old are gone, leaving only the reputation of a Sodom and Gomorrah. The modern tourism industry enthusiastically exploits this historical reputation, creating an expectation of revelry that perpetuates the reputation, leading to greater expectations. The result: Bourbon Street, go-cups, a bar on every corner, and otherwise decent citizens publicly indulging to excess. The high rate of bar listing in New Orleans, then, may simply reflect the city's huge tourism and convention industry, annually numbering over ten million visitors (pre-Katrina) and promoted by a crack professional marketing staff. It may also be a case of a numerator inflated by tourism divided by a relatively small denominator, since New Orleans had one of the smaller populations among the thirty-five major cities included in the study.

Hurricane Katrina changed all these numbers—of bars, population, tourism, liquor sales—but all signs indicate that the city's centuries-old reputation as a drinking town will, for better or worse, endure. Bars were among the very first businesses to reopen after the catastrophe—indeed, the only ones to remain open *during* the incident. Bars, nightclubs, and restaurants later in the autumn of 2005 reopened at a pace far brisker than any other business type, even those dealing in necessities.[569] Many New Orleanians imbibed liberally during the stressful and uncertain times following Katrina, when an open saloon was far easier to find than an open supermarket.

Whatever the fate of New Orleans, it is a safe bet that one of its last establishments will be a "grog house," and one of its more enduring reputations will be that of a drinking town.

On the Whitewashing of Tree Trunks

Some unscientific hypotheses about a curious tradition

Ordinary street scenes and cityscapes can serve as Rosetta Stones of culture and history. Consider, for example, the tradition of whitewashing the lower portions of tree trunks, seen throughout New Orleans and the Gulf Coast region. Little scholarly research has been conducted on this peculiar custom, but personal (unscientific) observations throughout the Americas suggest various hypotheses.[570]

Ask Louisianians why they do it and most will cite a pragmatic environmental reason: to keep potentially harmful borers off the tree. And this may well be true, especially if lime-based whitewash (toxic to insects) is used.

Others explain the coating as protection against wintertime freeze/thaw cycles and the effects of the sun. "The trunks of young trees," recommended a 1919

California newspaper column entitled *Good Orchid Practice,* "should be whitewashed as soon as they are planted in the orchid, to prevent sunscald and the drying of the buds…"[571] When telephone poles and lampposts are given the same treatment, public safety (marking of traffic obstacles) explains the phenomenon.

But there may also be a deeper significance here. Throughout Latin America, whitewashed tree trunks appear in *parques centrales,* along grand avenues, in school-yards, and in courtyards. Asked about the tradition, many Latinos will explain that it gives a clean, manicured, *bonito* appearance to vegetation that, if left unchecked, could become overgrown, unruly, and *feo.* French geographer Elisée Réclus seemed to pre-scribe to this aesthetic explanation in his 1853 critique of New Orleans society:

> Under the pretext of art, rich individuals limit themselves to whitewashing
> the trees in their gardens. This luxury has the double advantage of being
> pleasing to their sight and of costing very little.[572]

An 1897 article about a reunion of former slaves at a park in Waco, Texas mentioned that "the trunks of the trees were whitewashed for the occasion," as a festive backdrop for the barbecue picnic, fiddle players, and orators.[573] Another article from South Caro-lina in the same year also alluded to an aesthetic rationale for the tradition:

> One of the prettiest places in Columbia just now is the park…. [T[he trees
> have put on their green foliage[;] the undergrowth has been cut out and
> snakes no longer have a resort. This week Chairman Willis of the park com-
> mittee has been having the trunks of the trees and fences whitewashed and
> when the work is completed there will be *no neater or prettier place* in the
> whole city.[574]

Whitewashing tree trunks may represent a controlling of nature—a "neaten-ing up;" a taming of its ragged and potentially threatening edge. It may be a product of the same cultural instinct that makes Americans spend untold hours and countless dollars cutting grass and trimming hedges. Yet, unlike mowed lawns, whitewashed tree trunks are not evenly distributed throughout the United States. They are rare in the northern and central parts of the country, but common in certain neighborhoods in the urban Northeast, in the border country from Texas to California, in southern Florida and parts of the interior South, and in New Orleans and the Gulf Coast. They are also typical of societies of the Mediterranean region and other parts of Europe and Russia. The tradition may be a Mediterranean-region aesthetic trait which diffused primarily into areas colonized by France and Spain, and, later, into areas where immigrants from the Mediterranean region settled. This may explain why whitewashed tree trunks are found throughout the Latin world, in both cool, dry mountain environments and hot, moist, coastal environments, but less so in the Anglo world, regardless of environment. They are also found in many tropical East Asian societies.

Which brings us to the Vietnamese neighborhood of Versailles in eastern New Orleans, where whitewashed tree trunks also appear. Did these Catholic East Asian peoples adopt the tradition recently from their Louisiana neighbors? Did they pick it up long ago from French colonizers and bring it here when they immigrated to the

Catholic world of southern Louisiana, which *also* happened to have a French heritage? Or did they develop it independently for pragmatic environmental reasons? In one Versailles example, pine trees were painted the same pastel-blue-and-white colors used for the Virgin Mary statues standing in nearby front yards. Was this color scheme intended to deter insects or mark traffic obstacles? Not likely, or at least not entirely, as evidenced further by an example on North Carrollton Avenue, which incorporated a whitewashed tree trunk into a religious shrine: the mature live oak's whitened base rose out of a rock garden of white ornamental stones adorned with a Virgin Mary statue.[575]

In this seemingly mundane landscape feature, we may be seeing a centuries-old tradition that informs on topics ranging from European colonization and immigration, to the spatial extent of the Latin and Anglo worlds, to spiritually and public religious expression, to the relationship between humans and nature. Mapping this phenomenon might add to the understanding of the cultural geography of the United States. And it might well place New Orleans—Versailles and all—in the heart of America's Latin southern tier.

Devastating the Landscape

One day this city,
rapidly increasing as it is
in wealth and consequence,
will be swept into the Gulf of Mexico,
if the Mississippi happen to rise
[while] the south-east wind
raise the sea....

—James Edward Alexander, 1832

The Fortuitous Storm of 1722

Nature aids engineers in the initial planning of New Orleans

A few years of haphazard development following the spring 1718 founding of New Orleans inscribed an initial level of place-making into the "clean slate" of deltaic soil. One observer described the circa-1720 outpost as comprising

> about a hundred forty barracks, disposed with no great regularity, a great wooden warehouse, and…a few inconsiderable houses, scattered up and down, without any order or regularity… [they] would be esteemed common and ordinary buildings in a European village. *New Orleans*, in 1720, made a very contemptible figure…[576]

When engineers Le Blond de la Tour and Adrien de Pauger endeavored to rectify that "contemptible figure," the existing hodgepodge impeded their envisioned urban plan. Surely they would have eventually mustered official forces to clear away those first four years of unplanned cityscape, but nature beat them to it. Pauger wrote that at 9 a.m. on September 11, 1722,[577] "a great wind" swept the settlement,

> followed an hour later by the most terrible tempest and hurricane that could ever be seen…. It had overthrown at least two thirds of the houses here and those that remain are so badly damaged that it will be necessary to dismantle them. The church, the presbytère, the hospital and a small barracks building…are among [those] overthrown, without being, thanks to the Lord, a single person killed…. The river rose more than six feet and the waves were so great that it is a miracle that [all the boats] were not dashed to pieces.[578]

"With this impetuous wind came such torrents of rain," wrote Dumont years later, "that you could not step out a moment without risk of being drowned…. [T]his tempest was so terrible that it rooted up the largest trees, and the birds, unable to keep up, fell in the streets. In one hour the wind had twice blown from every point of the compass."[579] Not until 4 a.m. on the thirteenth of September did the winds abate, at which time "they set to work to repair the damage done."

New Orleans' first major hurricane proved to be a blessing in disguise. Wrote Pauger, who was responsible for surveying the new street system, "all these buildings were old and provisionally built, and not a single one in the alignment of the new city and thus would have had to be demolished. Thus there would not have been any great misfortune in this disaster except that we must act to put all the people in shelter."[580] Pauger prioritized for the unimpeded execution of his street plan and the orderly development of New Orleans. He once ordered the house of a man named Traverse demolished because it violated the grid; when Traverse petitioned the city for indemnification, Pauger personally beat him repeatedly with a stick, then had him bound by the feet in irons and imprisoned.[581]

Dumont described retrospectively the surveying of the street alignments in his *History of Louisiana*. La Tour "cleared a pretty long and wide strip [now Decatur Street] along the river, to put in execution the plan he [and Pauger] had projected." They

> traced on the ground the streets and quarters which were to form the new town, and notified all who wished building sites to present their petitions to the council. To each settler who appeared they gave a plot ten fathoms front by twenty deep [sixty by one-hundred-twenty English feet], and as each square was fifty fathoms front, it gave twelve plots in each, the middle ones being ten front by twenty-five deep. It was ordained that those who obtained these plots [must] inclose them with palisades, and leave all around a strip at least three feet wide, at the foot of which a ditch was to be dug, to serve as a drain for the river water in time of inundation.[582]

In this manner, the French swept away their own messy beginnings and imposed upon the newly emptied alluvial space a Cartesian sense of urban order. A built environment subsequently arose within the cells of Pauger's grid: the "palisade cabins" typical of Biloxi, built entirely of pine, transformed in the new New Orleans to ones build of "brick, or half-brick and half-wood," using cypress instead of pine. (Brick-between-post walls are still visible throughout the French Quarter and lower faubourgs.) Institutions of European order, both church and state, fronted the *Place d'Armes*, where once-wild nature would be controlled and aestheticized. Less than two months after the storm, "the streets of the old quarter had received the names they still bear."[583] Within several years, levees would be built by slave labor to control the river's natural flooding cycle. It was in 1722, according to Dumont, that "New Orleans began to assume the appearance of a city."[584]

A letter from a man named Devin in 1724 noted the effect of New Orleans' rise on a competing settlement: "Living in Mobile is beginning to be more disagreeable than ever. There is, so to speak, no more society." Prominent citizens, he noted, are all "going to reside at New Orleans.... There is no news here worthy of being written."[585] A short while later, Biloxi and Dauphin Island were recommended for evacuation and abandonment.[586]

New Orleans was on the rise, fortuitously assisted by the storm of 1722.

Transformation by Conflagration

The 1788 and 1794 fires and their impact on the cityscape

Densely populated, largely wooden, and nearly 300 years old, New Orleans understandably bears a lengthy history of terrible conflagrations. Two great fires within six years during the Spanish colonial era stand out for not solely for their severity, but for the lasting transformations they occasioned upon the cityscape.

According to Spanish colonial records, at 1:30 p.m. on March 21, 1788—Good Friday—a wooden cabinet caught fire in the home of State Treasurer José Vicente Nuñez, located at Chartres and Toulouse.[587] According to Chevalier Guy de Soniat du Fossat, who recorded his memories in 1791, the

> fire was caused by the negligence of a woman who thought of crowning her devotion by making a small altar.... She left several candles burning around it and went off to take her dinner. During her absence a candle fell on some ornaments which took fire, and the house in an instant was in flames....[588]

Adjacent buildings ignited, and winds swept the flames across streets and into abutting blocks. Wood was not the only fuel for the blaze:

> The powders which the merchants had in their stores for daily use, contributed largely to accelerate the conflagration, and rendered it more dangerous to those who wanted to save the remaining buildings.[589]

By late afternoon, recorded the Spanish authorities, "4/5 of the populated section of this City was reduced to ashes, [including] the Parish Church and House, Cabildo and Jail...." Worse yet, the destroyed district comprised not the peripheral shantytowns but "the part of the City most important and best situated."[590] At least twenty square blocks centered around the Royal/Toulouse intersection were charred utterly; the "Spaniards [estimated] their loss at twenty million of *piastres*."[591] In all, 856 "fine and commodious houses valued on an average at three thousand dollars each, were destroyed in that conflagration...."[592] Lost were most of the aging French colonial-era structures, noted for their raised construction, spacious galleries, and steep double-pitched roofs. That such structures are rarities in the French Quarter today speaks to the ferocity of the 1788 blaze.

"It would be difficult to depict the despair of the poor unfortunate persons whose properties had suffered from the fire," continued Soniat;

> [T]hese unhappy creatures, who, two hours before, enjoyed vast and commodious lodging with enough affluence to make one's life agreeable and easy, saw themselves and their children in a moment without resource. Some of them were obliged to take refuge in the woods, without necessary provisions and clothes. Some slept without cover under the broad canopy of the heavens.[593]

The disaster made news in the United States. "The misery of this place I shall not undertake to describe," wrote a New Orleanian in a letter published widely in American newspapers; "suffice it to tell you, that New-Orleans, which consisted of 1100 houses, was on Friday last, in the space of five hours, reduced by conflagration to 200.... [F]ew merchandize, household furniture, or clothing have been saved."[594]

Civic response to the disaster testifies to the common thread of humanity bonding survivors with fellow citizens in such times. Governor Estevan Miro took action immediately after the flames died down and the sun set: he "opened his house to all who were seeking shelter,...dispensed succor to the distressed families, caused the royal store, which had escaped the flames, to be opened, and...distributed the provisions therein...."[595] The Spanish Cabildo convened on Monday and issued two plans of action, already under way: "First...to aid [fire victims] with daily rations of food, and to build a cottage of pickets for their urgent shelter...," and second, to allot seven thousand pesos toward the immediate repair of the jail.[596] With remarkable progressiveness, the city government then conducted a fact-finding mission "to carefully inquire through public opinion and close investigations the most essential points which must be brought to the knowledge of his Royal consideration...."[597] Reported Soniat:

> Recourse was had to the surrounding country for help; permits were given
> to vessels to bring goods from abroad; in short, the Governor administered
> as a good pater familas ["father of the family"] and distributed that which he
> had gathered in the Colony [for] his numerous people, and he succeeded in
> making their provisions last up to the arrival of the relief from Havana and
> St. Domingo.... [Yet] poverty stared them in the face, and these conditions
> brought all the inhabitants to a state of consternation, which was followed
> by the death of 1 / 6 of the citizens.[598]

Loans payable over ten years were offered for the poor to rebuild. Later in April, as the remains were cleared away, the Cabildo considered how to avoid such a catastrophe in the future. A philosophy of fighting fires prevailed over preventing them, as the authorities submitted a request for "four pumps...60 leather buckets...two hooks with a chain...rope...and six hooks with long wooden handles."

Governor Miro's leadership, Don Andres Almonester y Roxas' financial aid, liberalization of trade regulations, a construction boom, and expansion into the city's first faubourg (*Ste. Marie*, today's CBD) rendered New Orleans remarkably resilient following its near annihilation—though not as quickly as residents might have wished. Wrote one observer soon after the first anniversary, in a tone of frustration recognizable to post-Katrina New Orleanians,

> inhabitants...are making some exertions to repair the losses of last year by
> fire. It will nevertheless be a considerable time before the town again exhib-
> its as elegant an appearance as formerly. Abundance of temporary buildings,
> or mere sheds, [have] been lately erected for the sake of convenience on lots
> that formerly supported very handsome edifices. It is a common thing here
> at present for a man worth four or five thousand pieces of eight to live in a
> shed under which you would scarcely lodge your servants.[599]

New houses soon replaced those temporary sheds, generally exhibiting the same local typological and stylistic traditions of earlier decades. Serendipitously, one of the best surviving examples of that first generation of French Creole domestic architecture—"Madame John's Legacy" at 632 Dumaine Street—is a product of the post-fire Spanish colonial era (and even had an American builder). It arose quite literally on the ashes of the previous edifice and incorporated some of its components. Although hundreds of French colonial structures disappeared in the Good Friday Fire of 1788, the French colonial architectural *tradition* survived. This would not quite be the case after New Orleans' next great blaze.

Governor Miro was replaced by the equally capable Governor Hector de Carondelet in 1792. The many municipal "firsts" achieved during the Carondelet administration—the city's first theater, newspaper, police force, and navigation canal, to name some—occurred amid three hurricanes and two fires during 1792-94. The worst disaster happened on December 8, 1794, when boys playing in a Royal Street courtyard (a few parcels away from the origin of the 1788 fire) ignited a blaze which swept southwardly with autumn winds. The fire eventually

> reduced to ashes one third of the best buildings of the Capital city, the greatest part of the department stores and other shops and groceries, leaving a large number of families of the well to do class ... in need[,] and some of them completely ruined and all the inhabitants stricken with horror....[600]

The conflagration destroyed 212 structures throughout "the most improved and opulent part of that city,"[601] the upriver/riverside quadrant. Combined with the deprivations of five hurricanes, two earlier fires, and numerous floods since 1779, the latest loss was almost too much to bear. In a manner similar to post-Katrina circumstances, the city warned Spanish royals that, "in order to rebuild the city," and in light of "the emigration of several useful residents [to] countries less exposed to ... detrimental risks[;] great and extraordinary aid is indispensable, which we can only expect of the powerful hand of our August kind Monarch ... to grant the loan of 1,000,000 pesos which distributed amongst the owners of the houses burnt in the last fire, will permit them to rebuild...."

While a loan from the King would help the victims rebuild, the Cabildo moved aggressively to *prevent* future fires (rather than concentrating on fighting them) by clearing the cityscape of fire hazards. First to go: clusters of makeshift straw huts erected legally by victims of the 1788 fire, which had since been rented out to non-victims and fallen into disrepair. Next to be removed: two small houses near the Plaza de Armas, "filled with combustible material and with almost no separation from one another," a lesson learned during the 1788 fire. Finally, the repeated fire losses motivated Spanish administrators to look to their own building traditions to foster a more resilient urban environment. Unlike after the 1788 fire, the Cabildo stipulated that new houses funded with the King's loan "must be built of bricks and a flat roof or tile roof," in the Spanish tradition.[602] The new building codes began to transform the cityscape, as evidenced by this record from February 20, 1795:

> The Cabildo grants permission to ... open a [new] street ... on the sole condition that all houses built thereon be of brick with flat roofs, and that on the extreme end of each house, two doors shall be built with a balcony over each, in order that the symmetry of the city will not be disregarded.[603]

The Cabildo further detailed the new construction codes on October 9, 1795. "[I]n order to prevent fires in the future, similar to those [of] 1788 and during the last year," read the Deliberations,

> Attorney General Don Miguel Fortier…is of the opinion that in the future…two story houses of two apartments…should all be constructed of brick or lumber filled with brick between the upright posts, the posts to be covered with cement of at least one inch thick, covered with a flat roof of tile or brick.

Those codes transformed wood to brick, clapboard to stucco exteriors, steep roofs to flat roofs, and wooden shingles to tile ones. The Cabildo further stipulated

> That the wooden houses covered with the same material must not be of more than 30 feet deep including the galleries.

> That all houses…must precisely have their front facing the street, and nobody is allowed to build them with the rear or sides to the street…

Those stipulations eliminated setback distances and brought the buildings right up to the banquettes, in the style of a Spanish city. Concluded the Cabildo,

> [All] citizens must comply with these rules whenever they wish to construct a new building.[604]

Other Spanish features unrelated to fire safety, such as arched openings on the ground floor, pilasters on outside walls, balconies above the *banquettes*, and courtyards in the rear, accompanied the architectural transformation. Soon, the fenced gardens and wooden galleries of a French village gave way to the stuccoed walls and wrought-iron balconies of a Spanish city. Christian Schultz noticed the new cityscape during his 1808 visit: "The houses of the principal streets nearest the river," he wrote, "are built of brick covered with slate, tile, or a fire-proof composition."[605] French geographer Elisée Réclus reflected on the transformation during his 1853 visit, even as the old Spanish city evolved again to an American city:

> For a long time, all the houses of New Orleans were simple huts made of wood, [giving] the whole city…the appearance of a huge fairground. Today, the houses of the two main districts are for the most part built with brick and stone.[606]

Evidence of the Spanish architectural transformation abounds throughout the "French" Quarter today: about 740 extant structures exhibit a Spanish-influenced, locally adapted style which may be described as "second-generation Creole" (see *Architectural Geography, 1710s to 1810s*). In addition, twenty-five edifices—about one of every 100 buildings in the Quarter—exhibit the pure Spanish Colonial style mandated after the 1794 blaze. Geographically, they cluster within two blocks of the intersection of Toulouse and Royal streets—not coincidentally the same blocks obliterated by the two great fires. They are particularly concentrated on the 600 block of Chartres Street—within a spark's leap of the origins of both great conflagrations.[607]

"May Heaven Avert Another Such Catastrophe!"

The Mississippi River as a flood threat to New Orleans

The Mississippi threatened New Orleans with hazards even as it blessed it with resources. The river's natural dynamism—to humans, its unacceptable uncontrollability—endangered the river-dependent port city seasonally through spring flooding, occasionally through bank erosion, and potentially through channel jumps.

Under natural conditions, the Mississippi River inundates the deltaic plain in two ways. During most springs, high waters overtop the crest of the natural levee and send over it a thin sheet of water (overbank flooding) toward the backswamp. A plantation owner recollected in 1740 one such event: "…New Orleans in its beginning was frightful, the river at its height spread out all over the land, and there were two feet of water in all the houses which caused general sickness and death."[608]

Alternately, a weak spot in the natural levee occasionally erodes into a *crevasse* ("crack"), which allows river water to surge through a focused flow toward the backswamp. Sometimes overbank and crevasse flooding occur simultaneously.

A complete chronology of floods in New Orleans resists easy compilation, because no single agency kept consistent, detailed records until the late 1800s. According to one 1882 report, "partial inundations by the river" afflicted New Orleans in 1719, 1735, 1785, 1791, 1799, 1816, 1849, and 1862, while "partial inundations by Lake Pontchartrain or by this lake aided by the river"[609] occurred in 1831, 1837, 1846, possibly in 1853 and 1854-55, 1856, 1861, 1868, 1869, 1871, and 1881. Data on lake floods prior to 1830 were either lost or never recorded, but the source states that such floods were "much more numerous" than direct overbank river flooding, which became increasingly rare as levee construction improved.[610] Gould's *Fifty Years on the Mississippi* adds 1780 to the list of colonial-era crevasse floods; Kendall's *History of New Orleans* (1922) adds 1813 to the record of crevasse floods and 1844 as a lake flood; and a recent Army Corps source adds 1850, 1858, 1865, 1867, and 1874 to the list of flood years.[611] In 1890, high river water topped the levee in the French Quarter and, via an upriver crevasse, raised the level of the lake which thence flooded the lakeside marshes up to the Metairie Ridge. Another study found that the river reached flood stage at New Orleans (but did not necessarily inundate the city) once every 4.07 years on average, from 1871 to the 1930s.[612]

"*Crevasse[s]*, the name given to a fissure or breaking of the Levée," wrote John

Adems Paxton in 1823, "are occasioned [firstly by] the yielding of the Levée; and secondly, the sinking of the bank of the river…"[613] That latter phenomenon was also called *éboulis* or *éboulemens*, meaning landslides of the river bank, or land cave-ins.[614] The resultant deluges accounted for the city's worst historical natural disasters. "The waters rush" through a Mississippi crevasse, wrote one visitor in the early 1800s, "with indescribable impetuosity, with a noise like the roaring of a cataract, boiling and foaming, and bearing every thing before them. Like the breaking out of a fire in a town, it excites universal consternation."[615] Indeed, *crevasse* was as dreaded a word in nineteenth-century Louisiana parlance as *fire, hurricane,* or *yellow fever.*

On May 6, 1816, a weak spot in the levee on Barthelemy McCarty's plantation in present-day Carrollton opened up into a crevasse, inundating the backswamp to the rear flanks of the city five miles downriver. "One could travel in a skiff from the corner of Chartres and Canal streets to Dauphin," read one account, "down Dauphin to Bienville, down Bienville to Burgundy, thus to St. Louis Street, from St. Louis to Rampart, and so throughout the rear suburbs."[616] Even with this destructive hazard came a valued river-borne resource: "the receding water," noted one historian, "filled the low terrain with alluvial deposits enriching the soil as well as elevating the swamp sections."[617] That summer also proved to be unusually healthy for the population—only 651 deaths occurred in New Orleans in 1816, compared to 1,252 in 1815 and 1,772 in 1817—probably due to the massive unplanned spring cleaning of the filthy port city.[618]

Thirty-three years later, a levee deteriorated on Pierre Sauvé's sugar plantation in the present-day River Ridge section of Jefferson Parish. Starting May 3, 1849, river water widened the crevasse to 150 feet long and six feet deep, slowly filling the hydrological basin between the river's natural levee and the Metairie Ridge. The deluge surpassed the New Basin Canal on May 8, reached Rampart Street on May 15, and peaked on May 30-June 1 at the intersection of Bourbon and Canal Street.[619] A few days later, a *Daily Picayune* journalist described the view from the 185-foot-high cupola of the St. Charles Hotel:

> Far away to…Carrollton [and up to] the Sauvé crevasse, the surface of the country on the left bank of the Mississippi is one sheet of water, dotted in innumerable spots with houses… barns, out houses, lofty trees and brushwood…. The whole of the streets in the Second Municipality… are now so many vast water courses, or aquatic highways, issuing as it were from the bosom of the swamp…. Indeed, there is no place with which we can compare New Orleans…, that would give the absent traveller so correct an idea of its topographical features, as the city of Venice.[620]

Volunteers heroically plugged the crevasse on June 20, but not before 220 city blocks, 2,000 structures, and 12,000 residents were flooded up to seventeen miles away. Within a few days, water receded from most city streets (though not yet from the backswamp or rural Jefferson Parish) by draining out through the New Basin Canal and Bayou St. John, or evaporating in the summer sun. Displaced citizens returned home to clean up and rebuild; pavement, gutters, wharves, levees, and city structures bore enough damage to warrant a special tax levied to fund repairs. The deluge left behind a "deposit of alluvion [with] vegetable and animal matter," concerning officials that "an active agent of disease—the *materies morborum*" threatened the population. Only months earlier, cholera had killed 3,176 New Orleanians. But heavy rains washed away the filth, and as in 1816, death rates actually declined after the flood.[621]

Other crevasse floods followed, including four at Bonnet Carré over the subsequent three decades. The Sauvé Crevasse of 1849 ranked as the worst inundation in the city's history until Hurricane Katrina and the levee failures of 2005, and remains the city's worst river-originated deluge. Yet, for all the damage, only 10 percent of the citizenry suffered flooding, and very few perished—compared to over 60 percent flooded and well over a thousand dead during Katrina. Nineteenth-century New Orleans endured natural disasters by accommodating their effects through its urban form, principally by building sturdy, raised structures in high density on elevated ground. And frequent the disasters were.

> May Heaven avert from us such another catastrophe! May our citizens, in their foresight and their intelligence, devise some means of raising an insuperable barrier to another inundation from [the Mississippi River]![622]

So implored the *Daily Picayune* journalist covering the Sauvé flood. His prayer was answered within a few decades: increasingly sophisticated levee construction following the federalization of flood control (1879) gradually reduced the river's threat to New Orleans. When the Great Mississippi River Flood of 1927 inundated the lower Mississippi Valley, federal riverfront levees succeeded in sparing New Orleans what could have been a catastrophic deluge. That a crevasse was intentionally dynamited in the Caernarvon levee below New Orleans, to guarantee the safety of the prosperous city at the expense of poor, rural Plaquemines Parish, remains one of the most controversial incidents in local history. The 1927 flood revealed the imprudence of the long-standing "levees only" policy for river flood control, and demonstrated the need to *accommodate* the will of the river. Afterwards, spillways—which are essentially controlled crevasses—were installed at Bonnet Carré and Morganza, to serve as "safety valves" in times of extremely high water: seventeen feet above sea level in stage, or 1,250,000 cubic feet per second in volume.

The Mississippi River still potentially threatens New Orleans—the Bonnet Carré Spillway has been opened in 1937, 1945, 1950, 1973, 1975, 1979, 1983, 1997, and 2008—but not in over a century has Mississippi River water significantly impinged directly upon Orleans Parish. Yet the legacy of the old threat lingers, affecting urban growth, influencing residential settlement patterns, spooking investment, and diverting scarce resources.

Riverfront levees in the twentieth century form the single most influential man-made feature in the deltaic landscape, protecting people, creating value, and encouraging urban development even as they occasion subsidence and coastal erosion. They held fast when Hurricane Katrina's residual Cateogry-5 surge raised the river's stage from four feet to sixteen feet above sea level. The same cannot be said of the slender levees and floodwalls lining the city's intricate network of drainage and navigation canals. Their failure formed the proximate (though not the ultimate) cause of the city's worst flood ever.

Geographies of Nuisance and Risk

A brief history of the back-of-town

The spatial distributions of that which made urban living more or less pleasant, safe, and opportune—and thus more or less costly—drove the residential settlement patterns of class, race, ethnicity, and nativity. These patterns are discussed in *Populating the Landscape*; investigated here are the underlying geographies of nuisance, risk, and inconvenience—or, alternately, of amenity, safety, and convenience.[623]

Although urban development in mid-nineteenth-century New Orleans occurred almost entirely on the natural levee, not all sections of that feature were equally valued. Those closest to the river boasted transportation advantages and the highest, best-drained elevations, but suffered from the environmental nuisances associated with riverfronts: smelly wharves and stockyards, unsightly warehouses, vermin, noisy railroads, traffic and activity at all hours, not to mention rough characters, saloons, "caravanserai" (inns for transients), and batture squatters. While ideal for commercial use and replete with low-skilled employment opportunities, riverfront blocks ranked less desirable for residential living and attracted housing stock accordingly.

Those areas farthest from the Mississippi avoided those riverfront nuisances, but suffered a different set of challenges. Lowest in elevation and closest to the mosquito-infested, flood-prone swamp, the so-called back-of-town ranked the riskiest, cost the least, exhibited the most primitive urban infrastructure, and inspired the humblest housing stock. Well into the twentieth century, "the deep black morass," as one official city document called the old backswamp, was remembered as "New Orleans' deadliest enemy," and its recent drainage hailed as a courageous "conquest."[624]

The perception of a back-of-town dates to the city's earliest years, when the higher blocks "fronting" the river developed first while the lower blocks in the "back" remained muddy and less desirable. In the front were the *Place d'Armes* and important structures, such as the Company warehouse, the governor's house, the manager's office, the planned church, the *presbytère*, and the residences of prominent colonists. In the back were less-desired features such as the hospital, cemetery, animal-processing facilities, weedy lots, and the abodes of commoners. Wrote the governor of the colony in 1728, "There is already a place reserved for a market *in the front of the city* and enough remains *in the rear to establish slaughter-houses there*...."[625] Sixty years later, the Spanish Cabildo made a similar decision regarding the original below-ground city cemetery at St. Peter and Burgundy, which, decades earlier, marked the uninhabited rear flanks of the city but now abutted developed blocks:

> [Such] a great number of people [are] buried in the cemetery...that there is
> no room for any more; and at the time of digging the graves, the remains of
> other deceased are found, which not only cause annoyance but [also] bad
> odor, which due to the *proximity to the City* may be the cause for *infection
> [and] epidemics of disease*.... [Thus] it was deemed necessary to establish
> another cemetery, *located further from the City... "*[626]

St. Louis Cemetery was created shortly thereafter, forty yards from another
perceived nuisance—Charity Hospital—which too was unwanted in the front-of-
town. Still active today, the famous St. Louis #1 Cemetery is a relic of the old colonial-
era back-of-town.

The racial segregation of public recreation also exhibited a front/back urban
geography. Free people on Sundays strolled riverfront promenades and the landscaped
gardens and squares of the front-of-town; slaves also had the day off, but were relegated
elsewhere:

> [A] walk in the rear of the town will...astonish [your] bewildered imagi-
> nations with the sight of twenty different dancing groups of the wretched
> Africans, collected together to perform their *worship* after the manner of
> their country. They have their own national music, consisting...of a long
> kind of narrow drum of various sizes, from two to eight feet in length, three
> or four of which make a band. The principal dancers or leaders are dressed
> in a variety of wild and savage fashions, always ornamented with...the tails
> of the smaller wild beasts, and those who appeared most horrible always
> attracted the largest circle of company. These amusements continue until
> sunset, when one or two of the city patrole show themselves with their cut-
> lasses, and the crowds immediately disperse.[627]

Thus concluded a spring evening at Congo Square, 1808, a few blocks away
from the cemetery, the mortuary, and the swamp.

The front-of-town/back-of-town spatial perception permeates New Orleans
history and remains evident in the lexicon and "mental maps" of present-day inhabitants. Exact locations and dividing lines vary depending on the era and the speaker.
Around 1800 the back-of-town would have lay lakeside of roughly Rampart Street; two
or three generations later, around Claiborne or Broad. A 1915 article described the
"back of town [as] that section lying between Esplanade avenue and Tulane avenue and
Claiborne avenue to the cemeteries" on the Metairie/Gentilly Ridge[628] Most other usages of the term implied a nebulous region with soft boundaries. One thing was certain:
if you were in the back-of-town, you knew it. That which was malodorous, offensive,
unsightly, or dangerous usually gravitated to the back (or downriver); that which was
attractive and agreeable generally blossomed toward the front. Yet the back-of-town
afforded certain working-class opportunities, particularly in the antebellum era. Canal
excavation, truck farming, railroad construction, tanneries, slaughterhouses, and similar operations dependent on unskilled labor and cheap real estate, which could not be
found in the city center, abounded here.

Desirability of land in historic New Orleans also varied with distance from the urban core. Lack of mechanized transportation made life on the urban periphery inconvenient and thus cheap, even more so for the abundant supply of land there. Life in or near the city center, on the other hand, was convenient but scarce and therefore valuable. The pattern is an ancient one—"in many medieval cities in Europe, the city centres were inhabited by the well-to-do, while the outer districts were the areas for the poorer segments of the population"[629]—and it carried over to most New World cities.

Desirability of land thus varied (1) *directly* with distance from the river, (2) *directly* with distance from the backswamp, and (3) *indirectly* with distance from the city center. In other words, areas too close to the river, too close to the backswamp, or too far from the central city, all constituted less-desirable zones. On the other hand, areas that lay farthest from sources of nuisance and risk, *and* closest to amenities and opportunities—the middle of the natural levee near the inner city—commanded the highest prices and attracted the greatest investments in infrastructure and housing. These areas comprise the present-day historic neighborhoods extending from the central French Quarter through the Central Business District and Coliseum Square and (later, with streetcar service) into the Garden District and up St. Charles Avenue.

With the introduction of mechanized transportation and later automobiles, the factor of distance became less weighty in influencing land values; wealthy areas thus developed farther uptown, close to the attractive new amenities of Audubon Park and the new university campuses of Tulane and (later) Loyola. Streetcars allowed these moneyed citizens to commute to the inner city. Still, the factors of nuisance and risk kept the prosperous area restricted to the middle of the natural levee, within a few blocks of St. Charles Avenue (not coincidentally the route of the original streetcar line).

With augmented levees on the Mississippi River and Lake Pontchartrain, plus a new municipal drainage system pumping out impounded swamp water, the ancient nuisances and risks of the backswamp lost their importance in the minds of early-1900s New Orleanians. Confident that technology had "fixed" this geographical problem, thousands of mostly white middle-class residents departed their historical front-of-town roost and "leapfrogged" over the mostly black back-of-town, settling in new whites-only subdivisions in Lakeview and Gentilly (see *"Two Centuries of Paradox"* and *The White Teapot*). After the Civil Rights Movement, many black families did the same, settling mostly in the modern Orleans Parish subdivisions east of City Park and eventually New Orleans East. The old front-of-town/back-of-town perception weakened, but it did not disappear entirely because those earlier geographies of nuisance and risk left behind an assortment of poor, troubled neighborhoods.

In addition to the front/back dimension to its urban geography, New Orleans also revolved around a riverine "up"-and-"down" axis. The inclination to keep the water source pure (relatively speaking) meant that objectionable operations tended to gravitate not only backward, but downriver, toward what is now the Lower Ninth Ward (see *How the Poor Third Became the Lower Ninth*). It was not by chance that the odious business of stocking and slaughtering animals ended up in the city's lowermost corner, after the state legislature mandated the consolidation of butchering activity in 1869. Nor was it a coincidence that the city's sewerage treatment plant ended up in back-of-town quadrant of the lowermost zone. That engineers sited the Industrial Canal in the Ninth Ward can also be partially attributed to the fact that it lay below the city proper and away from its more desirable sections. Slaughterhouses, railroad yards, canals, sewerage plants, petrochemical industries, and the like tended to get shoved downstream, where they deflated property values, drove away moneyed citizens, and attracted those who had to settle for less. This helps explain why the downriver half of the metropolis (downtown New Orleans and St. Bernard Parish) has always been poorer, in the aggregate, than the upper half (uptown New Orleans and Jefferson Parish)—just as the back-of-town ranks poorer than the front.

Perceptions of environmental safety that informed—and oftentimes misinformed—New Orleanians' residential settlement decisions were turned on their heads on August 29, 2005, when Hurricane Katrina reminded us that the old geographies of risk remained very real. Levees, drainage systems, and flood-control structures had in fact, we learned that day, only exacerbated the old risks; worse yet, they dangerously lured residents into the flood-prone areas and lulled them into complacency with a false sense of security.

Whatever the future of the flooded region, this much is certain: the geographies of nuisance and risk will continue to drive the human geography of New Orleans. One can only hope that, in the future, *perceived* levels of risk will match actual levels—and inspire people to settle out of harm's way.

The Great Storm of 1915

Why a big storm incurred relatively little damage

The hurricane that set the tone for early-twentieth-century New Orleans arrived fifty years before Betsy did the same for the late-twentieth-century metropolis, and ninety years before Katrina repeated the experience in the twenty-first century. Unnamed and uncategorized, the tempest became known locally as "the Great Storm of 1915."

Sailors first detected a tropical depression over the Lesser Antilles on September 22, only a month after a hurricane killed over 400 people in Galveston. A smooth arc-shaped track routed "the blow" (as newspaper writers called hurricanes in those days) between the Yucatan Peninsula and Cuba, with minimal land-induced weakening. By the time it leaned toward New Orleans, wind speeds topped 135 m.p.h.

An ominous "cirrus veil" clouded city skies Tuesday morning, September 28. The tense day ended with a "faint brick-dust" sunset; nighttime brought with it the system's outermost rainy feeder bands.[630] After making landfall over Grand Isle, the hurricane veered gently to the north northeast, positioning New Orleans in the storm's dreaded northeastern quadrant. By dawn on the twenty-ninth of September, winds in the city gusted at 40 m.p.h. and steadily increased. Lake Pontchatrain's waters swelled suddenly, in late morning, to five feet above normal—the highest recorded at the time—while coastal and gulf waters rose approximately fifteen to twenty feet. So abruptly did the tide rise that the last train through the eastern marshes, flagged down by desperate people seeking to evacuate, had to plow through violent surf to reach the city (see *Manuel's Dilemma*).

The surge overtopped the meager levees lining the lakeshore, adjoining outfall canals, the New Basin and Old Basin navigation canals, and Bayou St. John. "The over-flow from these sources, [plus] about 7¼ inches of rainfall, was a most discouraging feature of this day's development," wrote a Sewerage and Water Board engineer tasked with keeping the pumps operating.[631] Salt water filled the bottomlands from present-day Broadmoor to Lakeview (largely uninhabited at that time). "Over that portion of the city lying between the Old Basin Canal and Broadway and from Claiborne Avenue out to Lake Pontchartrain," wrote the famed forecaster Isaac Cline, "the water depth driven in by the storm ranged from 1 to 8 feet in depth."[632]

A bigger threat came from a crevasse (that old French term was still in use in this era) in the Florida Avenue rear protection levee, flooding sections behind St. Claude Avenue in the Seventh, Eighth, and Ninth wards. Meanwhile, the Mississippi River rose six feet above normal stage in uptown, and even higher in St. Bernard and Plaquemines parishes, where it spilled laterally over the riverfront levees and swept across the low country.

Winds blew to 86 m.p.h. at 5:10 p.m., with gusts easily topping 100 m.p.h. They then paused eerily and, around 6:35 p.m., reversed directions, as the eye passed twelve miles west of the city. A few hours later, a *Times-Picayune* reporter described "a peculiar lightening...flaring up in sheets not unlike the fire coming out of the mouths of serpents...."[633] The 300-mile-wide system proceeded northward along the western shore of Lake Pontchartrain, pummeling Tangipahoa and St. Tammany parishes even as their terrestrial surface robbed the system of energy. New Orleanians peered out their windows and surveyed their circumstances. "CITY CUT OFF FROM REST OF WORLD," read a worried headline in that evening's *Item*.[634] Nevertheless, the worst was over.

By Thursday morning, the sun shined over the Crescent City. Damage was extensive, mostly from wind. Wrote the *Times-Picayune* the day after,

> Numerous public buildings suffered and hundreds of homes were damaged severely, many being blown down. Scarcely a house in New Orleans escaped without a scratch. Several big churches seem to have been singled out as particular victims of the storm's fury. Department stores, hotels and other big buildings in the business district suffered. Street traffic was almost para-lyzed...and was rendered perilous by flying glass and debris...[635]

Over 25,000 structures experienced serious structural damage. Prominent landmarks seemed to suffer disproportionately: at least eleven major churches lost their steeples and adjoining towers; certain French Market pavilions were leveled; the Old French Opera House was severely damaged; and the famous St. Louis Hotel was so battered it was subsequently demolished. The deluge receded naturally everywhere except levee-encircled areas, where trapped water took four days to pump out via the recently installed drainage system. Damages exceeded $13 million region-wide, in unadjusted 1915 dollars, with roughly half occurring in New Orleans. At least 275 Louisianians perished. Within weeks of viewing the scientific data, the nation's top meteorologist described the storm as "the most intense hurricane of which we have record in history of the Mexican Gulf coast and probably in the United States."[636]

The marvel of the Great Storm of 1915 was not the extent of its damage, but its limit. " 'STORM PROOF!' *The Record Shows New Orleans*," crowed the *Item*'s editorial page the day after.[637] Indeed, the system arrived stronger and better positioned, compared to Hurricane Katrina in 2005, to devastate New Orleans utterly. Five reasons explain why it did not.

First, coastal wetlands spanned far more acreage and exhibited healthier conditions than they do today. An additional 2,000 square miles of marsh padded the populated regions of southern Louisiana in the early 1900s, acting as a buffer and absorber of gulf surges.

Second, no major modern navigation canals allowed gulf waters to penetrate the city's heart. The Industrial Canal was barely in planning stages; the Intracoastal Waterway did not yet exist; and the Mississippi River-Gulf Outlet Canal was not yet envisioned. No "funnel" existed in the eastern or southern marshes to allow the enemy to the heart of the fort. The extent of flooding that did occur happened in large part because of the two existing man-made navigation waterways, the New and Old Basin canals.

Third, a state-of-the-science municipal drainage system had just been installed to pump out standing water from within the bowl. That same system is now a century old.

Fourth, the drainage system, for all its effectiveness, had not yet had enough time to remove the water component from the soil body of the lakeside marshes. These areas, while slightly below sea level in some places in 1915, had not yet subsided nearly as deeply as they are today, after ninety additional years of sinkage. A less-deep bowl means shallower floodwaters.

Finally, urbanization of the lakeside marshes had barely begun by 1915; most New Orleanians remained on the higher ground closer to the Mississippi River. Rather than inhibiting the development of these areas, the Great Storm of 1915 paradoxically encouraged it, by inspiring what became the Lakefront Improvement Project (see "*Ornament to the City*") and other flood-control measures. This massive flood-protection project created new upraised land in an effort to protect the rapidly developing former marshland behind it. In the end, it demonstrated that, in coastal Louisiana and elsewhere, flood-control structures intended to protect people often end up drawing them into harm's way. Those very areas flooded severely during Hurricane Katrina, at a cost of hundreds of lives.

Manuel's Dilemma

Drama in the Rigolets during the Great Storm of 1915

Official records of historical hurricanes are replete with antiseptic meteorological data and generic descriptions of death and destruction. The searing first-hand experiences of everyday people usually went undocumented. But occasionally, often serendipitously, one comes across stories of the human dramas that play out during those apocalyptic moments. They serve to bind those long-gone lives with the region's latest generation of storm survivors, and perhaps teach lessons in need of learning. Manuel Marquez of the Rigolets tells one such story.

The Rigolets "land bridge," a marsh-impounded ridge created by an abandoned river distributary in extreme eastern Orleans Parish, is supremely vulnerable to gulf tempests. With enough warning, residents of this and other coastal marshes traditionally evacuated to the higher, levee-protected city of New Orleans when a hurricane approached.

Such a tropical system developed in the Caribbean during the last week of September 1915. Forecasting and communications as they were in that era, denizens of the Rigolets saw the odds in their favor and continued about their lives. But on Tuesday, September 28, reports from ships confirmed that the immense hurricane imminently threatened the Barataria and Terrebonne basins of southern Louisiana. New Orleans in general and the Rigolets in particular found themselves aligned with the system's dangerous northeastern quadrant. Feeder bands swirled over the metropolis by dusk.

Official warning of an unequivocal strike went out at 8:20 a.m. next morning from the Weather Bureau office of the famous hurricane forecaster Isaac M. Cline. A worried *Times-Picayune* reporter asked the chief about the fate of the Rigolets, where some acquaintances of his were staying at the Anglers' Club.[638]

"[You] had better telephone them at once[!]," admonished Cline, which the reporter did. Miraculously, the call went through—to Manuel Marquez, a fifty-one-year-old black Creole from the Seventh Ward who worked as the caretaker of the fishing lodge.[639] The reporter urged Manuel to gather all patrons and flag down the very next train, due at 10 a.m., for a last-minute evacuation to the city.

"[T]he train [will] not stop for [us]," Manuel countered, as if experienced in this rejection.

"[Then] put a cross tie on the track" and force them to stop!, pleaded the reporter.

"They will put me in jail," Manuel groused.

"You would be better off in jail than where you are now and for God's sake stop that train at all hazards and come to New Orleans[!]" shouted the reporter.[640]

Manuel had much to lose, the least of which were his job and responsibilities to the club members. His wife, sister, children, grandchildren, relatives, and friends, huddled nearby, also looked to him for salvation.[641]

Winds by this time surpassed 40 m.p.h., swelling the brackish waters of lakes Catherine, Borgne, and Pontchartrain to one, two, three feet above normal levels. Having squandered earlier evacuation opportunities and now seemingly out of options, "occupants of the Anglers' Club apparently considered it the wisest course to remain" in the coastal clubhouse.[642] Cline's interpretation of the members' decision differed: "absolute disregard of specific warnings and advice" to evacuate, he called it.[643]

Hope came in the form of the last train to New Orleans, the *Mobile Limited*, steaming through gusting surf along the Louisville & Nashville tracks from Alabama and the Mississippi Gulf Coast. Manuel flagged it down frantically, hoping for mercy but expecting to be bypassed. *"Put a cross tie on the track[!],"* he remembered the reporter saying. No need: the train, already filled with apprehensive passengers, screeched to a stop.

Manuel's salvation had arrived, but his kin and patrons remained scattered throughout the compound, hunkered down for safety. *Wait, wait!*, cried Manuel to the engineer as he raced away from the very train he worked so hard to summon. Anxious and bewildered faces gaped at him from the rain-splattered windows of the passenger cars, as he frantically ran off to seek his people.

Winds whipped up higher and wilder waves "with ever-increasing savageness,"[644] splashing salt water dangerously against the locomotive's hot boiler and greased pistols. Passengers hardly assured of their own survival grew agitated and then enraged at the seemingly endless delay. Every passing moment increased the odds that Manuel and his people would make it safely to the train, but decreased the chances that the train would ever arrive safely to the city. Consider the passengers' frenzied debate: At what point does the possibility of everyone surviving evaporate, leaving them to choose between *all* perishing, or *some* perishing? When the winds and surf suggest that point is about to pass, who among us would choose the former?

The passengers' dilemma pales in comparison to Manuel's. He could have boarded the train to save his own life, and, if circumstances permitted, his family's. But he convinced himself that all others could be saved if he were only granted a moment to gather and guide them to the train. Seemingly blocking out the fact that the passengers could easily trump his decision, off Manuel waded to search for his people. Who among us would not?

Colossal decisions—involving evacuating, relocating, hunkering down, giving up, resisting, conceding, fighting, accepting—confront citizens of New Orleans and southeastern Louisiana, oftentimes to the exasperated and impatient disbelief of Americans elsewhere. *Should we remain in eroding marshes and continue centuries of tradition, or end our way of life and move inland so that aggressive coastal restoration may commence? Should we maintain all low-lying, far-flung neighborhoods and trust that levees will protect us? Or should we concede these areas to nature and build only on higher ground? Should we try to save everyone, at the risk of losing everyone? Or should we ask some to sacrifice everything so that others may maintain something? Shall we strive toward the probable survival of half the society, or the possible survival of the entire society?* Manuel's dilemma, and that of the passengers, is Louisiana's dilemma.

Perhaps Manuel succeeded in finding some members of the group. Apparently he ran back to ensure the engineer would not move the locomotive before he gathered the others. But "the rising tide was jeopardizing the passengers on the train," Cline later wrote in his report, "which could not wait until the people could be collected from the houses. Manuel returned to his companions," and the train departed without them.[645]

History does not record the trip across the windswept marshes and surging Lake Borgne. We do know that "the last train in on the Louisville and Nashville [line] was the Mobile Limited, which reached the city at 11:50 o'clock a.m., [having gone] some distance…through water."[646] The passengers' decision to abandon their fellow citizens surely weighed heavily on them as their own fate played out. Some sense of guilt might have abated when, after departing the Anglers' Club, the passengers spotted a work train on a side track and a coal barge in a nearby canal, both of which eventually saved the lives of many stranded Rigolets denizens. Manuel and his people could have sought refuge there.[647]

What they in fact experienced late that afternoon was terrifying. Fierce surges fifteen to twenty feet high rendered the entire Rigolets marsh part of the Gulf of Mexico. Bridges and trestles along the Louisville and Nashville tracks were destroyed utterly. The "Anglers' Club…was literally splintered into kindling wood."[648] New Orleans itself suffered extensive wind damage and flooding.

When the Great Storm of 1915 had passed, Rigolets residents made their way back to their land. The physical environment endured the hurricane well; it might have even benefited, as gulf storms often deposit off-shore sediments upon coastal wetlands. Had the structures been built with appropriate strength and height, and had residents evacuated promptly, the hurricane would have represented a survivable inconvenience. Instead, it was a tragic disaster, to both the built environment and its humanity. Reported the *Time-Picayune* correspondent who telephoned Manuel the morning prior, "The survivors…were so distracted they did not know what to do with the bodies after they found them. Relatives of the dead were so downhearted and so "sick" of [this] place… they pleaded that the recovered bodies be buried elsewhere."[649]

But what of Manuel?

"[W]hen the storm was over," wrote Isaac Cline at the conclusion of his poignant scientific report, Manuel's "lifeless body, with 23 others of those who were in the club, were found strewn over the marshes." Among the dead were his wife, sister, at least two and possibly all five of his children plus four grandchildren, fellow employees, neighbors, and club members, whose own individual decisions collectively created Manuel's dilemma.

Hurricane Betsy

The unfinished business of the 1965 storm

In the late afternoon of August 26, 1965, a tropical depression formed 500 miles north of the South American nation of Surinam.[650] It grew to a tropical storm—the second of the season, named "Betsy"—as it moved northwestwardly over the Windward and Leeward islands, only to wobble and stall for two tense days north of Puerto Rico. Now a hurricane, the system slowly resumed a northwestward path on September 1, then stalled again 300 miles off the central Florida coast. Communities of the southeastern U.S. coast and island nations anxiously awaited the tempest's next move, while those in Miami and the Gulf Coast breathed easier. But on the night of September 5, Betsy wobbled southwardly, away from the East Coast, then darted straight west, striking between Miami and Key West in the wee hours of September 8. The system, sans any of its Atlantic indecisiveness, then swept northwestwardly across the Gulf of Mexico at an exceedingly fast clip of twenty knots. Given the forecasting technology of the time, Betsy's stunning bolt robbed coastal residents of precious hours needed for evacuation. Heroic efforts of individuals and local governments nevertheless aided 90 percent of the quarter-million people of the southeastern Louisiana coastal area to evacuate to shelters on higher ground.[651]

In metropolitan New Orleans, "evacuation" meant not the major metropolitan exodus practiced today, but micro-scale, intra-urban movement to sturdier structures such as old brick schoolhouses. With over 600,000 city residents (many without vehicles) and no modern interstates, a mass flight from the deltaic plain was neither possible, nor recommended, nor even envisioned. Most New Orleanians felt safe in the city and "rode out" the storm at home or in neighborhood schools or civic buildings; coastal residents evacuated *to* levee-protected New Orleans.

Betsy approached the southeastern Louisiana coast on what appeared to be, from New Orleans' perspective, a worst-case-scenario track. Radar systems based in the city first picked up the eye at 11:03 a.m. September 9; eleven hours later, Betsy made landfall directly over Grand Isle. The straight northwestward path, roughly parallel to the west bank of the lower Mississippi, meant the fiercest winds buffeted the Barataria Basin and the river towns of Venice, Buras, and Port Sulphur. Winds, swirling in from the north, peaked in Port Sulphur at 100 m.p.h. before the recorder failed; elsewhere they gusted to 140 and even 160 m.p.h. Areas east of the river saw only slightly weaker winds.

Betsy's low barometric pressure and winds lifted and pushed a dome of gulf water into southeastern Louisiana and coastal Mississippi. Coastal waters rose to 6.4 feet above mean sea level in Pascagoula, Mississippi; 8.6 feet in Biloxi; 10.7 feet in Gulfport; 10.6 feet at the Rigolets land bridge at the mouth of Lake Pontchartrain; 9.3 feet in the newly excavated Mississippi River-Gulf Outlet (MR-GO) Canal, five to seven feet at the mouth of the Mississippi, seven to nine feet in the lower Barataria Basin, and four feet at Morgan City. The swollen gulf backed the Mississippi River up upon itself, forcing water over the levees all along the river's lowermost fifty-three miles. In New Orleans proper, the river at the Carrollton Gauge rose from a normal late-summer stage of around three feet above sea level to 12.5 feet. Betsy's surge was, at the time, the highest ever recorded in the region, due in part to the sheer forward speed of the storm.

Hurricane Betsy pummeled New Orleans proper around midnight of Thursday-Friday, September 9-10, accompanied by 5.13 inches of rain falling over thirty hours. Winds in metropolitan New Orleans sustained at 75-85 m.p.h. and gusted to 110-125 m.p.h. Surge levels at the Seabrook and Paris Road bridges, which span the Industrial and Intracoastal Waterway/MR-GO canals, rose to six and ten feet.

After Betsy's weakening eye—roughly the size of Lake Pontchartrain—proceeded past Baton Rouge (which experienced 60-80 m.p.h. winds) at dawn Friday, it drifted up the Mississippi and Ohio river valleys and finally petered out in Ohio over the weekend.

Were an aerial image snapped as daylight broke on Friday, September 10, most of southeastern Louisiana—over 4,100 square miles over eleven parishes, from the Atchafalaya River to the Chandeleurs Islands and from Ponchatoula to South Pass— would have blended seamlessly with the Gulf of Mexico. Only the natural levees of the Mississippi River and Bayou Lafourche, plus the levee-protected western half of metropolitan New Orleans, remained dry. Those areas were home to the lion's share of the region's 1,171,800 people. Eastern regions were less fortunate: salt water inundated Plaquemines, St. Bernard, and eastern Orleans parishes, plus large expanses of mostly uninhabited zones of eight other coastal parishes. In all, 187,900 people, or 16 percent of the regional population, saw their homes flood. Depths region-wide varied by topographic elevation: populated portions of urbanized St. Bernard saw one to three feet of floodwater, while as-yet undeveloped lowlands saw seven to nine feet. Plaquemines and St. Bernard residents' homes inundated at the highest rates (96 and 61 percent of the population, respectively), while Orleans Parish had by far the most flood victims (141,600 out of 627,525, or nearly one of every four Orleanians.)[652] The disaster did not prevent President Lyndon B. Johnson from arriving directly into the flood zone on the day after Betsy to meet with Ninth Ward flood victims.

Flooding within New Orleans occurred mostly along—and on account of— three man-made navigation canals scoured into the eastern marshes during the previous five decades: the Industrial Canal, the Intracoastal Waterway (ICWW), and the adjoining Mississippi River-Gulf Outlet Canal (MR-GO), still under construction even as Betsy demonstrated its folly. Those waterways and their guide levees funneled wind-blown gulf waters into the heart of the metropolis. The surge penetrated five of the city's dozen or so hydrological sub-basins via levee-overtopping and levee-breaching, particularly along the west side of the Industrial Canal from Florida Boulevard and Claiborne Avenue. This sheet of water filled sections of the Seventh, Eighth, and Ninth wards lying within the hydrological sub-basin formed by the Gentilly Ridge, Esplanade Ridge, and natural levee of the Mississippi. These racially mixed back-of-town neighborhoods saw 6,350 homes and nearly 400 businesses flood, in places by as much as seven feet. The rising tide failed to surpass the Gentilly Ridge but nevertheless backed up the drainage canals that traverse that natural topographic crest, resulting in two to four feet of flooding in an all-white portion of Gentilly and the adjoining all-black neighborhood of Pontchartrain Park (opened nine years earlier as the city's first modern subdivision for African-American home-buyers). Over 200 homes and a dozen businesses were swamped in these two lakeside neighborhoods.

Overtopping of the ICWW and Industrial Canal levees accounted for the flooding of New Orleans East. At the time, most residential development there occupied the higher sections of Chef Menteur Highway and the lakeside Citrus and Little Woods enclaves along Hayne Boulevard, most of which were spared. Lower, mostly uninhabited areas ponded floodwaters at depths ranging from two to eight feet. The rural eastern marshes and St. Catherine community in the Rigolets, all unprotected by levees, witnessed fierce surges at the peak of the storm but did not suffer stagnating floods, because while no levees blocked water from coming in, neither did they prevent it from flowing out. About 1,330 homes and 140 businesses flooded by an average of three feet throughout the area east of the Industrial Canal and north of the ICWW.

Hardest hit of all was the Lower Ninth Ward. A series of Industrial Canal levee breaches along the Southern Railroad tracks, coupled with overtopping, deluged the poor, mostly black section of this neighborhood by three to five feet along St. Claude Avenue, and to nine feet along the back levee. Only the streets closest to the Mississippi River—present-day Holy Cross, a working-class, majority-white area at the time—evaded the flood. Severe flooding damaged or destroyed thousands of homes and hundreds of businesses throughout the Lower Ninth Ward, plus portions of Jackson Barracks. It would take over two weeks of pumping to remove the last of Betsy's surge from New Orleans.[653]

No floodwaters reached west of the Esplanade Ridge. The French Quarter, CBD, Uptown, Lakeview, urbanized Jefferson Parish, and the West Bank all endured only wind damage, though that too was extensive. Tens of thousands of homes suffered structural damage; historic churches lost steeples; old homes toppled by the score; and nineteenth-century roofing slates littered the streets of the French Quarter.

Hurricane Betsy and its flood claimed the lives of eighty-one Louisianians, injured 17,600, and caused $372 million 1965-value dollars in damage, about one-third in New Orleans proper. Its greatest cost, however, came in the form of unlearned lessons. As part of the Betsy-inspired Lake Pontchartrain and Vicinity Hurricane Protection Project, federal, state, and local efforts proceeded to build levees around the basins flooded by Betsy, expand residential developments into them, augment the very canals that ushered Betsy' surge inland, and build levees to standards that Betsy demonstrated to be obsolete.

Hurricane Katrina would reveal the folly of this effort forty years later, demonstrating a truism long recognized by hazard planners: the aftermath of one disaster becomes the prelude to the next.

Louisiana's Dilemma

Coastal erosion and challenges of reversing it

Louisiana has lost over 2,000 square miles of coastal wetlands—about one-third of the Louisiana deltaic plain—since the 1930s. Twenty-five to thirty-five square miles of marsh disappeared annually during the 1970s-80s, a pace of loss well over twenty times swifter than the Mississippi River took to build the wetlands in the previous 7,200 years. The rate slowed somewhat in the 1990s-2000s, not because the problem had been partially solved but because so little land was left to lose. Five interrelated factors drive coastal erosion.

First, the control of the Mississippi through the construction of artificial levees has starved the deltaic plain of annual deposits of replenishing freshwater and flood-borne sediments. Second, an extensive network of navigation, oil and gas, and drainage channels increased the extent of land/water interfaces and saltwater-intrusion routes, and thus opportunities for erosion and swamp die-off. Their attendant guide levees and spoil banks served to channelize storm surges and impound salt water. Third, soils drained of their water content, through municipal drainage or flood control, subside under their own weight (see *"Smile: Your House Is Sinking"*). Fourth, gulf waters are gradually rising, as global temperatures increase and ice sheets melt. Finally, the dying of coastal saltwater marsh grasses ("brown marsh"), destroyed by invasive nutria, salinity, or droughts, renders the dwindling land surface even more vulnerable to wind and water erosion. Geological faults and petroleum extraction may also play roles.

Human agency initiated these processes (some of which occur naturally to varying degrees) in the 1700s and 1800s, and accelerated them perilously in the 1900s with the emergence of modern river control, marsh reclamation, urban drainage, canal excavation, the petroleum industry, and fossil-fuel consumption. Debate rages in the scientific community as to whether levee constraint of the Mississippi, or the excavation of navigation, oil, and gas canals, weighs more heavily in the coastal-erosion equation. The stakes are high, because whichever factor proves more influential informs on who should foot the restoration bill. Most scientists agree that if current trends continue, the Louisiana deltaic plain will be mostly gulf water by the twenty-second century.

Coastal erosion makes New Orleans more vulnerable to hurricanes because approximately every 2.7 linear miles of wetland loss allows one extra vertical foot of seawater to surge inland in the face of a tropical storm. Some researchers put the ratio at one mile to one foot. The coastal land loss from hurricanes Katrina and Rita in 2005 totaled well over 200 square miles throughout southern Louisiana, or roughly ten years' worth of loss in two days. Worse yet, the loss was not proportionally distributed: nearly half came from the relatively small land area east of the lowermost Mississippi River, the buffer needed most for the protection of metropolitan New Orleans. In some areas, particularly the upper Breton Sound Basin around Lake Leary, nearly a half-century of erosion transpired in a matter of hours.

There is hope; this is a solvable problem. River diversions, siphons, crevasses, and "third deltas" must be deployed to re-create the historical tendency of the Mississippi to overflow and replenish the coastal wetlands with fresh water and sediment, without the deleterious effects of flooding. The Caernarvon (1991) and Davis Pond (2002) diversions have been successfully pushing back the saltwater wedge and creating some new land in the eroding wetlands. Caernarvon in particular serves the very area that suffered the most intense land loss during Katrina and Rita. The 2005 storms were not all bad for the coastal region: their surges mobilized offshore sediments and pushed them upon the wetlands, substantiating them in some areas.

Additional massive river diversions and uncontrolled crevasses are needed, but unfortunately, they will fall short of saving the coast. The reason why is alluded to in historical documents. Former French officer Soniat du Fossat reported in 1791 that, as the "extremely muddy Missouri" River joins the Mississippi, "the earthy substance contained in these waters" produces a "deposit ... about one-third of the volume of the water taken."[654] Christian Schultz wrote in 1810 that "the turbidness of the [Mississippi's] water is such as to prevent any thing being seen at a depth of six inches, [enough to] deposit a sediment of half an inch deep in a half pint tumbler..."[655] Joseph Holt Ingraham reported in 1835 that "a glass filled with [the Mississippi's] water appears to deposit in a short time a sediment nearly equal to one-twelfth of its bulk."[656] If one were to repeat these experiments today, a film of sediment immeasurably thin to the naked eye would settle to the bottom of the glass—revealing yet another very serious problem for the future of coastal Louisiana. Sediment levels in the river today are 60 to 80 percent lower than in historical times, because numerous dams and locks built upriver and on the sediment-bearing western tributaries since World War II have trapped vast quantities of the best suspended-sediment load (sand), while remaining particles spill out uselessly as bedload on the continental shelf. A levee-constrained river bearing less sediment means the river's land-building capability is handicapped even if diversions and crevasses are opened. To patch the shortfall, sediment-mining operations are needed locally to deliver this valuable resource from the river's bedload, or from offshore deposits, onto the fraying coastal wetlands. Dredging barges, siphons, diversions, and crevasses must be situated to disperse the sediments across the wetlands and fertilize them with the river's nutrient-rich fresh water.

Then there is the universal problem of global warming. While sea-level rise threatens levee-encircled New Orleans as it does all coastal cities, it does not neceessaily spell doom for the Louisiana coastal region on which New Orleans depends. Unlike other areas, Louisiana possesses a valuable tool to fight sea-level rise: the Mississippi River and its ability to build land. River diversions and sediment siphoning, if done at the requisite magnitude, can build up coastal marshes even upon rising seas. It's happened before: the entire Louisiana deltaic plain formed during a time of warming temperatures and rising seas. The current pace of rise, however, is troubling, as is the dearth of riverine sediments and the slow bureaucratic process behind major restoration projects.

Hurricanes Katrina and Rita convinced many scientists and managers that radical solutions are needed within the next generation if coastal Louisiana and New Orleans are to survive. Rerouting the Mississippi to create a new bird's foot delta in the Breton Sound, once the fantasy of extremists, is now recommended publicly by many experts.

Decisions of this magnitude may spell death for some of the very cultures and landscapes—namely in lower Plaquemines Parish—they are intended to save. Consider Louisiana's dilemma: What constitutes a culture worth saving? Worth sacrificing? How do we ask people who have lived sustainably off the land for generations to relocate, so that a city dweller may enjoy greater environmental security?

Then again, should we threaten the safety of a million people for the sake of a thousand?

"Smile: Your House Is Sinking"

Soil subsidence in the New Orleans metropolitan area

River-deposited sediments occupy a volume bloated by water content. If the water drains away, organic matter disintegrates and crevices open up, allowing particles to settle into the new air spaces and the soil body as a whole to become denser and more compact. The result: subsidence, "the lowering of the elevation of a land area in relation to sea level."[657] A natural process in a deltaic plain, subsidence is normally counterbalanced by incoming deposits of sediment-laden floodwaters, made at roughly the same pace. Deltaic regions maintain topographical equilibrium so long as the sustaining river does not meander away or otherwise cease to replenish its flanks.

Or so long as man does not intervene by constraining the river with artificial levees, which prevent inundation but also restrict new sedimentary deposits to the deltaic bank account. This is what has happened in southeastern Louisiana. New Orleans' topographic elevation is presently diminishing, in absolute terms and particularly in relation to sea level, which, in a conspiracy of factors partially of man's own doing, happens to be rising at increasing rates.

The prehistoric New Orleans landscape, unlike the cityscape today, lay *at* or *above* sea level; its lakeshore and eastern marshes communicated with saline water while interior ridges and natural levees rose five to fifteen feet above it. If any substantial areas lay below the level of the sea, they would inundate immediately to form tidal lagoons. Even as New Orleans developed, its urbanized surfaces remained almost entirely above sea level into the late nineteenth century. Period photographs of people recreating along the unleveed Lake Pontchartrain shore confirm this little-appreciated fact, as do nineteenth-century topographic maps and an 1853 account by visiting

French geographer Elisée Réclus:

> The districts far from the Mississippi are only a few centimeters above sea level, and people's homes are separated from alligator nests only by drainage pools of stagnant and always iridescent water.[658]

Twentieth-century levee and drainage manipulations subsequently allowed about 30 percent of the urbanized land surface to drop below sea level by 1935.[659] By century's end, that figure hovered around 50 percent; worse yet, those areas already below sea level had subsided further. An analysis of 1994 GPS elevation data indicates that the levee-protected terrestrial surfaces of Orleans Parish, from the Jefferson Parish line to the eastern hurricane-protection levees plus Algiers, are 53 percent at or above sea level, and 47 percent below. (The unprotected eastern marshes are mostly at or slightly above sea level.) Results are similar for the metropolitan area: circa-2000 LIDAR ("light detection and ranging" laser remote sensing technology) elevation data show that 51 percent of the terrestrial surface of the contiguous urbanized portions of Orleans, Jefferson, and St. Bernard parishes lie at or above sea level (with the highest neighborhoods ten to twelve feet above sea level), while 49 percent lies below sea level, in places to equivalent depths.[660] The "districts far from the Mississippi" that Elisée Réclus visited in 1853—probably today's Gentilly or Lakeview—now lie over eight feet below sea level in some areas.

Subsidence is not an arcane scientific preoccupation in New Orleans; it is a topic of everyday conversation. It became a household word during the oil-boom years of the 1970s, when rapid urbanization of recently drained Jefferson Parish resulted in widespread foundation and structural damage (including house explosions from severed gas lines) and landed the issue repeatedly in local news. Headlines tell the story of an unfurling environmental problem and a society grappling to adapt to it: "Rats, Nutria, Snakes, and Mosquitoes—Not to Mention Sinking Backyards" (1971), "Seeking Solutions to Kenner's Soil Subsidence" (1977), "Smile: Your House Is Sinking" (1977), "Soil Sinkage Plagues 84% of West Jeff" (1978), and "New Law Requires Pilings" (1979).[661]

Recent studies have calculated average subsidence rates of five to ten millimeters per year in and near the metropolis, and over double that rate at the bird's foot delta of the Mississippi.[662] Although its metropolitan effects—sunken cornerstones, buckled streets, cracked and leaning buildings—are visible to the eye, subsidence is difficult to measure precisely within cities because of its subtlety, complex causes, and high spatial variability. Factors including "geology, soils, hydrology, well locations and water withdrawal…levee locations, drainage pumping station sites…the history of drainage and settlement, application of fill and overburden, the bulk and density of buildings, [and] land use" all influence rates at any given spot.[663] Micro-scale subsidence measurements may thus vary widely with seemingly little rhyme or reason: some sites in the high-elevation CBD, for example, have paradoxically subsided faster in recent years than certain low-lying spots in Metairie and New Orleans East. However, the general rule is that higher-elevation lands with coarser soil particles and less organic matter subside at slower rates than low-lying former marshland with finer soil particles, higher water tables, more organic matter, and a more recent artificial-drainage history. Within the metro area, rates vary from two to three millimeters per year on the higher natural levees developed in historical times, to over ten millimeters annually in low-lying suburban subdivisions built on marsh soils and drained more recently.[664]

Comparison of circa-2000 LIDAR elevation data with nineteenth-century topographic maps helps capture the overriding trends and patterns of soil subsidence in New Orleans. Most historical efforts at elevation mapping were simply too limited, approximated, or inaccurate to be of any quantitative use today. There is, however, one exception: In 1893, the City Council directed the Engineering Committee of the Drainage Advisory Board to design a major pumping system to solve New Orleans' age-old drainage problem. Over the next two years, W. C. Kirkland and his staff, under the direction of city engineer L. W. Brown, ran hundreds of topographic surveys, tabulated the data, plotted one-foot contours on a detailed street network at a cartographic scale of one-inch-to-600-feet, and produced in 1895 ten large linen maps under the title *Topographical Map of New Orleans*.[665] The effort covered the heart of Orleans Parish, excluding rural areas east of Peoples Avenue and the Lower Coast of Algiers. Because the contours were based on the Cairo Datum, a now-obsolete cartographic standard calculated at the time as 21.26 feet above the mean level of the Gulf of Mexico, the Kirkland-Brown-D.A.B map shows elevations ranging from thirty-seven feet (16.74 above sea level) at the foot of Canal Street, to twenty feet (-1.26 below sea level) in present-day Mid-City. Adjusting for this vertical-datum difference allows for comparison to modern elevation data with respect to the levels of the sea which existed at the time. (Sea level has risen by roughly 4.7 inches since the late nineteenth century.[666])

The results are stunning (see map, "A Century of Soil Subsidence in New Orleans"). The natural levee of the Mississippi, measured from Claiborne Avenue to the river, subsided from an average of 5.1 feet above sea level in 1895 to 4.1 feet in 2000, while the Metaire/Gentilly/Esplanade ridge systems dropped from an average of two feet above sea level in 1895 to 0.76 feet in 2000. The basins (present-day Broadmoor and Mid-City, for example) between the river's natural levee and the ridge systems sunk from three inches below sea level in 1895 to 1.8 feet below sea level in 2000, while the former lakeside marshes now comprising neighborhoods such as Lakeview and Pontchartrain Park subsided from the level of the sea in 1895, to 4.4 below the sea on average in 2000. The mile immediately south of the original lakefront (present-day Robert E Lee Boulevard)—areas of finely textured, high-humus soils which once had a high water table—have subsided the most, by six to eight feet in one century.[667] Certain spots of urbanized New Orleans East (not included in this analysis) have dropped by nearly *double* that depth—in about *half* the time.

At the structural level, subsidence is an expensive nuisance. The mandated use of pilings for new construction in certain areas, the recommended use of flexible utility connections, and artificial fill by the truckload counter the worse effects of the phenomenon, but the problem itself may be unsolvable within urbanized areas. Homeowners respond by shoring up their raised houses with jacks and pilings, or, more desperately, watering the underlying soil with a garden hose during dry spells. Greater New Orleans is home to more shoring specialists per-capita than any other major American city; one, Abry Brothers, has been in business since the 1840s.

At the regional level, subsidence is deadly. Drainage-driven soil sinkage in collusion with levee construction transformed New Orleans' topography from a slightly above-sea-level plain interspersed with higher ridges, to a series of bowls half above and half below sea level, surrounded by high brims. When some of those brims breached during Hurricane Katrina, the water-trapping capacity of a hundred years' worth of soil subsidence helped turn a natural disaster into an unnatural catastrophe.

Hurricane Katrina

Paying the piper

I...awoke by the noise of the doors and windows violently agitated by the wind; it increased to the hurricane roar, lulled, and rose again, and blew with appalling force from the opposite point of the compass, rain at the same time deluging the city.

[Then] the sea rushed into Lake Pontchartrain [and] burst its banks, and the city was under water, the Levee only being dry.... Many houses were unroofed, and almost all damaged...many lives were lost...the unburied dead were laid in their coffins in the grave-yard, and floated about till the waters subsided[;] the stench was horrible....

[T]his led me to believe that one day this city, rapidly increasing as it is in wealth and consequence, will be swept into the Gulf of Mexico, if the Mississippi happen to rise [while] the south-east wind raise the sea.... [668]

—Scottish visitor Capt. James Edward Alexander,
New Orleans, September 1832

On Tuesday, August 23, 2005, tropical air fueled by unusually warm ocean water spiraled in an upward counterclockwise direction over the southeastern Bahamas. The westward-edging column of low pressure sucked increasing quantities of heated air into the system, growing it sufficiently for the National Hurricane Center to classify it as Tropical Depression 12, and by the next morning, as Tropical Storm Katrina. By late Thursday afternoon, Category-1 Hurricane Katrina approached the metropolis of southern Florida with 75 m.p.h. winds. The system and its torrential rains killed nine people in the north Miami area overnight, then, surviving the jaunt over the Florida peninsula, entered the Gulf of Mexico.

Although the 2005 hurricane season had been accurately predicted as an extraordinarily busy one, tropical activity had disarmingly abated during July and August, and most New Orleanians only passively took note of the seemingly weak and distant storm. But awaiting Katrina in the gulf was a gigantic source of storm fuel: a loop current of deeply layered warm water, pulsating in from the Caribbean between Cuba and the Yucatan and breaking off into eddies through the Gulf of Mexico before exiting into the Atlantic between Cuba and Florida. With sea surface temperatures around ninety degrees and more warmth below, a system that made it into the gulf at this particular time would strengthen dramatically without the reprieve of cooler sub-surface waters.

Computer models at first forecasted storm tracks up the Florida peninsula, then westward over the panhandle, then further westward to the Alabama border, where so many storms had landed during the recent ten-year surge in tropical activity. The farther west Katrina crept, the more energy it drew from the warm loop current, and the more seriously it threatened gulf coastal communities.

Yet as schools and offices closed down in New Orleans on Friday afternoon, most conversations and email communications concerned weekend plans and next week's meetings, not evacuations and possible closures, much less national calamity. It was not until that evening, by which time the forecast tracks started pointing to the Louisiana/Mississippi border and Governor Kathleen Blanco declared a state of emergency, that citywide attention turned to the heightening threat.

KATRINA PUTS END TO LULL;
STORM'S WESTWARD PATH PUTS N.O. ON EDGE
—*Times-Picayune* headline,
Saturday, August 27, 2005

With Katrina a strengthening Category-3 storm and the notoriously divergent computer models now all ominously concurring on a Louisiana landfall, the central Gulf Coast population finally mobilized on Saturday. Emergencies were declared at the state level in Mississippi and federal level in Louisiana, something rarely done before a disaster strikes. Officials activated the complex "contraflow" evacuation plan, allowing motorists to utilize incoming interstate lanes to flee the New Orleans metropolitan area. Many departed Saturday; more left Sunday, August 28, when the system strengthened to Category-4 and Category-5 levels within five hours.

KATRINA TAKES AIM
—*Times-Picayune* headline,
Sunday, August 28, 2005

By late Sunday morning, with Katrina's winds hitting 175 m.p.h., nearly all qualified observers were certain of a New Orleans-area landfall. Mayor C. Ray Nagin ordered a mandatory evacuation of the city, though no one seemed to know exactly what that meant and many could not comply even if they wanted to.

The evacuation window had all but closed by Sunday night, as the initial feeder bands whisked over the city; the only choices now were to "ride it out" at home or take refuge in the Superdome. Roughly 100,000 New Orleanians—one in every four to five—remained in the city, and of those, approximately 10,000 lined up outside the

Superdome, expecting at least a safe if uncomfortable night. A solemn and profoundly troubled air prevailed among the reporters and authorities on the local news stations that evening. No one could believe that the proverbial Big One, the topic of endless planning scenarios and stern authoritative admonitions, the butt of countless dooms-day jokes and glib clichés, was finally upon us, all within a weekend.

Overnight, Hurricane Katrina's low barometric pressure and high winds sucked up a dome of gulf water and blew it north- and northwestwardly into the Mississippi Gulf Coast and Louisiana deltaic plain. Under natural conditions, hundreds of square miles of wetlands would have absorbed or spurned the intruding tide. But a century of coastal erosion cost the region precious impedance, while a labyrinth of man-made canals served as pathways for the surge to penetrate inland. A "funnel" formed by two mid-twentieth-century navigation canals—the Intracoastal Waterway (ICWW) and the Mississippi River-Gulf Outlet (MR-GO) and their respective guide levees—allowed Katrina's surge to swell waters in the circa-1920 Industrial Canal transecting the very heart of the New Orleans metropolis.

GROUND ZERO
SUPERDOME BECOMES LAST RESORT
FOR THOUSANDS UNABLE TO LEAVE;
NEW ORLEANS BRACES FOR NIGHTMARE OF THE BIG ONE
—*Times-Picayune* headline,
Monday, August 29, 2005

At 4:30 a.m., August 29, with Hurricane Katrina a few miles offshore, canal water seeped through flood gates near Chef Menteur Highway. Minutes later, the tide in the funnel overwhelmed the guide levees of the MR-GO and rushed southward to within a few hundred feet of residential neighborhoods in the Lower Ninth Ward and St. Bernard Parish. The same thing happened around 6 a.m. to the guide levees along the Intracoastal Waterway to the north, and thirty minutes later, the surge inundated low-lying New Orleans East and its vast acreage of circa-1970s subdivisions.

Hurricane Katrina made landfall at 6:30 a.m. over Louisiana's Barataria Basin, between Grand Isle and the mouth of the Mississippi. The eye's center passed over the river towns of Empire and Buras, then the eastern St. Bernard Parish community of Hopedale, about twenty-five miles east of downtown New Orleans. The coiling mass of storm clouds spanned from central Louisiana to western Florida; the outermost feeder bands stretched from the Texas hill country to the Georgia coast, from the Yucatan to the Appalachians.

Although wind speeds had abated to Category-2 levels, Katrina's storm surge retained the momentum of the earlier Category-5 status. Gulf waters swelled ten to thirty feet above normal sea level, inundating 200 miles of coastline across four states. Lake Pontchartrain's waters swelled to almost nine feet above normal, while the Mississippi River, which gauged at a typically low late-summer stage of about four feet above sea level, rose to nearly sixteen feet and spilled over laterally in lower Plaquemines Parish.

In New Orleans, the front line of the unraveling drama was the Industrial Canal, where turbulent waters rose to twelve, thirteen, fourteen feet above normal level. Pressure built up upon layers of soft, organic marsh soils beneath the modest levees, while thin floodwalls anchored with insufficiently deep sheet pilings leaned landward with the weight of the water column. The first failure occurred at 6:50 a.m. on the western side of the canal, flooding the Florida Avenue corridor through the Upper Ninth, Eighth, Seventh, and Sixth wards. Then, at 7:45 a.m., a catastrophic failure on the eastern side of the Industrial Canal sent a torrent of water from a level of fourteen feet above sea level into adjacent blocks of the Lower Ninth Ward that lay as low as four feet below sea level. The violent rapids joined with other waters simultaneously overtopping the rear levee from the north, and a third source entering from the east via Bayou Bienvenue. By 8:30 a.m., nearly the entire Lower Ninth Ward of Orleans Parish plus Arabi, Chalmette, and Mereaux in adjacent St. Bernard Parish had drowned at a pace of ten feet of water within twenty minutes. Residents perished by the score.

The front line of the catastrophe then began to shift from the navigation-canal failures on the eastern edge of the metropolis to the slender drainage canals scoring the northern tier fronting Lake Pontchartrain. High seas in the brackish-water lake swelled their water levels and increased pressure on the canals' thin concrete walls and porous underlying marsh soils.

At 9:00 a.m., water began entering through a neglected low spot on the Orleans Avenue Canal west of City Park. Around the same time, small breaches opened in the London Avenue Canal east of the park, one of which widened at 9:30 and began to flood the low-lying sections of Gentilly. Then, at 9:45 a.m., a major failure occurred on the 17th Street Canal, violently inundating the prosperous, low-elevation subdivision of Lakeview. Within the next hour, another major breach opened on the London Avenue Canal.

By this time, Hurricane Katrina had made its second landfall near the mouth of the Pearl River along the Louisiana/Mississippi border. The Mississippi Gulf Coast towns of Waveland and Bay St. Louis, positioned in the northeastern quadrant of the track, bore the full strength of Katrina's 125+ mile-per-hour winds and twenty-nine-foot storm surge. Biloxi's surge measured the highest ever recorded in America. Neighborhoods within a half-mile of the beach were wiped off the face of the Earth within minutes. In New Orleans, winds peeled off the white surface coating of the Superdome and broke two six-foot holes in the roof, terrifying the thousands of frightened refugees within the darkened and sweltering interior. Denizens of higher ground who rode out the storm at home experienced the same moment-to-moment apprehension of winds rocking their houses and rattling roofs, windows, and doors. What none realized, of course, was that their fellow citizens on lower ground faced not only these same fierce gusts, but also deadly rising water.

The southern Mississippi landmass deprived Katrina of its warm-water fuel source, weakening the system to tropical-storm levels as it pushed inland, but not before it buffeted the southern half of the state as well as the eastern Florida parishes of Louisiana. Winds, now from a westerly direction, died down by late afternoon in New Orleans.

Many journalists, overly focused on Katrina' east-of-the-city track and diminishing intensity, mistakenly reported Monday afternoon that New Orleans, as the infamous cliché had it, "dodged the bullet." Many residents, evacuated and otherwise, went to bed prepared to return home, pick up the branches, fix the roof, and resume their lives. It was not until Tuesday that they learned a jolting new truth—one that, in fact, was as old as the city itself: the flood-protection and drainage system had *not* neutralized topography and hydrology; New Orleans' ancient geographies of risk, supposedly subjugated by technology a century ago, came rushing back to life. The various hydrological sub-basins comprising the New Orleans bowl were filling up.

CATASTROPHIC
STORM SURGE SWAMPS 9TH WARD, ST. BERNARD;
LAKEVIEW LEVEE BREACH
THREATENS TO INUNDATE CITY
—Times-Picayune headline,
Tuesday, August 30, 2005

Social unrest developed among the trapped, thirsty, hungry citizenry. Looting, sometimes out of genuine need for food and water, other times for opportunistic thievery or sheer vandalism, became so rampant that already overwhelmed police chiefs and politicians generally paid it lip service or ignored it entirely. Officials called for the immediate evacuation of the tens of thousands of people who remained in the city, but no mechanisms were in place to do so, nor were any immediately on the way. Crowds of the poorest citizens, which numbered about 10,000 in the Superdome Sunday night, swelled to as many as 45,000 at the damaged stadium and at the Morial Convention Center, both of which were completely unprepared for the crush. Scenes stereotypical of Haiti or Bangladesh, with all the ugliest of connotations, played out in downtown New Orleans and were broadcast worldwide. Elders, the infirm, and children suffered the most; some youths exploited the chaos, looting, brawling, and shooting at rescue workers.

UNDER WATER
LEVEE BREACH SWAMPS CITY FROM LAKE TO RIVER;
POPULATION URGED TO LEAVE; YEARS OF CLEANUP AHEAD
—Times-Picayune headline,
Wednesday, August 31, 2005

Efforts to plug the 17th Street Canal breach with helicopter-drops of sand failed utterly. Only when Lake Pontchatrain's high waters drained sufficiently back into the Gulf of Mexico on Wednesday and Thursday did water cease entering the city, allowing for the makeshift repair of the levees.

With Katrina's winds long gone and the floodwaters no longer rising, New Orleans now grappled with a third crisis: social disintegration. Police had to be called off search-and-rescue missions to control pillaging and chaos. Stranded crowds suffering deplorable conditions at the Superdome and later the Convention Center started making their way up exit ramps and onto interstates and bridges, in search of any alternative to the hell below. The line between victim and perpetrator blurred in the eyes of over-stressed authorities, occasionally leading to ugly confrontations and injustices. Buses to evacuate the desperate masses were few and slow in coming; the very first were able to depart for Houston on Wednesday. The shocking spectacle of a modern First World society coming apart at the seams, within the borders of the wealthiest and most powerful nation on Earth, was broadcast as lead story worldwide, repeatedly, for days and weeks.

HITTING BOTTOM
THE WATER HAS FINALLY STOPPED POURING IN BUT IT
COULD BE OCTOBER BEFORE THE CITY DRIES OUT
—*Times-Picayune* headline,
Thursday, September 1, 2005

Crises begin to multiply and intensify; what started as a disaster that turned into catastrophe was now starting to look like an apocalypse. Bandits and authorities engaged in shoot-outs from streets and rooftops. Gas bubbled up from floodwaters and burned like a scene in hell. Fires broke out citywide, which firefighters could neither reach nor douse. An anguished Mayor Nagin, his city at the darkest moment of its history and seemingly abandoned by the nation, issued a now-famous "desperate S.O.S." to the world via an emotional interview on WWL radio. "Don't tell me 40,000 people are coming here," he raged; "they're not here. It's too doggone late. Now get off your asses and do something, and let's fix the biggest goddamn crisis in the history of this country!" Federal responses in the form of armed troops, supplies, buses, medical attention, and most importantly, communication and coordination, finally began to trickle in late Thursday. It would take a full two to three days before they could stabilize the degenerative human conditions in the ravaged city (80 percent of which was under water), and evacuate the stranded to Houston or elsewhere.

"HELP US, PLEASE"
AFTER THE DISASTER,
CHAOS AND LAWLESSNESS RULE THE STREETS
—*Times-Picayune* headline,
Friday, September 2, 2005

By this time, pundits and the national press started to remark openly about what had been silently obvious to all viewers: the vast majority of the people stuck in the cauldron of the calamity were poor and black. A national conversation, conducted in tones ranging from cautious explanation to righteous indignation, ensued about race, poverty, history, and New Orleans society. The disaster-turned-catastrophe-turned-apocalypse was now becoming a troubling commentary about America.

FIRST WATER, NOW FIRE
BLAZES TURN PARTS OF BESIEGED CITY
INTO AN INFERNO
—*Times-Picayune* headline,
Saturday, September 3, 2005

The "lost September" of 2005 will be remembered by New Orleanians, scattered nationwide and humiliatingly dependent on the kindness of strangers, as among the most difficult times of their lives. Unknowns haunted every aspect of life, from food, clothing, and shelter in the near term, to the whereabouts of loved ones, to housing, finances, education, and employment in the long term. Backdropping this angst was the greatest unknown of all: the very survival of the metropolis. Once among the most diverse and colorful assemblages of humanity on the continent, regularly predicted to rank among the world's great cities, New Orleans in September 2005 stewed in its own filth, empty, broken, moldy, and silent.

HELP AT LAST
AFTER FIVE DAYS, THOUSANDS OF ANGUISHED STORM
VICTIMS FINALLY HAVE A REASON TO HOPE
—*Times-Picayune* headline,
Sunday, September 4, 2005

Restoring the Landscape

Time to move to higher ground.

—Timothy Kusky, September 2005

If you plan on shrinkage,
shrinkage is what you'll get.

—John Beckman, December 2005

Autumn in New Orleans

Heady days in troubled times

Only about one in four New Orleanians reinhabited their homes in the months following the Hurricane Katrina levee-failure catastrophe. For all the tragedy and uncertainty, life in New Orleans during that poignant and heady autumn of 2005 proved extraordinary.[669]

As the first cool fronts mercifully tempered that year's hyperactive hurricane season, citizens finally had a chance to assess how shockingly their city had changed. Beyond the vast physical wreckage, the society had transformed demographically and economically: once predominantly African-American and working-class or poor, residents were now more likely to be white, better-educated, and professional. Men outnumbered women, elders numbered few, children were practically non-existent, and transient laborers mostly from Latin America seemingly materialized out of nowhere, toiling off-the-books from dawn to dusk. Most schools remained closed. Violent crime, once pervasive, had disappeared almost entirely as its perpetrators, drawn disproportionately from the social classes affected most fundamentally by the catastrophe, remained evacuated. Military Humvees filled with M-16-toting soldiers, many fresh from combat in Iraq or Afghanistan, solemnly patrolled streets and enforced curfews — upon American citizens, in an American city.

At once reeling and resilient, the reconvening society exhibited the qualities of a bustling frontier village crossed with a dysfunctional Third World city. While mold and silence enveloped vast acreages of flooded ruins, higher areas buzzed with the sounds of saws and hammers. Locals reclaimed the once-touristy French Quarter as a place of importance, where one could conduct business, bank, worship, convene, eat, shop for groceries, recreate, and reside (albeit temporarily). Magazine Street became the "village's" bustling new main street, with 16 percent of its businesses reopening within six weeks of the storm and over 90 percent by Christmas.[670] "Welcome Home" banners draped from eager storefronts; proclamations of perseverance shouted from billboards; scornful graffiti rebuked FEMA and the Army Corps of Engineers; and placards offering house-gutting, shoring, roof repair, and legal services ("Saw Levee Breach? Call Us Now!") cluttered intersections to such a degree that local governments banned them for public safety. Patrons of local restaurants ordered staples off paper menus for cash only, waited patiently on short staffs, and took it in stride when blackouts interrupted their dinners. Housing, and thus labor, were scarce, driving up both rent and wages; immigrant laborers had no problem finding work but were forced to sleep in cars and tents for lack of affordable apartments. Flakey utilities, closed service stations, limited hours at scarce grocery stores, picked-over shelves, and other instabilities turned mundane errands into achievements and gave American citizens a sampling of how much of humanity lives.

Those fortunate enough to return home seemed to realize the history they were both living and making, and moved about with a sense of purpose. Human interaction was electric: emotional reunions erupted in crowded coffee shops, which, along with restaurants and churches, served as important nodes of social and civic engagement. Conversations began with *"So how'd you make out?!,"* continued with war stories and reconstruction visions, and ended with *"Stay safe!"* Strangers sitting at adjacent tables joined in conversations and debates, and left with exchanged phone numbers and email addresses. Patrons pecked away at wireless-enabled laptops—the unsung technological heroes of post-Katrina New Orleans—to reestablish social, educational, and professional networks or fight with insurance adjusters and FEMA. Office-less office workers convened in public spaces to strategize for their organizations' survival, but adjourned promptly at 4 p.m. to shop for food before understaffed grocery stores closed for the evening. Every story of determination, courage, and perseverance was matched by one of financial troubles, FEMA red tape, insurance grievances, excessive drinking, or stressed marital relations. Everyone, it seemed, dropped Dickens lines: *a tale of two cities… best of times, worst of times…* .

Best of times? In some strange ways, it was. Citizens were intensely engaged with each other toward overcoming tragedy and solving mutual problems. They worried about their neighbors and established new bonds with former strangers. Of course, those who lived in that *other* city, and who were suffering the *worst of times,* were largely absent from the inspiring postdiluvian tableau. Their stories played out beyond Orleans Parish limits. What passed for good news in their frozen-in-time neighborhoods were the moldy piles of personal possessions heaped unceremoniously in front of gutted houses—a sign, at the very least, of life.

Each dawn during the autumn of 2005 presented exasperating, unpredictable, high-stakes adventures through unchartered waters, and everyone knew only one source could reliably guide the way: a fresh copy of *Times-Picayune.* The venerable daily, long a target of local adoration as well as disdain, was now everyone's darling. It heroically covered the apocalypse first-hand ("We Publish Come Hell AND High Water") and reported on the recovery with journalistic objectivity blended with proactive investigation and steadfast demands for accountability. Citizens purchased "the T-P" at vending machines (home delivery was a rare luxury) or navigated the newspaper's Byzantine web site, and devoured the latest news like the figure in Richard Woodville's *War News from Mexico.*

The steady stream of new debates and dilemmas seemed to make everyone in New Orleans a policy-wonk, a disaster expert, a geographer, and above all, an urban planner. Most controversial of all was the so-called "footprint" question: Should the entire city come back? Or should the city redraw its urban footprint, permitting rebuilding on higher ground while allowing low-lying subdivisions to return to nature? If so, what methodology should be used to determine where that "build/no-build line" gets drawn?

A Proposed Rebuilding Methodology

Balancing urban values when you can't have it all

Note: An edited version of the following proposal appeared as a guest editorial in the Times-Pica-*yune* on November 13, 2005, during a time of passionate public debate about the reconfiguration of *the postdiluvian city. I previously presented it to the Bring New Orleans Back Commission, the City Planning Commission, and other forums; in 2006, it was published in the* Journal for Architectural Education. *Although it was never adopted (see next reading,* The Great Footprint Debate*), the proposed methodology—described as the first publicly proposed plan for determining the safest areas to rebuild[671]—helped frame the public discourse on what was at stake. It appears here in its original form.*

The number of commissions, panels, symposia, and workshops convened recently to discuss the rebuilding of New Orleans is exceeded only by the number of proposals offered on how to do it. Should certain neighborhoods be demolished? Should they be rebuilt? If so, how? What if residents want to return, but engineers recommend against it? What if the housing stock is severely damaged, but historically and architecturally significant?

Every New Orleanian, from layperson to professional, has ideas on how to resolve these colossal problems. Most are well worth discussing, and many are downright compelling. What has been lacking is a sound methodology through which these ideas may be passed, to ensure in a *fair, consistent,* and *repeatable* manner, that all stakeholders and values weigh in toward making the best decisions, and applying them to the right places.

As a geographer and long-time New Orleans historical researcher, I offer the following straightforward rebuilding methodology. It does not address important engineering issues such as levee reinforcement, sea wall installation, canal closures, or coastal restoration, but rather the mending of the city's urban fabric. The methodology is based on one overriding principle—*that the best decisions are based on solid, scientific data rather than emotions or politics*—and tries to balance four fundamental (and sometimes conflicting) values:

1. That all New Orleanians have the right to return to their city, and if at all possible, to their neighborhoods and homes;
2. That homes be structurally safe to re-inhabit;
3. That the historical and architectural character of the neighborhoods be maintained to the utmost degree possible; and
4. That the neighborhoods be environmentally and geographically as safe as possible from future floods, contaminants, and other threats.

Here it is:

Step 1. Determine Who Wants to Return, and to Where—Conduct a scientific survey of residents (both returned and evacuated) regarding their intent to return and remain in New Orleans. Record the respondents' pre-Katrina addresses, and map out the results by census tract. Code to red those with return rates of under 25 percent; code to yellow those with return rates of 25-50 percent, and code to green those with return rates of 50-100 percent.

Step 2. Determine Structural Safety—Conduct an engineering survey of all residential structures regarding their physical damage and salvageability, and map the results by census tract. Code to red those with over 75-percent condemnation rates, yellow those with 50- to 75-percent condemnation, and green those with under 50 percent condemnation.

Step 3. Determine Historical/Architectural Significance—Conduct a historical/architectural survey of all structures, and map the results by census tract. Code to red those deemed to be historically/architecturally less significant; code to yellow those deemed fairly significant, and code to green those deemed highly significant.

Step 4.   Determine Environmental Safety—Conduct a survey of elevation, vulnerability to flooding, subsidence, and environmental/human health conditions. Code to red those determined to be well below sea level and highly vulnerable or contaminated; yellow for those near sea level and somewhat vulnerable; and green those above sea level and relatively safe.

Step 5.   Tabulate Data—Take the results from all four surveys and map out the patterns. Some areas will be coded all or mostly green; some will be all or mostly red; and some will be mixed. Below are a set of potential recommendations for the most likely combinations:

For those tracts coded "Green" in all four surveys:
- These are safe, historic areas to which residents want to return. They will rebound on their own. The city should re-zone certain blocks to allow for intensified residential development and accommodate a higher population density.
- "New Urbanism," using traditional building styles and typologies (and recycled historical building materials), plus a healthy mix of modernism and new ideas, should be encouraged to fill open lots and mend the historical urban fabric.
- Historical structures from devastated areas should be moved here, whenever possible.
- Residents should be involved in all zoning and design decisions.

For those tracts coded "Red" in all four surveys:
- These are dangerous, heavily damaged, non-historic areas to which residents mostly do not want to return. Sad as it is for those few who do, it is not worth

the tremendous societal effort to rebuild in these unsafe areas. They should be bought out, cleared, and returned to forest, to serve as (1) flood-retention areas, (2) green space and wildlife habitat, and (3) Katrina memorial parks. Some may be used for appropriate commerce or industry, possibly as tax-free zones.

- Former residents of these areas who desire to return should have "first crack" at renting or buying parcels in nearby areas.
- Selected houses that survived in reasonable condition should be moved to other areas, to preserve their place in the architectural record.

For those tracts coded "Yellow" or "Green" in the Resident-Return Survey, but "Red" in all other surveys:

- The neighborhood should be cleared and then rebuilt, simply because a significant number of residents demand it.
- Experts and community representatives should meet and agree on new construction styles, designs, and typologies.
- All new structures should be raised on piers and reinforced for maximum flood and wind protection. Those few salvageable homes should be saved, to preserve architecture representation.
- Old street networks and names should be maintained in their entirety, but the lowest blocks should be reserved for green space and parks.

For those tracts coded "Yellow" or "Green" in the Architectural/Historical Survey but "Red" in all other surveys:

- The neighborhood should be saved at all costs, regardless of other factors. Historically and architecturally significant neighborhoods are absolutely critical to maintaining the city's character and tourism economy. Tax credits and other mechanisms should be established to encourage restoration.

Such a methodology offers numerous benefits. It respects and balances four fundamental values. It is easily communicable to the public. It provides a citable, accountable basis for difficult and controversial decisions. It relies on science and engineering, but not at the expense of humanistic, historical, and aesthetic values. The methodology's details, percentages, and proposed recommendations are all subject to rigorous debate. Perhaps the survey data should be aggregated by blocks, or by the seventy-odd official neighborhoods boundaries, rather than by census tracts. Certain elements are admittedly subjective, time-consuming, costly, susceptible to abuse, and overly simplistic. I offer this "road map" not as *the* methodology, but merely in the hope of convincing the powers-that-be of the need for *a* methodology.

The Great Footprint Debate

The fight for the fate of the flooded region, 2005-2006

High-stakes concerns about flood protection, soil contamination, health, education, residents' right to return, economic recovery, coastal restoration, and other issues drove energized public discourse in the months following Hurricane Katrina.[672]
In preparation, Mayor C. Ray Nagin formed, on September 30, 2005, the Bring New
Orleans Back (BNOB) Commission, inside what the *New York Times* described as
"the heavily fortified Sheraton Hotel on Canal Street, a building surrounded almost
constantly by cleanup crews as well as beefy private security guards armed with weapons."[673] That hotel, as well as the First Baptist Church in one of the few unflooded sections of Lakeview, would host scores of public meetings attended by thousands of concerned citizens in the upcoming months.

Committees and sub-committees tackled a wide range of topics, but one
topped the list and inspired the most passionate debate: Should the city's urban footprint, particularly its twentieth-century sprawl into low-lying areas adjacent to surge-
prone water bodies, be "shrunk" to keep people out of harm's way? Or should the entire footprint "come back," in the understanding that federal levee failure, not nature,
ultimately caused the deluge? That fundamental dilemma fell under the domain of the
BNOB's Urban Planning Committee.

As a geographer and long-time New Orleans researcher, I pondered the footprint question and sketched out a methodology to try to answer it (see previous reading). The proposal involved measuring four important variables—residents' desire to
return, structural safety, historical and architectural significance, and environmental and
geographical safety—and mapping out the results, to inform decisions on neighborhoods' futures. Encouraged by a stranger in a coffee-shop conversation—post-Katrina
civic engagement in its rawest form—I contributed the proposal to the email circuit. It
made its way to the chairman of the BNOB Commission, which yielded an invitation
to present it to the Urban Planning Committee and the City Planning Commission,
and, eventually, through a guest editorial in the *Times-Picayune*. The essay appeared
precisely as representatives from the Urban Land Institute (ULI) arrived in town to
advise the BNOB Commission on, among other things, the footprint issue.

I later learned that ULI members "hotly debated"[674] the proposed methodology, but decided not to endorse it, because of the difficulty of measuring the first variable
(desire to return). The proposal did, they told me, help frame the footprint question
as a balancing act between undeniable scientific realities on one hand, and cherished
cultural and humanistic values on the other. In other words, a classic dilemma.

Subsequent public meetings with capacity crowds and long lines of testifiers
indicated that the balancing act weighed heavily on everyone's mind. "In a city that has

seen a resurgence of civic activism since" Katrina, wrote the *Times-Picayune*,

> more than 200 people attended the [ULI] meeting to voice their opinions about what shape New Orleans should take in the future. The resounding refrain: Learn from our history.
>
> Many residents told the 37-member Urban Land Institute panel to use the original footprint of the city—along the Mississippi river and its high ridges—as a guide for land use.[675]

Those 200 people, however, mostly resided on those same "high ridges" they recommended for prioritization. Residents of low-lying areas, which mostly flooded, numbered few at the meeting, but nevertheless managed to engage through their political representatives, the Internet, and commuting. Their stance (shared by many in higher areas) was firm: the entire city will return; the footprint will remain precisely as before the storm.

When the ULI finally issued its recommendations to the BNOB Commission—via a long PowerPoint presentation that was at once wordy and carefully worded—it gently advocated footprint shrinkage through the allocation of recovery resources first to the highest and least-damaged areas, and only later to the depopulated flooded region. The news hit the front page of the *Times-Picayune* in the form of an intentionally confusing map of three purple-shaded "investment zones," in which "Investment Zone A," despite its optimistic label, was recommended for, at best, delayed rebuilding, and possibly for conversion to green space.[676]

The wordsmithing and mapsmithing fooled no one. "Don't Write Us Off, Residents Warn; Urban Land Institute Report Takes a Beating," scowled the headlines after the recommendations sunk in. The article continued,

> Elected officials and residents from New Orleans' hardest-hit areas on Monday responded with skepticism and, at times, outright hostility to a controversial proposal to eliminate their neighborhoods from post-Katrina rebuilding efforts.
>
> Even Mayor Ray Nagin...said he is reserving judgment on [whether] to abandon [some] lowest-lying ground.... During the meeting, Nagin reiterated his intention to ultimately "rebuild all of New Orleans."
>
> [City Council member Cynthia] Willard Lewis spoke with particular disdain for ULI's "color-coded maps" which divide the city into three "investment zones:" areas to be rehabilitated immediately, areas to be developed partially, or areas to be re-evaluated as potential sites for mass buyouts and future green space. Those maps, she said, are "causing people to lose hope," and others to stay away.[677]

Indicating the reductionist power of maps—a reoccurring theme in the footprint debate—another local politician, "noting that she was wearing a pink blouse... said sarcastically that she should have worn purple, the map color used by ULI for sections of the city that suffered the worst flood damage."[678]

Mayor Nagin found himself in a dilemma of his own, since the ULI offered its advice specifically for the benefit of his BNOB Commission. He assured agitated citizens that "once the recommendations are finalized … it will be up to the commission members and the community to 'evaluate it, kick the tires, say we like this and we don't like this'…."[679]

Kick it they did. The ULI report ratcheted up civic engagement in postdiluvian New Orleans markedly. It, as well as similar consultation from the Philadelphia-based design firm Wallace, Roberts & Todd (WRT), became gist for further rounds of highly attended and increasingly polemical BNOB meetings during December 2005 and January 2006.

Finally, on January 11, 2006, the Urban Planning Committee of the BNOB Commission unveiled its final recommendations. Like the ULI, the group (sometimes referred to as the Land Use Committee) communicated its findings again through a hefty PowerPoint presentation, rather than traditional literary methods. Entitled *Action Plan for New Orleans: The New American City*, the sixty-nine-page presentation's dizzying array of proclamations, factoids, bulletized lists, graphics and platitudes seemed eager to placate all sides while sacrificing lucidity in the process. Audience members hungry for a clear answer to the footprint question grew agitated at the recommendation of a moratorium on building permits for certain heavily damaged neighborhoods until May 2006. During those four months, residents themselves would have to demonstrate their neighborhood's "viability"—a requirement that cleverly placed the burden of proving neighborhood wherewithal on the backs of the most vocal full-footprint advocates. Further insight on the BNOB's position on the footprint question came in the form of a map, halfway through the presentation, entitled "Parks and Open Space Plan." It depicted Orleans Parish with the usual cartographic overlays of street networks and water bodies. At the bottom of its legend was a dashed-green line symbol indicating "Areas for Future Parkland," which corresponded to a series of six large perforated circles sprinkled throughout certain low-lying residential neighborhoods.[680]

The next morning, the *Times-Picayune* featured the map on its front page. The newspaper's adaptation transformed the dashed circles, which cartographically suggested a certain level of conjecture and abstraction, into semi-opaque green dots labeled as "approximate areas expected to become parks and greenspace." The green dots spanned so much terrain with such apparent cartographic confidence that many readers interpreted them to represent discrete polygons, rather than dimensionless abstractions merely suggesting the possibility of some new neighborhood parks. *If my house lies within those "green dots,"* many readers presumed, *it will be "green spaced" into wetlands.*

Just as citizens in November seized upon the ULI's "purple investment zone" map as the parapraxis of that organization's underlying footprint philosophy, citizens now clutched what quickly became known as the "Green Dot Map" as the Freudian slip of the BNOB Commission. The response was livid. Said one man to committee chairman Joseph Canizaro, whose day job as a major real estate investor was not viewed as coincidental by skeptical citizens, "Mr. Joe Canizaro, I don't know you, but I hate you. You've been in the background trying to scheme to get our land[!]"[681]

"4 MONTHS TO DECIDE," blared the *Times-Picayune* headline; "Nagin panel says hardest hit areas must prove viability; City's footprint may shrink."[682] The infamous "Green Dot Map" entered the local lexicon, even as it motivated residents of heavily damaged neighborhoods to commence demonstrating "viability" and save their neighborhoods. *Green space*, a benign notion elsewhere in urban America, became a dirty word in postdiluvian New Orleans.

What ensued, starting in late January 2006, was one of the most remarkable episodes of civic engagement in recent American history. Scores of grass-roots neighborhood associations and civic groups formed organically, sans professional expertise and usually with zero funding. Web sites went online; emails circulated; impromptu venues were arranged; signs popped up on once-flooded lawns (*Broadmoor Lives!; I Am Coming Home! I Will Rebuild! I Am New Orleans!*). One association in the heavily flooded Lake Bullard neighborhood, lacking a decent venue but not an ounce of determination, demurely asked attendees to "bring their own chairs"[683] to the group's next meeting. Despite their tenuous life circumstances and other responsibilities, New Orleanians by the thousands joined forces with their neighbors and volunteered to take stock of their communities; document local history, assets, resources, and problems; and plan solutions for the future.

So many grass-roots neighborhood planning groups formed that umbrella associations arose to coordinate them. One, the Neighborhood Partnership Network, listed at least seventy fully active neighborhood organizations within Orleans Parish alone, while many more in poorer areas strove to coalesce.[684] Their names formed a veritable *where's where* of famous New Orleans places—*French Quarter Citizens Inc., Audubon Riverside Neighborhood Association, Bouligny Improvement Association, Faubourg St. Roch Improvement Association, Algiers Point Association*—but also included less-famous modern subdivisions more likely to occupy lower ground and suffer higher flood risk—*Lake Bullard Homeowners Association Inc., Venetian Isles Civic and Improvement Association, Lake Terrace Neighborhood Property Owners Association*. In some cases, such as the stellar Broadmoor Improvement Association, professional help arrived from outside (Harvard University), and funding aided the planning process. Many associations eventually produced fine neighborhood plans, and, perhaps more importantly, empowered people to meet their neighbors and learn about their environs, past, present, and future, to degrees unimaginable a year earlier.

One crude way to measure this civic engagement is to compute the number of times the terms "civic association" or "neighborhood association" appear in *Times-Picayune* articles or announcements, as queried through the Lexis-Nexis news database. Before the storm, when roughly 450,000-455,000 people lived in the city, those key words appeared at a steady pace of forty to forty-five times per month. That rate dropped to zero during the "Lost September" of 2005, but returned to normal rates by early 2006 despite the dramatic drop in population. After January 2006—when the Green Dot Map inadvertently kick-started the grass-roots planning effort—the terms appeared over 100 times per month before stabilizing by summertime to around seventy per month. When normalized for population differences, neighborhood associations were literally "making news" in post-Katrina New Orleans at least four times, and up to seven times, the rate from prediluvian times—*despite* the new hardships of life in the struggling city.[685] A statistical sampling of 362 "Meetings" announcements posted in the *Times-Picayune* between November 2005 and April 2007 (from a total population of over a thousand) revealed that fully 48 percent represented neighborhood association meetings, and another 19 percent came from civic groups unaffiliated with specific neighborhoods.[686]

In an editorial on "the Curse of the Green Dot," *Times-Picayune* columnist Stephanie Grace reflected on the episode. "You know the Green Dot," she reminded her readers.

> In a move that will go down as one of the great miscalculations of post-Katrina planning, [the ULI and BNOB Commission] designated the off-limits areas with green dots.

> Around town, people picked up the paper that morning and saw, for the first time, that their neighborhoods could be slated for demolition. To say they didn't take the news well is an understatement.

> 'People felt threatened when they saw the green dot,' LaToya Cantrell, president of the Broadmoor Improvement Association, would say months later. 'All hell broke loose'....

> City Councilwoman Cynthia Willard-Lewis, who represents the hard-hit Lower 9th Ward and Eastern New Orleans, said the green dots made many of her African-American constituents flash back to the civil rights era, thinking they would need to fight for equal access all over again. *The maps*, she said soon after they were unveiled, *'are causing people to lose hope.'* [687]

Ironically, the very recommendations that motivated grass-roots associations to form—the Green Dot Map, the permit moratorium, and the threat of "green spacing" if neighborhood viability were not demonstrated by May 2006—ended up torpedoing the very commission that issued them. Mayor Nagin, embroiled in a nationally watched re-election campaign, rejected the politically volatile advice of his own BNOB Commission. Fatally undermined despite its worthwhile contributions beyond the footprint issue, the Commission disbanded unceremoniously. Footprint shrinkage became a radioactive topic among the mayoral candidates; anyone who supported the concept risked losing the votes of tens of thousands of flood victims. Engaged citizens and their representatives had, for better or worse, yelled the footprint debate off the table.

After Mayor Nagin cinched re-election in the mayoral campaign, the great footprint debate largely disappeared from public discourse. His *laissez-faire* repopulation and rebuilding stance, which was more of a default position than an articulated strategy, answered the footprint question by saying, in essence, *let people return and rebuild as they can and as they wish, and we'll act on the patterns as they fall in place.* Federal complicity bore responsibility as well: FEMA's updated Advisory Base Flood Elevation maps—which drive flood insurance availability and rates—turned out to be largely the same as the old 1984 maps, thus seemingly communicating federal endorsement (as well as actuarial encouragement) to homeowners deliberating on whether to rebuild in low-lying areas. Road Home monies imparted no special incentive to do otherwise, and no federal compensation fund awaited those homeowners and businesses that would have been affected by a hypothetical footprint-shrinkage decision.

The entire city *could* come back, but what that city would look and function like still remained an open question. Additional planning efforts, by the City Council-sponsored Miami-based Lambert/Danzey consultants and by the foundation-supported Unified New Orleans Plan (UNOP), provoked more civic engagement from meeting-weary New Orleanians during late 2006. UNOP's *Citywide Strategic Recovery and Rebuilding Plan* plus numerous district plans hit the streets in draft form in early 2007, about the same time that Mayor Nagin appointed renowned disaster-recovery expert Dr. Edward Blakely as chief of the city's Office of Recovery Management. In March 2007, "Recovery Czar" Blakely unveiled yet another plan—of seventeen "re-build," "re-develop," and "re-new" nodes throughout the city, marking spots for intensive infrastructure investment. Strikingly more modest and focused than the grandiose and sometimes radical visions of earlier plans, Blakely's plan aimed

> to encourage commercial investment—and with it stabilize neighbor-hoods—rather than defining areas that are off-limits to rebuilding. One such previous plan, advanced in early 2006 by Mayor Ray Nagin's Bring New Orleans Back Commission and backed by the widely respected Urban Land Institute, drew howls from residents who found their neighborhoods represented on maps by green dots that denoted redevelopment as perpet-ual green space.[688]

Once again, citizens convened to discuss and debate this latest proposal and how it may or may not relate to the earlier plans of UNOP, Lambert/Danzey, the numerous neighborhood associations, the BNOB Commission, WRT, and the ULI. Some wags described the parallel, overlapping, and sometimes competing planning efforts as "plandemonium." Citizens grew cynical, not because of lack of commitment, but because too many soft promises and uncoordinated efforts chased too little of the hard resources and inspirational leadership needed for genuine problem-solving.

Despite their noble intentions and the heroic civic engagement demonstrated by thoughtful and intelligent New Orleanians during a very busy and stressful era, the myriad public planning efforts of postdiluvian New Orleans face daunting odds of ever fully coming to fruition.[689] History indicates that, in the wake of urban disasters, the most ambitious and revolutionary rebuilding plans usually suffer the greatest likelihood of failure. Footprint renegotiation represented the most radical plan of all, and despite its compelling logic, suffered resounding rejection. The reason why can be found throughout this book, specifically in two words in the subtitle: *historical geography*.

The intricate layers of structures, infrastructures, legalities, economics, and social networks that form when humans cluster together for long periods all develop a great momentum which predisposes them to persist. Wars, changes of government, even revolutionary regime changes usually fail in erasing the importance of "past place" in the geography of the present and future. This urban momentum from the past explains why we have modern streets in uptown New Orleans that still limn the geometry of 300-year-old French surveying systems. It explains why we see certain ancient architectural styles in certain places, why certain industries cluster in certain locales, and why certain social groups reside in certain areas. It also explains why Louisiana has a mixed legal jurisdiction entailing elements of Napoleonic law, despite over two centuries of American dominion. It is axiomatic: *the past matters*. Patterns and precedences established in historical times become inscribed into the city and its society, and help create wealth—sometimes financial, sometimes humanistic—which people are inclined to maintain and protect. Thus they influence the present and future.

Despite its devastation, Hurricane Katrina's flood did not, by any means, "wipe the slate clean." The antecedent urban layers in the flooded zones (including land title, property value, commercial investments, social networks, and personal attachments) were in fact inscribed deeply and survived easily. In the absence of generous and immediate compensation for the loss of all those prior investments, most flooded homeowners—who understandably worried about *tomorrow*, not the distant and theoretical future—naturally gravitated to the default option of simply rebuilding in place. Local politicians, unable to guarantee an alternative and fearful of retribution at the polls if they proposed one, heard the keep-the-footprint consensus loud and clear and acted accordingly. Anti-shrinkage advocates cinched their victory by pointedly reminding critics that federal levee failure, not Hurricane Katrina *per se*, caused (or more accurately, failed to prevent) the flooding. What they ignored was the inconvenient geological truth beyond, and beneath, those levee walls.

In most cases, momentum from the past is good for landscapes and cityscapes. It creates value, generates wealth, and makes places distinctive and interesting: witness New Orleans' colorful street names, pedestrian-scale neighborhoods, and vast inventory of historical structures. But occasionally that momentum leads a community down a troubled path, in this case toward geological and environmental unsustainability.

The footprint controversy represented a genuine dilemma. Dilemmas demand decisions—difficult choices that yield unpleasant consequences—else they persist, and usually worsen. The Great Footprint Debate concluded when officials and society at large decided not to make the difficult decision of urban shrinkage. As often happens, the aftermath of this catastrophe may become the prelude to the next.

The Build/No-Build Line

Mapping out the philosophies on the future land use of New Orleans

Various philosophies have emerged on the rebuilding of New Orleans, each with its own logic, passion, experts, and dogma.[690] But all can be boiled down to a simple line on a map, separating areas recommended for rebuilding from those deemed best returned to nature. Where people locate their build/no-build line says as much about them—and how they view and weigh science, economics, social, and humanistic values—as it says about the geographical future of New Orleans.

One philosophy recommends the total abandonment of the metropolis. Its advocates essentially draw the build/no-build line at the metropolis' upper boundary, somewhere between rural St. Charles Parish and urbanized Jefferson Parish, or above Lake Pontchartrain's northern shore. St. Louis University geologist Timothy M. Kusky first voiced the "abandonist" philosophy in a *Boston Globe* editorial entitled "Time to Move to Higher Ground," which later earned him a national audience on CBS *60 Minutes*. He readily acknowledged:

> New Orleans is one of America's great historic cities, and our *emotional response* to the disaster is to rebuild it grander and greater than before. However this may not be the *most rational or scientifically sound* response and could lead to *even greater human catastrophe* and *financial loss* in the future.[691]

Abandonists like Kusky tend to be pragmatic and fiscally conservative; for them it is a rational question of hard science, hard dollars, and body counts. In making their case, they cite only the gloomiest scientific data on subsidence, coastal erosion, and sea-level rise, and dismiss humanist and cultural arguments as "emotional" or "nostalgic." Abandonists almost always have nothing to lose personally if the city does disappear, and feel no obligation to propose financial compensation plans for those who do. They are loathed in New Orleans, but occupy a seat at the table in the national discourse.

At the opposite end are those who advocate maintaining the urban footprint at all costs. Unlike abandonists, "maintainers" see this as primarily a humanist and cultural question, rather than a scientific or engineering one. To be against maintaining all neighborhoods is to be against people and against culture—worse yet, against *certain* peoples and *certain* cultures.

Maintainers tend to be passionate, oftentimes angry, and for good reason: many are flood victims and have everything to lose if the build/no-build line crosses their homes. If a levee can be built well enough to protect *them*, they reason, why not extend it around *us*? Among the most outspoken maintainers are social activists who interpret any postdiluvian adjustment to the urban perimeter as a conspiracy of "politically conservative, economically neoliberal power elites" who "are doing everything in their power to prevent [working-class African-Americans] from returning."[692] Ignoring scientific data and fiscal constraints, maintainers push the build/no-build line beyond the rural fringes of St. Bernard Parish, even all the way to the Gulf of Mexico.

In between fall the "concessionists," usually aficionados of the city, particularly its historical heart, and often residents of its unflooded sections. Concessionists struggle to balance troubling scientific data with treasured social and cultural resources. Their answer: concede certain low-lying modern subdivisions to nature—areas which, incidentally, they never found structurally appealing in the first place—and increase population density and flood protection in the higher, historically significant areas. Concessionists argue that, in the long run, this would reduce costs, minimize grief, protect the environment, and save lives. Concessionists sometimes failed to recognize, however, that footprint shrinkage itself costs money, in the form of fair and immediate compensation to homeowners.

Sensitive to accusations of elitism, concessionists soften their message with careful wordsmithing and confusing maps (see *The Great Footprint Debate*). They place their build/no-build line somewhere between those of the abandonists and the maintainers—sometimes near the Industrial Canal, sometimes between the Metairie/Gentilly Ridge and the lakefront, usually to the exclusion of the distant, charmless, low-lying subdivisions of New Orleans East. Concessionists enjoy widespread support among many educated professionals who live on high ground, but encounter fierce resistance among maintainers, who often accuse them being, at best, unrealistic utopian dreamers, and at worst, elitist, classist, racist land-grabbers.

Reports that rural, isolated lower Plaquemines Parish—home to only 14,000 people, or 2 percent of the region's population—may not receive full funding for levee maintenance seems to have spawned a fourth philosophy: push the build/no-build line down just past Belle Chasse, the only major community in upper Plaquemines Parish that adjoins the metropolitan area. Advocates include city dwellers, both concessionists and maintainers, who stand to benefit from the abandonment of lower Plaquemines because it would clear the path for aggressive coastal restoration while reducing the price tag on their own protection. Let the sediment-laden waters of the Mississippi River replenish those eroding marshes, they might contend; we need to restore them to buffer the metropolis against storm surges. What about the rural peoples who have called those marshes home for over a century? Well, as geologist Kusky put it in his now-famous abandonist editorial, it's "time to move to higher ground."[693]

Thus, social, cultural, and humanistic values, plus a sense of personal investment, tend to push the build/no-build line in a downriver direction, while scientific and financial values nudge the line upriver. What to make of all this?

First, even the most ardent lovers of New Orleans should refrain from loathing the abandonists. After all, concessionists (and those maintainers willing to sacrifice lower Plaquemines) are essentially making the same abandonist arguments that earned Kusky the enduring hatred of many New Orleanians. They're just applying them below different lines on the map.

Second, we should probably only pencil-in whatever build/no-build lines we draw, because we may well wish to change them if the going gets rough. Others have. Illinois Republican Rep. J. Dennis Hastert was among the first to hint at abandonment when he said rebuilding New Orleans "doesn't make sense to me. And it's a question that certainly we should ask." Shaken by angry responses, he later clarified his statement: "I am not advocating that the city be abandoned or relocated...."[694] Wallace, Roberts & Todd, a design firm hired to advise the BNOB Commission, at first professed a bold maintainer philosophy ("If you plan on shrinkage, shrinkage is what you'll get"[695]) but ended up recommending concessions in their final report to the Commission. Even Kusky softened his abandonist advice and suggested the possibility of "newer, higher, stronger seawalls" for "the business and historic parts of the city."[696]

I, too, as a geographer with both physical and cultural interests, have grappled with my concessionist recommendations when confronted by the tragic personal stories of individuals who desperately want to maintain the world they once knew and loved. Should another hurricane of the magnitude of Katrina strike New Orleans, we may see build/no-build lines erased and redrawn *en masse*: maintainers may become concessionists, concessionists may be willing to concede more, and abandonists will increase their ranks.

Finally, beware of those who claim to speak solely "for science," or "for the people." This is a complicated, interdisciplinary dilemma. The social scientist needs to be at the table as much as the physical scientist; the humanist deserves a voice as much as the economist; the poor renter of a shotgun house should be heard as much as the rich owner of a mansion. We should acknowledge that a tangle of personal, cultural, financial, nostalgic, emotional, practical, and scientific factors underlie which philosophy—abandon, maintain, or concede—we uphold for the future of New Orleans, and that *this is OK; this is acceptable.*

Postscript: Who prevailed?

Mayor Nagin, supported by most flooded homeowners and a vociferous cadre of local officials, opted for a politically safe *laissez-faire* repopulation and rebuilding policy. Abetting their victory, more through passivity than active support, was the federal government: FEMA's revised Advisory Base Flood Elevation maps, released in 2006, continued to make flood insurance available to heavily flooded areas, thus encouraging their rebuilding. And no federal buy-out plan promised compensation to homeowners and business owners who would be forced off their land in a concessionist (eminent domain) mandate coming from city, state, or federal levels. No sane person "concedes" his or her major life investment without fair compensation.

The apparent outcome: *Let people return and rebuild as they can and as they wish, and we'll act on the patterns as they fall in place.* The maintainers prevailed in drawing the build/no-build line along the existing, pre-Katrina urban edge (though the possibility of a lower-Plaquemines concession remains). Whether that line gets erased and redrawn again—by concessionists or by abandonists—will be determined by the

insurance industry, by mortgage companies, by property values, by federal intervention, by disappointed residents forced to re-address their initial post-Katrina rebuilding
stance, and ultimately, by nature.

Analyzing New Orleans' New Human Geography

Two years later, the patterns begin to fall in place

Note: An edited version of the following essay appeared as a guest editorial in the Times-Picayune *on
the second anniversary of Hurricane Katrina. Presented here in its original form, it offers a perspective
on New Orleans' postdiluvian repopulation patterns as of August 29, 2007.*

In autumn 2005, citizens of New Orleans engaged in what historians might
someday call "the Great Footprint Debate." Should the city shrink its urban footprint
and rebuild on higher ground? Or should the entire city come back? The Urban Land
Institute proposed its purple "investment zone" map; the Bring New Orleans Back
Commission suggested its "green dot map;" I myself proposed a methodology on this
editorial page.

By spring 2006, the matter was settled, by default more so than by decisive-
ness: the entire urban footprint would be allowed to rebuild. With new population data
recently released by GCR & Associates, Katrina's second anniversary is a good time to
assess how New Orleanians are reinhabiting that urban footprint.

Mapping the "population centroid"— the theoretical center of balance among
the distribution of households—is one way to do so. It's a little tricky to compute due
to the coarse nature of the data, but there is no doubt that East Bank Orleanians currently reside slightly more westward and closer to the river than before Katrina.

The 2000 East Bank population centroid was located in the central Seventh
Ward. That is, residents were distributed evenly lakeside, riverside, west, and east of
that locale. By August 2007, the centroid moved a mile to the southwest, into the central Sixth Ward. The westward movement mostly reflects the slower return rates east of
the Industrial Canal, while the southward movement signifies the much higher return
rates of the unflooded "sliver by the river."

Residents are not flocking to higher ground in massive numbers. However,
a higher percentage of New Orleanians are now living above sea level than in the past
half-century. In 1910, over 90 percent of city residents lived above sea level. That percentage dropped to 48 percent in 1960 and 38 percent in 2000. Today, it's back up to 50
percent. That means that both New Orleans' population and its urbanized land surface
now straddle the level of the sea—half above, half below.

When we divide up East Bank neighborhoods by their August 2007 return rates, we see the following patterns:

- 22,300 people live in areas in which less than one-third of residents have returned. With a mean elevation of three feet below sea level, these areas suffered flood depths averaging over five feet and structural damages averaging 49 on a 0-to-100 scale, in which 100 means total destruction. City records show that more building permits have been issued for these areas, relative to their current population, than anywhere else, indicating that many more intend to return.

- Areas that are currently one-third to two-thirds repopulated are home to over 107,200 residents—a substantial voting block. Located slightly higher than less-repopulated areas but still below sea level, these folks suffered three feet of flooding on average, and damage assessments of about 35/100. They have requested the most building permits in absolute numbers, again implying further repopulation. Many of these areas are historically significant: nearly six square miles of National Historic Register districts occur here.

- Areas over two-thirds repopulated are home to over 83,000 people on the East Bank plus more than 50,000 on the West Bank. Those on the East Bank reside at over three feet above sea level on average, suffered less than a foot of water if they flooded at all, and had damage assessments around 12/100. These areas comprise nearly eight square miles of National Historic Register districts.[697]

To what degree, then, is New Orleans "back?"

If we look at population, 60 to 65 percent of Orleans, 36 percent of St. Bernard, and nearly 100 percent of Jefferson and St. Tammany parishes have returned.

If we look at New Orleans' economic indicators such as labor force, employers, and tax revenues, return rates vary around three-quarters to four-fifths.

If we look at social and public-sector indicators like childcare and school enrollment, they're about one-quarter to two-fifths where they should be.

Consider all these metrics together, and a case can be made that New Orleans is roughly two-thirds back. When asked a year ago, I estimated it at half.

However, the notion of New Orleans "returning" implies that we can go back in time and recover the city we once knew. We can't. A new New Orleans will emerge, once Road Home monies are fully distributed, public housing issues are addressed, numerous other unknowns become known, and flood victims make their final residential decisions.

Assuming, of course, another hurricane does not strike—and force us to reopen the Great Footprint Debate.

"A Curious Town It Is"

*New Orleans' complex and conflicted relationship
with the United States of America*

I begin to understand the town a little ... and a curious town it is.[698]
—Benjamin Henry Boneval Latrobe, 1819

Interpreters of New Orleans' history generally fall into two camps. Both, I've
come to understand, play relevant roles in the city's future.

The "exceptionalists" see in New Orleans an enduring uniqueness, dating back
to its colonial origins and very much alive today. While they allow that some distinctiveness has disappeared—the French language, for example—exceptionalists view
modern New Orleans as a place with its heart still in the Franco-Afro-Caribbean world
from which it spawned, resigned only reluctantly to its American fate. This group sees
evidence for New Orleans' uniqueness in everything from music and food to attitudes,
race relations, linguistics, architecture, and politics. Exceptionalism is practically an article of faith among most New Orleans *aficionados* and city advocates, including many
lifelong local historical researchers. It forms the bedrock of local civic pride, and merely
questioning it can earn responses of consternation and reproach. Exceptionlists' pre-
disposition toward perceiving distinctiveness in all things related to New Orleans continually reinforces their stance that the city is axiomatically *sui generis*.

Nonsense, say the "assimilationists" (also known as "Americanists"). This
camp argues that two centuries of American dominion have enveloped New Orleans
almost entirely into the national fold, leaving only vestiges of distinction in such realms
as historical architecture, civic rituals such as Mardi Gras and second-line parades, and
in a smattering of linguistic and culinary traits. They point out that modern-day New
Orleanians in overwhelming numbers speak English, indulge in national popular culture, shop at big-box chains, and interact socially and economically with other Americans and the world on a daily basis. Assimilationists view the exceptionalists' insistence
of cultural uniqueness as an appealing mantra drummed up first by "local color" writers
in the late 1800s, and today by the industrial tourism machine.

Wherever the truth lies, one thing is certain: the prevailing narrative about
New Orleans communicated worldwide after Hurricane Katrina was that of the exceptionalists, and we should all be grateful for that. Their "uniqueness mantra" may well
have saved the city: allusions to cultural distinction played critical roles in persuading
the nation to invest taxpayer dollars in a place threatened with eroding coasts, sinking
soils, rising seas, and increasingly intense storms. If New Orleans were perceived as
interchangeable with any other American city, the pragmatic response of metropolitan
abandonment (see *The Build/No-Build Line*) might have won the day.

But the task of actually saving the city puts the exceptionalists in a philosophical dilemma, because the factors that they claim rendered New Orleans distinctive and charming also seem to have made it parochial, inefficient—and dangerous. This logical disconnect appears to be lost on many people. I've listened to countless speakers and panelists at post-Katrina conferences who commence their presentations with emotional tributes to New Orleans' cultural uniqueness, heterogeneity, and quirky independence, only to conclude them with strident calls for standardization, homogenization, and efficiency. Can we really have it both ways? Noble efforts to adopt national "green architecture" standards, build sustainable communities, unify parochial levee boards, consolidate rival port authorities, eliminate redundant tax assessors (a system unique in the nation), merge civil and criminal courts (one of few cities with separate systems), dispense with the state's insurance regulatory panel (only one in the country), and even to ban cockfighting (last state in the union to do so) are in fact outright *rejections* of exceptionalism in favor of national assimilation, even though most advocates of such measures purport to embrace the former and disdain the latter.

I grappled with this dilemma, sensing that a thoughtful person simply cannot pull on this one rope in two directions. But eventually I began to appreciate that both interpretations—regardless of their historical accuracy—have played important, complementary roles in the city's recovery. The exceptionalist interpretation helped persuade the nation to invest in rebuilding New Orleans, by rightfully portraying the city as an irreplaceable treasure. The assimilationist interpretation will guide actually saving it, by rightfully addressing the problems of inefficiency, parochialism, and unsustainability which, if left unchecked, would eventually destroy it.

May all New Orleans' dilemmas end as judiciously.

Notes

1 Peirce F. Lewis, *New Orleans: The Making of an Urban Landscape* (Cambridge, MA, 1976), 17.

2 As quoted by Joel K. Bourne Jr., "The Perils of New Orleans," *National Geographic* 212, No. 2 (August 2007): 61.

3 Frank Haigh Dixon, *A Traffic History of the Mississippi River System—National Waterways Commission, Document Number 11* (Washington, DC, 1909), 15.

4 *New Orleans Times*, November 23, 1866, p. 7, c. 1.

5 Ernst von Hesse-Wartegg, *Travels on the Lower Mississippi, 1879-1880: A Memoir by Ernst von Hesse-Wartegg*, ed. and trans. Frederic Trautmann (Columbia and London, 1990), 161.

6 For further details and sources on New Orleans' geological origins, see Richard Campanella, *Geographies of New Orleans: Urban Fabrics Before the Storm* (Lafayette, LA, 2006), 33-39, and *Time and Place in New Orleans: Past Geographies in the Present Day* (Gretna, LA, 2002), 16-18.

7 Basil Hall, *Travels in North America in the Years 1827 and 1828, Volume III* (Edinburgh and London, 1830), 317-18 (emphasis added).

8 Elisée Réclus, *A Voyage to New Orleans*, eds. John Clark and Camille Martin (Thetford, VT, 2004 translation of 1855 original), 42.

9 John McPhee, *The Control of Nature* (New York, NY, 1989), 5.

10 Robert T. Saucier, *Geomorphology and Quaternary Geologic History of the Lower Mississippi Valley*, 2 vols. (Vicksburg, MS, 1994), 1:276.

11 Samuel L. Clemens, *Life on the Mississippi* (New York, NY, 1958 reprint of 1883 original), 4.

12 "Letter from Father Vivier to the Society of Jesus, to a Father of the same Society," in *The Jesuit Relations and Allied Documents: Travels and Explorations of the Jesuit Missionaries in New France 1610-1791, Volume LXIX—All Missions, 1710-1756*, ed. Reuben Gold Thwaites (New York, NY, 1959), 210-13.

13 Identifying the highest and lowest points in New Orleans depends on what one regards as the legitimate topographic surface, so manipulated as it has been by man. Famous Monkey Hill at Audubon Zoo, built by the Works Progress Administration in 1933, rises 16.5 feet above a natural-levee surface that is eleven feet above sea level, for a total elevation of about 27.5 feet. A hill in the Couturie Forest Arboretum in City Park not only rises to about thirty feet, but starts at a lower base elevation (three feet below sea level). Some artificial levees, shored-up battures, and landscaping features measure over thirty feet above sea level. See Richard Campanella, *Time and Place in New Orleans: Past Geographies in the Present Day* (Gretna, LA, 2002), 52-53, for further information on elevation extremes in the city.

14 As quoted by Katy Reckdahl, "As Endymion Returns to Mid-City...," *New Orleans Times-Picayune*, February 1, 2008, p. A-6.

15 Le Page du Pratz, *The History of Louisiana*, ed. Joseph G. Tregle, Jr. (Baton Rouge, LA, 1976 reprint of 1758 original), 128 (emphasis added).

16 Elisée Réclus, *A Voyage to New Orleans*, eds. John Clark and Camille Martin (Thetford, VT, 2004 translation of 1855 original), 50.

17 Pierre Clément de Laussat, *Memoirs of My Life* (Baton Rouge and New Orleans, 1978 translation of 1831 memoir), 52-54.

18 Anonymous, *New Orleans As It Is: Its Manners and Customs* ("By a Resident, Printed for the Publisher," 1850), 20.

19 "Those marshes which have not acquired a sufficient consistency to produce trees, and shake...when trodden on, are in Louisiana called *prairies tremlantes*" [trembling prairies]. Edward Livingston, *An Answer to Mr. Jefferson's Justification of His Conduct in the Case of the New Orleans Batture* (Philadelphia, PA, 1813), footnote on 6.

20 Thomas Ashe, *Travels in America Performed in the Year 1806* (London, 1809), 304. Ashe goes on to say that disease "tarries only in [New] Orleans and the Natchez [region], where an overflowing population...render it powerful and contagious."

21 "From Swamp and Marsh," *New Orleans Times*, October 25, 1877, p. 7.

22 "Letter from Father Vivier to the Society of Jesus, to a Father of the same Society," in *The Jesuit Relations and Allied Documents: Travels and Explorations of the Jesuit Missionaries in New France 1610-1791, Volume LXIX—All Missions, 1710-1756*, ed. Reuben Gold Thwaites (New York, NY, 1959), 213.

23 Maj. Amos Stoddard, *Sketches, Historical and Descriptive of Louisiana* (Philadelphia, 1812), 175.

24 Basil Hall, *Travels in North America in the Years 1827 and 1828, Volume III* (Edinburgh and London,

1830), 344-45.

25 Benjamin Henry Boneval Latrobe, *Impressions Respecting New Orleans: Diary & Sketches 1818-1820*, ed. Samuel Wilson Jr. (New York, NY, 1951), 67-68.

26 The City Planning and Zoning Commission, *Major Street Report* (New Orleans, 1927), 26-28.

27 "A Description of the river Missisippi," *Salem Mercury* (Salem, Massachusetts), August 7, 1787, p. 4.

28 All flow rate data were extracted from the U.S. Geological Survey-Office of Surface Water stream-flow database (http://waterdata.usgs.gov/nwis/rt), and computed to determine average annual flow rates at selected gauges for as many years as data had been collected. Analysis by Richard Campanella, September 2003.

29 Charles Joseph La Trobe, *The Rambler in North America, Volume II* (New York, NY, 1835), 236.

30 "Letter from Father Vivier to the Society of Jesus, to a Father of the same Society," in *The Jesuit Relations and Allied Documents: Travels and Explorations of the Jesuit Missionaries in New France 1610-1791, Volume LXIX—All Missions, 1710-1756*, ed. Reuben Gold Thwaites (New York, NY, 1959), 207-09.

31 Fredrika Bremer, *The Homes of the New World: Impressions of America, Volume II* (New York, NY, 1853), 181.

32 Nathaniel H. Bishop, *Four Months in a Sneak-Box* (Boston, MA, 1879), 182-83.

33 Fredrika Bremer, *The Homes of the New World: Impressions of America, Volume II* (New York, NY, 1853), 193-94.

34 Anonymous, *New Orleans As It Is: Its Manners and Customs* ("By a Resident, Printed for the Publisher," 1850), 20.

35 Computed by Richard Campanella from 1992 bathymetric and bankline data from Bayou Manchac to Head of Passes.

36 "Letter from Father du Poisson, Missionary to Missionary to the Akensas, to Father * * *," in *The Jesuit Relations and Allied Documents: Travels and Explorations of the Jesuit Missionaries in New France 1610-1791, Volume LXVII—Lower Canada, Abenakis, Louisiana 1716-1727*, ed. Reuben Gold Thwaites (New York, NY, 1959), 287-97.

37 Pierre Clément de Laussat, *Memoirs of My Life* (Baton Rouge and New Orleans, LA, 1978 translation of 1831 memoir), 71.

38 Earlier stage data, held to different standards, record a low of −1.6 feet in 1872 and a high of 21.27 in 1922. U.S. Army Corps of Engineers, New Orleans District, Water Control Section, *Stage Data: Mississippi River At New Orleans, LA (Carrollton)*, http://www.mvn.usace.army.mil/cgi-bin/water-control.p1?01300.

39 Percentages computed by Richard Campanella from LIDAR digital elevation models of terrestrial surface of metropolitan area, from 90° 15' West, 29° 53' North to 89° 56' West, 30° 03' North (roughly from Westwego to Little Woods). This area is 44 percent above sea level, 49 percent below sea level, and 7 percent at sea level.

40 Basil Hall, *Travels in North America in the Years 1827 and 1828, Volume III* (Edinburgh and London, 1830), 319-20.

41 Charles Sealsfield, *The Americans As They Are; Described in A Tour Through the Valley of the Mississippi* (London, 1828), 165-66 (emphasis added). Sealsfield footnoted his endorsement with an additional observation: "Below New Orleans there is no place well adapted for the site of a large city."

42 Joseph Holt Ingraham, *The South-West by a Yankee*, 2 vols. (New York, NY, 1835), 1:62.

43 Pierre Clément de Laussat, *Memoirs of My Life* (Baton Rouge and New Orleans, LA, 1978 translation of 1831 memoir), 28.

44 Charles Joseph La Trobe, *The Rambler in North America, Volume II* (New York, NY, 1835), 238-39.

45 Data computed by Richard Campanella from various meteorological sources.

46 Anonymous, *New Orleans As It Is: Its Manners and Customs* ("By a Resident, Printed for the Publisher," 1850), 23.

47 Thomas Jefferys, *The Natural and Civil History of the French Dominions in North and South America* (London, 1760), 133.

48 "New Orleans is Getting Hotter—Increases in Temperature in Summer Attributed to the Drainage System," *Columbus Ledger-Enquirer* (Columbus, Georgia), June 13, 1918, p. 1, c. 3.

49 William Dunbar, "Meteorological Observations," *Transactions of the American Philosophical Society 6* (1809): 52-55.

50 Francisco de Garay, as quoted by Frederic Austin Ogg, *The Opening of the Mississippi: A Struggle for Supremacy in the American Interior* (New York and London, 1904), 16.

51 Father Zenobius Membré, "Narrative of La Salle's Voyage Down the Mississippi, By Father Zenobius

Membré," in *The Journeys of René-Robert Cavelier Sieur de La Salle, Volume I,* ed. Isaac Joslin Cox (Austin, TX, 1968 reprint of 1905 original), 131-59; quote on 143.

52 Pierre Le Moyne, Sieur d'Iberville, *Iberville's Gulf Journals,* ed. Richebourg Gaillard McWilliams (University, AL, 1991 translation of 1700 journal), 56.

53 Anonymous, "Historical Journal: or, Narrative of the Expedition Made by Order of Louis XIV, King of France, under Command of M. D'Iberville to Explore the Colbert (Mississippi) River and Establish a Colony in Louisiana," in *Historical Collections of Louisiana and Florida, Volume VII,* ed. B. F. French (New York, NY, 1875 translation of 1699 journal), 61.

54 Pierre Le Moyne, Sieur d'Iberville, *Iberville's Gulf Journals,* ed. Richebourg Gaillard McWilliams (University, AL, 1991 translation of 1700 journal), 63-64.

55 Anonymous, "Historical Journal: or, Narrative of the Expedition Made by Order of Louis XIV, King of France, under Command of M. D'Iberville to Explore the Colbert (Mississippi) River and Establish a Colony in Louisiana," in *Historical Collections of Louisiana and Florida, Volume VII,* ed. B. F. French (New York, NY, 1875 translation of 1699 journal), 74.

56 Pierre Le Moyne, Sieur d'Iberville, *Iberville's Gulf Journals,* ed. Richebourg Gaillard McWilliams (University, AL, 1991 translation of 1700 journal), 69.

57 William M. Denevan, "The Pristine Myth: The Landscape of the Americas in 1492," *Annals of the Association of American Geographers* 82, No. 3 (September 1992): 369.

58 Charles C. Mann, *1491: New Revelations of the Americas Before Columbus* (New York, NY, 2006), 321.

59 "Letter from Father du Poisson, Missionary to Missionary to the Akensas, to Father * * *," in *The Jesuit Relations and Allied Documents: Travels and Explorations of the Jesuit Missionaries in New France 1610-1791, Volume LXVII—Lower Canada, Abenakis, Louisiana 1716-1727,* ed. Reuben Gold Thwaites (New York, NY, 1959), 285.

60 Erhard Rostlund, "The Geographic Range of the Historic Bison in the Southeast," *Annals of the Association of American Geographers,* 50, No. 4 (December 1960): 405-07.

61 As quoted by William M. Denevan, "The Pristine Myth: The Landscape of the Americas in 1492," *Annals of the Association of American Geographers* 82, No. 3 (September 1992): 370.

62 Charles C. Mann, *1491: New Revelations of the Americas Before Columbus* (New York, NY, 2005), 321.

63 Pierre Le Moyne, Sieur d'Iberville, *Iberville's Gulf Journals,* ed. Richebourg Gaillard McWilliams (University, AL, 1991 translation of 1700 journal), 63.

64 Chevalier Guy de Soniat du Fossat, *Synopsis of the History of Louisiana from the Founding of the Colony to End of the Year 1791,* ed. and trans. Charles T. Soniat (New Orleans, 1903), 8.

65 William M. Denevan, "The Pristine Myth: The Landscape of the Americas in 1492," *Annals of the Association of American Geographers* 82, No. 3 (September 1992): 370.

66 Pierre Le Moyne, Sieur d'Iberville, *Iberville's Gulf Journals,* ed. Richebourg Gaillard McWilliams (University, AL, 1991 translation of 1700 journal), 60 (italics added).

67 Francisco de Garay, as quoted by Frederic Austin Ogg, *The Opening of the Mississippi: A Struggle for Supremacy in the American Interior* (New York and London, 1904), 16.

68 Álvar Núñez Cabéza de Vaca, *The Narrative of Cabeza de Vaca,* eds. Rolena Adorno and Patrick Charles Pautz (Lincoln, NE and London, 2003 translation of 1542 journal), 80.

69 Frederic Austin Ogg, *The Opening of the Mississippi: A Struggle for Supremacy in the American Interior* (New York and London, 1904), 27-28, 44.

70 "Letters Patent, Granted by the King of France to the Sieur de La Salle, on the 12th of May, 1678," in *On the Discovery of the Mississippi,* ed. Thomas Falconer (London, 1844 translation of 1678 original), Appendix: 18.

71 Father Zenobius Membré, "Narrative of La Salle's Voyage Down the Mississippi, By Father Zenobius Membré," in *The Journeys of René-Robert Cavelier Sieur de La Salle, Volume I,* ed. Isaac Joslin Cox (Austin, TX, 1968 reprint of 1905 original), 147. Membré made these observations of the same area after the expedition returned upriver on April 10.

72 M. de La Salle, "Account of the Taking Possession of Louisiana by M. De La Salle," in *The Journeys of René-Robert Cavelier Sieur de La Salle, Volume I,* ed. Isaac Joslin Cox (The Pemberton Press, Austin, TX, 1968 reprint of 1905 original), 159-70; quote on 165.

73 Marc de Villiers du Terrage, "A History of the Foundation of New Orleans (1717-1722)," *The Louisiana Historical Quarterly* 3, No. 2 (April 1920): 161.

74 Father Zenobius Membré, "Narrative of La Salle's Voyage Down the Mississippi, By Father Zenobius

Membré," in *The Journeys of René-Robert Cavelier Sieur de La Salle, Volume I*, ed. Isaac Joslin Cox (Austin, TX, 1968 reprint of 1905 original), 145.

75 M. Cavelier de La Salle, "Memoir of M. Cavelier de La Salle," in *On the Discovery of the Mississippi*, ed. Thomas Falconer (London, 1844 translation of 1680s original), Appendix: 3-4, 24-27.

76 Incredibly, La Salle's shipwreck and encampment were discovered in 1995.

77 Marcel Giraud, "France and Louisiana in the Early Eighteenth Century," *The Mississippi Valley Historical Review* 36, No. 4 (March 1950): 657, 665.

78 As quoted by Tennant S. McWilliams in *Iberville's Gulf Journals*, ed. Richebourg Gaillard McWilliams (University, AL, 1991 translation of 1700 journal), 4.

79 Pierre (born 1661) and Jean Baptiste (born 1680) were two of fourteen offspring of the prominent Le Moyne family of Montreal. They gained their landed titles of Iberville and Bienville during their youth, and it is by these names that the Le Moyne brothers are known to history. Iberville distinguished himself in French Canada with brilliant military exploits against the English during the 1680s and 1690s, a career shared by a number of his brothers. Teenaged Bienville seemed to be heading for a similar destiny until Iberville decided, "in true Le Moyne tradition," to bring him on his 1699 expedition to Louisiana. Iberville died of yellow fever in Havana in 1706, but not before successfully establishing a French colony in Louisiana. His decision to recruit his younger brother proved shrewd: Bienville led a long and eventful life, serving as governor of the Louisiana colony four times between 1701 and 1743 and founding New Orleans in 1718. He died in Paris in 1768. Philomena Hauck, *Bienville: Father of Louisiana* (Lafayette, LA, 1998), 1-8, 140-45.

80 M. de Pénicaut, "Annals of Louisiana, From the Establishment of the First Colony Under M. D'Iberville, to the Departure of the Author to France, in 1722," in *Historical Collections of Louisiana and Florida*, ed. B. F. French (New York, NY, 1869), 46. Pénicaut made this observation at the same site where Iberville first penetrated the river's mouth, but a few months later.

81 Pierre Le Moyne, Sieur d'Iberville, *Iberville's Gulf Journals*, ed. Richebourg Gaillard McWilliams (University, AL, 1991 translation of 1700 journal), 53.

82 Ibid., 89.

83 Charles R. Maduell Jr., *The Census Tables for the French Colony of Louisiana from 1699 to 1732* (Baltimore, MD, 1972), 1-3.

84 Anonymous, "Historical Journal: or, Narrative of the Expedition Made by Order of Louis XIV, King of France, under Command of M. D'Iberville to Explore the Colbert (Mississippi) River and Establish a Colony in Louisiana," in *Historical Collections of Louisiana and Florida, Volume VII*, ed. B. F. French (New York, NY, 1875 translation of 1699 journal), 57-58.

85 Ibid., 61.

86 Ibid., 61.

87 Pierre Le Moyne, Sieur d'Iberville, *Iberville's Gulf Journals*, ed. Richebourg Gaillard McWilliams (University, AL, 1991 translation of 1700 journal), 56.

88 Christopher G. Brantley and Steven G. Platt, "Canebrake Conservation in the Southeastern United States," *Wildlife Society Bulletin* 29, No. 4 (Winter, 2001), 1175-77.

89 Pierre Le Moyne, Sieur d'Iberville, *Iberville's Gulf Journals*, ed. Richebourg Gaillard McWilliams (University, AL, 1991 translation of 1700 journal), 57.

90 Paul du Ru, *Journal of Paul du Ru: February 1 to May 8, 1700*, ed. Ruth Lapham Butler (Chicago, IL, 1934), 16.

91 Pierre Le Moyne, Sieur d'Iberville, *Iberville's Gulf Journals*, ed. Richebourg Gaillard McWilliams (University, AL, 1991 translation of 1700 journal), 111-12 (emphasis added).

92 Susan Gibbs Lemann, *The Problems of Founding a Viable Colony: The Military in Early French Louisiana* (1982), reproduced in *The Louisiana Purchase Bicentennial Series in Louisiana History, Volume I: The French Experience in Louisiana*, ed. Glenn R. Conrad (Lafayette, LA, 1995): 360.

93 As quoted by Marc de Villiers du Terrage, "A History of the Foundation of New Orleans (1717-1722)," *The Louisiana Historical Quarterly* 3, No. 2 (April 1920): 174 (emphasis in original).

94 The register lists the resolution to establish New Orleans next to an incomplete date ("9th"). It is probable that the date was September 9, 1717, since the company received its charter on September 6 and made a clear reference to the proposed city on October 1, 1717. The register also called for a port at Ship Island, a town at Natchez, and forts in Illinois and Natchitoches country. Marc de Villiers du Terrage, "A History of the Foundation of New Orleans (1717-1722)," *The Louisiana Historical Quarterly* 3, No. 2 (April 1920): 174.

95 Bienville did not record or allude to the precise date of the foundation of the city; late March or

April 1718 is the closest the records indicate. In the 1960s, the City Council designated April 17 as "Founder's Day," which was commemorated in subsequent years with wreath-laying ceremonies and lectures. Selected on no specific historical basis, "Founder's Day" is all but unknown today.

96 Letter, Bienville to the Navy Council, June 12, 1718, *Mississippi Provincial Archives 1704-1743: French Dominion, Volume III*, eds. Dunbar Rowland and Albert Godfrey Sanders (Jackson, MS, 1932), 228.

97 As quoted by Shannon Lee Dawdy, *Madame John's Legacy (16ORS1) Revisited: A Closer Look at the Archeology of Colonial New Orleans* (New Orleans, 1998), 26-29.

98 Pierre François Xavier de Charlevoix, *Journal of a Voyage to North-America Undertaken by Order of the French King, Volume II* (London, 1761), 275-76.

99 Charles R. Maduell Jr., *The Census Tables for the French Colony of Louisiana from 1699 to 1732* (Baltimore, MD, 1972), 16-22.

100 Pierre François Xavier de Charlevoix, *Journal of a Voyage to North-America Undertaken by Order of the French King, Volume II* (London, 1761), 276.

101 Ibid., 289-90.

102 Ibid., 271-73.

103 Letter, Bienville to Pontchartrain, February 25, 1708, *Mississippi Provincial Archives 1704-1743: French Dominion, Volume III*, eds. Dunbar Rowland and Albert Godfrey Sanders (Jackson, MS, 1932), 122.

104 Like many employees on the heels of a workplace success, Bienville then asked for a promotion: "I entreat the Council very humbly to remember that I have thirty-three years of service in the navy twenty-five of which as commandant in this province, without having obtained any of those marks of distinction that are granted to persons who have been in an office for a long time…" Letter, Bienville to the Council, February 1, 1723, *Mississippi Provincial Archives 1704-1743: French Dominion, Volume III*, eds. Dunbar Rowland and Albert Godfrey Sanders (Jackson, MS, 1932), 343-44.

105 Memoir on Louisiana [by Bienville], 1726, *Mississippi Provincial Archives 1704-1743: French Dominion, Volume III*, eds. Dunbar Rowland and Albert Godfrey Sanders (Jackson, MS, 1932), 515-16.

106 Letter, Bienville and Salmon to Maurepas (emphasis added), March 20, 1734, *Mississippi Provincial Archives 1704-1743: French Dominion, Volume III*, eds. Dunbar Rowland and Albert Godfrey Sanders (Jackson, MS, 1932), 637-38.

107 M. Perrin Du Lac, *Travels Through the Two Louisianas… in 1801, 1802, & 1803* (London, 1807), 87-88 plus asterisked footnote. Despite his appreciation for New Orleans' challenges, Du Lac was not particularly impressed with the city. "New Orleans," he wrote, "does not merit a favourable description…."

108 Friedrich Ratzel, *Sketches of Urban and Cultural Life in North America*, trans. and ed. Stewart A. Stehlin (New Brunswick and London, 1988 translation of 1876 publication), 196 (emphasis added).

109 Henry Churchill Semple, ed. *The Ursulines in New Orleans 1727-1925* (New York, NY, 1925), 12, 222, and 226-27.

110 Grace King, *New Orleans: The Place and the People* (New York, NY, 1926), 56.

111 Letter of Sister Mary Madeleine Hachard of St. Stanislaus to Her Father, April 24, 1728, in *The Ursulines in New Orleans 1727-1925*, ed. Henry Churchill Semple (New York, NY, 1925), 224-25.

112 Letter of Sister Mary Madeleine Hachard of St. Stanislaus to Her Father, October 27, 1727, in *The Ursulines in New Orleans 1727-1925*, ed. Henry Churchill Semple (New York, NY, 1925), 193.

113 Ibid., 194-95.

114 Ibid., 195.

115 Letter of Sister Mary Madeleine Hachard of St. Stanislaus to Her Father, April 24, 1728, in *The Ursulines in New Orleans 1727-1925*, ed. Henry Churchill Semple (New York, NY, 1925), 225.

116 Henry Churchill Semple, ed. *The Ursulines in New Orleans 1727-1925* (New York, NY, 1925), 15.

117 "The Earliest Teachers," in *Publications of the Louisiana Historical Society, Volume III, Part 1* (New Orleans, 1902), 55.

118 Le Page du Pratz, *The History of Louisiana*, ed. Joseph G. Tregle, Jr. (Baton Rouge, LA, 1976 reprint of 1758 original), 53.

119 Ibid., 158.

120 Ibid., 53.

121 Ibid., 54.

122 Ibid., 54-55.

123 Ibid., 55.

124 Ibid., 55 and 157.

125 Malcolm Heard, *French Quarter Manual: An Architectural Guide to New Orleans' Vieux Carré* (New Orleans, 1997), 1.

126 Marcel Giraud, *A History of French Louisiana, Volume Five: The Company of the Indies, 1723-1731* (Baton Rouge, LA, 1987), 207.

127 Memoir on Louisiana [by Bienville], 1726, *Mississippi Provincial Archives 1704-1743: French Dominion, Volume III*, eds. Dunbar Rowland and Albert Godfrey Sanders (Jackson, MS, 1932), 509-10.

128 Ibid., 516.

129 Letter, De La Chaise and the Four Councillors of Louisiana to the Council of the Company of the Indies, April 26, 1725, *Mississippi Provincial Archives 1704-1743: French Dominion, Volume II*, eds. Dunbar Rowland and Albert Godfrey Sanders (Jackson, MS, 1929), 464.

130 Letter, King to Bienville and Salmon, February 2, 1732, *Mississippi Provincial Archives 1704-1743: French Dominion, Volume III*, eds. Dunbar Rowland and Albert Godfrey Sanders (Jackson, MS, 1932), 563.

131 Le Page du Pratz, *The History of Louisiana*, ed. Joseph G. Tregle, Jr. (Baton Rouge, LA, 1976 reprint of 1758 original), 239.

132 Letter, Périer and De La Chaise to the Directors of the Company of the Indies, January 30, 1729, *Mississippi Provincial Archives 1704-1743: French Dominion, Volume II*, eds. Dunbar Rowland and Albert Godfrey Sanders (Jackson, MS, 1929), 616-17; see also 259-60. For the origin of mulberry trees in Louisiana, see Edna F. Cambell, "New Orleans in the Early Days," *Geographical Review* 10, No. 1 (July 1920): 35.

133 Minutes of the Directors of the Company of the Indies, June 3, 1729, *Mississippi Provincial Archives 1704-1743: French Dominion, Volume II*, eds. Dunbar Rowland and Albert Godfrey Sanders (Jackson, MS, 1929), 656.

134 Letter, Committee of Louisiana to the Directors of the Company, November 8, 1724, *Mississippi Provincial Archives 1704-1743: French Dominion, Volume II*, eds. Dunbar Rowland and Albert Godfrey Sanders (Jackson, MS, 1929), 402, 408-09.

135 Letter, Périer and De La Chaise to the Directors of the Company of the Indies, November 3, 1728, *Mississippi Provincial Archives 1704-1743: French Dominion, Volume II*, eds. Dunbar Rowland and Albert Godfrey Sanders (Jackson, MS, 1929), 592.

136 Letter, King to Bienville and Salmon, February 2, 1732, *Mississippi Provincial Archives 1704-1743: French Dominion, Volume III*, eds. Dunbar Rowland and Albert Godfrey Sanders (Jackson, MS, 1932), 562.

137 This figure is for the New Orleans region. For the city proper, it was 60-40 free-slave. Charles R. Maduell Jr., *The Census Tables for the French Colony of Louisiana from 1699 to 1732* (Baltimore, MD, 1972), 16-22 and 81.

138 Capt. Philip Pittman, *The Present State of the European Settlements on the Missisippi* (Gainesville, FL, 1973 reprint of 1770 original), 10.

139 Ibid., 10.

140 Ibid., 10-11.

141 Ibid., 11.

142 Ibid., 12.

143 Francisco Bouligny, "The Memoria," in *Louisiana in 1776: A Memoria of Francisco Bouligny*, ed. Gilbert C. Din (New Orleans, 1977), 44-45.

144 Ibid., 44.

145 Ibid., 44-45.

146 Ibid., 44-45.

147 Ibid., 56.

148 John Pope, "Fontaine Martin, 93, Lawyer, Genealogist," *New Orleans Times-Picayune*, December 7, 2007, p. B-3.

149 William B. Knipmeyer had a somewhat different take on this: "Had those rivers [in southern Louisiana] been without natural levees, and had the land been completely flat but satisfactory for settlement, the land division would undoubtedly have been the same. If rivers had not been available for lines of departure, roads or canals would have served the purpose. The system was not devised to suit the particular topographic conditions, even though a system resembling it would probably have been invented if none had existed." William B. Knipmeyer, "Settlement Succession in Eastern French Louisiana" (Ph.D. dissertation, Louisiana State University, 1956), 32. For more on the environment-versus-culture debate on long lots, see Carl J. Ekberg, *French Roots in the Illinois Country* (Urbana, IL,

1998), 24-25.

150   "The Edict of Louis XV of October 12, 1716," translated by Henry P. Dart, "The First Law Regulating Land Grants in French Colonial Louisiana." *The Louisiana Historical Quarterly* 14, No. 3 (July 1931): 347.

151   Toponyms such as "40-Arpent Canal" or "Eighty Arpent Road" survive today throughout the region.

152   "Letter from Father du Poisson, Missionary to Missionary to the Akensas, to Father * * *," in *The Jesuit Relations and Allied Documents: Travels and Explorations of the Jesuit Missionaries in New France 1610-1791, Volume LXVII—Lower Canada, Abenakis, Louisiana 1716-1727*, ed. Reuben Gold Thwaites (New York, NY, 1959), 281-83.

153   I borrow the term "antecedent cadaster" from the late geographer Milton Newton Jr., *Louisiana: A Geographical Portrait* (Baton Rouge, LA, 1987), 211.

154   Angles measured by Richard Campanella using 1:6000-scale GIS coverages of New Orleans streets, from the New Orleans City Planning Commission.

155   Malcolm Heard, *French Quarter Manual: An Architectural Guide to New Orleans' Vieux Carré* (New Orleans, 1997), 119.

156   Bernard Lemann, *The Vieux Carré—A General Statement* (New Orleans, 1996), 11-30.

157   Bureau of Government Research, City of New Orleans, *Plan and Program for the Preservation of the Vieux Carré* (New Orleans, 1968), 19-35.

158   Lloyd Vogt, *New Orleans Houses: A House-Watcher's Guide* (Gretna, LA, 1985), 25-26.

159   This essay is partially based on a quantitative analysis of French Quarter architecture presented in my earlier book, *Geographies of New Orleans: Urban Fabrics Before the Storm* (Lafayette, LA, 2006).

160   Capt. Philip Pittman, *The Present State of the European Settlements on the Missisippi* (Gainesville, FL, 1973 reprint of 1770 original), 11.

161   See Jonathan Fricker, "The Origins of the Creole Raised Plantation House," *Louisiana History* 25 (Spring 1984): 142-44, for further discussion of "climatic determinism."

162   Jonathan Fricker, "The Origins of the Creole Raised Plantation House," *Louisiana History* 25 (Spring 1984): 146.

163   Jay D. Edwards, "The Origins of Creole Architecture," *Winterthur Portfolio: A Journal of American Material Culture* 29 (Summer/Autumn 1994): 156; Jay D. Edwards, "The Origins of the Louisiana Creole Cottage," in *French and Germans in the Mississippi Valley: Landscape and Cultural Traditions*, ed. Michael Roard (Cape Girardeau, MO, 1988), 21-22.

164   Pierre Clément de Laussat, *Memoirs of My Life* (Baton Rouge and New Orleans, LA, 1978 translation of 1831 memoir), 55.

165   Thomas Ashe, *Travels in America Performed in the Year 1806* (London, 1809), 311.

166   Malcolm Heard, *French Quarter Manual: An Architectural Guide to New Orleans' Vieux Carré* (New Orleans, 1997), 4.

167   Basil Hall, *Travels in North America in the Years 1827 and 1828, Volume III* (Edinburgh and London, 1830), 318.

168   Quantitative data on French Quarter architecture in this essay derive from the analysis presented in my earlier book, *Geographies of New Orleans: Urban Fabrics Before the Storm* (Lafayette, LA, 2006).

169   Lloyd Vogt, *New Orleans Houses: A House-Watcher's Guide* (Gretna, LA, 1985), 63.

170   Benjamin Henry Boneval Latrobe, *Impressions Respecting New Orleans: Diary & Sketches 1818-1820*, ed. Samuel Wilson Jr. (New York, NY, 1951), xiii.

171   Joseph G. Tregle Jr., "Creoles and Americans," in *Creole New Orleans: Race and Americanization*, eds. Arnold R. Hirsch and Joseph Logsdon (Baton Rouge and London, 1992), 152-57.

172   Malcolm Heard, *French Quarter Manual: An Architectural Guide to New Orleans' Vieux Carré* (New Orleans, 1997), 41.

173   Joseph G. Tregle Jr., "Creoles and Americans," in *Creole New Orleans: Race and Americanization*, eds. Arnold R. Hirsch and Joseph Logsdon (Baton Rouge and London, 1992), 155.

174   James Marston Fitch, "Creole Architecture 1718-1860: The Rise and Fall of a Great Tradition," in *The Past as Prelude: New Orleans 1718-1968*, ed. Hodding Carter (New Orleans, 1968), 86-87.

175   John Michael Vlach, "Sources of the Shotgun House: African and Caribbean Antecedents for Afro-American Architecture" (Ph.D. dissertation, Indiana University, 1975), 164.

176   Quantitative data on French Quarter architecture in this essay derive from the analysis presented in my earlier book, *Geographies of New Orleans: Urban Fabrics Before the Storm* (Lafayette, LA, 2006).

177   The earliest reference I have found appeared in a 1907 Texas newspaper, which used the term to de-

scribe a 14-by-32-foot bunkhouse used by foreigner workers employed in Fort Worth's meat-packing plants. "Anti-Foreign Feeling Quiet," *Fort Worth Star-Telegram,* December 22, 1907, p. 16.

178 John Michael Vlach, "Sources of the Shotgun House: African and Caribbean Antecedents for Afro-American Architecture" (Ph.D. dissertation, Indiana University, 1975), 29.

179 William Bernard Knipmeyer, "Settlement Succession in Eastern French Louisiana" (Ph.D. dissertation, Louisiana State University, 1956), 75.

180 Ibid., 81-87. Knipmeyer's dissertation primarily addressed settlement succession rather than the origin of house types.

181 James Marston Fitch, "Creole Architecture 1718-1860: The Rise and Fall of a Great Tradition," in *The Past as Prelude: New Orleans 1718-1968,* ed. Hodding Carter (New Orleans, 1968), 72.

182 John Michael Vlach, "Sources of the Shotgun House: African and Caribbean Antecedents for Afro-American Architecture" (Ph.D. dissertation, Indiana University, 1975), 80-155; quote on 189.

183 Fred B. Kniffen, "Louisiana House Types," *Annals of the Association of American Geographers* 26, No. 4 (December 1936): 191-92. See Vlach's response on pages 38-41 of Vlach's dissertation.

184 Among cities, Louisville, Kentucky has been described as second only to New Orleans in its number of shotguns.

185 Judy Walker, "Shotgun Appreciation," *New Orleans Times-Picayune,* March 1, 2002, Living section, p. 1.

186 John Michael Vlach, "Sources of the Shotgun House: African and Caribbean Antecedents for Afro-American Architecture" (Ph.D. dissertation, Indiana University, 1975), 60-63.

187 Jay D. Edwards, "The Origins of Creole Architecture," *Winterthur Portfolio: A Journal of American Material Culture* 29 (Summer/Autumn 1994): 155.

188 I borrow this observation from Craig E. Colten.

189 Pierre Le Moyne, Sieur d'Iberville, *Iberville's Gulf Journals,* ed. Richebourg Gaillard McWilliams (University, AL, 1991 translation of 1700 journal), 53.

190 Letter, Périer and De La Chaise to the Directors of the Company of the Indies, November 3, 1728, *Mississippi Provincial Archives 1704-1743: French Dominion, Volume II,* eds. Dunbar Rowland and Albert Godfrey Sanders (Jackson, MS, 1929), 592.

191 Charles F. Zimpel, *Topographical Map of New Orleans and Its Vicinity, 1834.* Original copy stored at Southeastern Architectural Archive, Tulane University Special Collections.

192 Gleaned from editions of the *Daily Orleanian,* 1849-50.

193 Louis C. Hennick and E. Harper Charlton, *The Streetcars of New Orleans* (Gretna, LA, 1965, reprinted 2000).

194 E. Robinson and R. H. Pidgeon, *Atlas of the City of New Orleans, Louisiana* (New York, NY, 1883).

195 Based on author's analysis of the 1910 and 1940 Census, at the enumeration district and census tract level.

196 Sewerage and Water Board of New Orleans, *Report on Hurricane "Betsy," September 9-10, 1965* (New Orleans, October 8, 1965), 32.

197 Based on author's analysis of the 1960 and 2000 Census, at the census-tract and block level.

198 Albert James Pickett, *Eight Days in New Orleans in February, 1847.* (Montgomery, AL, 1847), 17-18. I thank James D. Wilson for bringing this source to my attention.

199 The present-day Orleans/Jefferson parish line at Monticello Street also dates back to 1805, but had been changed to Felicity Street in 1812 and thence relocated throughout present-day uptown over the next six decades. Former upper boundaries of New Orleans include an old plantation line near St. Joseph Street (1797), Monticello Street (1805), Felicity Street (1812), an old plantation line between Foucher and Antonine streets (1818), Felicity Street again in 1833, Toledano Street (1852), Lowerline Street in 1870, and finally Monticello Street again in 1874, where it remains today. Sam R. Carter, *A Report on Survey of Metropolitan New Orleans Land Use, Real Property, and Low Income Housing Area* (New Orleans, 1941), "Growth in Area: New Orleans, Louisiana" fold-out map.

200 Gilbert Fowler White, "Human Adjustment to Floods" (Ph.D. dissertation, University of Chicago, 1942, published 1945), 2

201 Virginia R. Domínguez, "Social Classification in Creole Louisiana," *American Ethnologist* 4 (November 1977): 591

202 Letter, William C. C. Claiborne to James Madison, October 16, 1804, in *Interim Appointment: W. C. C. Claiborne Letter Book, 1804-1805,* ed. Jared William Bradley (Baton Rouge, LA, 2002), 39.

203 Benjamin Moore Norman, *Norman's New Orleans and Environs* (New Orleans, 1845), 73.

204 Joseph Holt Ingraham, *The South-West by a Yankee,* 2 vols. (New York, NY, 1835), 1:119 (footnote).

205 *Daily Orleanian*, March 9, 1849, p. 2, c. 4.

206 Thomas Ashe, *Travels in America Performed in the Year 1806* (London, 1809), 310.

207 Harriet Martineau, *Retrospect of Western Travel, Volume I* (London and New York, 1838), 263 and 271.

208 *Daily Orleanian*, February 19, 1849, p. 2, c. 3.

209 "From New Orleans—The Municipal Election," *New York Times*, June 4, 1856, p. 1.

210 Fredrika Bremer, *The Homes of the New World: Impressions of America, Volume II* (New York, NY, 1853), 240.

211 Mary Gehman, "The Mexico-Louisiana Creole Connection," *Louisiana Cultural Vistas* 11 (Winter 2000-2001): 72.

212 Barbara Leigh Smith Bodichon, *An American Diary 1857-8*, ed. Joseph W. Reed Jr. (London 1972), 98.

213 Joseph G. Tregle Jr., "Creoles and Americans," in *Creole New Orleans: Race and Americanization*, eds. Arnold R. Hirsch and Joseph Logsdon (Baton Rouge and London, 1992), 172.

214 Gwendolyn Midlo Hall, *Africans in Colonial Louisiana: The Development of Afro-Creole Culture in the Eighteenth Century* (Baton Rouge and London, 1992), 158.

215 Charles Gayarré, *The Creoles of History and the Creoles of Romance—A Lecture Delivered in the Hall of the Tulane University, New Orleans* (New Orleans, 1885), 3.

216 George Washington Cable, *The Creoles of Louisiana* (New York, NY, 1884), 41.

217 James H. Dormon, "Ethnicity and Identity: Creoles of Color in Twentieth-Century South Louisiana," in *Creole of Color of the Gulf South*, ed. James H. Dormon (Knoxville, 1996), 169-70.

218 Allan Katz, "The Seventh War: Mother of Mayors," *New Orleans Magazine* 28 (May 1994): 51 (emphasis added).

219 Jacques M. Henry and Carl L. Bankston, "Propositions for a Structuralist Analysis of Creolism," *Current Anthropology* 39 (August-October 1998): 558.

220 Mary Gehman, *The Free People of Color of New Orleans: An Introduction* (New Orleans, 1994), 103

221 "A Kaleidoscopic View of New Orleans," *Daily Picayune*, September 23, 1843, p. 2, c. 3.

222 Nathaniel H. Bishop, *Four Months in a Sneak-Box* (Boston, MA, 1879), 205.

223 Joseph Logsdon, "The Surprise of the Melting Pot: We Can All Become New Orleanians," in *Perspectives on Ethnicity in New Orleans*, ed. John Cooke (New Orleans, 1979), 8.

224 Treasury Department, Bureau of Statistics, *Tables Showing Arrivals of Alien Passengers and Immigrants in the United States from 1820 to 1888* (Washington, DC, 1889),108-09

225 Frederick Marcel Spletstoser, "Back Door to the Land of Plenty: New Orleans as an Immigrant Port, 1820-1860" (Ph.D. dissertation, Louisiana State University, 1979), vi.

226 Henry Bradshaw Fearon, *Sketches of America: A Narrative of a Journey of Five Thousand Miles Through the Eastern and Western States of America* (London, 1819), 273.

227 Richard W. Bailey, "The Foundation of English in the Louisiana Purchase: New Orleans, 1800-1850," *American Speech* 78 (2003), 365.

228 The subgroups were aggregated as (1) locally born; (2) born elsewhere in U.S.; (3) born in England, Wales, or Scotland; (4) born in Ireland; (5) born in Germany, Prussia, or Austria; (6) born in France; (7) born in Spain; (8) born in Italy; (9) free people of color; and (10) enslaved blacks. Analysis by Richard Campanella based on J. D. B. De Bow, *Statistical View of the United States—Compendium of the Seventh Census* (Washington, D.C.,1854), 395-99.

229 "Extracts from the Clockmaker," *The Madisonian*, 2, Issue 19, October 20, 1838, p. 1. Another version of this piece appears as "Sam Slick's Description of New Orleans," *Barre Gazette* (Barre, Massachusetts), 5, Issue 37, January 25, 1839, p. 1.

230 Ernst von Hesse-Wartegg, *Travels on the Lower Mississippi, 1879-1880: A Memoir by Ernst von Hesse-Wartegg*, ed. and trans. Frederic Trautmann (Columbia and London, 1990), 161. The figure for Anglo-Americans presumably includes tens of thousands of locally born descendents of Irish immigrants who arrived in the 1830s-50s.

231 "A Peep at New Orleans—Correspondence of the Boston Post," appearing in the *New Orleans Daily Delta*, February 5, 1863.

232 Frederick Law Olmsted, *A Journey in the Seaboard Slave States, With Remarks on Their Economy* (New York, NY, 1856) 593-94.

233 Ronald Van Kempen and A. Sule Özüekren, "Ethnic Segregation in Cities: New Forms and Explanations in a Dynamic World," *Urban Studies* 35 (1998): 1631.

234 Elisée Réclus, *A Voyage to New Orleans*, eds. John Clark and Camille Martin (Thetford, VT, 2004

translation of 1855 original), 50 (emphasis added).

235 J. D. B. De Bow, "Lafayette, Louisiana," *The Commercial Review of the South and West* 4 (1847): 262.

236 Charles Patton Dimitry, "Recollections of an Old Citizen," *Times-Democrat*, September 10, 1893.

237 Thomas K. Wharton, *Queen of the South—New Orleans, 1853-1862: The Journal of Thomas K. Wharton*, eds. Samuel Wilson Jr., Patricia Brady, and Lynn D. Adams (New Orleans, 1999), 60.

238 "A Kaleidoscopic View of New Orleans," *Daily Picayune*, September 23, 1843, p. 2, c. 3.

239 H. Didimus (Edward Henry Durell), *New Orleans As I Found It* (New York, NY, 1845), 7, published in 1845 based on observations from winter 1835-36.

240 A. Oakey Hall, *The Manhattaner in New Orleans; or Phases of "Crescent City" Life* (New York, NY, 1851), 35-36.

241 Ibid., 178.

242 Wrote Charles Lyell in 1846, "Ten years ago…all the draymen of New Orleans…and the cabmen… were colored. Now, they are nearly all white. The servants at the great hotels were formerly of the African, now they are of the European race. Nowhere is the jealousy felt by the Irish toward the negroes more apparent." Charles Lyell, *A Second Visit to the United States of North America*, 2 vols. (New York and London, 1849), 2:125; page numbers vary on subsequent editions.

243 "A Kaleidoscopic View of New Orleans," *Daily Picayune*, September 23, 1843, p. 2, c. 3.

244 Joseph C. G. Kennedy, *Population of the United States in 1860; Compiled from the Original Returns of the Eighth Census* (Washington, DC, 1864), 195; mapped by Richard Campanella in *Geographies of New Orleans: Urban Fabrics Before the Storm* (Lafayette, LA, 2006), 298.

245 In 1939, there were 5,941 dwelling units within the 2,204 surviving pre-1860 buildings, of which 4,605 were rented to tenants. Sam Carter, *A Report on Survey of Metropolitan New Orleans Land Use, Real Property, and Low Income Housing Area* (New Orleans, 1941), 36 and 52.

246 Paul Knox, *Urban Social Geography: An Introduction* (Essex, England and New York, 1987), 256.

247 David Ward, *Cities and Immigrants: A Geography of Change in Nineteenth Century America* (New York, London, Toronto, 1971), 106.

248 Ernest W. Burgess, "The Growth of the City: An Introduction to a Research Project," in *The City*, eds. Robert E. Park, Ernest W. Burgess and Roderick D. McKenzie (Chicago, IL, 1925), 47-62.

249 Brad Edmondson, "Immigration Nation: The New Suburbanities," *Preservation* 52, No. 1 (January-February 2000): 31.

250 Ibid., 31-32

251 Manuel Torres and Matt Scallan, "Outward Migration: Statistics Show Orleans Parish May Be Losing Its Appeal to Hispanics," *New Orleans Times-Picayune*, July 9, 2001, p. 1; and Joan Treadway and Coleman Warner, "East Meets West: Vietnamese Residents Have Put New Orleans on the Map as an Asian Cultural Center," *New Orleans Times-Picayune*, August 6, 2001, A7.

252 Coleman Warner and Matt Scallan, "Going to Extremes," *New Orleans Times-Picayune*, September 3, 2001, A-8.

253 Brian Thevenot and Matthew Brown, "School Segregation 50 Years Later: From Resistance to Acceptance," *New Orleans Times-Picayune*, May 19, 2004, A1.

254 Brad Edmondson, "Immigration Nation: The New Suburbanities," *Preservation* 52, No. 1 (January-February 2000): 31.

255 Larry Ford and Ernst Griffin, "The Ghettoization of Paradise," *Geographical Review* 69 (April 1979): 156-57. See also David T. Herbert and Colin J. Thomas, *Urban Geography: A First Approach* (Chichester, New York, Brisbane, Toronto and Singapore, 1982), 312-14.

256 "Emancipation at the South—Tolerance of Louisiana," *New York Times*, March 28, 1856, citing an article originally published in the *New-Orleans Bulletin*.

257 "A Kaleidoscopic View of New Orleans," *Daily Picayune*, September 23, 1843, p. 2, c. 3.

258 Dale A. Somers, "Black and White in New Orleans: A Study in Urban Race Relations, 1865-1900," *Journal of Southern History* 40, No. 1 (February 1974): 21.

259 John W. Blassingame, *Black New Orleans, 1860-1880* (Chicago, IL and London, 1973), 60-1.

260 Friedrich Ratzel, *Sketches of Urban and Cultural Life in North America*, trans. and ed. Stewart A. Stehlin (New Brunswick and London, 1988 translation of 1873 treatise), 214 (emphasis added).

261 Daphne Spain, "Race Relations and Residential Segregation in New Orleans: Two Centuries of Paradox," *The Annals of the American Academy of Political and Social Science* 441 (January 1979): 82.

262 Coleman Warner and Gwen Filosa, "UNANIMOUS: Council Votes to Raze 4,500 Units; Old Housing Model to Give Way to Mixed-Income Developments," *New Orleans Times-Picayune*, December 21, 2007, p. 1.

263 Analysis by Richard Campanella using Census 2000 demographic data and flood extent of September 8, representing deeply and persistently flooded areas.

264 Louisiana Department of Health and Hospitals, "2006 Louisiana Health and Population Survey Report—Orleans Parish," Louisiana Recovery Authority (Baton Rouge, January 17, 2007), 3, and U.S. Census Bureau, "American Community Survey—New Orleans City, Louisiana, ACS Demographic and Housing Estimates 2006: Demographic-Sex and Age, Race, Hispanic Origin, Housing Units," http://factfinder.census.gov (accessed 2008).

265 As quoted by Michelle Krupa, "It's Official: Katrina Chased Out a Huge Chunk of N.O. Voters, Remaking the Region's Electoral Landscape," *New Orleans Times-Picayune*, April 24, 2008, A1-A4.

266 Analysis by Richard Campanella using Census 2000 data. Post-Katrina figures cannot be computed precisely until the 2010 Census, but given the heavy flooding of mostly white Lakeview, an even higher percent of the city's white population may reside in the "teapot" after the storm.

267 Peirce F. Lewis, *New Orleans: The Making of an Urban Landscape* (Cambridge, MA, 1976), 46. Black males worked 57 to 60 percent of servant positions in New Orleans in 1870 and 1880, though they comprised 25 and 23 percent, respectively, of the labor force in those years. John W. Blassingame, *Black New Orleans, 1860-1880* (Chicago, IL and London, 1973), 61.

268 John Magill, "A Conspiracy of Complicity," *Louisiana Cultural Vistas* 17, No.3 (Fall 2006), 43.

269 H. W. Gilmore, *Some Basic Census Tract Maps of New Orleans* (New Orleans, 1937), map book stored at Tulane University Special Collections, C5-D10-F6.

270 Analysis by Richard Campanella, "Above-Sea-Level New Orleans: The Residential Capacity of Orleans Parish's Higher Ground," CBR Whitepaper funded by Coypu Foundation, http://kerrn.org/pdf/campanellaaslno.pdf, April 2007.

271 As quoted by Bruce Nolan, "Churches Celebrate 150 Years," *New Orleans Times-Picayune*, April 25, 2008, B1.

272 1960 data were processed at the coarser census tract level, while 2000 were analyzed at the more detailed census block level.

273 Analysis by Richard Campanella using August 2007 population figures released by GCR & Associates.

274 Analysis by Richard Campanella using block-level data on households receiving mail (as of February 2008) provided by the Greater New Orleans Community Data Center and Valassis, Inc. Because households may contain anywhere from one person to over a dozen, they cannot be viewed as a perfect surrogate for population data.

275 Analysis of most findings in this chapter by Richard Campanella, "Above-Sea-Level New Orleans: The Residential Capacity of Orleans Parish's Higher Ground," CBR Whitepaper funded by Coypu Foundation, http://kerrn.org/pdf/campanellaaslno.pdf, April 2007.

276 Peirce F. Lewis, *New Orleans: The Making of an Urban Landscape* (Cambridge, MA, 1976), 45-46.

277 Joseph C. G. Kennedy, *Population of the United States in 1860; Compiled from the Original Returns of the Eighth Census* (Washington, DC, 1864), 195; mapped by Richard Campanella, *Geographies of New Orleans: Urban Fabrics Before the Storm* (Lafayette, LA, 2006), 298.

278 Like all quantitative measures of social characteristics, the dissimilarity index is an oversimplification of a complex phenomenon, and may produce misleading results depending on the spatial scale, study area, and nuances of the input data.

279 "Large cities" means population over 400,000 within the city limits, excluding suburbs, in 2000. All dissimilarity indices presented here were computed for white and black populations (only two groups at a time can be tested against each other) at the block-group level. Indices will differ when computed for other units, such as census tracts or blocks. Calculated through the Social Science Data Analysis Network, University of Michigan, www.CensusScope.org ; www.ssdan.net. Indices computed in other studies may vary slightly because of differing input parameters; the University of Michigan Population Studies Center, for example, computed 68.8 for New Orleans at the block-group level.

280 N. M. Miller Surrey, *The Commerce of Louisiana During the French Régime, 1699-1763* (New York, NY, 1916), 155.

281 Ibid., 76-78 and 161-65.

282 Anonymous, "The Present State of the Country…of Louisiana…by an Officer at New Orleans to his Friend at Paris," in *Narratives of Colonial America 1704-1765*, ed. Howard H. Peckham (Chicago, IL 1971), 60-1.

283 Document 27, Michel to Rouillé, September 23, 1752, *Mississippi Provincial Archives: French Dominion, 1749-1763, Volume V*, eds. Dunbar Rowland and A. G. Sanders; revised by Patricia Kay Galloway

(Baton Rouge, LA and London, 1984), 114-17.

284   Capt. Philip Pittman, *The Present State of the European Settlements on the Missisippi* (Gainesville, FL, 1973 reprint of 1770 original), 22-23.

285   N. M. Miller Surrey, *The Commerce of Louisiana During the French Régime, 1699-1763* (New York, NY, 1916), 224, 289.

286   Francisco Bouligny, "The Memoria," in *Louisiana in 1776: A Memoria of Francisco Bouligny,* ed. Gilbert C. Din (New Orleans, 1977), 44-45.

287   Ibid., 55.

288   Ibid., 56.

289   Thomas Ashe, *Travels in America Performed in the Year 1806* (London, 1809), 309-10. Ashe might have engaged in hyperbole in estimating the increase of merchants between 1800 and 1806.

290   Fortescue Cuming, *Sketches of a Tour to the Western Country through the States of Ohio and Kentucky* (Pittsburgh, PA, 1810), 338.

291   M. Perrin Du Lac, *Travels Through the Two Louisianas... in 1801, 1802, & 1803* (London, 1807), 92.

292   Frank Haigh Dixon, *A Traffic History of the Mississippi River System—National Waterways Commission, Document Number 11* (Washington, DC, 1909), 12-13.

293   Pierre Clément de Laussat, *Memoirs of My Life* (Baton Rouge and New Orleans, LA, 1978 translation of 1831 memoir), 24-25.

294   Chevalier Guy de Soniat du Fossat, *Synopsis of the History of Louisiana from the Founding of the Colony to End of the Year 1791,* ed. and trans. Charles T. Soniat (New Orleans, 1903), 39.

295   Timothy Flint, *Recollections of the Last Ten Years... in the Valley of the Mississippi* (Boston, MA, 1826), 300.

296   Charles Lyell, *A Second Visit to the United States of North America,* 2 vols. (New York and London, 1849), 2:130 (emphasis added; page numbers vary on subsequent editions).

297   Richard Campanella, *Time and Place in New Orleans: Past Geographies in the Present Day* (Gretna, LA, 2002), 124-33.

298   John E. Dalton, *Sugar: A Case Study of Government Control* (New York, NY, 1937), 167-68.

299   Jaquetta White, "Business is Sour for La. Sugar Industry; Number of Farms, Mills Continues Slide," *New Orleans Times-Picayune,* January 30, 2005, Money section, p. 1.

300   Jeffrey Alan Owens, *Holding Back the Waters: Land Development and the Origins of Levees on the Mississippi, 1720-1845* (Ph.D. dissertation, 1999), quoted from abstract.

301   E.W. Gould, *Fifty Years on the Mississippi; Or, Gould's History of River Navigation* (St. Louis, MO, 1889), 224-25.

302   Le Page du Pratz, *The History of Louisiana,* ed. Joseph G. Tregle, Jr. (Baton Rouge, LA, 1976 reprint of 1758 original), 54.

303   Capt. Philip Pittman, *The Present State of the European Settlements on the Missisippi* (Gainesville, FL, 1973 reprint of 1770 original), 10.

304   Laura L. Porteous, trans., "Governor Carondelet's Levee Ordinance of 1792," *The Louisiana Historical Quarterly* 10, No. 4 (October 1927): 513-14.

305   Fred B. Kniffen, "The Lower Mississippi Valley: European Settlement, Utilization and Modification," *Geoscience & Man* 27 (1990): 6-7.

306   Adam Hodgson, *Remarks During a Journey Through North America in the Years 1819, 1820, and 1821* (New York, NY, 1823), 163.

307   Joseph Holt Ingraham, *The South-West by a Yankee,* 2 vols. (New York, NY, 1835), 1:78-79.

308   John M. Barry, *Rising Tide: The Great Mississippi River Flood of 1927 and How It Changed America* (New York, NY, 1997), 32-45.

309   Albert E. Cowdrey, *Land's End: A History of the New Orleans District, U.S. Army Corps of Engineers* (New Orleans, 1977), 9.

310   Ari Kelman, "A River and its City: Critical Episodes in the Environmental History of New Orleans" (Ph.D. dissertation, Brown University, 1998), 311.

311   Act 93 of the 1890 General Assembly of the State of Louisiana (July 7, 1890), as quoted in Orleans Levee District, *The Orleans Levee District—A History* and *The Mississippi River Levee* (New Orleans, 1999), pamphlet.

312   Ari Kelman, "A River and its City: Critical Episodes in the Environmental History of New Orleans" (Ph.D. dissertation, Brown University, 1998), 311-13.

313   Association of Levee Boards of Louisiana, *The System That Works to Serve Our State* (New Orleans, 1990), 44, and Orleans Levee District, *The Orleans Levee District—The Hurricane Levee System* (New

Orleans, 1999), pamphlet.

314 The government is not liable for the failure of flood-control devices such as the outfall canals and their levees and floodwalls, but can be held responsible for breaches on navigation waterways, such as the Industrial Canal, ICWW, and MR-GO.

315 Capt. Philip Pittman, *The Present State of the European Settlements on the Missisippi* (Gainesville, FL, 1973 reprint of 1770 original), 24.

316 Fortescue Cuming, *Sketches of a Tour to the Western Country through the States of Ohio and Kentucky* (Pittsburgh, PA, 1810), 338.

317 Frank H. Waddill, *Survey of the Right-of-Way of the Canal Carondelet, From Rampart Street to Hagan Avenue* (New Orleans, November 23, 1923), blueprint stored at Tulane University Special Collections, C5-D12-F8.

318 John Adems Paxton, *The New-Orleans Directory and Register*, 1822 (New Orleans, 1822), 37.

319 Christian Schultz, *Travels on an Inland Voyage Through the States of New-York, Pennsylvania, Virginia, Ohio, Kentucky and Tennessee; Performed in the Years 1807 and 1808*, Volume 2 (New York, NY, 1810), 202.

320 Maj. Amos Stoddard, *Sketches, Historical and Descriptive of Louisiana* (Philadelphia, 1812), 163.

321 "Domestic-New Orleans," *Middlesex Gazette* (Middletown, Connecticut), 39, Issue 2016, July 14, 1824, p. 2.

322 "New-Orleans—Sabbath in New Orleans," *New York Times*, April 12, 1853.

323 J. E. Alexander, *Transatlantic Sketches, Comprising Visits to the Most Interesting Scenes in North and South America, and the West Indies, Volume II* (London, 1833), 32 (emphasis added).

324 Thomas Ewing Dabney, *The Industrial Canal and Inner Harbor of New Orleans: History, Description and Economic Aspects of Giant Facility Created to Encourage Industrial Expansion and Develop Commerce* (New Orleans, 1921), 10-12.

325 U.S. Army Corps of Engineers New Orleans District, *Architectural and Archeological Investigations In and Adjacent to the Bywater Historic District* (New Orleans, 1994), 83. For an exact description of the site for the Industrial Canal, see Mayoralty of New Orleans, *New Orleans Industrial and Ship Canal: An Ideal Location for Shipyards, Factories and Warehouses* (New Orleans, May 21, 1918), pamphlet.

326 This problem was resolved by none other than Albert Baldwin Wood, who adapted his centrifugal pump impeller (designed to handle debris within the sewerage system) to the dredges. Thomas Ewing Dabney, *The Industrial Canal and Inner Harbor of New Orleans: History, Description and Economic Aspects of Giant Facility Created to Encourage Industrial Expansion and Develop Commerce* (New Orleans, 1921), 28.

327 Thomas Ewing Dabney, *The Industrial Canal and Inner Harbor of New Orleans: History, Description and Economic Aspects of Giant Facility Created to Encourage Industrial Expansion and Develop Commerce* (New Orleans, 1921), 17-30.

328 Anonymous, "The Marriage of Mississippi and Pontchartrain," *The Literary Digest*, Science and Invention section, April 14, 1923; and Thomas Ewing Dabney, *The Industrial Canal and Inner Harbor of New Orleans: History, Description and Economic Aspects of Giant Facility Created to Encourage Industrial Expansion and Develop Commerce* (New Orleans, 1921), 40-47.

329 As quoted by Gary A. Bolding, "The New Orleans Seaway Movement," *Louisiana History* 10 (1969): 53-54.

330 Gary A. Bolding, "The New Orleans Seaway Movement," *Louisiana History* 10 (1969): 56-57.

331 Brent M. Johnson, "Development of the Mississippi River-Gulf Outlet," *Journal of the Waterways Division, Proceedings of the American Society of Civil Engineers* (1969): 8-9.

332 U.S. Army Corps of Engineers, New Orleans District, *Water Resources Development in Louisiana* (New Orleans, 1995), 89-90.

333 U.S. Army Corps of Engineers, New Orleans District, *Water Resources Development in Louisiana* (New Orleans, 1995), 90 and *Waterborne Commerce of the United States, Part 2, Waterways and Harbors, Gulf Coast, Mississippi River System and Antilles* (Washington, DC, 1998), 165, 170, and 207.

334 Stanford E. Chaillé, "Inundations of New Orleans and Their Influence on Its Health," *New Orleans Medical and Surgical Journal* (July 1882), excerpt in Tulane University Special Collections Vertical File, Flooding folder, 13-16.

335 Mark Schleifstein, "Corps Moves to Close MR-GO," *New Orleans Times-Picayune*, November 17, 2007, p. 1.

336 "John Mitchell in New Orleans," *Sunday Delta* (New Orleans), April 18, 1858, p. 7, c. 1.

337 Basil Hall, *Travels in North America in the Years 1827 and 1828, Volume III* (Edinburgh and London,

1830), 318.

338 *Louisiana Advertiser*, "Opening of the Rail Road," April 25, 1831, p. 2, c. 4.

339 *Louisiana Advertiser*, September 18, 1832, p. 2, c. 4.

340 A. Oakey Hall, *The Manhattaner in New Orleans; or Phases of "Crescent City" Life* (New York, NY, 1851), 113.

341 Joseph Holt Ingraham, *The South-West by a Yankee*, 2 vols. (New York, NY, 1835), 1:171-73.

342 Ibid., 1:173-74.

343 J. S. Buckingham, *The Slave States of America*, 2 vols. (London and Paris, 1982), 294-95.

344 Charles Lyell, *A Second Visit to the United States of North America*, 2 vols. (New York and London, 1849), 2:90 (page numbers vary on subsequent editions).

345 Frederick Law Olmsted, *The Cotton Kingdom: A Traveler's Observations on Cotton and Slavery in the American Slave States*, 2 vols. (New York and London, 1861), 1:290-91.

346 William Howard Russell, *My Diary North and South* (Boston and New York, 1863), 228-29.

347 James S. Zacharie, *New Orleans Guide* (New Orleans, 1885), 99; all directions are Zacharie's.

348 "Pontchartrain Rail Line About To Be Abandoned," *New Orleans Times-Picayune*, August 26, 1930, p. 24, c. 3.

349 Ari Kelman, "A River and its City: Critical Episodes in the Environmental History of New Orleans" (Ph.D. dissertation, Brown University, 1998), 251-53, 267.

350 "Report on the Drainage of the City of New Orleans by the Advisory Board, Appointed by Ordinance No. 8327, Adopted by the City Council, November 24, 1893," as summarized by Ari Kelman, "A River and its City: Critical Episodes in the Environmental History of New Orleans" (Ph.D. dissertation, Brown University, 1998), 269.

351 George Washington Cable, "New Orleans Revisited," *The Book News Monthly* (April 1909): 564 and 560, as quoted by Ari Kelman, "A River and its City: Critical Episodes in the Environmental History of New Orleans" (Ph.D. dissertation, Brown University, 1998), 281.

352 The City Planning and Zoning Commission, *Major Street Report* (New Orleans, 1927), 75.

353 Sewerage and Water Board of New Orleans, *The Sewerage and Water Board of New Orleans: How It Began, The Problems It Faces, The Way It Works, The Job It Does* (New Orleans, 1998), 9-11.

354 "New Orleans is Getting Hotter—Increases in Temperature in Summer Attributed to the Drainage System," *Columbus Ledger-Enquirer* (Columbus, Georgia), June 13, 1918, p. 1, c. 3.

355 Judy A. Filipich and Lee Taylor, *Lakefront New Orleans: Planning and Development 1926-1971* (New Orleans, 1971), 7-13; Association of Levee Boards of Louisiana, *The System That Works to Serve Our State* (New Orleans, 1990), 43-44

356 Peirce F. Lewis, *New Orleans: The Making of an Urban Landscape* (Cambridge, MA, 1976), 65-66

357 Orleans Levee Board, *Building a Great City* (New Orleans, 1954, pamphlet.

358 Christian Schultz, *Travels on an Inland Voyage Through the States of New-York, Pennsylvania, Virginia, Ohio, Kentucky and Tennessee; Performed in the Years 1807 and 1808*, Volume 2 (New York, NY, 1810), 199.

359 Maj. Amos Stoddard, *Sketches, Historical and Descriptive of Louisiana* (Philadelphia, 1812), 164.

360 Pierre-Louis Berquin-Duvallon, *Travels in Louisiana and The Floridas in the Year 1802, Giving a Correct Picture of Those Countries*, trans. John Davis (New York, NY, 1806), 42. This was a common belief. Wrote Christian Schultz in 1808, "The waters of this river have the credit of being a powerful specific against sterility; and, from the many and well authenticated facts that were cited to me, I have great reason to believe there may be some truth in the relation." Christian Schultz, *Travels on an Inland Voyage Through the States of New-York, Pennsylvania, Virginia, Ohio, Kentucky and Tennessee; Performed in the Years 1807 and 1808*, Volume 2 (New York, NY, 1810), 199.

361 John H. B. Latrobe, *Southern Travels: Journal of John H. B. Latrobe 1834*, ed. Samuel Wilson Jr. (New Orleans, 1986), 47.

362 Albert James Pickett, *Eight Days in New Orleans in February, 1847* (Montgomery, AL, 1847), 26.

363 Julian Ralph, "New Orleans, Our Southern Capital," *Harper's New Monthly Magazine* 86 (February 1893): 370.

364 Walter L. Dodd, *Report of the Health and Sanitary Survey of the City of New Orleans* (New Orleans, 1918-1919), 94.

365 "Water Famine: Much Suffering in the City for Want of Water for Household Purposes," *Daily Picayune*, October 3, 1883, p. 2, c. 4.

366 When discharge is low and tides high, gulf waters sometimes intrude upriver and into the city's intake pipes, allowing salt water in the range of one-hundred parts per million to reach domestic taps.

A sand sill installed recently at River Mile 64 now impedes saltwater wedges (which sink, due to their heavier weight) from moving upriver.

367 Walter L. Dodd, *Report of the Health and Sanitary Survey*, 96-98; James S. Janssen, *Building New Orleans: The Engineer's Role* (New Orleans, 1987), 26-29; John Smith Kendall, *History of New Orleans*, 3 vols. (Chicago, IL and New York, NY, 1922), 1:113-14, 2:526-29, 2:580-84; George E. Waring Jr., *Report on the Social Statistics of Cities, Part II: The Southern and the Western States* (Washington, DC, 1887), 2:273; and *The New Orleans Book* (New Orleans, 1919), 45-46; The City Planning and Zoning Commission, *Major Street Report* (New Orleans, 1927), 16, 19, and 76.

368 Michelle Krupa, "Water Torture," *New Orleans Times-Picayune*, August 8, 2007, A1-A11; Sewerage and Water Board of New Orleans, *The Quality of Our Water,* http://www.swbnola.org/water_infor. htm; Sewerage and Water Board of New Orleans, *Quality Water 2006: A Report on the State of Tap Water in New Orleans,* pamphlet, 2007.

369 Michelle Krupa, "Water Torture," *New Orleans Times-Picayune*, August 8, 2007, A1-A11.

370 While New Orleans watches a half-million cubic feet of freshwater pass by every second, the Gulf Coast city of Tampa, Florida, just a few hundred miles away, struggles with a costly and problematic desalination plant to satisfy its water needs.

371 Erik Friso Haites, "Ohio and Mississippi River Transportation 1810-1860" (Ph.D. dissertation, Purdue University, 1969), 11-16.

372 L. Hirt, *Plan of New Orleans with perspective and geometrical Views of the principal Buildings of the City,* The Historic New Orleans Collection, assession number 1952.4.

373 *New Orleans Bee,* June 10, 1836, p. 2, c. 2.

374 John G. Clark, "New Orleans and the River: A Study in Attitudes and Responses," *Louisiana History* 8 (Spring 1967): 135.

375 Water L. Dodd, *Report of the Health and Sanitary Survey of the City of New Orleans* (New Orleans, 1918-1919), 15.

376 Merl E. Reed, "Boom or Bust: Louisiana's Economy During the 1830s," in *The Louisiana Purchase Bicentennial Series in Louisiana History,* Vol. 16, *Agriculture and Economic Development in Louisiana,* ed. Thomas A. Becnel (Lafayette, LA, 1997), 13.

377 Erik Friso Haites, "Ohio and Mississippi River Transportation 1810-1860" (Ph.D. dissertation, Purdue University, 1969), 11-16.

378 Ronald M. Labbé and Jonathan Lurie, *The Slaughterhouse Cases: Regulation, Reconstruction, and the Fourteenth Amendment* (Lawrence, KS, 2003), 19-20.

379 Erik Friso Haites, "Ohio and Mississippi River Transportation 1810-1860" (Ph.D. dissertation, Purdue University, 1969), 11-16.

380 These estimates reflect shipments from St. Paul, Minnesota to Liverpool, England as per the mid-1870s. Nathaniel H. Bishop, *Four Months in a Sneak-Box* (Boston, MA, 1879), 201.

381 John G. Clark, "New Orleans and the River: A Study in Attitudes and Responses," *Louisiana History* 8 (Spring 1967): 118.

382 Campbell Gibson, "Population of the 100 Largest Cities and Other Urban Places in the United States: 1790 to 1990," Population Division Working Paper No. 27, U.S. Bureau of the Census, Washington, DC, June 1998.

383 "New Orleans and Her Trade," *Daily Picayune*, September 8, 1850, p. 2, c. 2.

384 I borrow this observation from Lawrence N. Powell of Tulane University.

385 John G. Clark, "New Orleans and the River: A Study in Attitudes and Responses," *Louisiana History* 8 (Spring 1967): 135.

386 Alysia R. Kravitz, Richard Campanella, Lisa Schiavinato, and Aquatic Invasive Species Task Force, *State Management Plan for Aquatic Invasive Species in Louisiana* (Baton Rouge, LA, 2005).

387 "Navigation Impeded by Flowers," *Daily Republican* (Decatur, Illinois), August 1, 1895, p. 7, c. 2.

388 *Newark Daily Advocate* (Newark, Ohio), February 16, 1897, p. 1, c. 1.

389 Chris Kirkham, "Nutria Nation," *New Orleans Times-Picayune*, February 25, 2008, A1-A5.

390 Shannon Lee Dawdy, "La Ville Sauvage: 'Enlightened' Colonialism and Creole Improvisation in New Orleans, 1699-1769" (Ph.D. dissertation, The University of Michigan, 2003), 76.

391 Letter of Sister Mary Madeleine Hachard of St. Stanislaus to Her Father, Letter II, October 27, 1727, in *The Ursulines in New Orleans 1727-1925,* ed. Henry Churchill Semple (New York, NY, 1925), 192-93.

392 Letter of Sister Mary Madeleine Hachard of St. Stanislaus to Her Father, April 24, 1728, in *The Ursulines in New Orleans 1727-1925,* ed. Henry Churchill Semple (New York, NY, 1925), 228-29.

393 Anonymous, "Historical Journal: or, Narrative of the Expedition Made by Order of Louis XIV, King of France, under Command of M. D'Iberville to Explore the Colbert (Mississippi) River and Establish a Colony in Louisiana," in *Historical Collections of Louisiana and Florida, Volume VII*, ed. B. F. French (New York, NY, 1875 translation of 1699 journal), 67; M. de Pénicaut, "Annals of Louisiana, From the Establishment of the First Colony Under M. D'Iberville, to the Departure of the Author to France, in 1722," in *Historical Collections of Louisiana and Florida*, ed. B. F. French (New York, NY, 1869), 45, 49; Le Page du Pratz, *The History of Louisiana*, ed. Joseph G. Tregle, Jr. (Baton Rouge, LA, 1976 reprint of 1758 original), 138 and 368.

394 Gabriel Sagard, *Histoire du Canada et voyages que les Frères mineurs recollects y ont faicts pour la conversion des infidèles depuis l'an 1615* (Paris, 1866), 2:426.

395 Father Paul Le Jeune, "Relation of What Occurred in New France in the Year 1633," in *The Jesuit Relations and Allied Documents: Travels and Explorations of the Jesuit Missionaries in New France 1610-1791, Volume V—Quebec, 1632-1633*, ed. Reuben Gold Thwaites (New York, NY, 1959), 97 and 281-82 of Le Jeune's Relation, 1633.

396 Henri Joutel, *A Journal of the Last Voyage Perform'd by Monsr. de La Sale, to the Gulph of Mexico, to Find Out the Mouth of the Missisipi River* (London, 1714), 111 and 150.

397 Margaret Sargent, "Seven Songs from Lorette," *Journal of American Folklore* 63, No. 248 (April 1950): 175.

398 "Letter from Father du Poisson, Missionary to Missionary to the Akensas, to Father * * *," in *The Jesuit Relations and Allied Documents: Travels and Explorations of the Jesuit Missionaries in New France 1610-1791, Volume LXVII—Lower Canada, Abenakis, Louisiana 1716-1727*, ed. Reuben Gold Thwaites (New York, NY, 1959), 291-93.

399 Relation of the Saguenay, 1720 to 1730, by Reverend Father Pierre Laure, in *The Jesuit Relations and Allied Documents: Travels and Explorations of the Jesuit Missionaries in New France 1610-1791, Volume LXVIII—Lower Canada, Crees, Louisiana: 1720-1736*, ed. Reuben Gold Thwaites (New York, NY, 1959), 91.

400 Johann Georg Kohl, *Travels in Canada, and Through the States of New York and Pennsylvania, Volume I* (London, 1861), 175.

401 "Sagamite - Portable Food for Scouts," *Columbus Ledger-Enquirer* (*Daily Columbus Enquirer*, Columbus, Georgia), September 23, 1861, p. 2., c. 3.

402 George Washington Cable, "The Grandissimes," *Scribners Monthly* 19, Issue 1, November 1879: 105.

403 Grace King, *New Orleans: The Place and the People* (New York, NY, 1926), 67.

404 Anonymous, *The Present State of the Country and Inhabitants, Europeans and Indians, of Louisiana, on the North Continent of America* (London, 1744), 25.

405 I thank Marina Campanella, Shelley Meaux, Steven Meaux, and Carl Brasseaux for bringing some of these foods to my attention.

406 Janet C. Gilmore, "Sagamité and Booya: French Influence in Defining Great Lakes Culinary Heritage," *Material History Review* 60 (Fall 2004): 65 and 67.

407 The complex transformation of the meaning of *sagamité* recalls the similarly convoluted history of the word *Creole*.

408 Letter of Sister Mary Madeleine Hachard of St. Stanislaus to Her Father, Letter II, October 27, 1727, in *The Ursulines in New Orleans 1727-1925*, ed. Henry Churchill Semple (New York, NY, 1925), 192-93.

409 Gilbert Din and John E. Harkins, *The New Orleans Cabildo: Colonial Louisiana's First City Government 1769-1803* (Baton Rouge and London, 1996), 186.

410 *Records and Deliberations of the Cabildo, 1769-1803*, trans. Works Progress Administration, September 10, 1784, 7-A, p. 19 of second microfilm roll of Cabildo records, The Historic New Orleans Collection.

411 Ibid., p. 18 of second microfilm roll of Cabildo records, Historic New Orleans Collection.

412 Ibid., p. 19-20 of second microfilm roll of Cabildo records, Historic New Orleans Collection.

413 Gilbert Din and John E. Harkins, *The New Orleans Cabildo: Colonial Louisiana's First City Government 1769-1803* (Baton Rouge and London, 1996), 192-205

414 *Digest of the Acts and Deliberations of the Cabildo*, January 18, 1771, Book 1, p. 52.

415 Benjamin Henry Boneval Latrobe, *Impressions Respecting New Orleans: Diary & Sketches 1818-1820*, ed. Samuel Wilson Jr. (New York, NY, 1951), 101.

416 The Historic New Orleans Collection, *What's Cooking in New Orleans?: Culinary Traditions of the*

Crescent City, Exhibition and Guidebook, January 16-July 7, 2007.

417 "Sunday Morning in the Creole Market," *New Orleans Daily Crescent*, February 16, 1852, p. 1, c. 6.

418 Basil Hall, *Travels in North America in the Years 1827 and 1828, Volume III* (Edinburgh and London, 1830), 330-32.

419 "Sunday Morning in the Creole Market," *New Orleans Daily Crescent*, February 16, 1852, p. 1, c. 6.

420 Fredrika Bremer, *The Homes of the New World: Impressions of America, Volume II* (New York, NY, 1853), 213-14.

421 "The Old French Market," *Daily Picayune*, May 15, 1859, p. 2, c. 1.

422 Nathaniel H. Bishop, *Four Months in a Sneak-Box* (Boston, MA, 1879), 205.

423 The Historic New Orleans Collection, *What's Cooking in New Orleans?: Culinary Traditions of the Crescent City*, Exhibition and Guidebook, January 16-July 7, 2007.

424 "The Old French Market," *Daily Picayune*, May 15, 1859, p. 2, c. 1.

425 As quoted in Friends of the Cabildo, *New Orleans Architecture, Volume II: The American Sector* (Gretna, LA, 1972), 72-73.

426 *Soards' New Orleans City Directory* (New Orleans, 1887), 1047, and Friends of the Cabildo, *New Orleans Architecture, Volume II: The American Sector* (Gretna, LA, 1972), 74-75.

427 *Map of New Orleans Showing Street Railway System of the N.O. Railways Co.* (1904), as reproduced in John Churchill Chase, Hermann B. Deutsch, Charles L. Dufour, and Leonard V. Huber, *Citoyens, Progrès et Politique de la Nouvelle Orléans 1889-1964* (New Orleans, 1964), 8-9.

428 George W. Engelhardt, *New Orleans, Louisiana, The Crescent City: The Book of the Picayune* (New Orleans, 1903-04), 11-22 (emphasis added).

429 Edward McPherson, "Judicial Decisions and Opinions: The Louisiana Slaughter-House Cases." *Hand-Book of Politics for 1874: Being a Record of Important Political Action, National and State, from July 15, 1872 to July 15, 1874* (Washington, DC, 1874), 41.

430 Ronald M. Labbé and Jonathan Lurie, *The Slaughterhouse Cases: Regulation, Reconstruction, and the Fourteenth Amendment* (Lawrence, KS, 2003), 109-10.

431 Ibid., 120-22 and 163.

432 Michael A. Ross, "Justice Miller's Reconstruction: The *Slaughter-House Cases*, Health Codes, and Civil Rights in New Orleans, 1861-1873." *Journal of Southern History* 64, No. 4 (November 1998): 649-76, and Ronald M. Labbé and Jonathan Lurie, *The Slaughterhouse Cases: Regulation, Reconstruction, and the Fourteenth Amendment* (Lawrence, KS, 2003), 243.

433 Federal Writers' Project of the Works Progress Administration, *New Orleans City Guide* (Boston, MA, 1952 revision of 1938 original), 278.

434 Kate Moran, "Hospitals Engaging in Healthy Competition," *New Orleans Times-Picayune*, October 15, 2007, p. B1.

435 Anonymous, "The Present State of the Country...of Louisiana...by an Officer at New Orleans to his Friend at Paris," in *Narratives of Colonial America 1704-1765*, ed. Howard H. Peckham (Chicago, IL, 1971), 61-62.

436 Ibid., 68-69.

437 Ibid., 63

438 Chevalier Guy de Soniat du Fossat, *Synopsis of the History of Louisiana from the Founding of the Colony to End of the Year 1791*, ed. and trans. Charles T. Soniat (New Orleans, 1903), 29.

439 Francisco Bouligny, "The Memoria," in *Louisiana in 1776: A Memoria of Francisco Bouligny*, ed. Gilbert C. Din (New Orleans, 1977), 55-56.

440 Ibid., 57.

441 Ibid., 58.

442 Pierre-Louis Berquin-Duvallon, *Travels in Louisiana and The Floridas in the Year 1802, Giving a Correct Picture of Those Countries*, trans. John Davis (New York, NY, 1806), 42-44.

443 Ibid., 57.

444 Ibid., 42.

445 Ibid., 46.

446 Ibid., 47-48.

447 Ibid., 57.

448 Ibid., 62.

449 Ibid., 79-80.

450 Ibid., 81-84, 93.

451 Ibid., 49.

452 Ibid., 58.

453 Ibid., 59.

454 Ibid., 52.

455 Ibid., 60.

456 Ibid., 52-53.

457 Ibid., 180-81.

458 See, for example, Pierre Clément de Laussat, *Memoirs of My Life* (Baton Rouge and New Orleans, LA, 1978 translation of 1831 memoir), 92-95.

459 Pierre-Louis Berquin-Duvallon, *Travels in Louisiana and The Floridas in the Year 1802, Giving a Correct Picture of Those Countries*, trans. John Davis (New York, NY, 1806), 28-30.

460 Ibid., 29-30.

461 Anne Malena, "Louisiana: A Colonial Space of Translation," *Forum for Modern Language Studies* 40, No. 2 (2004), 205-09.

462 Pierre Clément de Laussat, *Memoirs of My Life* (Baton Rouge and New Orleans, LA, 1978 translation of 1831 memoir), 101-02.

463 Arnold R. Hirsch and Joseph Logsdon, *Creole New Orleans: Race and Americanization* (Baton Rouge and London, 1992), xi.

464 Shannon Lee Dawdy, *Madame John's Legacy (16OR51) Revisited: A Closer Look at the Archeology of Colonial New Orleans* (New Orleans, 1998), 26-29.

465 Pierre Clément de Laussat, *Memoirs of My Life* (Baton Rouge and New Orleans, LA, 1978 translation of 1831 memoir), 103.

466 Benjamin Henry Boneval Latrobe, *Impressions Respecting New Orleans: Diary & Sketches 1818-1820*, ed. Samuel Wilson Jr. (New York, NY, 1951), 35.

467 Ibid., 32.

468 Thomas Ashe, *Travels in America Performed in the Year 1806* (London, 1809), 310-11.

469 Charles Sealsfield, *The Americans As They Are; Described in A Tour Through the Valley of the Mississippi* (London, 1828), 154

470 Henry Bradshaw Fearon, *Sketches of America: A Narrative of a Journey of Five Thousand Miles Through the Eastern and Western States of America* (London, 1819), 273.

471 Charles Sealsfield, *The Americans As They Are; Described in A Tour Through the Valley of the Mississippi* (London, 1828), 147-48

472 Joseph Holt Ingraham, *The South-West by a Yankee*, 2 vols. (New York, NY, 1835), 1:93-94.

473 Ibid., 1:100-01.

474 Charles F. Powell, "New Orleans," *Barre Gazette* (Barre, Massachusetts) 9, Issue 12, July 29, 1842, p. 2 (emphasis added)

475 Frederick Law Olmsted, *The Cotton Kingdom: A Traveler's Observations on Cotton and Slavery in the American Slave States*, 2 vols. (New York and London, 1861), 1:291-92.

476 William Howard Russell, *My Diary North and South* (Boston and New York, 1863), 230-31.

477 Ibid., 230-49 (emphasis added)

478 Ernst von Hesse-Wartegg, *Travels on the Lower Mississippi, 1879-1880: A Memoir by Ernst von Hesse-Wartegg*, ed. and trans. Frederic Trautmann (Columbia and London, 1990), 156, 162-63.

479 Joseph G. Tregle Jr., "Creoles and Americans," in *Creole New Orleans: Race and Americanization*, eds. Arnold R. Hirsch and Joseph Logsdon (Baton Rouge and London, 1992), 153.

480 Robert Goodache, "Select Tales—New Orleans," *Macon Weekly Telegraph* (Macon, Georgia), May 19, 1828, p. 77, c. 4.

481 Elisée Réclus, *A Voyage to New Orleans*, eds. John Clark and Camille Martin (Thetford, VT, 2004 translation of 1855 original), 50-51.

482 "Letter from New Orleans," *The Sun* (Baltimore, Maryland), April 12, 1877, p. 4, c. 2 (emphasis added).

483 Benjamin Henry Boneval Latrobe, *Impressions Respecting New Orleans: Diary & Sketches 1818-1820*, ed. Samuel Wilson Jr. (New York, NY, 1951), 32 and 35.

484 U.S. Census, Fourth Count Summary Tape (Population), "Mother Tongue and Nativity," 1970. Data extracted and tabulated by Richard Campanella from digital files. Numbers do not include foreign-born residents.

485 Benjamin Henry Boneval Latrobe, *Impressions Respecting New Orleans: Diary & Sketches 1818-1820*, ed. Samuel Wilson Jr. (New York, NY, 1951), 35.

486 Similarly, Louisiana ranked highest among states: 79.4 percent of Louisianians were born in-state.

U.S. Census Bureau, "State of Residence in 2000 by State of Birth: 2000," January 31, 2005, http://www.census.gov/population/cen2000/phc-t38/phc-t38.xls

487 The six American cities reporting nativity rates of over 70 percent—Detroit, Cleveland, Baltimore, Philadelphia, Louisville, and New Orleans—tend to be economically troubled cities with large poor populations. Those with nativity rates at or below 40 percent—San Diego, Los Angeles, Denver, Washington, DC, Seattle, Tucson, Virginia Beach, Phoenix, San Francisco, and Las Vegas (by far the lowest at 20 percent)—mostly boast robust economies, some with a large government or military presence. Special thanks to Tulane University sociology student Laura Harris for census data-processing assistance.

488 Eric Weiner, *The Geography of Bliss: One Grump's Search for the Happiest Places in the World* (New York and Boston, 2007), 179.

489 This discussion limits the notion of "transplants" to American citizens who voluntarily relocate to New Orleans to live full-time, rather than to transferred military personnel, immigrants, extended-stay visitors, second-home owners, transients, college students, or others with no intention of remaining permanently.

490 U.S. Census Bureau, "County-to-County Migration Flow Files," August 11, 2003, http://www.census.gov/population/www/cen2000/ctytoctyflow.html.

491 Analysis by Richard Campanella using 2000 Census data on Louisiana nativity.

492 The figure of 86.4 percent nativity for St. Bernard Parish in 2000 was computed by averaging the average nativity rates at the block-group level within parish limits.

493 My own non-nativity to New Orleans surely influences how I interpret the city's historical geography in ways I may not fully appreciate. Being a transplant may make one more observant of things natives often take for granted; other times it makes one tone-deaf and oblivious.

494 John Shelton Reed, *One South: An Ethnic Approach to Regional Culture* (Baton Rouge, LA, 1982), 4.

495 Haya El Nasser and Paul Overberg, "Millions More Are Changing States," *USA Today*, November 30-December 2, 2007, p. 1.

496 Alison Stein Wellner, "The Mobility Myth: Pundits Love to Fret About Our "Increasingly Mobile Society," But Americans Are Actually More Likely Than Ever to Stay Put." *ReasonOnline* (April 2006), http://www.reason.com/news/show/33288.html

497 A few "LOUISIANA NATIVE" as well as "LOUISIANA TRANSPLANT" bumper stickers are circulating; I spotted both in the Faubourg Marigny, not coincidentally one of the city's premier transplant enclaves.

498 Alyson Papalia, "Smart and Smarter: America's Brightest Cities—New Ranking Identifies the 25 Best-Educated Cities in the U.S." *Forbes.com*, February 15, 2008.

499 Other variables, such as cost of living, crime rates, public education, housing, and "family friendliness," also play significant roles in American mobility. Senior citizens and immigrants relocate for very different reasons than young professionals.

500 Large cities also repel many would-be transplants for their high cost of living, congestion, and other factors. Those who do relocate to the nation's largest cities often settle in specific areas. Most American-born transplants to New York City, for example, live in Manhattan; the other four boroughs are overwhelming native-born or immigrant.

501 J. E. Alexander, *Transatlantic Sketches, Comprising Visits to the Most Interesting Scenes in North and South America, and the West Indies, Volume II* (London, 1833), vi, 12, 30, and 49; Charles Joseph La Trobe, *The Rambler in North America, Volume II* (New York, NY, 1835), 238.

502 New Orleans' numerous nicknames may also reflect the sheer volume of literature on this city. Writers tend to employ nicknames and other synonyms to avoid word repetition; the more written about a city, the more nickname usage occurs, and the greater the likelihood of a particular moniker catching on.

503 "Ancient Name of New Orleans," *Daily Picayune*, September 15, 1889, p. 7, c. 3.

504 As quoted by Marc de Villiers du Terrage, "A History of the Foundation of New Orleans (1717-1722)," *The Louisiana Historical Quarterly* 3, No. 2 (April 1920): 174 (emphasis in original).

505 Marc de Villiers du Terrage, "A History of the Foundation of New Orleans (1717-1722)," *The Louisiana Historical Quarterly* 3, No. 2 (April 1920): 175-76.

506 Pierre François Xavier de Charlevoix, *Journal of a Voyage to North-America Undertaken by Order of the French King, Volume II* (London, 1761), 275.

507 Marc de Villiers du Terrage, "A History of the Foundation of New Orleans (1717-1722)," *The Louisiana Historical Quarterly* 3, No. 2 (April 1920): 177.

508 U.S. Geological Survey, *Geographic Names Information System (GNIS)*, http://geonames.usgs.gov/domestic/index.html, and National Geospatial-Intelligence Agency/U.S. Board on Geographic Names. *NGA GEOnet Names Server (GNS)*, http://gnswww.nga.mil/geonames/GNS/index.jsp, accessed July 19, 2007.

509 *New-York Gazette & General Advertiser*, October 12, 1812, p. 2, c. 3.

510 *Independent Chronicle* (Boston, Massachusetts), September 25, 1815, p. 1, c. 4.

511 "Profanation of the Sabbath," *Boston Recorder*, September 25, 1819, p. 160, c. 4. The reputation continues into the Internet age: A Google search on "Sodom and Gomorrah" and "New Orleans" in spring 2007 yielded 29,200 hits, including articles entitled "An American Sodom & Gomorrah Is Destroyed" and "Hurricane Katrina and New Orleans: God's Judgment?" A search on "New Orleans" and "Queen City of the South," or "Queen of the South," on the other hand, yielded only 901 and 941 hits, respectively.

512 Timothy Flint, *Recollections of the Last Ten Years... in the Valley of the Mississippi* (Boston, MA, 1826), 305 and 309.

513 Anonymous, *New Orleans As It Is: Its Manners and Customs* ("By a Resident, Printed for the Publisher," 1850), 6.

514 Joseph Holt Ingraham, *The South-West by a Yankee*, 2 vols. (New York, NY, 1835), 1:91.

515 Marc de Villiers du Terrage, "A History of the Foundation of New Orleans (1717-1722)," *The Louisiana Historical Quarterly* 3, No. 2 (April 1920): 171.

516 Le Page du Pratz, *The History of Louisiana*, ed. Joseph G. Tregle, Jr. (Baton Rouge, LA, 1976 reprint of 1758 original), 157.

517 "From the Kentucky Gazette: New Orleans," *Adams Centinel* (Gettysburg, Pennsylvania), June 3, 1818, p. 2, c. 3.

518 Robert Goodache, "Select Tales—New Orleans," *Macon Weekly Telegraph* (Macon, Georgia), May 19, 1828, p. 77, c. 4.

519 The Historic New Orleans Collection, *Newspapers and Periodicals Relating to Louisiana* (Binder), 1840 section, 21.

520 Louis Fitzgerald Tasistro, *Random Shots and Southern Breezes, Volume II* (New York, NY, 1842), 9, 19, and 45.

521 *The United States Democratic Review* 11, Issue 49 (July 1842): 107.

522 Charles Lyell, *A Second Visit to the United States of North America*, 2 vols. (New York and London, 1849), 2:106 (page numbers vary on subsequent editions).

523 Elisée Réclus, *A Voyage to New Orleans*, eds. John Clark and Camille Martin (Thetford, VT, 2004 translation of 1855 original), 49.

524 "John Mitchell in New Orleans," *Sunday Delta* (New Orleans), April 18, 1858, p. 7, c. 1.

525 "Making of America" database, Cornell University, http://cdl.library.cornell.edu/moa/, accessed May 2007.

526 "America's Historical Newspapers, 1690-1922" database, Archive of Americana, accessed June 1, 2007 and updated March 7, 2008.

527 John T. Krumpelmann, "Ingraham's 'South-West' as a Source of Americanisms," *American Speech* 18, No. 2. (April 1943), 157-58.

528 *Scientific American* 2, Issue 46 (August 7, 1847): 366; "Memoir of Richard Yeadon, Esq.," *American Whig Review* 11, Issue 28A (May 1850): 485; *Scientific American* 6, Issue 13 (December 14, 1850): 98; and "The Upper Mississippi," *Harper's New Monthly Magazine* 16, Issue 94 (March 1858): 449.

529 "Cincinnati," *Harper's New Monthly Magazine* 67, Issue 398 (July 1883): 263-64.

530 *Harper's Weekly*, May 10, 1862, p. 303, c. 1.

531 David D. Porter, "The Opening of the Lower Mississippi," *The Century: A Popular Quarterly* 29, Issue 6 (April 1885): 949.

532 Robert C. Reinders, *End of an Era: New Orleans, 1850-1860* (Gretna, LA, 1964), 150.

533 *Daily Picayune*, February 9, 1912, section 3, p. 13.

534 *Des Moines Capital*, March 22, 1912, p. 15, c. 1; *Philadelphia Inquirer*, January 11, 1913, p. 15, c. 5.

535 St. Charles Hotel, New Orleans, *Souvenir of New Orleans: 'The City Care Forgot,'* Third Edition (New Orleans, 1917).

536 *Fort Worth Star-Telegram*; August 25, 1915, p. 2.

537 "Life Throbs Anew in Vieux Carre of City Care Forgot," *Dallas Morning News*, June 25, 1922, p. 15, c. 1.

538 New Orleans Federation of Clubs, *New Orleans: Key to America's Most Interesting City*. (New Orleans,

1926), 3.

539 Anthony Stanonis, *Creating the Big Easy: New Orleans and the Emergence of Modern Tourism, 1918-1945* (Athens and London, 2006), 28, citing the *New Orleans Association of Commerce News Bulletin* of July 25, 1922.

540 "The Old Crescent City," *Sunday Inter Ocean* (Chicago, IL), December 14, 1890, p. 1, c. 1.

541 Pops Foster, *Pops Foster: The Autobiography of a New Orleans Jazzman*, ed. Tom Stoddard (Berkeley, Los Angeles, and London, 1971), 26 and 79.

542 "Foster's Friends Wail Farewell," *Corpus Christi Times* (Corpus Chrisi, Texas), November 5, 1969, p. D6, c. 5.

543 Sid Moody, "Mardi Gras in New Orleans: Is It Worth It? Fat Tuesday in the Big Easy," *Lima News* (Lima, Ohio), April 2, 1972, p. D1-D5.

544 Daniel Carey, "'Big Easy': A Nickname from the Dawn of Jazz," *New Orleans Times-Picayune*, August 27, 1987, p. 1.

545 Ibid., p. 1.

546 Chris Rose, "The 60-Second Interview: Betty Guillaud," *New Orleans Times-Picayune*, May 15, 1999, p. E1.

547 Daniel Carey, "'Big Easy': A Nickname from the Dawn of Jazz," *New Orleans Times-Picayune*, August 27, 1987, p. 1.

548 Lexis-Nexis search conducted by Richard Campanella on May 28, 2007.

549 J. Mark Souther, *New Orleans on Parade: Tourism and the Transformation of the Crescent City* (Baton Rouge, LA, 2006), 262.

550 For an analysis of "uptown" and "downtown," see *Geographies of New Orleans: Urban Fabrics Before the Storm*, by Richard Campanella (Lafayette, LA, 2006), 157-67.

551 John Pope, "Evoking King, Nagin Calls N.O. 'Chocolate' City; Speech Addresses Fear of Losing Black Culture," *New Orleans Times-Picayune*, January 17, 2006, p. 1.

552 Michel Faulkner, as quoted by George Will, "Charter Schools Fight an Old Bigotry," *New Orleans Times-Picayune*, December 6, 2007, p. B-9.

553 I borrow this observation from St. Bernard Parish resident and Tulane University student Joseph Rodriguez.

554 Henry Bradshaw Fearon, *Sketches of America: A Narrative of a Journey of Five Thousand Miles Through The Eastern and Western States of America* (London, 1819), 278.

555 Richard Campanella, *Geographies of New Orleans: Urban Fabrics Before the Storm* (Lafayette, LA, 2006), 172.

556 Anonymous, "The Present State of the Country... of Louisiana ... by an Officer at New Orleans to his Friend at Paris," in *Narratives of Colonial America 1704-1765*, ed. Howard H. Peckham (Chicago, IL, 1971), 61-62.

557 As quoted by Shannon Lee Dawdy, *Madame John's Legacy (16OR51) Revisited: A Closer Look at the Archeology of Colonial New Orleans* (New Orleans, 1998), 122.

558 Pierre-Louis Berquin-Duvallon, *Travels in Louisiana and The Floridas in the Year 1802, Giving a Correct Picture of Those Countries*, trans. John Davis (New York, NY, 1806), 53-54.

559 "Extract of a Letter from an Emigrant in New-Orleans," *Newburyport Herald* (Newburyport, Massachusetts), October 17, 1817, p. 3, c. 2.

560 John H. B. Latrobe, *Southern Travels: Journal of John H. B. Latrobe 1834*, ed. Samuel Wilson Jr. (New Orleans, 1986), 42.

561 "Life in New Orleans," *Ohio Statesman* (Columbus, Ohio), May 7, 1847, p. 3, c. 2.

562 Elisée Réclus, *A Voyage to New Orleans*, eds. John Clark and Camille Martin (Thetford, VT, 2004 translation of 1855 original), 56-57.

563 Anonymous, *New Orleans As It Is: Its Manners and Customs* ("By a Resident, Printed for the Publisher," 1850), 52-55.

564 Ted Haigh and Phil Greene, as quoted by Pableaux Johnson, "Home of the Cocktail," *New Orleans Times-Picayune*, January 7, 2005, *Lagniappe*. p. 36; Ed Anderson, "Lawmaker Proposing a Toast to Sazerac," *New Orleans Times-Picayune*, March 18, 2007, p. A2.

565 Chris Rose, "Sazeracs and the City," *New Orleans Times-Picayune*, *Lagniappe* section, August 20, 2004, p. 23.

566 Rebecca Mowbray, "Mixed Vieux," *New Orleans Times-Picayune*, March 23, 2004, C1; Jaquetta White, "N.O. Tops for Food, Live Music, Poll Finds," *New Orleans Times-Picayune*, October 11, 2007, E1.

567 "Life in New Orleans," *Ohio Statesman* (Columbus, Ohio), May 7, 1847, p. 3, c. 2.

568 U.S. Department of Health and Human Services, Office of Applied Statistics, Table C8, "Alcohol Dependence or Abuse in Past Year," 2004, http://oas.samhsa.gov/substate2k6/alcDrugs.htm#ALL, accessed August 5 and October 26, 2007. Indian reservations partially account for the high alcohol use in the north central states.

569 Weekly survey of St. Claude Avenue, Magazine Street, and Carrollton Avenue business activity conducted by Richard Campanella during October 2005 through November 2006.

570 This essay is a revision of the original appearing in my earlier book, *Geographies of New Orleans: Urban Fabrics Before the Storm* (Lafayette, 2006).

571 "Whitewashing the Trunks of Young Trees Prevents Sunscald," *San Jose Mercury News* (San Jose, California), February 16, 1919, p. 15.

572 Elisée Réclus, *A Voyage to New Orleans*, eds. John Clark and Camille Martin (Thetford, VT, 2004 translation of 1855 original), 58.

573 "Ex-Slaves Meet at Waco," *Dallas Morning News*, August 12, 1897, p. 5.

574 "A Beautiful Park," *The State* (Columbia, South Carolina), April 22, 1897, p. 6, c. 1 (emphasis added)

575 The flood-stained Virgin Mary statue was removed after Katrina's deluge submerged it.

576 Thomas Jefferys, *The Natural and Civil History of the French Dominions in North and South America* (London, 1760), 148-49.

577 A footnote in Dumont's journal, as well as a number of tertiary sources, date this hurricane to September 11, 1721, but 1722 is the more likely date.

578 Adrien de Pauger, as quoted by Samuel Wilson Jr., *The Vieux Carre, New Orleans: Its Plan Its Growth, Its Architecture* (New Orleans, 1968), 13.

579 M. Dumont, "History of Louisiana, Translated from the Historical Memoirs of M. Dumont," in *Historical Memoirs of Louisiana, From the First Settlement of the Colony to the Departure of Governor O'Reilly in 1770*, ed. B. F. French (New York, NY, 1853), 24.

580 Adrien de Pauger, as quoted by Samuel Wilson Jr., *The Vieux Carre, New Orleans: Its Plan Its Growth, Its Architecture* (New Orleans, 1968), 13.

581 Diron d'Artaguiette, as quoted by Samuel Wilson Jr., *The Vieux Carre, New Orleans: Its Plan Its Growth, Its Architecture* (New Orleans, 1968), 13.

582 M. Dumont, "History of Louisiana, Translated from the Historical Memoirs of M. Dumont," in *Historical Memoirs of Louisiana, From the First Settlement of the Colony to the Departure of Governor O'Reilly in 1770*, ed. B. F. French (New York, NY, 1853), 23-24.

583 Heloise H. Cruzat, trans., "Allotment of Building Sites in New Orleans (1722)," *The Louisiana Historical Quarterly* 7, No. 4 (October 1924):564-65.

584 M. Dumont, "History of Louisiana, Translated from the Historical Memoirs of M. Dumont," in *Historical Memoirs of Louisiana, From the First Settlement of the Colony to the Departure of Governor O'Reilly in 1770*, ed. B. F. French (New York, NY, 1853), 41.

585 Letter, Devin to Pauger, August 29, 1724, *Mississippi Provincial Archives 1704-1743: French Dominion, Volume II*, eds. Dunbar Rowland and Albert Godfrey Sanders (Jackson, 1929), 395.

586 Letter, Committee of Louisiana to [the Directors of the Company], November 8, 1724, *Mississippi Provincial Archives 1704-1743: French Dominion, Volume II*, eds. Dunbar Rowland and Albert Godfrey Sanders (Jackson, MS, 1929), 410.

587 *Records and Deliberations of the Cabildo, 1769-1803*, trans. Works Progress Administration, March 26, 1788, 97-A/97-B, p. 13, second microfilm roll of Cabildo records, Historic New Orleans Collection.

588 Chevalier Guy de Soniat du Fossat, *Synopsis of the History of Louisiana from the Founding of the Colony to End of the Year 1791*, ed. and trans. Charles T. Soniat (New Orleans, 1903), 27.

589 Ibid., 27.

590 *Records and Deliberations of the Cabildo, 1769-1803*, trans. Works Progress Administration, April 3, 1788, 99-A/100, p. 19 of second microfilm roll of Cabildo records, Historic New Orleans Collection.

591 *The Times* (London, England), July 19, 1788, p. 2, c. 4.

592 Chevalier Guy de Soniat du Fossat, *Synopsis of the History of Louisiana from the Founding of the Colony to End of the Year 1791*, ed. and trans. Charles T. Soniat (New Orleans, 1903), 27-28.

593 Ibid., 27.

594 *Pennsylvania Mercury*, May 10, 1788, p. 4, c. 2.

595 Chevalier Guy de Soniat du Fossat, *Synopsis of the History of Louisiana from the Founding of the Colony to End of the Year 1791*, ed. and trans. Charles T. Soniat (New Orleans, 1903), 27-28.

596 *Records and Deliberations of the Cabildo, 1769-1803*, trans. Works Progress Administration, March 26, 1788, 97-B/98-A, p. 13-14 of second microfilm roll of Cabildo records, Historic New Orleans Collection.

597 *Records and Deliberations of the Cabildo, 1769-1803*, trans. Works Progress Administration, April 4, 1788, 99/99-A, p. 17 of second microfilm roll of Cabildo records, Historic New Orleans Collection.

598 Chevalier Guy de Soniat du Fossat, *Synopsis of the History of Louisiana from the Founding of the Colony to End of the Year 1791*, ed. and trans. Charles T. Soniat (New Orleans, 1903), 27.

599 *Pennsylvania Packet*, July 3, 1790, p. 2, c. 2

600 *Records and Deliberations of the Cabildo, 1769-1803*, trans. Works Progress Administration, December 19, 1794, 266/266-A, p. 180 of second microfilm roll of Cabildo records, Historic New Orleans Collection.

601 *Philadelphia Gazette*, February 3, 1795, p. 3.

602 *Records and Deliberations of the Cabildo, 1769-1803*, trans. Works Progress Administration, entries for mid-December 1794, 264-A/265, p. 177; 265/265-A, p. 178, 266/266-A, p. 180, and 266-A/267, p. 181, dated December 19, 1794, from second microfilm roll of Cabildo records, Historic New Orleans Collection.

603 *Digest of the Acts and Deliberations of the Cabildo*, February 20, 1795, Book 3, Volume 3, p. 198.

604 *Records and Deliberations of the Cabildo, 1769-1803*, trans. Works Progress Administration, Book 4, Volume 1, 18/18-A, p. 55 and 18-A/19, p. 56, October 9, 1795, Historic New Orleans Collection.

605 Apparently the standards did not reach everywhere. "The back part of the town," he continued, "is chiefly built of wood." Christian Schultz, *Travels on an Inland Voyage Through the States of New-York, Pennsylvania, Virginia, Ohio, Kentucky and Tennessee; Performed in the Years 1807 and 1808*, Volume 2 (New York, NY, 1810), 190.

606 Elisée Réclus, *A Voyage to New Orleans*, eds. John Clark and Camille Martin (Thetford, VT, 2004 translation of 1855 original), 52-53.

607 Richard Campanella, *Geographies of New Orleans: Urban Fabrics Before the Storm* (Lafayette, LA, 2006), 105-24.

608 Claude Joseph Villars Dubreuil, as quoted in Dawdy, Shannon Lee, "La Ville Sauvage: 'Enlightened' Colonialism and Creole Improvisation in New Orleans, 1699-1769" (Ph.D. dissertation, The University of Michigan, 2003), 67-68.

609 "This lake aided by the river" describes what occurred in 1871, when a crevasse at Bonnet Carre introduced river water to the lake, raising its level and inundating New Orleans from behind with waters that were generally clear of sediments.

610 Stanford E. Chaillé, "Inundations of New Orleans and Their Influence on Its Health," *New Orleans Medical and Surgical Journal* (July 1882), excerpt in Tulane University Special Collections Vertical File, Flooding folder, 3.

611 E.W. Gould, *Fifty Years on the Mississippi; Or, Gould's History of River Navigation* (St. Louis, MO, 1889), 225; Kendall, *History of New Orleans*, 1:167-69; Army Corps of Engineers, New Orleans District, *Bonnet Carré Spillway* (agency booklet, circa 2000), 3.

612 As cited by Richard Joel Russell, "Physiography of Lower Mississippi River Delta," *Lower Mississippi River Delta: Reports on the Geology of Plaquemines and St. Bernard Parishes*, Geological Bulletin 8 (New Orleans, 1936), 19.

613 John Adams Paxton, *The New-Orleans Directory and Register* (New Orleans, 1823), 138.

614 Pierre Clément de Laussat, *Memoirs of My Life* (Baton Rouge and New Orleans, LA, 1978 translation of 1831 memoir), 63.

615 As quoted by Adam Hodgson, *Remarks During a Journey Through North America in the Years 1819, 1820, and 1821* (New York, NY, 1823), 164.

616 George E. Waring Jr., *Report on the Social Statistics of Cities, Part II: The Southern and the Western States* (Washington, DC, 1887), 261.

617 Wilton P. Ledet, "The History of the City of Carrollton," *The Louisiana Historical Quarterly* 21, No. 1 (January 1938): 228.

618 Stanford E. Chaillé, "Inundations of New Orleans and Their Influence on Its Health," *New Orleans Medical and Surgical Journal* (July 1882), excerpt in Tulane University Special Collections Vertical File, Flooding folder, 5.

619 Ibid. Hurricane Katrina's maximum flood line also peaked at the Bourbon/Canal intersection.

620 "The Inundation," *Daily Picayune*, June 4, 1849, Monday evening edition, p. 2, col. 1.

621 Stanford E. Chaillé, "Inundations of New Orleans and Their Influence on Its Health," *New Orleans*

Medical and Surgical Journal (July 1882), excerpt in Tulane University Special Collections Vertical File, Flooding folder, 5, 9-12.

622 "The Inundation," *Daily Picayune*, June 4, 1849, Monday evening edition, p. 2, col. 1.

623 For further discussion of urban nuisances and hazards, see Craig E. Colten, *An Unnatural Metropolis: Wresting New Orleans from Nature* (Baton Rouge, LA, 2005).

624 The City Planning and Zoning Commission, *Major Street Report* (New Orleans, 1927), 16.

625 Letter, Périer and De La Chaise to the Directors of the Company of the Indies, November 3, 1728, *Mississippi Provincial Archives 1704-1743: French Dominion, Volume II*, eds. Dunbar Rowland and Albert Godfrey Sanders (Jackson, MS, 1929), 603 (emphasis added).

626 *Records and Deliberations of the Cabildo, 1769-1803*, trans. Works Progress Administration, October 17, 1788, 107/107-A, pp. 39-40 (emphasis added), second microfilm roll of Cabildo records, Historic New Orleans Collection.

627 Christian Schultz, *Travels on an Inland Voyage Through the States of New-York, Pennsylvania, Virginia, Ohio, Kentucky and Tennessee; Performed in the Years 1807 and 1808*, Volume 2 (New York, NY, 1810), 197.

628 "All 'Back of Town' Covered with Water," *New Orleans Item*, September 30, 1915, p. 7.

629 Ronald Van Kempen and A. Sule Özüekren, "Ethnic Segregation in Cities: New Forms and Explanations in a Dynamic World," *Urban Studies* 35 (1998): 1631.

630 Isaac M. Cline, "The Tropical Hurricane of September 29, 1915," *Monthly Weather Review* (September 1915): 457.

631 George G. Earl, *The Hurricane of September 29, 1915 and Subsequent Heavy Rainfalls: Report of George G. Earl, Gen'l Supt. to Sewerage and Water Board of New Orleans* (New Orleans, October 14, 1915), 7.

632 Isaac M. Cline, "The Tropical Hurricane of September 29, 1915," *Monthly Weather Review* (September 1915): 463.

633 As recorded by Isaac M. Cline, "The Tropical Hurricane of September 29, 1915," *Monthly Weather Review* (September 1915): 462.

634 "City Cut Off from Rest of World," *The New Orleans Item*, September 29, 1915 (evening edition), p. 1.

635 "Storm Takes Toll in Property Loss and Human Life," *New Orleans Times-Picayune*, September 30, 1915, p. 1.

636 Isaac M. Cline, "The Tropical Hurricane of September 29, 1915," *Monthly Weather Review* (September 1915): 456.

637 "'STORM PROOF!' The Record Shows New Orleans," *New Orleans Item*, September 30, 1915, p. 10.

638 The Anglers' Club was one of a number of fishing and hunting camps operating in the marshy periphery of circa-1900 New Orleans. Predating the age of automobiles, it was located not along present-day Highway 90 between lakes Pontchartrain and Catherine, but along the Louisville & Nashville (L & N) Railroad between lakes Catherine and Borgne, at the mouth of the Rigolets channel. The L & N transported recreational fishermen to these clubs every weekend in those days.

639 Population schedules from the 1910 Census, as well as city directories, other censuses, and the Louisiana Death Records Index, confirm that Manuel Marquez was born a "mulatto" in New Orleans' Seventh Ward around 1864. By 1891, he worked as a warehouseman and lived on North Derbigny between St. Anthony and Bourbon (now Pauger), an area settled largely by black Creoles. Manuel married Inez, two years his junior, probably in the late 1880s, and fathered five children between 1891 and 1900: Manuel, Emelia, Elma, Steven, and Veola. Manuel and his family resided at 1897 North Tonti Street according to the 1910 Census.

640 Isaac M. Cline, "The Tropical Hurricane of September 29, 1915," *Monthly Weather Review* (September 1915): 465.

641 "21 Lives Are Lost at Rigolets Flood," *New Orleans Item*, October 1, 1915 (page number not available due to document damage).

642 "Forty-Three Known Victims at Rigolets and Catherine," *New Orleans Times-Picayune*, October 1, 1915, p. 1.

643 Isaac M. Cline, "The Tropical Hurricane of September 29, 1915," *Monthly Weather Review* (September 1915): 465.

644 "Forty-Three Known Victims at Rigolets and Catherine," *New Orleans Times-Picayune*, October 1, 1915, p. 1.

645 Isaac M. Cline, "The Tropical Hurricane of September 29, 1915," *Monthly Weather Review* (September 1915): 465.

646 "Gale's Fury Ties Up All Railroad Traffic Into City," *New Orleans Times-Picayune*, September 30, 1915, p. 2.

647 "Storm takes Toll in Property Loss and Human Life," *New Orleans Times-Picayune*, September 30, 1915, p. 1; John T. Meehan, "Bodies Strewn Thick in Salt Gulf Marshes," *New Orleans Times-Picayune*, October 2, 1915, p. 1-2.

648 "24 Person Known to Have Lost Lives at the Rigolets," *New Orleans Times-Picayune*, October 2, 1915, p. 4.

649 John T. Meehan, "Bodies Strewn Thick in Salt Gulf Marshes," *New Orleans Times-Picayune*, October 2, 1915, p.2.

650 Data in this essay are drawn largely from two official reports and the graphs and maps therein: U.S. Army Engineer District, New Orleans. *Hurricane Betsy, September 8-11, 1965, Serial No. 1880* (New Orleans, November 1965), and U.S. Army Engineer District, New Orleans. *Hurricane Betsy, September 8-11, 1965: After-Action Report* (New Orleans, July 1966).

651 U.S. Army Engineer District, New Orleans. *Hurricane Betsy, September 8-11, 1965, Serial No. 1880* (New Orleans, November 1965), 13.

652 Ibid., 24.

653 Sewerage and Water Board of New Orleans. *Report on Hurricane "Betsy," September 9-10, 1965* (New Orleans, October 8, 1965), 32.

654 Chevalier Guy de Soniat du Fossat, *Synopsis of the History of Louisiana from the Founding of the Colony to End of the Year 1791*, ed. and trans. Charles T. Soniat (New Orleans, 1903), 8.

655 Christian Schultz, *Travels on an Inland Voyage Through the States of New-York, Pennsylvania, Virginia, Ohio, Kentucky and Tennessee; Performed in the Years 1807 and 1808*, Volume 2 (New York, NY, 1810), 167, 199.

656 Joseph Holt Ingraham, *The South-West by a Yankee*, 2 vols. (New York, NY, 1835), 1:60.

657 Roger T. Saucier, *Geomorphology and Quaternary Geologic History of the Lower Mississippi Valley*, 2 vols. (Vicksburg, MS, 1994), 1:53.

658 Elisée Réclus, *A Voyage to New Orleans*, eds. John Clark and Camille Martin (Thetford, VT, 2004 translation of 1855 original), 50.

659 "How Much of City is Below Sea Level?," *New Orleans Item*, April 13, 1948, p. 12.

660 Percentages computed from LIDAR digital elevation models covering from 90° 15' West, 29° 53' North to 89° 56' West, 30° 03' North (roughly from Westwego to Little Woods).

661 Christine Moe, *Soil Subsidence in the New Orleans Area* (Monticello, IL, 1979).

662 Kurt D. Shinkle and Roy K. Dokka, *NOAA Technical Report 50: Rates of Vertical Displacement at Benchmarks in the Lower Mississippi Valley and the Northern Gulf Coast*, National Oceanographic and Atmospheric Administration, July 2004.

663 David Hart and David Zilkoski, "Mapping a Moving Target: The Use of GIS to Support Development of a Subsidence Model in the New Orleans Region," *Urban and Regional Information Association (URISA) Proceedings*, 1994, http://libraries.maine.edu/Spatial/gisweb/spatdb/urisa/ur94049.html

664 Joel K. Bourne Jr., "The Perils of New Orleans," *National Geographic* 212, No. 2 (August 2007), map entitled "New Orleans is Sinking," 58.

665 The Historic New Orleans Collection, accession numbers 1987.116.1 through 1987.116.12.

666 Nathaniel L. Bindoff and Jurgen Willebrand, et al., "Observations: Oceanic Climate Change and Sea Level," in *Climate Change 2007: The Physical Science Basis*, eds. S. Solomon, et al. (Cambridge, 2007), 410.

667 GIS analysis by Richard Campanella, using LIDAR elevation data and 1895 elevation data derived and adjusted from L. W. Brown, "Contour Map of New Orleans," in *Report on the Drainage of the City of New Orleans* (New Orleans, 1895).

668 J. E. Alexander, *Transatlantic Sketches, Comprising Visits to the Most Interesting Scenes in North and South America, and the West Indies, Volume II* (London, 1833), 39-40.

669 This essay is drawn from Richard Campanella's contribution (entitled "'Bring Your Own Chairs:' Civic Engagement in Postdiluvian New Orleans") to *Civic Engagement in the Wake of Katrina*, edited by Amy Koritz and George Sanchez and planned for publication by The University of Michigan Press in 2009.

670 Richard Campanella, "Street Survey of Business Reopenings in Post-Katrina New Orleans," CBR

Whitepaper funded by National Science Foundation Award 0554937, www.kerrn.org/pdf/campan-ella2.pdf, May 2006 and January 2007.

671   Martha Carr, "Experts Include Science in Rebuilding Equation; Politics Noticeably Absent from Plan," *New Orleans Times-Picayune*, November 25, 2005, p. 1.

672   This essay is drawn from Richard Campanella's contribution (entitled "'Bring Your Own Chairs:' Civic Engagement in Postdiluvian New Orleans") to *Civic Engagement in the Wake of Katrina*, edited by Amy Koritz and George Sanchez and planned for publication by The University of Michigan Press in 2009. Portions are also scheduled to appear in a United Nations publication entitled *The Challenges of Sudden Natural Disasters for Land Administration and Management: The Case of the Hurricane Katrina in New Orleans*.

673   Gary Rivlin, "New Orleans Forms a Panel on Renewal," *New York Times*, October 1, 2005, p. A11.

674   Private conversation with ULI member, November 2005.

675   Martha Carr, "Citizens Pack Rebirth Forum; Experts Urged to Use N.O. history as Guide," *New Orleans Times-Picayune*, November 15, 2005, Metro section, p. 1.

676   Urban Land Institute, *New Orleans, Louisiana: A Strategy for Rebuilding—an Advisory Services Program Report*, November 12-18, 2005, map, p. 45 of PowerPoint file.

677   Frank Donze, "Don't Write Us Off, Residents Warn; Urban Land Institute Report Takes a Beating," *New Orleans Times-Picayune*, November 29, 2005, p. 1.

678   Ibid., p. 1.

679   Ibid., p. 1.

680   Bring New Orleans Back Commission, "Action Plan for New Orleans: the New American City, January 11, 2006," Parks and Open Space Plan map, p. 31 of PowerPoint file.

681   Gordon Russell and Frank Donze, "Rebuilding Proposal Gets Mixed Reception; Critics Vocal, But Many Prefer to Watch and Wait," *New Orleans Times-Picayune*, January 12, 2006, p. 1.

682   Frank Donze and Gordon Russell, "4 MONTHS TO DECIDE: Nagin Panel Says Hardest Hit Areas Must Prove Viability," January 11, 2006, p. 1.

683   "Meetings," *New Orleans Times-Picayune*, September 30, 2006, Metro section, p. 4.

684   Neighborhood Partnership Network, http://www.npnnola.com/associations. Many of these associations predate Katrina, but renewed their efforts after the storm.

685   Analysis by Richard Campanella using Lexis-Nexis to search for occurrence of "civic association" or "neighborhood association" in the full text of the *New Orleans Times-Picayune* from February 2004 through April 2007.

686   Analysis by Richard Campanella.

687   Stephanie Grace, "Will Plan Lift the Curse of the Green Dot?," *New Orleans Times-Picayune*, April 1, 2007, Metro- Editorial section, p. 7 (emphasis added).

688   Michelle Krupa and Gordon Russell, "N.O. Post-K Blueprint Unveiled; Plan Puts Most Cash in East, Lower 9th," *New Orleans Times-Picayune*, March 29, 2007, p. 1.

689   This is not to say that all post-Katrina "plandemonium" was for naught. Even beyond the rudimentary social benefits of civic engagement, the various planning efforts succeeded in spawning scores of fine ideas for the betterment of the city—*specific* ideas, with extensive documentation, ranging from bike lanes to green space to flood control and crime prevention. Many may eventually come to fruition, even if "the plan" as a whole (be it the UNOP or the BNOB Commission or any other) never ends up serving as the envisioned "blueprint" or "road map." Ed Blakely's Office of Recovery Management seemed to affirm this notion (of post-Katrina planning documents serving as handy rosters of project ideas rather than as genuine guiding documents) when, in early 2008, it described its 117 upcoming rebuilding projects as having mostly been "*gleaned* from post-flood neighborhood planning efforts, including the Unified New Orleans Plan." Michelle Krupa, "City Hall Begins a Building Boom," *New Orleans Times-Picayune*, February 23, 2008, B1-B3 (emphasis added).

690   Variations of this essay appeared as an editorial by Richard Campanella in the *New Orleans Times-Picayune*, and in an article in the journal *Technology in Society*.

691   Timothy M. Kusky, "Time to Move to Higher Ground," *Boston Globe*, September 25, 2005, p. D12 (emphasis added).

692   Jay Arena, as quoted by Gustavo Capdevila in "World Economic Forum: Davos and New Orleans, Neoliberal Twins." Inter Press Service News Agency, January 30, 2006, http://ipsnews.net/news.asp?idnews=31964, accessed May 26, 2006.

693   Timothy M. Kusky, "Time to Move to Higher Ground," *Boston Globe*, September 25, 2005, p. D12.

694   Jospeh B. Treaster and Deborah Sontag, "Despair and Lawlessness Grip New Orleans as Thousands

Remain Stranded in Squalor," *New York Times,* September 2, 2005, p. 1.

695 John Beckman, oral presentation on progress of WRT Design's investigation, New Orleans, Louisiana, December 2, 2005 (attended and recorded by Richard Campanella).

696 Timothy M. Kusky, "Time to Move to Higher Ground," *Boston Globe,* September 25, 2005, p. D12.

697 GIS analysis by Richard Campanella using GCR & Associates' August 2007 population estimates. Special thanks to Shelley Meaux for data-processing assistance.

698 Benjamin Henry Boneval Latrobe, *Impressions Respecting New Orleans: Diary & Sketches 1818-1820,* ed. Samuel Wilson Jr. (New York, NY, 1951), 40.

References

"21 Lives Are Lost at Rigolets Flood." *New Orleans Item*, October 1, 1915 (page number not available due to document damage).

"24 Persons Known to Have Lost Lives at Rigolets." *New Orleans Times-Picayune*, October 2, 1915, p. 4.

"A Beautiful Park." *The State* (Columbia, SC), April 22, 1897, p. 6.

"A Description of the river Missisippi." *Salem Mercury* (Salem, MA), August 7, 1787, p. 4.

"A Kaleidoscopic View of New Orleans." *Daily Picayune*, September 23, 1843, p. 2, col. 3.

Abbey, Kathryn T. "The Land Ventures of General Lafayette in the Territory of Orleans and State of Louisiana." *Louisiana Historical Quarterly* 16 (July 1933): 359-73.

Abbott, John S.C. *South and North; or Impressions Received During a Trip to Cuba and the South*. New York: 1860.

Alexander, J. E. *Transatlantic Sketches, Comprising Visits to the Most Interesting Scenes in North and South America and the West Indies, Volume II*. London, England: Richard Bentley, 1833.

"All 'Back of Town' Covered with Water." *New Orleans Item*, September 30, 1915, p. 7.

"America's Historical Newspapers, 1690-1922." Archive of Americana, accessed 2006-07.

"Ancient Name of New Orleans." *Daily Picayune*, September 15, 1889, p. 7, c. 3.

Anderson, Ed. "Lawmaker Proposing a Toast to Sazerac." *New Orleans Times-Picayune*, March 18, 2007, p. A2.

Anonymous. "The Marriage of Mississippi and Pontchartrain." *The Literary Digest*, Science and Invention section, April 14, 1923, archived at the Tulane University Special Collections-Vertical Files.

Anonymous. "Historical Journal: or, Narrative of the Expedition Made by Order of Louis XIV, King of France, under Command of M. D'Iberville to Explore the Colbert (Mississippi) River and Establish a Colony in Louisiana." In *Historical Collections of Louisiana and Florida*, ed. B. F. French. New York: Albert Masson, 1875 translation of 1699 journal.

Anonymous. "The Present State of the Country and Inhabitants, Europeans and Indians, of Louisiana ... by an Officer at New Orleans to his Friend at Paris." In *Narratives of Colonial America 1704-1765*, ed. Howard H. Peckham. Chicago, IL: The Lakeside Press, R. R. Donnelley & Sons Company, 1971): 53-70.

Anonymous. *New Orleans As It Is: Its Manners and Customs*. "By a Resident, Printed for the Publisher," 1850.

Anonymous. *The Present State of the Country and Inhabitants, Europeans and Indians, of Louisiana, on the North Continent of America*. London, England: J. Millan, 1744.

Anthony, Arthé Agnes. "The Negro Creole Community in New Orleans,1880-1920: An Oral History." Ph.D. dissertation, University of California-Irvine, 1978.

"Anti-Foreign Feeling Quiet." *Fort Worth Star-Telegram*, December 22, 1907, p. 16.

Arena Jay, as quoted by Gustavo Capdevila, World Economic Forum: Davos and New Orleans, Neoliberal Twins. Inter Press Service News Agency, January 30, 2006, http://ipsnews.net/news.asp?idnews=31964, accessed May 26, 2006.

Arfwedson, C.D. *The United States and Canada in 1832, 1833, and 1834*, 2 vols. London, England: Richard Bentley, Publisher, 1834.

Armstrong, Louis. *Louis Armstrong in His Own Words: Selected Writings*, ed. Thomas Brothers. Oxford, England: Oxford University Press, 1999.

Arnesen, Eric. *Waterfront Workers of New Orleans: Race, Class, and Politics, 1863-1923*. Urbana and Chicago, IL: University of Illinois Press, 1994.

Asbury, Herbert. *The French Quarter: An Informal History of the New Orleans Underworld*. Garden City, NY: Garden City Publishing Co., Inc., 1938.

Ashe, Thomas. *Travels in America Performed in the Year 1806*. London, England: Richard Phillips, 1809.

Associated Press. "Old Midwest, Northeast Cities Top List of Segregated Areas." *St. Louis Post-Dispatch*. January 29, 1997, 4A.

Association of Levee Boards of Louisiana. *The System That Works to Serve Our State*. New Orleans: Association of Levee Boards of Louisiana, 1990.

Bailey, Richard W. "The Foundation of English in the Louisiana Purchase: New Orleans, 1800-1850," *American Speech* 78 (2003), 363-84.

Barry, John M. *Rising Tide: The Great Mississippi River Flood of 1927 and How It Changed America*. New York: A Touchstone Book, Simon & Schuster, 1997.

Baudier, Roger. *The Catholic Church in Louisiana.* New Orleans: A.W. Hyatt, 1939.

Beckman, John. Oral presentation on progress of WRT Design's investigation. New Orleans, December 2, 2005 (attended and recorded by author).

Behrman, Martin. "New Orleans—A History of Three Great Public Utilities: Sewerage, Water, and Drainage." Paper delivered at the Convention of League of American Municipalities, Milwaukee, WI, 1914.

Bernhard, Duke of Saxe-Weimar-Eisenach. *Travels by His Highness Duke Bernhard of Saxe-Weimar-Eisenach Through North America in the Years 1825 and 1826,* trans. William Jeronimus, ed. C.J. Jeronimus. Lanham, MD: University Press of America, 2001.

Berquin-Duvallon, Pierre-Louis. *Travels in Louisiana and The Floridas in the Year 1802, Giving a Correct Picture of Those Countries,* trans. John Davis. New York: I. Riley & Co., 1806.

Bindoff, Nathaniel L., J. Willebrand, V. Artale, A. Cazenave, J. Gregory, S. Gulev, K. Hanawa, and C. LeQuéré. "Observations: Oceanic Climate Change and Sea Level." In *Climate Change 2007: The Physical Science Basis,* eds. S. Solomon, D. Qin, M. Manning, Z. Chen, M. Marquis, K. B. Averyt, M. Tignor and H. L. Miller. Cambridge, England: Cambridge University Press, 385-432.

Bird, Eric C. F. *Submerging Coasts: The Effects of a Rising Sea Level on Coastal Environments.* Chichester, NY, Brisbane, Toronto, and Singapore: John Wiley & Sons, 1993.

Bishop, Nathaniel H. *Four Months in a Sneak-Box.* Boston, MA: Lee and Shephard, 1879.

Blassingame, John W. *Black New Orleans, 1860-1880.* Chicago, IL and London, England: The University of Chicago Press, 1973.

Bodichon, Barbara Leigh Smith. *An American Diary 1857-8,* ed. Joseph W. Reed Jr. London, England: Routledge & Kegan Paul, 1972.

Bolding, Gary A. "The New Orleans Seaway Movement." *Louisiana History* 10 (1969).

Bossu, Jean-Bernard. *Travels in the Interior of North America 1751-1762.* Translated and edited by Seymour Feiler. Norman, OK: University of Oklahoma Press, 1962.

Bouligny, Francisco. "The Memoria," in *Louisiana in 1776: A Memoria of Francisco Bouligny,* ed. Gilbert C. Din. New Orleans: Jack D. L. Holmes, 1977.

Bourne, Joel K. Jr. "The Perils of New Orleans," *National Geographic* 212, No. 2 (August 2007): 32-67.

Bradley, Jared William, ed. *Interim Appointment: W. C. C. Claiborne Letter Book, 1804-1805.* Baton Rouge and London, England: Louisiana State University Press, 2002.

Brantley, Christopher G. and Steven G. Platt. "Canebrake Conservation in the Southeastern United States." *Wildlife Society Bulletin* 29, No. 4 (Winter, 2001): 1175-81.

Brasseaux, Carl A., trans. and ed. *A Comparative View of French Louisiana, 1699 and 1762: The Journals of Pierre Le Moyne d'Iberville and Jean-Jacques-Blaise d'Abbadie,* 2nd ed. Lafayette, LA: Center for Louisiana Studies, 1981.

Bremer, Fredrika. *The Homes of the New World: Impressions of America, Volume II.* New York: Harper & Brothers, 1853.

Briede, Kathryn C. "A History of the City of Lafayette." *Louisiana Historical Quarterly* 20, No. 4 (October 1937): 895-964.

Bring New Orleans Back Commission. *Action Plan for New Orleans: the New American City.* New Orleans, January 11, 2006.

Brooks, Jane S. *On the Avenue: A Plan to Revitalize the Lower St. Charles Corridor.* New Orleans: St. Charles Avenue Merchants Association and College of Urban and Public Affairs, University of New Orleans, 1996.

Brown, L. W. "Contour Map of New Orleans." In *Report on the Drainage of the City of New Orleans.* New Orleans: City of New Orleans, 1895.

Brown, Matthew. "Shrimp Fleet's Size Facing Caps." *New Orleans Times-Picayune.* April 17, 2005, B1.

Buckingham, J. S. *The Slave States of America,* 2 vols. London, England and Paris, France: Fisher, Son & Co., 1842.

Bureau of Governmental Research. *Plan and Program for the Preservation of the Vieux Carré: Historic District Demonstration Study.* New Orleans: City of New Orleans, 1968.

Bureau of Governmental Research. *Wards of New Orleans.* New Orleans: City of New Orleans, 1961.

Burgess, Ernest W. "The Growth of the City: An Introduction to a Research Project." In *The City.* eds. Robert E. Park, Ernest W. Burgess, and Roderick D. McKenzie, 47-62. Chicago, IL: University of Chicago Press, 1925.

Burkett, Virginia R., David B. Zilkoski, and David A. Hart. "Sea-Level Rise and Subsidence: Implications for Flooding in New Orleans, Louisiana." *Measuring and Predicting Elevation Change in the Mississippi*

River Deltaic System, Louisiana Governor's Office of Coastal Activities Conference, New Orleans, December 8-9, 2003.

Cabéza de Vaca, Álvar Núñez. *The Narrative of Cabeza de Vaca*, eds. Rolena Adorno and Patrick Charles Pautz. Lincoln, NE and London, England: University of Nebraska Press, 2003 translation of 1542 original.

Cable, George Washington. "Flood and Plague in New Orleans." *The Century, A Popular Quarterly* 26 (July 1883): 419-31.

Cable, George Washington. "The Grandissimes," *Scribners Monthly*, 19, Issue 1 (November 1879): 97-110.

Cable, George Washington. *The Grandissimes: A Story of Creole Life*. New York: Charles Scribner & Sons, 1880.

Cable, George Washington. *The Creoles of Louisiana*. New York: Charles Scribner & Sons, 1884.

Caldwell, Joan G. "Italianate Domestic Architecture in New Orleans 1850-1880." Ph.D. dissertation, Tulane University, 1975.

Caldwell, Joan G. "Urban Growth, 1815-1880: Diverse Tastes—Greek, Gothic, and Italianate." In *Louisiana Buildings 1720-1940*, eds. Jessie Poesch and Barbara SoRelle Bacot, 174-241. Baton Rouge and London, England: Louisiana University Press, 1997.

Cambell, Edna F. "New Orleans in the Early Days," *Geographical Review* 10, No. 1 (July 1920): 31-36.

Campanella, Richard. "Above-Sea-Level New Orleans: The Residential Capacity of Orleans Parish's Higher Ground," CBR Whitepaper funded by Coypu Foundation, http://kerrn.org/pdf/campanellaaslno. pdf, April 2007.

Campanella, Richard and Marina Campanella. *New Orleans Then and Now*. Gretna, LA: Pelican Publishing Company, 1999.

Campanella, Richard. *Geographies of New Orleans: Urban Fabrics Before the Storm*. Lafayette, LA: Center for Louisiana Studies, 2006.

Campanella, Richard. "Street Survey of Business Reopenings in Post-Katrina New Orleans," New Orleans: CBR Whitepaper/National Science Foundation Award 0554937, May 2006 and January 2007 (available www.kerrn.org/pdf/campanella2.pdf).

Campanella, Richard. *Time and Place in New Orleans: Past Geographies in the Present Day*. Gretna, LA: Pelican Publishing Company, 2002.

Carey, Daniel. "'Big Easy': A Nickname from the Dawn of Jazz," *New Orleans Times-Picayune*, August 27, 1987, p. 1.

Carr, Martha. "Citizens pack rebirth forum; Experts urged to use N.O. history as guide," *New Orleans Times-Picayune*, November 15, 2005, Metro section, p. 1.

Carr, Martha. "Experts Include Science in Rebuilding Equation; Politics Noticeably Absent from Plan." *New Orleans Times-Picayune*, November 25, 2005, p. 1.

Carter, Clarence Edwin. *The Territorial Papers of the United States*, vol. 9, *The Territory of Orleans, 1803-1812*. Washington, DC: United States Government Printing Office, 1940.

Carter, Sam R. *A Report on Survey of Metropolitan New Orleans Land Use, Real Property, and Low Income Housing Area*. New Orleans: Works Projects Administration, Louisiana State Department of Public Welfare, and Housing Authority of New Orleans, 1941.

Castellanos, Henry C. *New Orleans As It Was: Episodes of Louisiana Life*. New Orleans: L. Graham & Son, Ltd., 1895.

Chaillé, Stanford E. "Inundations of New Orleans and Their Influence on Its Health." *New Orleans Medical and Surgical Journal*, July 1882. Flooding folder, Special Collections Vertical File, Howard-Tilton Library, Tulane University, New Orleans.

Charlevoix, Pierre François Xavier de. *Journal of a Voyage to North-America Undertaken by Order of the French King, Volume II*. London, England: R. & J. Dodsley, 1761.

Charlevoix, Rev. P. F. X. de, S. J., *History and General Description of New France, Volume VI*, ed. John Gilmary Shea. New York: Francis P. Harper, 1900.

Chase, John Churchill, Hermann B. Deutsch, Charles L. Dufour, and Leonard V. Huber. *Citoyens, Progrès et Politique de la Nouvelle Orléans 1889-1964*. New Orleans: E. S. Upton Printing Company, 1964.

"Cincinnati," *Harper's New Monthly Magazine* 67, Issue 398 (July 1883), pp. 245-66.

"City Cut Off from Rest of World," *The New Orleans Item*, September 29, 1915 (evening edition), p. 1.

City Planning and Zoning Commission. *Major Street Report*. New Orleans: City Planning and Zoning Commission, 1927.

Clapp, Theodore. *Autobiographical Sketches and Recollections, During a Thirty-Five Years' Residence in New*

Orleans. Boston, MA: Phillips, Sampson & Company, 1858.

Clark, David. *Urban Geography: An Introductory Guide*. Baltimore, MD: Johns Hopkins University Press, 1982.

Clark, Emily, ed. *Voices from an Early American Convent: Marie Madeline Hachard and the New Orleans Ursulines, 1727-1760*. Baton Rouge and London, England: Louisiana State University Press, 2007.

Clark, John G. "New Orleans and the River: A Study in Attitudes and Responses." *Louisiana History* 8 (Spring 1967): 117-35.

Clark, Robert T. Jr. "The German Liberals in New Orleans (1840-1860)." *Louisiana Historical Quarterly* 20 (January 1937): 137-51.

Clemens, Samuel L. *Life on the Mississippi*. New York: Harper & Row, 1958 republication of 1883 original.

Cline, Isaac M. "The Tropical Hurricane of September 29, 1915." *Monthly Weather Review* (September 1915): 456-66.

Cohen's New Orleans Directory, Including Jefferson City, Carrollton, Gretna, Algiers, and McDonough. New Orleans, 1850, 1854.

Coleman, William H. *Historical Sketch Book and Guide to New Orleans and Environs*. New York: William H. Coleman, 1885.

Colten, Craig E. *An Unnatural Metropolis: Wresting New Orleans from Nature*. Baton Rouge and London, England: Louisiana State University Press, 2005.

Colten, Craig E., ed. *Transforming New Orleans and Its Environs: Centuries of Change*. Pittsburgh, PA: University of Pittsburgh Press, 2000.

Colten, Craig E. "Cypress In New Orleans: Revisiting The Observations of Le Page Du Pratz," *Louisiana History* XLIV, No. 4 (Fall 2003): 463-77.

Company of the West Ledger, as quoted in Marc de Villiers du Terrage, "A History of the Foundation of New Orleans (1717-1722)," *The Louisiana Historical Quarterly* 3, No. 2 (April 1920).

Conway, Alan A. "New Orleans as a Port of Immigration, 1820-1860." M.A. thesis, University of London, 1949.

Conway, Alan A. "New Orleans as a Port of Immigration, 1820-1860." *Louisiana Studies* 1 (Fall 1962): 1-22.

Cooke, John. *Perspectives on Ethnicity in New Orleans*. New Orleans: The Committee on Ethnicity in New Orleans, 1979.

Cowdrey, Albert E. *The Delta Engineers: A History of the United States Army Corps of Engineers in the New Orleans District*. New Orleans: U.S. Army Corps of Engineers, 1971.

Cruzat, Heloise H., trans. "Allotment of Building Sites in New Orleans (1722)," *The Louisiana Historical Quarterly* 7, No. 4 (October 1924):564-66.

Cuming, Fortescue. *Sketches of a Tour to the Western Country through the States of Ohio and Kentucky*. Pittsburgh, PA: Cramer, Spear & Eichbaum, 1810.

Cunningham, Robert, David Gisclair, and John Craig. "The Louisiana Statewide LIDAR Project." www.atlas.lsu.edu.

Cunningham, William P., and Barbara Woodworth Saigo. *Environmental Science: A Global Concern*. Boston, MA: McGraw Hill, 2001.

Curtis and Davis. *New Orleans Housing and Neighborhood Preservation Study*. New Orleans: Curtis and Davis, 1974.

D'Iberville, Pierre Le Moyne, Sieur. *Iberville's Gulf Journals*, edited and translated by Richebourg Gaillard McWilliams. University, AL: The University of Alabama Press, 1991.

Dabney, Thomas Ewing. *The Industrial Canal and Inner Harbor of New Orleans: History, Description and Economic Aspects of Giant Facility Created to Encourage Industrial Expansion and Develop Commerce*. New Orleans: Board of Commissioners of the Port of New Orleans, 1921.

Daily Delta, February 5, 1863, New Orleans, Louisiana.

Daily Orleanian, February 19, 1849, p. 2, col. 3.

Daily Orleanian, February 21, 1849, p. 2, col. 1.

Daily Orleanian, February 26, 1849, p. 2, col. 1.

Daily Orleanian, January 30, 1850, p. 2, col. 2.

Daily Orleanian, June 6, 1849, p. 2, col. 1.

Daily Orleanian, March 13, 1849, p. 2, col. 2.

Daily Orleanian, March 2, 1849, p. 2, col. 3.

Daily Orleanian, March 9, 1849, p. 2, col. 1-4.

Daily Orleanian, May 2, 1849, p. 2, col. 1.

Daily Orleanian, May 5, 1849, p. 2, col. 2.

Daily Orleanian, November 27, 1849, p. 2, col. 1.

Daily Picayune, February 9, 1912, section 3, p. 13.

Daily Picayune, January 26, 1866, p. 3, col. 2.

Daily Picayune, January 4, 1850, "City Intelligence" column, p. 2.

Daily Picayune, January 7, 1845, "City Intelligence" column.

Daily Picayune, July 7, 1852, "City Intelligence" column.

Daily Picayune, October 26, 1898, p. 9.

Dalton, John E. *Sugar: A Case Study of Government Control.* New York: The Macmillan Company, 1937.

Darby, William. *A Geographical Description of the State of Louisiana.* Philadelphia, PA: John Melish, 1816.

Dart, Henry P. "The First Law Regulating Land Grants in French Colonial Louisiana." *The Louisiana Historical Quarterly* 14, No. 3 (July 1931): 346-48.

Davis, Richard A. Jr. *The Evolving Coast.* New York: Scientific American Library, 1994.

Dawdy, Shannon Lee. "La Ville Sauvage: 'Enlightened' Colonialism and Creole Improvisation in New Orleans, 1699-1769," Ph.D. dissertation, The University of Michigan, 2003.

Dawdy, Shannon Lee. *Madame John's Legacy (16ORS1) Revisited: A Closer Look at the Archeology of Colonial New Orleans.* New Orleans: Friends of the Cabildo and Louisiana Division of Archeology, 1998.

Day, John W. Jr., Louis D. Britsch, Suzanne R. Hawes, Gary P. Shaffer, Denise J. Reed, and Donald Cahoon. "Pattern and Process of Land Loss in the Mississippi Delta: A Spatial and Temporal Analysis of Wetland Habitat Change." *Estuaries* 23 (August 2000): 425-38.

De Bow, J. D. B. "Lafayette, Louisiana," *The Commercial Review of the South and West* 4 (1847): 262.

De Bow, J. D. B. *Statistical View of the United States—Compendium of the Seventh Census.* Washington, DC: A.O.P. Nicholson, Printer, 1854.

De Bow, J. D. B. *The Commercial Review of the South and West,* 8 vols. New Orleans, LA: J.D.B. De Bow, 1846-50.

Deiler, Hanno J. "Germany's Contribution to the Present Population of New Orleans, with a Census of the German Schools." *The Louisiana Journal of Education,* May 1886. Special Collection Vertical File, Howard-Tilton Memorial Library, Tulane University, New Orleans, LA.

Denevan, William M. "The Pristine Myth: The Landscape of the Americas in 1492." *Annals of the Association of American Geographers* 82, No. 3 (September 1992): 369-85.

Des Moines Capital, March 22, 1912, p. 15, c. 1.

Desdunes, Rodolphe Lucien. *Our People and Our History.* Translated and edited by Sister Dorothea Olga McCants. Baton Rouge: Louisiana State University Press, 1973.

Didimus, Henry. *New Orleans As I Found It.* New York: Harper & Brothers, 1845.

Digest for the Acts and Deliberations of the Cabildo, January 18, 1771.

Dimitry, Charles Patton. "Recollections of an Old Citizen." *Times-Democrat.* September 10, 1893.

Din, Gilbert and John E. Harkins. *The New Orleans Cabildo: Colonial Louisiana's First City Government 1769-1803.* Baton Rouge and London, England: Louisiana State University Press, 1996.

Dixon, Frank Haigh. *A Traffic History of the Mississippi River System—National Waterways Commission, Document Number 11.* Washington, DC: Government Printing Office, 1909.

Dodd, Walter L. *Report of the Health and Sanitary Survey of the City of New Orleans.* New Orleans: City of New Orleans, Brandao Printing Company, 1918-19.

"Domestic-New Orleans," *Middlesex Gazette* (Middletown, Connecticut), 39, Issue 2016, July 14, 1824, p. 2.

Domínguez, Virginia R. "Social Classification in Creole Louisiana." *American Ethnologist* 4 (November 1977): 589-602.

Domínguez, Virginia R. *White by Definition: Social Classification in Creole Louisiana.* New Brunswick, NJ: Rutgers University Press, 1986.

Donze, Frank and Gordon Russell. 4 MONTHS TO DECIDE: Nagin Panel Says Hardest Hit Areas Must Prove Viability; City's Footprint May Shrink," January 11, 2006, p. 1.

Donze, Frank. "Don't Write Us Off, Residents Warn; Urban Land Institute Report Takes a Beating," *New Orleans Times-Picayune,* November 29, 2005, p. 1.

Dormon, James H. "Ethnicity and Identity: Creoles of Color in Twentieth-Century South Louisiana." In *Creole of Color of the Gulf South,* ed. James H. Dormon, 166-79. Knoxville, TN: University of Tennessee Press, 1996.

Drainage Advisory Board. *Report on the Drainage of the City of New Orleans.* New Orleans: T. Fitzwilliam

& Co. Printers, 1895.

"Dryades St. and Market." *Sunday States.* December 20, 1903, p. 20.

Dumont, M. "History of Louisiana, Translated from the Historical Memoirs of M. Dumont," in *Historical Memoirs of Louisiana, From the First Settlement of the Colony to the Departure of Governor O'Reilly in 1770,* ed. B. F. French. New York: Lamport, Blakeman & Law, 1853.

Dunbar, William. "Meteorological Observations." *Transactions of the American Philosophical Society* 6 (1809): 43-55.

Earl, George G. *The Hurricane of September 29, 1915 and Subsequent Heavy Rainfalls: Report of George G. Earl, Gen'l Supt. to Sewerage and Water Board of New Orleans.* New Orleans: Sewerage and Water Board, October 14, 1915.

Edmondson, Brad. "Immigration Nation: The New Suburbanities," *Preservation* 52, No. 1 (January-February 2000): 31-49.

Edwards, Jay D. "The Origins of Creole Architecture." *Winterthur Portfolio: A Journal of American Material Culture* 29 (Summer/Autumn 1994): 155-89.

Edwards, Jay Dearborn. "The Origins of the Louisiana Creole Cottage." In *French and Germans in the Mississippi Valley: Landscape and Cultural Traditions,* ed. Michael Roark, 9-60. Cape Girardeau, MO: Center for Regional History and Cultural Heritage, Southeast Missouri State University, 1988.

Edwards, Jay Dearborn. *Louisiana's French Vernacular Architecture: A Historical and Social Bibliography.* Monticello, IL: Vance Bibliographies, 1986.

Ekberg, Carl J. *French Roots in the Illinois Country.* Urbana and Chicago, IL: University of Illinois Press, 1998.

El Nasser, Haya, and Paul Overberg. "Millions More Are Changing States," *USA Today,* November 30-December 2, 2007, p. 1.

Engelhardt, George W. *New Orleans, Louisiana, The Crescent City: The Book of the Picayune.* New Orleans, 1903-04.

Erskine, Chris. "He left his heart…in New Orleans." *New Orleans Times-Picayune,* May 5, 2008, C1.

"Ex-Slaves Meet at Waco." *Dallas Morning News,* August 12, 1897, p. 5.

"Extract of a Letter from an Emigrant in New-Orleans." *Newburyport Herald* (Newburyport, MA), October 17, 1817, p. 3, c. 2.

"Extracts from the Clockmaker." *The Madisonian,* 2, Issue 19, October 20, 1838, p. 1.

Fearon, Henry Bradshaw. *Sketches of America: A Narrative of a Journey of Five Thousand Miles Through the Eastern and Western States of America.* London, England: Strahan and Spottiswoods, 1819.

Featherstonhaugh, G. W. *Excursion Through the Slave States, From Washington on the Potomac to the Frontier of Mexico.* New York: Negro Universities Press, 1968.

Federal Writers' Project of the Works Progress Administration. *New Orleans City Guide.* Boston, MA: Houghton Mifflin Company, 1952 revision of 1938 original.

Filipich, Judy A. and Lee Taylor. *Lakefront New Orleans: Planning and Development 1926-1971.* New Orleans, Urban Studies Institute, Louisiana State University in New Orleans, 1971.

Fisk, H. N. *Geological Investigations of the Alluvial Valley of the Lower Mississippi River.* Vicksburg, MS: U.S. Army Corps of Engineer, Mississippi River Commission, 1944.

Fitch, James Marston. "Creole Architecture 1718-1860: The Rise and Fall of a Great Tradition." In *The Past As Prelude: New Orleans 1718-1968,* ed. Hodding Carter, 71-87. Gretna, LA: Pelican Publishing Company, 1968.

Flint, Timothy. *Recollections of the Last Ten Years…in the Valley of the Mississippi.* Boston, MA: Cummings, Hilliard, and Company, 1826.

Fogelson, Robert M. *Downtown: Its Rise and Fall, 1880-1950.* New Haven, CT and London, England: Yale University Press, 2001.

Fontaine, Edward. "A Lecture on the Peculiarities of the Physical Geography of the Mississippi River and Its Delta." Washington, DC: Republican Job Office Print, 1874.

Ford, Larry R. "Reading the Skylines of American Cities." *Geographical Review* 82 (April 1992): 180-200.

Ford, Larry R. and Ernst Griffin. "The Ghettoization of Paradise." *Geographical Review* 69 (April 1979): 14-158.

Fort Worth Star-Telegram; August 25, 1915, p. 2.

"Forty-Three Known Victims at Rigolets and Catherine." *New Orleans Times-Picayune,* October 1, 1915, p. 1.

Fossier, Albert A. *New Orleans: The Glamour Period, 1800-1840.* New Orleans: Pelican Publishing Company, 1957.

Foster, Pops. *Pops Foster: The Autobiography of a New Orleans Jazzman*, ed. by Tom Stoddard. Berkeley, Los Angeles, and London, England: University of California Press, 1971.

"Foster's Friends Wail Farewell." *Corpus Christi Times* (Corpus Christi, Texas), November 5, 1969, p. D6, c. 5.

Frazier, D. E. "Recent Deltaic Deposits of the Mississippi River: Their Development and Chronology." *Transactions of the Gulf Coast Association of Geological Societies* 17 (1967): 287-315.

Freeman, Greg. "St. Louis Is Among Most-Segregated Cities—And Most of Us Are Comfortable With That." *St. Louis Post-Dispatch*. December 1, 2002, Metro Section, C3.

Freiberg, Edna B. *Bayou St. John in Colonial Louisiana, 1699-1803*. New Orleans: Harvey Press, 1980.

Fricker, Jonathan. "The Origins of the Creole Raised Plantation House." *Louisiana History* 25 (Spring 1984): 137-53.

Friends of the Cabildo. *New Orleans Architecture*, 8 vols. New Orleans and Gretna, LA: Friends of the Cabildo and Pelican Publishing Company, 1971-97 .

"From New Orleans—The Municipal Election." *New York Times*, June 4, 1856, p. 1.

"From Swamp and Marsh," *New Orleans Times*, October 25, 1877, p. 7.

"From the Kentucky Gazette: New Orleans." *The Adams Centinel* (Gettysburg, PA), June 3, 1818, p. 2, c. 3.

Gagliano, Sherwood M. "Mississippi River Sediment as a Resource." In *Modern Mississippi Delta—Depositional Environments and Processes*, ed. Ram S. Saxena, 103-25. New Orleans: New Orleans Geological Society, 1976.

Gagliano, Sherwood M., and Johannes L. Van Beek. *Geologic and Geomorphic Aspects of Delta Processes, Mississippi Delta System: Hydrologic and Geologic Studies of Coastal Louisiana*. Report 1, Louisiana State University, Center for Wetland Resources, Baton Rouge, 1970.

"Gale's Fury Ties Up All Railroad Traffic Into City." *New Orleans Times-Picayune*, September 30, 1915, p. 2.

Galloway, Patricia Kay, ed. *Mississippi Provincial Archives: French Dominion, 1749-1763, Volume V*, originally edited by Dunbar Rowland and A. G. Sanders. Baton Rouge: Louisiana State University Press, 1984.

Gardner, Charles. *Gardner's New Orleans Directory*. New Orleans: C. Gardner, 1858, 1859, 1861, 1869.

Gayarré, Charles. *The Creoles of History and the Creoles of Romance—A Lecture Delivered in the Hall of the Tulane University, New Orleans*. New Orleans: C.E. Hopkins, Publisher, 1885.

GCR & Associates, various post-Katrina population datasets.

Gehman, Mary. "The Mexico-Louisiana Creole Connection." *Louisiana Cultural Vistas* 11 (Winter 2000-2001): 68-75.

Gehman, Mary. *The Free People of Color of New Orleans: An Introduction*. New Orleans: Margaret Media, Inc., 1994.

Geology and Agriculture of Louisiana. Baton Rouge: Louisiana Geological Survey, 1892.

Gibson, Campbell. "Population of the 100 Largest Cities and Other Urban Places in the United States: 1790 to 1990," Population Division Working Paper No. 27, U.S. Bureau of the Census, Washington, DC, June 1998.

Gibson's Guide and Directory of the State of Louisiana, and the Cities of New Orleans and Lafayette. New Orleans: John Gibson, Publisher, 1838.

Gilmore, Janet C. "Sagamité and Booya: French Influence in Defining Great Lakes Culinary Heritage." *Material History Review* 60 (Fall 2004): 58-69.

Gilmore, H. W. *Some Basic Census Tract Maps of New Orleans*. New Orleans: Tulane University, 1937, stored at Tulane University Special Collections, C5-D10-F6.

Gilmore, H. W. "The Old New Orleans and the New: The Case for Ecology." *American Sociological Review* 9, No. 4 (August 1944), pp. 385-94.

Giraud, Marcel. "France and Louisiana in the Early Eighteenth Century." *The Mississippi Valley Historical Review* 36, No. 4 (March 1950): 657-74.

Giraud, Marcel. *A History of French Louisiana, Volume Five: The Company of the Indies, 1723-1731*. Baton Rouge and London, England: Louisiana State University Press, 1987.

Giraud, Marcel. *A History of French Louisiana, Volume One: The Reign of Louis XIV, 1698-1715*. Baton Rouge and London, England: Louisiana State University Press, 1990 reprint of 1953 original.

Giraud, Marcel. *A History of French Louisiana, Volume Two: Years of Transition, 1715-1717*. Baton Rouge and London, England: Louisiana State University Press, 1993 reprint of 1958 original.

Glazier, Captain Willard. *Peculiarities of American Cities*. Philadelphia, PA: Hubbard Brothers, Publishers,

1885.

Goldin, Claudia Dale. *Urban Slavery in the American South, 1820-1860: A Quantitative History*. Chicago, IL and London, England: University of Chicago Press, 1976.

Goodache, Robert. "Select Tales—New Orleans." *Macon Weekly Telegraph* (Macon, Georgia), May 19, 1828, p. 77, c. 4.

Gould, E. W. *Fifty Years on the Mississippi; Or, Gould's History of River Navigation*. St. Louis, MO: Nixon-Jones Printing Company, 1889.

Grace, Stephanie. "Will Plan Lift the Curse of the Green Dot?," *New Orleans Times-Picayune*, April 1, 2007, Metro- Editorial, p. 7.

Greater New Orleans Community Data Center, http://www.gnocdc.org, for various post-Katrina population datasets.

Hachard, Sister Mary Madeleine of St. Stanislaus. Letters dated October 27, 1727 and April 24, 1728. In *The Ursulines in New Orleans 1727-1925*, ed. Henry Churchill Semple (P. J. Kennedy & Sons, New York, 1925), 190-238.

Hair, William Ivy. *Bourbonism and Agrarian Protest: Louisiana Politics 1877-1900*. Baton Rouge: Louisiana State University Press, 1969.

Haites, Erik Friso. "Ohio and Mississippi River Transportation 1810-1860." Ph.D. dissertation, Purdue University, 1969.

Hall, A. Oakey. *The Manhattaner in New Orleans; or Phases of "Crescent City" Life.* New York: J. S. Redfield, Clinton Hall, 1851.

Hall, Basil. *Travels in North America in the Years 1827 and 1828, Volume III.* Edinburgh and London: Robert Cadell, and Simpkin and Marshall, 1830, Third Edition.

Hall, Gwendolyn Midlo. *Africans in Colonial Louisiana: The Development of Afro-Creole Culture in the Eighteenth Century*. Baton Rouge and London, England: Louisiana State University Press, 1992.

Hammer, David. "N.O. Airs Plans for Road Home Lots; 10-Year Strategy May Cost Millions," *New Orleans Times-Picayune*, November 28, 2007, p. 1.

Hankins, Jonn Ethan and Steven Maklansky, eds. *Raised to the Trade: Creole Building Arts of New Orleans*. New Orleans: New Orleans Museum of Art, 2002.

Hardee, T.S. *Topographical and Drainage Map of New Orleans and Surroundings, From Recent Surveys and Investigations* (1879). The Historic New Orleans Collection, New Orleans, accession number 1974.52.

Harper's Weekly, May 10, 1862, p. 303, c. 1.

Hart, David and David Zilkoski. "Mapping a Moving Target: The Use of GIS to Support Development of a Subsidence Model in the New Orleans Region." *Urban and Regional Information Association (URISA) Proceedings*, 1994, http://libraries.maine.edu/Spatial/gisweb/spatdb/urisa/ur94049.html

Hauck, Philomena. *Bienville: Father of Louisiana*. Lafayette, LA: Center for Louisiana Studies, 1998.

Heard, Malcolm. *French Quarter Manual: An Architectural Guide to New Orleans' Vieux Carré*. New Orleans: School of Architecture, Tulane University, 1997.

Hennick, Louis C. and E. Harper Charlton. *The Streetcars of New Orleans*. Gretna, Louisiana: Firebird Press Book/Pelican Publishing Company, 1965; reprinted 2000.

Henry, Jacques M., and Carl L. Bankston. "Propositions for a Structuralist Analysis of Creolism." *Current Anthropology* 39 (August-October 1998): 558-66.

Herbert, David T. and Colin J. Thomas. *Urban Geography: A First Approach*. Chichester, NY, Brisbane, Toronto, and Singapore: John Wiley & Sons, 1982.

Hesse-Wartegg, Ernst von. *Travels on the Lower Mississippi, 1879-1880: A Memoir by Ernst von Hesse-Wartegg*, ed. and trans. Frederic Trautmann. Columbia, MO and London, England: University of Missouri Press, 1990.

Hirsch, Arnold R., and Joseph Logsdon. "Introduction: Franco-Africans and African-Americans." In *Creole New Orleans: Race and Americanization*, eds. Arnold R. Hirsch and Joseph Logsdon. Baton Rouge and London, England: Louisiana State University Press, 1992.

Hirsch, Arnold R. "Simply a Matter of Black and White: The Transformation of Race and Politics in Twentieth-Century New Orleans," in *Creole New Orleans: Race and Americanization*, eds. Arnold R. Hirsch and Joseph Logsdon. Baton Rouge and London, England: Louisiana State University Press, 1992.

Hirt, L. *Plan of New Orleans with Perspective and Geometrical Views of the Principal Buildings of the City* (1841). The Historic New Orleans Collection, New Orleans, accession number 1952.4.

Hodgson, Adam. *Remarks During a Journey Through North America in the Years 1819, 1820, and 1821*. New

York: Samuel Whiting, 1823.

Horne, Jed. *Breach of Faith: Hurricane Katrina and the Near Death of a Great American City*. New York: Random House, 2006.

Houck, Oliver. "Can We Save New Orleans?" *Tulane Environmental Law Journal* 19, Issue 1 (Spring 2006), 2-67.

House Executive Documents. *Report on the Internal Commerce of the United States* (1887). 50th Congress, 1st Session, No. 6, Part II.

"How Much of City is Below Sea Level?" *New Orleans Item*. April 13, 1948, p. 12.

Independent Chronicle (Boston, MA), September 25, 1815, p. 1.

Ingraham, Joseph Holt. *The South-West by a Yankee*, 2 vols. New York: Harper and Brothers, 1835.

Jackson, Joy J. *New Orleans in the Gilded Age: Politics and Urban Progress 1880-1896*. Baton Rouge: Louisiana State University Press, 1969.

Janssen, James S. *Building New Orleans: The Engineer's Role*. New Orleans: Waldemar S. Nelson and Company, Inc., 1987.

Jefferys, Thomas. *The Natural and Civil History of the French Dominions in North and South America*. London, England: T. Jefferys, 1760.

"John Mitchell in New Orleans," *Sunday Delta* (New Orleans), April 18, 1858, p. 7, c. 1.

Johnson, A. Ivan. "Land Subsidence Due to Fluid Withdrawal in the United States—An Overview." In *Land Subsidence: Case Studies and Current Research*, ed. James W. Borchers, 51-60. Belmont, CA: Star Publishing Company, 1998.

Johnson, Brent M. "Development of the Mississippi River-Gulf Outlet." *Journal of the Waterways Division, Proceedings of the American Society of Civil Engineers* (1969).

Johnson, Jerah. "Colonial New Orleans: A Fragment of the Eighteenth-Century French Ethos." In *Creole New Orleans: Race and Americanization*, eds. Arnold R. Hirsch and Joseph Logsdon. Baton Rouge and London, England: Louisiana State University Press, 1992.

Johnson, Jerah. "Jim Crow Laws of the 1890s and the Origins of New Orleans Jazz: Correction of an Error." *Popular Music* 19 (2000): 243-51.

Johnson, Pableaux. "Home of the Cocktail." *New Orleans Times-Picayune*, January 7, 2005, *Lagniappe*. p. 37.

Joutel, Henri. *A Journal of the Last Voyage Perform'd by Monsr. de La Sale, to the Gulph of Mexico, to Find Out the Mouth of the Missisipi River*. London, England: A. Bell, 1714.

Jumonville, Florence M. *A Guide to the Vieux Carré Survey*. New Orleans: The Historic New Orleans Collection, 1990.

Kammerer, J. C. "Largest Rivers in the United States." *U.S. Geological Survey Water Fact Sheet*, Open File Report 87-242, 1990.

Katz, Allan. "The Seventh Ward: Mother of Mayors." *New Orleans Magazine* 28 (May 1994): 51-54.

Keim, De B.R. "The Mississippi River and Its Peculiarities." *Continental Monthly: Devoted to Literature and National Policy* 5 (June 1864): 629-49.

Kellogg, John. "Negro Urban Clusters in the Postbellum South." *Geographical Review* 67 (July 1977): 310-21.

Kelman, Ari. "A River and its City: Critical Episodes in the Environmental History of New Orleans." Ph.D. dissertation, Brown University, 1998.

Kendall, John Smith. *History of New Orleans*, 2 vols. Chicago and New York: Lewis Publishing Company, 1922.

Kennedy, Joseph C.G. *Population of the United States in 1860; Compiled from the Original Returns of the Eighth Census*. Washington, DC: Government Printing Office, 1864.

Kidder, Tristram R. "Making the City Inevitable: Native Americans and the Geography of New Orleans," in *Transforming New Orleans and Its Environs: Centuries of Change*, ed. Craig E. Colten. Pittsburgh, PA: University of Pittsburgh Press, 2000.

King, Grace. *Creole Families of New Orleans*. New York: The Macmillan Company, 1921.

King, Grace. *New Orleans: The Place and the People*. New York: The Macmillan Company, 1926.

Kirkham, Chris. "Nutria Nation," *New Orleans Times-Picayune*, February 25, 2008, A1-A5.

Klingler, Thomas A. *If I Could Turn My Tongue Like That: The Creole Language of Pointe Coupée Parish, Louisiana*. Baton Rouge: Louisiana State University Press, 2003.

Kniffen, Fred B. "Louisiana House Types." *Annals of the Association of American Geographers* 26, No. 4 (December 1936): 179-93.

Kniffen, Fred B. "The Lower Mississippi Valley: European Settlement, Utilization and Modification."

Geoscience & Man 27 (1990).

Kniffen, Fred B. and Sam Bowers Hilliard. *Louisiana: Its Land and People.* Baton Rouge and London, England: Louisiana State University Press, 1988.

Knight, Franklin W. *Slave Society in Cuba During the Nineteenth Century.* Madison, Milwaukee, and London, England: The University of Wisconsin Press, 1970.

Knipmeyer, William Bernard. "Settlement Succession in Eastern French Louisiana." Ph.D. dissertation, Louisiana State University, 1956.

Knox, Paul. *Urban Social Geography: An Introduction.* Essex, England and New York: Longman Scientific & Technical and John Wiley & Sons, 1987.

Kohl, Johann Georg. *Travels in Canada: and Through the States of New York and Pennsylvania, Volume I.* London, England: G. Manwaring, 1861.

Kolp, John Leslie. "Suburbanization in Uptown New Orleans: Lafayette City, 1833-1852." M.A. thesis, University of New Orleans, 1975.

Kravitz, Alysia R., Richard Campanella, Lisa Schiavinato, and Aquatic Invasive Species Task Force. *State Management Plan for Aquatic Invasive Species in Louisiana.* Baton Rouge, LA: Louisiana Department of Wildlife and Fisheries, July 2005.

Krumpelmann, John T. "Ingraham's 'South-West' as a Source of Americanisms." *American Speech* 18, No. 2. (April 1943): 157-58.

Krupa, Michelle. "City Hall Begins a Building Boom." *New Orleans Times-Picayune,* February 23, 2008, B1-B3.

Krupa, Michelle. "It's Official: Katrina Chased Out a Huge Chunk of N.O. Voters, Remaking the Region's Electoral Landscape." *New Orleans Times-Picayune,* April 24, 2008, A1-A4.

Krupa, Michelle. "Water Torture." *New Orleans Times-Picayune,* August 8, 2007, A1-A11.

Krupa, Michelle and Gordon Russell. "N.O. Post-K Blueprint Unveiled; Plan Puts Most Cash in East, Lower 9th." *New Orleans Times-Picayune,* March 29, 2007, p. A1.

Kuriloff, Aaron. "CARPetbaggers: The Appearance of Several Species of Asian Carp in Louisiana Has Scientists Worried." *New Orleans Times-Picayune.* June 23, 2003, National section, p. 1.

Kusky, Timothy M. "Time to Move to Higher Ground." *Boston Globe,* September 25, 2005, p. D12.

La Salle, M. de. "Account of the Taking Possession of Louisiana by M. De La Salle," in *The Journeys of René-Robert Cavelier Sieur de La Salle, Volume I,* ed. Isaac Joslin Cox. Austin, TX: The Pemberton Press, 1968 reprint of 1905 original.

La Salle, M. de. "Memoir of M. Cavelier de La Salle," in *On the Discovery of the Mississippi,* ed. Thomas Falconer. London, England: Samuel Clarke, 1844.

La Salle, M. de. "Memoir of the Sieur de La Salle Reporting to Monseigneur de Seignelay" (circa 1684), in *On the Discovery of the Mississippi,* by Thomas Falconer. London, England: S. Clarke, 1844.

Lafayette City Advertiser. January 29, 1842, p. 2, col. 2.

Labbé, Ronald M. and Jonathan Lurie. *The Slaughterhouse Cases: Regulation, Reconstruction, and the Fourteenth Amendment.* Lawrence, KS: University Press of Kansas, 2003.

La Trobe, Charles Joseph. *The Rambler in North America, Volume II.* New York: Harper & Brothers, 1835.

Latrobe, Benjamin Henry Boneval. *Impressions Respecting New Orleans: Diary & Sketches 1818-1820,* ed. Samuel Wilson Jr. New York: Columbia University Press, 1951.

Latrobe, John H.B. *Southern Travels: Journal of John H.B. Latrobe, 1834,* ed. Samuel Wilson, Jr. New Orleans: The Historic New Orleans Collection, 1986.

Laussat, Pierre Clément de. *Memoirs of My Life.* Baton Rouge and New Orleans: Louisiana State University Press and The Historic New Orleans Collection, 1978 translation of 1831 memoir.

Le Page Du Pratz, Antoine. *The History of Louisiana,* ed. Joseph G. Tregle, Jr. Baton Rouge: Louisiana State University Press, 1976 reprint of 1774 edition originally published in 1758.

Ledet, Wilton P. "The History of the City of Carrollton." *Louisiana Historical Quarterly* 21, No. 1 (January 1938): 220-81.

Lemann, Bernard. *The Vieux Carré—A General Statement.* New Orleans: School of Architecture, Tulane University, 1966.

Lemann, Susan Gibbs. *The Problems of Founding a Viable Colony: The Military in Early French Louisiana* (1982), reproduced in *The Louisiana Purchase Bicentennial Series in Louisiana History, Volume I: The French Experience in Louisiana,* ed. Glenn R. Conrad. Lafayette, LA: Center for Louisiana Studies, 1995.

Leonard, Irving A. "The Spanish Re-Exploration of the Gulf Coast in 1686." *The Mississippi Valley Historical Review* 22, No. 4 (March 1936): 547-57.

"Letter from New Orleans." *The Sun* (Baltimore, MD), April 12, 1877, p. 4, c. 2.

Lewis, Peirce F. *New Orleans: The Making of an Urban Landscape.* Cambridge, MA: Ballinger Publishing Company, 1976.

Lewis, Peirce F. *New Orleans: The Making of an Urban Landscape.* Santa Fe, NM, and Harrisonburg, VA: Center for American Places and University of Virginia Press, 2003.

Liebling, A.J. *The Earl of Louisiana.* New York, NY: Simon and Schuster, 1961.

"Life in New Orleans," *Ohio Statesman* (Columbus, OH), May 7, 1847, p. 3, c. 2.

"Life Throbs Anew in Vieux Carre of City Care Forgot." *Dallas Morning News,* June 25, 1922, p. 15, c. 1.

Literacy Volunteers of America. "1998 NALS Synthetic Estimates of Adult Literacy," http://www.literacyvolunteers.org/home/press/may1298/Lanals.html, accessed December 29, 2003.

Livingston, Edward. *An Answer to Mr. Jefferson's Justification of His Conduct in the Case of the New Orleans Batture.* Philadelphia, PA: William Fry, 1813.

Logsdon, Joseph, and Caryn Cossé Bell. "The Americanization of Black New Orleans 1850-1900." In *Creole New Orleans: Race and Americanization,* eds. Arnold R. Hirsch and Joseph Logsdon. Baton Rouge: Louisiana State University Press, 1992.

Logsdon, Joseph. "The Surprise of the Melting Pot: We Can All Become New Orleanians." In *Perspectives on Ethnicity in New Orleans,* ed. John Cooke. New Orleans: The Committee on Ethnicity in New Orleans, 1979.

Long, Alecia P. "Poverty Is the New Prostitution: Race, Poverty, and Public Housing in Post-Katrina New Orleans." *The Journal of American History* 94, No. 3 (December 2007): 795-803.

Louisiana Department of Health and Hospitals. "2006 Louisiana Health and Population Survey Report—Orleans Parish." Baton Rouge: Louisiana Recovery Authority, January 17, 2007.

Lutz, Brobson. "Water Whirled: How Safe Is Our Drinking Water? A Journey Through the Process." *New Orleans Magazine* 36 (November 2001): 45-52.

Lyell, Sir Charles. *A Second Visit to the United States of North America,* 2 vols. New York and London, England: Harper & Brothers and John Murray, 1849.

Mackay, Charles. *Life and Liberty in America, or, Sketches of a Tour in the United States and Canada in 1857-8.* New York: Harper & Brothers, Publishers, 1859.

Maduell, Charles R. Jr. *The Census Tables for the French Colony of Louisiana from 1699 to 1732.* Baltimore, MD: Genealogical Publishing Company, 1972.

Magill, John. "A Conspiracy of Complicity." *Louisiana Cultural Vistas* 17, No. 3 (Fall 2006): 43-53.

Magill, John. "A Legacy Lost—What Once Stood on the St. Thomas Site." *Preservation in Print* 27, No. 1 (February 2000).

Maggi, Laura. "What Price Justice? In N.O., $1 Billion." *New Orleans Times-Picayune,* November 6, 2007, p. 1.

"Making of America." Cornell University, http://library5.library.cornell.edu/moa, accessed 2005-08.

Malena, Anne. "Louisiana: A Colonial Space of Translation." *Forum for Modern Language Studies* 40, No. 2 (2004): 204-13.

Mann, Charles C. *1491: New Revelations of the Americas Before Columbus.* New York: Alfred A. Knopf, 2006.

Marshall, Bob. "City's Fate Sealed in Hours: Timeline Maps Course of Post-Katrina Deluge," *New Orleans Times-Picayune,* May 14, 2006, A-1.

Martin, John M. "The People of New Orleans As Seen By Her Visitors, 1803-1860." *Louisiana Studies* 6 (Winter 1967): 361-75.

Martineau, Harriet, *Retrospect of Western Travel, Volume I.* London and New York: Saunders and Otley, and Harper and Brothers, 1838.

Mayoralty of New Orleans. *New Orleans Industrial and Ship Canal: An Ideal Location for Shipyards, Factories and Warehouses,* New Orleans: Pamphlet No. 5098-Commission Council Series, May 21, 1918, archived in the Tulane University Special Collections Vertical File.

McPhee, John. *The Control of Nature.* New York: Farrar, Straus and Giroux, 1989.

McPherson, Edward. "Judicial Decisions and Opinions: The Louisiana Slaughter-House Cases." *Hand-Book of Politics for 1874: Being a Record of Important Political Action, National and State, from July 15, 1872 to July 15, 1874.* Washington, DC: Solomons & Chapman, 1874.

McQuaid, John and Mark Schleifstein. *Path of Destruction: The Devastation of New Orleans and the Coming Age of Superstorms.* Boston, MA: Little, Brown and Company, 2006.

Meade, Robert H. *Contaminants in the Mississippi River, 1987-1992.* Denver, CO: U.S. Geological Survey Circular 1133, 1995.

Meehan, John T. "Bodies Strewn Thick in Salt Gulf Marshes," *New Orleans Times-Picayune*, October 2, 1915, p. 1-2.

"Meetings," *New Orleans Times-Picayune*, September 30, 2006, Metro section, p. 4.

Melish, John. *A Geographical Description of the United States, with the Contiguous Countries, Including Mexico and the West Indies*. New York: A.T. Goodrich, New York, 1826.

Membré, Father Zenobius. "Narrative of La Salle's Voyage Down the Mississippi, By Father Zenobius Membré," in *The Journeys of René-Robert Cavelier Sieur de La Salle, Volume I*, ed. Isaac Joslin Cox. Austin, TX: The Pemberton Press, 1968 reprint of 1905 original.

"Memoir of Richard Yeadon, Esq.," *The American Whig Review* 11, Issue 28A (May 1850): 477-87.

Moe, Christine. *Soil Subsidence in the New Orleans Area*. Monticello, IL: Vance Bibliographies, 1979.

Moellhausen, Henry. *Norman's Plan of New Orleans & Environs 1845*. Baton Rouge and London, England: Louisiana State University Press, 1976.

Montulé, Edouard de. *Travels in America 1816-1817*. Translated by Edward D. Seeber. Bloomington, IN: Indiana University Press, 1951.

Moody, Sid. "Mardi Gras in New Orleans: Is It Worth It? Fat Tuesday in the Big Easy." *The Lima News* (Lima, Ohio), April 2, 1972, p. D1-D5.

Moran, Kate. "Hospitals Engaging in Healthy Competition," *New Orleans Times-Picayune*, October 15, 2007, p. B1.

Mossa, Joann. "Sediment Dynamics in the Lowermost Mississippi River." *Engineering Geology* 45 (1996): 457-79.

Mowbray, Rebecca. "Mixed Vieux." *New Orleans Times-Picayune*, March 23, 2004, C1.

National Geospatial-Intelligence Agency / U.S. Board on Geographic Names. *NGA GEOnet Names Server (GNS)*, http://gnswww.nga.mil/geonames/GNS/index.jsp, accessed July 19, 2007.

Natural Resources Defense Council. *What's On Tap? Grading Drinking Water in U.S. Cities: New Orleans, LA*. Published report, June 2003, http://nrdc.org/water/drinking/uscities/contents.asp.

"Navigation Impeded by Flowers." *Daily Republican* (Decatur, IL), August 1, 1895, p. 7, c. 2.

Neighborhood Partnership Network, http://www.npnnola.com/associations.

New Orleans Federation of Clubs. *New Orleans: Key to America's Most Interesting City*. New Orleans: Federation of Clubs, 1926.

"New Orleans," *Delaware Weekly Advertiser and Farmer's Journal*, March 27, 1828, p. 1, c. 4.

"New Orleans and Her Trade," *Daily Picayune*, September 8, 1850, p. 2, c. 2.

"New Orleans is Getting Hotter- Increases in Temperature in Summer Attributed to the Drainage System," *Columbus Ledger-Enquirer* (Columbus, Georgia), June 13, 1918, p. 1, c. 3.

"New-Orleans—Sabbath in New Orleans," *New York Times*, April 12, 1853.

Newark Daily Advocate (Newark, Ohio), February 16, 1897, p. 1, c. 1.

Newton, Milton B. Jr. *Louisiana: A Geographical Portrait*. Baton Rouge: Geoforensics, 1987.

New-York Gazette & General Advertiser, October 12, 1812, p. 2, c. 3.

Niehaus, Earl F. "Catholic Ethnics in Nineteenth-Century Louisiana." In *Cross, Crozier, and Crucible: A Volume Celebrating the Bicentennial of a Catholic Diocese in Louisiana*, ed. Glenn R. Conrad, 48-69. New Orleans and Lafayette: The Archdiocese of New Orleans and Center for Louisiana Studies, 1993.

Niehaus, Earl F. "The Irish in New Orleans." In *St. Patrick's of New Orleans, 1833-1958*, ed. Charles L. Dufour, 9-14. New Orleans: St. Patrick's Parish, 1958.

Niehaus, Earl F. *The Irish in New Orleans*. Baton Rouge: Louisiana State University Press, 1965.

Nolan, Bruce. "Churches Celebrate 150 Years," *New Orleans Times-Picayune*, April 25, 2008, B1

Norman, Benjamin Moore. *Norman's New Orleans and Environs*. New Orleans: B. M. Norman, 1845.

Nossiter, Adam. "Bit by Bit, Some Outlines Emerge for a Shaken New Orleans," *New York Times*, August 27, 2006, p. 1.

Ogg, Frederic Austin. *The Opening of the Mississippi: A Struggle for Supremacy in the American Interior*. New York and London, England: The MacMillan Company, 1904.

Olmsted, Frederick Law. *A Journey in the Seaboard Slave States, With Remarks on Their Economy*. New York: Dix & Edwards, 1856.

Olmsted, Frederick Law. *The Cotton Kingdom: A Traveler's Observations on Cotton and Slavery in the American Slave States*, 2 vols. New York and London, England: Mason Brothers and Sampson Low, Son & Co., 1861.

Orleans Levee Board. *Building a Great City*. New Orleans: The Orleans Levee Board Reports, 1954.

Orleans Levee District. *The Orleans Levee District—The Hurricane Levee System*. New Orleans: Orleans

Levee District, 1999.

Orleans Levee District. *The Orleans Levee District—A History*. New Orleans: Orleans Levee District, 1999.

Orleans Parish School Board. *The New Orleans Book*. New Orleans: Orleans Parish School Board, 1919.

Oszuscik, Philippe. "The French Creole Cottage and Its Caribbean Connection." In *French and Germans in the Mississippi Valley: Landscape and Cultural Traditions*, ed. Michael Roark, 61-78. Cape Girardeau, MO: Center for Regional History and Cultural Heritage, Southeast Missouri State University, 1988.

Owens, Jeffrey Alan. "Holding Back the Waters: Land Development and the Origins of Levees on the Mississippi, 1720-1845." Ph.D. dissertation, Louisiana State University, 1999.

Papalia, Alyson. "Smart and Smarter: America's Brightest Cities—New Ranking Identifies the 25 Best-Educated Cities in the U.S." *Forbes.com*, Feburary 15, 2008.

Paxton, John Adems. *The New-Orleans Directory and Register*. New Orleans: Benj. Levy & Co., Printers, 1822, 1823.

Pénicaut, M. de. "Annals of Louisiana, From the Establishment of the First Colony Under M. D'Iberville, to the Departure of the Author to France, in 1722," in *Historical Collections of Louisiana and Florida, Including Translations of Original Manuscripts Relating to Their Discovery and Settlement, Volume VI*, ed. B. F. French. New York: J. Sabin & Sons, 1869.

Penland, S., and R. Boyd. *Transgressive Depositional Environments of the Mississippi River Delta: A Guide to the Barrier Islands, Beaches, and Shoals in Louisiana*. Baton Rouge, LA: Louisiana Geological Society, 1983.

Penland, S., L. Wayne, L.D. Britsch, S.J. Williams, A.D. Beall, and V. Caridas Butterworth. *Geomorphic Classification of Coastal Land Loss Between 1932 and 1990 in the Mississippi River Delta Plain, Southeastern Louisiana*. Study sponsored by U.S. Geological Survey, University of New Orleans, and Army Corps of Engineers-New Orleans District, 1998.

Pennsylvania Mercury, May 10, 1788, p. 4, c. 2.

Pennsylvania Packet, July 3, 1790, p. 2, c. 2.

Perrin Du Lac, M. *Travels Through the Two Louisianas… in 1801, 1802, & 1803*. London, England: Richard Phillips, 1807.

Philadelphia Gazette, February 3, 1795, p. 3.

Philadelphia Inquirer, January 11, 1913, p. 15, c. 5.

Piazza, Tom. *Why New Orleans Matters*. New York: Harper Collins, 2005.

Pickett, Albert James. *Eight Days in New Orleans in February, 1847*. Montgomery, AL: Alabama Journal of Montgomery/S.I.), 1847.

"Pictures of the South: The French Market, New Orleans." *Harper's Weekly*, August 18, 1866, p. 526, col. 1.

Pierson, George Wilson. *Tocqueville in America*. Garden City, NY: Anchor Books, Doubleday and Company, 1959.

Pilié, Louis H. *Report on Drainage*. New Orleans: Common Council, City of New Orleans, 1857.

Pitot, James. *Observations on the Colony of Louisiana from 1796 to 1802*. New Orleans, Baton Rouge, and London, England: The Historic New Orleans Collection and Louisiana State University Press, republished 1979.

Pittman, Captain Philip. *The Present State of the European Settlements on the Missisippi*. Gainesville: University of Florida Press, 1973 facsimile of 1770 original.

Polk's New Orleans City Directory. New Orleans: R.L. Polk, 1940, 1947, 1954, 1955, 1962, 1969, 1971, 1977, 1979, 1981, 1986, 1991, 1994, 1991, 2001.

Pontchartrain Railroad Company, Minutes, vol. 1, June 8, 1830. Special Collections, Howard-Tilton Memorial Library, Tulane University, New Orleans.

Port of New Orleans. *About the Port of New Orleans*. www.portno.com/facts.htm.

Porteous, Laura L., trans. "Governor Carondelet's Levee Ordinance of 1792." *The Louisiana Historical Quarterly* 10, No.4 (October 1927).

Porter, David D. "The Opening of the Lower Mississippi." *The Century: A Popular Quarterly* 29, Issue 6 (April 1885), pp. 923-53.

Pope, John. "Evoking King, Nagin Calls N.O. 'Chocolate' City; Speech Addresses Fear of Losing Black Culture." *New Orleans Times-Picayune*, January 17, 2006, p. 1.

Pope, John. "Fontaine Martin, 93, Lawyer, Genealogist." *New Orleans Times-Picayune*, December 7, 2007, p. B-3

Post, Lauren C. "The Domestic Animals and Plants of French Louisiana as Mentioned in the Literature with Reference to Sources, Varieties, and Uses." *Louisiana Historical Quarterly* 16 (January-October 1933): 554-86.

Powell, Charles F. "New Orleans," *Barre Gazette* (Barre, MA) 9, Issue 12 (July 29, 1842): 2.

Powell, Lawrence N. "What Does American History Tell Us about Katrina and Vice Versa?" *The Journal of American History* 94, Volume 3 (December 2007), 863-76.

Price, Willard. *The Amazing Mississippi*. London, Melbourne, Toronto: Heinemann, Ltd., 1962.

"Profanation of the Sabbath," *Boston Recorder*, September 25, 1819, p. 160, c. 4.

Publications of the Louisiana Historical Society, Volume III, Part 1. New Orleans: Louisiana Historical Society, 1902.

Ralph, Julian. "New Orleans, Our Southern Capital." *Harper's New Monthly Magazine* 86 (February 1893): 364-86

Rankin, David C. "The Forgotten People: Free People of Color in New Orleans, 1850-1870." Ph.D. dissertation, The Johns Hopkins University, 1977.

Ratzel, Friedrich. *Sketches of Urban and Cultural Life in North America*, trans. and ed. Stewart A. Stehlin. New Brunswick and London, England: Rutgers University Press, 1988 translation of 1876 publication.

Reckdahl, Katy. "As Endymion Returns to Mid-City..." *New Orleans Times-Picayune*, February 1, 2008, p. A-6.

Réclus, Elisée. *A Voyage to New Orleans*, trans. and eds. John Clark and Camille Martin. Thetford, VT: Glad Day Books, 2004 translation of 1855 original.

Réclus, Elisée. "An Anarchist in the Old South: Elisée Reclus' Voyage to New Orleans, Part II," trans. Camille Martin and John Clark. *Mesechabe: The Journal of Surre(gion)alism* 12 (Winter 1993-94), 17-22.

Records and Deliberations of the Cabildo, 1769-1803, trans. Works Progress Administration, October 17, 1788, 107 / 107-A, pp. 39-40, second microfilm roll of Cabildo records, Historic New Orleans Collection.

Records and Deliberations of the Cabildo, 1769-1803, trans. Works Progress Administration, September 10, 1784, 7A, second microfilm roll of Cabildo records, Historic New Orleans Collection.

Records and Deliberations of the Cabildo, 1769-1803, trans. Works Progress Administration, March 26, 1788, 97-A / 97-B, p. 13, second microfilm roll of Cabildo records, Historic New Orleans Collection.

Records and Deliberations of the Cabildo, 1769-1803, trans. Works Progress Administration, March 26, 1788, 97-B / 98-A, p. 14 of second microfilm roll of Cabildo records, Historic New Orleans Collection.

Records and Deliberations of the Cabildo, 1769-1803, trans. Works Progress Administration, April 3, 1788, 99-A / 100, p. 19 of second microfilm roll of Cabildo records, Historic New Orleans Collection.

Records and Deliberations of the Cabildo, 1769-1803, trans. Works Progress Administration, April 4, 1788, 99 / 99-A, p. 17 of second microfilm roll of Cabildo records, Historic New Orleans Collection.

Records and Deliberations of the Cabildo, 1769-1803, trans. Works Progress Administration, December 19, 1794, 266 / 266-A, p. 180 of second microfilm roll of Cabildo records, Historic New Orleans Collection.

Records and Deliberations of the Cabildo, 1769-1803, trans. Works Progress Administration, entries for mid-December 1794, 264-A / 265, p. 177; 265 / 265-A, p. 178, 266 / 266-A, p. 180, and 266-A / 267, p. 181, dated December 19, 1794, from second microfilm roll of Cabildo records, Historic New Orleans Collection.

Redfern, Ron. *The Making of a Continent*. New York: Times Books, 1983.

Reed, John Shelton. *One South: An Ethnic Approach to Regional Culture*. Baton Rouge, Louisiana: Louisiana State University Press, 1982.

Reed, Merl E. "Boom or Bust: Louisiana's Economy During the 1830s." In *The Louisiana Purchase Bicentennial Series in Louisiana History*, vol. 16, *Agriculture and Economic Development in Louisiana*, ed. Thomas A. Becnel, Lafayette, LA: Center for Louisiana Studies, 1997.

Reed, Merl E. "Louisiana's Transportation Revolution: The Railroads, 1830-1850." Ph.D. dissertation, Louisiana State University, 1957.

Reed, Merl E. *New Orleans and the Railroads: The Struggle for Commercial Empire, 1830-1860*. Baton Rouge: Louisiana State University Press for the Louisiana Historical Association, 1966.

Reeves, William D. *De la Barre: Life of a French Creole Family in Louisiana*. New Orleans: Jefferson Parish Historical Commission / Polyanthos, 1980.

Regional Planning Commission. *History of Regional Growth of Jefferson, Orleans, and St. Bernard Parishes, Louisiana*. New Orleans: Regional Planning Commission, 1969.

Rehder, John B. *Delta Sugar: Louisiana's Vanishing Plantation Landscape*. Baltimore, MD: The Johns

Hopkins University Press, 1999.

Reinders, Robert C. *End of an Era: New Orleans, 1850-1860*. Gretna, LA: Pelican Publishing Company, 1964.

Renshaw, James A. "The Lost City of Lafayette." *The Louisiana Historical Quarterly* 2 (January 1919): 47-55.

Reps, John W. *The Making of Urban America: A History of City Planning in the United States*. Princeton, NJ: Princeton University Press, 1965.

Rice, Thomas D. and Lewis Griswold. *Soil Map, Louisiana, New Orleans Sheet*. Louisiana Agricultural Experiment Station, 1903.

Rice, Thomas D. and Lewis Griswold. *Soil Survey of the New Orleans Area, Louisiana*. Washington, DC: U.S. Department of Agriculture, Government Printing Office, 1904.

Ripley, Eliza. *Social Life in Old New Orleans, Being Recollections of My Girlhood*. New York and London, England: D. Appleton and Company, 1912.

Rivlin, Gary. "New Orleans Forms a Panel on Renewal." *New York Times*, October 1, 2005, p. A11.

Roberts, H. H. *A Study of Sedimentation and Subsidence in the South-Central Coastal Plain of Louisiana*. Final Report to the U.S. Army Corps of Engineers, New Orleans District, 1985.

Roberts, W. Adolphe. *Lake Pontchartrain*. Indianapolis and New York: The Bobbs-Merrill Company, 1946.

Robichaux, Albert. *Louisiana Census and Militia Lists, Volume I: German Coast, New Orleans, Lafourche, Below New Orleans*. Harvey, Louisiana, 1973.

Robinson, E. and R. H. Pidgeon. *Atlas of the City of New Orleans, Louisiana*. New York: E. Robinson, Publishers, 1883.

Rose, Chris. "Sazeracs and the City." *New Orleans Times-Picayune*, August 20, 2004, *Lagniappe*, p. 23.

Rose, Chris. "The 60-Second Interview: Better Guillaud," *New Orleans Times-Picayune*, May 15, 1999, p. E1.

Ross, Michael A. "Justice Miller's Reconstruction: The *Slaughter-House Cases*, Health Codes, and Civil Rights in New Orleans, 1861-1873." *The Journal of Southern History* 64, No. 4 (November 1998), 649-76.

Rostlund, Erhard. "The Geographic Range of the Historic Bison in the Southeast." *Annals of the Association of American Geographers* 50, No. 4 (December 1960): 395-407.

Roussève, Charles Barthelemy. *The Negro in Louisiana: Aspects of His History and His Literature*. New Orleans: Xavier University Press, 1937.

Rowland, Dunbar and Albert Godfrey Sanders, eds. *Mississippi Provincial Archives 1704-1743: French Dominion, Volume II*, Jackson, MS: Press of the Mississippi Department of Archives and History, 1929.

Rowland, Dunbar and Albert Godfrey Sanders, eds. *Mississippi Provincial Archives 1704-1743: French Dominion, Volume III*. Jackson, MS: Press of the Mississippi Department of Archives and History, 1932.

Russell, Gordon and Frank Donze. "Rebuilding Proposal Gets Mixed Reception; Critics Vocal, but Many Prefer to Watch and Wait." *New Orleans Times-Picayune*, January 12, 2006, p. 1.

Russell, R. J. "Quaternary History of Louisiana." *Geological Society of America Bulletin* 51 (1940): 1199-1234.

Russell, Richard Joel. "Physiography of Lower Mississippi River Delta." *Lower Mississippi River Delta: Reports on the Geology of Plaquemines and St. Bernard Parishes*, Geological Bulletin No. 8. New Orleans: Department of Conservation, Louisiana Geological Society, 1936.

Russell, William Howard, *My Diary North and South*, (Boston and New York: T. O. H. P Burnham and O. S. Felt), 1863.

"Sagamite-Portable Food for Scouts," *Columbus Ledger-Enquirer* (*Daily Columbus Enquirer*, Columbus, GA), September 23, 1861, p. 2., c. 3.

Sagard, Gabriel. *Histoire du Canada et voyages que les Frères mineurs recollects y ont faicts pour la conversion des infidèles depuis l'an 1615*. Paris, France: Librairie Tross, 1866.

"Sam Slick's Description of New Orleans." *Barre Gazette* (Barre, Massachusetts), 5, Issue 37, January 25, 1839, p. 1.

Sanborn Fire Insurance Maps. 1876, 1885-86, 1908-09.

Sargent, Margaret. "Seven Songs from Lorette." *The Journal of American Folklore* 63, No. 248 (April 1950): 175-80

Saucier, Roger T. *Geomorphology and Quaternary Geologic History of the Lower Mississippi Valley*, 2 vols.

Vicksburg, MS: U.S. Army Engineer Waterways Experiment Station, 1994.

Saucier, Roger T. *Recent Geomorphic History of the Pontchartrain Basin*. Coastal Studies Series 9. Baton Rouge: Louisiana State University Studies, 1963.

Saxon, Lyle, Edward Dreyer, and Robert Tallant. *Gumbo Ya-Ya*. Boston, MA: Houghton Mifflin Company, 1945.

Schleifstein, Mark. "Corps Moves to Close MR-GO." *New Orleans Times-Picayune*, November 17, 2007, p. 1.

Schleifstein, Mark. "No Single Decision Doomed Levees." *New Orleans Times-Picayune*, July 11, 2007, p. A1.

Schleifstein, Mark and Sheila Grissett. "The Best News Yet." *New Orleans Times-Picayune*, March 11, 2008, p. A1.

School of Architecture, Tulane University. *The Vieux Carré Survey: A Pictorial Record and a Study of the Land and Buildings in the Vieux Carré*. New Orleans: Edward G. Schlieder Foundation, 1966. 130 binders, Williams Research Center, The Historic New Orleans Collection, New Orleans, LA.

Scientific American 2, Issue 46 (August 7, 1847): 361-68.

Scientific American 6, Issue 13 (December 14, 1850): 97-104.

Sealsfield, Charles. *The Americans As They Are; Described in a Tour Through the Valley of the Mississippi*. London, England: Hurst, Chance, and Co., 1828.

Semple, Henry Churchill, ed. *The Ursulines in New Orleans and Our Lady of Prompt Succor: A Record of Two Centuries 1727-1925*. New York: P. J. Kennedy & Sons, 1925.

Severin, Timothy. *Explorers of the Mississippi*. New York: Alfred A. Knopf, 1968.

Sewerage and Water Board of New Orleans. *Report on Hurricane "Betsy," September 9-10, 1965*. New Orleans: Sewerage and Water Board, October 8, 1965.

Sewerage and Water Board of New Orleans. *The Quality of Our Water*, http://www.swbnola.org/water_info.htm.

Sewerage and Water Board of New Orleans. *The Sewerage and Water Board of New Orleans: How It Began, The Problems It Faces, The Way It Works, The Job It Does*. New Orleans: Sewerage and Water Board, 1998.

Sewerage and Water Board of New Orleans. *Quality Water 2006: A Report on the State of Tap Water in New Orleans*. Pamphlet, 2007.

Shinkle, Kurt D. and Roy K. Dokka. *NOAA Technical Report 50: Rates of Vertical Displacement at Benchmarks in the Lower Mississippi Valley and the Northern Gulf Coast*. Silver Spring, MD: National Oceanographic and Atmospheric Administration, July 2004.

Schultz, Christian. *Travels on an Inland Voyage Through the States of New-York, Pennsylvania, Virginia, Ohio, Kentucky and Tennessee; Performed in the Years 1807 and 1808*, Volume 2. New York: Isaac Riley, 1810.

Sitterson, J. Carlyle. *Sugar Country: The Cane Sugar Industry in the South, 1753-1950*. Lexington: University of Kentucky Press, 1953.

Snowden, J.O., W.C. Ward, and J.R.J. Studlick. *Geology of Greater New Orleans: Its Relationship to Land Subsidence and Flooding*. New Orleans: New Orleans Geological Society, 1980.

Soards' New Orleans City Directory. New Orleans: Soards' Directory Company, 1877, 1880, 1881, 1883, 1885, 1887, 1890, 1893, 1895, 1898, 1901, 1903, 1910, 1917, 1918, 1926, 1935.

Social Science Data Analysis Network. "CensusScope." Population Studies Center, University of Michigan, http://www.censusscope.org.

Somers, Dale A. "Black and White in New Orleans: A Study in Urban Race Relations, 1865-1900." *Journal of Southern History* 40, No. 1 (February 1974): 19-42.

Soniat du Fossat, Chevalier Guy de. *Synopsis of the History of Louisiana from the Founding of the Colony to End of the Year 1791*, ed. and trans. Charles T. Soniat. New Orleans: Louisiana Historical Society, 1903, pamphlet.

Soniat, Meloncy C. "The Faubourgs Forming the Upper Section of the City of New Orleans." *The Louisiana Historical Quarterly* 20 (January 1937): 192-211.

Soulé, Leon Cyprian. *The Know Nothing Party in New Orleans: A Reappraisal*. Baton Rouge: Louisiana Historical Association, 1961. South Central Bell Greater New Orleans White Pages, October 1990-91.

Souther, J. Mark. *New Orleans on Parade: Tourism and the Transformation of the Crescent City*. Baton Rouge: Louisiana State University Press, 2006.

Spain, Daphne. "Race Relations and Residential Segregation in New Orleans: Two Centuries of Paradox."

The Annals of The American Academy of Political and Social Science 441 (January 1979): 82-96.

Spletstoser, Fredrick Marcel. "Back Door to the Land of Plenty: New Orleans as an Immigrant Port, 1820-1860." Ph.D. dissertation, Louisiana State University, 1978.

St. Charles Hotel, New Orleans. *Souvenir of New Orleans: 'The City Care Forgot,'* Third Edition. New Orleans: Alfred S. Amer, 1917.

Stanonis, Anthony, *Creating the Big Easy: New Orleans and the Emergence of Modern Tourism, 1918-1945* (Athens, GA and London, England: University of Georgia Press, 2006).

Starr, S. Frederick. *Inventing New Orleans: Writings of Lafcadio Hearn.* Jackson: University Press of Mississippi, 2001.

Stoddard, Major Amos. *Sketches, Historical and Descriptive, of Louisiana.* Philadelphia, PA: Mathew Carey, 1812.

"Storm Takes Toll in Property Loss and Human Life." *New Orleans Times-Picayune*, September 30, 1915, p. 1.

"'STORM PROOF!' The Record Shows New Orleans." *New Orleans Item*, September 30, 1915, p. 10.

"Sunday Morning in the Creole Market." *New Orleans Daily Crescent*, February 16, 1852, p.1, c. 6.

Surrey, N. M. Miller. *The Commerce of Louisiana During the French Régime, 1699-1763.* New York: Columbia University Studies in History, Economics and Public Law, 1916.

Tasistro, Louis Fitzgerald. *Random Shots and Southern Breezes, Volume II.* New York: Harper & Brothers, 1842.

The Historic New Orleans Collection. *What's Cooking in New Orleans?: Culinary Traditions of the Crescent City.* Exhibition and Guidebook, January 16-July 7, 2007.

The Historic New Orleans Collection, *Newspapers and Periodicals Relating to Louisiana* (Binder), p. 21 of 1840 section.

"The Inundation." *Daily Picayune.* June 4, 1849, Monday evening edition, p. 2, col. 1.

"The Mississippi." *New Orleans Times.* November 23, 1866, p. 3, col. 1.

"The Old Crescent City." *Sunday Inter Ocean* (Chicago, Illinois), December 14, 1890, p. 1.

"The Old French Market." *Daily Picayune.* May 15, 1859, p. 2, c. 1.

The Times (London, England), July 19, 1788, p. 2, c. 4.

The United States Democratic Review 11, Issue 49 (July 1842): 106-08.

"The Upper Mississippi." *Harper's New Monthly Magazine* 16, Issue 94 (March 1858): 433-54.

Thwaites Reuben Gold, ed. *The Jesuit Relations and Allied Documents: Travels and Explorations of the Jesuit Missionaries in New France 1610-1791, Volume V—Quebec, 1632-1633.* New York: Pagent Book Company, 1959.

Thwaites Reuben Gold, ed. *The Jesuit Relations and Allied Documents: Travels and Explorations of the Jesuit Missionaries in New France 1610-1791,* Volume LXVII—Lower Canada, Abenakis, Louisiana 1716-1727. New York: Pagent Book Company, 1959.

Thwaites Reuben Gold, ed. *The Jesuit Relations and Allied Documents: Travels and Explorations of the Jesuit Missionaries in New France 1610-1791, Volume LXVIII—Lower Canada, Crees, Louisiana: 1720-1736.* New York: Pagent Book Company, 1959.

Thwaites Reuben Gold, ed. *The Jesuit Relations and Allied Documents: Travels and Explorations of the Jesuit Missionaries in New France 1610-1791, Volume LXIX—All Missions, 1710-1756.* New York: Pagent Book Company, 1959.

Tinker, Edward Larocque. *Creole City: Its Past and Its People.* New York: Longmans, Green & Co., 1953.

Torres, Manuel and Matt Scallan. "Outward Migration: Statistics Show Orleans Parish May Be Losing Its Appeal to Hispanics." *New Orleans Times-Picayune*, July 9, 2001, p. 1.

Trahan, Larry J. *Soil Survey of Orleans Parish, Louisiana.* Washington, DC: Soil Conservation Service, U.S. Department of Agriculture, 1989.

Treaster, Jospeh B. and Deborah Sontag. "Despair and Lawlessness Grip New Orleans as Thousands Remain Stranded in Squalor." *New York Times,* September 2, 2005, p. 1.

Treasury Department, Bureau of Statistics. *Tables Showing Arrivals of Alien Passengers and Immigrants in the United States from 1820 to 1888.* Washington, DC: Government Printing Office, 1889.

Treadway, Joan and Coleman Warner. "East Meets West: Vietnamese Residents Have Put New Orleans on the Map as an Asian Cultural Center." *New Orleans Times-Picayune*, August 6, 2001, A7.

Treat, Victor Hugo. "Migration into Louisiana, 1834-1880." Ph.D. dissertation, University of Texas at Austin, 1967.

Tregle, Joseph G., Jr. "Creoles and Americans." In *Creole New Orleans: Race and Americanization*, eds. Arnold R. Hirsch and Joseph Logsdon. Baton Rouge and London, England: Louisiana State

University Press, 1992.

Tregle, Joseph G., Jr. "Early New Orleans Society: A Reappraisal." *The Journal of Southern History* 18 (February 1952): 20-36.

Tregle, Joseph G., Jr. "On that Word 'Creole' Again: A Note." *Louisiana History* 13 (Spring 1982): 193-98.

Tregle, Joseph G., Jr. *Louisiana in the Age of Jackson: A Clash of Cultures and Personalities*. Baton Rouge: Louisiana State University Press, 1999.

Trudeau, Charles. *Plan of the City of New Orleans and Adjacent Plantations, Compiled in Accordance with and Ordinance Ministry and Royal Charter (Plano de la Ciudad de Nueva Orleans y de las habitaciones imediatas formado en virtud del decreto del Ill. Cabo)*, December 24, 1798.

University of Michigan. *CensusScope: Social Science Data Analysis Network*, http://wwwCensusScope.org.

U.S. Army Corps of Engineers New Orleans District. *Architectural and Archeological Investigations In and Adjacent to the Bywater Historic District, New Orleans, Louisiana*. New Orleans: R. Christopher Goodwin & Associates, Inc., 1994.

U.S. Army Corps of Engineers Water Resources Support Center, Navigation Data Center. *Tonnage for Selected U.S. Ports in 2000*, http://www.iwr.usace.army.mil/ndc/wcsc/portname00.htm.

U.S. Army Corps of Engineers, New Orleans District and State of Louisiana. *Louisiana Coastal Area: Most Efficient Comprehensive Coastwide Ecosystem Restoration Plans*. Agency document, 2003.

U.S. Army Corps of Engineers, New Orleans District, Water Control Section. *Stage Data: Mississippi River At New Orleans, LA (Carrollton)*, 2004, http://www.mvn.usace.army.mil/cgi-bin/watercontrol.pl?01300.

U.S. Army Corps of Engineers, New Orleans District. *Bonnet Carré Spillway*. Agency booklet, 2000.

U.S. Army Corps of Engineers, New Orleans District. *Freshwater Diversion*. Agency brochure, circa 2001.

U.S. Army Corps of Engineers, New Orleans District. *Old River Control*. Agency booklet, 1999.

U.S. Army Corps of Engineers, New Orleans District. *Water Resources Development in Louisiana*. Agency booklet, 1995.

U.S. Army Corps of Engineers, New Orleans District. *WaterMarks: Louisiana Coastal Wetlands Planning, Protection and Restoration News*. Agency periodical, August 2003.

U.S. Army Corps of Engineers. *Waterborne Commerce of the United States, Part 2, Waterways and Harbors, Gulf Coast, Mississippi River System and Antilles*, Washington, DC: U.S. Army Corps, 1998.

U.S. Army Engineer District, New Orleans. *Hurricane Betsy, September 8-11, 1965, Serial No. 1880*. New Orleans: Corps of Engineers, November 1965.

U.S. Army Engineer District, New Orleans. *Hurricane Betsy, September 8-11, 1965: After-Action Report*. New Orleans: Corps of Engineers, July 1966.

U.S. Census Bureau. "Aggregate Amount of Persons Within the United States in the Year 1810: Aggregate Amount of Each Description of Persons Within the Territory of Orleans, 1810." Government Documents, Howard-Tilton Memorial Library, Tulane University, New Orleans.

U.S. Census Bureau. "American Community Survey—New Orleans City, Louisiana, ACS Demographic and Housing Estimates 2006: Demographic - Sex and Age, Race, Hispanic Origin, Housing Units," http://factfinder.census.gov, accessed 2008.

U.S. Census Bureau. "American Community Survey—Ranking Tables, 2002: Percent of Population that is Foreign Born," http://www.census.gov/acs/www/Products/Ranking/2002/R15T160.htm, accessed 2002.

U.S. Census Bureau. "Census 2000 Full-Count Characteristics (SF1)," compiled by Greater New Orleans Community Data Center.

U.S. Census Bureau. "Census Tract Statistics—New Orleans, Louisiana." *1950 Population Census Report*, vol. 3, ch. 36. Washington, DC: U.S. Government Printing Office, 1952.

U.S. Census Bureau. "Profile of Selected Social Characteristics, 2000, Census 2000 Summary File 3 (SF 3) Sample Data," http://factfinder.census.gov/.

U.S. Census Bureau. *Census of 1820*. Washington, DC: Gales & Seaton, 1821.

U.S. Census Bureau. *Census of 1980*. Washington, DC: Bureau of the Census, 1981.

U.S. Census Bureau. *Fourteenth Census of the United States Taken in the Year 1920*, vol. 3, *Population 1920*. Washington, DC: Government Printing Office, 1922, especially Enumeration Districts 31, 34, and 35.

U.S. Census Bureau. Fourth Count Summary Tape (Population). "Mother Tongue and Nativity," 1970.

U.S. Census Bureau. *Louisiana 1910 Census: Orleans Parish (Part)*. Digital database of 1910 Census population schedules. North Salt Lake City, UT: HeritageQuest, 2003.

U.S. Census Bureau. *Population 1910: Reports by States, with Statistics for Counties, Cities, and Other Civil*

Divisions, Alabama-Montana. Washington, DC: Government Printing Office, 1913.

U.S. Census Bureau. *Population and Housing Statistics for Census Tracts—New Orleans, La.* Washington, DC: U.S. Government Printing Office, 1942.

U.S. Census Bureau. *Population and Housing, 1960: Census Tracts—New Orleans, La.* Washington, DC: U.S. Government Printing Office, 1961.

U.S. Census Bureau. Population Division. *Tech Paper 29, Table 4. Region and Country or Area of Birth of the Foreign-Born Population, With Geographic Detail Shown in Decennial Census Publications of 1930 or Earlier: 1850 to 1930*

U.S. Census Bureau. *Religious Bodies 1916: Part I Summary and General Tables.* Washington, DC: Governmental Printing Office, 1919.

U.S. Census Bureau. *Religious Bodies: 1926,* vol. 1, *Summary and Detailed Tables.* Washington, DC: Governmental Printing Office, 1930.

U.S. Census Bureau. *Religious Bodies: 1936,* vol. 1, *Summary and Detailed Tables.* Washington, DC: Governmental Printing Office, 1941.

U.S. Census Bureau. *Statistics of the Population of the United State at the Tenth Census.* Washington, DC: Government Printing Office, 1883.

U.S. Census Bureau. "State of Residence in 2000 by State of Birth: 2000," January 31, 2005, http://www.census.gov/population/cen2000/phc-t38/phc-t38.xls

U.S. Census Bureau. "County-to-County Migration Flow Files," August 11, 2003, http://www.census.gov/population/www/cen2000/ctytoctyflow.html

U.S. Congress. "An Act Respecting Claims to Land in the Territories of Orleans and Louisiana," March 3, 1807, as recorded on pages 1283-86 of *The Debates and Proceedings in the Congress of the United States,* printed 1852.

U.S. Department of Commerce. *Geographic Areas Reference Manual.* Washington, DC, November 1994.

U.S. Department of Health and Human Services, Office of Applied Statistics, Table C8. "Alcohol Dependence or Abuse in Past Year," 2004, http://oas.samhsa.gov/substate2k6/alcDrugs.htm#ALL, accessed August 5, 2007.

U.S. Geological Survey, *Geographic Names Information System (GNIS),* http://geonames.usgs.gov/domestic/index.html, accessed July 19, 2007.

U.S. Geological Survey, National Wetlands Research Center, and Louisiana Coastal Area Land Change Study Group. "100+ Years of Land Change for Coastal Louisiana," http://www.nwrc.usgs.gov/special/landloss.htm.

U.S. Geological Survey, National Wetlands Research Center. *Restoring Life to the Dead Zone: Addressing Gulf Hypoxia, A National Problem.* Agency brochure, circa 2000.

U.S. Geological Survey, Office of Surface Water. *Real-Time Data for the Nation,* http://waterdata.usgs.gov/nwis/rt.

U.S. Geological Survey. Nonindigenous Aquatic Species. "Zebra Mussel, *Dreissena polymorpha,*" http://nas.er.usgs.gov/zebra.mussel/docs/sp_account.html.

University of Virginia Geospatial and Statistical Data Center. *United States Historical Census Data Browser,* http://fisher.lib.virginia.edu/census, accessed 2002-07.

Urban Land Institute. "New Orleans, Louisiana: A Strategy for Rebuilding—an Advisory Services Program Report," New Orleans, November 12-18, 2005.

Usner, Daniel H. Jr. "The Frontier Exchange Economy of the Lower Mississippi Valley in the Eighteenth Century." *The William and Mary Quarterly* 44, No. 2 (April 1987): 165-92.

Uyeda, Seiya. *The New View of the Earth: Moving Continents and Moving Oceans.* San Francisco, CA and Reading, England: W.H. Freeman and Company, 1978.

Vale, Lawrence J and Thomas J. Campanella, eds. *The Resilient City: How Modern Cities Recover from Disaster.* Oxford and New York: Oxford University Press, 2005.

Van Heerden, Ivor and Mike Bryan. *The Storm: What Went Wrong and Why During Hurricane Katrina--the Inside Story from One Louisiana Scientist.* New York: Penguin, 2006.

Van Kempen, Ronald, and A. Şule Özüekren. "Ethnic Segregation in Cities: New Forms and Explanations in a Dynamic World." *Urban Studies* 35 (1998): 1631-56.

Villiers du Terrage, Marc de. "A History of the Foundation of New Orleans (1717-1722)." *The Louisiana Historical Quarterly* 3 No. 2, (April 1920): 157-251.

Viosca, Percy, Jr. "Flood Control in the Mississippi Valley in Its Relation to Louisiana Fisheries." Technical Paper No. 4. New Orleans: State of Louisiana Department of Conservation-Division of Fisheries, 1927.

Vlach, John Michael. "Sources of the Shotgun House: African and Caribbean Antecedents for Afro-American Architecture." Ph.D. dissertation, Indiana University, 1975.

Vogt, Lloyd. *New Orleans Houses: A House-Watcher's Guide.* Gretna, LA: Pelican Publishing Company, 1985.

Waddill, Frank H. *Survey of the Right-of-Way of the Canal Carondelet, From Rampart Street to Hagan Avenue* (New Orleans, November 23, 1923), blueprint stored at Tulane University Special Collections, C5-D12-F8.

Waldo, J. Curtis. *Illustrated Visitors' Guide to New Orleans.* New Orleans: J. Curtis Waldo, L. Graham, 1879.

Walk, Darlene M. *Pontchartrain Park Neighborhood Profile: City of New Orleans.* New Orleans: Office of Policy Planning, 1978.

Walker, Judy. "Shotgun Appreciation." *New Orleans Times-Picayune.* March 1, 2002, Living section, p. 1.

Ward, David. "The Emergence of Central Immigrant Ghettoes in American Cities: 1840-1920." *Annals of the Association of American Geographers* 58 (June 1968): 343-59.

Ward, David. *Cities and Immigrants: A Geography of Change in Nineteenth Century America.* New York, London, Toronto: Oxford University Press, 1971.

Waring, George E. Jr. *Report on the Social Statistics of Cities, Part II: The Southern and the Western States.* Washington, DC: Government Printing Office, 1887.

Warner, Coleman, and Matt Scallan. "Going to Extremes." *New Orleans Times-Picayune.* September 3, 2001, A8.

Warner, Coleman and Gwen Filosa. "UNANIMOUS: Council Votes to Raze 4,500 Units; Old Housing Model to Give Way to Mixed-Income Developments." *New Orleans Times-Picayune,* December 21, 2007, p. 1.

Weiner, Eric. *The Geography of Bliss: One Grump's Search for the Happiest Places in the World.* New York and Boston: Twelve Books, 2007.

Wellner, Alison Stein. "The Mobility Myth: Pundits Love to Fret About Our "Increasingly Mobile Society," But Americans Are Actually More Likely Than Ever to Stay Put." *ReasonOnline* (April 2006), http://www.reason.com/news/show/33288.html

Wharton, Thomas K. *Queen of the South—New Orleans, 1853-1862: The Journal of Thomas K. Wharton,* eds. Samuel Wilson Jr., Patricia Brady, and Lynn D. Adams. New Orleans: The Historic New Orleans Collection, 1999.

White, Gilbert Fowler. *Human Adjustment to Floods.* Chicago: University of Chicago Department of Geography, Research Paper No. 29, 1942, published 1945.

White, Jaquetta. "Business is Sour for La. Sugar Industry; Number of Farms, Mills Continues Slide." *New Orleans Times-Picayune,* January 30, 2005, Money section, p. 1.

White, Jaquetta. "N.O. Tops for Food, Live Music, Poll Finds." *New Orleans Times-Picayune,* October 11, 2007, E1.

"Whitewashing the Trunks of Young Trees Prevents Sunscald." *San Jose Mercury News* (San Jose, California), February 16, 1919, p. 15.

Williams, Leslie. "Katrina Left Many In Eastern N.O. Unscathed; 'Hard-Hit' Reputation Doesn't Always Fit," *New Orleans Times-Picayune,* May 7, 2007, p. 1.

Wilson, Samuel Jr. *The Vieux Carre, New Orleans: Its Plan Its Growth, Its Architecture.* New Orleans: Bureau of Government Research, 1968.

Winkler-Schmit, David. "The Long Road Ahead: The New Orleans Redevelopment Authority—NORA— is finally getting enough money to do its job. Is the agency ready?" *Gambit Weekly,* December 18, 2007, pp. 9-11.

Zimpel, Charles F. *Topographical Map of New Orleans and Its Vicinity,* 1834. Original copy stored at Southeastern Architectural Archive, Tulane University Special Collections.

INDEX